UNDERGRADUATE TEXTS IN COMPUTER SCIENCE

David R. Brooks

PROBLEM SOLVING WITH FORTRAN 90

FOR SCIENTISTS AND ENGINEERS

Springer

David R. Brooks
Department of Mathematics
    and Computer Science
Drexel University
Philadelphia, PA 19104
USA

Series Editors
David Gries
Fred B. Schneider
Department of Computer Science
Cornell University
405 Upson Hall
Ithaca, NY 14853-7501
USA

Library of Congress Cataloging-in-Publication Data
Brooks, David R.
    Problem solving with Fortran 90 : for scientists and engineers /
David Brooks.
        p.   cm. — (Undergraduate texts in computer science)
    ISBN 978-1-4612-7353-0   ISBN 978-1-4612-1952-1 (eBook)
    DOI 10.1007/978-1-4612-1952-1
    1. FORTRAN 90 (Computer program language)   2. Problem solving—
Data processing. I. Title. II. Series.
QA76.73.F25B754   1997
005.13´3—dc21   97-10929

Printed on acid-free paper.

Production managed by Lesley Poliner; manufacturing supervised by Johanna Tschebull.
Typeset in TEX from files supplied by the author.

9 8 7 6 5 4 3 2 1

ISBN 978-1-4612-7353-0

Preface

i.1 Overview for Instructors

The purpose of this text is to provide an introduction to the problem-solving capabilities of Fortran 90. The intended audience is undergraduate science and engineering students who have not previously taken a formal programming course. The focus is on the process of solving computational problems of interest to scientists and engineers, rather than on programming *per se*, which has several important implications for the contents of the text, as outlined later in the Preface.

Fortran has long been favored as an introductory programming language for engineering and science students because of its historical roots and continued prominence in the professional practice of these disciplines. The Fortran 77 standard has been taught, within an essentially mainframe context, to an entire generation of scientists and engineers. However, many of the science and engineering calculations that, a generation ago, could be done only on mainframe computers can now be done on desktop computers, often using applications that don't require any programming at all.

Students are certainly aware of the power of desktop computing, even when they are not prepared to use it effectively. They bring increasingly sophisticated expectations to even an introductory programming course, and they often have correspondingly less patience with the organizational overhead required to perform even the most trivial computational tasks. Nonetheless, there is a strong case to be made for learning how to write programs in a high-level procedural language, even when a student's major does not require that specific skill. Thus I believe that the continuing popularity of Fortran in science and engineering is due not to a reluctance to adopt more modern problem-solving tools, but to a deep understanding of the central role procedural programming plays in developing problem-solving skills that are independent of a particular language.

No matter how strong the argument for learning procedural programming, a new Fortran text should still justify itself on the basis of what it can offer to make an introduction to programming more rewarding for students and instructors alike. The Fortran 90 standard provides an opportunity for dramatically improving the content of introductory programming courses for science and engineering students because it is now possible to take advantage of the traditional strengths of Fortran and, at the same time, teach a language with features that have always been a part of other more "modern" languages such as C and Pascal.

i.1.1 The Case for Fortran 90

The basic problem with continuing to teach Fortran 77 is that the *standard* for this language has serious deficiencies relative to languages such as C, the other common choice for a first programming language taught to science and engineering students, and even Pascal, the use of which is now in decline and which never attracted a large following in the science and engineering community. One result of the aging of the Fortran 77 standard is that modern implementations of the language contain many nonstandard features to address its deficiencies. This is helpful to professional users of the language, but to the extent that Fortran texts have adhered to the language standard to ensure their marketability, students have for many years been taught a language that is far removed from what is actually used in practice.

Even for instructors who approach programming from a purely practical as opposed to a "computer science" point of view, the problems with standard Fortran 77 are clear from even a cursory comparison with other modern procedural languages. Among these are the lack of a way to enforce explicit typing of all variables, the restriction of variable names to six characters, limited syntax for constructing loops, no support for user-defined data types (other than arrays), and syntax possibilities that encourage the writing of "spaghetti code" that is not tolerated in modern procedural programming style.

Of course, many of these shortcomings have been addressed in nonstandard implementations of Fortran 77, and it is certainly possible to write well-structured programs by using appropriate syntax. However, this begs the question of whether to abandon the Fortran 77 standard in favor of a new one.

Fortran 90 has addressed many of Fortran 77's problems while retaining backward compatibility with Fortran 77 and older versions. It has incorporated many of the nonstandard features that are commonly included in Fortran 77 implementations. In addition, the new standard contains many features that make structured programs easier to write, which in turn makes Fortran much easier to teach and learn. To cite just a few examples, the new standard includes provisions for enforcing explicit data typing, DO WHILE. . . and SELECT CASE constructs, and user-defined data types (equivalent to structures in C or records in Pascal).

Finally, the increasing capabilities of personal computers have made it possible to put a full-featured Fortran compiler on a desktop, so it is now practical to consider Fortran not just in its traditional role as a mainframe language, but as an integral part of a personal computing environment that includes a variety of problem-solving tools. PC-based Fortran 77 compilers incorporate the same nonstandard language extensions as their mainframe relatives, but the compiler used to develop the programs in this text (see Section *i.1.5*) actually helped to define the Fortran 90 standard. Thus the case for Fortran 90 is made even more compelling by the availability of an implementation for desktop computers that represents, at least for a while, this new language as it is used in practice.

i.1.2 Structure of the Text

Introductory Material

Chapter 1 presents a brief historical review of electronic computing in mainframe and personal computing environments. I understand that this kind of material is often regarded as "fluff" by instructors and students alike. However, the pedagogical purpose of this chapter is to give students a chance, at the beginning of a course, to assess their general computing skills and address any weaknesses. To take a more proactive view, I would argue that it provides a good (and probably the only) opportunity for instructors to give their students a general introduction to the computing facilities they will be using to write Fortran programs.

Chapter 2 presents a detailed approach to problem solving and algorithm design. It is now common for introductory programming texts to emphasize the problem-solving process and to provide some formal or informal techniques. However, my experience is that the specific process required to develop algorithms and convert them into programs in any language remains a mystery to many students. Because at first there do not seem to be any rules to follow, it is difficult to know how to start—that is, how to develop algorithms without knowing what kinds of things programs should do.

Chapter 2 addresses this problem in two ways. First, it discusses the generic kinds of instructions and data used by and in computer programs written in a procedural language. Second, a syntax-free pseudocode language of "action commands" is presented. These commands are the means by which algorithms for a procedural programming language may be developed. I have tried to convey the message that despite the fact that this language is not in any way "standardized" (even though it is applied in a uniform way throughout the text), the actions implied by the language must be a part of any approach to developing algorithms. My practice is to discourage students from memorizing the commands; instead I encourage them to use the material in Chapter 2 to produce their own "language reference," which they can consult even during exams.

Students should be encouraged to use this pseudocode language (or their own version of it) to develop algorithms before they write source code because the process of applying such an informal language helps them separate the process of developing a logical solution to a problem from the syntax details of writing a program in a "real" language. In this text, I have encouraged this process by always presenting algorithms in pseudocode before implementing them in Fortran.

A few components of the pseudocode language deserve comment. Some instructors may prefer to use the ← symbol for the assignment operator, rather than the = sign used in this text. Obviously, this is OK; the symbol isn't as important as distinguishing the concept of assignment from that of equality in the relational or algebraic sense.

Note that the pseudocode language includes three different assignment commands: **ASSIGN**, **INITIALIZE**, and **INCREMENT**. (All references to the pseudocode language use this font.) Although each of these commands translates into an assignment statement, my experience is that students often do not understand the need for initializing variables or how and when to increment them, especially inside loop structures. Because of this, I have used separate commands to try to encourage proper algorithm design.

Another decision made about the pseudocode language concerns the command for repetition structures. No attempt is made at the algorithm design level to distinguish among pre-test, post-test, or count-controlled loops (as might be done when algorithms are developed with flowcharts, for example); the **LOOP...END LOOP** command represents all three, with conditions for loop termination written informally as part of the **LOOP** command.

The language used to express the terminating condition in English—"Do this 10 times," "Do this until you run out of data," "Repeat until this number is too large"—will determine how the loop is actually implemented in a procedural language. Being precise about the possibilities in plain English lays the groundwork for distinguishing among language-specific implementations for count-controlled, pre-test, and post-test loops. When this kind of pseudocode is later translated into a program, instructors are free to choose, for example, whether to encourage or discourage their students from using Fortran's STOP and EXIT statements to exit loops. (This text assumes that good programming style never requires multiple exit points from loops.)

A final point about Chapter 2 (and subsequent chapters) concerns the role of flowcharts. This is a teaching tool that has long been associated with programming in Fortran. It is certainly useful for visualizing the operation of certain language constructs such as **IF...THEN** statements, and it may be helpful for the top-level design of large and highly modularized programs. However, it is often a cumbersome way to design algorithms and has fallen out of favor in the teaching of other procedural languages. As a result, this text favors pseudocode as the basic algorithm design tool. Flowcharts are used as a supplement when they can convey useful information in a visually striking manner. That is, it is fair to say that flowcharts are treated as one way to convey information, rather than as an essential part of the programming process.

Because I understand that students are eager to begin the process of actually writing programs, Chapter 2 includes a simple program that can be copied and executed in a "rote" manner. This is useful for learning the mechanics of creating source code, compiling the code, and executing the resulting program.

Presentation of the Language

In Chapters 3 through 9, the syntax elements of Fortran are introduced, using what I would describe as a "show and tell" approach. New language features are often introduced through a problem that can't be solved with the tools available up to that time. A complete program to solve that problem will then be presented and examined in detail, moving from the specific to the general, rather than the other way around. Chapter 3 revolves almost entirely around a single simple program, which is used as a vehicle for examining many basic features of the Fortran language.

Each chapter after the second includes at least two complete programming applications drawn from typical problems found in introductory engineering and science courses. Whereas programs presented early in a chapter address conceptually simple problems and attempt to isolate the specific programming skill being developed in that chapter, the applications involve more challenging problems and integrate new material into a cumulative framework of developing programming skills. Some of the applications appear in more than one chapter, so students can see how increasingly sophisticated programming skills produce correspondingly more sophisticated solutions.

i.1.3 Decisions About Content

Compared to Fortran 77, Fortran 90 is a huge language, due to its backward-compatibility and its new features. This inevitably leads to making choices about what parts of the language are appropriate in an introductory text used for a one- or two-semester course. In every case where a conscious decision has been made, my motivation has been to choose those features of the language that are most essential for solving the kinds of problems science and engineering students are likely to encounter.

Some of the decisions are easy. Many syntax features of older versions of Fortran (arithmetic IFs and computed GO TOs, for example) are simply absent from this text because there is no justification for using them. It is harder to decide which new features of the language to include. To cite just two examples, pointers are *not* included in the text even though they are of great interest in computer science, and recursion *is* included because of the importance of recursively defined functions in science and engineering mathematics. The following topics all require decisions about content, and I hope my comments will help to explain how I have arrived at some of the choices that are evident in the text.

Program Layout

The text retains the "old-fashioned" Fortran line structure, with statements restricted to columns 7-72 and columns 1-5 reserved for line labels. Thus even though all the programs are written for compilation under Fortran 90's free format style, the program layout will be familiar to those who are used to previous versions of Fortran. This restriction on line length has the practical advantage of making source code listing fit more easily on the page of a textbook.

Because of their backward-compatibility with earlier versions, Fortran 90 compilers support Fortran 77 syntax. For example, the Fortran 77 statements

```
REAL pi
PARAMETER (pi=3.14159)
```

are still allowed in Fortran 90, even though the (free format) statement

```
REAL, PARAMETER :: pi=3.14159
```

is preferred Fortran 90 style. In the latter example, the PARAMETER *statement* has been replaced by the PARAMETER *attribute* appearing as part of a type declaration statement. I confess to not being rigorous about always insisting on the "correct" Fortran 90 implementation.

This program layout style should not be interpreted as a desire to make the programs look like Fortran 77. Although Fortran 90 can be used to write programs that look just like their Fortran 77 counterparts (and can be compiled under a "fixed format" option required for Fortran 90 compilers), that is certainly not the best use of this new language. I hope that instructors who are migrating from Fortran 77 will revise their teaching material (and their own programming style) to take advantage of Fortran 90's style and many new features. An excellent overview of important differences between Fortran 77 and 90 (as well as a definitive reference manual for the language) can be found in *Fortran 90 Handbook*, a complete reference for which is given at the end of this Preface.

Data Types

Even earlier versions of Fortran supplemented the basic REAL data type with DOUBLE PRECISION variables. Fortran 77 compilers typically include nonstandard variants of the INTEGER data type as well. Fortran 90 supports even more variants. It is possible, for example, to specify directly the minimum number of significant digits retained by a REAL variable. However, I believe these add nothing to an understanding of problem-solving methods or programming style. Therefore, the text uses only the basic data types and deals with increased precision only in Chapter 12.

One obvious place where this choice might have an impact is in numerical analysis algorithms, where DOUBLE PRECISION variables are typically used to improve the accuracy of calculations in older Fortran programs. I have chosen not to use the DOUBLE PRECISION data type at all because it adds nothing to the understanding of an algorithm and may even convey the dangerous message that the limitations inherent in numerical methods can be "fixed" just by using calculations with more significant figures. A brief discussion of enhanced precision variables is included in Chapter 12.

The COMPLEX data type is also dealt with only briefly in Chapter 12, based on the assumption that most students taking an introductory programming course will not yet have the mathematical sophistication to use complex numbers. Even if this isn't a good assumption, I still believe that bypassing this topic is a reasonable choice for an introductory programming text.

Derived Data Types

Derived data types are a major and welcome addition to Fortran 90, second in importance, in my view, only to the IMPLICIT NONE statement for enforcing explicit data typing. The ability to define multi-field records with the TYPE...END TYPE construct avoids the use of parallel arrays, which can make large programs written in older versions of Fortran quite cumbersome. Derived types can also be used to reduce the dimensionality of Fortran arrays. This simplifies programming and allows code to be more self-documenting because each field can be addressed by name rather than just by its array index. Although derived types aren't necessarily related to arrays, they are introduced in this text in the context of arrays of records, as this is the way they will most often be used in practice.

Pointers and Allocatable Arrays

Fortran 90 supports pointers, but they are not discussed at all in this text. In an introductory programming course taught in C, for example, pointers are often introduced early as a way to manipulate arrays and to provide "output" parameters with functions. Of course, Fortran's syntax makes pointers unnecessary for either of these purposes.

Pointers are also used to manage dynamically allocated data structures. These are important in computer science, and indeed some earlier Fortran texts have used static arrays and indices to simulate "pointer-like" operations on data structures such as stacks, queues, and other linked lists that are an important part of languages that support dynamic allocation. However, I do not believe these are essential topics for an introductory course aimed at science and engineering students.

Nonetheless, over several years of teaching Pascal, I have introduced pointers and dynamic memory allocation in the context of managing data structures without "wasting" memory resources. Even though there is usually no practical reason to worry about this problem, it *is* conceptually useful to be able to determine the size of data storage structures based on need at run time rather than compile time.

In Fortran, questions about how memory is used to store arrays arise when variably dimensioned arrays are used in subprograms. The Fortran syntax implies that such arrays are being dynamically allocated at the time the subprogram is called, but they are not. Instead, the variable dimension merely provides restricted access to a subset of the array space (through one or more subprogram parameters) that was statically allocated in the main program.

This arrangement is conceptually flawed because, whereas it is satisfactory for one-dimensional arrays, it doesn't work intuitively for multidimensional arrays. Typically, a subprogram must declare multidimensional arrays with the same dimensions used in the main program even though access is required only for a subset of that array. Thus both the maximum and the "working" sizes have to be passed to a subprogram to insure access to the desired subset of the array space. A failure to understand this fact leads to programs that look perfectly reasonable, but don't work properly; this kind of error is very difficult for students to find.

In Fortran 90, this awkward situation can often be eliminated by using `ALLOCATABLE` arrays. The Fortran implementation of an allocatable array isn't completely equivalent to dynamic allocation because it's not possible to use any element in such a structure until its maximum size has been allocated. That is, it's not possible to use allocatable arrays to build an expandable data storage structure "on the fly." Nonetheless, allocatable arrays give some of the flavor of dynamic memory allocation without the additional programming overhead of pointers and linked data structures. Therefore, they are included in the text.

Recursion

In contrast with earlier versions of the language, Fortran 90 supports recursive subprograms as part of the standard. I have included a brief discussion of this topic because some recursively defined functions, such as the Legendre polynomials, are important in science and engineering, and I believe that seeing them evaluated in a natural way is worth the difficulties students have with this concept. Another justification is that it is then possible to discuss the important Quicksort algorithm in its usual recursive version; this is impossible with previous standard versions of Fortran. A nonrecursive Quicksort algorithm is so unwieldy that it is usually not included at all in Fortran texts, with the result that students see only the inefficient $O(N^2)$ algorithms instead of the much more efficient $O(Nlog_2N)$ Quicksort algorithm.

Explicit vs. Implicit Typing

Because explicit data typing is obviously good programming practice, its use is uniformly stressed in Fortran 77 texts, even though there is no way to enforce explicit typing under the Fortran 77 standard. However, Fortran 90 supports the IMPLICIT NONE statement, which is available only as a nonstandard feature in some Fortran 77 compilers. I believe inclusion in Fortran 90 of a means to enforce explicit typing is the single greatest improvement over earlier versions of Fortran. In this text, an IMPLICIT NONE statement is part of every program and subprogram.

Programs compiled with IMPLICIT NONE will automatically generate messages for misspelled variables and other variables that are not included in type statements, and, depending on the compiler, may also generate warnings for variables that are declared but not used in a program. This information is invaluable to students when they debug their programs.

COMMON Blocks

In previous versions of Fortran, information not appearing in parameter lists could be shared among subprograms only by using COMMON blocks. This is a persistent source of problems because of the burden placed on the programmer to ensure that references to variables passed through a COMMON block in one program segment match the references to variables passed through that same block to other segments. The problem arises because the data types of variables referred to in COMMON blocks are almost without exception intended to be the same in all segments using that block, but they don't *have* to be. This is because information in COMMON blocks is "storage associated" rather than "name associated." That is, a COMMON block occupies a certain range of memory locations based on the data types of items in the original definition of the block. In another part of the program, the information in those memory locations can be accessed in a variety of ways, including ways not originally intended.

This problem can be remedied by using Fortran 90 MODULEs, which can be referenced in the main program and other subprograms through the USE statement. Information in the modules must be accessed specifically by name. (Local aliases can be defined.) Modules can consist simply of data type specifications and PARAMETER statements or attributes, but they have other uses too, such as making selected subprograms and derived data types available to other program units. For these reasons, I believe there is no reason for new programmers to use COMMON blocks, and I have not used them in any of the programming examples in this text. However, because COMMON blocks appear so frequently in earlier versions of Fortran, I have included a brief introduction to their use, and potential misuse, in Chapter 12.

Program Modularization

An important decision to be made in any introductory programming course concerns the appropriate place to introduce program modularization. In C, for example, the fact that even the "main program" is nothing more than a function naturally leads to an early discussion of this topic. In this text, I have deferred introducing functions and subroutines in Fortran—basically until students are writing programs that are worth modularizing. Programs that implement a single programming concept—IF...THEN... statements, for example—are generally restricted to one task and do not really need to be modularized as part of the top-down process of dividing a large task into several smaller tasks. To give students some feeling for modularizing tasks, I have included statement functions along with the discussion of intrinsic functions in Chapter 4, even though some Fortran 90 programmers believe statement functions should no longer be used.

My decision to delay a discussion of subroutines and functions until Chapter 7 is also motivated by the fact that Fortran 90 has greatly increased the level of effort required to write subprograms that take full advantage of the features provided by the language. The MODULE and INTERFACE constructs, and the INTENT attribute for parameters, are welcome additions to the language, but they require more teaching and learning time. Consequently, I have delayed their introduction past the point that I might feel was appropriate in some other language.

Obviously, instructors who wish to discuss modularization early in their course can easily rewrite many of the examples presented in the text to include functions and subroutines called from a main program. It is even possible to use subprograms in the "old-fashioned" way, without MODULEs, although this practice is discouraged.

Arrays

Arrays are introduced in Chapter 8. Again, Fortran 90 presents new opportunities and challenges. In addition to allocatable arrays, as discussed earlier, the availability of elemental functions, operations on whole arrays (or subsets of arrays), and the several array manipulation and reduction functions greatly increases the teaching and learning load without introducing any concepts and capabilities that I consider absolutely essential. However, it is certainly convenient to be able to reduce the number of loops that must be written for manipulating arrays, so I have attempted to find a workable compromise. Some of Fortran 90's array manipulation features are used in Chapter 8 and subsequent chapters, and some are deferred to Chapter 12, which presents a miscellany of Fortran 90 features that I believe are not essential for an introductory programming course.

One result of making the kinds of content decisions discussed here is that this text is not, and does not try to be, a Fortran 90 reference manual. I believe the level of detail and sheer volume required to create such a manual is inappropriate for an introductory text and may not even be compatible with *any* text devoted to developing problem-solving skills rather than programming *per se*. My own questions about details of the Fortran 90 language standard have been answered by two excellent references, which are given near the end of this Preface.

i.1.4 Pedagogical Features

Obviously, this text mirrors my own ideas about how an introductory programming course should be taught, and it draws on my experiences with teaching C, Pascal, and Fortran to a wide range of students in science, engineering, and other disciplines.

A Formal Problem-Solving Process Is Followed Throughout the Text

Chapter 2 describes a five-step problem-solving process and a pseudocode language for algorithm development. What distinguishes this text is that the process is followed rigorously for all substantive programs throughout the text. I hope that my own determination to adhere to a specific problem-solving plan will motivate students to develop the same habit in their own programming.

Some Applications and Problems Appear More Than Once

Some of the applications and exercises in early chapters are revisited in later chapters, when more sophisticated programming skills can be applied. For example, both algorithm design applications in Chapter 2 are presented as programming problems in later chapters, and new versions of both applications in Chapter 3 are discussed in later chapters. Some of the programming exercises in Chapter 3 reappear in expanded versions in later chapters. I believe that returning to the same problems will give students a sense that they are progressing and that programs are dynamic entities that can grow in response to new demands and developing skills.

Programs and Exercises

The text contains many complete programs in addition to the end-of-chapter applications. The source code listings have been copied directly from the original source code files, although in a few cases comments have been added and lines have been continued to fit the source code onto the textbook page.

Every program has been written "from scratch" for this text. Especially in the later chapters, some of the source code implements well-known algorithms. However, the resulting code often differs significantly from similar code appearing in older (Fortran 77) texts, in order to take advantage of Fortran 90 features.

The exercises are subdivided into three categories. "Self-testing" exercises are intended to help students test their own understanding of the problem-solving and programming concepts and Fortran syntax covered in the chapter. "Basic programming" exercises often include modifications to programs presented in the text. This provides practice in reading and understanding someone else's code and should also provide incentives to study programs in the text more thoroughly than might otherwise be the case.

"Programming applications" involve writing complete programs based on the material presented in the chapter. Such exercises are cumulative in the sense that they assume all programming skills learned up to the present can be brought to bear on the problem. Complete source code listings for the programming applications are available to instructors (see Section *i.1.6*), and I hope my solutions to these exercises will be useful for your lectures and classroom discussions.

Nearly all the exercises are related to the kinds of problems students will encounter in introductory science, engineering, and mathematics courses. Some of the problems use discipline-specific terminology, and I do not think it is practical or necessary to try to eliminate all jargon from every problem. In some cases, I have provided representative output to help students verify the operation of their programs. Programming in the real world often takes place in an environment where programmers don't understand all the subtleties of the problems they are being asked to solve, and it is important for students to develop confidence in their skills even when faced with this kind of uncertainty.

I have tried to order the programming exercises roughly by increasing difficulty, although I assume that my ideas about this won't always match yours or your students'. This progression in difficulty is as often related to mathematical skills as it is to programming skills. Especially in the later chapters, some of the exercises will make more sense if a student has some familiarity with calculus or basic numerical analysis, even though the programming itself may not be difficult.

I have marked such problems with an appropriate message, but I have still attempted to provide enough information about the problem so that students can write the code even if they don't completely understand the underlying mathematics.

i.1.5 The Compiler Used to Prepare Programs for This Text

At the time the first drafts of this text were written, there was, at least as far as I knew, only one commercially available Fortran 90 compiler for MS-DOS-based PCs, the platform I chose for convenience in developing the programs. This was the Numerical Algorithms Group (NAG)/Salford Software FTN90 compiler, which is also available for other computing platforms. As a result, all the programs were written for this compiler—initially using the MS-DOS version and later the Windows 95 version.[1] Because this compiler actually helped define implementation of the Fortran 90 standard, it is practically by definition a compiler that embraces that standard, and I have not felt a need to test the programs on any other compiler.[2]

To the extent that programs in the text make full use of the Fortran 90 standard, which supports syntax from earlier versions of Fortran, it is certain that many programs will be incompatible with compilers that, in an effort to simplify the language, use a restricted subset of the Fortran 90 standard and consciously avoid supporting certain syntax forms. For example, such compilers may support PARAMETER used as an attribute in a type declaration statement, but not a separate PARAMETER statement. Although it would not be difficult to bring the programs in this text into conformity with such language subsets, I have chosen not to do so, as that seems to me to place unreasonable restrictions on students' use of the language.

---

[1]It is somewhat misleading to refer to FTN90 as a "Windows 95" compiler because it is not a Windows application. Rather, it runs comfortably as a DOS application under Windows 95, without the memory management problems that plagued earlier versions.

[2]I would like to think that this loyalty to the NAG/Salford Software compiler has not been inappropriately influenced by the fact that Numerical Algorithms Group, Inc. generously provided both MS-DOS and Windows versions of its FTN90 compiler while this text was being written.

i.2 Overview for Students

i.2.1 The Purpose of This Text

Over the past few years, there has been a growing realization among your instructors that traditional introductory programming courses have not been meeting your needs. In response, many introductory programming texts have shifted their emphasis away from a computer-science-oriented approach to programming and toward an approach that emphasizes the problem-solving applications of high-level programming languages.

Fortran texts were the first to make this welcome change, as Fortran has long been associated with practical computing applications in engineering and science. However, the Fortran 77 language standard, which has been taught to the generation of students preceding you, has some deficiencies when compared to more modern languages such as C and Pascal. Without going into the details (you can read Section i.1 of this Preface, the Overview for Instructors, if you are curious), the new Fortran 90 standard has revitalized Fortran by providing many of the features that are expected of a modern high-level procedural programming language. Thus the purpose of this text is to introduce you to this new language standard in a way that meets the problem-oriented needs of science and engineering students.

i.2.2 The Approach Taken by the Text

When I started to write this text, I tried to think carefully about my own learning strategy. How do I learn a new programming language? For me, the answer to this question seemed clear: "Show me an example." Once I see a program that works, I can apply the lessons contained in that example to other situations.

Not surprisingly, then, this text is based on the premise that the best way to learn how to solve problems on a computer is to follow a step-by-step procedure and to study good examples. Chapter 2 presents a five-step approach to problem solving and an "action command" language that you can use to solve computational problems in any high-level procedural programming language, of which Fortran is one. This "pseudocode" language doesn't have any grammar rules, so you can concentrate on the solution to a problem rather than the details of a new language.

I understand that you are eager to start seeing results from your own Fortran programs, so Chapter 2 includes a simple program you can copy and execute. However, my own teaching experience has demonstrated that time spent thinking about how to organize programs away from a computer will be time very well spent.

Starting in Chapter 3, the details of the Fortran language are presented. At this point, as you can probably guess, grammar rules suddenly become very important. New programming concepts are often introduced by posing a computational problem, presenting a solution, and then generalizing from this specific solution to a broader understanding of programming concepts and their Fortran implementation. I have chosen the approach of moving from the specific to the general because it matches my own style of learning by example. I understand that this may not match your learning style, but I hope it will help at least to be aware of why this text is written the way it is.

Solutions to problems are always implemented using the five-step approach presented in Chapter 2. Each chapter starting with the third includes at least two complete programming applications to help you integrate new material into your expanding programming skills. These applications are drawn from topics you will encounter in introductory science, engineering, and mathematics courses. Some of the applications appear more than once, when new programming skills can provide a better or more comprehensive solution.

In keeping with my belief that examples are important learning tools, this text contains many complete programs in addition to the applications. To get the most out of the text, you should study *every* program carefully and try to understand the purpose of every line of code. You can—and should—download the source code and data files, where applicable, from the World Wide Web site given in Section *i.1.6* of this Preface. However, you should not overlook the fact that the physical act of entering programs yourself, from a computer keyboard, is a process that will help you develop the mechanical skills required for efficient programming.

"Style" is an important part of programming, but it's difficult to explain and teach except by example. For reasons having to do with its historical development, Fortran is a language that can easily be abused to produce programs that do not meet widely accepted standards of modern programming style. I have tried to make every example in this text a model of good programming style. In order to attain this goal, many choices have been made about how Fortran should be used. These choices often will not be obvious to a beginning programmer; for example, some forms of Fortran syntax simply don't appear in the text because their use is inconsistent with good programming style.

Not everyone—including your instructor—will agree with every stylistic choice I have made. Fortran 90 is a much more flexible language than its predecessors, so there is more room for personal preferences. Thus you should expect programs from other sources to look somewhat different, and it's certainly possible that your instructor may have different ideas. However, some of the choices are so important that I don't believe they should be negotiable as matters of personal style. (I have tried to be clear about these when they occur.) Until you are confident in your own ability to write programs that are easy to understand, debug, and modify, I encourage you to imitate the style used in this text.

In each chapter you will find three kinds of exercises:

1. "Self-testing" exercises that test your basic understanding of the concepts and syntax presented in the chapter.

2. "Basic programming" exercises that often involve modifications to programs in the text. The purpose of such exercises is to encourage you to study the programs in the text more thoroughly than you might otherwise do.

3. "Programming applications" that involve writing complete programs dealing with the kinds of engineering, science, and mathematics problems you are likely to encounter in other courses.

I have tried to arrange these programming exercises roughly in order of increasing difficulty. The more difficult exercises may require more sophisticated mathematical skills even though the programs themselves may not be particularly difficult to write. You should spend as much time as possible with these exercises.

i.2.3 What Does This Textbook Expect from You...

Every textbook incorporates some assumptions about the students who will use it, and this one is no exception. It assumes that you are a freshman or a sophomore in a science or engineering curriculum or that, for whatever other reason, you need an introduction to the problem-solving and computing skills required for such disciplines. No previous programming experience is required, but the text assumes that you already have, or will be able to acquire quickly on your own, a working knowledge of computers; to use the cliché, it assumes that you are already "computer literate." The truth of the matter is that if you are not comfortable working with computers, you will be at a disadvantage in *any* programming course.

The examples, applications, and exercises in the text assume that you are familiar with algebra and trigonometry and are comfortable thinking about mathematical problems at that level. Many of you will already have been exposed to some fundamental concepts of calculus or will be taking a first course in calculus at the same time you are taking a course that uses this text; some of the applications and exercises later in the text will make more sense if this is true.

Because this is a text intended for science and engineering students, the programs in the text and the programming exercises naturally involve problems from science and engineering. This means that the terminology required to state a problem may sometimes be unfamiliar. The reality is that problem solving and computer programming often have to be done in an environment that includes a little uncertainty and insecurity, and I must assume that you won't be discouraged.

In return, I have tried to give you enough information to understand a problem without overwhelming you with too much detail. In some cases, I have included representative output to help you verify your program's operation.

Learning a new programming language requires thought and practice. Some students seem to believe that they can learn to write programs just by reading *about* programming. Obviously, it is a good idea to read and study this text carefully. However, the only way to become proficient at using any programming language is to write programs. The bottom line is that you can't learn to program in Fortran without practice any more than you can learn to speak a foreign language without practice.

i.2.4 ...and What Does It Offer in Return?

Too often, students approach programming as an activity unrelated to their other courses. I hope this text will prevent that from happening by providing you with the problem-solving skills you will need to use a computer effectively throughout your college and professional career. The skills required to use a language such as Fortran are essential not just for writing programs, but also for understanding other computer applications, and even for solving problems without computers. In summary, unlike the details of a specific programming language, the problem-solving skills you can learn from this text will never be out of date.

On a more general level, I believe that learning how to program really *is* good for your character. In my own teaching of freshmen, I often see students who have excellent mathematics backgrounds and extensive experience with computers. They *should* do well in a programming course. However, they often have poor study habits and lack the self-discipline to manage their time effectively in a learning environment that offers more personal freedom than they had in high school. For these students, learning how to succeed in college is as much a personal challenge as an intellectual one. A programming course is an excellent (if arguably perverse) environment in which to develop these skills.

Finally, when you learn to write programs with Fortran 90, you get all the traditional advantages of Fortran, which is still the most widely used language in science and engineering. At the same time, you will be learning a language that has much in common with other languages, such as C, that you may want to learn later.

i.3 Useful References for Fortran 90

For reasons discussed earlier in this Preface, this text is not intended to take the place of a Fortran reference manual. I have found two books useful for filling this need:

Adams, J. C., W. S. Brainerd, J. T. Martin, B. T. Smith, and J. L. Wagener (1992). *Fortran 90 Handbook: Complete ANSI/ISO Reference*. Intertext Publications, McGraw-Hill Book Company, New York.

Metcalf, M., and J. Reid (1996). *Fortran 90/95 Explained*. Oxford Science Publications, Oxford University Press, Oxford. (This book is included with the FTN90 compiler used for the programs in this text.)

i.4 Contacting the Author

I look forward to hearing your comments and constructive criticism about this text and being informed of any typographical and other errors you might find, as well as receiving feedback on your classroom experiences as a student or as an instructor. I can be reached on the Internet at brooksdr@duvm.ocs.drexel.edu.

i.5 Obtaining Source Code and Data Files for Programs in this Text

The source code and data files for all programs in the text can be downloaded from the publisher's World Wide Web site:

http://www.springer-ny.com/supplements/dbrooks

Also available at this site are sample data files for all exercises that require them. Instructors using the text are invited to contact Customer Service at Springer-Verlag, 175 Fifth Avenue, New York, N. Y. 10010, in writing on department letterhead, to obtain source code and data files for all programming exercises in the text. The source code file names are given in brackets following each problem statement in the exercises.

i.6 Acknowledgments

I would like to thank Dr. Martin Gilchrist, Computing Editor at Springer-Verlag, for his interest in and support of this project, and Numerical Algorithms Group, Inc. for the use of its MS-DOS and Windows 95 FTN90 compilers since the earliest versions of this text were being written. Also, I would like to thank my partner, Susan Caughlan, for her editorial oversight and her many allowances for the time required to complete this project.

Contents

1

Computing Environments for Problem Solving

This chapter offers a very brief history of electronic computing and an equally brief description of some of the features of computing environments you are likely to encounter during a course based on this text. It also includes a discussion of the role of Fortran and programming in the problem-solving process.

1.1 A Brief History of Electronic Computing

1.1.1 The First Generation

The **electronic computer**[1] has existed for only about half a century. The ENIAC (Electronic Numerical Integrator and Computer), built at the University of 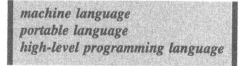 Pennsylvania with funding from the U.S. Army in 1946, is generally considered to be the first successful programmable electronic computer. It was a one-of-a-kind research tool designed to perform calculations for the military, but by 1951 its descendant, the UNIVAC I, became the first mass-produced electronic computer. This was the beginning of the first generation of computing. In 1953, International Business Machines (IBM) began manufacturing computers, and it soon dominated the scientific and business market with its model 650.

The ENIAC could be programmed only by rewiring its circuits manually through large "patch panels," a lengthy process that clearly limited its general usefulness. Later, computers were (and continue to be) programmable with **machine language** instructions specific to a particular kind of computer. During the first generation of computing, the concept of a standardized **portable language** was developed. This allowed programmers to write programs that would work on more than one kind of computer. Specialized **high-level programming languages** such as

---

[1]All words or phrases printed in bold italics are defined in the Glossary at the end of this text.

FORTRAN (the original spelling, adopted from FORmula TRANslation) and COBOL (COmmon Business-Oriented Language) were developed for scientific and business applications.[2]

1.1.2 The Second and Third Generations

First-generation computers used vacuum-tube technology. They were large and heavy and consumed a great deal of power. The ENIAC weighed 30 tons, used about 18,000 vacuum tubes, and lined the walls of a large room. The limitations of vacuum-tube technology spurred research into solid-state electronics, which led to the invention of the transistor in 1948. In 1959, the first transistorized computers marked the beginning of computing's second generation. Again, IBM dominated the market and produced several successful series of computers targeted at users ranging from small businesses to large scientific research institutions.

The third generation of computing started in the mid 1960s, as computer manufacturers switched from discrete transistors to even smaller integrated circuits. By this time, computer systems and their peripheral equipment had become sufficiently complicated that they needed to be managed by teams of professionals. These computers were amazingly fragile devices that consumed large amounts of power, generated a lot of waste heat, and therefore required special environmental controls to function reliably. As a result, during this period of **centralized computing** using **mainframe computers**, scientists, engineers, and other computer users were physically isolated from the machines that served their needs. Besides learning a high-level programming language such as Fortran, computer users also needed to learn how to maneuver around sometimes daunting institutional barriers; the computer centers at colleges, universities, large corporations, and research laboratories could be as difficult to master (in the organizational sense) as programming itself.

However, a revolution was about to take place. The introduction of **minicomputers**— simple enough to be maintained by one or two people, yet powerful enough for all but the largest and most complex computing tasks—brought a new level of direct involvement by engineers and scientists in the computing process. By using minicomputers to decrease their reliance on a central computing facility, computer users could set their own priorities and accumulate the hardware and software that was best suited

centralized computing
mainframe computers

minicomputers
decentralized computing

---

[2]Much has been made of whether Fortran should be spelled FORTRAN (*i.e.*, with all uppercase letters). Earlier versions of the language used the latter spelling, but Fortran is now the preferred spelling.

for their own research tasks. This was the start of serious *decentralized computing*. In some organizations, computer managers engaged in bitter infighting against the proponents of decentralized computing in an attempt to maintain the prestige and funding that accompanied control over computing equipment and facilities; eventually, they lost the battles and the war, and the rest, as they say, is history.

Remote access to large mainframe computers through electronic terminals also brought computing closer to people who were interested in solving science 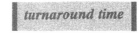 and engineering problems rather than in the details of the computers themselves. It was now possible to use computers without ever traveling to the computer center. This greatly reduced the *turnaround time* for computational tasks.[3]

Another significant computing milestone was the development of BASIC (Beginners All-Purpose Symbolic Instruction Code). Even though it was never intended to challenge Fortran as a "serious" programming language, BASIC introduced the problem-solving capabilities of a high-level language to nonspecialists from many disciplines, including those whose professional interests could not justify the investment of time required to learn a more complex language.

1.1.3 The Fourth Generation

In view of BASIC's success as a "personal" programming language, it was inevitable that hardware appropriate for *personal computers* would also be developed. This part of the computer revolution began in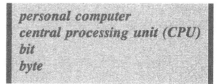

---

[3]Author's note: when I was working at the National Aeronautics and Space Administration's Langley Research Center during the 1970s, the presence of a remote access terminal on a researcher's desk was perceived by coworkers as a status symbol and viewed with great suspicion by supervisors. Among coworkers, the terminal advertised the fact that its owner would no longer have to use "punch card machines" to generate programs and would no longer have to make the long walk to the computer center to submit and retrieve "batch jobs." To supervisors, the sight of research personnel working at terminals looked too much like "typing," an activity they considered unworthy of skilled professionals! However, the advantages of being able to write, edit, and debug programs in electronic form were so overwhelming that these terminals soon became a permanent feature in every researcher's office.

Later, when personal and distributed computing appeared to be on its way to diluting the power accumulated by computing professionals, NASA refused to allow researchers to buy computing equipment for their own use. At one time, it was possible to circumvent this ban by referring to computers as "electronic calculators," but this ruse was not successful for long.

1971 when Intel released the first microprocessor—a complete *central processing unit (CPU)*, the 4004, on a single chip. Its basic unit of storage was a "word" consisting of four *bits*, each bit representing the "on" or "off" state of an electronic circuit or some other kind of storage device. This CPU was followed the next year by Intel's 8008 and in 1973 by the 8080. These CPUs used an eight-bit word (a storage unit now universally referred to as one *byte*). These chips were the predecessors of Intel's 8086/8088, 80286, 80386, 80486, and Pentium chips that drove much of the personal computing revolution in the 1980s and into the 1990s.

The first microprocessors were used for "pocket" calculators, which were actually a little too bulky to fit in pockets. However, in January 1975, the first widely available *microcomputer*, the Intel 8080-based Altair, was the cover story in *Popular Electronics* magazine. It consisted basically of a CPU in a box. It had no keyboard, no monitor, no external storage device, just 256 bytes of *random access memory* (RAM) and no *read-only memory* (ROM). It was hailed as a "real" computer because it could be programmed, but only by setting switches on its front panel. The Altair 8080 was offered in kit form for about $400, and 2000 of them—ten times the original estimate—were quickly sold.

> *microcomputer*
> *random access memory (RAM)*
> *read-only memory (ROM)*
> *personal computer*

At that time, traditional computer users were interested only in larger and larger computers, not in what appeared to be no more than an interesting toy. It's interesting that, far removed from the influence of the military, commercial, and scientific forces that had always driven the development of computing, the first personal computer was sold to amateur electronics experimenters.

The pivotal event that started the personal computer revolution is widely recognized as the development in the late 1970s of the *Apple II*. This computer quickly developed a huge following among hobbyists and in the educational market, but it was virtually ignored by commercial and scientific computer users. Significant inroads into these markets began with IBM's introduction in 1981 of the *IBM-PC*. The original PC was quickly replaced by the more powerful IBM-XT and IBM-AT series of machines. The backing of the world's foremost computer manufacturer guaranteed the rapid integration of this new technology into a wide range of computing activities, including tasks traditionally reserved for mainframe computers and new applications designed specifically with personal computing in mind.

> *Apple II*
> *IBM-PC*

IBM's decision to compete against Apple's proprietary hardware and operating system by developing an "open architecture" using readily available components led virtually overnight to the development of an entire industry devoted to

> *IBM-clone*
> *IBM-compatible*
> *graphical interface*
> *text-based interface*

producing *IBM clones*—computers compatible at the hardware and software level with IBM's personal computers. A highly competitive environment drove down prices and accelerated development of increasingly powerful systems. It is difficult to overestimate the influence of these products on the development of computing. Even though IBM quickly lost its dominant role in the development and marketing of personal computers, *IBM-compatible* hardware and software continued to define the development of the personal computer industry. Even after the IBM-PC itself became obsolete in terms of computing power, market forces required software to be "backward compatible" with the IBM-PC standard until the development of *graphical interfaces* (as opposed to *text-based interfaces*) in the late 1980s. These new interfaces imposed hardware requirements that were simply beyond what could be supported by the original IBM-PC. Even then, however, the concept of IBM compatibility continued to drive the development of software and hardware for personal computing.

There were only a few other important ventures in the early days of personal computing. In the late 1970s, Radio Shack (Tandy), Atari, and Commodore developed relatively inexpensive personal computers. These were widely accepted as "home" computers and were used mostly for games, although Commodore (with its famous Commodore 64) developed a modest following in the educational market. However, these computers lacked the power and flexibility to make significant inroads in the commercial and scientific workplace.

Of the early contenders, only Apple, with its Macintosh computers, developed "serious" computers that managed to cut significantly into the near-monopoly enjoyed by IBM-compatible computers for scientific and business uses during the 1980s. Apple developed a user-friendly graphical interface that was especially attractive to the educational market. These same IBM and Macintosh systems also monopolized the home market, as more and more people wanted a computer at home that worked just like the one they used in the office.

The differences between IBM-compatible and Macintosh computers are fundamentally hardware-based, but they are seen most clearly in their *operating systems*—the "invisible" software that manages the basic functions of a computer. Apple and Macintosh computers use a proprietary operating system. When IBM needed an

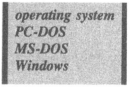

operating system for its new PC, it turned to a then obscure company, Microsoft, which developed the first version of *PC-DOS* and its "clone" version, *MS-DOS*, perhaps the most famous computer operating systems ever developed. Since then, almost all IBM-compatible personal computers have used a version of MS-DOS. More recently, Microsoft developed *Windows*, a graphical interface that competes head-on with (and, some might say, flagrantly attempts to imitate) the Apple/Macintosh operating system.

It is definitely a cliché to marvel at the "exponential growth" in the power of personal computers. At least the cliché is justified. Figure 1.1 shows the growth in three important specifications for typical PCs available during the decade starting around 1985–86: CPU speed, RAM size, and hard drive size.[4] At the beginning of this period, 8088-based PCs were being replaced by computers using Intel's 80286 CPU chip. Computers based on this chip could run only a single application at a time, and the character-based interface placed relatively small demands on system memory. At the beginning of this period, 1.2-MB floppy diskette drives (using the 5¼" format) were standard on mainstream systems and hard drives were an expensive luxury.

As shown in Figure 1.1, each of these three measures of computing power has undergone exponential growth since 1986. CPU speed has increased by a factor of about 40 over the decade, driven by the demands of increasingly large and sophisticated software. Typical RAM specifications have also increased by a factor of approximately 40, from under 500 KB to 16 MB; these increases are due to operating systems that allow several tasks to run simultaneously as well as larger and more sophisticated graphically based applications that require a great deal of memory. Growth in the size of graphically based software—both the applications themselves and the large files they produce—has driven the dramatic increase in permanent magnetic storage capacity from the "luxury" of 10- and 20-MB hard drives to typical drives in excess of 2 GB.

What has *not* increased exponentially is the cost of mainstream personal computing. Complete systems with the specifications shown in Figure 1.1 have been available throughout the entire decade at a remarkably consistent price of approximately $2500–$3000. This is even more remarkable because, taking into account the effects of inflation, $3000 represents a significantly smaller investment in 1996 than it did in 1986. Thus the real cost of a mainstream personal computer has actually decreased substantially at the same time that its capabilities have undergone the meteoric growth shown in Figure 1.1.

1.2 The Academic Computing Environment

There is perhaps no undertaking so certain to make an author look foolish and out of date as describing the "current" computing environment, since any such description is sure to be on its way to obsolescence even as it is written. Nonetheless, it is worthwhile to try to follow up to the present the historical progression outlined briefly in this chapter.

---

[4]These data come from the specifications of typical, not state-of-the-art, systems advertised and reviewed in *PC Magazine*, a magazine devoted to Intel-based PC computing.

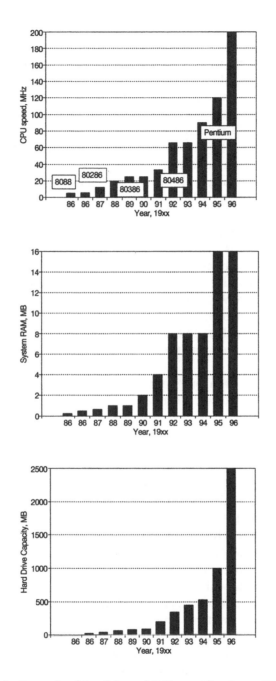

Figure 1.1. Growth of Intel-based PC specifications, 1986–1996

First of all, the historical division of labor between mainframes and minicomputers has little current relevance. Historically, mainframes monopolized scientific and engineering applications for the simple reason that only large computers were adequate for the computational tasks of interest to scientists and engineers. To a certain extent, this remains true today. Some of the most important scientific and engineering challenges of our time, such as global climate modeling and aeronautical design, still tax the capabilities of even the largest *supercomputers*. These are characterized by their support of specialized operating systems and languages (including high-performance versions of Fortran for advanced scientific and engineering computing). However, the role of the traditional mainframe computer has been greatly diminished by dramatic increases in the power of desktop computers.

supercomputer

The traditional minicomputer, which freed an entire generation of scientists and engineers from centralized computing, has essentially ceased to exist. Now the needs of relatively small communities of computer users are met with personal computers, *workstations*, and computers whose capabilities defy easy categorization as either mainframes or minicomputers. All these computers are typically interconnected through a *network* that provides communication between hardware and multiple users and thereby greatly extends the capabilities of single machines.

workstation network

How will you learn programming within this highly decentralized and rapidly evolving environment? There are basically two possibilities.

1.2.1 The Department-Based Computing Environment

Most academic computing is now done at the department level with machines that typically use the *UNIX* operating system, support remote access and *multitasking* for many simultaneous users, have shared *peripherals*, and are managed by a department-financed support staff. Basically, such systems are designed to meet all the computing needs of a specific community of users; a large university will have many such systems as well as a campus-wide network that links at least some parts of all these systems together.

UNIX multitasking peripherals

Typically, such systems can allocate their resources among many users so that no single user is even aware of the presence of others. Only with large computational tasks, or when human intervention is required, are individual users aware of limitations to *throughput*—the rate at which a computer system completes all the computational and related tasks associated with a particular job. In fact, you will probably never experience any significant throughput or turnaround time delays with the kinds of

programs you will write in an introductory programming course. Any delay of more than a few seconds in executing a program is much more likely to be a sign of problems with that program than a sign of throughput limitations.

If your institution maintains a traditional mainframe computer, it probably supports Fortran (although perhaps not Fortran 90). However, it is unlikely that you will use a mainframe for an introductory programming course. Faculty tend not to use such computers for their own research; these machines are more likely to be used for administrative purposes than for research and teaching.

On a department computer, you will be assigned an *account ID* and a unique *password*.[5] Typically, you will be able to access the computer from a terminal in a computer center or lab, or from your own personal computer *via* a

modem. If you live in a dormitory, you may be able to connect your personal computer to a campus-wide network simply by plugging a cable into a wall jack.

You will probably be given an electronic mail (*e-mail*) account and access to the *Internet*. You may be able to participate in electronic discussion groups that deal with course-related matters or allow you to communicate directly with your instructor. Course notes

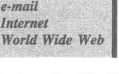

and homework assignments may be distributed electronically through a *World Wide Web* page.

The sequences of instructions required to *logon* to a department computer, create and edit a program, execute that program, and *logoff* the computer vary widely among computer

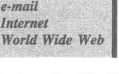

systems and institutions. Even institutions with the same kind of computer hardware may have rules and procedures that apply only at that institution, so it's pointless to try to give even a typical scenario beyond telling you that you will need to provide an account ID and a password. Later in the text, we will describe the general steps required to create and execute a Fortran program, but the specific procedures applicable to the computing environment you will be using must be provided by your instructor.

1.2.2 The Personal Computing Environment

One milestone during the personal computer revolution was the point at which the capabilities of PCs allowed traditional mainframe languages such as Fortran to be

---

[5]There is an important distinction between an account ID and a password. An account ID is public information that identifies you to the computer system and other users. A password is private information that protects your work from other users. You should *never* share your password with anyone!

implemented on a desktop computer. This was almost exclusively an IBM-compatible phenomenon. The migration of Fortran from mainframes and minicomputers to the desktop has been successful, and it is entirely possible that you will learn to program in Fortran on a PC.

Unlike many other PC applications, Fortran doesn't depend on a graphical interface. Although it is certainly possible to "package" a Fortran programming environment within a graphical interface, the language itself is text-based, contains no graphics capabilities as part of the language standard, and is therefore perfectly at home in the text-based MS-DOS environment. Nonetheless, Windows-based PCs are the current standard, so you will probably develop Fortran programs from within this environment.

1.3 What Do You Need to Know About Your Computing Environment?

One of the major reasons to learn a language such as Fortran is to isolate the programmer from the system-level operation of a particular computer. However, regardless of the kind of computer system you use to learn how to program in Fortran, there are several things that you need to know about that system.

1. What kind of operating system does the computer have?
Is it UNIX, Windows, or something else? Will you be writing Fortran programs in an MS-DOS environment even if your PC is running Windows?

2. How do you perform basic file-related tasks?
Do you know how to name, create, search, and maintain directories? Do you know how to name, create, examine, edit, and delete files?

3. Do you understand how to use storage capabilities on your system?
Do you know how to examine and modify your PC's hard drives and other electronic storage media, such as backup tapes and CD-ROMs? Do you understand the directory structure and memory limitations of your department's computer?

4. Do you understand how to use telecommunications?
Can you attach your PC to a campus network? Do you know how to send and receive e-mail and how to manage your e-mail directory? Do you know how to communicate electronically with your instructor? Do you know how to access an electronic class folder or course-related material on a World Wide Web page?

The exercises at the end of this chapter provide more suggestions for things you should know about the computer systems you will use.

1.4 Fortran and the Personal Computing Environment

It is clear that PCs are now essential tools for scientists and engineers. This would be true even if Fortran were not available for PCs because of the availability of a wide range of sophisticated computing tools. However, the development of personal computing has been driven by a basically commercial market, and it has not always been obvious that PCs would, or could, play a major role in serious scientific and engineering computing.

Historically, Fortran has been the essential interface between scientists or engineers and a computer, and this relationship continues in many areas of research and applications. However, the availability of fully functional versions of Fortran for PCs requires a re-examination of the role of Fortran relative to other languages and other kinds of software.

Fortran was invented for doing numerical calculations. Its primary advantages for science and engineering are that it provides powerful and flexible computational and data-handling capabilities and it represents a stable, well-defined language standard. Its primary shortcoming, which it shares with some other high-level languages, is that it was developed for use in a text-based computing environment and it includes no intrinsic graphics capabilities.[6] The previous standard, Fortran 77, was adopted by an international committee in 1978 and remained in place until the adoption of Fortran 90 in 1991. Many enhancements and changes have been added to versions of Fortran 77 in actual use, but the standard itself has remained unchanged in the sense that *every* Fortran 77 implementation includes, or at least *should* include, the standard as a subset.

The new Fortran 90 language accepts the entire Fortran 77 standard as a subset. Because Fortran 77 in turn accepts the entire previous Fortran version (Fortran IV) as a subset, Fortran 90 provides a programming standard that is backward-compatible with programs written decades ago. Most important, Fortran 90 contains many new features, including many of the nonstandard enhancements developed for Fortran 77 programming environments.

Fortran's problem-solving competition includes three major classes of software: *spreadsheets* such as Excel, Lotus 1-2-3, and Quattro Pro; *computer algebra systems* such

> *spreadsheet*
> *computer algebra system*
> *data analysis and statistics software*

as Maple and Mathematica; and *data analysis and statistics software* such as SPSS and Statistica. These have all been developed, at least in commercial versions, within the shadow of the PC revolution, and most didn't even exist when the previous Fortran standard was adopted in 1978. All provide powerful

---

[6]There are many different "add-in" graphics packages available for Fortran compilers, but they are not part of the language standard.

capabilities for solving particular kinds of problems and include sophisticated graphical interfaces and display capabilities. Of these three, spreadsheets are generally recognized as the "killer app(lication)" that turned the personal computer from an interesting toy into an essential commercial and scientific tool.

A major potential disadvantage of these powerful applications is their lack of standardization. Indeed, because of the competitive nature of the commercial software market, there are actually strong disincentives to standardization; from a marketing perspective, it may be more important to have unique capabilities than to adhere to a standard. Nowhere is this conflict more evident than with spreadsheets, the most widely used problem-solving software. Attempts by some companies to make their products work just like their more successful competitors have led to legal battles over whether duplicating the "look and feel" of someone else's software is desirable in the sense that it promotes standardization in an important class of PC applications or whether it constitutes a theft of intellectual property.

In contrast with Fortran's development, the pace of change in the commercial software market has been so rapid that a company's latest version may not even completely support its own previous versions. It is even less likely that applications from one company will be compatible with those from another company. These incompatibilities became especially severe in the PC environment as software companies switched from MS-DOS to Windows products.

A lack of standardization in problem-solving software can be especially alarming to scientists and engineers. With Fortran, programs written many years ago will still work today, often without even minor modification. This is extremely important for large and complex programs, as it is difficult and time-consuming, and therefore expensive, to reinvent solutions to the kinds of complex computing problems Fortran is often used to solve. Reworking algorithms for new computing environments is always a risky undertaking, and it is even more of a problem to guarantee the performance of algorithms that *appear* to work in a software environment that lacks widely accepted performance standards.

There have been some attempts by the dominant software companies in the commercial PC software market to make at least the files generated by their products translatable by and for their competitors. As the marketplace has weeded out the less robust competitors and despite legal challenges, the capabilities and even the "look and feel" of the remaining spreadsheet products have come closer together. In spite of the corporate desire to maintain a unique identity, spreadsheets are so similar that even casual users shouldn't have much trouble making the transition from one product to another. However, there is still no equivalent of the international standardization that Fortran enjoys. For algebra and statistics software, there is even less standardization. Files are generally incompatible and the commands required to achieve similar objectives differ from one product to the next. In critical problem-solving applications, it is the details that count, and it is not sufficient to have merely "similar" products.

Scientists and engineers are faced, then, with two completely different kinds of problem-solving environments. The Fortran environment provides the standardization and stability required for complex calculations, but it suffers from its "old-fashioned" mainframe heritage. The other environment makes better use of PC and workstation capabilities, but presents a bewildering jumble of incompatible and volatile products.

The migration of Fortran to PCs provides one obvious way to maximize the return from both these problem-solving environments. This is surely a better idea than what would be widely viewed as the backward step of bringing PC-based applications to large computers, including traditional mainframes. (There has, in fact, been relatively little migration of PC applications to mainframe computers, but a massive migration in the other direction.) One obvious link between Fortran and other applications is spreadsheets. We can ask Fortran to perform the kind of computationally intensive tasks at which it excels and then to produce output data in a format that can be accepted as input to spreadsheets. This allows us to do complex calculations in the stable programming environment provided by Fortran. In particular, we will be able to use the vast libraries of "canned" Fortran software that is available for solving a wide range of computational problems.

If we then "import" the output from Fortran programs into a spreadsheet, graphics display capabilities are immediately available. Although it is possible to add graphics to Fortran, it is reasonable to ask if this is worth the effort for any but the most specialized problems. We can use spreadsheets to visualize results and even perform simple analyses, and we won't have to worry about trying to ask Fortran to do something that requires a software "add-in" to the language standard. This is entirely feasible, especially for analyzing and displaying "static" data, and some typical results are evident in the spreadsheet-generated graphics for many of the applications and exercises you will find throughout this text. If the required graphics become more sophisticated—for example, if you require visualizations for dynamic data—then you will have to use more specialized tools.

The danger in building synergistic relationships among computer applications lies in the volatility of these applications. The rate of change in computer hardware and software has been driven by commercial forces that far exceed those acting on scientific computing and formal programming languages. For commercial applications, success is measured by market share. For scientific applications, measures such as professional credibility and language stability retain their importance. Regardless of the driving forces, rapid changes in any part of the computing environment can pose a significant problem for students, professionals, and the authors and publishers of texts such as this one.

By the time you purchase this text, it is certain that the kinds of hardware and problem-solving software available when the text was being written will have been replaced with new versions. Because of the rapid pace of change in computing technology, students and professionals must constantly upgrade their skills just to stay even.

Fortunately, rapid change won't be much of a problem for this text. Because Fortran is the most stable programming environment in history,[7] and because the Fortran 90 standard is new, specific details of the material in this text will not be quickly outdated. You should be able to use the language you will learn from this text without modification on any computer that supports the Fortran 90 standard. Unlike commercial PC applications, there are no version-dependent tricks, no flashy user interfaces, and nothing about learning Fortran that will be fundamentally altered by having a CPU that's ten times faster and more powerful than the one your computer is using now. If you're using Fortran on a department computer, you may never perceive *any* changes in your operating environment even though changes may be occurring at the system level.

In addition, this text stresses basic problem-solving principles that will continue to apply *regardless* of the computing tools you are using. If the text is successful, the skills you learn will be easily transferable to any new problem-solving environment.

1.5 Is Programming Necessary Anymore?

As programming developed as an activity that could be undertaken not only by computer scientists, but also by others who needed computers for their professional work, the question arose as to who should teach programming to students outside the computer science curriculum. In many colleges and universities, such courses have traditionally been taught by computer science faculty. In the extreme, faculty with a computer science background may approach this task with the attitude that the problems programs are written to solve are of negligible interest compared to the art and science of programming *per se*.

Such an attitude annoys scientists and engineers, for whom programming serves a fundamentally practical role as a problem-solving tool. From that perspective, computer programming conducted as an activity for its own sake has no great intrinsic value, even though it is common to find scientists and engineers who are highly skilled programmers.

The view that computers can and should serve practical, task-oriented ends has gained respectability due to the availability of problem-specific software for meeting many needs that used to require custom-written programs. Do you need to analyze some data? Use a statistics application. Need to plot a graph? Use a graphics application. Need to summarize a lab experiment? Use a spreadsheet.

---

[7]COBOL (Common Business-Oriented Language) might be the other contender for this title.

Need to solve an equation? Use a symbolic algebra application. With this much computing power available, is there any need to learn a traditional computer programming language that often requires a significant effort to learn and that is almost certainly not optimized to solve the problem you wish to solve? It is tempting to answer, no, not anymore.

However, it remains true that the process of learning how to write logically, and even elegantly, constructed computer programs encompasses a formal approach to solving problems whose value extends far beyond computer programming itself. For example, the process required to write a program to solve a system of linear equations is merely the formalization of the process required to solve that same problem by hand. A programmed solution even provides some extra benefits because the demands of writing a computer program that works correctly under a wide range of input conditions force the programmer to think carefully and in great detail about the computational demands of the problem.

Many engineers, scientists, and computer scientists continue to maintain that a complete reliance on "canned" software is a mistake because it discourages the development of independent problem-solving skills. In fact, they would argue, easy access to powerful computing tools makes these skills more important than ever before. The applicability of the old programming axiom "garbage in, garbage out" increases in proportion to the ease with which "garbage out" can be produced. The only way to minimize this problem is to be increasingly aware of the process as well as the answers being produced.

As a result of these considerations, there has been a growing realization on the part of those who teach programming that more attention should be paid to helping students apply the skills they learn in introductory programming courses. Computer science courses that just a few years ago would have dealt *only* with learning Pascal (the traditional first computer science language for an entire generation of computer science students) now place more emphasis on underlying problem-solving strategies and their application to disciplines other than computer science. A textbook that might have been titled, tongue-in-cheek, something like *Learning Pascal for Its Own Sake Regardless of Your Major* is now more likely to be titled, seriously, *C for Scientists and Engineers*. (The C programming language, or its derivative C++, has now replaced Pascal as a first language in nearly all computer science departments.)

This text tries always to avoid presenting programming as an end in itself. At the same time, it reasserts a traditional conviction that programming continues to be a valuable activity because of the broadly applicable problem-solving skills that are required to be successful in that endeavor. So you should not be surprised to find that the conclusion of this section is that computer programming is still a necessary skill for any student who aspires to a career in science or engineering.

1.6 Exercises

The purpose of the exercises in this chapter, which admittedly aren't exciting engineering applications, is to encourage you to assess your general computing skills and improve them where necessary. Even if an introductory course based on this text claims, as courses often do, that "no prior programming knowledge is assumed," you will still find yourself at a disadvantage if you are unfamiliar with computer hardware, standard applications such as word processors and spreadsheets, and telecommunications. Time spent on this chapter will give you a short but critical window of opportunity in which to address your shortcomings in these areas.

Exercise 1. Ask a computer support person for general information about your institution's or department's computer. What kind of computer is it? What kind of operating system does it have? Which languages and applications does it support? What kinds of access modes does it support?

Exercise 2. Find out if your institution's computer center offers "short courses" on using its facilities and sign up for one.

Exercise 3. If you don't already have an account on your institution's or department's computer, you may wish to get one even if you will do your programming on a PC. Ask your instructor or a computer support person about getting an account. Find out whether the account is temporary—for as long as you're enrolled in a particular course, for example—or "permanent"—for as long as you're enrolled as a student. If it's temporary, make sure you understand when it terminates and how you can avoid losing access to files stored under the account. Make sure you know how to access this computer from your computer center, home, or dormitory room.

Exercise 4. If you have a computer account and don't already know how to use e-mail, ask your instructor or computer support person for documentation on setting up and using e-mail. Together with a classmate, make sure you know how to send and receive messages and files, how to save messages for future reference, and how to erase old messages that you don't wish to save.

Exercise 5. Your institution probably provides a great deal of useful online information through such means as department networks, anonymous ftp, Gopher, or the World Wide Web. If you don't know what these terms mean, ask a computer support person and learn how to use them!

Exercise 6. Inventory the software applications that reside on the computers available to you. For each application, list the kinds of courses in which you could use that application. For example, a word processor will be useful in all your courses. A statistics package will be useful in a course that involves the analysis of laboratory data.

Exercise 7. Data files used for programming examples and exercises discussed later in the text can be downloaded from the World Wide Web site mentioned in Section i.5 of the Preface. These files were created on an MS-DOS-based system and have a .DAT file name extension. "Import" one of these files into a spreadsheet. Create a graph that helps you visualize the data in the file. You will have to import the data as a text file and "parse" the file to assign numerical and character data to columns. Consult your spreadsheet documentation. If you have never used a spreadsheet before, this will probably be a difficult exercise, but it will certainly be worthwhile to learn how to do it.

2

Solving Problems with a
High-Level Programming Language

This chapter presents a general approach to using computers to solve certain kinds of computational problems. It describes instructions and data types common to structured programming with high-level procedural languages and defines a specific strategy for developing algorithms that can easily be translated into a language such as Fortran. It includes a short Fortran program that you can copy and execute on the computer you will be using for a course based on this text.

2.1 Structured Programming and Problem Solving

2.1.1 A High-Level Programming Language Provides the Tool

Structured programming with a high-level language is an important technique for solving certain kinds of computational problems. It involves the process of writing computer

structured programming
control structures

programs that consist of English-like instructions written in the framework of a few **control structures** that determine the order in which those instructions are executed. Languages such as BASIC, C, Fortran, and Pascal are examples of high-level languages in which program instructions consist of words and a symbolic language of operators that, in many cases, resemble algebraic operators. To cite just two examples:

(1) Many high-level languages contain the instruction "print" or "write," and the words mean just what you expect—they display output from a program.

(2) The "+" sign is the addition operator in high-level programming languages, with the same meaning that it has in mathematics.

The **source code** of a program written in a high-level language is a sequence of instructions created according to a detailed set of rules. These rules define the **language syntax** that describes how instructions must be

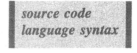

source code
language syntax

written in the same sense that the syntactic rules of the English language define the components and organizational structures of our written and spoken communication.

Source code that is free from syntax errors does not necessarily constitute a well-written or usable program. The instructions in a correctly written program must describe a logical, unambiguous, step-by-step approach to solving a clearly defined computational problem. Structured programming reflects a certain approach to organizing and writing such programs that makes them easy to understand, maintain, and modify.

Any of the programming languages mentioned above *can* be used to write structured programs, but not all programs written in these languages are necessarily "well structured." For example, there are many features of BASIC and older versions of Fortran that encourage a careless style of programming that cannot be called structured. Carelessly designed programs are more likely to contain *bugs* (mistakes). When bugs are found, either when the program can't be executed or when it produces output that doesn't make sense, the mistakes must be found and corrected. This process is called ***debugging***. Carelessly written programs are difficult to debug, and they are also difficult and expensive to maintain and modify.

Even though languages such as C, Pascal, and Fortran 90 are designed to encourage well-structured programs, it is certainly possible to write very poor programs in any of these languages. In summary, it is not the programming language itself that makes programs "structured," but the way that language is used.

Criticism of older Fortran programs for their sometimes unstructured style isn't entirely fair because the concepts of structured programming—and, for that matter, most of what is now called computer science—were developed only after Fortran had been invented. Many of the features found in Fortran 90, the new Fortran standard, have been strongly influenced by other languages, especially Pascal, which was developed specifically as a result of a more formal approach to structured programming. As a result, it is much easier to write structured programs in Fortran 90 than in its predecessors.

All the programming examples in this text strive to demonstrate a structured style worthy of emulation in your own programs. This emphasis on a particular style means that some features of the Fortran 90 language left over from earlier versions won't even be mentioned in this text. As a result, this text isn't intended as a complete reference for Fortran 90, but rather as an introduction to those parts of the language that are especially applicable to solving problems in science and engineering in a way that meets the stylistic standards expected of a modern programming language. One result of this approach is that you will find additional high-level languages easier to learn because they all share common standards of good programming style.

Once a program has been written in a high-level language, in the form of a source code file, a *compiler*—a separate program that is part of the programming environment—is used to start the process of translating the source code into a language that can be understood directly by a computer. For example, computers don't know how to interpret a high-level programming instruction to "print" something without a detailed set of hardware-specific instructions for sending the contents of certain memory locations to a particular device or output port on your computer. One job of the compiler is to provide these instructions.

Starting with the source code file, the compiler produces a *binary file* called an *object file*. This file contains translations into machine-level instructions of all the source code instructions; the file is no longer in a "human readable" form, and it is no longer portable to some other kind of computer. Next, a *linker*—another program that is part of the programming environment—is used to connect (link) the object file to other files that are necessary for the program to run. These include computer-specific translations of commands such as "print."

The result of the compiling and linking operation is an *executable file* that works only on the kind of computer 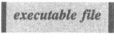 that was used to generate it. A Fortran source code file can be compiled on any computer that has an appropriate Fortran compiler, but an executable file generated on an IBM-compatible PC won't work on a Macintosh or a supercomputer, for example. Figure 2.1 illustrates the process of creating an executable file. Some details of this process will be discussed in Chapter 3.

One of the major advantages of programs written in a high-level language is their portability at the source code level. For the most part, source code written on one computer will work equally well on a variety of computers. If we use the "print" instruction as an example, any computer that has a Fortran compiler will know how to translate a "print" instruction to display output from your program. The computer-specific differences occur not at the source code level, but at the executable code level.

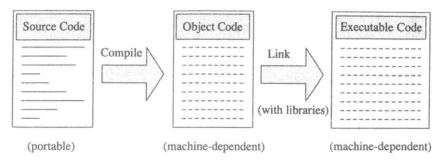

Figure 2.1. Compiling and executing a source code file

Minor changes in source code may sometimes be required when programs are executed on computers other than the one on which they were written. For example, if a Fortran source code file contains a reference to a *data file*, the syntax of that file's name must be recognizable by the computer system on which the program is being executed. Except for this kind of detail, the language compiler on each computer, not the programmer, is responsible for translating source code into appropriate machine-level instructions. Without this arrangement, it would be impractical to put sophisticated computing power directly in the hands of individuals who are interested in solving problems rather than in the operating details of computer systems.

In conclusion, the advantage of using a portable, high-level language for problem solving should be clear: you are free to concentrate on solving problems, rather than on the details of how a computer operates. The source code files for programs in this text have been written on an IBM-compatible PC. However, they should be directly transferable (except, in a few cases, for changing the names of data files, as noted above) to *any* computer that supports a standard Fortran 90 compiler.

2.1.2 Developing a Formal Approach to Problem Solving

A high-level programming language is of no value without a specific plan for applying it to solving problems. Such a plan can be stated as a sequence of five steps:

1 *Define the problem.*

2 *Outline a solution.*

3 *Design an algorithm.*

4 *Convert the algorithm into a program.*

5 *Verify the operation of the program.*

The process described by these steps is fundamental to quantitative problem solving in all areas of science and engineering (as well as other disciplines). The computational tools have changed over the years—slide rules and pocket calculators have been replaced by computers—but the process itself has remained essentially unchanged. These steps do not describe a process that is at all theoretical. Rather, they provide a practical guide to solving problems that is useful because it works. Learning how to apply the process requires practice. Consequently, these five steps will be applied to every programming example that appears in this text, even when one or more of the steps appear trivial.

Note that of the five steps, only the fourth—translation of an *algorithm* (a term we will define more formally in our discussion of Step 3) into a specific programming language—necessarily depends on the details of a particular programming language. In fact, most of the process applies equally, if less formally, to problems you solve in your head or with a pencil and paper.

When you first start to learn a programming language, it is easy to confuse the problem-solving process with the syntax and structural requirements of the language you are learning. This is a natural reaction because learning the details of a new programming language is a demanding undertaking, and because you don't yet have the experience to understand that problem-solving strategies can apply equally to any of several languages as well as other computer-based problem solving tools. With this in mind, however, you should try as much as possible to separate the task of learning the details of a particular language—the fourth step in the problem-solving process—from the other four steps.

Having made the distinction between programming and problem solving, you must also recognize that, especially when you are first learning to write programs, it will sometimes be necessary to combine the two. In order to minimize the potential difficulties, new programming concepts in this text are usually introduced in the context of a problem that is simple enough to allow you to concentrate on the programming details.

On the other hand, the focus of the programming applications that appear in every chapter (as well as the programming exercises at the end of each chapter) is always on solving realistic problems that will be relevant to your other science and engineering courses. In this case, the content of the problem becomes more important, and the Fortran language becomes simply a tool to solve that problem. The process of solving such problems in Fortran—including thinking about the capabilities and limitations of this particular problem-solving tool—will help you solve other kinds of problems even when they don't require a computer program.

Now we will examine each of the five problem-solving steps in more detail. Along the way, we will solve a simple programming problem.

1 *Define the problem.*

It is well known that cold weather feels even colder when the wind is blowing. This effect gives rise to what is commonly described as the windchill temperature—the temperature of still air that produces the same feeling of "coldness" as a person experiences when exposed to a combination of temperature and wind. Assuming that the windchill temperature depends only on the actual air temperature and the wind speed, develop an algorithm for calculating the windchill temperature.

A formula commonly used to compute the windchill temperature T_{wc} in °F, for ambient temperature T in °F and wind speed V in miles per hour, is

$$T_{wc} = (0.279\sqrt{V} + 0.550 - 0.0203\,V)(T - 91.4) + 91.4$$

where T < 91.4° F and V ≥ 4 mph. Write a program that accepts as input the temperature and wind speed and then calculates and displays the windchill temperature.

Especially in an introductory course, the problem definition may already have been done for you, as has been done here. The examples in this text and the end-of-chapter exercises involve problems that have been framed in a way that illustrates a particular point or tests your understanding of how to achieve a well-defined goal. After all, this is a text about solving problems with programs written in Fortran, so it doesn't make sense to ask you to solve a problem that can't reasonably be solved in this way. Nonetheless, it is always worthwhile to test your understanding of a problem by restating it in your own words, with additional elaboration as necessary.

If you have questions about the meaning of a problem, you need to resolve them before you can proceed to the next step. It may seem obvious that you can't solve a problem you don't understand, but it is common for beginning programming students to write programs that work, but that don't address part or all of the problem they were asked to solve.

In the "real world," it is often very difficult to define a problem and state it clearly. In order to formulate a problem in a useful way, you must understand not only the problem itself, but also the means available to solve it. If you don't understand something about the principles of structured programming and the capabilities of high-level programming languages, you can neither formulate nor solve computational problems. By the time you finish a course based on this text, you will have the experience you need to formulate computational problems so they can be solved in any of several high-level procedural programming languages. This experience will be of great value in solving other kinds of computational problems, no matter what tools you are using.

2   *Outline a solution.*

This problem has been chosen because the concept of "windchill" is widely known, but the formula for computing the windchill temperature is relatively obscure.[1] Also, the calculation is interesting because the formula exhibits some perhaps unexpected behavior. Your thought process for solving this problem, which is conceptually very simple, might be something like this:

> "Even though I don't understand the derivation of this formula, I will simply translate it directly into my algorithm and eventually into my program. My program will ask the user to provide the temperature and wind speed (by typing it at the keyboard?). I will be careful to let the user know what units to use. Then the program will do the calculations and display the results (on the computer monitor?)."

This outline doesn't have to be anything more than a rough, plain-English version of how you will solve the problem. You may not even have to write down this step after you gain more experience in designing algorithms. Your goal at this point is to organize your thoughts about the problem and its solution, not to worry about the implementation details.

If you don't understand how to solve a problem, you might need to have a discussion with your instructor to make sure you understand what is required and to get a general idea of how to proceed. You might have to look up formulas if they're not given as part of the problem statement, or you might need to rewrite formulas in a more convenient form.

It's important at this stage to clarify the nature of the input required and the output provided by the program you will eventually write. What information does the program need to do its job? Where does it come from? What should be included in the output? Where and how will the output be displayed? Will additional input or output, beyond what is called for in the problem statement, help to clarify the program's operation or verify its performance?

If you're like most students, you probably underestimate the value of simply thinking and talking about a difficult problem, especially when you're

---

[1] Author's note: It may be interesting to note that I found this formula in less than five minutes on the World Wide Web by searching for "windchill" at the www.yahoo.com site.

under time pressure to complete an assignment. If your instructor allows or encourages you to discuss assignments with your peers, you should set aside some time to "brainstorm" and trade ideas. It's often helpful just to "sleep on" a problem; if you think this is silly, just ask any good programmer how often solutions to a problem magically appear after a good night's sleep (or during a poor night's sleep)!

3 Design an algorithm.

An algorithm appropriate for implementation in a high-level procedural language consists of a complete set of instructions that can be followed step by step to achieve a well-defined computational objective. The instructions must be written so they can be executed one at a time, starting at the beginning. Here is an algorithm for solving this problem, using a format that we will follow throughout this text:

DEFINE *(all values as real numbers:*
       INPUT: temperature, wind_speed;
       OUTPUT: wind_speed_temperature)
WRITE *("Give the temperature in deg F and the wind speed in mi/hr:")*
READ *(temperature, wind_speed)*
ASSIGN *wind_chill_temperature =*
      0.0817(3.71$\sqrt{V}$ + 5.81 - 0.25V)(temperature - 91.4) + 91.4
WRITE *(wind_chill_temperature)*

The intent of this algorithm, which is written in a somewhat formal way, should be clear; it is nothing more than a straightforward translation of Step 2 of the problem-solving process. The terms appearing in bold type will be given specific definitions shortly, but their meaning essentially matches their obvious "plain English" meaning.

Writing down an algorithm prior to writing a program, especially for a problem this simple, may seem like a waste of time. However, many difficulties with computer programs can be traced to algorithms that can't be followed sequentially or that, when followed in sequence, don't lead to the intended solution. For example, it's possible, and a common error in computer programs, to write an instruction using information that's not yet available. A program containing such instructions can't possibly work because the instructions can't be followed in sequence. So, one purpose of writing an algorithm is to avoid these kinds of problems in programs, where they are harder to correct.

Initially, the instructions in your algorithm can be general. "Calculate the deflection on a beam supported at both ends" is an instruction with a clearly defined goal, even if the implementation details aren't obvious. Later on, as the general outline of your algorithm becomes clear, you will return to general statements and convert them to more specific instructions.

In this algorithm design example, the *variables*—the symbolic names by which quantities will be identified in a program—are given readable, meaningful names. This is an important part of making algorithms and programs easy to understand. You *could* have named the variables T, V, and T_wc. After all, those are the symbols used in the formula, and those choices would probably be clear enough. However, as a matter of style, it is better to choose longer descriptive names.

The rather formal algorithm designs we will use in this text are sometimes referred to as *pseudocode* because algorithms will often look very similar to the source code instructions you will finally write. For example, generic instructions such as "read" or "write" will often be required in your algorithms. These instructions, with similar or identical names, are common to Fortran and other high-level languages. The similarity between pseudocode and programming languages is not an accident. By incorporating just a few pseudocode "action commands," you can write algorithms in a form that can easily be translated into language-specific source code. Later in this chapter, we will describe a complete set of such action commands.

As you become more familiar with a particular programming language, the algorithms you design may start to look more and more like the actual syntax of that language. However, you should try to retain a language-independent algorithm design style so that you develop and practice the habit of separating problem-solving details from language implementation details.

4 Convert the algorithm into a program.

Program P-2.1 gives a translation of the algorithm from Step 3 into Fortran 90 source code. Even though you are not expected to understand the details of this source code, the correspondence between the algorithm from Step 3 and the code should nonetheless be clear. This example is given as *one* possible translation of the algorithm. As you will see in later chapters, there are many choices that can be made about the details of Fortran programs so that even very simple programs won't always look exactly the same.

P-2.1 [WINDCHIL.F90]

```
      PROGRAM WindChill
!
! Program file name WINDCHIL.F90.
! Given a temperature (deg F) and wind speed (mi/hr), calculate
! the equivalent windchill temperature (deg F).
!
! Variable declarations...
      IMPLICIT NONE
      REAL :: temperature,wind_speed,wind_chill_temperature
!
! Get input...
!
      WRITE(*,*)&
        'Give temperature in deg F and wind speed in mi/hr...'
      READ(*,*)temperature,wind_speed
!
! Do calculation...
!
      wind_chill_temperature=0.0817*(3.71*SQRT(wind_speed)+ &
        5.81 - 0.25*wind_speed)*(temperature-91.4)+91.4
!
! Display output...
!
      WRITE(*,*)wind_chill_temperature
!
      STOP
      END PROGRAM WindChill
```

At this point, your instructor may show you how to enter this source code into the computer system on which you are learning Fortran. Type the code *exactly* as shown. Your instructor will also provide you with instructions on how to execute the program. In this way, you can start to become familiar with the purely mechanical process of using Fortran.

In general, the steps required to translate an algorithm into source code range from trivial to difficult, depending on your familiarity with the 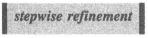 programming language you are using. You may find that you will have to cycle through Steps 2 through 4 several times in response to changes in the way you think about a problem or to the demands of a particular language. This process is called *stepwise refinement*.

As you become more comfortable with Fortran syntax, you may often be tempted to write the program first and the algorithm later (or ignore the algorithm design altogether). This is a mistake! For all but the most trivial problems, it is a better use of your time to refine your approach to a problem at the pseudocode design level, when you don't have to worry about the details of implementing your solution in a particular language. Here's a test you can apply to your own work:

> **If you find yourself making major structural changes in your program as you write it, you should leave the programming environment and return to the algorithm design environment.**

If you try to bypass the algorithm design and refinement process, you will often find yourself struggling simultaneously with two difficult tasks—developing a logically correct algorithm and writing an error-free program—that can and should be kept largely separate.

As an example of a situation in which some stepwise refinement of an algorithm might be needed, consider the task of finding an item in a list of related items. In most high-level languages, you must write your own algorithm for searching a list. When you first start to design the algorithm, you might include a statement such as "Find item X in this list." Later on, you must be more specific about the implementation of this instruction.

Preliminary "algorithm"
Find X in list.

Algorithm after some stepwise refinement
Assume X "not found."
Start at beginning of list.
Look at each item in list, in order.
When you find X, set item "found" and stop.

If you have never written a list-searching algorithm before, this may represent a programming problem that you need to think through in detail. For example, you should consider the possibility that you won't find what you're looking for in the list. This possibility isn't accounted for in the algorithm as it is now stated because it says "*When* you find what you're looking for..." and not "*If* you find what you're looking for..." Rewrite the algorithm to account for this possibility:

Algorithm after additional stepwise refinement
Assume X "not found."
Start at beginning of list.
Look at each item in list, in order.
If you find X, set item "found" and stop.
If you get to the end of the list, stop.
Provide output indicating whether X was found.

If you have written a searching algorithm many times, this problem may not require any thought at all and may not even warrant writing more detailed instructions; it may even be possible to "borrow" the required code from a program you have written previously.

5 *Verify the operation of the program.*

Try to find a published table of windchill temperatures (on the World Wide Web?) to use as a check against the results produced by this program.

Problem Discussion

Figures 2.2 and 2.3 show two different views of the windchill temperature. In Figure 2.2, the values are calculated as a function of ambient air temperature for several values of wind speed. In Figure 2.3, the windchill temperatures are calculated as a function of wind speed for two temperatures, 0°F and 32°F.

These two figures demonstrate that there is ample reason to be suspicious of the answers provided by the formula. You can see that for small values of the wind speed the formula produces a windchill temperature that is *higher* than the ambient air temperature. There is perhaps a plausible explanation for this result: when there is no wind, your body warms the layer of air next to your skin so the air feels warmer than it actually is. However, this is an insufficient reason to accept the values provided at low wind speed without further investigation. Actually, as is typically the case with engineering formulas, there are easily overlooked restrictions on this formula: it applies only to wind speeds of no less than 4 mph and to temperatures less than 91.4°F. You will be aware of these restrictions only if you examine the source of the formula.[2]

When you first start writing programs, you may be so relieved to create a program that executes successfully that you will be eager to assume that the answers it produces are correct. This particular problem *should* warn you against making that assumption!

First of all, what do we mean by a "correct" program? One definition is that the algorithm on which the program is based is logically consistent and the program implements that algorithm without errors. It is not always possible to "prove" that a computer program is correct in this sense. Therefore, verification of a program's correct operation by means other than the program output itself is extremely important. Implementation errors in programs are sometimes easy to find and sometimes very elusive. If you're lucky, logical programming errors, as

---

[2]The original reference is: Court, A., 1948: Windchill. *Bull. Amer. Meteor. Soc.*, **29**, 487-493. Note that some atmospheric scientists believe that the concept of windchill has little scientific value.

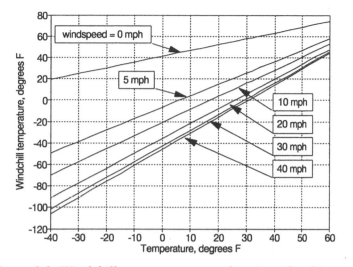

Figure 2.2. Windchill temperature as a function of ambient air temperature

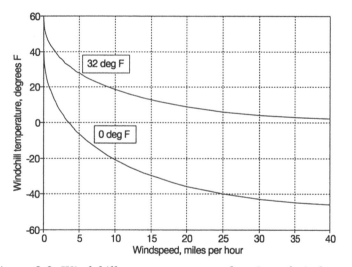

Figure 2.3. Windchill temperature as a function of wind speed

opposed to syntax errors detected by the programming environment, will cause your program to "crash" or produce answers that are wrong. Unfortunately...

> **It is not unusual even for apparently simple programs to produce output that looks perfectly reasonable, but is in fact wrong.**

A second definition of "correct" is that you have asked your program to do something that makes sense. With respect to the windchill temperature problem, you might argue that, as a programmer, it is your responsibility only to guarantee that your program correctly implements the formula given in the problem statement. However, as a scientist or engineer, your responsibility extends to making sure that what you have asked your program to do is reasonable. This is often a problem when your program uses engineering formulas, especially when their derivation is unknown and their range of applicability is uncertain, as in this case. Do you really think that it feels nearly 60°F on a still day when the ambient air temperature is 32°F, as indicated by Figure 2.3? In summary, the "garbage in, garbage out" rule means that you must...

> **Assume that all programs produce incorrect output until they have been thoroughly tested. Even when you are convinced that a program is error-free and *always* does what you intend, don't assume that the output from that program must therefore be correct.**

2.1.3 Beware of Logical Errors

To illustrate the kinds of logical errors that can creep into programs, consider this typical problem for an introductory programming course.

> An income tax is collected according to the following rule: for incomes less than or equal to $50,000, the tax is 7% of the income. The tax is 3% on any income in excess of $50,000. Write a program that will calculate the tax for a user-supplied income.

You might design an algorithm that looks like this:

```
READ (income)
IF income ≤ 50000 THEN
        ASSIGN tax = income•0.07
ELSE
        ASSIGN tax = income•0.03
WRITE (tax)
```

A program that implements this algorithm will produce numbers that look reasonable and are in fact correct for incomes less than $50,000. However, it *should* be obvious that the **IF...** statement must read:

IF *income* ≤ *50000* **THEN**
        ASSIGN *tax = income•0.07*
ELSE
        ASSIGN *tax = 50000•0.07 + (income - 50000)•0.03*

If you used the first **IF...** statement in the above example and it occurred to you to calculate the tax on incomes of $50,000 and $50,001 as part of your program testing, you might have been alerted to the fact that something was wrong.

    Here's another problem that can easily result in logical errors:

The time T required for a satellite in orbit around the earth to travel once around the earth (its period) is $T = 2\pi a(a/G)^{1/2}$, where the quantity "a" is the average distance from the center of the earth to the satellite and G is the earth's gravitational constant, $398,601.2 \text{ km}^3/\text{s}^2$. The earth's radius is approximately 6378 km. What is the period of a satellite at an average altitude of 600 km above the earth's surface?

Your algorithm might perform this calculation:

$$T = 2\pi\, 600 \sqrt{\frac{600}{398601.2}} = 146 \text{ s}$$

instead of adding the satellite's altitude to the earth's radius and performing the correct calculation:

$$T = 2\pi\, 6978 \sqrt{\frac{6978}{398601.2}} = 5801 \text{ s}$$

A program based on the first calculation will work perfectly well, and the answer may or may not appear "obviously" wrong; not everyone knows that satellites do not travel around the earth in 2.4 minutes! (This one takes about 97 minutes.) In this case, by the way, you should be alerted by the fact that the first calculation doesn't make use of the earth's radius. While it's certainly not true that all information supplied with a problem is necessarily useful (especially in the "real world"), you need at least to examine all information for its possible relevance.
    It's not possible to give a foolproof set of rules for eliminating logical errors in algorithms and their associated programs. In the tax problem given above, testing incomes of $50,000 and $50,001 would have detected the error in the first algorithm (because the tax on $50,001 would be less than the tax on $50,000, which is inconsistent with the problem statement). For the orbiting

satellite problem, however, you would have to find an answer you knew was correct and compare that value with the output from your program. Without this kind of "reality check," you may never detect the error in this program.

Another verification strategy is to try to force your program to fail. Test it under all possible input conditions, even conditions that should never exist under "normal" operation. Sometimes, however, it isn't easy to force a calculation literally to fail. In the satellite problem, there are plenty of "unreasonable" input values (satellites won't stay in orbit at any altitude less than about 100 km, for example), but no input values other than negative altitudes greater than 6378 km will actually force the calculation to fail (because the number under the square root will be negative).

Obviously, verifying the performance of a program implies that you can determine in some other way not only what a correct answer looks like, but also what appropriate input is. This is not always easy. For many kinds of problems, if you could calculate representative answers by hand, you wouldn't have needed a program in the first place. However, for many science and engineering problems, it's possible to test the output from a program with nothing more than common sense and a hand calculator.

2.2 Designing Algorithms for Procedural Programming Languages

2.2.1 Getting Started

The goal of algorithm design in programming is to produce a step-by-step problem-solving plan that can be implemented in a programming language. Making a smooth transition from designing an algorithm to writing a program is a skill you will need to practice. On the one hand, algorithm development should be generic and not associated too closely with just one language. On the other hand, you cannot design algorithms without understanding what kinds of tools are available.

As an example, think about describing the trajectory of a projectile under the influence of the earth's gravitational field. You cannot develop a detailed algorithm to describe this motion without some understanding of the capabilities of the mathematical tools—algebra, as a minimum, and calculus, in general—available for solving this kind of problem.

The purposes of this section are to:

1. Outline the generic capabilities of high-level procedural programming languages.

2. Describe a specific language for designing algorithms that can be converted easily into programs.

We will start by discussing the kinds of instructions available in procedural languages and the kinds of data they can manipulate.

2.2.2 Executable Instructions

An **executable instruction** written in source code is a "plain English" instruction that can be translated by a compiler into instructions that can then be
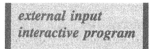
carried out directly by your computer. There are five categories of executable instructions available for writing programs in a high-level procedural programming language. These are listed in Table 2.1, and each of them will be discussed briefly here and in more detail later in the text.

Table 2.1. Instruction categories for high-level programming

Instruction Category	Example
1, Input/output	"Read (write) a value."
2. Assignments	"Set A equal to 3."
3. Calls to subprograms	"Determine the moment of inertia...."
4. Comparisons (conditional)	"Is A greater than B?"
5. Repetitive calculations (loops)	"Perform these calculations 10 times."

1. Input/output

Often programs need **external input** before they can perform calculations. On personal computers or computers accessible from a terminal, input is often entered directly from the keyboard when the program is running. This is called an **interactive program**. The other common source of input is a data file accessed and processed by the program.

The output from programs is usually sent by default to the monitor screen. Other possibilities include sending output to a printer or a data file for use by another program. The actual process of interpreting input and directing output may be quite complicated at the basic computer hardware level, but high-level languages use simple goal-oriented instructions to represent these processes. Fortran 90's specific implementation of input and output will be discussed in several places throughout the text, starting in Chapter 3.

2. Assignments

Assignment statements allow a program to manipulate values and evaluate expressions. When one or more assignment statements are performed one after the other, in order, they become part of a

> assignment statement
> sequence structure

control structure called a *sequence structure*. Often assignment statements look a lot like algebraic expressions. For example, the algebraic expression x = 3a + 4b + 6c is easily translated into Fortran:

```
x = 3*a + 4*b + 6*c
```

where clearly the * implies multiplication. However, there is much more to assignment statements than this, as we will see when we discuss them in detail in Chapter 3.

3. Calls to subprograms

A *subprogram* is a separate set of instructions that performs a single task as part of a larger program. Subprograms are not required as part of a programming language's structure or syntax, but

> subprogram
> program modularization

the structured programming approach to problem solving encourages *program modularization*. Hence subprograms are required as a matter of style in all but the simplest programs. The Fortran implementation of subprograms will be discussed in Chapter 7.

4. Comparisons (conditionals)

Computers can't make decisions the same way that humans do, but high-level languages contain instructions that allow a program to compare values and to take action based on the result of the

> conditional (statement)
> selection structure

comparison. This kind of instruction is called a conditional statement, or *conditional*. Comparisons are often made in the context of a *selection structure* that allows a program to execute some instructions and ignore others. The Fortran implementation of selection structures will be discussed in Chapter 6.

5. Repetitive calculations (loops)

Problem-solving algorithms often involve repetitive calculations. In high-level languages, a *repetition structure* can be used to control repetitive calculations.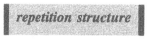
"Count-controlled" loops repeat a group of instructions a predetermined number of times. "Conditional" loops repeat a group of instructions until (or as long as) one or more specified conditions are met. These terms will be described in more detail when the Fortran implementation of repetition structures is discussed in Chapter 6.

2.2.3 Data Types and Variables

Data types

There are four basic data types used in languages such as Fortran. These are given in Table 2.2.

Table 2.2. Data types used in high-level languages

Data Types	Examples
1. Numbers (real or integer)	17, 3.33, 1.01×10^{-7}, -32768
2. Characters and strings of characters	a, Z, $, Fortran, Laura
3. Logical (boolean) values	true, false
4. User-defined types (data structures)	arrays, records

1. Numbers

Most high-level languages differentiate between *integers* and *real numbers* (also called *floating point* numbers). Here are some examples:

integers: 10, 0, -32768
real numbers: 3.3, 1.555×10^{-17}, -33.17, 17.0

Integers are whole numbers, expressed without a decimal point or fractional part. Real numbers always have a fractional part, even if that part is 0. That is, 1.0 is considered a real number in Fortran just because of the way it is written.

The reason for differentiating between integers and real numbers is that the **internal representation** of integers and real numbers (that 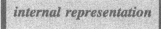 is, the way they are stored in your computer's memory), is different, with sometimes important consequences. (Some details are given in Chapter 12.)

2. Characters and strings of characters

The set of all individual characters that most computers can represent constitutes the so-called *ASCII* (American Standard Code for Information Interchange, pronounced *ask*-ee) *collating sequence* of characters. The first 128 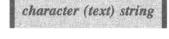 characters represent the uppercase and lowercase letters of the alphabet, punctuation marks and other symbols, the digits 0-9, and some nonprintable "control" characters. The remaining 128 characters vary from system to system; on IBM-compatible PCs, for example, these include graphics characters, foreign language letters, and other special characters. You can find lists of ASCII characters in textbooks (including this one—see **Appendix 2**) and in documentation for other computer applications and programming environments.

Some computers use a different collating sequence. The so-called EBCDIC (Extended Binary Coded Decimal Interchange Code, pronounced *eb*-si-dik) sequence used by IBM mainframe computers is a notable example.

When several characters are combined, the result is called a *character string*, or text string. For example, C is a character, whereas computer is a  character string. An individual character can always be stored in just one byte of memory, but character strings can be of variable length. Therefore, high-level languages sometimes have separate data types for characters and character strings. However, Fortran supports just one basic data type for characters and strings of characters; in particular, Fortran treats a single character as a character string of length 1.

3. Logical (boolean) values

When a high-level language compares two values, the result of that comparison can have one of only two possible outcomes—true or false. That is. the statement "A is less than B" is either true or false.[3] Some high-level languages, including Fortran,[4] support a separate data type to represent these logical or so-called **boolean values**.

4. User-defined types

In many programming languages, the basic data types can be combined into user-defined data structures. The most common of these structures are arrays and records. Fortran includes strong support for arrays because of their importance in scientific and engineering computing. Fortran 90 also supports other kinds of composite data structures that were not available in earlier versions of Fortran. We will defer definition of arrays and records until Chapter 8, where they will be discussd in detail. As we will see, user-defined data types are important because they can greatly simplify the organization and manipulation of data in programs.

Variables

A basic function of high-level languages is to allow programmers to refer symbolically by name to locations in computer memory. These symbolic names are called variables or variable names. Recall the algebraic equation x = 3a + 4b + 6c mentioned previously in the brief discussion of assignment statements. If this expression becomes an assignment statement in a program, x, a, b, and c will become variables in the program. (The numbers 3, 4, and 6 will become constants, most likely expressed as real numbers.) Variables are always associated with a particular data type; in this case, these four variables would probably represent real numbers.

In programming, there is no distinction between "independent" and "dependent" variables as there is in mathematics. In the equation x = 3a + 4b + 6c, a, b, and c might be considered independent variables and x a dependent variable. That is, x might be considered to be a function of a, b, and c. However, all four of these quantities have the same status as "variables" in programming.

Throughout the rest of this text, we will refer to variables with the understanding that they are symbolic names associated with locations in computer memory that will be assigned values in a program. Sometimes the values will be assigned directly, perhaps by asking a program user to provide the value. At other times, the values will be assigned as a result of evaluating an expression. If the above equation were expressed as a statement in a program, the implication would

---

[3]The assertion that "A is less than B" must be true or false implies that A and B actually have values that can be compared because they are both of the same or compatible data types.

[4]C is a notable exception.

be that there were already values in the memory locations associated with the names a, b, and c, and the value of x would be obtained by evaluating the expression on the right side of the = sign using those known values.

2.2.4 Designing Algorithms for Solving Problems

When we combine what we have learned about instructions and data types with a step-by-step approach to solving problems, the result is a powerful problem-solving tool. In the five-step approach outlined earlier in this chapter, the critical step of designing an algorithm that can be translated into a computer program is usually the hardest to master; in fact, most programming students find that algorithm design is much more difficult than learning the syntax of a language. It can be frustrating to try to design an algorithm when there don't appear to be any specific rules about how to proceed. This section will describe an approach that should help you get started.

Defining a pseudocode language

One way to develop algorithm design skills is to use a generic language consisting of "action commands" that provide specific expressions for the kinds of executable instructions discussed in Section 2.2.2. This language needs only a small vocabulary because the list of instructions that a high-level language can execute directly is not very long.

An informal action command language offers major advantages over a "real" programming language for algorithm development. It is easy to be lulled into believing that programming languages "understand" English, with all its subtleties and ambiguity, just because their commands sometimes look like English words. Nothing could be further from the truth, as every struggling programmer knows! The syntax and structural requirements of procedural languages are very strict, and especially before you are thoroughly familiar with their requirements, their rigidity can be an impediment to the problem-solving process. An intermediate design process can't protect you from sloppy thinking, but at least it can free you from worrying about syntax errors that your computer refuses to explain in any helpful way.

The pseudocode language presented in this section isn't a "real" language with a set of syntax rules. It's possible that you or your instructor will choose different words for the commands or use an entirely different method of describing the actions implied by the commands. You may even develop your own unique algorithm design style. However...

> **A pseudocode language must describe all actions that can be taken by a program written in a high-level procedural language.**

In any event, you should be free to apply a pseudocode language without worrying about making the kinds of syntax mistakes that plague students attempting to learn a new programming language. It is a mistake to treat this language as just one more list of things to memorize; it's intended simply as a tool to help you organize your thoughts and facilitate the design of your programs.[5]

The algorithm design language we will use in this text consists of the following commands, in alphabetical order. In some cases the terms used to explain the commands will themselves need additional explanation, which will be provided as needed in the text.

ASSIGN

Set a variable equal to another variable, constant value, or expression. See also the **INCREMENT** and **INITIALIZE** commands.

CALL subprogram_name (with a list of parameters)

Invoke another set of commands that, when given a specific set of input values, executes a list of instructions and produces a set of output values. A carefully planned list of input parameters (quantities needed for the subprogram to do its job) and output parameters (the results of operations performed inside the subprogram) is critical to well-structured program design.

CHOOSE (from a list of possibilities)

From a list of possible courses of action, select just one action based on the value of a single variable or expression.

CLOSE (data file)

Close an external data file when you're done with it.

DEFINE (a list of variables, constants, and data structures)

Define the names and kinds of variables, constants, and user-defined data structures your program will need. Some of the variables will have values provided by the user, others will be used internally by the program, and others will be output from the program.

---

[5]Author's note: I never ask my students to memorize the components of this pseudocode language, and I try not to impose my own style preferences; there's plenty of time for that when they're writing real code! I encourage students to make their own list of commands, operators, and functions and to have it available whenever they write programs—even on exams.

IF (something is true) **THEN** *(take action)* **ELSE** *(take a different action)*

Take one course of action or another based on the value of a logical expression. The **ELSE** part of the command is optional because sometimes no alternative action may be required if the "something" isn't true.

INCREMENT

This is a command for assignments such as $x = x + 1$. It is given a separate name because of its importance in **LOOP** structures.

INITIALIZE

This is an assignment command used to emphasize the necessity of initializing the value of a variable before it can be incremented. For example, if **INCREMENT** $x = x + 1$ appears inside a loop, x must first be **INITIALIZE**d outside the loop.

LOOP (continuation or termination conditions)...END LOOP

Define a structure inside of which lists of instructions can be executed repetitively until (or as long as) certain conditions are met.

OPEN (data file)

Open an external data file for use within a program.

READ (list of values)

Provide input for a program.

SUBPROGRAM (list of input and output parameters)

This contains an algorithm to produce one or more output values using one or more specified input values. It is used in conjunction with **CALL**.

WRITE (list of values)

Generate and/or display output from a program.

Appendix 3 contains a table of all these pseudocode commands along with examples of their implementation in Fortran. It should be clear even from a brief glance at **Appendix 3** that despite the many implementation details, Fortran commands closely resemble their corresponding pseudocode commands.[6]

---

[6]Author's personal note: While I was working on early drafts of this text, my daughter Laura, who had just turned one, learned her first pseudocode command. She picked up a book and said "Read!" Even though she had no understanding of the mechanics of reading, she had learned enough about the function of language to realize that her parents could translate this command into a complex sequence of events without her having to worry about the implementation details.

In addition to "action commands," an algorithm development language needs a collection of operators, such as shown in Table 2.3.

Table 2.3. Mathematical and logical operators

Arithmetic Operator	Operation	Relational Operator	Meaning
+	addition	=	equal
-	subtraction	>	greater than
*	multiplication	<	less than
/	division	≤	less than or equal to
superscript	exponentiation	≥	greater than or equal to
		≠	not equal to
Logical Operator	**Meaning**		
AND	logical "and"		
OR	logical "or"		
NOT	logical "not"		

The *arithmetic* and *relational operators* should be familiar to you from mathematics. Exponentiation doesn't have a separate symbol; it is indicated by a superscript: x^2 means "x raised to the second power," or "x squared." We will return to the *logical operators* in Chapter 6.

arithmetic operator
relational operator
logical operator

Finally, every language provides some built-in functions to perform frequently needed calculations. To cite just two examples, many languages provide functions to calculate the trigonometric sine of a quantity x or the square root of x. Computer science-oriented languages such as C provide relatively few of these functions as part of their language definitions. Because of its science and engineering origins, Fortran provides many such functions.

The functions provided with a particular language will have a major impact on your programs, but less on your algorithm design. For example, if a problem requires a quantity y to be set equal to the arcsine (inverse sine) of x, you should simply assume that you can write

ASSIGN $y = sin^{-1}(x)$

Later, when you implement this algorithm, you may find that your language doesn't include this function. Then you will have to provide your own source code. Depending on your familiarity with trigonometric functions, additional algorithm design may or may not be required to guide your construction of appropriate code. (Don't worry about Fortran, which includes this and many other trigonometric functions.)

The point is that, at the design level, you should write mathematical and other operations with the expectation that you will be able to implement them in a programming language without too much trouble. If this task later proves too cumbersome, then you need to seek a better match between your problem and an appropriate problem-solving tool.

The three basic program control structures

The pseudocode language components we have discussed so far are equivalent to words and sentences in English. In the same sense that you have to develop a plot framework before you can combine English sentences into a coherent story, you need to develop a strategy for organizing the pseudocode components into a complete algorithm. In principle, this isn't difficult because there are only three basic strategies, or control structures, for combining these components into structured algorithms: sequence, selection, and repetition. These three, which have been mentioned briefly in the discussion of pseudocode commands, are illustrated in Figure 2.4.

In a sequence structure, instructions are executed in order, starting at the "top." Each instruction is executed once and only once. In a selection structure, one group of instructions from a group of two or more possibilities is chosen to be executed and the remaining possibilities are ignored. In a repetition structure, a group of instructions is executed repeatedly until (or as long as) certain conditions are satisfied. The relationship between the three control structures and the pseudocode commands for algorithm design are given in Table 2.4.

Computer science has as one of its basic principles that any algorithm can be written in terms of these three simple control structures. From the pseudocode commands listed above, it should be clear that the **IF...THEN...[ELSE...]** and **CHOOSE** commands will be used to implement the Selection structure and the **LOOP...END LOOP** structure will implement the Repetition structure. The other

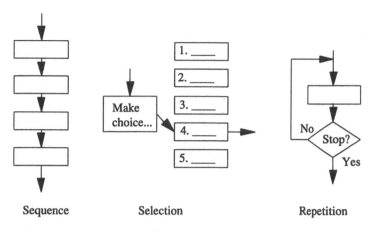

Figure 2.4. The three basic program control structures

commands (except for **DEFINE**, which isn't an "executable" statement, as discussed in Chapter 3) are all used to form statements that will be part of a sequence structure.

Table 2.4. Program control structures and pseudocode commands

Control Structure	Pseudocode Command(s)
Sequence	*ASSIGN, CALL, CLOSE, INCREMENT, INITIALIZE, OPEN, READ, WRITE*
Selection	*CHOOSE, IF...THEN...[ELSE...]*
Repetition	*LOOP...END LOOP*

Adding to your pseudocode vocabulary

From time to time you may wish to add your own commands to the pseudocode language discussed in this chapter. For example, a programming problem may require that two values be exchanged. The first time you perform this task, you could write instructions to implement the exchange:

```
(exchange variable1 and variable2)
ASSIGN temp = variable1
        variable1 = variable2
        variable2 = temp
```

Later, you may feel confident enough to replace this pseudocode with a new action command, such as **SWAP** *(variable1, variable2)*.

There are other useful "higher level" commands that could be added. Consider the common tasks of searching for an item in a list or putting a list into a particular order. At a certain point in your algorithm design, these tasks could be represented by action commands that provide a shorthand representation of what actually may be a complicated set of instructions:

SEARCH *(list for a specified item)*
SORT *(list in specified order)*

In most high-level languages, these actions must be implemented through algorithms written by the programmer. These commands are good examples of the kinds of interactive relationships that need to exist between algorithm design and a working program. The stepwise refinement process implies a gradual transition from the general to the specific, where broadly stated actions become more specific as the process progresses.

Flowcharts: another way to visualize algorithms

Some programmers prefer to design an algorithm more visually, using a *flowchart*. This is a diagram that describes an algorithm using a standard set of symbols, illustrated in Figure 2.5. (This flowchart doesn't actually accomplish anything other than to demonstrate the symbols.)

The terminal symbol is used to mark the beginning and end of an algorithm. The parallelogram-shaped input/output symbol represents input and output operations, including prompts for user input. The rectangular process symbol contains calculations that are performed sequentially. The "predefined" process symbol indicates code that has already been written for some particular task or that isn't specifically relevant to the algorithm under discussion. Points at which decisions are required are represented by the diamond-shaped symbol. These will be found in, for example, a flowchart representation of the pseudocode **IF...THEN... ELSE...** command. There are two possible exits from the decision symbol: one when a condition is true, and one when the condition is false.

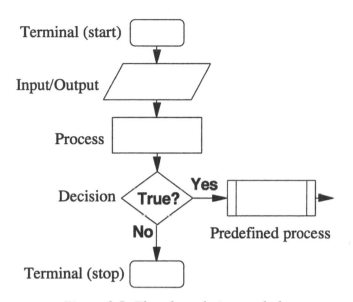

Figure 2.5. Flowchart design symbols

All the symbols in a flowchart are connected by lines. Arrows at the ends of lines indicate the direction of "flow" for the algorithm; the direction of a flowchart is usually from the top down and from left to right.

Some programmers, especially Fortran programmers, believe that all algorithms should be represented as flowcharts. Others believe that pseudocode is a better choice for designing algorithms and that flowcharts are better for describing existing programs, especially to nonprogrammers. This text will sometimes use flowcharts as a visual aid to help clarify certain program control structures. However, flowcharts are often a cumbersome way to describe long or complicated algorithms, so this text generally favors the use of pseudocode commands as described above. Regardless of your or your instructor's preference, the important point to remember is that pseudocode and flowchart representations can be used interchangeably to design and describe algorithms and programs.

2.3 Program Modularization

Top-down design is a concept at the heart of structured programming. The purpose of top-down design is to divide large problems into several smaller problems, each 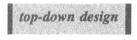 of which can be solved separately. Solutions to these smaller problems can often be developed within self-contained program modules called subprograms. When you design algorithms, the top-down design philosophy is implemented through the **CALL** and **SUBPROGRAM** pseudocode commands.

Consider a typical computer application—a program to manage a checking account. Such a program needs to be able to perform at least the following tasks:

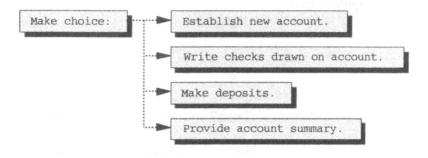

Using top-down design, the main program could consist of no more than some code to present the user with this menu of choices and a way to respond to a choice from the menu. That is, the program would be "menu-driven."

Each menu choice would then be implemented as a call to a separate subprogram. Each subprogram would be responsible for handling one menu task. Within each of the modules, other menus and lower-level subprograms might be required. For example, consider the second choice—writing checks. Its functions could be outlined as follows:

```
SUBPROGRAM - Write checks drawn on account.
1. Determine current account balance.
2. Determine current check number.
3. Request information for writing check.
4. Update balance.
5. Update check number.
```

At least some of these tasks—the third one, in particular—could be implemented in an additional subprogram that would be called from this subprogram.

When you design modularized programs, it's important to think carefully about how information flows between the main program and various subprograms. Consider, for example, the information flow between the check-writing subprogram and an additional subprogram to request information for writing a check:

SUBPROGRAM *WriteCheck(IN: Current balance, Last check number;*
OUT: Payee name, Check amount,
Memo (optional),
Check category (optional),
Write check? (yes or no))

Why does this subprogram need the current balance as input? Suppose the check you are planning to write will overdraw the account. You need to offer the user the chance of changing her mind or writing the check. (Maybe the account has overdraft privileges, in which case it would still be OK to write the check.)

Depending on what kind of account summaries you would like to provide, you may wish to categorize each check so that you can later provide a summary of your expenses by category. Also, you may need to provide a "flag" to let the calling subprogram know whether you actually wrote a check. An exercise at the end of this chapter will give you a chance to design an algorithm for this part of the subprogram.

The justification for top-down design done at the algorithm level is that it is much easier to organize your programs by tasks at this stage, when you're not actually writing source code. For many kinds of problems, the programming details are relatively easy once the tasks and the flow of information between tasks have been defined clearly. Conversely, it is often difficult to modify the structure and information flow of a program once you have started writing it. The important lesson is that when programs consist of several tasks, it is essential to design separate subprograms for each task and to plan carefully how information will be shared among those subprograms.

2.4 Applications

In this section we will design algorithms for two typical engineering problems. We will return to both these applications later in the text to consider their Fortran implementation.

2.4.1 Maximum Deflection of a Beam Under Load

1 Define the problem.

A beam L feet long is supported at each end. A downward load of F pounds is concentrated at the midpoint of the beam. This arrangement is shown schematically in Figure 2.6. The maximum deflection of a beam under such a load

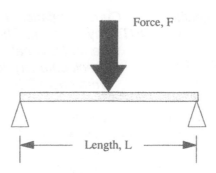

Figure 2.6. A supported beam
subject to a central load

(at its midpoint) is $-FL^3/(48EI)$, where the negative sign denotes a downward deflection. The elasticity E is a property of the material from which the beam is made, and the moment of inertia I is a property of the shape of the beam.

Write a program that accepts as input the elasticity, moment of inertia, and concentrated midpoint load on a beam and then calculates and displays the maximum deflection of the beam in inches.

2 *Outline a solution.*

First of all, do you understand enough about the terminology to solve the problem? For a "beam...supported at each end," think of a 2"×6" piece of lumber lying horizontally and supported by a brick at each end. For a "downward load of F pounds...concentrated at the midpoint...," think of a person standing in the middle of the board. The problem asks how much that board will deflect in the middle.

The elasticity and moment of inertia are properties of the beam. If you haven't had an introductory engineering course in materials, you probably won't know precisely what they mean. All you really need to know to write a program is some representative values for these quantities.

Here are the steps required to solve the problem:

1. Provide values for the elasticity, moment of inertia, beam length, load, and deflection, with appropriate units.

2. Convert beam length to inches.

3. Calculate the deflection in inches and display the result.

3 *Design an algorithm.*

Convert your plan for solving this problem into a formal algorithm:

DEFINE *(All quantities as real numbers;*
IN: elasticity, lb/in² ; moment_of_inertia, in⁴ ; length, ft; load, lb;
OUT: deflection, in)
READ *(elasticity, moment_of_inertia, length, load in specified units)*
(Don't forget to convert feet to inches.)
ASSIGN *deflection =-load•(length•12)³/(48•elasticity•moment_of_inertia)*
WRITE *(deflection)*

4 *Convert the algorithm into a program.*

Defer this step for now. This problem appears again as an application in Chapter 3 and in an expanded version in Chapter 6.

5 *Verify the operation of the program.*

Do you have a sense of what a reasonable beam deflection is for a specified load? One constraint is that for any acceptable use of a beam in a structure, the maximum deflection should be *much* less than the length of the beam. In any case, you can check results by hand for a specified loading force and beam length, using tabulated values for the properties of beams. Because this calculation involves just a series of multiplications and divisions, you can be confident that if the results are correct for one set of values, there won't be any computational problems with other values as long as the elasticity and moment of inertia have nonzero values, expressed in the proper units. Some representative input values are given in Chapter 3, where the Fortran implementation of this problem is given as an application.

Problem Discussion

This is an example of a problem whose statement is longer than its solution, which requires only the evaluation of a single formula. However, it is necessary to be careful about 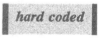 the physical units assumed for, and values assigned to, the input variables. The elasticity and moment of inertia are different for different types of beams, so they should be represented symbolically in the subprogram's parameter list. That is, values for a certain beam shouldn't be written as constants (*hard coded*) in the program.

The formula applies only to the special case in which the loading force is concentrated at the center of the beam, as opposed to being distributed along the entire length of the beam. (Remember the image of someone standing in the middle of a board supported by a brick at each end; that's a concentrated load.)

The units used in the problem statement aren't consistent. The problem asks that the deflection be given in inches, and the elasticity and moment of inertia are specified in units that involve inches. However, the problem also asks that the length of the beam be supplied in units of feet. Therefore, the length value used in the formula must be $L \cdot 12$; this step in the calculation is easy to forget.

This calculation could be done in a subprogram that will become part of a larger program. Also, a program could ask the user to select a beam from a table of choices. With this information, the program could select appropriate values of elasticity and moment of inertia from a table of values stored within the program. (See Exercise 15 in Section 2.6.2 at the end of this chapter.)

If the algorithm is rewritten in a more general  way, you can use the subprogram in any program that requires this calculation just by providing the subprogram with an appropriate list of values (the *calling arguments*) without having to rethink the details of the calculation. This kind of modularization is an important part of structured programming and can save you countless hours of "reinventing the wheel."

However, it is always important to be aware of two potentially serious problems:

(1) Formulas—especially engineering formulas—are often approximations that give usable results only over a restricted (and perhaps unknown) range of values. In this case, for example, a sufficiently large load will cause a beam to deform or collapse rather than just deflect. Consequently, when you use such formulas, it is important to understand the conditions under which they are applicable.

(2) Formulas produce correct answers only when all the required values are expressed in appropriate units. The requirement might be obvious when you first design an algorithm, but it might not be obvious to someone else using your algorithm, or even to you at some time in the future. Be sure to include a discussion of units in Step 2 of the problem-solving process. This discussion should also be included in comments in your algorithm as well as when you write source code that implements the algorithm.

Problems associated with the misuse of engineering formulas are notoriously difficult to detect. In many cases, numerical values will continue to look reasonable even when the conditions under which a formula applies have been exceeded or when inconsistent units are used. It is important to document *all* algorithms in order to provide a record of the (hopefully) careful thought that went into their original creation. Once that has been done, only vigilance and common sense can prevent their misuse!

2.4.2 Oscillating Frequency of an LC Circuit

1 Define the problem.

An electrical circuit that contains an inductance L (units of henrys, H) and a capacitance C (units of farads, F) in series (see Figure 2.7) oscillates at a characteristic frequency:

$$f = \frac{1}{2\pi\sqrt{LC}}$$

Design an algorithm that generates a table of oscillating frequencies for a two-dimensional table of L and C values. Let the L values form the rows of the table and the C values form the columns. Such a circuit can be used to "tune" radios or TVs. The table for this problem should include values for a circuit to be used in a radio that receives AM-band radio stations—on the order of 1000 kHz. A circuit containing an inductance of 2.5 mH (0.0025 H) and a capacitance of 10 pF (10×10^{-12} F) oscillates at about 1000 kHz.

2 Outline a solution.

Like the previous problem, this one contains some terminology that may be unfamiliar unless you have had an introductory physics or engineering course that covered this topic. However, the unfamiliarity of the jargon shouldn't deter you from solving the problem. After all, you don't need to manipulate these quantities in any other than a completely specified way.

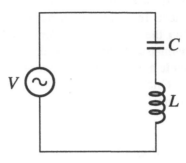

Figure 2.7 An LC circuit

The table holding the output could be laid out like this:

```
        C (pF)
L (H)   2     4     6     8    10    12    14    16    18    20
0.0010
 .0015
 .0020
 .0025
 .0030
 .0035
 .0040
```

Each position in the two-dimensional table is identified by its row and column, and the frequency is calculated from the L and C values for that row and column. For example, the frequency value in row 2, column 3 is calculated for a circuit with an inductance of 0.0015 H and a capacitance of 6 pF. These values are chosen to include 2.5 mH and 10 pF.

To generate the inductance and capacitance values for the table, use "nested" loops. The outer loop generates the inductance values and the inner loop generates the capacitance values. Initialize the inductance to 0.0005 H and increment it in steps of 0.0005 H for each trip through the outer loop. Initialize the capacitance to 0 pF and increment it in steps of 2 pF in the inner loop.

3 *Design an Algorithm.*

DEFINE *(inductance (henrys), capacitance (farads), frequency (Hz)*
   as real numbers; π as a real constant; row and col as integers)
INITIALIZE *inductance = 0.0005*
WRITE *(all table headings, with loop to print capacitance values)*

(outer loop for rows...)

```
LOOP (for row = 1 to 7)
   INCREMENT inductance = inductance + 0.0005 (H)
   WRITE (inductance) (no "carriage return")
   INITIALIZE capacitance = 0
   (inner loop for columns...)
   LOOP (for col = 1 to 10)
         INCREMENT capacitance = capacitance + 2 (pF)
         ASSIGN frequency  = 1/[2π•(inductance•capacitance•10⁻¹²)¹ᐟ²]
         WRITE (frequency for this row and column)
   END (inner) LOOP
   ("carriage return" to start new row goes here)
END (outer) LOOP
```

ASSIGN frequency $= 1/[2\pi \cdot (\text{inductance} \cdot \text{capacitance} \cdot 10^{-12})^{1/2}]$

4   *Convert the algorithm into a program.*

Defer this step for now. The Fortran implementation of this problem is discussed in Chapter 6.

5   *Verify the operation of the program.*

Check several calculations with a hand calculator. Make sure that the row and column labels correspond to the values actually used to calculate the frequency for that row and column.

Problem Discussion

The potential difficulties with this problem are primarily organizational. First you must plan a suitable tabular layout, as shown. This will be easier if you have used a spreadsheet, for which a two-dimensional table is the basic paradigm. To solve this problem in a programming language, you must design an algorithm that uses nested **LOOP** structures to perform the calculations one row at a time. Each row corresponds to one "trip" through the outer loop. The calculations in the inner loop fill the columns of that row.

Be sure you understand which commands go inside or outside which loop structure. For example, the commands to generate the table headings must be outside the outer loop so they will be printed only once. The initialization for the inductance goes outside the outer loop because it must be done only once. The initialization for the capacitance must be done every time the inner loop is executed, so it goes inside the outer loop, but just before the inner loop. The initializations use values that will produce the desired value the first time they are incremented inside their respective loops. Thus the inductance is initialized to a value of 0.005 so that its first printed value will be 0.010 when it is incremented by 0.005 inside the outer loop, as required by the problem statement.

Note the comments concerning the location of "carriage returns" inserted in the algorithm. These are to remind you that later, when you implement this algorithm, you will have to pay attention to how the output is generated. For now, don't worry about it.

Finally, don't forget that the problem requires the tabulated values of capacitance to be expressed as picofarads. However, the formula for frequency assumes that capacitance is expressed in farads; this is the source of the multiplication by 10^{-12} in the **ASSIGN** statement that calculates frequency. This problem is certainly much more difficult than the previous application. The design of the algorithm may require some study, especially because of its use of the probably unfamiliar nested loop structure. It's easy to assume that examples in a text have simply appeared "as is" and that you should be able to recreate them in their finished form in a single step. To avoid endless frustration, you must understand that this is not true! Many of the examples in this text have been rewritten several times. Ideally, they should represent the best possible solution to a particular problem. To the extent that this is true, they are models to be emulated. Unfortunately, however, the dynamic nature of the process by which they were created is lost when they appear as finished products on a printed page.

2.5 Debugging Your Algorithms

2.5.1 Algorithm Style

The ideal algorithm should solve a problem in as straightforward a manner as possible. Without exception, a simple and direct algorithm is preferred over a clever but more obscure one. Names of variables and constants should always be descriptive. If there is *any* possibility for confusion, the nature of each quantity (whether, for example, it is a real number or integer), and its physical units if appropriate) should be stated clearly. Calculations should be written in clear algebraic notation. Usually, algebraic simplifications that result in fewer mathematical operations (which might provide a computational advantage in some programs) should be avoided in favor of clarity. If there is any possibility of confusion about your algorithm design, you should include enough comments so that anyone who understands the problem you are trying to solve should also be able to understand your algorithm without additional explanation.

Even though there aren't any syntax rules for the command language described in this chapter, you should develop and adhere to a consistent physical layout that makes your algorithms easy to read. For example, all commands inside a loop should be indented the same amount. Generally, you should avoid putting multiple commands and assignments on the same line.

For large problems, or for calculations that must be repeated several times with different input values, algorithms should be modularized so that each subprogram performs a single well-defined task. The inputs and outputs for each subprogram should be clearly stated. As a result of this modularization, the "main program" part of your algorithm can define the overall structure of the problem solution, without distracting detours into the details of complicated calculations.

2.5.2 Problems with Your Algorithms

It is important to try to find errors during the algorithm design phase of solving a computational problem. Of course, it's often difficult to check the correctness of an algorithm before it is actually implemented in a program that produces output. Nonetheless, you can follow the steps in your algorithm manually, and you can sometimes do calculations by hand or with a hand calculator. You should try to imagine conditions for which your algorithm will fail even if those conditions are "unreasonable." Another useful means of verification is to let someone else try to follow the steps in your algorithm.

There are no rules for "perfect" algorithms. As a result, not all acceptable algorithms will look exactly the same. However, it is easy to write algorithms that *look* OK, but are wrong because they contain logical flaws or don't solve all of a problem. Obviously, such algorithms will lead to programs that won't work properly (or at all, if you're lucky).

2.6 Exercises

These exercises provide an opportunity to apply to a range of problems the concepts and techniques of algorithm design discussed in this chapter. For each of these exercises, carry out Steps 2, 3, and 5 of the problem-solving procedure described in this chapter. If you find it helpful, use Step 1 to restate the problem in your own words. Don't worry about Step 4 except in Exercise 13. Be sure you use Step 5 to indicate specific steps that could be taken to verify the operation of the algorithm when it is converted to a program. Include a flowchart if requested by your instructor or if you find it helpful to visualize algorithms in this way.

2.6.1 Self-Testing Exercises

The exercises in this section are intended to test your basic understanding of the material discussed in this chapter.

Exercise 1. Define an "algorithm" in your own words.

Exercise 2. Discuss "top-down design" in your own words.

Exercise 3. Make your own list of "action commands" and provide an example of each. Although these pseudocode commands don't have any syntax requirements, establish some style guidelines of your own to use when you design algorithms.

Exercise 4. Make a list of mathematical or other "action commands" you would like your pseudocode language to have. (For example, see the *SWAP* command in the "You can add to your pseudocode vocabulary" subsection of Section 2.2.4.)

Exercise 5. Take a problem from one of your other courses and rewrite it and its solution according to the pattern of Steps 1–3 in the problem-solving process defined in this chapter. How will you verify the operation of a program based on your algorithm (Step 5 of the problem-solving process)?

Exercise 6.
(a) Design a loop that counts backwards from 10 to 0. When the counter equals 0, print "FIRE!" instead of 0.
(b) Draw a flowchart for this problem.

Exercise 7.
(a) Design a loop that will choose a different action for each day of the week from Monday through Sunday. (The actions can be anything you like.)
(b) Draw a flowchart for this problem.

Exercise 8.
(a) Design a loop that will increment a counter in steps of 5, starting at 0 and ending at 100.
(b) Draw a flowchart for this problem.

Exercise 9. A ball bearing is supposed to have a diameter of 5 mm.
(a) Design an *IF...* test that will reject a ball bearing if its diameter differs from the required diameter by more than ±0.005 mm.
(b) Draw a flowchart for this problem.

Exercise 10.
(a) Design an algorithm that will test the value of $b^2 - 4ac$ (recall the formula for calculating the roots of a quadratic equation). If it is positive, calculate its square root. If it is zero or negative, print an appropriate message.
(b) Draw a flowchart for this problem.

2.6.2 Basic Algorithm Development Exercises

The exercises in this section involve modifications or extensions to algorithms developed earlier in the chapter.

Exercise 11. Refer to the income tax problem given in Section 2.1.3 and design a complete algorithm to carry out the required calculation. The algorithm should include steps for input and output. Be sure to describe how you would test your algorithm.

Exercise 12. Refer to the orbiting satellite problem given in Section 2.1.3 and design a complete algorithm to carry out the required calculation. The algorithm should include steps for input and output. Be sure to describe how you would test your algorithm.

Exercise 13. Modify program P-2.1 so that it will calculate the windchill temperature in degrees centigrade when the ambient temperature is expressed in degrees centigrade and the wind speed is expressed in kilometers per hour. The formula is

$$T_{wc} = (0.417\sqrt{V} + 0.550 - 0.0454\,V)(T - 33) + 33$$

where $T < 33°C$ and $V \geq 1.79$ m/s. Make sure that the answer produced by this modified program is consistent with the original program. If you are ambitious, you could incorporate conversions for temperature and wind speed from one set of units to the other in one or both programs.

Exercise 14. Construct a flowchart for the LC circuit application discussed in Section 2.4.2.

Exercise 15.
(a) Modify the algorithm discussed in Section 2.4.1 so the calculations are done in a subprogram that accepts as input the properties of the beam, its length, and the load, and that provides the deflection as output.
(b) Modify the algorithm discussed in Section 2.4.1 so that it presents the user with a table of steel I-beam properties. (You don't have to provide values at this point.) When the user makes a selection from the table, the algorithm should then select and use the appropriate values without the user having to enter them manually.

Exercise 16. For the check-writing problem discussed at the end of Section 2.3, design the part of the algorithm that allows a program user to decide whether to write a check that results in an overdraft.

2.6.3 Algorithm Development Applications

Exercise 17. Student data are maintained in an external data file. The information includes first and last name, social security number, the number of credit hours completed by the student, and the student's grade point average (GPA).

(a) Design an algorithm that prints two separate lists. The first list should print all available information for students whose GPA is 3.5 or above. The second list should print all available information for students whose GPA is less than 1.5.

(b) Construct a flowchart for this problem.

Exercise 18. An object falling freely under the influence of gravity attains a speed gt and travels a distance $gt^2/2$ as a function of time, where the gravitational acceleration g=9.807 m/s^2. (See Figure 2.8.) Design an algorithm that calculates and displays the speed and distance travelled by a freely falling object for the first 20 seconds after it is released, in one-second increments.

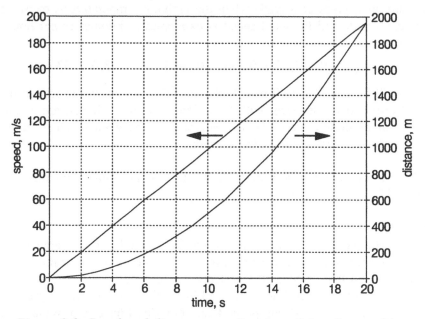

Figure 2.8. Speed and distance as a function of time for an object falling under the influence of gravity

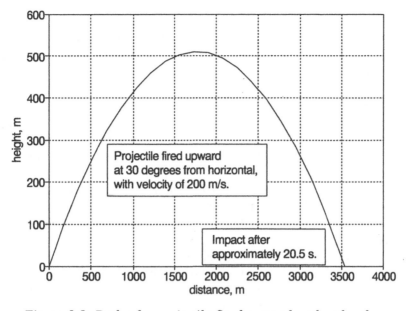

*Figure 2.9. Path of a projectile fired upward and under the
influence of gravity*

Extra Credit

Assume the object starts at the ground and is projected upward with a user-specified velocity. Modify the algorithm so that it calculates speed and distance from the ground in one-second increments until the object hits the ground. It is OK if the last time increment results in a negative position for the object. That is, you do not have to solve the equation of motion for the exact moment at which the object returns to the ground. (See Figure 2.9.)

Exercise 19. The change in length ΔL when an object of length L is subjected to a change in temperature ΔT is $\Delta L = \alpha L \Delta T$. The coefficient of linear thermal expansion α is material dependent and is independent of the units used to express the length. For example, if the length is expressed in meters and temperature changes are expressed in degrees centigrade, then the coefficient of linear expansion has units of (m/m)/°C. The value doesn't change if the length units are different, *e.g.*, in/in, but it does change if temperature changes are expressed in degrees Fahrenheit. Typical values are 23×10^{-6} m/m/°C for aluminum and 8.5×10^{-6} m/m/°C for glass.

Design an algorithm for a subprogram that accepts as input a coefficient of linear thermal expansion, a length measured at some initial temperature, and a temperature change in degrees Fahrenheit, and that returns as output the new length as a result of the temperature change.

Notes for Exercise 19

1. It is essential that you be clear about what units the subprogram will expect. In particular, if you prefer (or are required) to work in metric units, your algorithm should reflect that fact.

2. The phrase "accepts as input," which will often appear in the context of designing subprograms, should be taken to mean that variables appear in the subprogram's parameter list and that you may assume appropriate values are provided when the subprogram is used. As a result, the subprogram algorithm itself doesn't need to provide a means of obtaining these values from the user.

The phrase "returns as output" should be taken to mean that the calculations performed inside the subprogram are passed back to the calling program, with the assumption that they don't need to be printed inside the subprogram.

By making these assumptions, you can concentrate on developing algorithms for the subprogram without worrying about getting input and displaying output. Subprograms will often work this way, with input and output tasks being assigned to the calling program or another subprogram.

Exercise 20. In a collision between two objects, linear momentum and the total energy of the system are conserved. Assume that a bullet of known mass is fired horizontally with a known speed into a wood block of known mass and remains embedded in the block, which is suspended from a long string. As a result of the collision with the bullet, the block acquires kinetic energy that is then converted to potential energy as the block swings on its string. How high (relative to its initial position) will the block swing? (Refer to Figure 2.10.)

Conservation of momentum can be used to determine the speed of the block and bullet just after the collision:

$$m_1 v_1 = (m_1 + m_2) v_2$$

where m_1 and m_2 are masses in kg and v_1 and v_2 are speeds in m/s. Then conservation of energy can be used to determine how high the block swings:

$$(m_1 + m_2)gh = (m_1 + m_2)v_2^2/2$$

where g is the gravitational constant 9.807 m/s^2 and h is the height in meters.

Design an algorithm that asks the user for the mass of the bullet and the block and the initial speed of the bullet and then calculates the maximum height reached by the block.

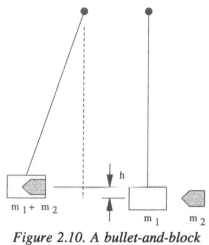

*Figure 2.10. A bullet-and-block
system before and after impact*

Exercise 21. Radioactive elements decay at a rate that is characterized by their "half life," defined as the time required for the original amount of radioactive material to be diminished by half. For example, radon, a colorless, odorless radioactive gas that can contribute to the development of lung cancer in humans, has a half life of 3.8 days. If there are originally 100 mg of radon gas in an enclosed container, there will be 50 mg after 3.8 days, 25 mg after 7.6 days, and so forth. (See Figure 2.11.) This is a process of exponential decay that can be expressed by the formula

$$A = A_o e(-t/t_o)$$

where A_o is the initial amount, A is the amount after time t, and t_o is proportional to the half life:

$$A_o/2 = A_o e(-\text{half life}/t_o)$$
$$t_o = -\text{half life}/\ln(1/2)$$

For radon, t_o is about 5.48 days.

Design an algorithm that calculates the amount of radon remaining from a user-supplied original sample mass after each of 20 consecutive days. Also, let the user provide the half life so your program won't be restricted just to radon. (Because half lives vary over a wide range, days won't always be a good choice

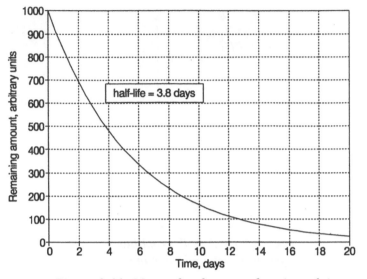

Figure 2.11. Mass of radon as a function of time

of units.) For now, don't worry about how to take e to a power or calculate the logarithm. These are implementation details that you can address later.

Exercise 22. Newton's algorithm is a well-known method for estimating the square root of any positive number. It works as follows:
(a) Make an initial guess for the square root. If the number is A, then an initial guess of X = A/2 is reasonable.
(b) Calculate a new guess using the formula X = (X + A/X)/2.
(c) Repeat (b) until the absolute value of X - A/X is less than some specified error limit.

Design a pseudocode algorithm to implement Newton's algorithm. If you like, you may design the pseudocode as a subprogram that accepts a number as input and returns the square root of the number as output. What happens to Newton's algorithm if the original number A equals zero?

Exercise 23. Remote access to computer systems often requires both a user ID and a password. Usually, a potential user is given only a limited number of attempts to "log on" correctly.

Design an algorithm that simulates the process whereby a computer system asks a user for an ID and a password. The user's responses are checked against a file of users, and access is granted if both the ID and the password are OK. A user is given three chances to enter an ID and password correctly. If the third attempt is unsuccessful, the connection with the computer is terminated and the program ends. In this problem, you can make up a pseudocode command—something like **SEARCH** *(list, for what?)*—to represent the operations required to search for an ID in a list of users.

Exercise 24. This exercise will make more sense if you have had or are taking an elementary calculus course. However, you should be able to write the algorithm in any case. The derivative of a function f(x) at any point x can be approximated by

> An understanding of elementary calculus will be helpful.

$$\frac{d\,f(x)}{dx} = \frac{[f(x+dx) - f(x)] + [f(x) - f(x-dx)]}{2\,dx} = \frac{f(x+dx) - f(x-dx)}{2\,dx}$$

for small values of dx. Design an algorithm in the form of a **SUBPROGRAM** for approximating the derivative of a specified function f(x) for any user-specified value of x. You can assume any convenient function. When you consider Step 5 of the problem-solving process, it should be obvious that the best way to verify the performance of a program is to use a function whose derivative you already know. For example, if f(x)=sin(x), then the derivative of f(x) is cos(x).

At this point, you do not have to determine how small dx should be to produce acceptable accuracy; that's the point of representing its value symbolically during algorithm development. We will return to this problem in a later chapter and give some suggestions for determining the size of dx and verifying the operation of the algorithm.

Hint: define a second **SUBPROGRAM** called *Value_of_Function* that requires a single input argument. The subprogram returns a numerical value equal to a specified function evaluated at the value of its input argument. Assume that you can use this subprogram as you would any other mathematical function. For example, you can write *y = Value_of_Function(z)* just as you would write the expression y = sin(z), where z is any appropriate quantity or expression. For this algorithm, the function will be called twice, once with argument z = x + dx and once with z = x - dx.

In Figure 2.12, the plain line represents the polynomial $0.1x^3 - x^2 + 2x$ plotted over the range [0,10]. Its analytic derivative is $0.3x^2 - 2x + 2$. The symbols represent the derivative estimated by applying the above formula, using steps of 0.25 in x. The line that appears to connect the symbols is the analytic derivative plotted as a function of x. For this very smooth and "well-behaved" function, the approximation to the analytic derivative is very good—essentially indistinguishable from the analytic derivative. Other than for illustrative purposes, there is no need to use numerical methods to estimate the derivative of this function because the analytic derivative is simple to calculate.

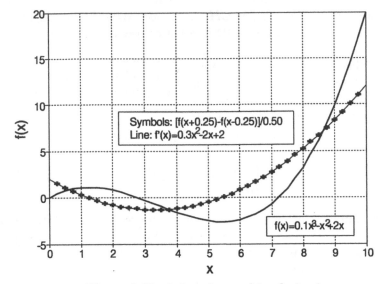

Figure 2.12. A function and its derivative

Exercise 25. Like the previous problem, this one will make more sense if you have had or are taking a calculus course. The integral of a function f(x) can be thought of

> An understanding of elementary calculus will be helpful.

graphically as the area under the curve y = f(x). Some functions can't be integrated analytically, in which case numerical methods are required. One simple way to approximate the value of an integral is to divide the area under f(x) into small trapezoidal areas. This is called "trapezoidal rule" integration. Given the lower and upper limits of x, x_1, and x_2, over which the integral is to be evaluated, the integral I can be approximated by

$$I = \sum_{i=1}^{n}[f(x_1+i \cdot dx)+f(x_1+(i-1) \cdot dx)]dx/2$$

where the "step size" dx is $(x_2 - x_1)/n$ and n is the number of equal intervals into which the range $[x_2-x_1]$ is divided.

Design an algorithm in the form of a **SUBPROGRAM** that uses trapezoidal rule integration to approximate the integral of a function that will be hard coded into a program. The user specifies the lower and upper boundaries of the integration interval and the number of intervals into which to divide that range.

Hint: use a loop to perform the summation indicated in the formula for the integral I. A loop counter i should count from 1 to n. Inside the loop, calculate

the corresponding value of x and then evaluate the function twice—once for
x_i + i•dx and once for x_i − (i − 1)•dx. The multiplication by dx/2 in the formula
can be done just once, after the loop terminates; there is no need to perform these
two operations repeatedly inside the loop.

The function in Figure 2.13 shows sin(x) between 0 and π radians (0° and
180°), which has an easily determined analytic integral of 2. This example divides
the range of x into just six equal intervals, simply for illustration, and the
approximation to the integral calculated in this way is 1.954. Normally, many
more than six intervals would be used. However, trapezoidal rule integration will
always underestimate the value of this integral no matter how small the step size.[7]

When you write a program to perform trapezoidal rule integration (see
Chapter 11), you will need to verify its operation by testing it with a simple
function such as sin(x).

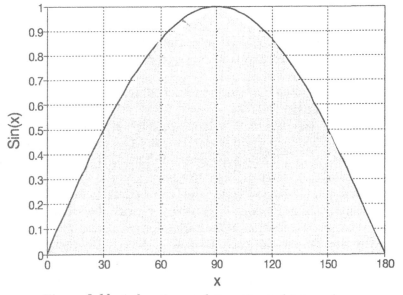

Figure 2.13. A function and its estimated integral

---

[7]This is because sin(x) is convex everywhere.

Exercise 26. There are many ways to encode text messages. One simple scheme is to replace each letter with another letter in the alphabet according to an encoding key that is randomly generated ahead of time. Here's an example:

```
ABCDEFGHIJKLMNOPQRSTUVWXYZ (original alphabet)
WKGLREUSPBTNQIFAMVHXOZYCJD (encoded alphabet)
```

Here's a message:

Roses are red;
Violets are blue.
I love programming,
And I hope you do too.

Here it is in the above code:

VFHRHWVRVRL
ZPFNRXHWVRKNOR
PNFZRAVFUVWQQPIU
WILPSFARJFOLFXFF

All the spaces and punctuation have been removed, and uppercase and lowercase letters are treated the same. This assumes that someone given the code key should be able to interpret the reconstructed message even if the original spacing can no longer be retrieved.

Design an algorithm to create such a coding key and then read and encode a text file using that key.

Hint: one way to create a code sequence is to store the letters of the alphabet in a table and then shuffle them around. Construct two tables. (For design purposes, lay one out right below the other.) Fill the first table with the uppercase letters of the alphabet in order. Copy this table into the second table. Start with the first position in the second table, which now contains the letter "A". Select a location in that table at random. Swap the "A" with the letter in that position. Proceed to the second position in the table. Select another random location and swap two letters. Do this for each position in the table. When you're done, the alphabet in the second table will be shuffled and the two tables will look like the example shown above (with the characters in the second table in different random positions, of course). Each character in the shuffled table is used as the coded character to represent the character directly above it in the original alphabet table.

Getting Started with Fortran: Writing Simple Programs

This chapter describes some basic elements of the Fortran language and lays the foundation for every Fortran program you will write. It includes Fortran implementations of the *ASSIGN*, *DEFINE*, *INCREMENT*, *INITIALIZE*, *READ*, and *WRITE* pseudocode commands from Chapter 2. By the time you finish this chapter, you will be able to write simple Fortran programs that accept input from your computer keyboard, perform some calculations, and display output on your monitor.

3.1 A Simple Problem and a Fortran Program to Solve It

We will start our discussion of Fortran by stating a very simple computational problem and applying the five-step problem-solving process presented in Chapter 2. We will continue to follow each step of this process throughout the text, even though you may think some problems are too simple to warrant that much attention. Later, when the problems you are asked to solve are more complicated, it will be very important to be familiar with a process that will help you develop solutions in an organized way, one step at a time.

1 *Define the problem.*

Given a radius, determine the circumference and area of a circle.

2 *Outline a solution.*

Your "plain English" outline for this problem is very simple:

1. Prompt the program user to supply a radius (from the keyboard?).
2. The circumference and area of a circle are given by:

$$\text{circumference} = 2\pi r$$
$$\text{area} = \pi r^2$$

3. Display the results (on the monitor?).

3 *Design an algorithm.*

DEFINE *(radius, circumference, area, and π as real numbers)*
WRITE *(prompt user to enter radius)*
READ *(radius)*
ASSIGN *circumference = 2π•radius*
          area = π•radius²
WRITE *(circumference and area)*

This algorithm defines a typical and straightforward sequence of steps: input → calculations → output.

4 *Convert the algorithm into a program.*

Here is a complete Fortran program that implements this algorithm. Files containing source code for this and all other complete Fortran programs in this text can be downloaded from the World Wide Web site mentioned in Section i.5 of the Preface. The file name for each program is given in square brackets.

> **The two italicized lines at the beginning of the program are *not* part of the program, which starts with the line containing the words** PROGRAM **Circle. These lines are there just to show how the statements in the program are placed on the line. In subsequent programs, this "ruler" will not be shown.**

For P-3.1 and most other programs in this text, some sample output will be included to give you a better idea of what the program actually does. Program P-3.1 is an interactive program that requires the user to provide a value for the radius. In this case, the user has typed the value 3. User input typed on the keyboard will always be printed in bold type even though this is not a distinction that will be made on your monitor.

We will discuss the details of P-3.1 (at great length!) in this chapter, so it's not necessary at this time to understand the significance of every detail. However, especially if you have successfully executed program P-2.1 from Chapter 2, you should be able to create or copy P-3.1 and execute it on your computer system.

If you type the program yourself, it is a good idea to copy it *exactly* as shown (except for the ruler line that, as explained above, is not part of the program) because you do not yet know what is essential and what isn't.

P-3.1 [CIRCLE.F90]

```
         1         2         3         4         5         6
123456789012345678901234567890123456789012345678901234567890123456
      PROGRAM Circle
!
! Purpose: Calculate the circumference and area of a circle.
!
! variable declarations...
!
      IMPLICIT NONE !Forces explicit typing of all variables.
      REAL radius, circumference, area
      REAL, PARAMETER :: pi=3.1415927 !Defines pi as a constant.
!
! get input...
!
      PRINT*,' Give radius of a circle: '
      READ*,radius
!
! do calculations...
!
      circumference=2.0*pi*radius
      area=pi*radius*radius
!
! display output...
!
      PRINT*,' circumference=',circumference,'  area=',area
!
! terminate program...
!
      END
```

Running P-3.1

```
 Give radius of a circle:
3
 circumference=    18.8495560      area=    28.2743340
```

Study Tip

You should be able to associate the parts of P-3.1 with the pseudocode commands in Step 4 even if you don't understand all the details.

Programming Tip

Remember that the source code file for CIRCLE.F90, and all other programs in this text, can be downloaded from the World Wide Web site mentioned in Section i.5 of the Preface. These files were created on an MS-DOS-based system. If you are programming in some other environment, your instructor may need to show you how to transfer source code files to that environment.

The MS-DOS source code files will be readable on any Macintosh computer with hardware/software that enables it to recognize the format of IBM-compatible diskettes. There is no basic file compatibility problem because source code files are purely "text" files that can be interpreted properly by any computer system. However, there are some minor differences between IBM-compatible and Macintosh text files that must be resolved when you translate IBM-compatible files into the Macintosh environment. Consult with your instructor if you use a Macintosh computer.

5 *Verify the operation of the program.*

The operation of P-3.1 is easy to verify with a hand calculator. Run the program several times and compare answers for several values of the radius. You can use almost any radius value to check your program. However, a value of 1 is clearly a poor choice. Why? Suppose you mistakenly wrote area=pi*radius. If the radius equals 1, the program will produce the correct numerical answer even though the code is wrong.

Because this is the first Fortran program in this text, we will examine it in great detail. By the time you finish this chapter, you should be able to write and execute programs similar to P-3.1 on your own. In fact, P-3.1 can serve as a model for many simple programs that involve nothing more complicated than input, a few calculations, and output. We will divide the discussion of P-3.1 into six topics, listed in Table 3.1.

Table 3.1. Programming topics in Chapter 3

Programming Topic	Section
Program layout	3.2
Variable declarations	3.3
List-directed input and output	3.4
Arithmetic operators, assignment statements, and calculations	3.5
Program termination	3.6
Compiling and executing a program	3.7

3.2 Program Layout

3.2.1 What Is "Source Code?"

P-3.1 constitutes the source code for a single Fortran 90 **program unit.** The source code file, in the form of a "human-readable" file stored on your computer, contains all the 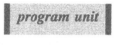 information required for a Fortran compiler to translate your problem-solving algorithm into a set of instructions your computer can understand. Large programs typically contain one main program and several subprograms, and they may also include other subprograms stored in one or more additional program units. For now, your programs will consist of one main program stored in a single source code file.

It's important to understand that source code is machine independent because the Fortran language is standardized. This means that the file CIRCLE.F90 can be used as the source code on *any* computer that has a Fortran 90 compiler. Machine independence is an essential feature of any high-level language.

It is possible for source code to contain **nonstandard extensions**—features that are not part 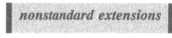 of the language standard—that will work with one compiler but not with others. Such extensions can compromise the portability of source code. This is a major problem with Fortran 77 compilers, almost all of which contain many nonstandard features.[1] However, all the programs in this text should execute with any Fortran 90 compiler because they all conform to the Fortran 90 standard.[2]

Even though it is common to refer to source code as a "program," this isn't completely accurate. A source code file is just an interface between you and the Fortran environment—a way to transmit instructions—and its creation is only the first step in creating a program. As you will see later in this chapter, the Fortran environment generates additional files, including a so-called "executable" file that contains the translation into computer-specific machine language of all the instructions from possibly several source code program units.

As previously noted in Chapter 2 (see Figure 2.1), although the source code file is transferable to any other computer that supports a Fortran 90 compiler, the

---

[1]Potential problems with nonportable extensions explain why Fortran 77 texts usually restrict themselves to the language standard and therefore have, for many years, taught a version of Fortran that is increasingly irrelevant to the way this language is used in practice.

[2]Some programs later in the text require input from an external data file. When the names of such files are included as part of the source code, they may need to be changed to correspond to the file-naming syntax for your computer.

additional files that your Fortran environment creates are not. The executable file produced by an IBM-compatible personal computer won't work on a mainframe or Macintosh computer, for example. To "port" a program to another computer, you have to transfer the source code file and compile it on the new computer. The new executable file will be different from the executable file on the original computer, but the advantage of using a high-level language to write source code is that you shouldn't have to worry about those differences.

It's no accident that the source code in P-3.1 is so easy to understand in general terms that its purpose should be clear even to someone who doesn't understand the Fortran language. That is, after all, one of the main reasons for using a high-level programming language. Some of the words appearing in uppercase letters are commands that don't look much different from the pseudocode commands used to develop the algorithm in Step 3 of the problem-solving process. Throughout the program, there are other lines of text beginning with a " ! " that appear to be explanatory comments; in fact, they are. The calculations look very similar to algebraic expressions even though, as we will see, there are some important differences between how Fortran uses the familiar "=" sign and its meaning in algebra.

However, just because you can interpret this source code doesn't mean that you are ready to create your own programs. There are many general questions to be answered about the layout and structure of Fortran programs before you can write an equivalent one on your own. The elements of the Fortran language are simple. However, source code must conform to syntax rules that are very specific and rigid compared to, for example, the flexible and sometimes vague rules for effective human communication.[3]

The smallest building blocks of Fortran source code are characters:

(blank, sometimes represented as Ⱦ)

```
!      "      $      %      &      '      (      )      *
+      ,      -      =      .      /
0-9  (the digits)
:      ;      <      =      >      ?
A-Z  (all the uppercase letters)
_  (underscore)
a-z  (all the lowercase letters)
```

Meaningful characters or combinations of characters, called *tokens*, are defined by the Fortran language. Fortran tokens include line labels, keywords, names, constants, operators, and separators. We will deal with the meaning of each

tokens
statements

---

[3]Rigid syntax rules are a property of all procedural languages, not just Fortran.

of these tokens as we encounter them in the text. Sequences of tokens form *statements*. Statements usually occupy one line. In P-3.1, the first statement,

```
PROGRAM Circle
```

consists of two tokens, the keyword `PROGRAM` and the name `Circle`. The statement

```
X=A*B
```

consists of five tokens, X, =, A, *, and B. (Although the meaning of this statement appears obvious because of its similarity to an algebraic expression, we will later discuss the meaning and use of each of these tokens in great detail.)

Tokens may be separated by one or more spaces, but a Fortran 90 compiler will not accept spaces embedded within tokens.[4] For example, X = A * B is equivalent to X=A*B, but P R O G R A M Circle is not equivalent to PROGRAM Circle.

Fortran statements may contain extra spaces at the beginning of lines and *between* tokens. That is, the statements

```
PRINT*,' User prompt: '
            PRINT              *,          ' User prompt: '
```

are equivalent.

A collection of statements forms source code, which is contained in a program unit that includes a main program and often one or more subprograms. Figure 3.1 illustrates the components of a source code file. An entire program may include subprograms from one or more additional program units. P-3.1 consists of one program unit, containing just a main program. In Chapter 7, several modifications of P-3.1 will be presented to illustrate how to use subprograms.

3.2.2 Where Does Source Code Come From?

Source code for a program written in a high-level language can be created with a text editor or word processor. Some programming environments, especially those written for use on desktop computers, include special text editors that are

---

[4]This restriction actually applies only to Fortran 90 compilers in their default "free format" mode, as will be described later in this section. Older versions of Fortran and Fortran 90 compilers used in their "fixed format" mode will accept blanks within keywords, although there is no good reason to put them there. Even within "free format" Fortran 90, there are a few exceptions. For example, the keyword `ENDIF`, which we will discuss in later chapters, can also be written with an embedded space, as `END IF`.

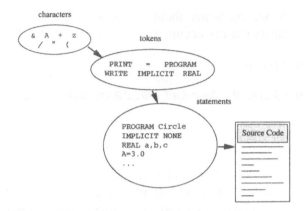

Figure 3.1. Components of source code

integrated into that environment. A completely integrated programming environment can provide some shortcuts. For example, when you write source code, the environment may check each statement for syntax errors as you write it.

Your Fortran environment may not be as "user-helpful" in this regard. On most systems, you must first create a separate file containing the source code, using whatever kind of text processing or editing capability you have available. Then you must ask your Fortran compiler to try to convert that source code file into an executable program. The first step in the compilation process is to check your source code for syntax errors—combinations of characters, tokens, or statements that your compiler cannot interpret as part of a valid Fortran program. If the compiler finds errors, you must edit the source code file to remove the errors and repeat the compilation process.

Programming Tip

If you use a word processor to create source code, don't save that file as a word-processing document. Such documents contain not only the text you have written, but also other information about the document that your Fortran compiler will not be able to interpret. If you use a word processor, you must save the source code as a "text only" or "ASCII text" file. If your word processor won't allow you to do this, you need a different word processor!

Regardless of your programming environment, you can create source code for Fortran using any available text editor. Your instructor will provide specific instructions for doing this, based on the software available at your institution.

Because the source code files in this text were written in an MS-DOS environment, their file names consist of no more than eight characters, a period, and an extension of no more than three characters. Other computing environments place fewer restrictions on file names, and you may wish to take advantage of that fact.

Some Fortran compilers assume that, by default, source code files will be identified by a particular file name extension. Possibilities include `.F77` or `.FOR` for Fortran 77 code and `.F90` for Fortran 90 code. In this text, we will assume that all source code files have an `.F90` extension. Once you determine an appropriate file name extension for your programming environment, use it consistently for source code files and for no other purpose. Then it is easy to locate Fortran source code files by performing a directory search for files with a particular extension.

3.2.3 Why Do the Fortran Statements All Start in Column 7?

You might not have noticed it, but all the lines in P-3.1 except for those beginning with a `!` start in column 7. This is basically a style choice that you and your instructor may disagree with. Prior to the Fortran 90 standard, this layout

fixed format comment line

was a requirement for every Fortran program. Each line in a Fortran program contained 80 positions, corresponding roughly to the number of characters that can be typed on one line of a piece of 8½"×11" paper. The 80 positions were used according to a *fixed format*. If the first position contained a c, C, or *, the line was interpreted as a *comment line*, as described in Section 3.2.4. Otherwise, the first five positions were reserved for line labels, which were either convenient or required, depending on the context. The sixth position was reserved for a symbol to indicate that a previous line was being continued onto the current line, and positions 7–72 were reserved for Fortran statements.

In the early days of Fortran, programs used to be stored on "punch cards" rather than electronically. If you were unfortunate enough to drop a large "deck" of these cards, you would have a difficult time putting them back into the proper order! Therefore, positions on these cards 73-80 were reserved for a card number.

Even after source code files could be created and stored in a much safer electronic form, the 80-column card format was retained for Fortran source code. Although the Fortran 90

free format

standard no longer requires this layout and allows *free format* lines of up to 132 characters starting in any column, we will continue to use the Fortran 77 standard 72-column layout in this text. It makes programs easy to display in a textbook format, and your source code will be recognizable to anyone who uses either the new (Fortran 90) or old (Fortran 77) standard. Most monitor screens still display only 80 characters on a line, so you may find little advantage in being able to write lines 132 characters long. However...

> **It is important to remember that the physical layout of the source code in this text is a matter of style and not a Fortran 90 language requirement.**

3.2.4 Inserting Comments in Source Code Files

Any line that contains a ! as its first nonblank character or contains nothing but blank characters is treated as a comment line and is ignored by the compiler. Comment lines are used to separate sections of your program and explain what you're doing. Comments aren't required for Fortran programs to work, but they *are* required as a matter of good programming style. Because they are ignored by the compiler, they can appear anywhere in a program. In this text, we will always put the ! in column 1 of any line intended to be blank or to contain nothing but a comment. This style restriction isn't really necessary, but it makes source code easy to read.

A comment initiated by a ! character can also follow a statement on the same line. Earlier versions of Fortran did not allow comments on the same line as a statement, although some Fortran 77 compilers have a nonstandard implementation of this feature. In this text, we will use a combination of separate and in-line comments as required to clarify source code.

In programs written in older versions of Fortran, you will see comment lines indicated by a c, C, or * in the first column. These characters, which mean something else when they appear elsewhere on a line, could always be interpreted correctly because older versions of Fortran required a fixed format line that eliminated any possibility of misinterpretation. However, because characters can appear anywhere on a Fortran 90 line, it's not possible for the compiler to make assumptions about the meaning of a character just because it appears in the first column.

To solve this problem, the Fortran 90 standard uses a ! character to indicate the start of a comment in free format code. This works because this is the only use allowed for the ! character. (The exception is that the ! character can be part of a string constant, as defined later in this chapter.)

Programming Tip

The Fortran 90 standard requires compilers to include options for interpreting *both* fixed format and free format source code, but not within the same program module. (Free format is the default option.) That is, your entire source code file can use *either* fixed format or free format style, but not a mix of the two. All the source code in this text should be compiled under the free format option even though it retains, purely as a matter of style, the "old-fashioned" column allocations of the Fortran 77 standard. Because of the way comment lines are constructed, the source code in this text cannot be compiled in the fixed format mode of a Fortran 90 compiler. (However, some Fortran 77 compilers have nonstandard extensions that allow Fortran 90-style comment lines.)

If you want to use older code that contains pre-Fortran 90-style comment lines within a program written in free format, it's easy to make them compatible.

Simply use a text editor to perform a search-and-replace operation to change comment characters to !, making sure not to alter c, C, or * characters when they appear in other contexts.

3.2.5 How Much of P-3.1 Is Absolutely Necessary and How Much Is a Matter of Style?

In order to develop a sense of source code "style," you must first know what is necessary and what is discretionary. Consider the minimum contents of a file that can be recognized as Fortran 90 source code:

```
END
```

That is, the only absolutely necessary component of such a file is a statement telling the compiler where the end of the program is. Of course, such a program doesn't do anything!

Another way to learn about style is to rewrite P-3.1. P-3.1(a) produces the same results as P-3.1 even though the physical layout of the source code is very different. Note that the PROGRAM statement is optional, as are all the comment lines. The significance of the missing statement beginning with REAL will be discussed in the next section. The descriptive variable names used in P-3.1 have been replaced with the one-letter names a, c, and r. Some individual statement lines have been strung together on the same line, and use a semicolon as a statement separator.

P-3.1(a) [CIRCLE1A.F90]

```
parameter (pi=3.1415927)
print*,' Give radius of a circle:';read*,r;c=2.*pi*r;a=pi*r*r
print*,' circumference=',c,'  area=',a;end
```

The source code in P-3.1(a) is perfectly acceptable to a standard Fortran 90 compiler, but it is much harder for humans to read than P-3.1. A long program written in this style would be virtually unreadable and would not be allowed in any professional programming application. In programming, clarity is almost always preferred over brevity. As your programs become more complex, a consistent, readable style for writing source code becomes increasingly important. Therefore, as a matter of style, P-3.1(a) is unacceptable.

3.2.6 Fortran Keywords

Note that some of the words in P-3.1 are in all caps. These words, called *keywords*, all have specific meanings in Fortran. Each keyword is a Fortran token. Some of them are the direct Fortran implementation of the pseudocode commands defined in Chapter 2. We will be consistent about capitalizing keywords even though, as P-3.1(a) demonstrates...

> **Fortran compilers are case-insensitive.**

Even though PROGRAM, program, Program, and even pROGRAM are all the same as far as your Fortran compiler is concerned, we will always use PROGRAM. Some programmers prefer to use lowercase letters and may consider the use of uppercase spellings an old-fashioned style choice, but it has been chosen for this text to make the keywords stand out in the program listings.

The first keyword we encounter in P-3.1 is PROGRAM. Even though it's optional, it's a good idea to use a PROGRAM statement in your source code. Every Fortran keyword has to be used within an appropriate syntax framework, and we will describe the syntax for each keyword as it is first encountered. A summary of syntax for all keywords discussed in the text is found in **Appendix 2**. The general syntax for the PROGRAM keyword is:

```
PROGRAM program_name

Examples:
      PROGRAM Model_1

      PROGRAM My_Program
!
!     This program is stored in file MY_PROG.F90
```

In this and all subsequent syntax descriptions, *italicized_text* always means that some information, most often a single word, must be chosen and supplied by the programmer. The *program_name* can contain up to 31 characters. It shouldn't be the same as a Fortran keyword—it's possible to name a program program, but it's certainly not a very good idea—and it can't be the same as a variable name (as defined in the next section) you will use elsewhere in your program. If the PROGRAM keyword appears, it must be followed by a valid name; that is, PROGRAM can't appear by itself on a line. It makes sense for the program name to be the same as the file name under which the source code is stored on your computer system.

Study Tip

You should start writing your own annotated list of basic Fortran syntax, with examples. Will it be more helpful to organize this list alphabetically or by function?

Programming Tip

The fact that computer operating systems place restrictions on file names may be irritating. If you are using such a system (MS-DOS, for example) and you would like your program to have a longer descriptive name, include the system file name in a program comment line. (See the second example in the PROGRAM syntax box.)

3.2.7 What If a Statement Is Too Long to Fit on a Single Line?

All the statements in P-3.1 fit easily on a single line, but long statements can be a problem when complicated expressions are translated into Fortran. Consider this algebraic expression for calculating one root of the quadratic equation $ax^2 + bx + c = 0$:

$$\text{root} = \frac{-b + \sqrt{b^2 - 4ac}}{2a}$$

Its Fortran equivalent, assuming $(b^2 - 4ac) \geq 0$, is: [5]

```
root=(-b+(b*b-4.0*a*c)**0.5)/(2.0*a)
```

This statement will make more sense after we have discussed arithmetic operators later in this chapter. Even though the statement still isn't too long for a single line, we could, just for demonstration purposes, separate it into several lines of code like this:

```
root=                             &
      (-b+(b*b-4.0*a*c)**0.5) &
      /(2.0*a)
```

The ampersand (&) is the Fortran 90 line continuation mark. It is appended to any partial statement that is continued onto the next line. It can go anywhere on the line after the partial statement to be continued, and, of course, it does not become part of the statement itself. (To put it another way, the ampersand has no

---

[5]This statement also assumes that a, b, c, and root all have appropriate data types, as discussed later in the chapter.

possible interpretation other than as a line continuation mark.[6]) A single statement can occupy as many as 40 lines, using up to 39 line continuations.

Programming Tip

If your programs need to retain as much compatibility with Fortran 77 code as possible, you can improve compatibility by using an alternative form for line continuations. In Fortran 90, the continued line normally starts with the first nonblank character, but, optionally, it starts with the first nonblank character following a continuation mark on the continued line. In Fortran 77 (and earlier versions), continuation marks can be any character, but they have to appear in column 6. This fact can be combined with the fact that Fortran 77 ignores characters in columns 73-80. This version of the above statement is compatible with both Fortran 90's free format style and Fortran 77:

```
         1         2         3         4         5         6         7
1234567890123456789012345678901234567890123456789012345678901234567890123
   root=                                                                &
   &    (-b+SQRT(b*b-4.0*a*c))                                          &
   &    /(2.0*a)
```

The ampersand at the end of a continued line will be ignored by a Fortran 77 compiler because it's in column 73. Fortran 77 requires a continuation character to appear in column 6 of the continued line. If that character is an ampersand, this statement will be accepted by both Fortran 77 and 90 compilers.

3.2.8 Executable and Nonexecutable Statements

Fortran source code consists of a combination of *executable* and *nonexecutable statements*. The layout of a simple program's source code looks like this:

> *executable statements*
> *nonexecutable statements*

```
[PROGRAM name]
[specification statements]
[executable statements]
END [PROGRAM [name]]
```

In this and all subsequent syntax definitions, any quantity enclosed in brackets [...] is optional. (Recall from Section 3.32.5 that END is the only required statement in a Fortran program.)

---

[6]The exception is that an ampersand can appear as a character in a string constant.

The PROGRAM statement and the specification statements are nonexecutable statements. They are essentially "bookkeeping statements" that tell your Fortran compiler how to allocate space in your computer's memory. The nonexecutable statements are followed by the executable statements that do the actual work of the program. In this text, every program will include a nonexecutable PROGRAM *name* line. Remember that the keyword PROGRAM cannot appear on a line by itself without a name. When the keyword PROGRAM appears in conjunction with the END statement, a name is optional. This text will not include the optional PROGRAM [*name*] as part of the END statement, although you are free to do so in your own programs.

3.3 Declaring Variables and Defining Constants

3.3.1 Variable Names and Data Type Declarations

Recall that the first task in designing an algorithm—Step 3 of the problem-solving process—is to assign names to the quantities needed to solve the problem, using the ***DEFINE*** command. You should take this opportunity to think about the nature of the information needed to solve the problem and the output provided by the program.

When you write a program in any high-level language, including Fortran, the names of these quantities become variable names that must be associated with data of a particular type. Variable names give you a symbolic way to access values in your computer's memory without having to worry about the details of where those memory locations actually are. For all practical purposes, the memory location and the variable name by which you access information in that location are the same thing.

The association of a variable name with a specific data type is called ***type declaration***. This is a 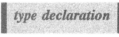 nonexecutable specification statement that must appear at the beginning of your program, before that program can make any calculations. The general syntax for a type declaration statement is

```
data_type[, attributes] [::] <list of variables,
                            separated by commas>
```

The *data_type* name is optionally followed by one or more *attributes*. If no attributes are present, the double colon is optional. If attributes are present, the double colon is required. Finally, a list of variables to be associated with this data type is given. We will show examples of several data type and attribute declarations later in this section.

For P-3.1, the type declarations are

```
REAL radius, circumference, area
REAL, PARAMETER :: pi=3.1415927 !Defines pi as a constant.
```

The program requires four numerical quantities, all of which should be declared as real numbers rather than integers. No distinction is made between "input" (radius) and "output" (area and circumference) to and from a program; it is up to you to keep track of the *purpose* of each variable you declare. However, there is one important distinction you can ask a program to make. In P-3.1, the variable pi contains the value of the constant π, and it has been defined in such a way that its value cannot be changed while the program is running. (More will be said about this later.)

The Fortran 90 rules for naming variables are:

1. Names may contain up to 31 characters, including uppercase and lowercase letters, digits, and the underscore character _.
2. The first character must be a letter.
3. Embedded blanks aren't allowed.

Here are some allowed variable names:

TAXES   Final_Grade   Y1993   i

In older versions of Fortran, variable names could contain no more than six characters. They had to start with an uppercase letter, and the rest of the name could consist only of other uppercase letters or digits. This is why you will often see strange-looking variable names in older programs or texts that use the Fortran 77 standard. RADIUS looks reasonable, but circumference had to be abbreviated to something like CIRCUM. Most Fortran 77 compilers have nonstandard features that allow longer and more descriptive variable names as well as a mixture of uppercase and lowercase letters.

In this text we will make full use of the variable-naming features of Fortran 90 to make names as clear and descriptive as possible. For example, we will usually consider such shortcuts as naming the radius r to be unacceptable style because such abbreviated variable names make programs harder to read and understand. Exceptions might be made in cases where a well-known equation is used in a program. For example, in the ideal gas equation pV=μRT, the variable names for the pressure p, volume V, and temperature T might be retained because their interpretation should be clear in context. The symbol μ would have to be given some other name, such as mu.

Although the ability to mix uppercase and lowercase letters is useful to make variable names easier to read, remember that Fortran compilers don't distinguish between uppercase and lowercase letters. So R and r are interpreted as the same variable name. If a program happened to involve the universal gas constant, often represented as R in formulas, as in the previous paragraph, as well as a linear correlation coefficient, often represented as r, then you will have to choose a different variable name for one of these two quantities.

Programming Tip

As a matter of style, it might be acceptable to use single-letter symbols for variable names in simple calculations involving well-known scientific or engineering formulas if the meaning of each symbol is clear in context. However, if such calculations are embedded in a larger program with many variable names and/or formulas, it is better programming style to use longer and more descriptive variable names. Whenever there is any chance of misinterpretation, it is up to you to make the calculation in question as clear as possible. Calculations that seem perfectly clear when you're writing a program have a way of becoming obscure when you look at the program a few weeks later.

3.3.2 Intrinsic Data Types

Type declarations for intrinsic data types

The most common type declarations in Fortran involve the basic data types supported by the language. There are five such data types, called *intrinsic data types*, as described in Table 3.2.

intrinsic data types

Table 3.2. Fortran intrinsic data types

Intrinsic Data Type	Fortran Type Declaration
integer numbers	INTEGER
real numbers	REAL
logical values	LOGICAL
characters and strings of characters	CHARACTER
complex numbers	COMPLEX

All variables used in a program must be given a data type. For now, all variables in the programs you will write will be declared as one or the intrinsic data types. Your compiler uses the declarations to set aside an appropriate amount of, computer memory to store the values needed by your program while it's running. Data declaration statements appear at the beginning of your program, after the PROGRAM statement and before the first executable statement. Executable statements contain your programming instructions. In P-3.1,

```
PRINT *,' Give radius of a circle: '
```

is the first executable statement.

In this section, we will describe type declarations for the first four intrinsic data types listed in Table 3.2. We will return to the COMPLEX data type later in the text.

Type declarations for numbers

For the purpose of programming, there are two basic kinds of numbers: integers and real numbers. An integer is a "whole" number—any number that does not contain a decimal point. The values 1, -1, 0, and 17 are integers. A real number, whether rational or irrational, contains a decimal part. The values 0.333, -0.5, 14.1, and 1.3×10^{-9} are real numbers. Fortran recognizes both real and integer numbers. In common with other languages, real numbers and integers are stored differently, with important implications about how arithmetic operations are performed in programs.

An important distinction must be made between an integer value such as 1 and the apparently equivalent real number 1.0. Although these values may be equivalent in the numerical or algebraic sense, expressing the value 1.0 with decimal notation means that it will be stored differently in a Fortran program from the integer value 1. As a result, these values may not be interchangeable in a program.

When you use numerical variables associated with numbers in a Fortran program, you must distinguish between *real variables*, which hold real numbers, and *integer variables*, which hold integer values. You do this by giving the variables a REAL or INTEGER data type.

real variable
integer variable
implicit typing

Traditionally, Fortran programs have made use of *implicit typing* for numerical variables. All variables beginning with letters I through N are implicitly typed as INTEGER. (Because of Fortran's mathematical origins, this convention is related to the common mathematical use of letters such as i for indices or counters that can have only integer values.)

Variables beginning with any other letter are implicitly typed as REAL numbers. Other kinds of variables, such as characters, must always be given an explicit data declaration. If P-3.1 had been written in an earlier version of Fortran, the REAL statement would not be required. All four variables would be implicitly typed as REAL numbers because none of the names assigned to the four variables used in that program begins with the letters I through N. (The IMPLICIT NONE statement in P-3.1 would not appear in programs written in earlier versions of Fortran. Can you guess its purpose? We will discuss this statement later in this section.)

Fortran 90 still allows implicit typing. However, as a matter of good programming style, we will insist on *explicit typing* for *every* variable. Explicit typing means that every 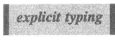 variable name used in a program (plus names for a few other things, as we will see later in the text) must appear in a data type declaration statement. Why is this important? Because explicit typing makes programs less prone to errors and easier to read, debug, and modify, and also because explicit data typing is consistent with requirements imposed by other high-level languages, such as C.

A somewhat simplified syntax for REAL and INTEGER data type declarations is:

```
REAL [::] variable_name[, variable_name] ...
INTEGER variable_name[, variable_name]

Examples:
      REAL x_value, y_value, radius, angle
      INTEGER i,j,k
```

The double colon is optional for this kind of declaration. (The double colon will be required in some circumstances that will be discussed later in this chapter.) A single data declaration statement may contain as many variable names as you wish.

The REAL and INTEGER data types also define, by implication, the allowed range of integers and real numbers. It is possible within the Fortran 90 standard to change those ranges, but we will not usually need to do that for the problems in this text.[7]

Type declarations for logical variables

The LOGICAL data type is used for declaring variables that can have one of only two possible values: .TRUE. or .FALSE.. (The periods preceding and following the words TRUE and FALSE are required.) We will discuss the use of these variables later in the text. The syntax is

---

[7]For some kinds of calculations, you may wish to know what the size and range restrictions actually are because if you exceed the allowed ranges, your progam can "crash." These values are available from Fortran 90 intrinsic functions, which we will discuss in a later chapter.

```
LOGICAL variable_name[, variable_name]
```

Type declarations for characters and strings of characters

Historically, Fortran was concerned largely with arithmetic calculations. Now, however, text manipulation may comprise a significant portion of the

character variable

tasks performed by many programs. Modern high-level programming languages include data types to manipulate *character variables*, and they may distinguish between single characters and sequences of more than one character. In Fortran, no distinction is made between single characters and strings of characters. That is, a variable that will be assigned a "value" of a single character is treated as a character string of length 1. The CHARACTER data type is used to define such variables. (The name is somewhat misleading, because the data type applies basically to *strings* of characters.) The maximum number of characters that will be assigned to a variable must be stated explicitly. There are two syntax forms for CHARACTER data type declarations:

```
CHARACTER[([LEN=]n)] variable_name[*n][, variable_name[*n]] ...
CHARACTER[*n] variable_name[*n][, variable_name[*n]] ...
   where n is an integer constant.

Examples:
     CHARACTER a, b, c, d*3
     CHARACTER*10 name1, name2
     CHARACTER*20 Name, Street*30, City*25, State*2
     CHARACTER(20) Name, Street*30, City*25, State*2
```

In the first form, the LEN= is optional. The constant *n* defines the length of the character string. Its presence after any variable name overrides the value following the CHARACTER declaration. A CHARACTER declaration without a value for the length implies that the variables declared in that statement are of length 1 unless that length is overridden as shown in the syntax examples. Any combination of these declaration statements can be used interchangeably within a single program.

In the first example, a, b, and c contain just one character, but d contains three characters. In the second example, name1 and name2 each contains 10 characters. In the last two examples, Name contains 20 characters, but this value is overridden for the other three variable names by their individual length specifiers.

The PARAMETER attribute and statement

Sometimes "variables" really need to be constants that shouldn't be changed while your program is running. Fortran allows you to associate a constant value with a name *either* by using a PARAMETER statement or by assigning the PARAMETER attribute as part of a type declaration statement. In P-3.1, the variable holding the value of π (pi) is given the PARAMETER attribute:

```
REAL, PARAMETER :: pi=3.1415927
```

In this kind of type declaration statement, which includes both type and attribute declarations, the double colon is required. Once a quantity has been given the PARAMETER attribute, it becomes a ***named constant*** that can't be changed anywhere else in your program; any attempt to do so will generate an error message when you try to compile the program. An alternative way to achieve the same result is first to declare a variable and then to include it in a separate PARAMETER statement. For example:

named constant

```
REAL pi
PARAMETER (pi=3.1415927)
```

The general syntax forms for giving a variable the PARAMETER attribute are

```
PARAMETER (variable_name=value[, variable_name=value] ...)
data_type,PARAMETER :: variable_name=value
                       [, variable_name=value] ...

Examples:
(using a PARAMETER statement)
     INTEGER MaxSize
     PARAMETER (MaxSize=1000)
(using the PARAMETER attribute)
     REAL,PARAMETER :: pi=3.1415927, Deg_to_Rad=0.0174532
```

The first syntax form is retained from Fortran 77. When a PARAMETER statement is used, as in the first syntax form, it is assumed that each variable name has previously been included in a type declaration statement. The preference for Fortran 90 is to use the PARAMETER attribute within a type declaration statement.

When you give a variable PARAMETER status, it might be helpful to think of the result as being similar to a "search and replace" operation in a word processor. The effect is the same as if you searched through your program and replaced every occurrence of that variable name with the characters appearing to the right of the = sign in the PARAMETER or type declaration statement. That is, the = sign has the meaning of "replace with" rather than "is equal to" in either the algebraic sense or the "assignment" sense, as we will discuss later in this chapter. If you maintain this mental image of what's happening, you will be less likely to misuse a variable that has been given PARAMETER status. In particular, you won't be tempted to try to give such a variable a different value.

Enforcing explicit typing

In earlier versions of Fortran, a style requirement of explicit typing imposed a significant burden on programmers because there was no way to enforce that requirement. However, Fortran 90 and some Fortran 77 compilers, through a nonstandard extension, provide a means of forcing explicit typing of all variables. The syntax is

```
IMPLICIT NONE
```

This is a nonexecutable statement that must appear before the type declaration statements. It "turns off" implicit typing and forces you to declare explicitly the data type of every variable you use in your program; if you don't, your compiler will generate an error message.

The IMPLICIT statement can also be used with other parameters to alter Fortran's default implicit typing rules. We will not give the general syntax for the IMPLICIT statement because the programs presented in this text will always use the IMPLICIT NONE statement to enforce explicit data typing of every variable name, as in P-3.1.

It may seem that asking you to include the IMPLICIT NONE statement in every program is an unnecessary imposition. However, this style requirement prevents program errors that can be very difficult to find. As an example, suppose you are writing a program to calculate taxes. You select a variable name Taxes to represent the result of a calculation and explictly type it as a REAL variable. Now suppose that, at some point in your program, you misspell the variable name Taxes as Texas. This will certainly lead to problems in your program's operation. However, a Fortran program that allows implicit typing will be perfectly happy with this variable name. It will create another memory location for this new, implicitly REAL variable and perform whatever operations you ask it to perform when you refer to its name. However, if your program contains an IMPLICIT NONE statement, the Fortran compiler will flag the variable named Texas as an undeclared variable and will generate an error message.

Programming Tip

Your compiler may issue a warning message concerning variable names that are included in data type declaration statements, but not used anywhere in your program. (This feature isn't required by the Fortran 90 standard.) The message is given only as a warning because these "extra" variables may not represent a problem; perhaps you are still developing a program and haven't yet written the code that uses the variable(s) in question.

The implications of type declaration

When you declare a variable's type by including it in a Fortran declaration statement, three important things happen:

1. The variable name is "reserved" and can't be used for any other purpose in the main program or subprogram in which it is declared.

However, the same name can be reused in a different program unit or in a different subprogram within the same program unit.

2. The kinds of values that can be assigned to the variable name are specified.

Each data type is associated with a certain collection of appropriate values. Variables declared as having that data type can have any one of those values, but the variable cannot be assigned an inappropriate value. For example, you can't assign a CHARACTER value to an integer.

3. The kinds of operations that can be performed on the variable name are specified.

Arithmetic operations can be performed on numerical variables, but these operations make no sense for a CHARACTER variable, for example.

As you can see, type declaration has important implications that extend beyond simply providing a way to ensure that all variables have been associated with a particular data type. Explicit type declaration allows your compiler to perform several different kinds of "error checking" on your source code to prevent you from assigning values and performing operations that are inappropriate for a particular variable name.[8]

---

[8]Not all languages are as strict as Fortran about interpreting these kinds of rules. C is a notable example.

Using nonexecutable statements in programs

So far, we have identified several nonexecutable statements that should, or may, appear in source code:

1. a PROGRAM statement
2. one or more comment lines, marked with a !
3. an IMPLICIT NONE statement
4. one or more data type declaration statements: REAL, INTEGER, CHARACTER, or LOGICAL
5. one or more PARAMETER statements to identify quantities whose value cannot be changed while the program is running
6. an END statement that terminates the program

Of these, Fortran requires only the END statement, but as a matter of good programming style, programs in this text will always include the first four kinds of nonexecutable statements. The appearance of the PARAMETER statement is determined by the nature of the program.

All the specification statements—including the IMPLICIT NONE statement, data type declaration statements, and PARAMETER statements—must appear in your program *after* the PROGRAM statement and *before* the first executable statement in your program. In P-3.1, remember that

```
PRINT*,' Give radius of a circle:
```

is the first executable statement. Comment lines are ignored during compilation and can appear anywhere.

3.3.3 Constants

Fortran supports several kinds of constants that correspond to the intrinsic data types. These may be either named constants, such as result from using a PARAMETER 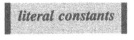 statement or attribute, or *literal constants* (or "literals"). We will discuss four kinds of literals: integers, real numbers, characters, and logical.

Integers and real numbers

INTEGER constants are signed or unsigned integer values. The allowed range is determined by your compiler, not by the language standard. Default ranges can be overridden by using additional data type specifiers, but we will defer a discussion of this topic until Chapter 12. As mentioned previously, you can determine the default range on your system, and we will return to this point later. Some `INTEGER` constants (or literals) are

```
1          0          +17          32767          -333
```

    `REAL` constants consist of some or all of the following: a signed or unsigned integer part; a decimal point; a fractional part; an exponent part consisting of the letter `E` (or `e`) followed by a signed or unsigned integer. Some `REAL` constants are

```
1.    -0.0037    +.17        1E+20 1.0E+20      -3.777e-7
7e6   7.e6
```

A plus sign is always optional for a positive number, but a minus sign is required if you wish to represent a negative number. Note that 1 (without a decimal point) is an `INTEGER` constant. Either `1.` or `1.0` is a `REAL` constant. Remember that 1 and 1. or 1.0 are treated differently by your program. Numbers expressed in scientific notation (with `e` or `E`) are always `REAL` and don't require decimal points. Thus `1E+20` and `7.e6` are `REAL` constants, corresponding to 1×10^{20} and 7×10^6. The numbers `1E+20`, `1E20`, `1.E20`, `1.0E20`, and `1.E+20` are all equivalent.

    You may sometimes forget that the conventional way of writing numbers with commas or $ signs in some contexts won't work in Fortran, or other languages, for that matter. Thus these "values" contain special characters and won't be recognized as numerical constants:

```
$1000              3,777.78          1,222,333
```

You should help the user of your programs avoid entering inappropriate numerical values by supplying helpful prompt messages prior to `READ` statements. For example,

```
PRINT *,' How much is in your account?  $'
PRINT *,' Enter a large number, without commas or spaces:'
```

Logical constants

As noted above, there are only two logical values and hence only two possible logical constants, `.TRUE.` and `.FALSE.`. The periods at each end of the word are required, and you may use either uppercase or lowercase letters, or a mixture of the two.

Character constants

Character constants (or string literals) consist of strings of zero or more characters enclosed in a pair of single quotation marks (apostrophes) or double quotation marks. Any displayable character supported by your computer is allowed. For example, a "#" can appear in a character constant even though it isn't one of the Fortran special characters. Here are some examples of character constants:

```
' ' (a space)
'Laura'
"C"
"This is a Fortran string constant!"
```

Note that it's OK to use the ! character as part of a string constant. Blank spaces and distinctions between uppercase and lowercase letters are significant in strings. The strings `'David'`, `'DAVID'`, `'        David'`, `'David       '`, and `' D a v i d '` are all different. A single quotation mark may be included in a character string by using double quotation marks to enclose the entire string or by using two single quotation marks embedded in a string surrounded by single quotes:

```
"Here's a string constant"
'Here''s a string constant.'
```

These two are equivalent, as are

```
'Here is a "string constant."'
"Here is a ""string constant."""
```

Programming Tip

One way to create a source code file is to use a word processor and save the document as a text file. However, some word processors have a "smart quotes" option that is turned "on" by default. When you type a double or single quotation mark, the smart quotes option will try to "help" by inserting typographical symbols, "..." or ', which are different from the symbols "..." and '. Typographical quotation marks and apostrophes will *not* work in Fortran source code.

Long string constants may take more than one line to express, in which case a specific line continuation form is required in order to allow the ampersand and exclamation point characters to be part of string constants. These characters might otherwise be interpreted as a line continuation or the initiation of an in-line comment. Here's an example:

```
Poem_String='Roses are red, &
              && Violets are blue.  &
              &I love Fortran &
              &But I don''t expect you to!'
```

A line to be continued may not contain a trailing comment, and each continuation line must have a continuation mark as its first nonblank character. The trailing blanks before the continuation mark at the end of a line are part of the string, but the leading blanks before the continuation marks in the continued lines are not. The ampersands are not part of the string. The second ampersand in the first continuation line is *not* a misprint. If a program printed this string constant, it would look like this:

```
Roses are red, & Violets are blue.   I love Fortran But I don't
expect you to!
```

(It won't all fit on one line here, either.)

3.3.4 Initializing Values with the DATA Statement

Programs often require that variables be "initialized" to a particular value at the beginning of a program. One way to do this is with the DATA statement. A simplified version of the syntax is

```
DATA variable_list/constant for each variable,
     separated by commas/
DATA variable_list/n*constant/
DATA variable_name/constant/[,variable_name/constant/] ...

  where n is an integer that specifies the number
  of repetitions of the constant

Examples:
     DATA x,y,z/1.1,2.2,3.3/
     DATA x/1.1/,y/2.2/,z/3.3/
     DATA a,b,c/0,0,0/
     DATA a,b,c/3*0/
```

The DATA statement is a nonexecutable statement that should appear after all type declaration and PARAMETER statements and before the first executable statement in your program. Any variable initialized in a DATA statement must appear in a type declaration statement, assuming that the IMPLICIT NONE statement is included prior to the data declaration statements.

The significant difference between variables initialized in a DATA statement and quantities given PARAMETER status is that initialized variables retain their "variable" status and can be reassigned other values while the program is running.

However, because the DATA statement is nonexecutable, it cannot be used to "reinitialize" variables later in a program.[9] Note that the DATA statement is one implementation of the pseudocode *INITIALIZE* command.

In the third syntax form, the first `variable_name/constant/` can be, but doesn't have to be, followed by additional `variable_name/constant/` specifications, separated by commas.

3.4 List-Directed Input and Output

Program P-3.1 has three functions: to accept user input, to perform some calculations, and to display the results of the calculations. The first and third of these provide the critical input/output (I/O) interface between the program and a user. Fortran includes extensive and sometimes complicated I/O capabilities. Fortunately, it also includes some provisions for simple I/O operations that are well suited to simple programs such as P-3.1.

3.4.1 Reading and Displaying Numerical Values

Displaying a prompt for user input

The first task of P-3.1 is to obtain information from the user—specifically the radius required to calculate the circumference and area:

```
!
!     get input...
!
      PRINT *, ' Give radius of a circle: '
      READ *, radius
```

This is an example of an interactive program that requires the user to provide input while the program is running. Most of the programs in this

| standard output device |

text will contain some user-provided input. A user prompt should always precede a request for input in an interactive program. This isn't necessary from Fortran's point of view, but it is certainly necessary from the user's point of view. The PRINT * statement prints the message

```
 Give radius of a circle:
```

---

[9]This fact has important implications in subprograms, as we will discuss later in the text.

on the computer's ***standard output device***. This is almost always a terminal or computer screen. Recalling the output from P-3.1, consider what would happen if you executed a version of P-3.1 that did not include the prompt for input. When the program was executed, it would wait for you to enter a value for the radius, but you would have no way of knowing what the program expected. The program would wait, you would stare at the screen, waiting for something to happen.

The presence of an asterisk in P-3.1's `PRINT` statements identifies this as ***list-directed output***. This is a kind of "shorthand" output instruction for displaying

list-directed output

program output on your monitor screen. When you use list-directed output, the Fortran compiler, rather than the programmer, decides how to display the output, and the results will vary from compiler to compiler. A simplified syntax for list-directed output using the `PRINT` statement is

```
PRINT *[,list of variables, expressions, functions,
        or constants, separated by commas]
Examples:
    PRINT*,'This prints a string constant.'
    PRINT* ! This prints a blank line.
    PRINT*, 'The two sides are ',x,' and ',y, &
            '.  The hypotenuse is ',hypotenuse,'.'
    PRINT*,'The average of x and y is ',(x+y)/2.0
```

A more complete description of syntax for the `PRINT` statement is given in **Appendix 2**, to which we will refer when we discuss the `PRINT` statement again in Chapter 5. The output list is optional. Without such a list, a blank line is printed, as in the second example. The last example demonstrates that expressions can be evaluated and printed directly from within the `PRINT` statement.

Getting input from the keyboard

Following the user prompt provided by the first `PRINT` statement in P-3.1, the `READ *,radius` statement requests input from the keyboard—the default input device. When a `READ` statement is encountered, the program's operation is suspended until the user presses the `Enter` key at least once. In order for the program to continue, the user must provide *all* the information expected by the `READ` statement. As noted previously, without a prompt message in a `PRINT` statement immediately preceding a `READ` statement, a program will be suspended indefinitely while it waits for a user to respond. Without an *appropriate* prompt message, the program may still be suspended indefinitely, waiting for the user to guess the required response.

A simplified syntax for the list-directed READ statement is

```
READ *[, list of variable names, separated by commas]

Example:
      READ *,a,b,c
```

A list of variables is optional, although almost always present. Even without a list, a response is required: press the Enter key.

Just as an asterisk in a PRINT statement provides a convenient way to produce output in simple programs, an asterisk in a READ statement specifies *list-directed input*. Fortran compilers are relatively forgiving about how you enter numbers in response to a request for list-directed input. For example, you can precede the number with blank spaces, although there is no reason to do this.

list-directed input

Here's a new problem to demonstrate some features of list-directed I/O. One difference is that more than one input value is required.

1 *Define the problem.*

Given the height, width, and length of a box, calculate its surface area and volume.

2 *Outline a solution.*

1. Prompt the program user to supply the height, width, and length.
2. The equations for surface area and volume of a rectangular box with height, width, and length h, w, and l are

$$\text{surface area} = 2(lw + lh + hw)$$
$$\text{volume} = lwh$$

3. Display the results.

3 *Design an algorithm.*

DEFINE *(length, width, height, surface area, and volume as real numbers)*
WRITE *(prompt user to enter length, width, and height)*
READ *(length, width, height)*
ASSIGN *surface area = 2•(length•width + length•height + height•width)*
            volume = length•width•height
WRITE *(surface area and volume)*

4 *Convert the algorithm into a program.*

P-3.2 [BOX.F90]

```
      PROGRAM box
!
! Purpose: Calculate surface area and volume of a rectangular box.
!
      IMPLICIT NONE
      REAL height, width, length, SurfaceArea, volume
!
      PRINT *,'Give the height, width, and length of a box: '
      READ *,height,width,length
!
      SurfaceArea=2.0*(height*width+height*length+length*width)
      volume=height*width*length
!
      PRINT *,' surface area = ',SurfaceArea,'    volume = ',volume
!
      END
```

Running P-3.2

```
Give the height, width, and length of a box:
2.0 5.0 9.0
 surface area =        1.4600000E+02  volume =         90.0000000
```

5 *Verify the operation of the program.*

Check values by hand or with a calculator.

Problem Discussion

Program P-3.2 shows that a single READ statement can process several values typed on your keyboard. Suppose the box has a height, width, and length of 3.2, 4.2, and 5.2, respectively. The units are unimportant for this discussion. In general, however, your prompt message should indicate the physical units of all values a user is expected to supply. After the prompt message appears on your screen, there are several acceptable ways to provide the three desired values for list-directed input, including:

```
3.2 4.2 5.2<Press the Enter key.>

3.2, 4.2, 5.2<Press the Enter key.>
3.2  ,     4.2        5.2<Press the Enter key.>

3.2/4.2/5.2<Press the Enter key.>

3.2<Press the Enter key.>
4.2<Press the Enter key.>
5.2<Press the Enter key.>
```

Numerical values can be separated by spaces, commas, slashes, end-of-line marks (put there by pressing the Enter key or, on some computers, the Return key), or even combinations of these separators. There is usually no good reason to use slashes to separate numerical values, and their use could be confusing, as though you were trying to imply a division operation. So as a matter of style and habit, you should not use slashes as separators. As a practical matter, you should develop the habit of consistently using either commas or spaces as value separators.

In all cases, keyboard input must be terminated by pressing the Enter key; we have indicated that action specifically in these examples only to clarify the matter. Your program will not do anything else until you enter at least the required number of values. If you enter more values than are required, your program will ignore the extra values.

Suppose, for P-3.2, the dimensions of a box are 2.0×3.0×4.0 inches. If you are diligent about representing REAL numbers correctly, you will type

```
2.0 3.0 4.0
```

or

```
2. 3. 4.
```

when you enter the values. However, it is OK to type

```
2 3 4
```

This will result in an INTEGER-to-REAL *type conversion*, which means that the whole numbers 2, 3, and 4 will be stored internally as though they were real numbers instead  of integers (because the variables that are receiving the values are REAL). This won't cause problems in this context, but there are other situations in which type conversions should be avoided; we will discuss them later in this chapter.

If you enter some characters that can't be interpreted as a number, your program will crash. Suppose that you intend to type 3.1, but type 3.q instead (because the q key is just below the 1 key on the keyboard). Your program will crash and your Fortran implementation will print a message that tries to explain the problem—perhaps something mysterious like "Invalid List-Directed Input."

It is possible for a program to read a line of keyboard input as a character string, check it for characters that don't belong there, and then either remove the unwanted characters or ask the user to try again. As a practical matter, this is rarely worth the effort for programs you write to use yourself. If your program crashes because you make a mistake when you're typing input on the keyboard, just start over again. If the input your program requires is too long or complicated for keyboard input to be a reasonable option, then you should consider reading input data from some other source, as we will discuss in Chapter 9.

Programming Tip

If you have programmed in BASIC, you may be accustomed to using commas as value separators. If you have programmed in C, you may be accustomed to using spaces. Either style is OK for list-directed input in Fortran, but you should pick one and stick with it.

Displaying output

As mentioned above, when you use list-directed output, your Fortran environment decides how the output will appear on your screen. The output of string constants, as for the user prompts in P-3.1 and P-3.2, is usually perfectly reasonable. However, the output of numerical values may be confusing or arbitrary. The Fortran 90 compiler used to develop the programs in this text produces screen output for P-3.2 that looks like this:

```
Give the height, width, and length of a box:
3.2 4.2 5.2
  surface area =    1.0384000E+02    volume =    69.8879929
```

For no apparent reason, numbers larger than 100 are displayed in *scientific notation* (as a number times a power of 10). Also, the list-directed output displays many more *significant figures* than is reasonable for the calculation. (The output also demonstrates that Fortran arithmetic operations aren't always exact, but that's another topic.)

Other Fortran compilers will produce list-directed output that looks different from this example. List-directed output is OK for simple programs written for your own use, but you will eventually wish to gain more control over the appearance of your output. We will cover this topic in detail in Chapter 5.

3.4.2 Manipulating Text Information

So far, nothing has been said about providing non-numerical information to your program. Consider this example:

P-3.3 [NAMES.F90]

```
        PROGRAM names
!
        IMPLICIT NONE
        CHARACTER*20 name
        INTEGER age
!
        PRINT *,' What is your first name? '
        READ *, name
        PRINT *,' How old are you? '
        READ *,age
        PRINT *,name,age
!
        END
```

Running P-3.3

```
  What is your name?
David
  How old are you?
34
  David                   34
```

With list-directed input of a character string, you can enter a single name, as shown. However, suppose you wanted to enter a complete name such as Susan Anthony or Anthony, Susan. If you enter either of these inputs, the READ*, name statement in P-3.3 will not work as you intended because the space after Susan or the comma after Anthony will be treated as a separator between two string variables. The result will be that the "full name" you intended to enter will be the single name Susan or Anthony, depending on which one you entered first. The easiest solution to this problem is to read the first name and last name in different statements:

```
PRINT *,' What is your first name?'
READ *, first_name
PRINT *,' What is your last name?'
READ *,last_name
```

Note that if your name is Susan B. Anthony and you enter `Susan B.` in response to the request for your first name, this code will ignore the middle initial, so you may also need to provide a separate prompt for the middle initial.

It is possible to modify P-3.3 so that the complete name and age can be provided in response to a single `READ *` statement:

```
      ...
      CHARACTER*20 last,first,MI
      INTEGER age
!
      PRINT *, &
      ' Give your first name, middle initial, last name, and age,'
      PRINT *,' separated by a space or comma:'
      READ *,first,MI,last,age
      PRINT*,last,', ',first,MI,age
      ...
```

The problem with this code is that not everyone has a middle initial. If the user enters *just* a first name, last name, and age:

```
David Brooks, 33
```

then the program will think that the middle initial is `Brooks`, the last name is the character string `33`, rather than the number 33, and that the age has not yet been entered. Even worse, if you declare the strings more reasonably as

```
CHARACTER*20 last,first,MI*2
```

the program's response to entering `David Brooks, 33` will *not* be useful. (Try it and see.)

Because of these potential problems with reading text, it is good programming style, at least for inexperienced programmers, to read numerical and string information in *separate* statements, as has been done in P-3.3, and to specify in the user prompt that strings entered should contain no spaces or commas.

3.5 Arithmetic Operators, Assignment Statements, and Calculations

3.5.1 Arithmetic Operators, Expressions, and the Assignment Operator

We will now return to the P-3.1, the first program in this text, to examine the part of the program that calculates the area and circumference of a circle with a specified radius. The two statements are

```
! do calculations...
!
     circumference=2.0*pi*radius
     area=pi*radius*radius
```

It's easy to understand what these two calculations do because the statements look very similar to their algebraic equivalents. However, we need to examine statements like this in the broader context of how Fortran evaluates expressions and performs calculations.

Fortran supports several arithmetic operators, as shown in Table 3.3. The first five are familiar from algebra, although you may be accustomed to using the symbol × or • instead of a * for multiplication. The algebraic expressions a•b or ab must be represented as a*b in Fortran. The characters a•b can't even be translated into source code because the • symbol doesn't exist as a "keyboard character" and it wouldn't be recognized by Fortran even if it did. The characters ab will be interpreted not as "a times b," but as a variable named ab—not at all what you intended.

The exponentiation operator is used for raising a constant, variable, or expression to an integer or real power. The power may be a constant, variable, or expression. The algebraic expression x^3 is represented in Fortran by x**3; the square root of x can be represented by x**0.5 or x**(1./2.).

The first five operators in Table 3.3 are called **binary operators**, which means that there must be a variable, constant, or expression on each side of the operator. Therefore expressions such as *a or a*/b 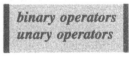 aren't allowed. (They don't make any algebraic sense, either.) The last two operators are **unary operators**. This means that they need a variable, constant, or expression only on the right side of the operator. Therefore, expressions such as -z, -3.5+x, -(a+b), or +(a*b) are perfectly reasonable. In the last of these, the + sign is optional and the expression is equivalent to a*b.

Table 3.3. Fortran arithmetic operators

Operation	Symbol
Binary Operators	
Addition	+
Subtraction	-
Multiplication	*
Division	/
Exponentiation	**
Unary Operators	
Multiply by +1	+
Multiply by -1	-

In Fortran, statements can contain expressions consisting of a combination of constants, variable names, and operators. Algebraic expressions such as

$$x = a + b$$
$$x = y + 3$$

can be translated directly into Fortran. Consider program fragment P-3.4. A and B are first assigned values of 2 and 4. Then X is assigned the value A+B. The value of X is now 6. In the next line, Y is assigned the value of X; Y now has the value 6. In the final line, X is assigned the value Y+3. X now has the value 9.

P-3.4 (fragment)

```
      . . .
      REAL X, Y, A, B
!
      A = 2.0
      B = 4.0
      X = A + B
      Y = X
      X = Y + 3.0
      . . .
```

In the examples in P-3.4, the = sign means "assign the value of the expression to the right of the = sign to the variable name to the left of the = sign." The = sign is called an *assignment operator*. A statement containing an assignment operator is called an *assignment operation* or an *assignment statement*. The general syntax of the assignment statement is

> *assignment operator*
> *assignment operation*
> *assignment statement*

```
variable_name = expression consisting of constants,
                variables, functions, and operators
```

(We haven't discussed "functions" yet, but we will in Chapter 6.) The executable statements in P-3.4 are all examples of assignment statements. Note that the only thing that can appear on the left side of an assignment operator is a single variable name.

"Assigning" a value has an obvious English-language interpretation that is not too different from the technical programming-language interpretation. However, the fact that the Fortran assignment operator is an = sign (it could easily be something else) does *not* mean that an assignment operation is the same thing as an algebraic equality. The specific programming-language interpretation of an assignment operation is very important.

> **An assignment statement means: Evaluate the expression on the right side of the assignment operator and place the result in the computer memory location associated with the variable name on the left side of the assignment operator.**

Because of this interpretation, you need to be careful about how you think about and write assignment statements.

First of all, it is a serious mistake to associate the = sign in Fortran with its meaning of "equality" in the algebraic sense. For one thing, only a single variable name can appear on the left side of an assignment operator. So, for example, the algebraic expression x + y = z + 3 is perfectly reasonable because it expresses the symbolic equality between x + y and z + 3, but the Fortran statement

```
X + Y = Z + 3 !makes no sense
```

makes no sense at all and is not allowed under any circumstances.

There's another important difference between an assignment statement and an algebraic expression. Note that the variables A and B are assigned

> *uninitialized variable*

numerical values in P-3.4 *before* the statement X=A+B. This is because it is necessary for A and B to have values in order for the assignment statement to be executed correctly. To put it another way, the assignment statement X=A+B doesn't express a symbolic relationship between A and B in the algebraic sense; rather, it indicates an operation whereby the sum of the memory locations associated with A and B will be placed in the memory location associated with the variable X. If A and B don't have values, they are "uninitialized," and the results can be unpredictable. Sometimes a programming language or a particular compiler will assume that *uninitialized variables* have the value 0, but you should never assume that this will be the case. The programming rule, to which you should *NEVER* make exceptions, is

> **Variables should not appear on the right side of an assignment operator until they have been given a value as a result of a previous statement.**

Variables may be given a value by appearing on the left side of an assignment operator, by being given the PARAMETER attribute, by appearing in a DATA statement, or as a result of a READ statement.[10] In P-3.4, A and B have been assigned values by placing them on the left side of an assignment operator. You could also let the user provide values for A and B in response to a READ statement.

3.5.2 Assignment Statements That Increment Variables

Because of the way the assignment operation is defined, the code fragment in P-3.5 makes perfect sense in Fortran, even though the second assignment statement doesn't make algebraic sense:

P-3.5 (fragment)

```
INTEGER x
...
x = 3
x = x + 1
```

First x is assigned the integer value 3. In the second statement, the expression on the right side of the assignment operator is evaluated—it has a value of 4. Then this result is placed in the memory location represented by x.

---

[10]A and B could also be given a value as output from a subroutine, as we will discuss in Chapter 7.

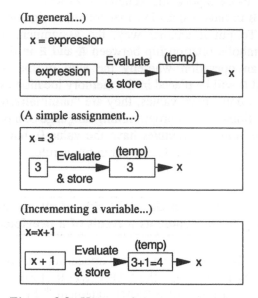

*Figure 3.2. How assignment statements are
used to initialize and increment a variable*

That is, the original value of x, 3, is replaced (or "overwritten") by the new value. This process is illustrated in Figure 3.2.

Incrementing a variable (not always just by 1) is a very common assignment operation in programs, and we will use it often in problems throughout the text. Recall that we defined two pseudocode commands in Chapter 2—***INITIALIZE*** and ***INCREMENT***—to emphasize the special purpose of these two kinds of assignment statements. In pseudocode, the statements in P-3.5 would be written

INITIALIZE *index = 3*
INCREMENT *index = index + 1*

We will use the ***INITIALIZE*** and ***INCREMENT*** pseudocode commands again when we discuss loop structures in Chapter 6. Note that the ***INCREMENT*** command also includes "decrementing" a variable in an assignment statement. The Fortran statements

```
index = 3
index = index - 1
```

result in `index` having a value of 2.

3.5.3 Mixed-Mode Calculations

The observant reader will notice that the numerical constants in P-3.4 are expressed as real constants; for example, "2.0" rather than "2". This is because you must be careful to distinguish between real numbers and integers in Fortran. All the variables in P-3.4 are declared as REAL and therefore all the operations involve real, as opposed to integer, arithmetic.

Assuming X and Y are REAL variables, as they are in P-3.4, the Fortran statement

```
X = Y + 3
```

will produce the same result as

```
X = Y + 3.0
```

However, the first of these two statements is a *mixed-mode expression* that combines two different data types, INTEGER (the constant 3) 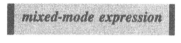 and REAL (the variable Y), in the same expression. This statement requires your compiler to convert the integer constant on the right side of the assignment operator to a real number when it is added to Y.

Consider also the statement

```
A = 2
```

from P-3.4. This statement, too, will produce the same result as

```
A = 2.0
```

Again, in the first of these two statements, your compiler is required to perform a type conversion to convert the integer constant on the right side of the assignment operator to a real number when it is assigned to the REAL variable A on the left.

In almost all cases, it is preferable to avoid mixed-mode expressions. Why? Because these operations can cause problems! Consider P-3.6, which contains several examples of mixed-mode calculations.

P-3.6 [MIXED.F90]

```
      PROGRAM mixed
!
      IMPLICIT NONE
      INTEGER i,j
      REAL x,y
!
      i=5
      j=2
      x=i/j
!
      PRINT *,i,j,x
      x=3.3
      y=1.5
      i=x/y
      PRINT *,i
      x=2/3*4.
      PRINT *,x
      x=2*4./3
      PRINT *,x
!
      END
```

Running P-3.6

```
 5 2    2.0000000
 2
  0.0000000E+00
  2.6666667
```

How do you determine what value will be printed for x in the first PRINT statement? The variables i and j are integers, but x is real. With i=5 and j=2, the result of the division is 2, not 2.5, because the remainder is lost in integer division. Therefore, even though x is real, it has a value of 2.0 after the type conversion, not 2.5! This result is due to the fact that the first step in an assignment operation is to evaluate the expression on the right side of the assignment operator. At the time this evaluation is carried out, Fortran doesn't "know" that you intend to store the result of the evaluation in a location associated with a REAL variable. Hence it has no way of knowing that you probably wish the division operation 5/2 to be treated as an operation involving REAL constants. Similarly, the statement i=x/y results in i being assigned a value of 2 because i is an integer and can't have a value of 2.2.

What results will be displayed by the third and fourth PRINT statements? Clearly, the statements x=2/3*4. and x=2*4./3 are "algebraically" equivalent, but they do not produce the same value! The integer division 2/3 in the first of these statements is truncated to 0, so x eventually will be assigned a value of 0. In the second statement, the result of the multiplication operation 2*4. is the real value 8.0. When this real value is divided by the integer value 3, the result is the real value 2.666667.

Programming Tip

The interpretation of mixed-mode expression varies from language to language. In Fortran and C, the data types of the numerator and denominator determine the result of division; 5/2 equals 2 because 5 and 2 are both INTEGER constants. In Pascal, for example, the operator and not the operand determines the data type of the result. Hence, in Pascal, 5/2 yields a value of 2.5 rather than 2 and the assignment of this result to an integer data type isn't allowed. This kind of language dependency is another good reason to be careful about using mixed-mode expressions carelessly.

Although this discussion may seem a bit theoretical, the way Fortran evaluates mixed-mode expressions and performs type conversions can have important practical consequences. Consider these Fortran statements intended for converting back and forth between centigrade (C) and Fahrenheit (F) degrees, assuming both C and F have been declared as type REAL:

```
C = 5/9*(F - 32)  !wrong!
F = 9/5*C + 32     !wrong!
```

These statements look like straightforward translations of algebraic expressions. However, both statements produce incorrect results. The conversion from Fahrenheit to centigrade gives a value of 0 for *every* value of F because the division operation 5/9 equals 0. The second expression is equivalent to F=C+32 because the division operation 9/5 equals 1. These expressions *should* be written[11]

```
C = 5./9.*(F - 32.)
F = 9./5.*C + 32.
```

Although it is possible to develop a set of rules for determining the results of mixed-mode calculations, it is not worth the effort for a beginning programmer. It is easy to make mistakes with these kinds of calculations, and the resulting errors are very hard to track down in a program because, from Fortran's point of view, there is nothing wrong with them. To avoid these kinds of errors, it is usually a much better idea to avoid mixed-mode calculations. This means

---

[11]Actually, writing *either* the 9 or the 5 as a REAL constant will produce the desired result, but it is better style to write all the values as REAL constants.

Usually, all the variables, functions, and constants appearing in a Fortran assignment statement should have the same data type.

There are a few reasonable exceptions to this rule. Program P-3.7 illustrates a typical example in which the average of three real numbers is calculated by dividing the sum of the three numbers by the integer value 3; this mixed-mode calculation won't cause any problems.

P-3.7 [AVERAGE.F90]

```
      PROGRAM average
!
      IMPLICIT NONE
      REAL x,y,z,avg
      INTEGER n
!
      PRINT *,' Give three numbers: '
      READ *,x,y,z
      n=3
!
      avg=(x+y+z)/n
!
      PRINT *,'The average of these three numbers is ',avg
!
      END
```

Running P-3.7

```
  Give three numbers:
 3.3 5.2 4.9
  The average of these three numbers is     4.4666667
```

The number of values n is an INTEGER. However, the mixed-mode expression (x+y+z)/n is evaluated properly because x, y, and z are REAL variables and the result, avg, is also a real number. That is, the result of dividing a REAL variable by an INTEGER variable is a real number.[12]

---

[12]The interpretation of mixed-mode expressions through "type coercion" is a topic of interest in a more theoretical study of programming languages. For our purposes, it is sufficient to understand the examples given in P-3.6 and P-3.7. When we discuss Fortran intrinsic functions in Chapter 4, you will see that the mixed-mode expression in P-3.7 could be rewritten as (x+y+z)/REAL(n), which might be a better choice because the INTEGER-to-REAL conversion is done explicitly.

Programming Tip

Remember that the statement

```
PRINT *,'The average of these three numbers is ',(x+y+z)/n
```

in P-3.7 is permissible. In that case, the variable name `avg` need not be declared and the assignment statement in which it appears is not required. Whether this kind of "short cut" is a good idea depends on the program in which it is used.

3.5.4 Using Compatible Constants

As we have indicated in the previous discussion of mixed-mode expressions and type conversions, some mixing of data types is allowed in Fortran regardless of whether this is a good idea. However, some incompatible assignments simply aren't allowed. Consider Fortran program fragment P-3.8:

P-3.8 (fragment)

```
...
REAL a
CHARACTER*8 b
a='computer' !Syntax error.
b=3.0          !Syntax error.
...
```

It should be obvious that the code in P-3.8 doesn't make any sense. If `a` is a REAL variable, then it cannot be assigned the value of a character constant. Similarly, `b` can't be assigned a numerical value. These assignments will cause your program to crash because it cannot perform the requested operation.[13] However, some incompatible assignments are acceptable to your Fortran compiler even when they can cause problems in your program. Consider code fragment P-3.9:

P-3.9 (fragment)

```
...
REAL a
INTEGER b
a=3
b=3.3
```

---

[13]If you study the C programming language, you will find that assignment statements in that language allow type conversions that don't "make sense" in Fortran.

The assignment a=3 won't cause any problems in a program because the integer value 3 will be converted to a real value, but b=3.3 results in 3.3 being truncated to 3; this is almost surely not what you wish to happen. This problem was noted previously in the discussion of keyboard input. Remember:

In general, constants should be assigned only to identically typed variables.

In some cases Fortran will object if you try to make incompatible assignments with constants, but in other cases Fortran will be perfectly happy to return answers that won't be what you expect. Be careful!

3.5.5 Operator Precedence

Expressions evaluated as part of an assignment statement can sometimes be quite complicated. When Fortran evaluates an expression, the process follows specific rules so that there can never be any ambiguity about what the value of the expression should be. Fortunately, the rules are similar to what you should have learned in algebra. Consider code fragment P-3.10:

P-3.10 (fragment)

```
      REAL X,Y,A,B
!
      X=3.0
      A=2.0
      B=4.0
      Y=A+B*X
      . . .
```

What is the value of Y? The answer depends on the order in which Fortran performs the indicated arithmetic operations. If all the operations are performed in order from left to right, then in algebraic notation, $y = (2 + 4)3 = 18$. However, this is not the case. In fact, $y = 2 + 12 = 14$. Why? Because in the same sense that the algebraic expression $y=a+bx$ implies a specific order of operations in which the multiplication is done first, Fortran assigns priorities to operators and, if there are no parentheses present, evaluates operators with the highest priority first. The evaluation priorities for arithmetic operators are given in Table 3.4.

First Fortran reads through an expression from left to right and performs all the exponentiation operations. Then it reads through the expression again and performs all the multiplications and divisions. Finally, it reads the expression again and performs all the additions and subtractions. In P-3.10, the operation B*X is performed first. The result of that operation, the value 12.0, is temporarily stored, and on the second pass through the expression, the operation A + 12.0 is performed.

Table 3.4. Priority for Arithmetic Operator Evaluation

Operator	Evaluation Priority
**	First
*, /	Second
+, -	Third

Here is another Fortran statement that involves all the operators:

```
Y = A+B*X**2/A-B
```

Using Table 3.4 and the values in P-3.10, try to calculate the value of Y yourself now. After the first pass through the expression, the exponentiation operation has been completed and the expression is equivalent to the algebraic expression

$$y = a + (9b/a) - b$$

During subsequent passes, the expressions are equivalent to

$$y = a + (36/2) - b = a + 18 - b = 2 + 18 - 4 = 16$$

Parentheses can be used to alter the order in which Fortran evaluates expressions. For example, the Fortran assignment statement

```
Y = (A+B)*X
```

is not the same as

```
Y = A+B*X
```

for the same reason that the algebraic expression $y = (a + b)x$ is different from $y = a + bx$. In both algebra and Fortran, the parentheses force the addition operation inside the parentheses to be performed first. Fortran expressions are always evaluated from the innermost set of parentheses outward. For $y=(a+b)x$, $y = (2 + 4)3 = (6)3 = 18$, and not 14, for the values used in P-3.10. Similarly, the Fortran assignment statement

```
Y = A+(B*X)**2/A-B
```

is not the same as

```
Y = A+B*X**2/A-B
```

because, in the former case, B*X is evaluated first and this product, not just X, is squared.

Whenever you convert algebraic expressions into their Fortran equivalents, you must be careful to use pairs of parentheses when they are required to produce the desired result. Use of parentheses in a statement such as

```
Y = A+(B*X)
```

is unnecessary because the multiplication will be performed first even if the parentheses aren't there, but they may make your intentions more clear. However, if you wish to translate the algebraic expression $y = (a + b)x$ into Fortran, the parentheses in the statement Y = (A+B)*X are essential because you are asking Fortran to evaluate this expression in a way that overrides the normal operator precedence.

Algebraic expressions are often written on more than one line; for example,

$$x = \frac{a+b}{c+d}$$

Remember that the translation of this algebraic expression into a Fortran expression must occupy just one line. If you rewrite the algebraic expression as $x = (a + b)/(c + d)$, the Fortran translation is more obvious:

```
x = (a+b)/(c+d)
```

All of these Fortran expressions are perfectly legal, but none of them gives the same result or correctly translates the above algebraic expression:

```
x = a+b/c+d
x = (a+b)/c+d
x = a+b/(c+d)
```

It is easy to misrepresent algebraic expressions in Fortran. Consider this expression for one real root of a quadratic equation:

$$r = \frac{-b+\sqrt{b^2-4ac}}{2a}$$

Which of these Fortran implementations is correct, assuming that the expression under the square root sign $b^2 - 4ac$ is greater than or equal to zero?

(a) `Root=-B+(B*B-4.0*A*C)**0.5/2.0*A`
(b) `Root=(-B+(B*B-4.0*A*C)**0.5)/2.0*A`
(c) `Root=(-B+(B*B-4.0*A*C)**0.5)/(2.0*A)`
(d) `Root=(-B+(B*B-4.0*A*C)**0.5)/2.0/A`

(a) is wrong because the entire numerator needs to be enclosed in parentheses. This problem is corrected in (b), but both (a) and (b) are wrong because although the A appears to the right of the /, it is still not part of the denominator of the expression, as required. Either (c) or (d) will give the correct result.

A common syntax error in Fortran is to leave sets of parentheses unbalanced in complicated expressions. The rule is that

> **In any expression, the number of left parentheses must equal the number of right parentheses.**

The Fortran statement

    Y=((A+B)*X+3.0*C

cannot be evaluated because a right parenthesis is missing. You might intend

    Y=((A+B)*X)+3.0*C

or

    Y=((A+B)*X+3.0)*C

or even

    Y=((A+B)*X+3.0*C)

even though the outer parentheses serve no purpose in the first and third possibilities. In any event, you cannot expect your Fortran compiler to guess your intentions!

Here's one final point about operator precedence. When two or more exponentiation operations appear consecutively in an expression, the operations are performed in *right-to-left* order rather than in left-to-right order. This is "backward" relative to the usual order in which operators are evaluated and can cause problems if you're not careful. The expression `a**b**c` is equivalent to `a**(b**c)` and, in general, is not equal to `(a**b)**c`. For example, `2**(3**3)` evaluates as `2**27`, but `(2**3)**3` becomes `8**3`. In such cases, it would be a good idea to use parentheses to make clear the order in which you wish the exponentiations to be performed.

3.6 Program Termination

As noted earlier in this chapter, the END statement, which marks the end of a source code file, is the only required statement in a Fortran program. The general syntax is

```
END [PROGRAM [program_name]]
```

The keyword PROGRAM is optional. If the PROGRAM keyword is present, then *program_name* may also appear. We will not use the PROGRAM keyword option in this text.

The STOP statement terminates program execution. It can appear anywhere in a program before the END statement, and a program can include more than one STOP statement. The syntax forms for the STOP statement are

```
STOP
STOP ddddd
STOP 'string constant'
```

where ddddd is an integer of up to five digits.

If an integer of up to five digits or a string constant is included in the statement, it is printed after the word STOP. Hence the STOP statement can be used not just to terminate a program, but also to generate a message that indicates where termination occurred. For example, the statement

```
STOP 'Normal program termination.
```

at the end of a program could be used to indicate that the program executed and terminated normally.

In the complete programs given in this text, we will rarely use a STOP statement because good programming style should make it unnecessary to terminate a program anywhere except at the end. (One example of an appropriate use appears in Program P-6.13 in Chapter 6. In that case, a STOP statement is used to terminate a program and print a message when a user enters inappropriate input.)

However, the STOP statement is extremely useful for developing and debugging programs. Initially, you can include PRINTs to display intermediate results at several critical points in your program. Follow each such PRINT or group of PRINTs by a STOP statement, perhaps including an explanatory message about where you are in your program. Then, as you verify the operation at each one of these critical points, you can remove the PRINTs and the STOP. Of course, you can approach this the other way around. If your completed program doesn't work, you can temporarily insert PRINTs and STOPs anywhere you think they might be useful in locating the problem. For completed programs, however, multiple STOPs should be avoided as a matter of programming style.

3.7 Compiling and Executing a Program

3.7.1 Source Code Portability

As you now know, Fortran source code must be written according to a very rigid set of syntax rules. The unforgiving nature of source code syntax often seems excessively burdensome for beginning programmers. However, the advantage of these rules in a standardized language is that source code is highly portable from one computer and compiler to another. As noted earlier in this chapter and previously in Chapter 2, any Fortran 90 source code you write during a course based on this text can probably be compiled and used with no (or very minor) changes on any other computer that has a Fortran 90 compiler.

Why is your source code only "probably" portable to another computer? To answer this question, consider the Fortran's predecessor, Fortran 77, which has been around for a long time—as you would guess, since the late 1970s. Since then, the authors of compilers have added many new features to Fortran 77, some to meet specific programming needs and others in response to concepts implemented in newer languages such as Pascal and C. These nonstandard extensions differ from compiler to compiler, so that a program written to take advantage of extensions available on one compiler will not work on a compiler that does not have those same extensions. Some extensions, such as those allowing variable names to be written in both uppercase and lowercase letters and to be longer than six characters, are almost universal, but others are not.

With the implementation of a new Fortran standard, compatibility is at least temporarily less of an issue for programs written in the Fortran 90 language. Therefore, all the programs in this text *should* execute on *any* computer equipped with a Fortran 90 compiler, although it is not practical to guarantee 100 percent compatibility. The only likely incompatibility lies in the syntax of file names, which arises from the fact that the syntax for naming files is system dependent.

However, the "programmer's market" demands that led to extensions to Fortran 77 will eventually be applied to Fortran 90. Although this new standard undoubtedly has its own weaknesses, not nearly enough time has elapsed for either its weaknesses or its strengths to be fully determined or appreciated; even though it is called Fortran 90, compilers were not commercially available until 1993. It is inevitable that extensions to the Fortran 90 standard will cause the same kinds of compatibility problems that are now evident in Fortran 77. Likely areas for extensions include object-oriented programming and, especially for large science and engineering applications, language extensions to take advantage of parallel processing and supercomputers.

There are two additional points of interest about language compatibility. First it is typical for Fortran texts to adhere to the language standard in order to ensure their widespread adoption. However, this means that the Fortran 77 language students have been taught for the past several years is only a restrictive subset of the language as it is used in practice. It will be several years before this will be a significant problem for Fortran 90 texts.

Finally, Fortran 77 language extensions affect the compatibility between Fortran 77 programs and Fortran 90 compilers. Although the standard requires that Fortran 90 compilers accept Fortran 77 programs, this requirement applies *only* to programs that adhere to the Fortran 77 standard. As a practical matter, this means that many programs written with nonstandard pre-Fortran 90 compilers will require modification before they can be compiled under Fortran 90.

3.7.2 Compilation and Execution

As mentioned briefly earlier in this chapter, a source code file is often referred to as a "program." This is somewhat misleading because the contents of a source code file need to be translated into computer-specific machine instructions before your computer can actually perform any operations. It is this translated file that might more properly be called a program because this is the set of instructions that is used directly by your computer.

Regardless of what kind of a computer system you are using, you and your Fortran environment will need to perform several specific tasks in order to "run" a program. These are shown schematically in Figure 3.3.

First, the Fortran compiler checks your source code for syntax errors. If it finds errors, it prints (sometimes helpful) messages and stops. You must then fix the errors and recompile the source code. When the compilation is successful, the Fortran environment creates an object file. It links this object file with any Fortran libraries needed by your program, as well as with object files from other program units. (Most of the programs in this text will not need to access other program units.)

Finally, the Fortran environment creates an executable file and loads it into computer memory, where the program executes. Your instructor will provide you with specific instructions for carrying out this process on the computer you are using for this course. For the purposes of a course based on this text, you do not need to understand any more than the mechanics of compiling and executing a program. The details are more appropriate for later courses in computing.

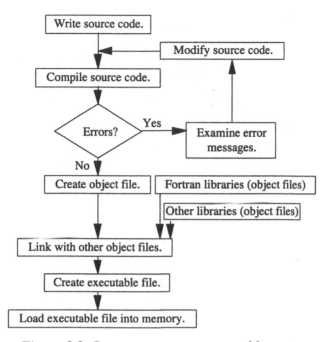

Figure 3.3. Steps to create an executable program

If you have written programs in other languages in PC-based environments, you may wonder how those environments make compiling and executing a program look so easy. The answer is that the required steps are still the same, but they are taken care of automatically. In some environments, for example, your source code is automatically checked for syntax errors as you write it. Code may be compiled "on the fly" as you write it, and a link to other program libraries may have been done ahead of time. This makes compilation and generation of an executable program file appear virtually instantaneous. With Fortran, you may have to perform each of these steps manually by typing an appropriate sequence of commands. In some cases, you may be able to use "batch" files that simplify the process.

3.7.3 Saving Output from Your Programs

The programs we have discussed up to now produce simple output, and you can certainly transcribe the results by hand when you need to save them. However, it is much more useful 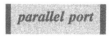 to be able to save a permanent record of a program's activities, including your typed responses to prompts for input. An easy way to do this is to "dump" the contents of your screen to a printer. On PCs, this is accomplished by pressing the PrtScr key, usually located near the upper righthand corner of your keyboard. This action assumes that your computer is connected to a printer at the default port (usually the *parallel port* at address LPT1). On a UNIX system, you can use the script command to copy everything that appears on the screen into a text file; check the online documentation by typing man script.

The PC method is adequate when the entire output from a program fills no more than one screen on your computer's monitor, and it is a convenient way to record your work when you hand in programming assignments. It will be less satisfactory when your programs get larger and generate more output than will fit on one screen. In Chapter 5 we will discuss how to save the output from programs in a permanent file.

3.8 Applications

In this section, and in similar sections in later chapters, we will develop programs that use and sometimes extend the material discussed in the chapter. Hopefully, even these relatively simple programs will help you solve the kinds of problems you will encounter in your other introductory science, engineering, and mathematics courses. It will always be helpful for you to read the problem statement and then try to design the algorithm and write the program on your own. The two applications in this chapter follow the simple input→calculations→output format used in P-3.1 at the beginning of this chapter.

3.8.1 Maximum Deflection of a Beam Under Load

1 *Define the problem.*

Consider a beam of length L feet supported at each end and subject to a downward force of F pounds concentrated at the middle of the beam. The maximum downward deflection of the beam (at its middle) is $-FL^3/(48EI)$. Write a program to calculate the maximum deflection if L, F, E, and I are specified as input. For a particular steel I-beam (a beam with an I-shaped cross section), $E=30\times10^6$ lb/in^2 and $I=797$ in^4. The deflection of such a beam as a function of length is illustrated in Figure 3.4. (This problem appeared previously as an algorithm design application in Chapter 2.)

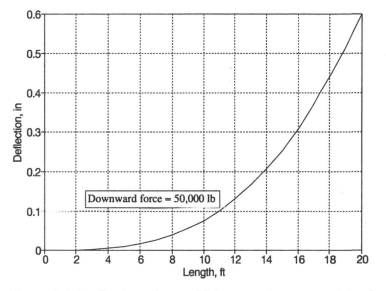

Figure 3.4. Deflection of a steel I-beam under a central load

2 *Outline a solution.*

1. Specify L, F, E, and I as user input. Convert length from feet to inches.
2. Calculate deflection according to the above formula. The sign of the deflection can be either positive or negative as long as it's understood that the deflection is in the downward direction.
3. Display the output.

3 *Design an algorithm.*

DEFINE *(L, F, E, I, and deflection as real numbers.)*
WRITE *(Give length (ft), force (lb), elasticity (lb/in^2)*
and moment of inertia (in^4))
READ *(L,F,E,I)*
ASSIGN *L = L•12.0 (convert to inches)*
deflection = -F•L^3/(48EI)
WRITE *(deflection)*

4 *Convert the algorithm into a program.*

P-3.11 [BEAM.F90]

```
      PROGRAM beam
!
! Calculate maximum deflection of a beam supported at both ends,
! with the load concentrated at the middle of the beam.
!
      IMPLICIT NONE
      REAL length, force, elasticity, moment_of_inertia,deflection
!
      PRINT *,' Give length (ft), force (lb): '
      READ *,length,force
      PRINT*,' Give elasticity (lb/in^2), mom. of inertia (in^4):'
      READ *,elasticity,moment_of_inertia
!
      length=length*12.0
      deflection=&
        -force*length**3/(48.0*elasticity*moment_of_inertia)
!
      PRINT *,'The deflection (in) is: ',deflection
!
      END
```

Running P-3.11

```
 Give length (ft), force (lb):
20 50000
 Give elasticity (lb/in^2), moment of inertia (in^4):
30e6 797
 The deflection (in) is:    -0.6022584
```

5 *Verify the operation of the program.*

You probably don't have an intuitive feel for what the answer should be for a beam having the values of elasticity and moment of inertia specified in the problem statement. As indicated in the sample output, and according to Figure 3.4, the maximum downward deflection of a 20-foot section of such a beam when it is subjected to a load of 50,000 pounds concentrated at the middle is about 0.6 inches. What would you think about using this formula if it returned an answer of 0.001 inches? How about 10 inches? See this application in Chapter 2 for additional discussion.

Problem Discussion

P-3.11 is a straightforward program, but there is one interesting Fortran-related detail. In the expression for calculating the deflection, the expression length³ is translated as `length**3` rather than `length**3.` or, equivalently, `length**3.0`. Is there any difference between these two Fortran expressions? Both will give the same answer, but the first choice makes it possible for a Fortran compiler to calculate (length)³ the "easy" way, just by multiplying length by itself two times, because the power is expressed as an integer. The other two expressions, in which 3 is expressed as a real number, will force Fortran to invoke a more sophisticated, and hence more time-consuming, algorithm to evaluate the expression. Such an algorithm is required when a power can't be expressed as an integer, but should be avoided when it can. That is, $x^{3.2}$ can't be calculated by multiplying x by itself an integer number of times, but x^3 can. Thus $x^{3.2}$ must be represented as `x**3.2`, but `x**3` is preferable to `x**3.0`.[14] If x is negative, then *only* integer exponents are allowed.

3.8.2 Relativistic Mass and Speed of an Electron

This program requires some minor algebraic manipulation of the equations given in the problem to solve for the required values. This particular problem has been chosen specifically because the quantities involved may be unfamiliar. Hopefully, this unfamiliarity will encourage you to be careful when you translate this and every other problem statement into a program, and to be especially diligent when you verify that program's operation.

1 Define the problem.

An electron accelerated by a voltage V in an electron gun acquires an energy of $Ve = mc^2 - m_0c^2$, where

charge on an electron	$e = 1.602 \times 10^{-19}$ coulomb
rest mass	$m_0 = 9.109 \times 10^{-31}$ kg
speed of light	$c = 2.9979 \times 10^8$ m/s

The speed v of an electron of relativistic mass m kg is obtained from $m/m_0 = 1/\sqrt{1-(v/c)^2}$. Write a program that prompts the user to supply a voltage and calculates the relativistic mass and speed of an electron. (Sample answer: for a voltage of 1.5×10^6 V, m=3.58×10^{-30} kg and v=2.9×10^8 m/s. See Figure 3.5.)

---

[14]The expression x^n can be evaluated as $e^{[n \cdot \ln(x)]}$. The expressions $\ln(x)$ and $e(z)$ can both be evaluated by using a series expansion.

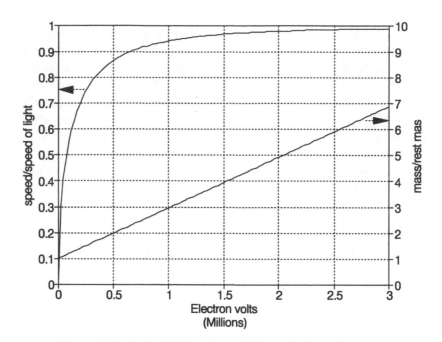

Figure 3.5. Relativistic mass and speed of an electron

2 *Outline a solution.*

The terminology of this problem may be unfamiliar, but the algebraic manipulations required are straightforward. The "relativistic mass" is a consequence of relativity theory, which predicts that mass is not a constant property of matter, but increases with speed.

1. Specify the voltage of the electron gun.
2. Calculate the mass first, then the speed, using the equations given in Step 1. Solve the first equation for mass. Then solve the second equation for speed.
3. Display the output.

3 *Design an algorithm.*

DEFINE *(All variables are real numbers. The rest_mass,*
      charge e, and speed of light c are constants)
WRITE *(prompt for voltage)*
READ *(voltage)*

ASSIGN *mass = (voltage•e + rest_mass•c²)/c²*
        velocity = c[1 − (rest_mass/mass)²]¹ᐟ²
WRITE *(mass and velocity)*

4 Convert the algorithm into a program.

P-3.12 [REL_MASS.F90]

```
      PROGRAM Rel_Mass
!
! Calculate relativistic mass and speed of an electron.
!
      IMPLICIT NONE
      REAL rest_mass,relativistic_mass ! kg
      REAL voltage                     ! volt
      REAL speed                       ! m/s
      REAL e                           ! electron charge, Coulomb
      REAL c                           ! speed of light, m/s
      PARAMETER (e=1.602e-19, c=2.9979e8, rest_mass=9.109e-31)
!
      PRINT *,' Give electron gun voltage in volts: '
      READ *,voltage
!
      relativistic_mass=(voltage*e+rest_mass*c**2)/c**2
      speed=c*(1.-(rest_mass/relativistic_mass)**2)**0.5
!
      PRINT *,'relativistic mass (kg) and speed (m/s): ', &
              relativistic_mass,speed
      END
```

Running P-3.12

```
 Give electron gun voltage in volts:
1e6
  relativistic mass and speed:    2.6933944E-30    2.8212490E+08
```

5 Verify the operation of the program.

These calculations are easy to implement in Fortran, but it is imperative to check them by hand, using a calculator to do the arithmetic. Be careful when you calculate the exponents on powers of 10. It is easy to accept wrong answers when the numbers are so large, or small, that it is difficult to develop a "feel" for them. If you have never had an introductory physics course (or even if you have!), the numbers may be essentially meaningless, so a wrong answer will look as reasonable, or unreasonable, as the right one.

3.9 Debugging Your Programs

3.9.1 Programming Style

It's important to pay attention to details in even the simplest program. Every Fortran program should have a descriptive name and, when reasonable, that name should be the same as the file name under which the source code is stored on your computer. (This is easier on some systems than others.) Explicit typing for every variable should be enforced through use of the IMPLICIT NONE statement. Comments should be used to describe and give units for all variable names corresponding to physical quantities. The PARAMETER attribute should be used to define basic physical and mathematical constants, as well as other values that can be determined ahead of time and shouldn't be changed while the program is running. Input, calculation, and output sections of the program should be clearly separated, often by blank comment lines. Comments should be used liberally to explain what the program does.

Algebraic expressions should be translated into Fortran in a straightforward manner. Although it is sometimes possible to simplify algebraic expressions, it is not usually worth sacrificing clarity for brevity just to save a few arithmetic operations. Parentheses can sometimes help to clarify algebraic expressions even when they're not required.

Straightforward implementation of an algorithm is always preferred over "clever" but more obscure solutions. Although it is sometimes possible to improve the performance of large and computationally intensive programs by optimizing the source code, this is wasted effort for the kinds of programs you will be writing in a course based on this text (even if you knew how to do it).

When a program requests input from the user, the prompt for input should describe specifically what actions are expected, including a description of the appropriate physical units. Output statements should contain a description of what the output means, including physical units, where appropriate.

While a program is being developed, it can contain several temporary PRINT statements that "echo" program input and display the results of intermediate calculations. As a trivial example, you could add the line

```
PRINT*,'New length: ',length
```

after the statement length=length*12.0 in P-3.11, just to make sure that the conversion from feet to inches has been done properly. You won't find many examples of these temporary statements in this or any other text because they are removed when the program is complete. Nonetheless, they are as essential to good programming style as the code remaining in the final version of any program you write.

3.9.2 Your Programs Will Often Contain Errors

There is no shortage of problems that can arise in Fortran programs. You can minimize errors by being careful with algorithm design and following good programming practice as described in this chapter and summarized in the previous section. However,

> **No amount of planning can prevent errors in programs.**

This fact will never change, no matter how proficient a programmer you become.

The kinds of errors beginning programmers worry about the most are those that prevent their programs from compiling or executing successfully. It is discouraging to write programs that don't work, and it probably isn't very comforting to be told that even experienced programmers expect only the simplest programs to work the first time they try to compile and execute them.

A generation ago, when Fortran programs were written on punch cards and submitted in "batch" mode to a mainframe computer at a (perhaps remotely located) computer center, a single misplaced character could mean a delay of hours or days. With the nearly instantaneous error detection and feedback provided by modern interactive computing environments, it is no longer worth the extra effort required to write a program that is correct in every syntax detail before you try to compile and execute it for the first time. It is usually more efficient to write source code using reasonable care and then fix whatever errors the compiler detects.

3.9.3 Some Common Errors

After you have discovered that your program doesn't work, what then? First you need to be aware of the difference between *compile-time errors* and *run-time errors*. Compilation errors result from using incorrect syntax when you create your program's source code. Execution (run-time) errors can occur only after your program is free from syntax errors. They occur once your program is running and attempts to execute an instruction that doesn't make sense in context, or that results in an illegal operation.

compile-time errors
run-time errors

Here are some common programming errors, grouped as compilation, execution, or logical errors. It is a mistake to think of this list as a place to look only *after* you have a problem. You can save yourself a lot of time and prevent future problems by reading through this list *before* you write your next program.

Compilation Errors

1. Using unbalanced parentheses

Whenever you use parentheses to clarify an expression or to force your compiler to evaluate an expression in a particular way, the number of left parentheses must equal the number of right parentheses.

2. Undeclared variables

This is a "good" error because it helps you find misspelled variable names and variables that you have not yet associated with an appropriate data type. You can expect this helpful error message only if you *always* use the IMPLICIT NONE statement, as discussed in this chapter.

3. Misspelled keywords

Because your compiler doesn't know how to interpret statements with misspelled keywords, it may not have anything helpful to say about how to fix the statement. If you are using the IMPLICIT NONE statement, your compiler may interpret the keyword as an undeclared variable. Remember that spaces embedded in most keywords are not allowed.

4. Nonexecutable statements appearing after executable statements

Even if individual statements you write are free from syntax errors, they can still generate errors if they are placed inappropriately within your program. Remember that nonexecutable statements must precede all executable statements. (Comment lines can appear anywhere.)

Execution Errors

1. Arithmetic errors

By far the most common arithmetic error is dividing by zero. For example, the statement Y=A/B cannot be evaluated if B equals 0. Of course you didn't mean for B ever to equal zero. Perhaps you haven't yet given B any value at all; in that case, your compiler may assume that B equals zero. Some compilers may actually "allow" division by zero, but won't allow the resulting value, which is meaningless, to be used for anything. In this case, the error may be harder to isolate.

2. Finding illegal data during a READ

The most common action that produces this error is responding with an inappropriate numerical value. For example, if you write a program that asks a user to respond to this prompt,

```
How much money do you have in your account?
```

and the user responds, $1000, this will generate an error because Fortran doesn't understand that $1000 is a number. You can minimize this problem by changing the prompt to read,

```
How much money do you have in your account? $
```

so the user will understand that the $ sign shouldn't be typed as part of the response.

Another potential source of trouble is using punctuation in numbers. For example, if you have $10,000 in a bank account, you might type 10,000 in response to the above prompt instead of 10000. Usually, your program will assume that you have entered two numbers instead of one—10 and 0—separated by commas, and it will simply ignore the extra value. As a result, your program will assume that you have $10 in your account instead of $10,000. Obviously, this is a potentially serious problem for a program that processes financial transactions!

3. Not finding enough data.

This occurs when you don't provide as many values as your program expects. If you're reading data from an external file, as we will discuss later in the text, your program will crash and produce a message something like "attempt to read past end of file." When you are providing keyboard input, your program won't crash. This can be a very puzzling error because your computer doesn't provide any kind of error message. Instead it simply waits patiently for you to complete the required response. You can avoid this problem by remembering that a prompt for information must clearly reflect the program's demands.

Note, by the way, that it's OK—from Fortran's point of view, at least—to provide too many values. Your program will simply ignore the extra ones.

Logical Errors

Are your problems over after your programs are free from compilation and execution errors? Possibly not. The most dangerous kinds of programming errors are logical (algorithm design) errors. Programs with logical errors often run smoothly and appear to be working properly. It is up to you to determine, based on your examination of the program's output, whether the answers are actually correct.

Even if you assume that your algorithm design is logically correct, there are still ways for errors to creep into your programs. It's not possible to list them all, because students have an uncanny ability to devise new logical programming errors. However, here are some common pitfalls:

1. Giving incorrect information in a prompt for keyboard input

In science and engineering problems, physical units are always important. Therefore, a prompt for input should always indicate the units of quantities to be supplied by the user. Fortran doesn't care about these kinds of inconsistencies, but you should if you want your calculations to be correct!

2. Using improper units in calculations

This is related to the previous logical pitfall. As everyone who has taken an introductory engineering or science course knows, one of the most frequent causes of wrong numerical solutions to problems is improper or inappropriately mixed units. It's bad enough to make these kinds of errors with a pencil and paper, but the problem is compounded when they are embedded in programs. Then, instead of making the mistakes just once, you can make them every time you run the program.

It is this kind of error that makes validating the performance of your program so important. Whenever you incorporate calculations with physical quantities into a program, there is absolutely no substitute for comparing that program's output with sample calculations worked out carefully by hand or with known results.

3. Using mixed-mode arithmetic and type conversions

Errors can arise from unanticipated results of mixed-mode arithmetic operations and type conversions. (Recall program P-3.6.) Because of Fortran's automatic type conversions, mixed-mode arithmetic is allowed even when it produces unintended results. As noted in the text, the best way to avoid these problems is to avoid mixed-mode arithmetic and type conversions unless you make a conscious choice to use them for a specific reason.

4. Using variables that have not been initialized or assigned a value

You should *never* expect a compiler to assume a value for an uninitialized or unassigned variable appearing on the right side of an assignment operation. The most common assumption is that an uninitialized value will be zero, but you should never assume that this will be true.

5. Providing a real number in response to a prompt for an integer

Consider this code:

```
INTEGER radius
...
PRINT *,'Give radius: '
READ *,radius
...
```

Clearly, the program expects the radius to be given as an integer (because radius is of type INTEGER), even though the prompt message doesn't make this clear. So 3 is an appropriate response, but 3.3 isn't. Your compiler will truncate 3.3 to 3; this will keep your program running, but it will produce answers that are wrong.

One way to avoid this kind of error is to restrict your use of the INTEGER data type. Many beginning programmers assume that just because numbers are conveniently expressed as whole numbers without decimal points (in algebraic expressions, for example), they should be declared as type INTEGER. Usually, unless a variable is specifically intended to count events or "things," it should be declared as REAL. For example, suppose your program is intended to calculate the average of three test grades. Your prompt might look like this:

```
Enter three test grades in the range 0-100:
```

and you might respond 83, 91, 77. These look like integers, but variables to hold these values should be REAL. (Just let your program perform the type conversion.) Why? Because, in general, the average of a list of whole numbers won't be a whole number (the average of these three numbers is 83 2/3, or about 83.66667), so all the calculations involving these numbers involve real arithmetic.

To summarize, it's OK to enter REAL numbers without a decimal point, but

> **You should never enter INTEGER numbers as values with a decimal point and digits to the right of the decimal point even if your compiler lets you get away with it.**

3.9.4 Forcing Your Programs to Fail

Part of verifying the proper operation of any program is trying to devise conditions under which it will fail. Forcing your program to fail is analogous to performing destructive testing on a physical mechanism; only by going through this process can you be convinced that the mechanism, or program, will perform reliably when it is used properly. In the same sense that a bridge is built to withstand a specified maximum load, calculations in science and engineering applications can often be made appropriately only within a specific range of input values.

Once you have encoded a formula, however, a Fortran program is usually perfectly willing to perform calculations with any set of input values; the only common exception occurs when input values result in dividing by zero. If you wish to limit the range of calculations, you may need to instruct your program to reject certain input values. Later in the text, we will discuss the kind of syntax that will make this possible. Within the constraints of the programming skills you have now, the best you can do is include limits for input values when you write prompts for keyboard input. For example, the prompt

```
PRINT*," Enter a positive integer >0, NOT=0:"
```

is certainly more informative, and restrictive, than

```
PRINT*," Enter an integer:"
```

and the former statement should certainly motivate a user of your program to be careful about the value she enters.

In general, you should always consider the maximum and minimum possible values that your program might encounter, regardless of whether those values are "reasonable." You should also consider the effects of assigning a variable a value of 0 even if you never intend that to happen, as well as the effects of negative values in a program that is expecting positive values (or *vice versa*). Only by trying these "unreasonable" values can you gain confidence in the output produced by your program under "reasonable" conditions.

3.10 Exercises

3.10.1 Self-Testing Exercises

These exercises are intended to make sure you have a basic understanding of material—especially the Fortran syntax—presented in this chapter. When the exercises ask for Fortran statements or code fragments, it is good practice to test your answers by trying them in a complete program. You should review appropriate parts of the chapter if you have problems with any of these exercises.

Exercise 1. Referring to the table of ASCII characters in **Appendix 1**, find some printable characters that cannot be part of a Fortran token.

Exercise 2. Design some comment lines to appear at the beginning of each of your programs. These could include a course number and description, your instructor's name, and your name.

Exercise 3. Which of these are legal variable names? If they aren't legal, why not?

(a) X/Y   (f) Y1995
(b) First Name   (g) last;
(c) right angle   (h) The first day of the new calendar year

(d) `2001_year`   (i) `x_003`
(e) `_radius_`   (j) `print`

Exercise 4. For each item, choose an appropriate data type and decide whether the value could reasonably be given the PARAMETER attribute.

(a) e (the base of natural logarithms)
(b) the period of an orbiting satellite
(c) social security number
(d) weight per foot of a steel I-beam
(e) your grade on an exam

(f) Avogadro's number
(g) daily production of widgets
(h) telephone number
(i) number of hours in a week
(j) number of days in a month

For each item, write an appropriate type declaration statement and, where appropriate, a PRINT statement to prompt a program user for input. The prompt message should help the user enter the value correctly.

Exercise 5. Declare appropriate variables for a program that processes transactions in a bank account. The quantities of interest include the date, the amount of the transaction, and the type of transaction—"deposit," "withdrawal," or "service charge."

   Hints: use a character "flag" to tell the program what kind of transaction is to be processed. Write list-directed PRINT and READ statements that will help the program user enter information correctly.

Exercise 6. Declare appropriate variables for entries on an order form. The required information includes customer name, telephone number, credit card number, item number, quantity required, and unit price. Write list-directed PRINT and READ statements for obtaining this infomation from a customer. The information about the customer needs to be given only once, but the customer might wish to order several items.

   You haven't learned how to implement loop structures in Fortran, so you can use a combination of pseudocode commands (*LOOP...END LOOP*) and Fortran statements for this problem.

Exercise 7. Which of these algebraic expressions can be translated *directly* into Fortran assignment statements in their present form, assuming that the variables x, y, and c have previously been given values?

(a) $z = (x^2 + y^2)^2$
(b) $z^3 = x^2 + y^2$
(c) $z = 2x + 3y + c$
(d) $z - 1 = 4x/3y$

For those expressions that can't be written as Fortran assignment statements, how could you rewrite them to "solve for z" in the algebraic sense so they *can* be written as Fortran assignment statements?

Exercise 8. Translate the following algebraic expressions into Fortran statements.

(a) $C = \dfrac{KA}{4\pi d}$

(b) $\lambda = 3646\dfrac{N^2}{N^2 - 4}$

(c) $M_B = \dfrac{P_2 - P_1}{\left(\dfrac{v_1 - v_2}{v_1}\right)}$

(d) $f = \dfrac{1}{2\ell}\sqrt{\dfrac{T}{m}}$

3.10.2 Basic Programming Exercises

Exercise 9. Write a source code "shell" that can serve as the starting point for all your other programs. What three statements should be included in this shell?

Exercise 10. Modify program P-3.1 so that it also calculates and prints the surface area and volume of a sphere with the specified radius. The surface area of a sphere is $4\pi r^2$ and the volume is $4\pi r^3/3$.

Exercise 11. Modify program P-3.2 so that it also calculates and prints the area of the material required to construct an *open* rectangular container with the same dimensions. That is, the container doesn't have a top.

Exercise 12. Modify program P-3.3 so that it also asks the user to supply a birth date in the format mm dd yyyy, e.g., 01 01 1977. You can print the birth date in the format mm/dd/yyyy, but there will be extra spaces because of the list-directed output. (You might wish to modify this program when you have learned to use formatted output.)

Exercise 13. Using the following code, write a complete program that will assign values to x, j, b, and c and print the results of the calculations as shown. You may either "hard code" the values using assignment statements within the program or ask the program user to supply them. Be sure to use values that make it easy to check the program's output with a hand calculator. Some of the expressions involve mixed-mode calculations. Which ones give answers that might not be what you expect or desire? What happens if b or c equals zero?

```
      . . .
      REAL x,b
      INTEGER j,c
!   (Assign values here.)
      . . .
      PRINT *,x**0.5,x**(-1./b),x**(-1/b)
      PRINT *,j**0.5,j**(-1./b),j**(-1/b)
      PRINT *,        x**(-1./c),x**(-1/c)
      PRINT *,        j**(-1./c),j**(-1/c)
      PRINT *,        x**(1./b),x**(1/b)
      PRINT *,        j**(1./b),j**(1/b)
      PRINT *,        x**(1./c),x**(1/c)
      PRINT *,        j**(1./c),j**(1/c)
      END
```

Exercise 14. Based on material from other courses you are taking, state a computational problem and write a complete program to solve it.

3.10.3 Programming Applications

These programming applications should include Steps 2–5 of the problem-solving process described in Chapter 2: a written outline of the solution, including formulas, an algorithm design using the pseudocode language from Chapter 2, a working Fortran program, a description of how the program's operation has been verified, and representative input and output to document your program's operation. You may also wish to restate the problem for yourself (Step 1 of the problem-solving process) to make sure you understand what is required.

The name in brackets given at the end of each exercise refers to a source code file that is available to instructors who are using this text. (See Section i.5 of the preface.)

Exercise 15. Write a program that calculates and prints the total resistance of three resistors connected (a) in series and (b) in parallel (as illustrated in Figure 3.6). When n resistors are connected in series, the total resistance of the connected resistors is $r_T = r_1 + r_2 + r_3 + ... + r_n$. When they are connected in parallel, the total resistance is $1/r_T = 1/r_1 + 1/r_2 + 1/r_3 + ... + 1/r_n$. Prompt the user to enter values in ohms, the usual unit of resistance. [RESISTOR.F90]

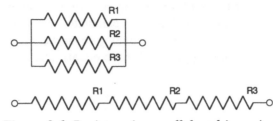

Figure 3.6. Resistors in parallel and in series

Exercise 16. Consider the reliability of a system consisting of three components connected in series or parallel. If the reliability of the components is given as R_1, R_2, and R_3, where $0 \leq R \leq 1$, then the reliability of a system with the components wired in series is $R_1 R_2 R_3$. If the same components are wired in parallel, and if the system remains functional as long as any one of the components is working, then the system reliability is $1 - (1 - R_1)(1 - R_2)(1 - R_3)$. Write a program to calculate the reliability of such systems for three user-specified values of reliability.

Systems using components in series are vulnerable to failure even if the individual components are very reliable. On the other hand, "redundant" systems, with components in parallel, are very reliable even if the components aren't individually very reliable. For example, if each component has a reliability of 0.900, a system with these components in series has a reliability of only 0.729. If the same components are in parallel, then the system reliability is 0.999. [RELIABLE.F90]

Exercise 17. Write a program that calculates and displays the volume and surface area of a cylinder, given the radius and height in meters. The volume of such a cylinder is $\pi r^2 h$ and its surface area is $2\pi r^2 + 2\pi rh$. [CYLINDER.F90]

Extra Credit
1. Assuming that the cylinder is solid and that the density (kg/m^3) of the material is specified as input, calculate the mass of the cylinder. Use an engineering handbook to find densities for one or more materials. Your program output should indicate what materials you have used.
2. Assuming that the cylinder is an empty container made of thin sheets of material with a specified thickness, calculate the mass of the cylinder. Is it appropriate to assume that this value is just the surface area times the mass per unit area of the material?

Exercise 18. Write a program that asks the user to supply the mass and velocity of an object and then calculates and displays the kinetic energy and momentum of that object. The kinetic energy is $mv^2/2$ and the momentum is mv. Use SI units (mass in kilograms, velocity in meters per second, energy in Joules). [KINETIC.F90]

Extra Credit
Include source code that will convert the kinetic energy and momentum into their British system equivalents. The British unit of energy is foot-pounds and the unit of momentum is slug-feet per second. 1 foot-pound = 1.356 Joule; 1 slug = 14.59 kilogram; 1 foot/second = 0.3048 meters/second.

Exercise 19. Write a program that requests as input the clock time in hours (0-24), minutes, and seconds, in the format hh mm ss, and displays the time in seconds and fractions of a day. One day contains 86,400 seconds. For example, 12 00 00 is 43,200 seconds, or 0.5 days. [TIME.F90]

Exercise 20. Write a program that requests as input an angle expressed in degrees, minutes, and seconds, in the format dd mm ss, and converts it to whole and fractional degrees. There are 60 minutes in a degree and 60 seconds in a minute. For example, 30 15 04 equals 30.25111°. [ANGLES.F90]

Exercise 21. Write a program that requests as input the time in seconds required to cover a distance of one mile and calculates the speed in units of feet per second, meters per second, and miles per hour. For example, a 4-minute (240-second) mile is run at an average speed of 22 feet per second, 6.7 meters per second, or 15 miles per hour. There are 5,280 feet in one mile and 3.2808 feet in one meter. [SPEED.F90]

Exercise 22. A mass swinging at the end of a massless string (a simple pendulum) undergoes simple harmonic motion as long as the displacement of the mass from the vertical is very small compared to the length of the string. The period T of a simple pendulum is independent of its mass and is given by $T = 2\pi(L/g)^{1/2}$, where the length L is given in meters and $g = 9.807$ m/s^2. (See Figure 3.7.) Write a program that will determine (a) the period of a pendulum with a specified length and (b) the length a pendulum must have to produce a period of 1 second. [PENDULUM.F90]

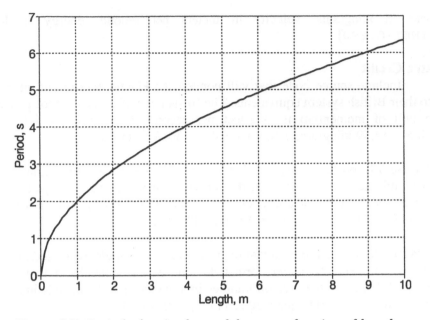

Figure 3.7. Period of a simple pendulum as a function of length

Exercise 23. Write a program that calculates and prints the energy of a photon the wavelength of which λ is given in centimeters. Energy=hf Joule, where $h = 6.626 \times 10^{-34}$ Joule-s (Planck's constant); $f = c/\lambda$, where $c = 2.9979 \times 10^{8}$ m/s (the speed of light) and wavelength is given in meters. (See Figure 3.8.)

   Hint: declare the speed of light and Planck's constant with a PARAMETER attribute, using "E" notation, e.g., 2.9979e8. [PHOTON.F90]

Extra Credit
   A 1 eV (electron volt) photon has an energy of 1.602×10^{-19} Joule. Modify your program so it will also calculate the wavelength of a photon with an energy of 1 eV. (Answer: about 1240×10^{-9} m. This is in the infrared part of the electromagnetic spectrum.)

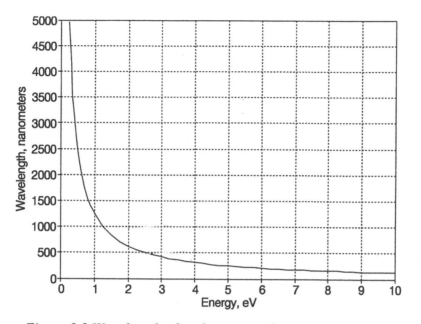

Figure 3.8 Wavelength of a photon as a function of energy.

Exercise 24. Write a program that asks for a student's name, ID, and cumulative grade point average (GPA). Print this information on a single line. NOTE: You may find that if you enter a GPA as 3.9, for example, your program will print something different, such as 3.900000, 3.900001 or 3.899999. This isn't your fault. It is a consequence of how Fortran stores REAL numbers and the limitations of list-directed output. You can't change the appearance of this number until you learn how to specify your own output format in a later chapter. [GPA.F90]

Extra Credit

Modify your program so it asks the user to provide the total number of credit hours she has accumulated through last semester. Calculate the total number of grade points by multiplying the number of credit hours by the GPA. Now ask the user to supply information about a new course she has just completed. This information should include the number of credit hours for the course and the number of points for each credit hour—4 for an A, 3 for a B, 2 for a C, 1 for a D, and 0 for an F. Multiply the credit hours by this number and add the result to the old number of total grade points. Add the new credit hours to the old credit hours. Divide the new number of grade points by the new total credit hours to recalculate the GPA. Display this value.

Exercise 25. Given the (x,y) coordinates of two points in a plane, write a program that calculates (a) the shortest distance between the two points and (b) the (x,y) coordinates of a point halfway between the two points, lying on a straight line joining the points. (See Figure 3.9.)

Hint: you will need to calculate a square root in your program. In Chapter 4 we will discuss how to use a standard Fortran function to do this: $y=SQRT(x)$ assigns a value to y equal to the square root of x, where x represents any non-negative number, expression, or variable. You can use this function or you can calculate the square root of any number, variable, or expression by using the exponentiation operator with a value of 0.5. For example, $x^{1/2}$ can be expressed as `x**0.5`. [POINTS.F90]

Extra Credit:

If you have had a precalculus course, you should understand the concept of a line slope. (The derivative of a function that produces a straight line is the constant slope of that line.) Modify your program so that it also calculates the slope of the line joining two points in a plane. What restriction will this calculation impose on the location of the two points?

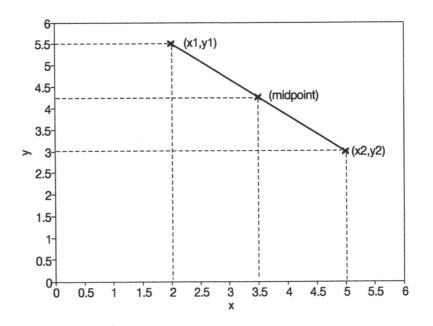

Figure 3.9. Distance between two points in a plane

Exercise 26. The ideal gas law describes the relationships among pressure (p), volume (V), and temperature (T) of an ideal gas,

$$pV = \mu RT$$

where μ is the number of kilomoles of gas and R is the universal gas constant. For volume in m^3, temperature in kelvins, and pressure in Newtons/m^2 (Pascals), R = 8314.3 Joule/kilomole-K and 1.0132×10^5 Pascals = 1 standard atmosphere (atm). Write a program that calculates the volume occupied by a specified number of kilomoles of an ideal gas at temperature T (kelvins) and pressure p (atm). (Sample answer: under standard conditions of T = 273.15 K (0° C) and a pressure of 1 atm, 1 kilomole of an ideal gas occupies a volume of about 22.4 m^3.) [GAS.F90]

Extra Credit
1. If you were trying to determine the validity of the ideal gas law experimentally, it would make more sense to use the law to calculate pressure for a specified volume and temperature. Modify the program to do this calculation instead of the calculation specified in the original problem statement.

2. Because molecules occupy volume and exert intermolecular (bonding) forces on each other, the ideal gas law becomes less accurate as density increases; that is, as more molecules occupy the same volume. The van der Waals modification to the ideal gas law attempts to take this into account with the following empirical formula,

$$(p + a/v^2)(v - b) = RT$$

where v is the specific volume (m^3/kilomole, for example). The constants a and b are different for each gas and are experimentally derived. Table 3.5 contains data for several gases. Figure 3.10 shows some calculations for nitrogen. Over an appropriate range of specific volumes, for which v > b, the van der Waals pressure is less than the ideal gas pressure.

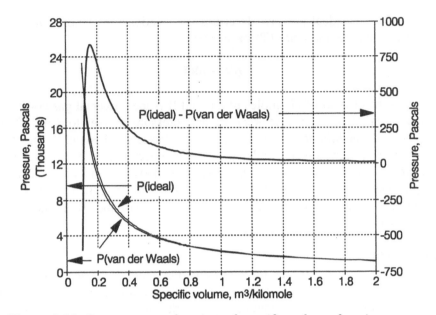

Figure 3.10. Pressure as a function of specific volume for nitrogen at T=273.15 K

Table 3.5. Molar masses and van der Waals coefficients for selected gases.

	Molar mass, gm/mole	van der Waals coefficients			
Gas		a, kPa-m^6/ kg^2	b, m^3/kg	a, l^2-atm/ mole^2	b, l/mole
air	28.97	0.1630	0.001270	1.350	0.0368
ammonia	17.03	1.4680	0.002200	4.202	0.0375
carbon dioxide	44.01	0.1883	0.000972	3.600	0.0428
helium	4.00	0.2140	0.005870	0.034	0.0235
hydrogen	2.02	6.0830	0.013200	0.245	0.0267
methane	16.04	0.8880	0.002660	2.255	0.0427
nitrogen	28.02	0.1747	0.001380	1.354	0.0387
oxygen	32.00	0.1344	0.000993	1.358	0.0318
propane	44.09	0.4810	0.002040	9.228	0.0899

Source: M. C. Potter and C. W. Somerton (1993). *Schaum's Outline Series: Theory and Problems of Engineering Thermodynamics*, Tables B-3, B-8.

Modify your program (the extra credit one, not the original one) to do calculations for both the ideal gas law and the van der Waals modified law.

   Hint: be careful with units. 1 liter/mole is numerically identical to 1 m³/kilomole. If the pressure is calculated in Pascals, then the tabulated value for a must be multiplied by 101320. Use Figure 3.10 to check your answers. [GAS2.F90]

Using Functions to Expand the Power of Fortran

Much of the power of Fortran is due to its dozens of predefined functions for performing mathematical and other calculations. This chapter describes many of these functions and introduces one way to create your own functions.

4.1 Fortran Intrinsic Functions

4.1.1 Intrinsic Functions for Arithmetic Calculations: Arguments and Ranges

You shouldn't be surprised to find that a programming language designed specifically for solving scientific and engineering problems includes many of the important basic mathematical functions used in these disciplines. In this section, we will discuss mathematical and other functions that are part of the Fortran language. These "built-in" functions are called *intrinsic functions*.[1]

Fortran intrinsic functions are related to what you normally think of as a "function" in mathematics, as defined generically for functions of one variable by the algebraic expression $y = f(x)$, but with some specific programming-related details. In the mathematical interpretation of the expression $y = f(x)$, f is a symbolic name for the function, the argument x represents a value of the independent variable at which the function is evaluated, and y is equal to the value of the function at argument x. For example, the expression $y=\sin(x)$ means that y is equal to the trigonometric sine evaluated at the angle x.

In Fortran, an intrinsic function is a built-in subprogram that accepts, through an *argument list*, one or more input values in the form of constants, variable names, expressions, or other functions and returns a single value as output. In source code, an intrinsic function is "called" or "invoked" when it appears on the right-hand side of an assignment operator (either alone or as part of a larger

---

[1]Fortran intrinsic functions are sometimes referred to as intrinsic procedures. However, "functions" is a preferable description based on how these terms are used in other programming languages.

expression) or in an output statement such as the PRINT statement. That is, functions are treated just like values.

Code fragment P-4.1 shows how an intrinsic function is used in a Fortran program.

P-4.1 (fragment)

```
REAL Z,Y,DegToRad
...
DegToRad=3.1415927/180.
Z=0.5
Y=SIN(Z)
PRINT *,Y,SIN(Z/2.)
PRINT *,SIN(30.*DegToRad)
...
```

A Fortran compiler knows what SIN(Z)means because SIN is an intrinsic function that is supported by all Fortran compilers as part of the language standard. So, in the same sense that a pocket calculator knows how to evaluate the sine of an angle, your Fortran program will be able to evaluate SIN(Z). (As always, Fortran isn't case-sensitive, so SIN, Sin, and sin are all equivalent and equally acceptable. This text will adopt the convention of spelling the names of intrinsic functions with uppercase letters.)

Once the variable Z has the value 0.5 assigned to it in P-4.1, the assignment statement Y=SIN(Z) results in the variable Y having a value of 0.4794255. In order to understand this result, you need to know that the Fortran SIN function expects as its argument an angle expressed in radians, not degrees. Thus the value of 0.5 used in P-4.1 is interpreted as 0.5 radians, or about 28.6°. All the Fortran trigonometric functions that have angles as arguments require that the angles be expressed in radians. Functions that return an angle as output (the inverse trigonometric functions) return that value in radians.

The second and third calls to the SIN function in P-4.1 illustrate the fact that the argument(s) of a function can be expressions as well as variables (or constants). Pay special attention to the third call to SIN (in the second PRINT statement). If you forget to convert an angle to radians before using it as an argument in a trigonometric function, you will get results that often appear reasonable but will be wrong. For example, SIN(30.) is *not* the correct way to calculate the sine of 30°. The value of this argument will be interpreted as 30 radians (equivalent to about 278.9°), not 30°.[2] So (because 180° equals π radians),

---

[2]30 radians is $(30 \times 180)/\pi$ = 1718.873387°, which equals 4×360° plus approximately 278.9°.

> **When an angle is given in degrees, multiply it by $\pi/180.0$ to convert it to radians before using it as the argument in a Fortran intrinsic trigonometric function.**

In P-4.1, this conversion factor is stored in the variable DegToRad.

What happens in P-4.1 if the statement Z=0.5 is not included? That is, what happens if Z is not given a value before it is used as an argument? Your compiler will probably assume that Z equals zero. (Try it and see.) However, no matter what the result of this experiment,

> **It is unacceptable programming practice to use an uninitialized variable as an argument for any intrinsic function.**

Why is this so important? Because even though uninitialized variables often don't prevent your program from executing, the results are compiler-dependent and unpredictable. In general, regardless of the language you are using, you should *never* allow a compiler to make assumptions about values you wish to use!

There are many intrinsic functions in Fortran. In order to use one, it's necessary to know its name, its purpose, the restrictions on its argument(s), and the data type and range of the value it returns. For example, you need to know that when you use the SIN function, the argument must be an angle in radians, expressed as a type REAL numeric constant, expression, or variable, and that the function returns a REAL value in the range [-1.0,1.0]. (Following conventional mathematical usage, a bracket means that the limit includes the value to the right or left of the bracket and a parenthesis means that the limit excludes the value to the right or left of the bracket. Thus, for example, a range (-1.0,1.0) means that the range includes values between -1 and +1, but excludes the values -1 and +1 themselves.)

As another example, in order to use the inverse trigonometric function, ASIN, you need to know that the argument must be a REAL numeric constant, expression, or variable in the range [-1.0,1.0] and that the function returns a REAL angle expressed in radians, in the range $[-\pi/2,\pi/2]$. In this case, and with many other intrinsic functions, an argument outside the allowed range will cause your program to crash, as there is no built-in protection against the effects of providing inappropriate arguments.

Table 4.1 contains a partial list of Fortran intrinsic functions that return values of type REAL or INTEGER. We will use only a few of these functions in this chapter, but Table 4.1 will be important for future reference.

Table 4.1. Selected intrinsic Fortran functions for arithmetic operations

4.1 (a) Mathematical functions

Trigonometric [1]	Fortran Usage	Argument Type(s) and Range	Result Type and Range
sin(x)	SIN(X)	REAL, any	REAL, [-1,1] [2]
cos(x)	COS(X)	REAL, any	REAL, [-1,1]
tan(x)	TAN(X)	REAL, any	REAL, $(-\infty,\infty)$ [3]
$\sin^{-1}(x)$	ASIN(X)	REAL, [-1,1]	REAL, $[-\pi/2,\pi/2]$
$\cos^{-1}(x)$	ACOS(X)	REAL, [-1,1]	REAL, $[0,\pi]$
$\tan^{-1}(x)$	ATAN(X)	REAL, any	REAL, $[-\pi/2,\pi/2]$
$\tan^{-1}(y/x)$ [4]	ATAN2(Y,X)	REAL, any	REAL, $(-\pi,\pi]$
Hyperbolic			
sinh(x) [5]	SINH(X)	REAL, any	REAL, $(-\infty,\infty)$ [3]
cosh(x) [6]	COSH(X)	REAL, any	REAL, $[1,\infty)$ [3]
tanh(x) [7]	TANH(X)	REAL, any	REAL, [-1,1]
Transcendental			
$\sqrt{x}$	SQRT(X)	REAL, ≥ 0	REAL, $[0,\infty)$ [3]
e^x	EXP(X)	REAL, any	REAL, $(0,\infty)$ [3]
ln(x)	LOG(X)	REAL, >0	REAL, $(-\infty,\infty)$ [3]
$\log_{10}(x)$	LOG10(X)	REAL, >0	REAL, $(-\infty,\infty)$ [3]

[1] For all trigonometric and inverse trigonometric functions, angles are expressed as radians.

[2] For any values x and y given as limits on a range, "[x" means that the lower limit of the range includes x, "(x" means that the lower limit excludes x, "y]" means that the upper limit includes y, and "y)" means that the upper limit excludes y.

[3] "Infinite" values are limited by the range of REAL numbers.

[4] The ATAN2 function calculates the arctangent of Y/X. By using information about the sign of both X and Y, it preserves the quadrant associated with the coordinates X and Y. The values of X and Y may not both be zero.

[5] $\sinh(x) = (e^x - e^{-x})/2.$ [6] $\cosh(x) = (e^x + e^{-x})/2.$ [7] $\tanh(x) = \sinh(x)/\cosh(x).$

4.1 (b) Numeric functions

Purpose	Fortran Usage	Argument Type(s) and Range(s)	Result Type
`INTEGER` result			
Truncate to integer	`INT(X)`	REAL, any	`INTEGER`
Round to integer	`NINT(X)`	REAL, any	`INTEGER`
Least integer $\geq X$	`CEILING(X)`	REAL, any	`INTEGER`
Greatest integer $\leq X$	`FLOOR(X)`	REAL, any	`INTEGER`
`REAL` result			
Truncate toward zero	`AINT(X)`	REAL, any	`REAL`
Nearest whole number	`ANINT(X)`	REAL, any	`REAL`
Convert to real	`REAL(X)`	INTEGER, any	`REAL`
Result type depends on argument(s) [1]			
Absolute value	`ABS(X)`	Numeric	`REAL` or `INTEGER`
Maximum difference [2]	`DIM(X,Y)`	Numeric	`REAL` or `INTEGER`
Maximum	`MAX(X1,X2` `[,X3,...])`	Numeric	`REAL` or `INTEGER`
Minimum	`MIN(X1,X2` `[,X3,...])`	Numeric	`REAL` or `INTEGER`
Remainder of X1 modulo X2, with `INT` [3]	`MOD(X1,X2)`	Numeric	`REAL` or `INTEGER`
Remainder of X1 modulo X2, with `FLOOR` [4]	`MODULO(X1,X2)`	Numeric	`REAL` or `INTEGER`
Sign transfer [5]	`SIGN(X1,X2)`	Numeric	`REAL` or `INTEGER`

[1] If there are multiple arguments, they must all be of the same type.
[2] Returns the maximum of X-Y or 0.
[3] Returns `X1-INT(X1/X2)*X2`. Results are undependable (compiler-dependent) if X2=0.
[4] Returns `X1-FLOOR(X1/X2)*X2` if X1 and X2 are REAL,
`X1-FLOOR(REAL(X1)/REAL(X2))*X2` if X1 and X2 are INTEGER. Results are undependable (compiler-dependent) if X2=0.
[5] Returns absolute value of X1 times the sign of X2. If X2=0, its sign is considered positive.

Programming Tip

Some of the intrinsic function names, for example, INT and AINT, follow Fortran implicit data typing conventions. Hence INT returns an INTEGER value and AINT returns a REAL value. However, you may not recognize this convention because it is part of an old-fashioned Fortran programming style specifically avoided in this text. Based on implicit typing, any function name beginning with a letter I through N returns an INTEGER value, and a name beginning with any other letter returns a REAL value.

Functions that don't follow implicit type conventions include, for example, the CEILING and FLOOR functions, which are implicitly of type REAL, but which return INTEGER results (and didn't exist in older versions of Fortran), and the last seven functions in Table 4.1(b), which return results of the same type as their argument(s). Also, the LOG and LOG10 functions return REAL results even though their names are implicitly INTEGER. In older versions of Fortran, these functions are named ALOG and ALOG10 in order to conform to implicit typing rules.

It's important to remember that the name X and other argument names used in Table 4.1 are just "place holders" used to illustrate how a particular function should be used. In your programs, function arguments can be constants, variable names, other functions that return a value of the appropriate data type, or expressions that evaluate to the appropriate data type.

The difference between the MOD and MODULO functions in Table 4.1(b) is subtle. Suppose, for example, X1= -5.55 and X2= 3.1. INT(-5.55/3.1)=-1, so MOD(X1,X2)=-5.55-(-1)(3.1)= -2.45. However, FLOOR(-5.55/3.1) =-2, so MODULO(X1,X2)= -5.55-(-2)(3.1)= 0.65. The MOD and MODULO functions return the same value if both arguments are either positive or negative, but if one of the arguments is negative, you need to make sure you choose the appropriate function for your program.

The MIN and MAX functions in Table 4.1(b) are unique because they accept a variable number of arguments (two or more).

As long as you understand the mathematical purpose of these functions, their application in Fortran is straightforward. However, you must always be careful to provide arguments of the proper data type and within the allowed range. To give just two examples, your program will crash (terminate with a run-time error) if you try to evaluate ACOS(2.0) (because the cosine of an angle can't possibly have a value of 2) or if you use the SQRT function with a negative argument. Whenever you provide a constant value, a variable name, or an expression to be evaluated as an argument for a function, it is up to you to guarantee that the value falls within the allowed range. (Fortran syntax discussed in Chapter 6 will provide you with some programming tools for performing checks on values before you use them as function arguments.)

Table 4.1(a) contains the ranges for arguments and for the results returned by the mathematical functions. As noted in footnote 3 to Table 4.1(a), functions that become either positively or negatively infinite at an endpoint of the range for their argument can't actually return an infinite value. The largest value (in absolute magnitude) they can return depends on the range of REAL numbers. This restriction can sometimes cause problems when such functions are used in numerical calculations.

It is worth reiterating the very important and not always obvious restriction on the use of the mathematical intrinsic functions: the arguments must have the expected data type. It's tempting to think that, for example, SQRT(2) is an appropriate use of the SQRT function even though Table 4.1 indicates that the argument must be REAL. You might make this assumption because, for example, the assignment X=2 is OK (even though it is not usually good programming practice) because Fortran will make an appropriate type conversion. In principle, there is no reason why a compiler shouldn't be able to perform the required type conversion from the integer value 2 to the real value 2.0, but under the Fortran 90 standard, it is *not* supposed to do this.[3] Therefore, an INTEGER variable, constant, or expression used in a function that expects a REAL argument *should* generate a run-time error. This is important enough to state as a rule:

> **Never use INTEGER arguments in an intrinsic function that calls for REAL arguments, or *vice versa*.**

4.1.2 Intrinsic Functions for Character and String Manipulation

In addition to intrinsic functions for arithmetic operations, Fortran 90 also includes several functions for manipulating individual characters and "strings" of characters. Table 4.2 lists these functions.

The first four functions in Table 4.2 perform conversions back and forth between characters and their position in a system-dependent table of characters called a collating sequence. The most common collating sequence is the ASCII sequence, given in **Appendix 1**. The functions ACHAR and IACHAR produce values based on this sequence, regardless of whether the computer you are working on uses the ASCII sequence. The functions CHAR and ICHAR *assume* that your computer uses the ASCII sequence. On most computers, these functions are equivalent because such computers do in fact use the ASCII collating sequence. However, assuming that you wish to perform these conversions based

---

[3]This was not true in earlier versions of Fortran. Fortran 77 compilers would allow SQRT(2), for example.

Table 4.2. Fortran intrinsic functions for manipulating characters and strings.

Purpose	Fortran Usage	Argument Type and Range	Result Type
Character-Integer Conversions			
Character in ASCII collating sequence	ACHAR(I)	INTEGER, [0,127]	CHARACTER
Character in processor collating sequence	CHAR(I)	INTEGER, [0,n-1]	CHARACTER
Position in ASCII sequence	IACHAR(C)	CHARACTER	INTEGER
Position in processor sequence	ICHAR(C)	CHARACTER	INTEGER
String Manipulation and Inquiry Functions			
Remove leading blanks [1]	ADJUSTL(S)	CHARACTER	CHARACTER
Remove trailing blanks [2]	ADJUSTR(S)	CHARACTER	CHARACTER
Leftmost [rightmost] starting position of substring (SS) in string (S) [3]	INDEX(S, SS[,BACK])	CHARACTER	INTEGER
Length of string [4]	LEN(S)	CHARACTER	INTEGER
Length of string, not counting trailing blanks	LEN_TRIM(S)	CHARACTER	INTEGER
Concatenate n copies of S [4,5]	REPEAT(S,n)	CHARACTER, INTEGER	CHARACTER
Position of character included in string SET [3]	SCAN(S, SET[,BACK])	CHARACTER	INTEGER
Remove trailing blanks [4]	TRIM(S)	CHARACTER	CHARACTER
Returns 0 if each character in S appears in SET, or position in S of first character that does not [3]	VERIFY(S, SET[,BACK])	CHARACTER	INTEGER

[1] Inserts the same number of trailing blanks.
[2] Inserts the same number of leading blanks.
[3] Returns leftmost value if BACK is absent or present with a value of .FALSE.; otherwise returns the rightmost value. INDEX and SCAN functions return 0 if search string or character isn't found.
[4] Accepts only scalar arguments. (See discussion of arrays in Chapter 8.)
[5] See discussion of the concatenation operator later in this section.

on the ASCII sequence, use of the ACHAR and IACHAR functions will make your programs portable even to systems that use another collating sequence (such as some IBM mainframe computers).

The ACHAR function produces a truly portable result only if the argument does not exceed 127 because the ASCII collating sequence standardizes only those characters in the range [0,127]. For values in the range [128,255], the result is system-dependent. On IBM-compatible PCs, for example, these characters include the so-called "IBM graphics" characters, mathematical symbols, and characters from nonEnglish languages (including Greek characters for use in mathematical expressions).

In addition to the string manipulation functions described in Table 4.2, Fortran also provides an operator for "adding" strings. The  symbol for the *concatenation operator* is a double slash (//), and it is the only intrinsic operator for data of type CHARACTER. For two CHARACTER variables A and B, the result of A//B is a new string that contains all characters of B appended to the end of the characters of A.

If the result of the concatenation is stored in another CHARACTER variable, that variable should be long enough to hold all the characters. If it's not, no error message is generated, but the resulting string is truncated from the right to fit the declared length of the variable.

Program P-4.2 demonstrates the concatenation operator and the TRIM, LEN, and LEN_TRIM functions.

P-4.2 [STRING.F90]

```
      PROGRAM string
!
! Demo program for string operations.
!
      IMPLICIT NONE
      CHARACTER *10 first_name,last_name,name*15
!
      first_name='Laura'
      last_name='Brooks'
      name=first_name//last_name
      PRINT *,name
      PRINT *,'untrimmed length: ',LEN(name)
      name=TRIM(first_name)//' '//TRIM(last_name)
      PRINT *,name
      PRINT *,'untrimmed length: ',LEN(name)
      PRINT *,'trimmed length: ',LEN_TRIM(name)
!
      END
```

Running P-4.2

```
Laura      Brook
untrimmed length:   15
Laura Brooks
untrimmed length:   15
trimmed length:   12
```

When values are assigned to first_name and last_name, they are "right-padded" with enough blanks to make up the declared length of 10 characters, as demonstrated by the result from the LEN function. When the concatenated value of name is printed, only the leftmost 15 characters are printed because the variable name has a declared length of only 15 characters. When the TRIM function is used twice in a new concatenation operation, three trailing blanks are still added to Laura⌀Brooks to fill name, and the LEN function still returns a value of 15. However, the LEN_TRIM returns a more useful value of 12 characters, the length of the string ignoring the trailing blanks.

The fact of the matter is that string manipulation is *relatively* unimportant for the kinds of problems Fortran is most often called upon to solve. However, the functions in Table 4.2 can sometimes be used to solve tricky problems when you must interpret the contents of a data file. Suppose a file contains information about monthly snowfall recorded at a weather station. Most of the time, the value for a month will be 0 or some other numerical value for the recorded snowfall. Occasionally, a "trace" level will be recorded (perhaps as the character T) when snow fell, but there was not a measurable accumulation. How can the information in such a file be interpreted if it is not possible to know ahead of time whether the data fields will contain numbers or characters?

If the fields containing these values can first be read as character strings, the presence of certain characters can be detected by using the INDEX function. If the appropriate characters aren't found, then the (presumed) numerical information in the string can be processed. We will discuss the details of the kind of code required to do this in Chapter 9.

As a final example, consider the problem of converting lowercase characters to uppercase characters. This might be required when you want a text search to be case-insensitive. (Normally such a search will be case-sensitive.) Here is a statement that performs this operation:

```
upper_ch = ACHAR(IACHAR(ch)-32)
```

The statement assumes that the variables upper_ch and ch are declared as type CHARACTER, and it makes use of the fact that, in the ASCII collating sequence, the lowercase alphabet starts at position 97 and the uppercase alphabet starts at position 65, a difference of 32. Assuming only that every uppercase and lowercase letter is separated by the same numer of positions in the collating sequence, you can generalize this statement for nonASCII systems:

```
upper_ch = ACHAR(IACHAR("A")+(IACHAR("a")-IACHAR(ch)))
```

4.1.3 Examples of Calculations Using Intrinsic Functions

Polar/Cartesian conversions

First we will present a complete program that uses Fortran intrinsic functions to convert between Cartesian and polar coordinates. Figure 4.1 shows the relationship between these two coordinate systems.

1 Define the problem.

Given a point expressed in polar coordinates (r,θ), calculate the corresponding Cartesian coordinates (x,y), or the other way around.

2 Outline a solution.

For the polar coordinates (r,θ), the corresponding Cartesian coordinates are

$$x = r \bullet \cos(\theta)$$
$$y = r \bullet \sin(\theta)$$

For the Cartesian coordinates (x,y), the corresponding polar coordinates are

$$r = \sqrt{x^2 + y^2}$$
$$\theta = \tan^{-1}(y/x)$$

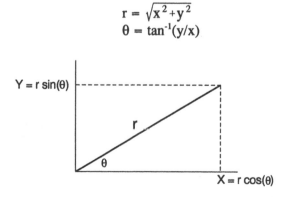

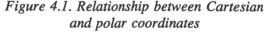

Figure 4.1. Relationship between Cartesian and polar coordinates

3 *Design an algorithm.*

This algorithm converts specified Cartesian coordinates to polar coordinates and back again.

DEFINE *(x, y, r, theta (in degrees))*
From polar to Cartesian:
WRITE *(prompt for input)*
READ *(r,theta)*
ASSIGN *x = r•cos(theta)*
         y = r•sin(theta)
WRITE *(x,y)*
Back to polar:
ASSIGN $r = (x^2+y^2)^{1/2}$
         theta = $tan^{-1}(y/x)$ (Be sure to get the quadrant right,
                        based on the signs of x and y.)
WRITE *(r,theta)*

In this algorithm, the details of a **WRITE** command that tells the user what kinds of input values to provide have been left out. We will often omit this detail in future algorithms even though it is essential in a program. By now, you should know that such prompts are always required whenever keyboard input is required.

This algorithm design has also omitted the conversions between degrees and radians that will be required in the Fortran implementation. It would certainly be acceptable to include those calculations, but they represent an implementation detail that need not be part of the algorithm design.

4 *Convert the algorithm into a program.*

P-4.3 [POLAR.F90]

```
      PROGRAM polar
!
!     Convert polar coordinates to Cartesian and check the
!     results by converting them back to polar coordinates.
!
      IMPLICIT NONE
      REAL X,Y,r,theta,pi,DegToRad
!
      pi=4.0*ATAN(1.0)
      DegToRad=pi/180.0
```

```
      PRINT*,' Give polar coordinates r, theta (deg): '
      READ*,r,theta
!
      X=r*COS(theta*DegToRad)
      Y=r*SIN(theta*DegToRad)
!
      PRINT*,' x and y: ',X,Y
!
!     Recalculate values of r and theta...
!
      r=SQRT(X*X+Y*Y)
      theta=ATAN2(Y,X)/DegToRad
!
      PRINT*,' recalculated r and theta: ',r,theta
!
      END
```

Running P-4.3

```
   Give polar coordinates r, theta (deg):
5.0 30.0
   x and y:      4.3301272   2.5000000
   recalculated r and theta:      5.0000000  29.9999981
```

When you implement the algorithm for this problem in Fortran, you must include conversions between radians and degrees to use the ATAN, SIN, COS, and ATAN2 functions appropriately. Remember that the ATAN2 function is required in order to return the original value of θ.

5 *Verify the operation of the program.*

Program P-4.3 has been designed to check its own calculations. When the user gives a set of polar coordinates, the program calculates the corresponding Cartesian coordinates and then converts these Cartesian coordinates back to polar coordinates. Because of the way Fortran does arithmetic with real numbers, conversion of the x and y coordinates back to radius and angle may not yield precisely the original value. This apparent problem, or at least its appearance in displayed output, can be minimized by exerting more control over the form of program output, as will be discussed in Chapter 5.

It's especially important to verify the operation of the program at angles of 90° and 270° because the tangent is undefined at these two angles.[4] What will Fortran produce for $r = 10$ and $\theta = 90°$, for example? The calculated x-coordinate will be small, but not exactly 0, and the y-coordinate may not be exactly 10.

---

[4]Because the tangent is defined as y/x in Cartesian coordinates, the tangent approaches infinity whenever x approaches 0.

Although the definition of the ATAN2 function implies that a division by zero may occur if x=0, this will not actually occur within the function, and your program will not crash. Try some potentially troublesome values on your system and see what happens. You may or may not see anything that looks strange, depending on the number of significant figures displayed by your compiler's list-directed output format.

Problem Discussion

There are several points worth mentioning about P-4.3's solution to this apparently simple problem. Recall that, in program P-3.1 from Chapter 3, pi was defined as a constant (by giving it the PARAMETER attribute) when π was needed to calculate the area and circumference of a circle. In P-4.3, π is defined as a variable and calculated by making use of the fact that $\pi/4$ radians (45°) is the arctangent of 1. In this way, pi is automatically calculated to as many significant digits as your compiler supports for REAL numbers. You may use whichever method you or your instructor prefers.

Another important point concerns the conversion back and forth between degrees and radians. The program user is asked to provide angles in degrees, and angular output is expressed in degrees. However, remember that Fortran trigonometric functions require arguments expressed in radians. Multiply an angle by $\pi/180$ to convert from degrees to radians and by $180/\pi$ to convert from radians to degrees. It's easy to forget this conversion, and the error can be difficult to detect, especially in programs where the results of trigonometric calculations are used internally and never printed as part of the program's output.

Program P-4.3 uses the ATAN2 function rather than the ATAN function to calculate θ. Suppose, for example, the Cartesian coordinates are $(x,y) = (1,2)$. If the Fortran argument X for the ATAN function is set equal to y/x, or 2.0, then ATAN returns a value of 1.107 radians, or 63.43°. For the same arguments used in the ATAN2 function, the same correct value is returned. Now, however, suppose the Cartesian coordinates are $(-1,-2)$. For the ATAN function, X still equals 2.0, and the value returned is still 1.107 radians. However, this isn't the correct answer. Only the ATAN2 function knows how to interpret the signs of x and y to return the correct value for θ, 4.249 radians, or 243.43°, an angle in the third quadrant. Also, it is essential to remember the order in which the two arguments for the ATAN2 function must be given: first y, then x.

Finally, remember that intrinsic functions can be used in PRINT statements just like other expressions, and they can be used as arguments in other functions. This means that the code for recalculating r and θ could reasonably be rewritten as:

```
PRINT*, SQRT(X*X+Y*Y), ATAN2(Y,X)/DegToRad
```

Just to demonstrate how functions can be used in expressions that are arguments of other functions, `theta` could also be recalculated in terms of itself, like this:

```
theta=ATAN2(r*SIN(theta*DegToRad),r*COS(theta*DegToRad))/DegToRad
```

However, substituting these expressions for Y and X doesn't make sense except as a demonstration.

Calculating the absolute value

Programs are often required to compare the absolute magnitude of the difference between two numbers. Consider the algebraic expression $d = |y - x|$. A Fortran translation of this expression is

```
abs_dif = ABS(y-x)
```

The remainder from integer or real division

As a final example, consider this question: if today is the fourth day of the week (Wednesday), what day of the week will it be 53 days from now? The answer is the integer remainder of dividing 53 + 4 by 7, or 1 (Sunday). Use the MOD function for this calculation:

```
MOD(53+4,7)
```

The function `MOD(n,m)` returns a value between 0 and m - 1. In this example, it returns a value between 0 and 6. If it returns a value of 0, this must be interpreted as day 7 (Saturday).

A similar function is available for real numbers. Here's an example. Full moons occur every 29.53 days. If a full moon occurred 3.7 days ago, how many days after full will it be 144.7 days from now? Use the AMOD function (the REAL version of the MOD function) for this calculation:

```
AMOD(3.7+144.7,29.53)
```

The answer is the remainder from dividing 3.7 + 144.7 by 29.53, or 0.025 days.

4.2 Fortran Statement Functions

The large number of intrinsic functions supported by Fortran is an essential reason for its continuing popularity. However, it is often convenient to be able to  define your own functions in programs that require the same calculation to be performed many times with different arguments. In Fortran, you can define such functions, called *statement functions*, at the beginning of your program. Once defined, these functions can be used just like the intrinsic functions.[5] An important difference is that, unlike intrinsic functions, statement functions exist only within the program or subprogram in which they are defined. If you need them in another program or subprogram, you have to write or copy the code again. The types of calculations that can be performed with statement functions are restricted by the fact that they must consist of one and only one Fortran statement, which may be continued onto more than one line. Chapter 7 will present additional ways to define more complicated functions as separate subprograms.[6]

A statement function definition is not an executable Fortran statement. It must appear after the specification (data declaration) statements and before the first executable statement in the program unit. The general syntax for a statement function is

```
function_name(one or more "dummy" parameters) = expression

Example:
      REAL BoxVolume,l,w,h
      BoxVolume(l,w,h)=l*w*h
```

There is no specific Fortran keyword that identifies a statement function. This means that your program must be able to interpret a statement as a statement function based only on its syntax and position prior to executable statements in your program.

The statement function definition includes a *parameter list* of one or more quantities needed as "input" to the function. The parameter list defines the number and data type of the arguments expected by the function. The *expression* uses these parameters and can also contain references to constants, PARAMETERs,

---

[5]There is an important exception. Intrinsic functions can be used as arguments in a call to a subprogram, as will be discussed in Chapter 7, but statement functions cannot.

[6]It is worth noting here that some Fortran programmers believe statement functions, which have been supported in older versions of Fortran, should no longer be used in Fortran 90 programs. Alternatives will be discussed in Chapter 7.

Fortran intrinsic functions, and even other statement functions that have already been defined in the source code. (It cannot contain references to statement functions that have not yet been defined in the source code.)

When you define a calculation in pseudocode that will later become a statement function, you can put that definition anywhere you want. However, when you convert the pseudocode to Fortran, you must follow the syntax rules. Here they are.

1. The data type of the result produced by a statement function is determined by the data type of its name, which must be explicitly declared in a previous type declaration statement.
2. The dummy parameter(s) used in defining the statement function must appear in a type declaration statement.[7]
3. The number and type of the argument(s) used when the function is invoked should match the number and type of the function's parameter list. The arguments may be constants, variables, or expressions.
4. The names of variables in an argument list that calls a statement function may be, but don't have to be and usually aren't, the same as the names of dummy variables used in the function's parameter list.

As an illustrative example, consider this problem:

1 Define the problem.

Write a program to calculate the area of a circular ring with a user-specified inner and outer radius.

2 Outline a solution.

1. Provide the inner and outer radius.
2. Subtract the area of the circle with the inner radius from the area of the circle having the outer radius.

---

[7]Saying that a statement function and its arguments "must" appear in explicit type declaration functions assumes that the program in which they appear includes an IMPLICIT NONE statement.

3 Design an algorithm.

DEFINE *(inner radius, outer radius, π, ring area as real numbers; a function to calculate area)*
READ *(inner and outer radius)*
(Assume that the "Area" subprogram will be defined.)
ASSIGN *ring area = Area(outer radius) – Area(inner radius)*
WRITE *(ring area)*

SUBPROGRAM *Area(IN: radius; OUT: area of a circle)*
       ASSIGN *Area = π•radius²*
(end subprogram)

4 Convert the algorithm into a program.

P-4.4 [RING.F90]

```
        PROGRAM Ring
!
!       Calculate the area of a circular ring.
!
        IMPLICIT NONE
        REAL Inner_Radius,Outer_Radius,AREA,radius
        REAL, PARAMETER :: pi=3.1415927
        AREA(radius)=pi*radius*radius
!
        PRINT*,' Give outer radius, then inner radius: '
        READ*,Outer_Radius,Inner_Radius
!
        PRINT*,' The area of the ring is: ',&
               AREA(Outer_Radius)-AREA(Inner_Radius)
!
        END
```

Running P-4.4

```
   Give outer radius, then inner radius:
5.3 2.1
   The area of the ring is:    74.3929214
```

5 *Verify the operation of the program.*

Check the calculations with a hand calculator.

Problem Discussion

In P-4.4, the statement

```
AREA(radius)=pi*radius*radius
```

appearing just after the type declaration statements defines the statement function the purpose of which is to calculate the area of a circle of specified radius. It requires a single input parameter, symbolically referred to as `radius`, and calculates the area of the circle corresponding to the value of that argument. The value for π doesn't have to appear in the parameter list because `pi` is defined as a constant in a `PARAMETER` statement.

Note that the data type of `AREA` must be declared. As long as you include the `IMPLICIT NONE` statement in your program, you won't be allowed to use implicit typing for statement function names and arguments.[8] As usual, it wouldn't be a good idea to rely on implicit typing even if you could get away with it.

It is especially important to understand the relationship between the parameter used in `AREA`'s definition, radius, and the arguments used when the function is used, `Outer_Radius` and `Inner_Radius`. Obviously, the names of the arguments don't match the name appearing in the parameter list. What is essential is only that `radius`, `Outer_Radius`, and `Inner_Radius` all have the same data type.

The Fortran implementation of the algorithm in P-4.4 results in adding some items associated with the statement function definition to the data specifications that didn't appear in the *DEFINE* section of the algorithm. Also, there is no variable corresponding to "ring area" because the `PRINT` statement displays the desired result without assigning its value to a separate variable name. These discrepancies between the algorithm and the source code are due to the way the algorithm was implemented in Fortran and are not an inherent part of the problem solution. There is no reason to try to change the algorithm to match these details of the Fortran implementation, or *vice versa*.

---

[8]In Section 3.3.2 of Chapter Three, it was mentioned that every variable name plus "a few other things" must appear in a data type declaration statement. The names and parameters of statement functions are some of those "other things."

4.3 Applications

4.3.1 Refraction of Light

1 *Define the problem.*

Snell's law describes the refraction (bending) of light as it passes from one medium to another. If the refractive index of the incident medium is n_i and that of the refracting medium is n_r, the angles of incidence i and refraction r of a ray of light, measured from the perpendicular to the boundary between the two mediums, are related by

$$n_i \sin(i) = n_r \sin(r)$$

Figure 4.2 illustrates the geometry and Figure 4.3 gives some typical data.
Write a program that asks the user to provide two refractive indices and the angle of an incident ray and then calculates the angle of a refracted ray.

2 *Outline a solution.*

1. Prompt the user to supply two indices and an incident angle.
2. Apply Snell's law to determine the angle of the refracted ray:

$$r = \sin^{-1}\left(\frac{n_i}{n_r}\sin(i)\right)$$

Table 4.3 gives the angles of refraction when a light ray is directed from air ($n_i = 1$) into some common materials. (They are the data shown in Figure 4.3.)

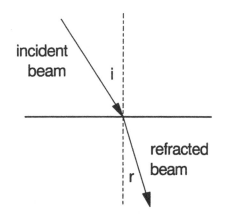

Figure 4.2. Geometry for Snell's law of refraction

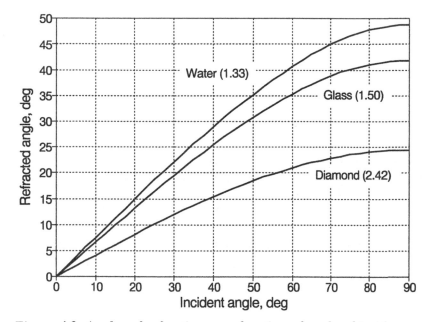

Figure 4.3. Angles of refraction as a function of angle of incidence

Table 4.3. Calculations for Snell's law

Angle of Incidence (from air)	Refractive Index of air=1 For refractive index of:		
	1.33 (Water)	1.50 (Glass)	2.42 (Diamond)
0	0.00	0.00	0.00
10	7.50	6.65	4.11
20	14.90	13.18	8.12
30	22.08	19.47	11.92
40	28.90	25.37	15.40
50	35.17	30.71	18.45
60	40.63	35.26	20.97
70	44.95	38.79	22.85
80	47.77	41.04	24.01
90	48.75	41.81	24.41

3   *Design an algorithm.*

DEFINE *(n_i, n_r, incident_angle, refracted_angle as real numbers,*
      π and DegToRad (conversion from angles to radians) as real)
ASSIGN *DegToRad = π/180*
WRITE *("Give index of refraction for incident and refracting medium:")*
READ *(n_i, n_r)*
WRITE *("Give incident angle, in degrees:")*
READ *(incident_angle)*
(Convert to radians before doing trig calculations.)
ASSIGN *refracted_angle = $\sin^{-1}$(n_i /n_r•sin(incident_angle•DegToRad))*
(Display output in degrees.)
WRITE *("Refracted angle is", refracted_angle/DegToRad)*

This algorithm explicitly includes the conversions back and forth between degrees and radians. As noted previously, this is optional for the algorithm design, but essential for a Fortran program.

4

Convert the algorithm into a program.

P-4.5 [REFRACT.F90]

```
      PROGRAM Refract
!
! Calculate angle of refraction for an incident ray,
! using Snell's Law.
!
      IMPLICIT NONE
      REAL ni,nr            ! indices of refraction (dimensionless)
      REAL incident,refracted ! angles from perpendicular (deg)
      REAL DegToRad           ! required for trig functions
      REAL, PARAMETER :: pi=3.1415927
!
      DegToRad=pi/180.
      PRINT*,' Give indices for incident and refracting medium:'
      READ *,ni,nr
      PRINT*,' What is the angle of incidence?'
      READ *,incident
!
! Convert refracted angle to degrees before displaying its value.
!
      refracted=ASIN(ni/nr*SIN(incident*DegToRad))
      PRINT *,' refracted angle = ',refracted/DegToRad
      END
```

Running P-4.5

```
 Give indices of refraction for incident and refracting medium:
 1.0 1.5
 What is the angle of incidence?
 30
 refracted angle =    19.471221
```

Note how in-line comments in P-4.5 are used to explain the variables, including their units.

5

Verify the operation of the program.

Check your results with a hand calculator. Compare your values with those in Table 4.3.

4.3.2 Inverse Hyperbolic Functions

1 Define the problem.

Although Fortran includes the hyperbolic functions among its intrinsic functions, it doesn't include the inverse hyperbolic functions

$$\sinh^{-1}(x) = \ln(x + \sqrt{x^2+1})$$
$$\cosh^{-1}(x) = \ln(x + \sqrt{x^2-1})$$
$$\tanh^{-1}(x) = \frac{\ln\left(\dfrac{1+x}{1-x}\right)}{2}$$

Write a program that calculates the hyperbolic functions and their inverses, using statement functions. Based on results from your program, make a table for the inverse hyperbolic functions that shows the theoretical range for arguments and the range of values returned for each function. These three functions are illustrated in Figure 4.4.

2 Outline a solution.

1. Ask the user to provide a real number.
2. Display the intrinsic hyperbolic functions.
3. Use each of the results as the argument in the corresponding inverse hyperbolic function and display the results.

3 Design an algorithm.

DEFINE *(x, hyperbolic_sin, hyperbolic_cos, hyperbolic_tan as real numbers)*
WRITE *("Give any real number.")*
READ *(x)*
ASSIGN *hyperbolic_sin = sinh(x), hyperbolic_cos = cosh(x)*
        hyperbolic_tan = hyperbolic_sin/hyperbolic_cosine
WRITE *(hyperbolic_sin,hyperbolic_cos,hyperbolic_tan)*
WRITE *(InvSinh(hyperbolic_sin),InvCosh(hyperbolic_cos),*
     InvTanh(hyperbolic_tan))
(Define functions for inverse functions—see problem statement.)

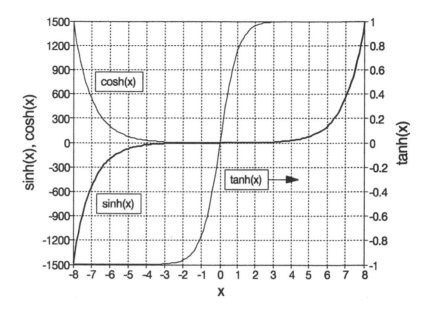

Figure 4.4(a). Hyperbolic functions

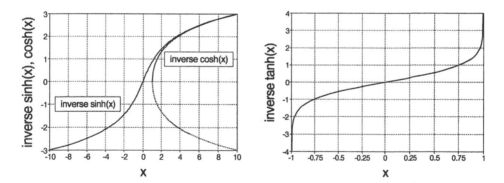

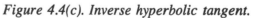

Figure 4.4(b). Inverse hyperbolic sine and cosine

Figure 4.4(c). Inverse hyperbolic tangent.

4

Convert the algorithm into a program.

P-4.6 [HYPERBOL.F90]

```
     PROGRAM hyperbol
!
! Calculate inverse hyperbolic functions.
!
     IMPLICIT NONE
     REAL x,hyperbolic_sin,hyperbolic_cos,hyperbolic_tan
     REAL z,InvSinH,InvCosH,InvTanH !for statement functions
     InvSinH(z)=LOG(z+SQRT(z*z+1.0))
     InvCosH(z)=LOG(z+SQRT(z*z-1.0))
     InvTanH(z)=LOG((1.0+z)/(1.0-z))/2.0
!
     PRINT*,' Give any real number: '
     READ*,x
     hyperbolic_sin=SINH(x)
     hyperbolic_cos=COSH(x)
     hyperbolic_tan=hyperbolic_sin/hyperbolic_cos
     PRINT*,' Hyperbolic sin,cos,tan:', &
            hyperbolic_sin,hyperbolic_cos, hyperbolic_tan
     PRINT*,' Inverse hyperbolic sin, cos, tan: ', &
       InvSinH(hyperbolic_sin),                    &
       SIGN(InvCosH(hyperbolic_cos),x),InvTanH(hyperbolic_tan)
!
     END
```

Running P-4.6

```
  Give any real number:
  1.5
  Hyperbolic sin, cos, tan:    2.1292794   2.3524096   0.9051482
  Inv. hyper. sin, cos, tan:   1.5000000   1.5000000   1.4999998
```

5

Verify the operation of the program.

You can assume the Fortran hyperbolic functions work correctly. With this assumption, your program should return the original input if the inverse hyperbolic calculations are done correctly and the functions are used appropriately.

In response to the second part of the problem, Table 4.4 presents argument and function ranges for the inverse hyperbolic functions. Make sure you understand these ranges and that they are consistent with results from your program.

Table 4.4. Argument and value ranges for inverse hyperbolic functions. (See Table 4.1 for ranges of hyperbolic functions.)

Function	Argument Range	Function Range
sinh(x)	(-∞,∞)	(-∞,∞)
cosh(x)	(-∞,∞)	[1,∞)
tanh(x)	(-∞,∞)	(-1,1)
sinh⁻¹(x)	(-∞,∞)	(-∞,∞)
cosh⁻¹(x)	[±1,±∞)	[0,∞)
tanh⁻¹(x)	[-1,1]	(-∞,∞)

Problem Discussion

This is an excellent example of a problem that appears very simple, but actually contains several potential programming problems. First of all, $\cosh^{-1}(x)$ requires that its argument be greater than or equal to 1, and it always returns a non-negative value. Because $\cosh(x)$ is always greater than or equal to zero, regardless of the sign of x, $\cosh^{-1}(\cosh(x))$ will always return a positive result even if x is negative. This means that the inverse function won't give back the original value of x unless the SIGN function is used, as shown in the final PRINT statement; it makes the sign of the displayed result dependent on the sign of the original value of x.

A more serious problem concerns the accuracy of the underlying computations for numbers of type REAL. An obvious trouble spot is the calculation for the inverse hyperbolic tangent, which contains 1 - z in the denominator, where z = tanh(x) when the function is used in the program. How big (in absolute magnitude) does x have to be before tanh(x) is so close to 1 that the 1-z in the denominator results in an apparent division by zero, or before it's so close to 1 that the calculation is no longer sufficiently accurate? The answer is "Not very big!" Why? Because tanh(x) is very close to 1 for any value larger than about 3. Table 4.5 gives some representative values for the hyperbolic functions.

With the compiler used for the programs in this text, x = 4 produces $\tanh^{-1}(\tanh(x))$=3.99998. For x = 8, the calculation produces 8.11503—a significant error. For slightly larger values, the calculation is either completely unreliable or causes the program to crash.

Table 4.5. Values for hyperbolic functions

x	sinh(x)	cosh(x)	tanh(x)
0	0.00000	1.00100	0.00000
1	1.17520	1.54308	0.76159
2	3.62686	3.76220	0.96403
3	10.01787	10.06766	0.99505
4	27.28992	27.30823	0.99933
5	74.20321	74.20995	0.99991
6	201.71316	201.71564	0.99999
7	548.31612	548.31704	1.00000

Similar computational problems also arise in the sinh and cosh calculations because the exponential function e^x causes an ***arithmetic overflow*** error for large values of x. With the compiler used for the programs in this text, arithmetic overflows occur for the sinh and cosh functions when x reaches a value of about 90.

These kinds of computational problems result from the fact that the accuracy of arithmetic calculations is limited by the accuracy with which real numbers are represented in Fortran. Their onset can be delayed by using Fortran data type declarations that allow more accurate calculations, which we will discuss briefly in Chapter 12, but in general they can't really be solved in Fortran, or any other procedural language, for that matter. As is so often the case, *you* are responsible for appropriate use of a programming language. In many situations, a loss of accuracy in calculations means that you should reformulate your problem, rather than worrying about the limitations imposed by the programming language. This topic, which is covered in courses on numerical analysis, is beyond the scope of this text.

Programming Tip

If you're curious about the kinds of computational problems that might occur in programs similar to P-4.6, you can investigate limitations on the REAL and INTEGER data types by using Fortran 90's intrinsic

arithmetic overflow

numeric inquiry function

numeric inquiry functions. Program P-4.7, offered without additional comment, shows how to use some of these functions. For additional details, consult a Fortran 90 reference manual. With the compiler used for the programs in this text, the `Huge` function returns 3.4028235E+38 as the largest `REAL` number. An examination of the properties of `REAL` and `INTEGER` data types on your computer system would make an excellent extra-credit project!

P-4.7 [NUMBERS.F90]

```
    PROGRAM Numbers
!  Performs some tests on default REAL and INTEGER values.
    IMPLICIT NONE
    REAL x
    INTEGER i
!
    x=1. !can be any value of type REAL
    i=1   !can be any value of type INTEGER
    PRINT *,' For real numbers...'
    PRINT *,' Digits(x) ',Digits(x)
    PRINT *,' Huge(x) ',Huge(x)
    PRINT *,' Tiny(x) ',Tiny(x)
    PRINT *,' MaxExponent(x) ',MaxExponent(x)
    PRINT *,' MinExponent(x) ',MinExponent(x)
    PRINT *,' Precision(x) ',Precision(x)
    PRINT *,' Epsilon(x) ',Epsilon(x)
    PRINT *,' For integers...'
    PRINT *,' Digits(i) ',Digits(i)
    PRINT *,' Huge(i) ',Huge(i)
    END
```

4.4 Debugging Your Programs

4.4.1 Programming Style

Your programs should use intrinsic functions whenever possible. There is hardly ever any justification for writing your own code to duplicate the capabilitites of these functions. Whenever you need to perform simple calculations several times, typically with different input values each time, your program can use statement functions to perform the calculations. These functions should be descriptively named and given appropriate type declarations. Comments should be included to describe their output and the nature of the input required to use them.

4.4.2 Problems with Programs

Major sources of errors when using functions include using inappropriate input arguments and misusing output values. (See the discussion of P-4.6.) If you're lucky, inappropriate arguments will result in compilation or execution errors. If you're not, your program will appear to work, but your answers will be wrong. Here are some problems to watch for whenever you include functions in your programs.

1. Trigonometric calculations give strange answers. A very common programming error is forgetting to convert angles expressed in degrees to radians when you use them as arguments in Fortran trigonometric functions. This sometimes produces odd-looking answers, but all too often the answers look OK even when they are wrong. Similarly, inverse trigonometric functions return values in radians. Be sure to convert from radians to degrees if you wish to see angles displayed in degrees as part of your program's output. When trigonometric functions are used internally in your program, it is often easier simply to retain the values in radians.

2. Misuse of the ATAN function. Trigonometric calculations are often a source of elusive problems. The ATAN function returns values in the range ±90°. Many practical problems require an arctangent function that returns angles in the proper quadrant based on the value of the x and y coordinates. (For example, if x and y are both negative, the angle must be in the third quadrant.) In these cases, you should use the ATAN2 function. (Review the use of the ATAN2 function in P-4.3 earlier in this chapter.)

3. Misuse of the LOG and LOG10 functions. Although there are no "rules" for knowing whether to use natural (base e) or common (base 10) logarithms, mathematical formulas usually use natural logarithms. Common logarithms are often used when the range of numerical results to be plotted on a graph spans many orders of magnitude. For example, values in the range 10^{-6} to 10^{+6} can be plotted conveniently on a common log scale with values in the range -6 to +6.

4. Statement functions generate compilation errors. Remember that statement function definitions are nonexecutable statements and must appear before all executable statements in your program.

5. Your program crashes when you run it. Run-time errors can often be traced to inappropriate use of functions. As discussed throughout this chapter, functions must be used with an understanding of their limitations. Remember that function arguments that exceed the allowed range will produce run-time errors rather than compile-time errors. This is because your Fortran compiler has no way to know during compilation that an input argument eventually will be given an inappropriate value. When these kinds of errors occur, you may need to re-evaluate the source of the function's arguments or rethink how the function is being used.

4.5 Exercises

4.5.1 Self-Testing Exercises

Exercise 1. Describe in your own words the two most important concepts you have learned from this chapter.

Exercise 2. Describe in your own words how you could use in your own programs a problem-solving skill demonstrated in a program described in this chapter.

Exercise 3. Use Fortran 90 intrinsic functions to translate these definitions or algebraic expressions into Fortran statements.

(a) The hypotenuse of a right triangle is equal to the square root of the sum of the squares of the two perpendicular sides.

(b) The height as a function of time reached by a projectile fired with speed v at an elevation angle θ is $h = vt\sin(\theta) - gt^2/2$.

(c) $X = V\cos(\theta)(1-e^{-k/t})/k$

(d) $Y = F/(2W) \cdot (e^{WX/F} + e^{-WX/F}) + Y_o - F/W$

Exercise 4. Create statement functions for the following:

(a) The definitions or expressions in Exercise 3

(b) Cartesian coordinates x and y as a function of the polar coordinates r and θ, where $x = r \cdot \cos(\theta)$ and $y = r \cdot \sin(\theta)$ (see P-4.3)

(c) Trigonometric functions (sine, cosine, and tangent) for angles expressed in degrees[9]
(d) Inverse trigonometric functions (arc sine, arc cosine, and arc tangent) that return angles in degrees

---

[9]In earlier versions of Fortran, some compilers included such functions as a nonstandard extension.

Exercise 5. Create statement functions for the following conversions:

(a) Fahrenheit to centigrade

(b) Fahrenheit to kelvins

(c) Newtons/m^2 to pound/in^2

(d) a lowercase ASCII character to uppercase (see the discussion at the end of Section 4.1.2)

(e) an uppercase ASCII character to lowercase

4.5.2 Basic Programming Exercises

Exercise 6. Using P-4.4 as a model, write a program that defines a statement function to calculate the volume and mass of a sphere. Use this statement function to calculate the volume and mass of the wall of a hollow sphere with a user-specified outer radius, wall thickness, and material density. Use metric units of kg and kg/m^3.

Extra Credit
Suppose all the air could be removed from a hollow sphere without it collapsing. For some reasonable material (aluminum, for example), how thin must the walls be before a sphere with an outer diameter of 50 m will "float" in air at standard pressure and temperature?

Exercise 7. Modify program P-4.5 so the calculation for the refracted angle is contained in a statement function.

Exercise 8. Suppose a light ray passes from a medium of higher refractive index to a medium of lower refractive index. For some critical angle θ_c, measured from the local perpendicular to the plane that separates the two mediums, the light ray will be reflected internally, with no light passing into the medium of lower refractive index. Modify program P-4.5 to calculate the critical angle for the two mediums defined by the indices of refraction you provide as input.
Hint: the critical angle occurs when the refracted angle is 90°. If the medium with the lower refractive index is air, the critical angles are given as the last refraction angle in each column of Table 4.3.

Exercise 9. Based on material from other courses you are taking, state a computational problem and write a complete program to solve it. Make sure the problem involves the use of one or more Fortran intrinsic functions or a statement function.

4.5.3 Programming Applications

Exercise 10. Radioactive elements decay at a rate characterized by their "half-life," defined as the time required for the original amount of radioactive material to decrease by half. (The decayed material doesn't disappear, of course. The process produces decay products that may themselves be stable or unstable.) For example, radon has a half-life of 3.8 days. If there are originally 100 mg of radon gas in an enclosed container, there will be 50 mg after 3.8 days, 25 mg after 7.6 days, and so forth. The process of radioactive decay can be described by the formula

$$A(t) = A_o\, e^{-t/t_o}$$

where A_o is the initial amount, $A(t)$ is the amount after time t, and t_o is proportional to the half-life t_{half}. To relate t_o to t_{half}, set $A(t)=A_o/2$ and take the logarithm of both sides:

$$A/2 = A_o\, e^{-t_{half}/t_o}$$
$$t_o = -t_{half}/\ln(1/2)$$

For radon, t_o is about 5.48 days. Figure 4.5 shows a radioactive decay curve for radon.

Write a program that calculates and prints the amount of radon remaining from a given original sample mass after a specified number of days. Include the calculation for t_o in the program rather than doing it by hand ahead of time.

Note: You may already have done the algorithm design for this problem when it appeared as Exercise 21 at the end of Chapter 2. [HALFLIFE.F90]

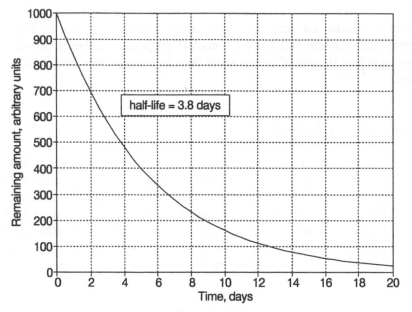

Figure 4.5. Radioactive decay of radon

Extra Credit

(a) Half-lives vary over a wide range, from small fractions of a second to thousands of years. Modify your program so it will let the user provide both the half-life, in appropriate time units, and the elapsed time in the same units, so the program will work for elements other than radon. (This would be a better way to write the original program, too, because it represents a more general approach to the problem.)

(b) You may prefer to write $A = A_o(1/2)^{t/t_{half}}$ to calculate radioactive decay. Modify your program accordingly.

Exercise 11. Write a program that asks the user to enter a currency amount and then calculates how many dollar bills, quarters, dimes, nickels, and pennies are required to return this amount in change. Assume that the minimum total number of coins should be returned. This means that your program should return first the maximum number of quarters, then the maximum number of dimes, and so forth.

That is, even though you obviously could return \$0.66 in change as, for example, six dimes and six pennies, the program should tell you to return this change as two quarters, one dime, one nickel, and one penny. This "restriction" actually makes the problem easier to solve.

Hint: first convert the currency to cents and then use integer division and the MOD function, starting with the fact that one dollar equals 100 cents, one quarter equals 25 cents, and so forth. [CHANGE.F90]

Exercise 12. Write a program that calculates the volume and surface area of a cylinder, given the radius and height in inches. The volume of such a cylinder is $\pi r^2 h$ and the surface area is $2\pi r^2 + 2\pi rh$. Use a statement function for each calculation. (For comparison, see Exercise 17 in Chapter 3.) [CYLINDR2.F90]

Exercise 13. Write a program that asks the user to supply the mass and velocity of an object and then calculates and prints the kinetic energy and linear momentum of that object. The kinetic energy is $mv^2/2$ and the momentum is mv. Use SI units (mass in kilograms, velocity in meters per second, energy in joules). Use a statement function for each calculation. (For comparison, see Exercise 18 in Chapter 3.) [KINETIC2.F90]

Extra Credit

Include code for statement functions that will convert the kinetic energy and momentum into their British system equivalents. The British unit of energy is foot-pounds and the unit of momentum is slug-feet/seconds. 1 foot-pound=1.356 joule; 1 slug=14.59 kilogram; 1 foot/second=0.3048 meters/second. Use statement functions for the conversion calculations.

Exercise 14. Under natural conditions of ample food supplies, adequate living space, and a stable environment, animal populations grow exponentially, as illustrated for the global human population in Figure 4.6. That is, the projected population at some future time will be proportional to the current population. A simple single-parameter model for extrapolating an initial population P_o n years into the future is:

$$P = P_o \bullet (1+g)^n$$

where g is the net annual growth rate as determined by the difference between births and deaths.

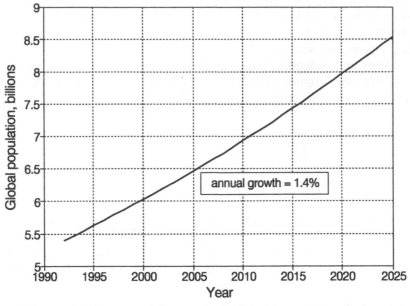

Figure 4.6. Exponential growth of global human population

Write a program that uses this formula to calculate the growth rate needed to achieve a specified population at some time in the future. In 1992, the global human population was about 5.4×10^9 people. Some estimates predict that global population will be about 8.5×10^9 in the year 2025. It is not at all clear that the "natural" conditions required to support exponential growth will continue to exist for the human population. Food shortages, overcrowding, poor economic conditions, war, and environmental degradation can significantly affect both birth and death rates. [POPULATN.F90]

Exercise 15. The loudness of a sound is measured in decibels (dB) on an arbitrary scale that relates perceived loudness to the ratio of the intensity of a sound to the intensity of the weakest audible sound I_o, which is about 10^{-12} W/m²:

$$\text{Loudness} = 10\log_{10}(I/I_o)$$

Intensity is a physically measurable quantity, but loudness is a subjective human perception. The perception of loudness has approximately the logarithmic relation indicated by the equation, but it varies among individuals. Write a program that calculates and displays the intensity and loudness for sounds 10, 100, and 1000 times more intense than the weakest audible sound. [NOISE.F90]

Extra Credit

Modify your program to calculate and display the intensity of a sound with a specified dB value. What is the intensity of a sound of 100 dB, which is loud enough to cause permanent hearing damage?

Exercise 16. The efficiency of solar energy systems depends critically on the ability to track the sun's position. One required value is the solar elevation angle ε, the angle to the sun measured upward from the local horizontal. It depends on the latitude of the subsolar point (solar declination) δ, the observer's latitude λ, and the hour angle β, where hour angle is the angle from the observer's meridian to the subsolar meridian. ($\beta = 0°$ occurs at local "high noon," which generally differs from clock noon by a few minutes. One hour of clock time corresponds to approximately 15° of hour angle. A meridian is a line of constant longitude running from the north pole to the south pole.) The latitude of the subsolar point is seasonally dependent, with a range of $\pm 23.4°$. The largest positive value occurs at northern hemisphere midsummer, and the largest negative value occurs at northern hemisphere midwinter. The solar elevation angle for any solar declination, latitude, and hour angle is given by:

$$\varepsilon = 90° - \cos^{-1}(\cos\delta\cos\lambda\cos\beta + \sin\delta\sin\lambda)$$

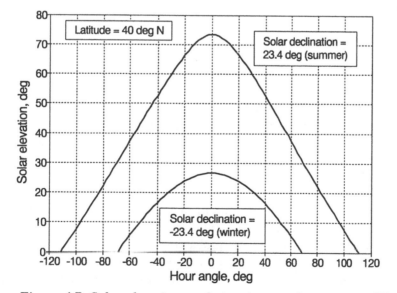

Figure 4.7. Solar elevation angle in winter and summer at 40°N latitude

Write a program that asks the user to supply an observer's latitude and the solar declination and then calculates and displays solar elevation angle for hour angles of 60°, 30°, and 0° (corresponding approximately to 8am, 10am, and noon in clock time). Use your program to determine the range of high noon (maximum) elevation angles as a function of season at a specified latitude. What happens in the polar regions, when the sun may not shine at all during part of the year? Figure 4.7 shows the elevation angle for 40°N latitude in the summer and winter. [ELEVATIN.F90]

Exercise 17. The well-known factorial function n! is defined as

$$n! = n•(n - 1)•(n - 2)•...•2•1$$

For example, $5! = 5•4•3•2•1 = 120$. For large values of n, this is a very impractical calculation. However, n! can be approximated for large values of n with Stirling's formula:

$$n! \approx (n/e)^n (2n\pi)^{1/2}$$

Write a program that requests a value of n and calculates n! using Stirling's approximation. How close is Stirling's approximation for values of n! you can calculate yourself by hand? This approximation is especially useful when calculating the ratio of two large factorials, as required for certain problems in probability theory.

Hint: declare n as REAL. [STIRLING.F90]

Extra Credit
What is the largest value of n for which n! can be calculated from its definition when n is declared as the default INTEGER data type? Can you comment on the applicability of Stirling's formula for larger values of n? In order to answer this question, you could look ahead to the part of Section 3 in Chapter 12 that deals with declaring numbers with greater precision and range than the default REAL data type.

Exercise 18. Suppose a single measurement is taken from a standard normal (Gaussian) distribution. For such a distribution, the mean (arithmetic average) is 0 and the standard deviation is 1. The probability that a single measurement will be no greater than some specified value z is equal to the area under the curve defined by the standard normal probability density distribution function, integrated from -∞ to z.

The standard normal probability density function cannot be integrated analytically. One solution is to approximate the integral with a polynomial:

$$\text{cumulative probability} \approx 1 - r(a_1t + a_2t^2 + a_3t^3)$$

where

$$r = e^{-z^2/2}/\sqrt{2\pi} \qquad t = (1 + 0.3326z)^{-1} \qquad a_1 = 0.4361836$$
$$a_2 = -0.1201676 \qquad a_3 = 0.9372980$$

The error resulting from using this approximation is less than 10^{-5}.

Write a program that will calculate cumulative probability for some specified value z using this approximation. [NORMAL2.F90]

Extra Credit

The standard normal variable z is related to measurements of normally distributed quantities taken from populations whose sample mean and standard deviation m and s have values other than 0 and 1 by

$$z = \frac{x - m}{x}$$

Modify your program so that it will calculate the probability that a single measurement from a normally distributed population with sample mean m and standard deviation s will not exceed the mean by more than some specified amount.

Gaining Control Over Program Output

This chapter discusses techniques for supplementing the list-directed output formats used in the previous chapters with formats that provide a wide range of options for controlling the appearance of displayed output from your programs.

5.1 The Formatted PRINT Statement

5.1.1 Introduction to Formatted Output

In the previous two chapters, output from programs in the text and programs you wrote yourself was generated by using the PRINT *,... statement. This list-directed output is easy to use because your Fortran compiler decides how the output will be displayed on your computer's default output device, usually a monitor. List-directed output is very convenient for "quick and dirty" programming, or as an intermediate step when you're developing a complicated programming project.

Eventually, however, you will wish to make use of Fortran's extensive features for controlling the appearance of your programs' output. These *formatted* 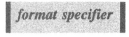 *output* features can be implemented either with the PRINT statement, which has been used in previous chapters to produce list-directed output, or the WRITE statement, which will be described in this chapter.

First consider the PRINT statement. The list-directed output from the PRINT *,... statement syntax can be modified by including a *format specifier* that describes how the programmer wants output to appear. An expanded syntax for the PRINT statement now looks like this:

```
PRINT *[, list of variables, expressions, functions,
           or constants, separated by commas]
PRINT label[, list...]
PRINT format string[, list...]
```

The first form is the familiar syntax for list-directed output and the other two are for formatted output. As an introduction to how the PRINT statement is used to produce formatted output, consider program P-5.1, which involves a minor modification of program P-4.3 from Chapter 4.

P-5-1 [POLAR2.F90]

```
      PROGRAM polar2
!
!     Convert polar coordinates to Cartesian and check the
!     results by converting them back to polar coordinates.
!     Demonstrates formatted output.
!
      IMPLICIT NONE
      REAL X,Y,r,theta,pi,DegToRad
!
      pi=4.0*ATAN(1.0)
      DegToRad=pi/180.0
      PRINT *,' Give polar coordinates r, theta (deg): '
      READ *,r,theta
!
      X=r*COS(theta*DegToRad)
      Y=r*SIN(theta*DegToRad)
!
      PRINT 1000,X,Y
!
!     Recalculate values of r and theta...
!
      r=SQRT(X*X+Y*Y)
      theta=ATAN2(Y,X)/DegToRad
!
      PRINT 1001,r,theta
!
!     FORMAT statements...
!
 1000 FORMAT(1x,'x and y: ',2f6.2)
 1001 FORMAT(1x,'recalculated r and theta: ',2f7.3)
      END
```

Running P-5.1

```
 Give polar coordinates r, theta (deg):
5, 30.
 x and y:    4.33  2.50
 recalculated r and theta:    5.000 30.000
```

Compare this output with that from program P-4.3, which used list-directed output. The results of the calculations are the same in each case. However, the output from P-5.1 is easier to read and makes more sense in the context of how the input values are expressed because the extraneous digits in the output of P-4.3 are no longer present in this output.

Program P-5.1 differs from program P-4.3 in the syntax of its two PRINT statements and the addition of two FORMAT statements; these four statements are printed in bold italics. In place of the asterisk that specifies list-directed output, each PRINT statement now contains a reference to a line containing a FORMAT statement that controls how the output is displayed.

FORMAT statements are identified by *line labels* in the form of numbers. This is the first time we have used such labels. In older versions of Fortran, columns 1-5 were reserved for line labels and we will continue to follow this style even though it's not required in the free-format environment of Fortran 90. All that is required by Fortran 90 is that the label appear first on the line containing the statement to which it refers.

The syntax of the format statement is :

```
label FORMAT(format descriptors)

Example:
1000   FORMAT(1x,'x and y: ',2f6.2)
```

Here are some rules for using FORMAT statements:

1. A line label can be any positive integer up to five digits. That is, lines can be labelled from 1 to 99999.

2. You can't use the same label for more than one FORMAT statement in a single program unit.[1] However, the labels don't have to be numbered consecutively, and they don't have to appear in any particular numerical order.

3. FORMAT statements can appear anywhere in a program after the nonexecutable statements.

4. More than one PRINT statement can reference the same FORMAT statement.

5. It is an error to reference a FORMAT statement label that does not actually appear in the program.

In this text, FORMAT statements will always appear at the end of a program and always with their labels in ascending numerical order because that makes the code easier to read.[2] The first FORMAT statement label will usually be 1000, but this is just a style choice and not a Fortran requirement.

---

[1]As you will see in later chapters, FORMAT statement labels can be reused in subprograms.

[2]This is a personal preference. Some programmers prefer to put FORMAT statements directly after the output statements that refer to them.

Although the differences in the output produced by P-4.3 and P-5.1 may seem minor, the ability to control the appearance of output is an important feature of Fortran. We will make extensive use of these capabilities in many of the programs in this text.

5.1.2 Format Descriptors for Numbers and Character Strings

The FORMAT statements labeled 1000 and 1001 in P-5.1 include the string constants that formerly were part of the list-directed output statement. They also

format descriptors

include other *format descriptors*, which may be grouped in three classes: numerical, character, and control. Table 5.1(a) includes a listing of several descriptors. A program including examples of each descriptor, DESCRIPT.F90, is included in the files available from the World Wide Web Site mentioned in Section i.5 of the Preface, but it will not be discussed in the text.

For the A, I, E, EN, ES, and F descriptors, the total number of characters allocated for the output, the *field width*, is given by the positive integer constant w. Some general rules for using descriptors include:

field width

(1) Any descriptor can be repeated by including an optional repeat count specifier n.
(2) Descriptors in a FORMAT statement are always separated by a comma.
(3) Descriptors must always match the data type of values being printed under that descriptor.

INTEGER descriptors

The Iw descriptor is used to display INTEGER values. If the field width w isn't wide enough to display the entire value, asterisks will be displayed. Numbers are always right-justified in the field specified by w.

REAL descriptors

The basic descriptor for REAL (or "floating point") numbers is Fw.d. The field width w must be wide enough to include a space for a sign, all required digits to the left of the decimal point, the decimal point itself, and the specified number of digits to the right of the decimal point, as specified by d. If w is too narrow, asterisks will be displayed. If the number is positive, the default action calls for the "+" sign not to be displayed. It is possible that your compiler will require one space for a sign regardless of whether it is actually displayed. Because of this, and for general readability of your output, it's always a good idea to leave at least one extra space in the field width. Numbers printed using the F descriptor are always right-justified in the field specified by w.

Table 5.1. Format descriptors

Table 5.1(a) Numerical and character descriptors

Data Type	Descriptor Syntax[1]	Example[2]	Output
INTEGER	[n]Iw [n]Iw.m	4i4 i5.4	øø17øøø3øø-3ø567 ø0099 (Inserts leading zeros)
REAL	[n]Fw.d [n]Ew.d [3] [n]ENw.d [4] [n]ESw.d [5]	2f6.2 e13.4 en13.4 es13.4	øø1.41ø-1.41 øøø0.2998E+09 ø299.7900E+06 øø-2.9979E+08
CHARACTER	[n]A [n]Aw	a a10 a4	Fortran øøøFortran Fort (Assuming a character variable of length 10)
LOGICAL	[n]Lw	L3	øøT
General	[n]Gw.d	3g5.0	ø1994ø1995ø1996
String constant	'...' "..."	'Fortran' "Fortran"	Fortran (String may contain any printable character.)

[1] d, m, n, and w are unsigned (positive) integer constants. The repeat count specifier [n] is optional in all cases. A repeat count of 1 is allowed but extraneous.

[2] Either lowercase or uppercase letters can be used.

[3] The absolute magnitude of the significand (digits to the left of the decimal point) is less than 1.

[4] The absolute magnitude of the significand is greater than or equal to 1 and less than 1000. The exponent is evenly divisible by 3.

[5] The absolute magnitude of the significand is greater than or equal to 1 and less than 10.

Table 5.1(b) Control descriptors

Control Function	Descriptor Syntax	Example/Comment
Carriage control [1]	character embedded in a string constant	ɓ start new line + remain on same line 0 skip a line 1 skip to new page
Skip spaces	nX	10x
Sign display	SS SP S	suppresses + sign displays + sign returns to default [2]
New line	[,n]/ [3]	,3/ is equivalent to ///
Tabulation	Tn TRn TLn	tab to column n tab right n spaces [4] tab left n spaces
Terminate format	[,]:[,]	stops processing format when I/O list is empty

[1] See text for description of carriage control functions.

[2] Default condition (suppress or print + sign) is system-dependent.

[3] The comma is required only when the slash descriptor is preceded by another edit descriptor.

[4] Tn is an "absolute" tab to a specified position in the line. TRn and TLn are "relative" tabs from the current position; TRn is equivalent to nX.

For a REAL number less than 10, as in the first line of output from P-5.1, a descriptor of F4.2 might work, but F5.2 might be required. A descriptor of F3.2 would not work because a minimum of four characters is required. Assuming that your compiler will accept an F4.2 descriptor for the first line of output from P-5.1, the repeated descriptor 2F4.2 would display the confusing output 8.665.00, which is another reason to make sure w is wide enough so that all your output is easily readable. The total field width should be at least three more than d, including a space for a sign.

The E descriptors display REAL numbers in "exponential" or "scientific" format, as a value times a power of 10. For Ew.d, w must be at least seven more than d: one space for a sign, two spaces for the 0 and decimal point, and four spaces for the exponent.

The E, EN, and ES descriptors differ in the number of nonzero digits they place to the left of the decimal point, as explained in the notes accompanying Table 5.1(a). For the same value of d, the EN descriptor may require a field width up to nine more than d, depending on the size of the number being displayed.

CHARACTER descriptors

The A descriptor is used to display character data. It displays the value using the number of characters in the string. The Aw descriptor will right-justify the character string in a field of width w if w is greater than the number of characters in the type declaration and will truncate characters from the right if w is less than the number of characters in the string.

LOGICAL descriptor

The Lw descriptor prints a T or an F for the logical value .TRUE. or .FALSE., right-justified in a field of width w.

General descriptor

The G descriptor can be used to display any of the data types discussed above. Its use of w or w.d follows the rules for the data type being displayed.

String constant descriptors

String constants (literals) are displayed by including them in statements enclosed in single or double quotes. The constants may include any printable character.

5.1.3 Control Descriptors

Carriage control

In the early days of Fortran, the standard output device was a mechanical printer, so the concepts of "line" and "page" had a very specific physical interpretation. The carriage control descriptors controlled the position of the printer's printhead and the motion of paper past the printhead. The first character generated as a result of a PRINT statement was not actually printed, but was used to control the motion of the paper and the printhead. As shown in Table 5.1(b), these controls included characters to start a new line (β), to remain on the same line (+), to skip a line (0), and to advance to the beginning of a new page (1). The "new page" control was especially insidious, as it could turn a short printed output into hundreds of mostly empty pages if you happened to be unlucky enough to print lots of numbers starting with a "1" in the first column.

In modern Fortran implementations, the standard output device is a monitor screen rather than a printer. The IBM-compatible PC-based compiler used to develop the programs for this text doesn't even recognize carriage control characters, and it prints all characters, even the first one, directly on the monitor screen. You can test the performance of your own version of Fortran by running the DESCRIPT.F90 program mentioned at the beginning of Section 5.1.2.

Regardless of how your version of Fortran treats control characters, you can avoid potential problems by developing the habit of including one blank space as the first printable character in every output statement, unless you are using a system that interprets these characters and you wish to use them. For example, when a formatted output statement is used to display a string constant, the first character should always be blank. When data are displayed using unformatted (list-directed) output, the compiler-generated default field width is always wide enough so that the first space is blank. The compiler used to develop programs for this text always starts list-directed output in the second column. That is, the statement PRINT *, 'message' displays βmessage rather than message. Thus if you run sample programs from this text on a different system, spacing may sometimes differ by one column.

Skipping spaces

The nX descriptor prints blank spaces. For example, including 1X as the first descriptor in a FORMAT statement generates a space, which avoids unintentional carriage control problems as described in the previous section. For this descriptor, a value for n must be included even if it is 1.

Sign display

As mentioned previously, your system may or may not print a + sign in front of positive numbers, and your system may or may not require your format specification statement to include a space for this sign. In any case, you can use the S descriptors to force the + sign to be displayed (SP) or suppressed (SS), or to revert to the default condition for your system (S).

New lines

The slash (/) descriptor is used to force a *line feed* and *carriage return*. By using this control, you can create several lines of output within a single PRINT statement. The slash descriptor does not have to be separated from 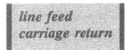 previous descriptors with a comma unless the n/ syntax is used. Multiple slashes can appear together. As noted in Table 5.1(b), /// is equivalent to , 3/.

Tabulation

The T descriptors generate "tabs" on a printed line. They may be relative (TRn and TLn) or absolute (Tn). An absolute tab counts n spaces from the beginning of the line. The relative tab counts n spaces from the current position on the line. Hence TRn is equivalent to nX. The T descriptors are useful for printing output in columns, although it is hardly ever necessary to use them because uniform columns can also be generated by adjusting the field width in data format descriptors. Note that the tabulation descriptors don't actually generate "tab" characters, as word processors do. Rather, they simply move the "printhead" an appropriate number of blank spaces. This distinction may be important in some applications. For example, suppose you used the T descriptors in a Fortran program that saved its output in a data file. If you tried to use that data file as input to an application that was expecting "tab-delimited" values (a spreadsheet, for example), the Fortran-generated file would not meet that requirement.

Programming Tip
    You might be tempted to think that you could use the TL descriptor to create multiple-character overstrikes. This won't work. Instead only the last character printed in a space is retained.

Format termination

The colon (:) descriptor terminates processing of the contents of a format statement as soon as there are no more items to be read or written in the input/output list. A practical application is to prevent output of unwanted string constants used for annotating output. For example, the statements

```
      a=5
      b=1776
      PRINT 1000,a,b
1000  FORMAT(' a=',i5,' b=',i5,' c=',i5)
```

produce the output

```
 a=    5 b= 1776 c=
```

even though no value for c is being displayed. However, replacing the PRINT statement with

```
      PRINT 1000,a,b
1000  FORMAT(' a=',i5,:,' b=',i5,:,' c=',i5)
```

produces the output

```
 a=    5 b= 1776
```

In some circumstances, use of the colon terminator can significantly reduce the number of different format statements you must create for a program.

5.1.4 Repeating Groups of Descriptors

It is clear from Table 5.1 that individual descriptors can be repeated n times by placing n in front of the descriptor. It is also possible to repeat groups of descriptors by enclosing them in parentheses. For example, the FORMAT statements

```
      FORMAT(1x,3(f6.2,i5))
      FORMAT(1x,2(f4.1,3(a6)),f10.5)
```

are equivalent to

```
      FORMAT(1x,f6.2,i5,f6.2,i5,f6.2,i5)
      FORMAT(1x,f4.1,a6,a6,a6,f4.1,a6,a6,a6,f10.5)
```

Especially with repeated groups of descriptors, it is important to make sure that the data types of the values being printed agree with the descriptors; if they don't, your program will issue an error message.

5.1.5 Producing Formatted Output without a FORMAT Statement

As noted previously in the syntax definition for formatted output, it is possible to replace a reference to a labeled FORMAT statement with a string that contains the format description. Some programmers prefer this approach because they believe line labels should be avoided whenever possible. The format string may be either a string literal or a CHARACTER constant declared with an appropriate length. Consider the two PRINT statements in program P-5.1:

```
      PRINT 1000,x,y
      PRINT 1001,r,theta
      . . .
1000  FORMAT(1x,'x and y: ',2f6.2)
1001  FORMAT(1x,'recalculated r and theta: ',2f7.3)
```

These can be written as

```
      PRINT "(1x,'x and y: ',2f6.2)",x,y
      PRINT "(1x,'recalculated r and theta: ',2f7.3)",r,theta
```

and also as

```
      CHARACTER*40 F1,F2
      . . .
      F1="(1x,'x and y: ',2f6.2)"
      F2="(1x,'recalculated r and theta: ',2f7.3)"
      . . .
      PRINT F1,x,y
      PRINT F2,r,theta
```

Note the use of quotation marks to delimit the format strings. These, rather than single quotation marks, are necessary because the string itself contains single quotation marks. The format string must include parentheses as shown.

This text favors the use of labeled FORMAT statements over the use of character strings for defining formats. We will be consistent about placing these statements in numerical order at the end of a program—or subprogram, when we get to that later in the text. String literals embedded within output statements often make those statements more cluttered and harder to read. Also, defining CHARACTER constants seems like a waste of time when done *just* for the purpose of avoiding line labels.[3]

There is one circumstance in which the use of string constants to describe formats can be very helpful. Suppose a program needs to read an external data file—a topic that will be covered in Chapter 9. If the file is originally created with a Fortran program in mind, the first line in the file can contain a string that gives the format for the file. Then a program can construct its own format based on the information provided in the file.

---

[3]Author's note: this style is purely a personal preference and some Fortran programmers will disagree. However, I find nothing objectionable about using line labels for this purpose, and I believe the use of appropriately placed FORMAT statements at the end of a program or subprogram usually makes source code easier to read.

5.2 The WRITE **Statement**

5.2.1 Syntax of the WRITE *Statement and the Standard Output Unit*

The PRINT statement always directs its output to the standard output device for a particular Fortran implementation. In the early days of Fortran, this standard device was a mechanical printer. In modern Fortran usage, the standard output device is almost always a monitor screen. However, it is often necessary to direct Fortran output to some other destination. Typically, this destination is a data file that will contain a permanent record of the output generated by a program. In order to direct output to anywhere other than the standard output device, you must use a WRITE statement in place of a PRINT statement. A simplified syntax for the WRITE statement is

```
WRITE(u,*)[list of variables, expressions, functions,
           or constants, separated by commas]
WRITE(*,*)[list...]
WRITE(u,[FMT=]label,[ADVANCE='NO'])[ list...]
WRITE(u,[FMT=]format string,[ADVANCE='NO'])[ list..]
```

where u represents a **unit number**. A unit number is used to create an association between a programmed I/O operation and a physical device. In particular, a unit number can be used to 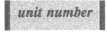 direct output to a specified output device, including the standard output device. We will discuss a simple application of this concept in the next section of this chapter, and we will discuss the use of unit numbers in detail in Chapter 9. For now, it is sufficient to know that for output to a monitor screen, the unit number in a WRITE statement that directs output to the standard output device can be either an asterisk or, on most systems, a 6. If the 6 has to be replaced with some other unit number on your system, your instructor will tell you what value to use.

The WRITE statement can be used for either list-directed or formatted output. An asterisk in place of a format specification indicates list-directed output. The FMT= text for the format specification is optional as long as the label or format string occurs immediately after the unit number. The format specification can be either a label or a string constant. The optional ADVANCE='NO' specifier, available only with formatted output, produces "nonadvancing output" that prevents a carriage return from being added to the end of the output line. With nonadvancing output, the output from more than one WRITE statement can appear on the same line. This is often useful when displaying output from inside DO... loops, for example.

As a simple example of using nonadvancing output, consider this common code using PRINT:

```
PRINT *,'Type an integer: '
READ *,i
```

If you enter a value of 10, your screen will look like this:

```
 Type an integer:
10
```

That is, the message from PRINT appears on one line and the response appears on the next line. It's a minor point, but it might be convenient to have your screen look like this:

```
 Type an integer: 10
```

You can produce this result by using a formatted WRITE statement and the ADVANCE='NO' specifier:

```
WRITE(6,'("Type an integer: ")',advance='no')
READ *,i
```

In addition to providing the option of nonadvancing output, there is at least one more significant advantage to using WRITE instead of PRINT. The unit number u can be a constant, an integer variable, or an expression that returns an appropriate positive value. How could you make use of this fact? Suppose you are developing a program. During the development process, you can direct all the output to your monitor screen by assigning u a value of 6 at the beginning of your program. When the program is complete, you can redirect the output to a data file just by opening that data file from within your program and associating it with an appropriate value of u. We will demonstrate this process in the next section of this chapter.

5.2.2 *Format Descriptors for the* WRITE *Statement*

The good news about format descriptors for the WRITE statement is that they are the same as for the PRINT statement. Therefore, Table 5.1 applies to both PRINT and WRITE. For formatted output, the only difference in the syntax of PRINT and WRITE statements is that WRITE provides the option of nonadvancing output.

5.3 Saving Program Output

As noted in the previous section, the default output destination for program output is probably your monitor screen. On some systems, you can save the output from a program simply by "dumping" the contents of your computer's monitor screen to a printer. However, what you usually wish to do is create a permanent electronic record of your program's output.

Fortunately, it is easy to direct output from a program to other destinations, including a data file that captures a permanent electronic record of all the output from your program. This is an excellent way to record your work on homework assignments, but the major advantage is that data generated by a Fortran program can be saved in a file that can then be "imported" into a variety of other computer applications, including word processors, spreadsheets, and graphing applications.

To demonstrate the process of creating a permanent electronic file, consider program P-5.2, which is a modification of P-5.1. P-5.2 is identical to P-5.1 (POLAR2.F90) except for the addition of several statements printed in bold italics. It even produces the same output on your computer monitor, so its displayed output isn't duplicated here.

After the data declarations, an OPEN statement is used to create an association between a data file called POLAR3.OUT and unit number 1. This unit number is a label that can be referenced later by the program. Any WRITE statement that refers to unit number 1 will send output to this file.

The choice of a value of 1 for the unit number is somewhat arbitrary. As noted in the previous section, unit number 6 is "preconnected" to the default output device of many Fortran systems. Similarly, on most systems, unit number 5 is preconnected to the default input device. There may also be restrictions on other unit numbers; ask your instructor. However, assuming that 5 and 6 are the preconnected unit numbers, the values 1–4 should be available.[4]

P-5.2 [POLAR3.F90]

```
      PROGRAM polar3
!
! Convert polar coordinates to Cartesian and check the
! results by converting them back to polar coordinates.
! Demonstrates formatted output and creation of an output
! data file.
!
      IMPLICIT NONE
      REAL X,Y,r,theta,pi,DegToRad
!
      OPEN(1,file='polar3.out')
!
      pi=4.0*ATAN(1.0)
      DegToRad=pi/180.0
      PRINT *,' Give polar coordinates r, theta (deg): '
      READ *,r,theta
      WRITE(1,*)' For r and theta = ',r,theta
!
```

---

[4]It may actually be possible to reassign the preconnected unit numbers 5 and 6 to an external file. but there is no reason to do this.

```
        X=r*COS(theta*DegToRad)
        Y=r*SIN(theta*DegToRad)
!
        PRINT 1000,X,Y
        WRITE(1,1000)X,Y
!
!       Recalculate values of r and theta...
!
        r=SQRT(X*X+Y*Y)
        theta=ATAN2(Y,X)/DegToRad
!
        PRINT 1001,r,theta
        WRITE(1,1001)r,theta
        CLOSE(1)
!
!       FORMAT statements...
!
1000    FORMAT(1x,'x and y: ',2f6.2)
1001    FORMAT(1x,'recalculated r and theta: ',2f7.3)
        END
```

The file that your program will create can have any name that is legal for your system. Use of the .OUT extension (which is a typical choice for MS-DOS systems, for example) is an arbitrary but reasonable choice in the context of P-5.2. If the requested output file name does not already exist on your computer, Fortran will create such a file. If the file name already exists, program output will be sent to that file and will *overwrite* existing information on that file.

Statements that prompt the user of a program to provide input while it is executing must still be directed to the monitor screen; there is usually no reason to send copies of such directions to a file. This isn't a problem because output not specifically sent to a file will continue to be sent to the monitor screen. Also, responses that a user types at the computer's keyboard won't be recorded in the output file. For this reason, an extra WRITE statement has been added to P-5.2 to "echo" the input values to the output file.

Later in P-5.2, each PRINT statement is followed by a corresponding WRITE statement that sends duplicate copies of the output to POLAR3.OUT. Thus output from this program continues to appear on the monitor screen, but identical output is also recorded in a permanent file. When the output is complete, a CLOSE statement closes POLAR3.OUT.

Another approach to saving program output is to use WRITE statements with a unit number for all output except for that which must appear on the monitor screen to direct user responses. For output that should always appear on the screen, use either a PRINT or a WRITE with an asterisk (for the default output unit) instead of a unit number.

For output that may later be directed to a file, declare the unit number as a variable and assign it an initial value of 6 so that output from WRITE statements using that unit number will be directed to the screen. (See, for example, P-5.4 in Section 5.4.2 below.) Later, the unit number variable can be assigned a different value, and statements can be added to open and close a file associated with that unit number.

Figure 5.1 summarizes the use of PRINT and WRITE statements to send output to various destinations (including a printer, which will be discussed in the next part of this section). The characters fffff represent either a label for a FORMAT statement or a complete format specification given as a string constant. The solid arrow from the upper box to the monitor icon indicates that these output options send output *only* to the default output device. It is only by using the WRITE statement with a unit number that output can be directed optionally to the default device, a printer, or an external data file. (The diskette icon represents storage on any electronic medium—typically a hard drive on your PC or other computer.) We will discuss unit numbers and the syntax of the OPEN and CLOSE statements in more detail in Chapter 9. For now, you can use P-5.2 and the other suggestions in this section as a "cookbook" model for saving program output in a permanent electronic form.

Programming Tip

On MS-DOS systems, you can use the OPEN statement to send output from a program directly to a printer by replacing the name of an output file with the DOS "file name" for a printer, usually LPT1. The most convenient way to do this is to modify your program so that it asks the user to provide the name of the output file when the program executes. Then you can provide the name LPT1 instead of a "real" file. For an example, see the program POLAR4.F90 available from the World Web Site mentioned in Section i.5 of the Preface.

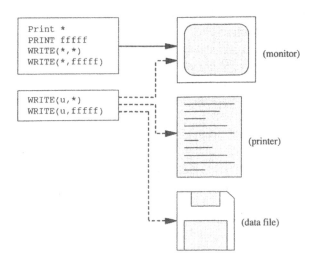

Figure 5.1. Summary of options for directing program output

5.4 Applications

5.4.1 Stellar Magnitude and Distance

1 *Define the problem.*

The absolute magnitude M of a star is related to its relative magnitude m and the distance to a star r measured in parsecs, where 1 parsec = 3.26 light years, by the equation

$$M = m + 5 - 5\log_{10}(r)$$

According to this equation, a star with relative magnitude of +1 at a distance of 10 parsecs has an absolute magnitude of +1. The larger the magnitude, the dimmer the star. Sirius is a very bright star, with a relative magnitude of -1.58. Stars visible to the naked eye range mostly from about +1 to +6 in relative magnitude. The dimmest star that can be seen with the 200-inch Hale telescope has a magnitude of about +23. Write a program to calculate and display the absolute magnitude of a star based on user-supplied values for its distance and relative magnitude. Display the results using appropriate formatted output.

2 *Outline a solution.*

The calculations are straightforward, but be sure to use base 10 logarithms.

3 *Design an algorithm.*

DEFINE *absolute and relative magnitudes and distance as real numbers.*
WRITE *(Give relative magnitude and distance in parsecs.)*
READ *(m,r)*
ASSIGN *M = m + 5 − 5•log₁₀(r)*
WRITE *(M)*

4 Convert the algorithm into a program.

Remember that Fortran is case-insensitive. Therefore, the symbols m and M used in the problem statement and algorithm must be given distinct names in a program.

P-5.3 [STARMAG.F90]

```
      PROGRAM StarMag
! Calculates absolute stellar magnitude based on relative magnitude
! and distance.
!
      IMPLICIT NONE
      REAL abs_mag,rel_mag,parsecs
!
      WRITE(6,"(' To calculate absolute stellar magnitude:')")
      WRITE(6,"(' Give relative mag. and distance in parsecs: ')"&
               ,advance='no')
      READ *,rel_mag,parsecs
!
      abs_mag=rel_mag+5.0-5.0*LOG10(parsecs)
!
      WRITE(6,1000)rel_mag,parsecs,abs_mag
!
1000  FORMAT(' A star with relative magnitude ',f6.2/&
             ' at a distance of ',f5.1,' parsecs'/&
             ' has an absolute magnitude of ',f6.2)
      END
```

Running P-5.3

```
To calculate absolute stellar magnitude:
Give relative magnitude and distance in parsecs: 10 3
A star with relative magnitude  10.00
at a distance of   3.0 parsecs
has an absolute magnitude of  12.61
```

5 Verify the operation of the program.

The best way to verify the operation of this program is to look up the absolute and relative magnitudes of some stars in an astronomy textbook. Other than that, your only recourse is to check some calculations by hand.

Problem Discussion

Note how the / descriptor in P-5.3 is used to divide the output into several lines. It would also be OK to use formatted PRINT statements instead of WRITEs in P-5.3. One alternative to the first two WRITE statements is:

```
WRITE(6,"(' To calculate absolute stellar magnitude:'/&
         ' Give relative mag. and distance in parsecs: ')"&
         ,advance='no')
```

Another alternative is:

```
      PRINT 1001
      ...
1001  FORMAT(' To calculate absolute stellar magnitude: '/&
             ' Give relative magnitude and distance in parsecs:')
```

With the second alternative, the only difference is that the values you type in response to the prompt appear on the third line rather than at the end of the second line because the nonadvancing input option isn't available with PRINT.

5.4.2 Relativistic Mass and Speed of an Electron

Refer to the application in Chapter 3, Section 3.8.2, and to program P-3.12, a program that calculates the relativistic mass and speed of an electron. We will modify that program so that it produces neatly formatted output that looks like this:

```
  For an electron gun voltage of: 1.0000E+06 V
            rest mass of electron: 9.1090E-31 kg
       relativistic mass and speed: 2.6934E-30 kg   2.8212E+08 m/s
  ratio of relativistic to rest mass: 2.9568E+00
     ratio of speed to speed of light: 9.4108E-01
```

You will need to include two new calculations for the specified ratios, but you can include them as expressions within a PRINT or WRITE statement rather than assigning the values to two new variables. It is essential to use the E descriptors whenever numbers are very large or very small, and it is often helpful to use them when you're not sure what the magnitude of calculated values will be.

We will not bother to follow a formal problem-solving procedure for this problem, as the algorithm design changes relative to P-3.12 are minor. The major modifications deal with the implementation details required to replace the list-directed output with formatted output. Here is the modified program. Compare its output against the values in Figure 3.5 from Chapter 3.

In P-5.4, the unit number is declared as a variable and assigned a value of 6, so output is directed to the monitor screen. An end-of-chapter exercise will ask you to modify this program according to the discussion in Section 5.3 so that its output will be directed to some other destination.

P-5.4 [RELMASS2.F90]

```
      PROGRAM RelMass2
!
! Calculates relativistic mass and speed of an electron.
!
      IMPLICIT NONE
      REAL rest_mass,relativistic_mass ! kg
      REAL voltage                     ! volts
      REAL speed                       ! m/s
      REAL e                           ! electron charge, Coulomb
      REAL c                           ! speed of light, m/s
      INTEGER u                        ! output unit
      PARAMETER (e=1.602e-19, c=2.9979e8, rest_mass=9.109e-31)
      u=6 !output to monitor
!
      PRINT *,' Give electron gun voltage in volts: '
      READ *,voltage
!
      relativistic_mass=(voltage*e+rest_mass*c**2)/c**2
      speed=c*SQRT(1.-(rest_mass/relativistic_mass)**2)
!
      WRITE(u,1000)voltage
      WRITE(u,1001)rest_mass
      WRITE(u,1002)relativistic_mass,speed, &
                   relativistic_mass/rest_mass
      WRITE(u,1003)speed/c
!
1000  FORMAT('      For an electron gun voltage of: ',es10.4,' V')
1001  FORMAT('               rest mass of electron: ',es10.4,' kg')

1002  FORMAT('        relativistic mass and speed: ',es10.4, &
             ' kg',es12.4,' m/s'/&
             ' ratio of relativistic to rest mass: ',es10.4)
1003  FORMAT('   ratio of speed to speed of light: ',es10.4)
      END
```

Running P-5.4

```
   Give electron gun voltage in volts:
1e6
      For an electron gun voltage of: 1.0000E+06 V
               rest mass of electron: 9.1090E-31
        relativistic mass and speed: 2.6934E-30 kg   2.8212E+08  m/s
 ratio of relativistic to rest mass: 2.9568E+00
   ratio of speed to speed of light: 9.4108E-01
```

5.5 Debugging Your Programs

5.5.1 Programming Style

Formatted output should be used to produce output that is readable and reflects the accuracy of the quantities being calculated. Descriptions of the output should be concise but complete. When appropriate, numerical values should be formatted so that their decimal points are in the same column. You should resist the temptation to display output with a large number of significant figures. A quantity that is calculated from measurements accurate to, for example, only three significant figures usually is not displayed with more than three significant figures.

A carefully planned program should contain a mixture of PRINT and WRITE statements organized so that prompts for user input are displayed on the monitor screen and program output can be saved in a data file or printed.

5.5.2 Problems with Programs

There are two common problems with output formats:

(1) The format descriptor doesn't match the data type of the value being displayed.

This kind of error will cause your program to crash.

(2) The specified field width is too narrow for the value being displayed.

Your program will run, but it will fill the inappropriately formatted field with asterisks.

Solutions to these problems are usually self-explanatory. When a field width is too narrow, it may be not because you have written an inappropriate field descriptor but because an error in your program is producing a value much larger than you expected.

Problems with WRITE statements containing unit numbers can arise when the unit number's value conflicts with a preconnected input or output unit, or when the unit number isn't preconnected and hasn't been connected with an OPEN statement. Preconnected unit numbers that work on one system may not work on all systems.

When you wish, at least initially, to display output on a monitor screen, there is a tradeoff in convenience between using an asterisk to direct output to the default output device and using a unit number variable assigned the value associated with the preconnected output device. In the first instance, the program will be completely portable to other systems, but you will have to manually replace all the asterisks if you later wish to direct output to some other device. In the second instance, redirection to another device can be accomplished simply by changing the value of the unit number variable; however, the original program may not be portable to all systems.

5.6 Exercises

5.6.1 Self-Testing Exercises

Exercise 1. Describe in your own words the two most important concepts you have learned from this chapter.

Exercise 2. Describe in your own words how you could use in your own programs a problem-solving skill demonstrated in a program described in this chapter.

Exercise 3. What format(s) could be used to produce these outputs?

(a)
```
33.33E+09
0.3333E+11
3.333E+10
```

(b)
```
You have won a grand total of $ 99999.00.  Congratulations!
```

(c) Assume an address consists of four separate character strings containing the street address, city, state postal abbreviation, and ZIP code.

```
123 Main St., Anytown, PA 19000-1234
```

(d)
```
Yearly total sales: 1990 17.7
                    1991 23.3
                    1992 22.9
                    1993 24.1
                    1994 26.9
                    1995 28.0
                    1996 29.3
                    1997 31.5 (projected)
```

Exercise 4. Define these terms in your own words:

(a) default output device
(c) external output device
(e) formatted output
(g) format descriptor

(b) preconnected unit number
(d) list-directed output
(f) format specification

5.6.2 Basic Programming Exercises

Exercise 5. What happens to the output of program P-5.3 if you replace all the format descriptors with G descriptors?

Exercise 6. Write a short program that prints several numbers, including very large and very small numbers that require the use of scientific notation, using E, EN, ES, F, and G formats.

Exercise 7. Modify program P-5.3 to include a conversion of stellar distance from parsecs to meters or kilometers. A light year is the distance light travels in 1 year. There are approximately 86,400×365.25 s/year. The speed of light is 2.9979×10^8 m/s. Use an appropriate format for the output.

Exercise 8. A more useful application of the relationship between absolute and relative stellar magnitude is to compute stellar distances. This is possible because the absolute magnitude of a star can be inferred from its spectral characterstics (essentially, from its color). Modify program P-5.3 so that the inferred absolute magnitude and the observed relative magnitude can be used to determine the distance of a star from the observer.

Exercise 9. Modify program P-5.4 so that program output is sent to an appropriately named output file.

Exercise 10. Modify program P-5.4 so that all the output is produced with a *single* WRITE statement. The appearance of the output should be unchanged.

Exercise 11. Modify program P-5.4 so that program output can be sent *either* to an output file or to the monitor, based on a user-supplied file name.

Exercise 12. Based on material from other courses you are taking, state a computational problem and write a program to solve it. Use formatted output and save the output from your program in an external file.

5.6.3 Programming Applications

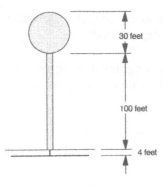

Figure 5.2. Layout of a
water tower

Exercise 13. A tower 100 feet high supports a spherical water tank with a diameter of 30 feet. What is the range of pressures, measured in pounds per square inch (psi), available from this storage tank at a water line located four feet below ground level? See Figure 5.2. The density of water is 62.43 pounds per cubic foot. [TOWER.F90]

Exercise 14. A water company regularly tests its residential meters for accuracy against laboratory standards. It often finds that the meters slightly underestimate the actual flow at low rates, are more accurate in the mid range of flow rates, and slightly overestimate the actual flow at high rates. In order to assess the overall performance of a particular meter, it calculates a weighted accuracy A_w based on measured accuracies and estimates of the percentage of total water usage at low, middle, and high flow rates:

$$A_w = \frac{\%_L \cdot A_L + \%_M \cdot A_M + \%_H \cdot A_H}{100}$$

Write a program that asks the user to provide estimated percentages of total water usage in each range, the actual accuracy of a meter at each range, and the weighted accuracy for the meter.

Some sample measurements are given in Table 5.2. Use your program to reproduce the values in this table and to fill in the missing values for weighted accuracy. [METERS.F90]

Table 5.2. Measured accuracies for residential water meters.

Meter Number	Low Range (30%)	Mid Range (45%)	High Range (25%)	Weighted Accuracy
1	98.7	99.6	100.3	
2	99.2	100.1	101.4	

Exercise 15. The weight and muzzle velocity of bullets for several firearms are given in Table 5.3. Write a program that will reproduce the values in the table and fill in the missing muzzle energy values in the table. The muzzle energy is $mv^2/2$ foot-lbf where lbf indicates pound-force rather than pound-mass. There arc 7000 grains in one pound. [BULLETS.F90]

Table 5.3. Bullet weights, muzzle velocities, and muzzle energies for several firearms.

Bullet	Weight (grains)	Speed (fps)	Muzzle Energy (ft-lbf)
.38 special	95	1175	
.357 Magnum	125	1450	
.308 Winchester	150	2533	
.223 Remington	55	3240	
.22 long rifle	40	1150	

Exercise 16. Suppose you are a highway engineer designing an intersection that will be controlled by a traffic light. When the light turns yellow, a driver approaching the intersection must have time to decelerate safely to a stop before the light turns red. If you know the speed limit for cars approaching the intersection (in miles per hour), how long must the light stay yellow? You must know the driver's reaction time—the time that elapses between when the light turns from grccn to yellow and when brakes are applied—and the average deceleration (ft/s^2). See Figure 5.3.

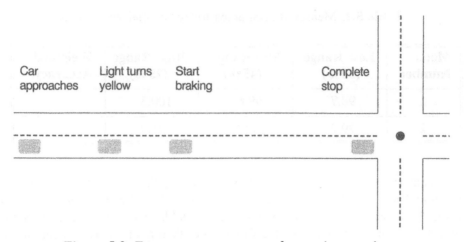

Figure 5.3. Events as a car approaches an intersection

Write a program to solve this problem. Your output should appear in a table that looks something like this:

```
    Approach speed, mph:
    Approach speed, fps:
       Reaction time, sec:
     Distance covered, ft:
         Braking time, sec:
     Distance covered, ft:
   Total stopping time, sec:
Total distance covered, ft:
```

The equation describing the distance covered by the car is

$$\text{distance} = \text{speed} \cdot t_{\text{reaction}} + at^2_{\text{braking}}/2$$

where a is a constant acceleration and the time t during which brakes are applied is $t_{\text{braking}} = v/a$. See Figure 5.4 for some representative stopping distances.

You must make several assumptions to solve this problem. First of all, ignore the possibility that a driver within some critical distance of an intersection may decide not to stop at all. As a rough estimate, assume that a car can be decelerated at a constant average rate in the range 10–15 ft/s^2 and that a driver's reaction time to start braking is a few tenths of a second. How much of a safety margin do you want to design into the system to allow, for example, safe stopping when roads are wet? [STOPLITE.F90]

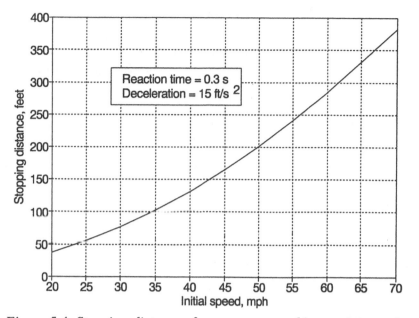

Figure 5.4. Stopping distances for a car approaching an intersection

Exercise 17. When you were in grade school, you may have made a "shoebox" solar system with models of the planets, and you may even have kept the size of the planets to scale. As instructive as this might have been, it badly distorts spatial scales within the solar system. Write a program that allows you to specify the diameter of a model earth and then calculates the size of a model sun and all the other planets, along with the average distance of each model planet from the sun, all to the same spatial scale. Calculate the diameter of the model sun and planets in inches and their distance from the model sun in feet. (You can use comparable metric units if you prefer.)

A pea-sized (1/4" diameter) model earth is a reasonable value to start with. Table 5.4 contains the actual diameters and average orbital distances of the planets from the Sun. Your program should create a table that includes the data in this table plus the scaled diameters (in inches or centimeters) and distances (in feet or meters). [PLANETS.F90]

Table 5.4. Diameters and distances for sun and the planets.

Object	Diameter (km)	Average Orbital Distance from Sun (million km)
Sun	1,392,000	
Mercury	4,878	57.9
Venus	12,102	108
Earth	12,760	150
Mars	6,786	228
Jupiter	142,800	778
Saturn	120,660	1,427
Uranus	52,400	2,870
Neptune	50,460	4,500
Pluto	2,200	5,900

Program Control: Branching and Repetitive Calculations

The chapter begins with a discussion of Fortran 90's implementation of program control constructs, including the *IF...THEN...* and *CHOOSE...* pseudocode commands and the *LOOP...END LOOP* pseudocode command. Fortran implementation of the relational operators and the LOGICAL data type is discussed.

6.1 Using Program Control Structures

As noted in Chapter 2, all computer algorithms can be implemented with just three basic program control structures: sequence, selection, and repetition. The programs presented so far in Chapters 3 through 5 have required only sequential structures. That is, each executable statement has been executed once, in order. Many algorithms require more sophisticated controls. These include selection or branching structures, which provide the ability to execute certain statements and not others, and repetition structures, which allow groups of statements to be executed repetitively.

In the pseudocode language presented in Chapter 2, branching structures are represented by the *IF...THEN...* and *CHOOSE* commands and repetition constructs by the *LOOP...END LOOP* command. We will now examine these two commands in more detail.

6.1.1 The *IF...THEN...(ELSE...)* Pseudocode Construct

Consider the common computing task of taking the square root of a number. In Fortran, you would use the SQRT intrinsic function. However, there's a catch: if the argument of the SQRT function is negative, your program will crash. In some situations, this doesn't represent a serious problem. The worst that can happen is that the crash is due to a mistake in input and you will simply have to start your program over again. However, in larger programs that involve many complex and interrelated calculations, it may be important to keep the program running and, more important, to prevent inappropriate calculations from being made in the first place.

With respect to using the SQRT function, you might wish your program to respond like this: "Here is a potential argument for the SQRT function. If it's non-negative, it's OK to take the square root. Otherwise, I won't try to take the square root, and instead I'll send an appropriate message." This is easy to implement in pseudocode. Suppose the potential argument is X and Y will contain the square root of X:

IF $X \geq 0$ **THEN**
    ASSIGN Y = SQRT(X)
ELSE
    WRITE ("I can't take this square root!")
    WRITE ("Instead I will set Y = 0.")
    ASSIGN Y = 0
(end **IF**...)

In this particular pseudocode example, Y is assigned a value of 0 if the square root function can't be applied. You can take any action you like; giving Y a negative value might also be a good choice because the SQRT function always returns a positive value. However, as a matter of style, it's not a good idea to leave Y unassigned. Another way to achieve this result in pseudocode, without the explanatory messages, is:

ASSIGN Y = 0
IF $X \geq 0$ **THEN ASSIGN** Y = SQRT(X)

In this case, too, Y always has an assigned value. The important feature shared by these algorithms is that they test the value of X before attempting to take the square root. Clearly, this algorithm *won't* work:

ASSIGN Y = SQRT(X)
IF $X < 0$ **THEN WRITE** ("I can't take this square root!")

In this case, the test on X is made too late—a program based on this algorithm will crash before the message is printed.

The pseudocode solutions to this problem are typical examples of a selection construct. A *logical expression* (such as $X < 0$) is evaluated, and the result controls the subsequent action. Later in this chapter, we will discuss in detail what it means for Fortran to be asked to answer questions such as "Is x greater than or equal to 0?"

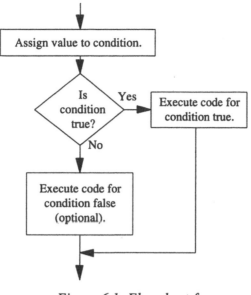

Figure 6.1. Flowchart for an
IF...THEN...ELSE... *construct*

The operation of the ***IF...THEN...ELSE...*** pseudocode command can be visualized in terms of a flowchart using the symbols discussed briefly in Chapter 2, as in Figure 6.1. First one or more values are assigned—for example, A=0, B=1. Then a condition involving those values is evaluated—for example, "Is A equal to B?" The diamond symbol represents a decision point. If the condition is true, then the "yes" branch is taken. If the expression is false, then the "no" branch is taken. For the example given, A is not equal to B, so the "no" branch is taken. Rectangular symbols represent blocks of statements that are executed sequentially. As noted, statements associated with an ***ELSE...*** branch are optional; in some cases nothing should happen if the condition is false.

6.1.2 The **CHOOSE** *Pseudocode Command*

Another kind of branching structure involves choosing a course of action from a list of possibilities. In the pseudocode command language described in Chapter 2, this structure is represented by the ***CHOOSE*** command. To investigate the use of this command, we will reconsider the application originally presented in Section 2.4.1—determining the maximum deflection of a beam under a load.

In that application, a formula was given for the maximum deflection at the center of a beam when it is supported at each end and a concentrated force is applied to the center of the beam. However, there are several other possibilities for loading a beam. Table 6.1 presents four, including the original, with formulas for calculating the maximum deflection:

Table 6.1. Maximum deflection of a beam subject to various support and loading conditions

Support and Loading	Schematic	Maximum Deflection
Supported at each end, concentrated force F [1]	F ↓ /\ <------- L -------> /\	$-FL^3/(48EI)$ at L/2
Supported at each end, distributed weight W	W ↓↓↓↓↓↓↓↓↓↓ /\ /\	$-5WL^3/(384EI)$ at L/2
Supported at one end, concentrated force F at free end	F ↓	$-FL^3/(3EI)$ at free end
Supported at one end, distributed weight W	W ↓↓↓↓↓↓↓↓↓↓	$-WL^3/(8EI)$ at free end

[1] Force F and weight W have units of lb; length L has a unit of in, elasticity E has a unit of lb/in^2, and moment of inertia has a unit of in^4.

Here is one way this table might be incorporated into an algorithm, assuming that values for F, L, E, and I are already available, as defined in Table 6.1.

WRITE (menu describing four possible support systems, user prompt)
READ (choice of support system 1-4)
CHOOSE (based on support/load ID)
       1: ASSIGN deflection = $-FL^3/(48EI)$
       2: ASSIGN deflection = $-5WL^3/(384EI)$
       3: ASSIGN deflection = $-FL^3/(3EI)$
       4: ASSIGN deflection = $-WL^3/(8EI)$
       anything else: WRITE ("Input error.")
(end CHOOSE)
WRITE (deflection)

Although the **CHOOSE** command could be represented as a flowchart with a series of decision symbols, such flowcharts are rather cumbersome.

6.1.3 The **LOOP...END LOOP** Pseudocode Command

Repetition is the third program control construct, represented by the **LOOP...END LOOP** pseudocode command. Repetition constructs are divided into two basic types: ***count-controlled loops*** and ***conditional loops***. In this section, we will discuss these loops, and later in the chapter, we will discuss their Fortran implementations.

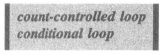

Count-controlled loops

Count-controlled loops are appropriate when you know ahead of time, or your program can calculate, how many times the statements inside the loop will be executed. The execution of the loop is controlled by a ***loop counter variable*** that is initialized to a specified lower limit and incremented by a specified amount for each "trip" through the loop. When the loop counter reaches a specified upper limit, the loop terminates. The command

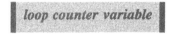

LOOP *(for counter = 1 to 10)*

is typical pseudocode for a count-controlled loop. It is also possible to construct loops in which the counter is initialized to an upper limit and decremented; the loop continues to execute as long as the counter is greater than or equal to a lower limit.

Figure 6.2(a) shows a basic flowchart for a count-controlled loop. The boxes shown with dotted outlines and the assignments in parentheses mean that when these kinds of loops are implemented in a language such as Fortran, the initial assignment of the counter variable and the incrementing of the counter are managed *automatically* by the loop syntax. This fact makes count-controlled loops very easy to write, and we will often use them in programs throughout the rest of this text.

Figure 6.2(b) shows another way of drawing a flowchart for count-controlled loops. The loop control conditions are gathered together in one place and the initialization and incrementing steps are not shown specifically.

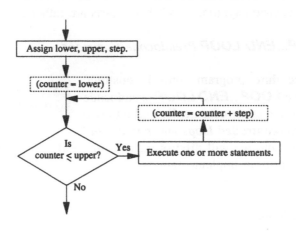

Figure 6.2(a). Basic flowchart for a count-controlled loop

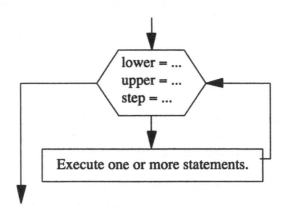

Figure 6.2(b) Alternate flowchart for a count-controlled loop

Conditional Loops

Conditional loops are appropriate when the number of times the statements inside a loop will be executed is unknown or can't be determined ahead of time. This kind of loop is often required for *iterative calculations*, in which successive estimates of a desired quantity improve until a specified

iterative calculation
convergence criterion
pre-test loop
post-test loop

convergence criterion is met. Conditional loops may be either *pre-test* or *post-test* loops. The difference is that the conditions under which the statements inside a loop are executed are determined either before (pre-test) or after (post-test) those statements have been executed at least once. To put it another way, the terminating conditions are evaluated at the "top" of the loop for a pre-test loop and at the "bottom" for a post-test loop.

LOOP (until a condition is true) is a generic pseudocode statement of a post-test loop. It indicates that statements inside a loop will be executed at least once before the program determines whether the loop will terminate. *LOOP (as long a condition is true)* is generic pseudocode for a pre-test loop. It implies that the test for continuing, or starting, the loop is done before the statements inside the loop are executed.

By definition, statements inside a post-test loop are always executed at least once, whereas statements inside a pre-test loop might not be executed at all. In principle, conditional loops can be designed as either pre-test or post-test loops. As a practical matter, the way a problem is stated will often determine the easiest way to implement the loop.

Figure 6.3 illustrates the operation of the two kinds of conditional loops. In a pre-test loop, some condition is initialized before the loop begins. Then, if the condition is "true" (however the particular problem requires that test to be evaluated), one or more statements are executed and the condition is modified. Depending on the initial value of the condition, the statements inside the loop may never be executed. In a post-test loop, statements inside the loop are executed at least once. Only after they have been executed once is the terminating condition evaluated. At this point, the statements inside the loop may or may not be executed again.

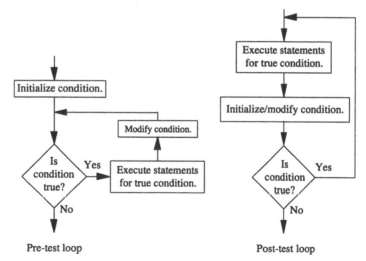

Pre-test loop   Post-test loop

Figure 6.3. Flowcharts for pre-test and post-test loops

A difference between count-controlled loops and conditional loops is that count-controlled loops are controlled, as the name implies, by "counting" something; this usually means that the counter variable is an integer to be incremented, or decremented, by some specified integer value during each "trip" through the loop.[1] The operation of conditional loops is more flexible. Their terminating conditions *may* be set by counting something, but they may also be controlled by other kinds of terminating conditions.

6.2 Relational and Logical Operators and the Fortran IF... Construct

Now that we have completed a discussion about using program control structures in pseudocode, we will examine their implementation in Fortran, starting with the relational and logical operators.

6.2.1 Relational and Logical Operators

Let's look again at the **IF...THEN...ELSE...** pseudocode example from Section 6.1.1:

IF X ≥ 0 **THEN**
    ASSIGN Y = SQRT(X)
ELSE
    WRITE ("I can't take this square root!")
    WRITE ("Instead I will set Y = 0.")
    ASSIGN Y = 0
(end **IF...**)

Here's one way to translate this pseudocode into English: "If it is true that $X \geq 0$, then assign y a value equal to the square root of x. Otherwise, assign y a value of 0." In this expression, the ≥ sign is one of the relational operators previously defined in Table 2.3. The result of evaluating the logical expression $X \geq 0$ is a logical (or "boolean") value of true or false. If the expression has a value of true, then the **THEN...** branch of the **IF...THEN...ELSE...** statement is taken. If the value is false, then the **ELSE...** branch is taken; only *one* branch of the structure can be taken.

---

[1]As you will see when the text discusses the implementation of count-controlled loops in Fortran, the counter variable doesn't *have* to be an integer number, although we will require this as a matter of good programming style.

It's easy to translate this pseudocode into source code because the Fortran language includes syntax nearly identical to the **IF...** pseudocode command. Table 6.2 contains the Fortran 90 symbols for the relational and logical operators given previously in Table 2.3.

Table 6.2. Fortran implementation of relational and logical operators

Relational or Logical Operator	Meaning	Fortran Implementation
=	equal	== or .EQ.
>	greater than	> or .GT.
<	less than	< or .LT.
≤	less than or equal to	<= or .LE.
≥	greater than or equal to	>= or .GE.
≠	not equal to	/= or .NE.
and	logical "and"	.AND.
or	logical or	.OR.
not	logical not	.NOT.

There are no special characters in the Fortran language that allow single-character representations equivalent to, for example, the ≤ symbol from mathematics; in Fortran 90, this symbol is represented by the two-character symbol <=. Note that the symbol for equality is == and not just =; this symbol serves as a reminder that a test for equality is not the same thing as an assignment statement. The implementations that use these more familiar mathematical symbols are new to Fortran 90. The implementations using letters, such as .EQ., were used in older versions of Fortran and are still supported under the Fortran 90 standard. You may use whichever representation you like, but the Fortran 90 symbols are probably a better choice.

Fortran also includes intrinsic functions for comparing strings. A list of these boolean lexical comparison functions is given in Table 6.3.

Table 6.3. Lexical string comparison functions

Function Name	Description
LGE(string_a,string_b)	Returns .TRUE. if string_a is equal to or follows string_b in the ASCII collating sequence, .FALSE. otherwise.
LGT(string_a,string_b)	Returns .TRUE. if string_a follows string_b in the ASCII collating sequence, .FALSE. otherwise.
LLE(string_a,string_b)	Returns .TRUE. if string_a is equal to or precedes string_b in the ASCII collating sequence, .FALSE. otherwise.
LLT(string_a,string_b)	Returns .TRUE. if string_a precedes string_b in the ASCII collating sequence, .FALSE. otherwise.

When strings are compared, "greater than" or "less than" means that one string follows or precedes another relative to some character collating sequence. The purpose of these lexical comparison functions is to force all computer systems, even ones that don't use the ASCII collating sequence, to compare strings relative to the ASCII sequence. For systems that *do* use the ASCII sequence, the two statements

```
IF (a<b) THEN
IF (LLT(a,b)) THEN
```

are equivalent. Otherwise, the results *might* be different. When strings are compared in this way, the comparisons are always case-sensitive, with the result that, for example, 'David' is "less than" 'david' because the uppercase alphabet comes before the lowercase alphabet in the ASCII collating sequence.

6.2.2 The IF... Construct

As indicated above, the pseudocode **IF...** command is easy to translate into Fortran, using the IF... construct. Program fragment P-6.1(a) gives Fortran code that checks the value of a variable before taking its square root. Note how close the syntax of this Fortran code fragment is to the corresponding pseudocode. However, the parentheses around the logical expression X >= 0 are required as part of the Fortran syntax. The modification of P-6.1(a) given in P-6.1(b) provides more insight into the implementation of logical expressions.

P-6.1(a) (fragment)

```
IF (X >= 0) THEN
  Y=SQRT(X)
ELSE
  PRINT *,'I can''t take this square root!'
  PRINT *,'Instead, I will set Y=0.'
  Y=0.0
END IF
```

P-6.1(b) (fragment)

```
LOGICAL X_test
...
X_test = (x >= 0)
IF (X_test) THEN
  Y=SQRT(X)
ELSE
  PRINT *,'I can''t take this square root!'
  PRINT *,'Instead, I will set Y=0.'
  Y=0.0
END IF
```

In P-6.1(b), the variable `X_test` is declared as having type `LOGICAL`. Such variables can have only two values, true or false, represented in Fortran by `.TRUE.` or `.FALSE.`. The evaluation of the expression `(x >= 0)` yields one of these values, depending on the value of x. There isn't much point in rewriting the simple example in P-6.1(a) as we've done in P-6.1(b), but in more complicated programs, the value of `X_test` might be assigned as the result of several statements, or it might be returned as the output from a function. It's also possible to give a logical variable such as `X_test` a value of `.TRUE.` or `.FALSE.` directly by using an assignment statement such as `x=.TRUE.`, assuming x has been declared as type `LOGICAL`.

Again, the parentheses around the logical expression in the assignment statement `X_test = (x >= 0)` are required as part of its syntax. In the `IF...` statement, the logical expression consists solely of the logical variable `X_test`, but it must still be enclosed in parentheses. The value of `X_test` determines which branch of the `IF...` statement is executed. This example demonstrates that an `IF...` statement decides which branch to execute by examining the logical expression and proceeding according to whether the value of that expression is true or false.

Beginning programmers often write the `IF` test in P-6.1(b) like this:

```
IF (X_test==.TRUE.) THEN
  ...
```

This is OK, but redundant. Remember that the variable X_test contains the result of determining whether x is greater than or equal to zero, so if X_test has a value of .TRUE., then the expression X_test==.TRUE. must also have a value of .TRUE..

Compound relational expressions can be formed with the three logical operators given in Table 6.2. Program fragment P-6.2 gives an example:

P-6.2 (fragment)

```
LOGICAL raining
REAL temperature
CHARACTER YesNo
...
PRINT *,' Is it raining (y/n)?'
READ *,YesNo
raining=.false.
IF (YesNo='y') raining=.TRUE.
PRINT *,' How hot is it? '
READ *,temperature
IF ((.NOT. raining) .AND. (temperature>85.0)) THEN
  PRINT *,'Time to go swimming.'
ELSE
  PRINT *,'Stay inside.'
END IF
```

The .NOT. operator is a unary operator that operates on the logical value of the expression that follows it by converting a value of .TRUE. to a value of .FALSE. and *vice versa*. The .AND. and .OR. operators are binary operators that produce a value of .TRUE. or .FALSE. depending on the value of expressions on either side of the operator. In order for the message "Time to go swimming." to be printed by P-6.2, the expressions on both sides of the .AND. operator must have a value of .TRUE.. The results of applying the .AND. and .OR. operators to two expressions are shown in the "truth tables" given in Table 6.4. The expression (A .AND. B) is true only if both A *and* B are true. The expression (A .OR. B) is true if either A *or* B is true.

Table 6.4. "Truth tables" for logical expressions "A" and "B"

.AND.	B is true.	B is false.
A is true.	true	false
A is false.	false	false
.OR.	B is true.	B is false.
A is true.	true	true
A is false.	true	false

There are several forms of the Fortran IF... construct. The general syntax is:

```
Syntax
form

(1)   IF (logical expression) action_statement

(2)   [name:] IF (logical expression) THEN
              statement block
         END IF [name]

(3)   [name:] IF (logical expression) THEN
              statement block
           ELSE [name]
              statement block
           END IF [name]

(4)   [name:] IF (logical expression) THEN
              statement block
           [ELSE IF (logical expression) THEN [name]
              statement block]...
           [ELSE [name]
              statement block]
           END IF [name]
```

In the first and simplest form, the THEN... is implied. The action consists of a single statement following the logical expression, which must be enclosed in parentheses. As an example, the statement

```
IF (YesNo=='y') THEN
   raining=.true.
END IF
```

can be written more compactly as

```
IF (YesNo=='y') raining=.TRUE.
```

In the other forms, there can be multiple statements, forming a statement block, in each branch of the construct. The third form is the `IF...THEN...ELSE...` form—a two-branch construct. The fourth form shows multiple branches using the `ELSE IF...` syntax.

Note that `IF...` constructs and their parts can be given names. (Remember that the brackets around *name*: are not part of the syntax, but an indication that using a name label is optional.) In all cases, the name must be the same. In the third and fourth examples, the `ELSE` and `ELSE IF` statements may be named only if the corresponding `IF` and `END IF` statements are named. In this text, we will not use names as "labels" in `IF...` statements. We will rely on in-line comments if needed to clarify the purpose of `IF...` constructs.

Programming Tip

The `END IF` Fortran keywords can also be spelled as one word, `ENDIF`.

Here's one more important point about evaluating logical expressions. What does it mean to ask Fortran to evaluate the expression (`A == B`) when `A` and `B` are `REAL` variables? Suppose `A` and `B` have both been assigned the value 10.0. Clearly, `A` is equal to `B`. However, when the values of `A` and `B` are produced through arithmetic operations, problems can arise. For example, what is the value of `A` as a result of the Fortran assignment `A=10.0/3.0*3.0`? In the algebraic sense, it is obvious that `A` is equal to 10. However, Fortran doesn't care about algebra. It just evaluates expressions by performing operations from left to right, following the precedence rules. The results of arithmetic operations are limited by the numerical accuracy of your computer system and compiler. In this case, it will produce 10.0/3.0=3.3333333... and then perhaps 9.9999999... rather than 10 as the result of multiplying the intermediate result by 3. If so, the expression (`A == B`) will then have a value of `.FALSE.` because 9.9999999... is not exactly equal to 10. In fact, some compilers will produce the "algebraic" result of 10 for this particular example. (Try it with your compiler.) However, it is inevitable that similar kinds of operations will eventually cause unexpected results in your programs.

The solution is never to test `REAL` variables for equality. In this case, it would be better to compare the values of `REAL` variables `A` and `B` like this, using the `ABS` intrinsic function:

```
IF (ABS(A-B) <=  error limit) THEN...
```

For the expression to have a value of "true," the difference between A and B must be smaller than some number that you select. Its value should bear some relationship to the internal accuracy of calculations done by your compiler or the requirements of your problem. Often, for calculations involving physical quantities, 10^{-6} or 10^{-7} is more than sufficiently small. An error limit as small as 10^{-9}, for example, is unreasonable for calculations involving default REAL numbers, because such calculations are probably not performed to this degree of accuracy.

The same problem applies to testing values for equality when they have different data types. Suppose A is REAL and B is INTEGER. The code

```
A=10.
B=10
IF (A == B) THEN
...
```

will work as expected here, but it may not work if A is the result of arithmetic operations. One way to fix this would be to modify the IF... test:

```
IF (NINT(A) == B) THEN
...
```

This forces a type conversion and will give the expected result of .TRUE.. Because of these potential problems—and for basically the same reasons they should be avoided in assignment statements—it's a good idea to avoid mixed-mode expressions in logical expressions.

6.2.3 Using the IF... Construct in Programs

Here's a typical problem that uses an IF... construct.

1 Define the problem.

Write a program that asks the user to supply a numerical grade and then converts it to a letter grade according to this table:

```
90-100      A
80- 89      B
70- 79      C
60- 69      D
<60         F
```

2 *Outline a solution.*

Prompt the user to supply the numerical grade and then use an IF construct to control the translation of the numerical grade into a letter grade

3 *Design an algorithm.*

DEFINE *(numerical grade as a real number)*
WRITE *("Give a numerical grade:")*
READ *(grade)*
IF *(grade >= 90)* **THEN**
    WRITE *(A)*
ELSE IF *(grade >= 80)* **THEN**
    WRITE *(B)*
ELSE IF *(grade >= 70)* **THEN**
    WRITE *(C)*
ELSE IF *(grade >= 60)* **THEN**
    WRITE *(D)*
ELSE
    WRITE *(F)*
(end IF)

Here's a question you might have about this pseudocode. Suppose the numerical grade is 91. This is greater than 90, so the **WRITE** *(A)* command will be executed. However, 91 is also greater than 80, so will the **WRITE** *(B)* command, and all the other commands, also be executed? As you would hope, the answer is "No." A selection construct executes only *one* branch—in particular, the first branch for which the relational expression is true—and then ignores all the others; this is true for the pseudocode conception of the **IF...** command and also for its language implementation. Even though you may be tempted to rewrite the first **ELSE IF...** command, for example, to be "more restrictive," like this:

ELSE IF *((grade >= 80) and (grade < 90))* **THEN**

This is not necessary and probably means that you don't really understand the operation of the **IF...** command.

4 *Translate the algorithm into a program.*

P-6.3 [GRADES.F90]

```
      PROGRAM Grades
!
! Convert a numerical grade to a letter grade.  Demonstrates
! compound IF... statements.
!
      IMPLICIT NONE
      REAL grade
!
      PRINT *,' Give a numerical grade 0-100: '
      READ *,grade
!
      IF (grade .GE. 90.0) THEN
         PRINT *,' Letter grade: A'
      ELSE IF (grade .GE. 80.0) THEN
         PRINT *,' Letter grade: B'
      ELSE IF (grade .GE. 70.0) THEN
         PRINT *,' Letter grade: C'
      ELSE IF (grade .GE. 60.0) THEN
         PRINT *,' Letter grade: D'
      ELSE
         PRINT *,' Letter grade: F'
      END IF
!
      END
```

Running P-6.3

```
  Give a numerical grade 0-100:
87
  Letter grade: B
```

For demonstration purposes, this program uses the older style (.GE.) representation for the "greater than or equal to" relational operator. It is better Fortran 90 style to use the >= representation, which is completely equivalent.

5 *Verify the operation of the program.*

Run the program with numerical grades that will produce all possible outputs. It's especially important to think carefully about the structure of IF... constructs at the algorithm design level *before* you implement them in Fortran because logical errors in this kind of code are often very difficult to find.

6.3 The SELECT CASE Construct

Recall that the pseudocode **CHOOSE** command allows your program to select from a limited number of specified options. In Fortran, the **CHOOSE** pseudocode command is implemented with the SELECT CASE construct. Its general syntax is

```
[name:] SELECT CASE (expression)
        [CASE (list of nonoverlapping values and ranges
                with same data type as expression) [name]
         statement block]...
        [CASE DEFAULT
         statement block]
        END SELECT [name]
```

Based on the value of expression, the statement block following one of the CASE selectors is executed. The [   ]... notation means that the code represented inside the brackets may appear one or more times. Therefore, there may be one or more CASE selectors containing a list of nonoverlapping values and ranges of values. As noted, the values and ranges must have the same data type as expression.

The CASE DEFAULT statement allows action to be taken for any possible value of expression not specifically included in the CASE selectors; it is often given as the last CASE selector, but it and the other choices can appear in any order. A name can be given to the individual CASE statements only if the SELECT CASE statement and the END SELECT statements are named, and all must have the same name. In this text, we will not use names in this way. The CASE expression must be type CHARACTER, LOGICAL, or INTEGER. It may *not* be REAL. Each value in the list of values and ranges of values in the various CASE statements must have the same type as expression.

The restrictions on the type of expression and the 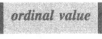 CASE selector values basically mean that these values must be *ordinal*; that is, enumerable. Integers are ordinal, but real numbers are not. The exception is that if expression is of type CHARACTER, then the lengths of the values given as CASE selectors don't have to be the same. That is, strings of differing numbers of characters are allowed even though strings of characters aren't ordinal.[2]

---

[2]Single characters are ordinal—B comes after A, for example—but strings of characters are not because there is no way to enumerate strings in the sense that it's not possible to specify which string comes "after" some other string. Other languages—Pascal, for example—may enforce this distinction by allowing their equivalent of the SELECT CASE to use characters but not strings as a controlling expression.

A range of ordinal values may be included in the list of CASE selectors using the format *low*: *high*. The range is [low,high] in the mathematical sense; that is, the range is inclusive of the end points. Either low or high may be absent, in which case the remaining value acts as a limit. For example, the range of CASE (:0) is all integers less than or equal to 0 and the range of CASE (1:) is all positive integers. The CASE selectors must not overlap, either within the range of a single selector or with other selectors in the same SELECT CASE construct.

As an example of how to use the SELECT CASE construct, consider program P-6.3 from the previous section. It might seem that the problem addressed in this program—to convert a numerical grade into a letter grade—is an ideal situation in which to use a SELECT CASE construct because the letter grade choices are taken from a relatively small list of possibilities. In fact, a SELECT CASE construct is a good idea, but it can be used *only* if the grade value used in the SELECT CASE expression is converted to an integer. This can be accomplished by rounding the grade, or truncating it, depending how generous a grader you wish to be. Program P-6.4 offers a solution to the grade assignment problem using a SELECT CASE construct.

P-6.4 [GRADES2.F90]

```
      PROGRAM Grades2
!
! Converts a numerical grade to a letter grade.  Demonstrates
! SELECT CASE statements.
!
      IMPLICIT NONE
      REAL grade
!
      PRINT *,' Give a numerical grade 0-100: '
      READ *,grade
!
      SELECT CASE (NINT(grade))
        CASE (90:100)
          PRINT *,' Letter grade: A'
        CASE (80:89)
          PRINT *,' Letter grade: B'
        CASE (70:79)
          PRINT *,' Letter grade: C'
        CASE (60:69)
          PRINT *,' Letter grade: D'
        CASE DEFAULT
          PRINT *,' Letter grade: F'
      END SELECT
!
      END
```

Just as in the compound IF... construct used in P-6.3, the SELECT CASE construct executes only *one* of the possibilities; that's why the ranges of the CASE values must not overlap. (The output is identical with that of P-6.3 for the same input values, so it is not repeated here.) Note that the first CASE range could be given as (90:) and the last could be given as (0:59) or (:59) rather than CASE DEFAULT, depending on how you wish to treat grades outside the range 0-100. For example, giving the first CASE range as (90:) would allow for grades over 100 as the result of extra credit.

6.4 Fortran Loop Constructs

In this section, we will discuss Fortran implementations for repetition constructs, and we will use count-controlled and conditional loops to solve some typical programming problems.

6.4.1 Count-Controlled (DO . . .) Loops

Count-controlled loops are often used to generate tables of values. Here is a typical problem.

1 *Define the problem.*

Write a program to generate a table of sin(x), cos(x), and tan(x) for 5° increments of x, in the range 0°-180°.

2 *Outline a solution.*

Use a count-controlled loop to generate the values. The program will not require any user input. Be sure to take into account the fact that tan(90°) is undefined.

3 *Design an algorithm.*

DEFINE *(x as real number)*
WRITE *(column headings)*

LOOP *(for x = 0 to 180 in steps of 5)*
  IF x ≠ 90° THEN
    WRITE (x, sin(x), cos(x), tan(x))
  ELSE
    WRITE (x, sin(x), cos(x))
END LOOP

Pay special attention to the way the terminating condition in the *LOOP...*
END LOOP command is written. It gives an initial value (0), a final value (180),
and an increment (5) for a value that will be incremented inside the loop. Even
though this text has previously stated (several times!) that pseudocode can and
should be language-independent, you probably wouldn't express the terminating
condition in exactly this way unless you had some idea about how count-
controlled loops work. You might think that in order to supply the values of x
implied by the comment about the loop's operation, this pseudocode needs to be
given in more detail, something like this:

INITIALIZE *x=0*
LOOP *(until x > 180)*
  IF x ≠ 90° THEN
    WRITE (x, sin(x), cos(x), tan(x))
  ELSE
    WRITE (x, sin(x), cos(x))
  INCREMENT x = x + 5
END LOOP

This pseudocode is logically correct, but you will see that it's not required in
situations where a count-controlled loop can be used. When the pseudocode for
a count-controlled loop is converted to real code, the corresponding program
statements will automatically initialize and increment the loop variable (*x*, in this
case).

4 *Convert the algorithm into a program.*

  Count-controlled loops are implemented in Fortran with a DO . . . END DO
statement. It has several syntax forms:

```
Syntax
form
(1)     [name:] DO n = limit1,limit2[,step]
                statement block
                END DO [name]

(2)             DO label n = limit1,limit2[,step]
                statement block, except for...
        label   last line of statement block

(3)             DO label n = limit1,limit2[,step]
                statement block
        label CONTINUE
```

The values *limit1*, *limit2*, and *step* are INTEGER constants, variables, or expressions. The **loop counter** *n* is automatically initialized to *limit1* when the loop begins, is 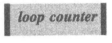 incremented by the amount *step*, and ends after *statement block* is executed for *n* equal to *limit2*. A specified step size is optional, but it must be nonzero when it is present. When *step* isn't present, the default increment is 1. Usually, *step* is set so that it evenly divides the interval from *limit1* to *limit2*, with the last value of the loop counter being *limit2*. For example, n=0,100,5 results in n having the values 0, 5, ..., 95, 100. However, *step* can also be set so that the last value taken by a loop counter is less than the upper limit. For example, n=1,20,3 results in n having the values 1, 4, 7, 10, 13, 16, 19.

The loop can be made to execute "backward" by having *limit1* greater than *limit2* and step less than 0. If *limit1* is greater than *limit2* and *step* is specified as positive, or has its default value of 1, the loop isn't executed at all. That is, it's not an error to have *limit1* greater than *limit2*, although it's not usually what you intend.

In the first syntax form, an END DO statement marks the end of the loop. That is, the *statement block* consists of all statements between the DO... and END DO statements. The *name* labels are optional and, as in earlier cases, we will not use them in this text.

In earlier versions of Fortran, the DO... statement required a reference to a line label in the form of an integer of one to five digits. This line could reference either the last line of the statement block, as shown in the second syntax example, or a line containing the CONTINUE keyword. These three DO... loops are equivalent:

```
     DO i=1,10
       statement block
     END DO

     DO 10 i=1,10
       statement block except for the...
10   last statement

     DO 10 i=1,10
       statement block
10   CONTINUE
```

In Fortran 90, the DO...END DO syntax is preferred, as modern programming languages tend to avoid line labels whenever possible; in this text, we will always use the DO...END DO syntax.[3]

Program P-6.5 implements the count-controlled loop algorithm to generate a table of trigonometric functions defined in Step 3.

P-6.5 [TRIGTABL.F90]

```
     PROGRAM TrigTabl
!
! Generate a table of trig values.  Demonstrates count-controlled
! loops.
!
     IMPLICIT NONE
     REAL angle,deg_to_rad
     INTEGER i !loop counter
!
     deg_to_rad=4.0*ATAN(1.0)/180.0
     PRINT *,'  x    sin(x)   cos(x)    tan(x)'
     PRINT *,' ---------------------------'
!
     DO i=0,180,5
       angle=REAL(i)*deg_to_rad
       IF (i .NE. 90) THEN
         PRINT 1000,i,SIN(angle),COS(angle),TAN(angle)
       ELSE
         PRINT 1001,i,SIN(angle),COS(angle)
       END IF
     END DO
!
1000 FORMAT(1x,i3,3f9.4)
1001 FORMAT(1x,i3,2f9.4,'   undef.')
     END
```

---

[3]Author's note: some Fortran 90 programmers will accuse me of seriously understating this point. They feel so strongly that line labels should be avoided that they consider the labelled DO... loops unacceptable.

Running P-6.5

```
    x    sin(x)    cos(x)    tan(x)
  - - - - - - - - - - - - - - - - - -
    0    0.0000    1.0000    0.0000
    5    0.0872    0.9962    0.0875
   10    0.1736    0.9848    0.1763
   15    0.2588    0.9659    0.2679
   20    0.3420    0.9397    0.3640
   25    0.4226    0.9063    0.4663
   30    0.5000    0.8660    0.5774
   35    0.5736    0.8192    0.7002
   40    0.6428    0.7660    0.8391
   45    0.7071    0.7071    1.0000
   50    0.7660    0.6428    1.1918
   55    0.8192    0.5736    1.4281
   60    0.8660    0.5000    1.7321
   65    0.9063    0.4226    2.1445
   70    0.9397    0.3420    2.7475
   75    0.9659    0.2588    3.7321
   80    0.9848    0.1736    5.6713
   85    0.9962    0.0872   11.4300
   90    1.0000    0.0000    undef.
   95    0.9962   -0.0872  -11.4300
  100    0.9848   -0.1736   -5.6713
  105    0.9659   -0.2588   -3.7321
  110    0.9397   -0.3420   -2.7475
  115    0.9063   -0.4226   -2.1445
  120    0.8660   -0.5000   -1.7321
  125    0.8192   -0.5736   -1.4281
  130    0.7660   -0.6428   -1.1918
  135    0.7071   -0.7071   -1.0000
  140    0.6428   -0.7660   -0.8391
  145    0.5736   -0.8192   -0.7002
  150    0.5000   -0.8660   -0.5774
  155    0.4226   -0.9063   -0.4663
  160    0.3420   -0.9397   -0.3640
  165    0.2588   -0.9659   -0.2679
  170    0.1736   -0.9848   -0.1763
  175    0.0872   -0.9962   -0.0875
  180    0.0000   -1.0000    0.0000
```

5

Verify the operation of the program.

These calculations are straightforward. However, remember that the tangent funtion is undefined for an angle of 90°. The IF...THEN...ELSE... statement prevents this calculation from being done. The expected result of actually trying to calculate tan(90°) is that your program will crash.

It should be noted that the DO... loop values *limit1*, *limit2*, and *step* do not actually have to be integers. In principle, they can be real numbers.

In practice, however, this is not a good idea because computed limits are subject to numerical limitations, including roundoff errors. As a result, you can never be certain that a DO... loop with a REAL loop counter will terminate properly. In P-6.5, the loop counter is used to generate integer values between 0 and 180. Then the statement angle=REAL(i)*deg_to_rad converts these values to angles expressed in radians. Even if the values 0.0, 5.0, 10.0, and so forth, could be used directly in the loop calculations, the loop counter itself should still be an INTEGER variable and the required values should be obtained by using the REAL function.

If you study P-6.5 carefully, you will notice that, as discussed above, the initialization and incrementing of the loop counter i are, in fact, done "automatically" by the loop structure. That is, it is necessary neither to initialize i to zero before the loop starts nor to increment i by writing something like i=i+5 inside the loop. Beginning programmers often write code that looks like this:

```
i=0
DO i=...
```

There's nothing wrong with this code, but it indicates that the programmer doesn't understand how DO... loops work. The statement i=0 has no effect in the program because i is initialized to the specified lower limit when the loop starts.

Values of the loop counter can be used inside the loop, as they are in P-6.5, but they don't *have* to be used for anything except to control the execution of the loop. You should *never* reassign loop counters inside the loop. Suppose, for example, you write code that looks like this, because you've forgotten that loop counters are automatically incremented in loops:

```
i=0
DO i=1,10
  i=i+1
  other statements
END DO
```

The statement i=i+1, or any other similar incrementing or decrementing assignment, is *not* allowed, and your compiler should generate an error message. To put it another way,

> **The loop counter variable should never appear on the left side of an assignment operator inside the loop.**

What do you suppose the value of a loop counter is after the loop is completed? This code

```
DO i=1,10
  PRINT *,i
END DO
PRINT *,i
```

will print the values

```
1
2
3
4
5
6
7
8
9
10
11
```

The fact that i equals 11 when the loop is terminated indicates that the loop counter is incremented before it is tested against the second limit value, that is, that a DO... loop is a form of pre-test loop. You may be tempted to rely on the loop counter value having a value one "step size" greater than the value that terminates the loop, but it is very poor programming practice to make this assumption.

It is proper programming practice to treat the value of a loop counter as undefined anywhere except inside its loop.

In the above example, if you wished to save the last value of the loop counter in order to get a value of 11, you should use this code:

```
last=10
DO i=1,last
  print *,i
END DO
last=last+1
```

The programs in this text will *never* use the value of a loop counter anywhere except inside the loop. However, it's perfectly OK to reuse a loop counter in another loop, or even to reuse the loop counter variable for an entirely different purpose, even though the latter practice can be confusing and therefore isn't very good programming style. Beginning programmers often define a different loop counter for every loop in their program even though this isn't usually necessary and results in the declaration of unnecessary variables.

6.4.2 Pre- and Post-Test Conditional Loop Constructs

Recalling the discussions in Section 6.1, we know that it is not always possible to determine ahead of time how many times the statements inside a loop must be executed. This situation occurs, for example, in certain kinds of mathematical problems requiring iterative solutions in which a calculation is repeated until a specified accuracy goal is met. In such situations, conditional rather than count-controlled loops must be used. There are two kinds of conditional loops, pre-test and post-test.

Pre-test loops

Here is a typical problem that can use a pre-test conditional loop.

1 Define the problem.

For $x^2<1$, the arctangent function $\tan^{-1}(x)$ may be calculated in terms of the following infinite series:

$$\tan^{-1}(x) = x - \frac{1}{3}x^3 + \frac{1}{5}x^5 - \frac{1}{7}x^7 + \dots$$

Design an algorithm that will use this series to approximate $\tan^{-1}(x)$ for a specified value of x, using all terms greater than or equal to some specified small value.

2 Outline a solution.

1. Supply the value of x and a lower limit on the size of the last term included in the series. (The latter value can be specified as a constant within the algorithm rather than as user input.)
2. Initially, let $\tan^{-1}(x)$=x, term=x, and denominator=1.
3. Inside a loop, increment the denominator by 2, set the power for x equal to the denominator, and change the sign on "term."
4. Increment the value of $\tan^{-1}(x)$.
5. Repeat steps 3 and 4 as long as the current value of "term" is greater than or equal to the specified lower value.

3 *Design an algorithm.*

DEFINE *(arctan, term, denominator as real numbers;*
    sign as +1 or -1, error_limit as real)
WRITE *("Give value of x, x^2<1.")*
ASSIGN *error_limit = ? (choose a reasonable small value)*
READ *(x)*
INITIALIZE *arctan = x*
    term = x
    denominator = 1
ASSIGN *sign = 1*
LOOP *(as long as term ≥ error_limit)*
    INCREMENT *denominator = denominator + 2*
    ASSIGN *sign = -sign*
        term = sign•$x^{denominator}$/denominator
    INCREMENT *arctan = arctan + term*
END LOOP
WRITE *(arctan)*

4 *Convert the algorithm into a program.*

In Fortran, a pre-test conditional execution loop is implemented with a DO WHILE... loop. This loop evaluates a relational/logical expression *before* executing statements inside the loop. That is, the statement block is executed if and only if the relational/logical expression being evaluated is true. The general syntax of the DO WHILE... construct is

```
[name:] DO WHILE (relational/logical expression)
        statement block
        END DO [name]
```

As usual, the *name* label option will not be used in this text. Program P-6.6 implements the algorithm for calculting the arctangent.

P-6.6 [ARCTAN.F90]

```
      PROGRAM tan_1
!
! File name ARCTAN.F90.
! Uses conditional loop to estimate tan^1(x) from its series
! expansion.
!
      IMPLICIT NONE
      REAL x,term,arctan,sign
      INTEGER denominator
      REAL,PARAMETER :: error_limit=1e-7
!
      PRINT *,' Give x, where x^2<1'
      READ *,x
!
      arctan=x
      term=x
      denominator=1
      sign=1
      PRINT *,' Intermediate values...'
      DO WHILE (ABS(term)>error_limit)
        sign=-sign
        denominator=denominator+2
        term=sign*x**denominator/REAL(denominator)
        arctan=arctan+term
        PRINT *,denominator,term,arctan
      END DO
      PRINT *,' Estimated = ',arctan,' Intrinsic = ',ATAN(x)
!
      END
```

Running P-6.6

```
 Give x, x^2<1
 .35
 Intermediate values...
 3   -1.4291666E-02   0.3357083
 5    1.0504375E-03   0.3367588
 7   -9.1913273E-05   0.3366669
 9    8.7572917E-06   0.3366756
 11  -8.7771946E-07   0.3366747
 13   9.0978993E-08   0.3366748
 Estimated =      0.3366748  Intrinsic =      0.3366748
```

Algorithms that require conditional execution loops can, in principle, be implemented using either pre- or post-test loops even though one or the other often seems more logical. In an exercise at the end of this chapter, you will be asked to modify P-6.6 to use a post-test loop instead of a pre-test loop.

5 *Verify the operation of the program.*

When this algorithm is implemented in Fortran, the results can be compared with the intrinsic ATAN function.

Post-test loops

With a post-test loop, the terminating condition is tested at the end of a loop rather than at the beginning. This is sometimes the most natural way to implement a particular algorithm. Here is a typical problem.

1 *Define the problem.*

An adhesive needs to be cured in an oven by raising its temperature gradually from room temperature to 150°C. Write a program that will request the user to specify proposed temperature increases. For each proposed increase, the program must check to make sure that the oven temperature never exceeds 150°C. Terminate the program when the temperature has been raised to 150°C.

2 *Outline a solution.*

1. Assume that room temperature is 20°C. Let the user supply the desired final oven temperature rather than "hard-coding" this value.

2. Design a post-test loop that asks the user for a proposed temperature increase and checks whether it is allowed. Provide "feedback" to the user after each temperature increase by displaying the difference between the current temperature and the final temperature.

3. Keep count of the number of increases and print a summary report after the loop terminates.

4. Assume that temperatures and increases are always given as whole numbers so integer variables can be used.

3 *Design an algorithm.*

DEFINE *(All integers: room_temperature, final_temperature,*
               proposed_increase, current temperature, counter)
ASSIGN *room_temperature = 20*
        current_temperature = room_temperature
WRITE *(Give final oven temperature.)*
READ *(final_temperature)*
INITIALIZE *counter = 0*

LOOP *(until final temperature is reached)*
   INCREMENT *counter = counter + 1*
   WRITE *(Give proposed temperature increase.)*
   READ *(proposed_increase)*
   IF *(current_temperature + proposed_increase) > final_temperature* **THEN**
      WRITE *(This increase is too large!)*
   ELSE
      INCREMENT *current_temperature =*
                           current_temperature + proposed_increase
      WRITE *("This is how far you have to go:",*
                  final_temperature – current_temperature)
   (end IF...)
END LOOP
WRITE *("It took",counter,"increases to reach the final oven temperature.")*

4 *Convert the algorithm into a program.*

In Fortran, there is no special syntax for post-test loops, but they can still be implemented by using a DO WHILE... loop and the EXIT keyword. The structure of such a loop looks like this:

```
DO
   <statement block>
   IF (terminating condition is true) EXIT
END DO
```

When the terminating condition is true, the EXIT command transfers program control to the first executable statement after the END DO. Otherwise, the loop continues to execute.

Program P-6.7 gives one possible implementation of the algorithm in Step 3, using a post-test loop.

5 *Verify the operation of the program.*

Because of the printout that displays the current temperature and the number of degrees remaining between the current and final temperatures, you can check the operation of the program just by trying various combinations of proposed temperature increases. The sample output includes a proposed temperature increase that is too large.

P-6.7 [CURE.F90]

```
      PROGRAM Cure
!
! Control temperature increases in a curing oven.
!
      INTEGER final_temperature,proposed_increase
      INTEGER current_temperature
      INTEGER, PARAMETER :: room_temperature=20
      INTEGER counter
!
      PRINT *,' Give final oven temperature...'
      READ *,final_temperature
      counter=0
      current_temperature=room_temperature
      DO
        counter=counter+1
        PRINT *,' Give proposed temperature increase...'
        READ *,proposed_increase
        IF ((current_temperature + proposed_increase) > &
                                   final_temperature) THEN
          PRINT *,'This increase is too large!'
        ELSE
          current_temperature = &
                   current_temperature + proposed_increase
          PRINT *, 'This is how far you have to go: ', &
                   final_temperature - current_temperature
        END IF
        IF (current_temperature >= final_temperature) EXIT
      END DO
      PRINT *, 'It took ',counter, &
        ' increases to reach the final oven temperature.'
!
      END
```

Running P-6.7

```
  Give final oven temperature...
150
  Current temperature is:  20
  Give proposed temperature increase...
30
  Current temperature is:  50
  This is how far you have to go:  100
  Give proposed temperature increase...
75
  Current temperature is:  125
  This is how far you have to go:  25
  Give proposed temperature increase...
30
  This increase is too large!
  Give proposed temperature increase...
25
  Current temperature is:  150
  This is how far you have to go:  0
  It took  4  increases to reach the final oven temperature.
```

Problem Discussion

Note that P-6.7 uses all integer variables even though we have previously suggested that REAL variables are usually a better choice for physical quantities. In this case, integers are OK as long as we are willing to restrict temperatures to whole numbers. Using integers will make it easier to write a simple loop terminating condition. (Recall that comparisons of REAL numbers for equality can cause problems.)

6.4.3 Nested Loops

As mentioned in the discussion of the application in Section 2.4.2 (generating oscillating frequencies for an LC circuit), loop structures can be nested. We will write a Fortran program to solve that problem as an application in Section 6.6.2 of this chapter. As a preliminary exercise, consider this output:

```
1
1234
2
1234
3
1234
4
1234
5
1234
```

Program P-6.8 gives the Fortran code for generating this output:

P-6.8 [LOOP.F90]

```
    PROGRAM loop
!
    IMPLICIT NONE
    INTEGER i,j
!
    DO i=1,5
      WRITE(*,'(1x,i1)')i
      WRITE(*,'(1x)',advance='no')
      DO j=1,4
        WRITE(*,'(i1)',advance='no')j
      END DO
      WRITE(*,*)
    END DO
    END
```

Note the use of WRITE statements with the advance='no' option to control the placement of the output generated by the inner loop.

6.4.4 Loop Design Considerations

From the point of view of programming style and code readability, it's important to follow a consistent plan for indenting code inside loops. In P-6.8, each DO... statement lines up with its corresponding END DO statement and the statement block for each loop is indented.

It is more than a matter of style to make sure that loop counter variables in nested DO... loops don't overlap. In P-6.8, for example, it would be a serious logical error, as well as a syntax error, to try to use the same loop counter variable for both loops. As a matter of algorithm design, it can't possibly be (or shouldn't be!) what you really intended. As a matter of syntax, the inner loop would redefine the outer loop counter inside the loop, which isn't allowed.

In P-6.8, the output demonstrates that the loop on the counter j is executed completely for each "trip" through the loop on i. This a logical way for nested loops to work; in fact, it's hard to think of any other way that would make sense. However, this logic works only if the range of an interior loop is contained entirely within the statement block of its exterior loop. Loops can be nested several layers "deep." Although there may be some implementation-specific maximum allowed number of layers, it is unlikely that this restriction will ever cause problems in practice.

Conditional execution loops can be nested just as DO... loops can, and the different kinds of loops can even be intermixed without syntax restrictions.

There are two potential pitfalls to avoid. First, make sure that counter variables, whether as part of a count-controlled loop or incremented inside conditional execution loops, are distinct. Second, make sure that interior loops are contained entirely within exterior loops. The presence of overlapping, as opposed to properly nested, loop structures is certainly a design error, and in most cases will generate a syntax error. Finally, it should be obvious, as a matter of algorithm design, that your Fortran source code shouldn't try to enter any kind of loop except at the beginning. In fact, this is not allowed as a matter of syntax for the DO . . . and DO WHILE . . . loops.

Fortran's support of an EXIT command raises the question whether it's a good idea to exit a loop anywhere except at the end. As a matter of syntax, an EXIT command can appear anywhere in a loop. However, as a matter of style, we will restrict the use of EXIT to situations where it appears *only* at the end of a post-test loop construct.

With respect to "infinite loops," note that count-controlled (DO . . .) loops can never execute indefinitely, but that any conditional execution loop is potentially infinite if its terminating conditions are never met. There are no syntax prohibitions against writing conditional loops that will never terminate. This is an algorithm design problem the solution of which is left completely to you when you write programs!

Although you may be tempted to believe these design considerations are just irksome Fortran implementation details, they are almost always algorithm design details that should be worked out before the first line of Fortran code is written.

6.5 Using Implied DO . . . Loops in Output Statements

The DO . . . loop is a comprehensive count-controlled repetition construct. However, Fortran also provides an extremely useful "shortcut" way of implementing a count-controlled loop within an output statement. Suppose you are creating a table and need to provide numerical values as column headers, similar to this:

```
value:    2    4    6    8   10   12   14   16   18   20
```

Consider the code fragment in P-6.9. First this heading is produced with a DO . . . loop, using the advance='no' option in a WRITE statement. There is certainly nothing wrong with this approach, but it seems an unwieldy way to produce a very simple result. An alternative is given in the WRITE and PRINT statements printed in bold italics, each of which produces with a single statement the same line of output as the original loop structure. In both cases, printing the values for value is controlled by an implied DO . . . loop matched with an appropriate format description. (The FORMAT statement could also be referenced with a line label instead of being given as a string constant.)

P-6.9 (fragment)

```
      INTEGER label
!
      WRITE(*,"(' value: ')",advance='no')
      DO label=2,20,2
        WRITE(*,"(i4)",advance='no')label
      END DO
      WRITE(*,*)
!
! Using implied DO... loops...
      WRITE(*,"(' value: ',10i4)")(label,label=2,20,2)
      PRINT "(' value: ',10i4)",(label,label=2,20,2)
```

The general syntax possibilities for implied DO... loops include

```
PRINT *,loop
PRINT fffff,loop
WRITE(*,*)loop
WRITE(*,fffff)loop

where loop is
  (variable_name,variable_name=lower,upper,step)
or
  (array_name(index),index=lower,upper,step)
and fffff is
  format label or format description in the form of
  a string constant
```

In P-6.9, the value printed in the implied DO... loop is the value of the implied loop counter itself. However, any appropriate value or expression can be printed here. For example, implied DO... loops are especially useful for displaying the contents of arrays, which we will discuss in Chapter 8. Implied DO... loops can also be used in input statements, as we will discuss in Chapter 9.

6.6 Applications

6.6.1 Refraction of Light

1 Define the problem.

Refer to Section 4.3.1 for a discussion of Snell's Law, which gives the angle of a refracted ray of light as a function of the angle of the incident ray with respect to a perpendicular to the plane that forms the interface between two materials with different refractive indices:

$$n_i \sin(i) = n_r \sin(r)$$

Table 4.3 in that section gives angles of refraction for a ray of light passing from air into three different materials over a range of incident angles ranging from 0° to 90°. Write a program that duplicates the calculations in that table.

2 Outline a solution.

1. Specify the refractive index for each of the three materials in Table 4.2; they can be "hard-coded" within the program.
2. Use a count-controlled loop to generate the incident angles. Within the loop, calculate refracted angles for an air-material interface with the three materials.

3 Design an algorithm.

DEFINE *(incident_angle, water_angle, glass_angle, diamond_angle, as real numbers; pi and DegToRad (conversion from angles to radians) as real numbers; water_index, glass_index, diamond_index, air_index as real numbers)*
ASSIGN *DegToRad = pi/180*
  water_index = 1.33
  glass_index = 1.50
  diamond_index = 2.42
  air_index = 1.00
WRITE *(headings)*

LOOP *(incident_angle = 0 to 90, steps of 10)*
      ASSIGN *incident_angle = incident_angle•DegToRad*
         water_angle =
            $sin^{-1}[(air\_index/water\_index)•sin(incident\_angle)]$
         glass_angle =
            $sin^{-1}[(air\_index/glass\_index)•sin(incident\_angle)]$
         diamond_angle =
            $sin^{-1}[(air\_index/diamond\_index)•sin(incident\_angle)]$
   (Display angles in degrees.)
      WRITE *(incident_angle,water_index/DegToRad,*
              glass_index/DegToRad, diamond_index/DegToRad)
END LOOP

4

Convert the algorithm into a program.

P-6.10 [REFRACT3.F90]

```
      PROGRAM refract3
!
! Creates table of refracted angles for light ray in air incident
! on water, glass, and diamond.
      IMPLICIT NONE
      REAL air_index,water_index,glass_index,diamond_index
      REAL water_angle,glass_angle,diamond_angle
      REAL angle,DegToRad
      REAL ni,nr,incident,Refract ! for statement function
      INTEGER i
      PARAMETER (air_index=1.00,water_index=1.33,glass_index=2.50)
      PARAMETER (diamond_index=2.42)
! Function to calculate refracted angle...
      Refract(ni,nr,incident)=ASIN(ni/nr*SIN(incident))
!
      DegToRad=4.0*ATAN(1.0)/180.0
      WRITE(*,*)'          Refracted angle........'
      WRITE(*,*)' inc.    water    glass   diamond'
      WRITE(*,1001)water_index,glass_index,diamond_index
      WRITE(*,*)'-------------------------------'
      DO i=0,90,10
        angle=REAL(i)*DegToRad
        water_angle=Refract(air_index,water_index,angle)/DegToRad
        glass_angle=Refract(air_index,glass_index,angle)/DegToRad
        diamond_angle= &
          Refract(air_index,diamond_index,angle)/DegToRad
        WRITE(*,1000)i,water_angle,glass_angle,diamond_angle
      END DO
!
1000  FORMAT(1x,i5,3f9.2)
1001  FORMAT(1x,'angle',3(3x,'(',f4.2,')'))
      END
```

Running P-6.10

```
          Refracted angle.......
  incident water     glass   diamond
  angle    (1.33)   (2.50)   (2.42)
  ----------------------------------
      0      0.00     0.00     0.00
     10      7.50     3.98     4.11
     20     14.90     7.86     8.12
     30     22.08    11.54    11.92
     40     28.90    14.90    15.40
     50     35.17    17.84    18.45
     60     40.63    20.27    20.97
     70     44.95    22.08    22.85
     80     47.77    23.20    24.01
     90     48.75    23.58    24.41
```

Problem Discussion

In P-6.10, separate PARAMETER statements have been used to specify the several values of refractive index. They could also be given in assignment statements or, with minor modification of the program, obtained as user input from the keyboard. In this program, π isn't needed except to calculate the variable DegToRad, so it's never declared or defined separately. Be sure you understand how and why the INTEGER loop counter is used inside the loop to generate the angle needed for the calculations. It would be OK to use the mixed-mode expression angle=i*DegToRad instead of angle=REAL(i)*DegToRad, but the latter code makes the required type conversion perfectly clear.

5 Verify the operation of the program.

Verify the tabulated values with a hand calculator in addition to comparing your results with Table 4.2. Textbooks can make mistakes, too!

6.6.2 Oscillating Frequency of an LC Circuit

This problem statement and its solution developed in pseudocode have been given in Section 2.4.2 and will not be repeated here. P-6.11 uses nested DO... loops to generate resonant oscillating frequencies for seven values of inductance (L) and 10 values of capacitance (C) in an LC circuit.

P-6.11 [OSCILLAT.F90]

```
      PROGRAM Oscillat
!
! Generates resonant frequency table for LC circuit.
!
      IMPLICIT NONE
      REAL inductance      ! Henrys
      INTEGER capacitance  ! pico Farads
      REAL f               ! frequency, kHz
      INTEGER row          ! loop index
      INTEGER u
      REAL, PARAMETER :: pi=3.1415927
!
      u=6
!     OPEN(u,file='oscillat.out')
      WRITE (u,"('Frequency, kHz')")
      WRITE (u,"('         C (pF)')")
      WRITE (u,"('   L (H)',10i5)")(capacitance,capacitance=2,20,2)
      WRITE (u,"('----------------------------------------&
         &---------------')")

      DO row=1,7
        inductance=(row+1)*.0005
        WRITE (u,'(f7.4)',ADVANCE='NO') inductance
        DO capacitance=2,20,2
! NOTE: Express frequency in kHz by dividing by 1000.
!       Convert pico Farads to Farads by multiplying by 10^-12.
        f=1./(2.*pi*SQRT(inductance*REAL(capacitance)*1e-12))/1000.
          WRITE (u,'(i5)',ADVANCE='NO') NINT(f)
        END DO
        WRITE (u,'()') ! line feed
      END DO
!     CLOSE(u)
!
      END
```

Running P-6.11

```
Frequency, kHz
       C (pF)
   L (H)    2    4    6    8   10   12   14   16   18   20
   -----------------------------------------------------------
  0.0010 3559 2516 2055 1779 1592 1453 1345 1258  186 1125
  0.0015 2906 2055 1678 1453 1299 1186 1098 1027  969  919
  0.0020 2516 1779 1453 1258 1125 1027  951  890  839  796
  0.0025 2251 1592 1299 1125 1007  919  851  796  750  712
  0.0030 2055 1453 1186 1027  919  839  777  726  685  650
  0.0035 1902 1345 1098  951  851  777  719  673  634  602
  0.0040 1779 1258 1027  890  796  726  673  629  593  563
```

Problem Discussion

The output from P-6.11 is sent to the default output device. This is why the OPEN and CLOSE statements have been changed to comment lines. To send the output to the data file OSCILLAT.OUT, "uncomment" the OPEN and CLOSE statements by removing the ! character. It would be a good idea to change the unit number assignment to a value other than the preconnected value of 6, but it's not required.

The advance='no' option (either uppercase or lowercase is OK) is required to control the position of "carriage returns" when you're writing the results. Remember that PRINT and WRITE statements automatically move to the start of a new line and only WRITE offers the possibility of preventing this action.

P-6.11 contains a typical use of an implied DO... loop to generate column headings. (See the line printed in bold italics.)

6.6.3 Calculating Radiation Exposures for a Materials Testing Experiment

1 Define the problem.

This problem is similar to the heat curing problem discussed in Section 6.4. The new feature is the use of a random number generator to select radiation doses instead of having these values provided by user input.

In a test of the effects of radiation on materials, an experiment protocol requires that:

(1) a sample be subjected to several bursts of radiation of random intensity, each of which must not exceed some specified maximum value;
(2) the sum of the intensities must never exceed a specified limit for total exposure.

Write a program to simulate this experiment by generating a sequence of random exposure levels that satisfy this protocol.

2 Outline a solution.

1. Ask the user to supply the maximum intensity for a single exposure and the limit on total cumulative exposure; the former must be less than the latter.
2. Initialize the cumulative exposure to 0 and generate a random exposure value; call this value the "current value."
3. Construct a loop that allows the execution of statements inside the loop only if the cumulative exposure plus the current value doesn't exceed the allowed total cumulative exposure.

4. Inside the loop, add the current value to the cumulative exposure. Print the current and cumulative exposures. Generate a new current exposure value.
5. Outside the loop, after it terminates, print the current exposure value along with a message indicating that this exposure would have exceeded the allowed maximum.

3 Design an algorithm.

It would be a good idea to try to design your own algorithm before studying this one. Think carefully about how to satisfy the demands of the problem statement. For this problem, the flowchart shown in Figure 6.4 might be helpful.

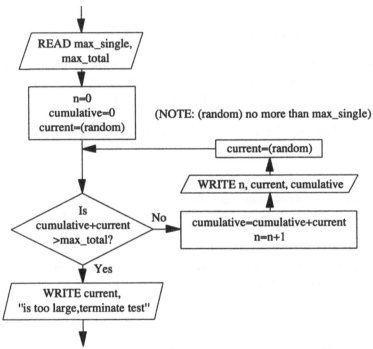

Figure 6.4. Flowchart for radiation exposure problem

DEFINE (max_single, max_total, current_exposure,
            cum_exposure as real numbers;
            number of exposures (n) as integer)
WRITE ("What are the maximum single intensity and maximum
            total exposure?")
READ (max_single, max_total)
INITIALIZE n = 0
            cum_exposure = 0
(Select an initial exposure.)
ASSIGN current_exposure = random value, no more than max_single
LOOP (while cum_exposure + current_exposure doesn't exceed max_total)
        INCREMENT cum_exposure = cum_exposure + current_exposure
                    n = n + 1
        WRITE (n, current_exposure, cum_exposure)
        (Get a new exposure to try.)
        ASSIGN current_exposure = random value, ≤ max_single
END LOOP
WRITE (current exposure, "is too big")

4

Convert the algorithm into a program.

P-6.12 [EXPOSE.F90]

```
      PROGRAM Expose
!
! Generate a random radiation exposure history for a sample
! so that the total exposure doesn't exceed a specified maximum.
!
      IMPLICIT NONE
      REAL current_exposure !the proposed current exposure
      REAL max_single        !maximum single exposure
      REAL cum_exposure      !cumulative exposure
      REAL max_total         !maximum allowed total exposure
      INTEGER n_exposures    !number of exposures
      REAL x                 !0<=x<1
      INTEGER Count(1)       !current value of system clock
!
      PRINT *,' What is the total allowed exposure?'
      READ *,max_total
      PRINT *, &
        ' What is the largest allowed single exposure (< total)?'
      READ *,max_single
!
      CALL System_Clock(Count(1))
      CALL Random_Seed(Put=Count)
      CALL Random_Number(x)
      current_exposure=max_single*x
      cum_exposure=0.0
      n_exposures=0
```

```
!
      DO WHILE ((cum_exposure+current_exposure)<=max_total)
         n_exposures=n_exposures+1
         cum_exposure=cum_exposure+current_exposure
         PRINT 1000,x,n_exposures,current_exposure,cum_exposure
! Get a new exposure value to try...
         CALL Random_Number(x)
         current_exposure=Max_single*x
      END DO
      PRINT 1001,current_exposure
!
1000  FORMAT(f10.5,i3,2f8.1)
1001  FORMAT(' The next proposed exposure of ',f5.1, &
              ' is too large.'/' Terminate the experiment.')
!
      END
```

Running P-6.12

```
   What is the total allowed exposure (0-1000)?
1000
   What is the largest allowed single exposure (0-500)?
500
   max single and max total are     5.0000000E+02    1.0000000E+03
   0.27609  1    138.0    138.0
   0.31017  2    155.1    293.1
   0.98066  3    490.3    783.5
   0.01780  4      8.9    792.4
   0.22745  5    113.7    906.1
   The next proposed exposure of 411.6 is too large.
   Terminate the experiment.
```

5 *Verify the operation of the program.*

The goal of your program testing must be to ensure that the specified maximum limit is never exceeded. The simplest way to do this is to observe the operation of the program several times. However, it is also worth temporarily replacing the random levels generated in the program with user-supplied levels. That way you can test specific combinations of levels. What happens if the first proposed intensity is greater than the maximum allowed intensity? What happens if the cumulative exposure exactly equals the total allowed exposure? These are questions that are difficult to answer when each exposure is chosen randomly, but easy if you can select the exposures yourself.

Problem Discussion

There are several features of P-6.12 that are worth studying. First, each variable is declared on a separate line, with a comment about its purpose. This is good programming style whenever there could be confusion about the purpose of some variables. No physical units have been specified in the problem statement or program. From the point of view of writing the code for this simulation, the units don't matter as long as they are consistent.

Second, this program requires a sequence of random numbers. Computers can't generate truly random numbers, but Fortran, and other high-level languages, include a

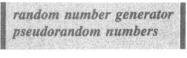

random number generator pseudorandom numbers

software-based *random number generator* that can be used to produce sequences of *pseudorandom numbers* that appear to be random. The statements required to generate random numbers are printed in bold italics in P-6.12.

For now, don't worry about the syntax of the CALL statements; they access built-in subprograms that you can use whenever a program needs a sequence of random numbers. (We will discuss the CALL statement in Chapter 7.) Briefly, the CALL System_Clock(Count(1)) statement obtains an integer value from your computer's internal (system) clock. The INTEGER Count(1) declaration is required for this CALL statement. The statement

```
CALL Random_Seed(Put=Count)
```

uses the integer retrieved from the system clock to "seed" a random number generator. Because the value obtained from the system clock is essentially a random number, this "seed" generates a different sequence of random numbers every time the program runs.

The CALL Random_Number(x) generates a random REAL value x uniformly distributed on the range [0,1). (Remember that this notation means that x may be exactly 0, but it will never be exactly 1.[4]) The value of x is then used to calculate an exposure that will always be less than the maximum single exposure; this is OK because the problem definition states only that the maximum value of a single exposure is limited by a specified maximum intensity, without stating specifically how the limit should be imposed. In this case, the code will generate values arbitrarily close to a specified limit.

---

[4]The reason for this is obscure; however, it is sometimes helpful to know that a value of exactly 1 will never be generated.

6.6.4 Maximum Deflection of a Beam with Various Support/Loading Systems

The pseudocode for this problem, using the **CHOOSE** command, has been discussed in Section 6.1.2, so only Steps 4 and 5 of the problem-solving process will be discussed here. Recall that the **CHOOSE** pseudocode command is implemented in Fortran with the SELECT CASE... construct.

4 Convert the algorithm into a program.

P-6.13 [BEAM2.F90]

```
      PROGRAM Beam2
!
! Calculates beam deflection for four different
! support/loading systems.
!
      IMPLICIT NONE
      REAL elasticity         !lb/in^2
      REAL moment_of_inertia  !in^4
      REAL length             !ft
      REAL load               !lb
      REAL deflection         !in
      INTEGER systemID  !1 - supported at each end, concentrated load
                        !2 - supported at each end, distributed load
                        !3 - supported one end, concentrated at free end
                        !4 - supported one end, distributed
      CHARACTER YesNo
!
! (begin post-test loop)
10    PRINT *, &
          ' Give elasticity (lb/in^2) and moment of inertia (in^4).'
      READ *,elasticity, moment_of_inertia
      PRINT *,' Give the beam length in ft.'
      READ *,length
      PRINT *,' Choose one of these support/loading systems: '
      PRINT *,' 1 - supported at each end, concentrated load'
      PRINT *, &
          ' 2 - supported at each end, uniformly distributed load'
      PRINT *, &
          ' 3 - supported at one end, concentrated load at free end'
      PRINT *,' 4 - supported at one end, distributed load'
      READ *,systemID
      SELECT CASE (systemID)
        CASE (1,3)
          PRINT *,' Give the concentrated force.'
        CASE (2,4)
          PRINT *,' Give the distributed weight.'
        CASE DEFAULT
          STOP 'Program termination due to input error.'
      END SELECT
      READ *,load
!
      length=length*12.0
```

```
         SELECT CASE (systemID)
         CASE (1)
           deflection= &
             -load*length**3/(48.0*elasticity*moment_of_inertia)
         CASE (2)
           deflection=&
             -5.0*load*length**3/(384.0*elasticity*moment_of_inertia)
         CASE (3)
           deflection= &
             -load*length**3/(3.0*elasticity*moment_of_inertia)
         CASE(4)
           deflection= &
             -load*length**3/(8.0*elasticity*moment_of_inertia)
         END SELECT
!
         PRINT 1000,deflection
         PRINT *,'More? (y/n)'
         READ *,YesNo
       IF (YesNo=='y') GO TO 10
! (end post-test loop)
!
1000   FORMAT(1x,es10.3)
       END
```

Running P-6.13

```
 Give elasticity (lb/in^2) and moment of inertia (in^4).
30e6 797
 Give the beam length in ft.
20
 Choose one of these support/loading systems:
 1 - supported at each end, concentrated load
 2 - supported at each end, uniformly distributed load
 3 - supported at one end, concentrated load at free end
 4 - supported at one end, distributed load
3
 Give the concentrated force.
10000
-1.927E+00
 More? (y/n)
n
```

5 *Verify the operation of the program.*

Refer to Figure 3.4 in Chapter 3, which shows the maximum deflection of a beam supported at both ends as a function of load when the load is concentrated in the center. For additional verification, you will have to look elsewhere!

Problem Discussion

P-6.13 contains several interesting features. The input section, which consisted of one **WRITE** and one **PRINT** command in the pseudocode, has been expanded to provide better control over input. It includes a SELECT CASE construct that prompts the user to supply either a concentrated force or a distributed weight, depending on which support and loading system is chosen. All the program's executable statements are included in a post-test loop so you can calculate the deflection for many different conditions without having to re-execute the program; the loop continuation test (IF (YesNo=='y') GO TO 10) looks at the value of a character entered by the user in response to a prompt. You might wish to make this test a little more foolproof by modifying the IF... statement to read

```
IF ((YesNo=='y') .OR. (YesNo=='Y')) GO TO 10
```

to allow for either an uppercase or a lowercase y.[5]

Finally, note the use of the STOP statement in the first SELECT CASE construct. This is the first time this statement has been used in a program in this text. It terminates the program and prints an appropriate message if the user enters an inappropriate value for systemID. This prevents the program from trying to execute the next SELECT CASE construct with an inappropriate value of systemID. It is possible to rewrite the program so that the prompt for systemID is repeated, using another post-test loop, until the user provides an appropriate value in the range 1–4, but it doesn't seem worth the trouble in this case.

6.7 Debugging Your Programs

6.7.1 Programming Style

In well-written programs, control structures need to be carefully planned to make sure that all problem requirements are considered. In selection constructs, it is important to make sure that all possible branches, even "abnormal" ones, are accounted for. If you know which branch of an IF... statement is most likely, it is a good idea for this branch to appear first. IF... statements should never test REAL variables directly for equality. Choices in a SELECT CASE statement should be arranged in a logical order.

Your choice of loop constructs should reflect what you know about the calculations that must be done. If you know, or your program can calculate, how

---

[5]Remember that even though Fortran is case-insensitive in its interpretation of source code, the character constant 'y' is not the same as 'Y'.

many times the statements inside a loop will be executed, always use a count-controlled loop to reflect that knowledge. Conditional loops should always be written in a way that makes the terminating condition(s) as clear and simple as possible.

In DO... loops, you should not use REAL loop control variables. Calculations that need to be done only once should never be done repetitively inside a loop even if the answers are unaffected.

6.7.2 Logical Problems

Potential problems with selection and repetition structures often are related to algorithm design rather than language syntax. These problems can be difficult to isolate because it is not easy to guarantee that you have tested all possible conditions under which IF... and SELECT CASE statements may fail to operate, or under which DO..., DO WHILE... loops may not terminate properly (or at all). Nonetheless, here are some suggestions.

1. For the kinds of programs discussed in this chapter, a reasonable execution time is no more than a few seconds. If a program doesn't terminate within a few seconds, it is almost certainly due to the program being trapped inside a conditional loop for which the terminating condition is never met. Check your algorithm, and if you're convinced that the logic is OK, make sure that your program actually implements this logic. If a loop doesn't include a PRINT or WRITE statement, put one there temporarily so you will see some output displayed for each "trip" through the loop.

2. When you test a program containing an IF... or SELECT CASE statement, make sure that you try it with input that will force it to execute the code associated with every possible branch or CASE selector. It may be helpful to include temporary PRINT statements inside each branch to let you know when statements in that branch are being executed.

3. A common logical error is to use a conditional loop when a count-controlled loop would have sufficed. Count-controlled loops are easier to write and less prone to logical errors, so you should use them whenever you can.

4. Make sure that IF... statements don't have overlapping conditions. Here's an example:

```
IF (A>=0) THEN
  ...
ELSE IF (A=0) THEN
```

```
ELSE
 . . .
END IF
```

The condition `A=0` overlaps the condition `A>=0`. Fortran won't detect this as a syntax error, but it can't possibly be logically correct.

6.7.3 Syntax and Execution Problems

1. Syntax problems with `IF...` statements sometimes lead to error messages that aren't very helpful because your Fortran compiler is trying unsuccessfully to understand what you are asking it to do. One common error is to forget to include the `END IF` statement at the end of an `IF...` statement. It may be helpful to "label" each `END IF` statement with an inline comment to indicate which `IF...` statement it is terminating. Consistent use of indented statements will make debugging easier. Each `END IF` statement should begin in the same column as its corresponding `IF...` statement.

2. A common error with the `SELECT CASE` statement is to forget the `END SELECT` statement. Again, consistent use of indenting will make these statements easier to understand and debug.

3. Remember that you're not allowed to reassign loop counter variables inside a `DO` loop. This means that nested loops must each use a different name for their counter variables.

4. If a program containing a `SELECT CASE` statement sometimes works and sometimes "crashes," it may mean that the `CASE` expression has a value not included in the list of `CASE` selectors. You should determine which value is causing the problem and either include it in the list of `CASE` selectors or include a `CASE DEFAULT` statement.

6.8 Exercises

6.8.1 Self-Testing Exercises

Exercise 1. Describe in your own words the two most important concepts you have learned from this chapter.

Exercise 2. Describe in your own words how you could use in your own programs a problem-solving skill demonstrated in a program described in this chapter.

Exercise 3. How does the statement

```
IF ((.NOT. raining) .AND. (temperature>85.0)) THEN...
```

differ from the statement

```
IF ((.NOT. raining) .OR. (temperature>85.0)) THEN...
```

6.8.2 Basic Programming Exercises

Exercise 4. Create a flowchart for the beam deflection example in Section 6.1.2.

Exercise 5. Create a flowchart for P-6.7.

Exercise 6. Include code fragment P-6.1(a) in a complete program that asks the user to supply a number and then calculates and displays the square root of that number if it's non-negative and prints an appropriate message if it's not.

Exercise 7. Modify program P-6.13 so that it tests the deflection against some specified maximum and prints an informative message if the maximum deflection appears to be unreasonably large. You will have to decide what "unreasonably large" means; is a 12-inch deflection unreasonably large for a 20-foot beam?
    Hint: you could express the maximum reasonable deflection as a percentage of the length of the beam.

Exercise 8. Modify Program P-6.6 so that it uses a post-test loop syntax as described in Section 6.4.2.

Exercise 9. Write pseudocode for a loop to print the values 1–20 in steps of 0.5. That is, the loop should print

```
1.0
1.5
2.0
```
(and so forth)

Implement the pseudocode first as a DO... loop, then as a DO WHILE... loop, and finally as a post-test loop using a GO TO statement at the end. Do *not* use a REAL variable for the counter in the DO... loop.

Exercise 10. A wage tax is collected according to the following rule: the tax is 7 percent on income less than or equal to $50,000 and 3 percent on income in excess of $50,000. Write a program that will calculate the tax for a user-supplied income. (See Section 2.1.3 for a brief discussion of this problem.)

Exercise 11. Refer to Exercise 19 in Chapter 3. Modify that program so that it will display seconds and fractions of a day when the input time is given in am and pm time. Take into account the fact that 12:00 am should be interpreted as 0h0m0s and 12:00 pm as 12h0m0s.

Exercise 12. Based on material from other courses you are taking, state a computational problem and write a complete program to solve it. Make sure the problem requires the use of either a conditional or a count-controlled loop or a SELECT CASE construct.

6.8.3 Programming Applications

Exercise 13. The quadratic equation $ax^2 + bx + c = 0$ has roots $\dfrac{-b \pm \sqrt{b^2 - 4ac}}{2a}$

The expression $b^2 - 4ac$ is called the discriminant. If it is positive, there are two real roots—one calculated using the + sign and the other using the − sign. If the discriminant is zero, there is one real root. If the discriminant is negative, there are no real roots. Write a program to find the real roots, if any, for specified values of a, b, and c. Your program's output should include an informative message concerning the number of real roots it found. [QUADRAT1.F90]

Exercise 14. Electric utility rates in the Philadelphia area are among the highest in the country. In 1994, charges for residential customers who use electric resistance heating or an electric heat pump were calculated as follows:

Service Charge:	$5.08
Energy Charge	
Winter:	$0.1345/kWh for first 600 kWh
	$0.0679/kWh for additional kWh
Summer:	$0.1345/kWh for first 500 kWh
	$0.1530/kWh for additional kWh

The service charge is always added to each month's bill. The energy charge is different in the summer and the winter. Summer months are defined as June through September. The rest are winter months. Write a program that asks the user for the month and number of kWh (kilowatt hours) used during that month and then calculates her monthly basic charges.

Hints: use a `SELECT CASE` construct to control calculation of charges for winter and summer months. Use a `CHARACTER*9` specification for a variable to hold the month because September, the longest month name, contains nine letters.) [`PECO.F90`]

Exercise 15. A tray is formed from a sheet of metal by cutting the same size square from each corner and bending up the sides. Given the length and width of the original sheet, what is the size of the square cut that gives a tray with maximum volume? Write a program that will provide an approximate answer to this question by assuming a user-specified size for the sheet and then calculating the volume based on a series of cut sizes in increments of 0.1". Ignore the fact that because the sheet has a finite thickness, bending it results in a small loss in the height of the sides. [`TRAY_VOL.F90`]

Extra Credit
If you have had an introductory course in differential calculus, you should be able to determine the exact answer for this problem. Compare it with the result from your program.

> An understanding of elementary calculus is required.

Exercise 16. (a) The population of a certain animal is 1,000,000 at the beginning of the year. During each year, 6 percent of the animals alive at the beginning of the year die. The number of animals born during the year that survive to the end of the year is equal to 1 percent of the population at the beginning of the year. Write a program that prints out the births, deaths, and total population at the end of each year and stops when the population falls to 10 percent or less of the original population.

Hint: populations can have only integer values.

(b) Assuming that the death rate stays the same as in part (a), what birth rate is required for the population to double in 20 years? Starting with the original population of 1,000,000, print the births, deaths, and total population at the end of each year for 20 years, using the newly calculated birth rate. The population after 20 years will be twice the original population when $2=(1+r)^{20}$, where r is the overall population growth rate—birth rate minus death rate.

You may include both parts of the problem in a single program. [`POPULATN.F90`]

Exercise 17. The average temperature of the earth/atmosphere system as viewed from space depends on the solar constant S_o, which is about 1368 W/m², and the earth's albedo (reflectivity). Assuming the earth acts like a "blackbody" (i.e., it radiates 100 percent of the radiation that strikes it), the temperature is related to the solar constant by

$$S_o(1 - \alpha)/4 = \sigma T^4$$

where σ is the Stefan-Boltzmann constant, 5.67×10^{-8} W/(m$^2 \cdot$K^4), and α is the earth's albedo, about 0.30. (Albedo is a dimensionless measure of the fraction of incoming solar energy reflected by the earth/atmosphere system.)

Write a program that calculates the temperature as a function of changes in the solar constant over the range ±10 percent. Note that the temperature of the earth/atmosphere system as viewed from space is *not* the same as the average surface temperature of the earth, which is about 33°C warmer because of the well-known "greenhouse" effect of the Earth's atmosphere. [EARTHATM.F90]

Exercise 18. The resistivity ρ of tungsten wire is roughly 100×10^{-6} ohm-cm at the operating temperature of a lightbulb filament. Suppose a lightbulb consumes 100 W of power on a 110-volt circuit. The power can be expressed in terms of the voltage V and resistance R of the filament as

$$\text{Power} = V^2/R = V^2/(\rho L/A)$$

where L is the length of the filament in cm and A is the cross-sectional area in cm^2.

Write a program that generates a table of *reasonable* lengths and diameters that will give the required resistance. It is up to you to decide what "reasonable" means. [TUNGSTEN.F90]

Exercise 19. The wavelengths of the Balmer series of lines in the hydrogen spectrum are given by

$$\lambda = \frac{3646 \cdot n^2}{n^2 - 4}$$

where n is an integer having values greater than 2. Write a program that generates the first 10 wavelengths in the Balmer series. [BALMER.F90]

Exercise 20. One of the concerns about global warming is that the average sea level may rise. Suppose you are a civil engineer who has been asked to estimate the loss of land along a coastline. Write a program that relates a sealevel rise of R cm to loss of land, given in units of km^2/km and acres/mile along a coastline with a specified range of grades. A grade of 0.1 percent–10 percent with respect to the sea, in increments of 0.1°, is reasonable.

If the coastline makes an angle θ with the sea, the distance lost from the original coastline, measured along the sloping ground, is R/sin(θ). The grade is defined as $100 \cdot \tan(\theta)$ percent. Suppose the sea level rises 10 cm (about 4 inches). A 1° slope (about 1.75 percent grade) means that the coastline will recede about

5.7 m, with a loss of about 0.0057 km^2 per kilometer of coastline, or about 2.3 acres per mile of coastline. (There are 1609.3 m/mile and 640 acres/mile^2.) [SEA_LEVL.F90]

Exercise 21. Simulation studies in science, mathematics, and engineering often require random numbers from a so-called "normal distribution." Such numbers have a mean of 0 and a standard deviation of 1. (The standard deviation is a measure of the "spread" of values in a distribution.) Fortran includes a random number generator (recall the application from Section 6.6.3), but it generates *uniformly* distributed numbers in the range [0,1) rather than normally distributed numbers.

Fortunately, there is a simple way to generate a pair of normally distributed numbers x_1 and x_2 from a pair of uniformly distributed numbers u_1 and u_2:

$$x_1 = \sqrt{-2\ln(u_1)}\cos(2\pi u_2)$$
$$x_2 = \sqrt{-2\ln(u_1)}\sin(2\pi u_2)$$

Write a program that uses this formula to generate a sample of 200 normally distributed numbers. You can check the numbers to see if they actually appear to be normally distributed by calculating their mean and standard deviation:

$$m = \Sigma x/n$$
$$s^2 = \frac{\Sigma x^2 - (\Sigma x)^2/n}{n-1}$$

Accumulate the sums of x and x^2 inside the loop and use the sums to calculate the mean and standard deviation when the loop is complete. The mean and standard deviation, or the average of the means and standard deviations from several sets of numbers, will be "close" to 0 and 1, but they won't be exactly 0 and 1. There are quantitative statistical tests for a normal distribution, but they are beyond the scope of this problem. **Hint:** remember that a DO... loop from 1 to 100 generates 200 random numbers, not 100.

The formulas given above for generating normally distributed numbers require uniform numbers in the range (0,1] because ln(0) is undefined. Fortran's random number generator produces numbers in the range [0,1). The upper limit can be arbitrarily close to 1, so that end of the range is of no concern. However, it's possible that a value of exactly 0 might be generated. Your program should protect against this possibility, even though it is unlikely, by testing u_1 and replacing it with a very small number if its generated value is exactly 0. [NORMAL.F90]

Exercise 22. One way to estimate the square root of a number is to use Newton's algorithm. Given a number n, guess its square root. For the purposes of the algorithm, the value of the initial guess is relatively unimportant; guess=n/2 is a reasonable choice. Then calculate a new estimate by calculating a new guess:

$$guess = (guess + n/guess)/2$$

Continue to make new estimates until the absolute value of the difference between n and the guess multiplied by itself differs from the original number by less than some specified small amount. [NEWTON.F90]

Exercise 23. The Internal Revenue Service acknowledges that the value of equipment used in manufacturing and other businesses declines as that equipment ages. Therefore, businesses can gain a tax advantage by depreciating the value of new equipment over an assumed useful lifetime of n years. At the end of n years, the equipment may have either no value or some small "salvage" value. Depreciation can be computed in three ways:

1. Straight-line depreciation. The value of an asset minus its salvage value depreciates by the same amount over its useful life of n years.
2. Double-declining depreciation. Each year, the original value of an asset minus previously declared depreciation (its "book value") is diminished by 2/n.
3. Sum-of-digits depreciation. Add the integers from 1 through n. The depreciation on the original value of an asset minus its salvage value allowed in year i is $(n - i) + 1$ divided by the sum of the digits.

Write a program that calculates the depreciation available for years 1 through n. Assume that the salvage value is some small percentage (perhaps a value in the range 5 percent–10 percent) of the original value. Here is a depreciation table for an asset originally valued at $1000 with a useful lifetime of 7 years and an assumed salvage value of $100.

```
        Original value   $1000
        Salvage value    $ 100
        Lifetime             7 years
```

Year	Straight line	Asset value	Double-declining	Asset value	Sum-of-digits	Asset value
1	128.57	871.43	285.71	714.29	225.00	775.00
2	128.57	742.86	204.08	510.20	192.86	582.14
3	128.57	614.29	145.77	364.43	160.71	421.43
4	128.57	485.71	104.12	260.31	128.57	292.86
5	128.57	357.14	74.37	185.93	96.43	196.43
6	128.57	228.57	53.12	132.81	64.29	132.14
7	128.57	100.00	37.95	94.86	32.14	100.00

Note that the double-declining method doesn't depend at all on the salvage value. This means that not all the depreciation in the seventh year could actually be taken if the asset really has a salvage value of $100 at the end of seven years. [DEPRECIA.F90]

Extra Credit

Businesses often like to maximize depreciation when equipment is new in order to maximize their tax advantage. Which method should they choose? If businesses can change the method by which they calculate depreciation at any time during the life of an asset, when, if ever, should they change methods? (The answer to this questions depends on the salvage value of the asset.)

Exercise 24. In orbital mechanics, the angular position of an orbiting object is calculated as a function of time. For a circular orbit, the calculation is simple because the position is directly proportional to time. For noncircular orbits, the calculation is more complicated.

First, some definitions. The time required for an orbiting object to complete one revolution is called its period. The mean anomaly is the angular position that an object would have in its orbit if it were in a circular orbit with the same period. Mean anomaly is directly proportional to time.

The eccentric anomaly E_c is related to the mean anomaly M through the transcendental equation

$$M = E_c - e \sin(E_c)$$

where both angular quantities must be expressed in radians rather than degrees and the eccentricity e is a measure of the shape of the orbit. The range of e is $0-1$, with circular orbits having an eccentricity of 0. The true anomaly θ is related to the eccentric anomaly through the algebraic equation

$$\cos(\theta) = \frac{\cos(E_c) - e}{1 + e \cos(E_c)}$$

Therefore, true anomaly can be related to mean anomaly, and hence to time, through the eccentric anomaly. The geometry is illustrated in Figure 6.5.

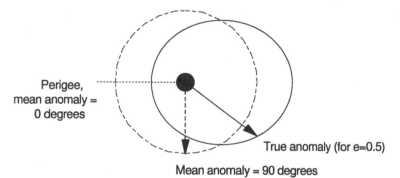

Figure 6.5. Geometry of noncircular orbits

The equation involving M (Kepler's equation) can't be solved directly for eccentric anomaly, but it can be solved iteratively:

1. As a first guess, assume $E_c = M$.
2. Replace E_c with a new value: E_c: $E_c = M + e \cdot \sin(E_c)$.
3. Calculate a new M using the new value of E_c: $M_{new} = E_c - e \cdot \sin(E_c)$.
4. Repeat steps 2 and 3 until the absolute magnitude of M minus M_{new} is less than some specified small value (10^{-5} is a reasonable choice).

Write a program that calculates true anomaly as a function of mean anomaly for values of mean anomaly in the range 0°–360°, in steps of 5°, for these values of eccentricity: 0.1, 0.25, 0.50, 0.75, and 0.90.

Hints
1. Remember that all angular calculations must be done in radians and converted to degrees if you like only when the values are displayed as output.
2. Arithmetic errors can occur when the mean anomaly is 180° because the argument of the arccosine function must never exceed 1. As the eccentric anomaly approaches 180°, the calculation for $\cos(\theta)$ might produce a value slightly greater than 1. Account for this possibility by testing the value of $\cos(\theta)$ before you take its arccosine. Also, the arccosine function doesn't produce values in the range 0–2π or 0°–360°. Use the values of mean anomaly to make sure your program produces answers in the appropriate range. [KEPLER2.F90]

Exercise 25. A satellite flies over a cloudless desert. The satellite contains an instrument that measures the longwave radiance emitted in the direction of the instrument from a particular spot on the desert's surface. The instrument records the radiance L as a function of zenith angle θ relative to the spot on the surface. A series of such measurements leads to an empirical model of the radiance as a function of zenith angle and the radiance L_0 that would be measured from a satellite passing directly over the site:

$$L = L_0 \sec(\theta)^x, \quad \theta \leq 60°$$
$$L = L_0 \sec(\theta)^x - a[\sec(\theta) - \sec(60°)], \quad \theta > 60°$$

The secant of the zenith angle is proportional to the amount of atmosphere between the satellite and the ground (the atmospheric "path length"). The model reflects the fact that a satellite view of a site on the surface undergoes "limb darkening" because the satellite must look through more atmosphere as the zenith angle increases. At large zenith angles, an additional term is required to account for the rapidly decreasing transparency of the atmosphere to longwave radiation.

Table 6.5 gives empirical model parameters for three desert surfaces derived from measurements taken in January. This is winter in the northern hemisphere, which explains why the value of L_o is higher for Australian deserts than it is for the two northern hemisphere deserts; because the satellite measures longwave radiance, a larger radiance means that the surface is warmer. Figure 6.6 shows predicted radiances for these surfaces.

Table 6.5. Model parameters for longwave radiance from deserts

Desert Location	Overhead Radiance, W/m²/ster	x	a
Australia	110	-0.2116	3.184
Sahara	85	-0.0998	1.854
Saudi Arabia	90	-0.0974	1.241

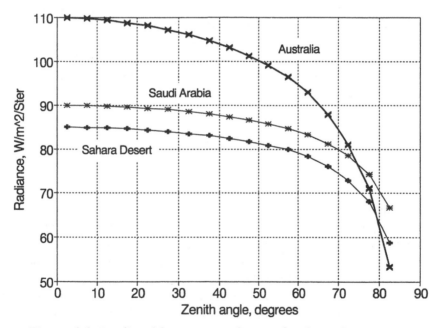

Figure 6.6. Predicted longwave radiances for three desert sites.

Write a program that will calculate predicted values of radiance as a function of satellite zenith angle for the three sets of model parameters given in Table 6.5. What happens as the zenith angle approaches 90°? What can you conclude about the validity of the model as the satellite approaches the horizon? What might you conclude about the fact that as the zenith angle increases, the differences in radiances observed from different surfaces tend to decrease? [LIMBDARK.F90]

Exercise 26. A rectangular container with specified length, width (as viewed from the side), and depth contains a liquid (molten metal, for example). The container is rotated about an axis parallel to the depth dimension at a constant angular rate, and the contents of the container spill into a mold. Write a program that will calculate the total volume of liquid that pours into the mold as a function of container angle. Also, calculate an approximation to the "instantaneous" rate at which liquid pours from the container.

Hints: rotate the container in equal angular increments and calculate the resulting volume that has been emptied from the container. Subtract the volume at the previous angular value and divide by the angle increment. If the angle changes at a constant rate with respect to time, this calculation gives an approximation of the changing volume rate with respect to time.

Divide the calculations into two parts. The first part calculates the angles from the beginning of the rotation to the time when the liquid level reaches the bottom corner of the container. The second calculates the angles for this point to 90°, at which time the container is empty. The angle at which this transition occurs is given by

$$\tan(\theta) = \text{height/width}$$

[POURING.F90]

Extra credit

1. Suppose you need to pour liquid at a constant rate. Modify your program to calculate how the angle must change with respect to some arbitrary time unit. One way to visualize this problem "discretely" rather than continuously is to imagine that the molten metal is used to fill 100 identical molds; that is, each mold uses 1 percent of the liquid. How much should the angle increase to fill each mold? Clearly, the change in angle required to fill each mold is *not* constant.

2. Suppose the container is cylindrically shaped rather than rectangular. The equations for emptying the first half of the container are easy because the volume at any angle is just half a cylinder with height equal to the intersection of the liquid with the side. However,

> A good understanding of integral calculus is required.

after the liquid reaches the upper bottom corner of the container, the volume becomes a conic section, and this volume is harder to calculate.

Exercise 27. A simple model of population growth assumes that a new population p' is linearly related to the current population p; that is, p' = rp. Such a population will increase or decrease monotonically, depending on the value of r. Biologists have long recognized that populations are usually bounded in some way. For example, as an animal population reproduces and grows, limited food resources may constrain its growth. Conversely, when a population shrinks, those same limited food resources may be able to support a population that starts to grow again.

Here is a simple equation that models this "bounded" behavior:

$$p' = rp(1 - p)$$

where, for simplicity, the population has a normalized value in the range [0,1]. Clearly, this model has the desired properties of bounding p'. As p grows, 1 − p shrinks, and vice versa. Suppose r = 2. Here are the first few values derived from iterating this equation from an initial value of p = 0.2:

```
cycle  p          p'
       1   0.20       0.32000
       2   .32        .43520
       3   .4352      .49160
       4   .4916      .49986
       5   .49986     .50000
```

One remarkable property of this function is that for r = 2, the population stabilizes at a value of 0.5 for any value of initial population p in the range (0,1)—that is, for any value between, but not including, 0 and 1.

For many years, however, some interesting properties of this disarmingly simple equation went unnoticed. Suppose r = 3.2. Iterate on the equation, starting with p = 0.5:

```
cycle  p          p'
       1   0.50000    0.80000
       2   .80000     .51200
       3   .51200     .79954
  ...
      12   .79946     .51304
      13   .51304     .79946
      14   .79946     .51304
      15   .51304     .79946
```

Now the population no longer stabilizes at a single value. Instead it cycles back and forth between two values.

For r = 3.5, the population cycles among four different values. For a slightly higher value, it cycles among eight values. For r just in excess of 3.57, the population oscillates randomly. At even larger values of r, other cycles emerge, only to disappear into randomness as r continues to increase. The discovery that an apparently simple dynamic system could produce this odd kind of "random" behavior gave birth to what is now known as chaos theory and, some would say, has had as profound an effect on our view of the natural world in the second half of the 20th century as relativity theory had in the first half.

Fortunately, it is easy to investigate the behavior of this remarkable equation. Write a program that requests a value for r between 0 and 4 and for p between 0 and 1 and then performs multiple iterations. What happens if r is greater than 4?

Hint: there is no simple way to terminate the iteration if it is implemented as a conditional loop because there is, in general, no way to predict future values of the population. [POPCHAOS.F90]

Program Modularization

This chapter describes how to design modularized Fortran programs. It begins with a discussion of algorithms that use the **CALL** and **SUBPROGRAM** commands from the pseudocode language of Chapter 2. It then shows how to implement these algorithms using Fortran subroutine and function subprograms.

7.1 Designing Modularized Algorithms with the **CALL** and **SUBPROGRAM** Pseudocode Commands

Modularized programs are an integral part of structured programming and problem solving. The basic idea is simple: it is easier to solve difficult problems when they are divided into smaller and potentially more manageable parts. As a valuable byproduct, solutions you develop for one problem can often be reused in similar problems. This is especially important for programming in science and engineering, where algorithms designed to solve complex computational problems often represent enormous investments of time and expertise; it would be very wasteful to have to "reinvent" such solutions for each new application.

Some authors and instructors would have preferred a discussion of program modularization earlier in this text. In a computer science course based on C or Pascal, for example, program modularization is often introduced even before discussing some basic language syntax. However, this text has taken the approach that program modularization can be postponed until your programs are worth modularizing. There is little practical reason to modularize programs that perform only one task, and the programming overhead required isn't worth the effort. The programs you have written so far fall into this category. On the other hand, many of the calculations those programs perform could later become part of more complex programming tasks. We will illustrate this point by rewriting some previous programs with subprograms that can be incorporated into larger programs.

The **CALL** and **SUBPROGRAM** pseudcode commands introduced in Chapter 2 define, in a generic way, a framework within which to design modularized programs. They imply that procedural programming languages will encourage the division of a large problem into several smaller parts. The purpose of using **CALL** and **SUBPROGRAM** in your algorithms is to encourage you to think carefully about how to define the tasks your program must perform and how information will flow among those tasks.

When you design a subprogram, you can think of it as a "black box."[1] One or more inputs go in one end of the box, and one or more outputs come out the other end. The box processes the input in a prescribed way, and it is not necessary for you to understand the details of the box's contents. This model is illustrated in Figure 7.1. When you write an entire program yourself, including the subprograms, presumably you understand everything that happens inside the subprograms. However, it's not always necessary for the user of a subprogram to understand the details of what happens inside. It's only necessary for the user to understand the requirements for the input and how to interpret the output. That is, the user must understand the information interfaces.

Beginning programmers often concentrate first on the *contents* of subprograms. However, your first task should always be to concentrate on the "ends" of the subprogram; that is, to design an information interface for the subprogram. Begin by asking yourself these questions:

1. Do I understand what the subprogram is supposed to do?
2. What information is required for the subprogram to complete its assigned task?
3. What information will be returned as output from the subprogram?

You cannot answer the second and third questions until you know the answer to the first question. Even if you do not know precisely how the calculations in the subprogram will be done, you must at least understand the nature of the task. Once you have answered the first question, you can decide how information should flow into and out of the subprogram. Only when you have answered all these questions should you concern yourself with details of the calculations that are performed inside each subprogram.

The place to ask these questions is in Step 2 of the problem-solving process. You can start to answer them when you write **DEFINE** commands into

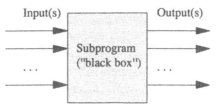

*Figure 7.1. "Black box" model of a
subprogram*

---

[1]The "black box" analogy comes from electronics, where a device to process a signal may literally be constructed inside a black box.

demonstrate this process, consider again P-3.1 from Chapter 3. The very simple problem was: *given a radius, calculate the area and circumference of a circle.* The user is prompted to provide a radius, and the program calculates and displays the circumference and area of a circle with this radius. In pseudocode, an algorithm to modularize this calculation could be written like this:

(main program)
DEFINE *(radius, area, and circumference as real numbers)*
WRITE *(prompt user to provide radius of a circle)*
READ *(radius)*
CALL *CircleStuff(IN: radius; OUT: area,circumference)*
WRITE *(area and circumference)*

The **CALL** *CircleStuff* command implies that there is a subprogram that, given a value for the radius as its input, will calculate the area and circumference as its output. The **CALL** command defines an information interface between your algorithm and the subprogram. It specifies which values are input to the subprogram and which are output. The list of values in the **CALL** command is called the argument list or sometimes the actual parameter list. (The argument list was introduced in Chapter 4's discussion of intrinsic functions.)

When you write a program based on this algorithm, you will provide specific values in the **CALL** to the subprogram. Some of the input information may be in the form of variables, and some may be in the form of constants. When you design the **SUBPROGRAM**, you should further define the information interface by

(1) selecting an appropriate data type for each piece of information entering or leaving the subprogram, and
(2) designating each piece of information as input to or output from the subprogram.

The resulting list is called the formal parameter list, or just the parameter list (as opposed to the argument list).[2] This parameter list and its description should contain all the information a potential user needs to know to use the subprogram. For the circle problem, the subprogram's parameter list could look like this:

SUBPROGRAM *CircleStuff(IN: radius, a real number;*
                       OUT: area and circumference, real numbers)

---

[2]This text will always use the terminology "argument list" and "parameter list."

In this example, the parameter list tells the user of this subprogram that three arguments are required and that they must all be either real numbers or variables associated with real numbers. The first argument should be the radius of a circle—the input. The second and third arguments will contain the output from the subprogram—the area and circumference.

As a matter of style, it often makes sense to describe the input first and then the output. However, the order doesn't make any difference, especially at this initial design state. In fact, parameters can appear in any convenient order in algorithms and, as you will see later in this chapter, in programs.

The names in this parameter list—*radius*, *area*, and *circumference*—are the same as those used in the **CALL** statement, but it's important to understand that they don't have to be. For example, this version of the **SUBPROGRAM** parameter list definition is perfectly OK even though the variable names are less descriptive:

SUBPROGRAM *CircleStuff(IN: r, a real number;*
OUT: a and c, real numbers)

Essentially, the names in a subprogram's parameter list are "place holders" for the actual values or variables that will be associated with them in an argument list when a program uses the subprogram.

In some cases, information in a subprogram's parameter list needs to be treated as both input and output. That is, a parameter associated with a variable having a certain value when the subprogram is **CALL**ed may be modified in the subprogram so that, when the subprogram is complete, the value of the argument associated with that parameter will be changed. You may indicate such a parameter by specifying it as *IN/OUT*, or some similar terminology, in the subprogram's parameter list.

This text will be consistent about writing pseudocode **CALL** commands and **SUBPROGRAM** definitions in the format shown here (with varying degrees of detail), but don't worry about trying to duplicate every nuance in your own algorithms. Unlike a real programming language, pseudocode imposes no rigid syntax rules and restrictions! The important point to remember is that the **CALL** command and the **SUBPROGRAM** definition are organizational aids that should clearly define the data type and intended use of each quantity needed as input or produced as output. As you gain more programming experience, you may not need to define this list at the algorithm design stage in as much detail as you should now.

Now that the information interface has been established in pseudocode for the new version of P-3.1, you can think about the contents of the subprogram. In this case, the required definitions and calculations are simple:

DEFINE (*π, a real constant*)
ASSIGN area = *π•radius²*
        circumference = *2π•radius*
(end of subprogram)

Within the code of the subprogram, the names must match the names in the parameter list. In this case, the names *radius, area,* and *circumference* indicate that these names, and not *r, a,* and *c ,* for example, are used in the parameter list. Although there isn't any pseudocode "syntax rule" that requires the names to be the same, this is just a common sense rule that you would be foolish to ignore. When you translate the algorithm into Fortran, this name association will be enforced through use of the IMPLICIT NONE statement.

Not surprisingly, all the pieces from the design of P-3.1 are still present in its redesign, but they are rearranged. The significant difference is that the calculations of area and circumference are performed inside a subprogram rather than in the main program. Information required for this calculation, the radius, flows into the subprogram and the answers, area and circumference, flow back out, as indicated by the *IN:* and *OUT:* specifiers in the subprogram's parameter list.

You might have noticed that the value of π isn't included in the parameter list. This is because π is needed only for the calculations performed in the subprogram. In that sense, it's neither "input" nor "output," but a constant value that is needed only locally within the subprogram. In some other situation, you might choose to define π in the main program and make its value available to one or more subprograms. In general, subprograms will contain a mixture of values passed through the parameter list and locally defined variables and constants.

Because of the simplicity of the pseudocode **CALL** command, it's easy to underestimate both the power of subprograms and the problems that can arise when you are careless about their design and use. For example, consider these two uses of the *CircleStuff* subprogram:

CALL *CircleStuff(3,area,circumference)*
CALL *CircleStuff(radius,10,circumference)*

The first use of *CircleStuff* is OK because the first item in the **SUBPROGRAM** *CircleStuff* parameter list is specified as input in the algorithm design. In this case, the calling program is providing a number, rather than a variable name, that the subprogram will then use in its calculations.

The second use of *CircleStuff* is inappropriate. Why? Because the second item in **SUBPROGRAM** *CircleStuff*'s parameter list is designated as output. This means that the subprogram will calculate a value and then expect to associate this value with a variable name from the calling program that will hold the calculated value. Instead the *10* in the second use of *CircleStuff* looks like input *to* the subprogram; this does not make sense for this algorithm. Even after we describe details of how subprograms are implemented in Fortran and the problems that can arise when argument lists contain inappropriate quantities, it will be important to remember that using appropriate choices for values and variables in argument lists is fundamentally a matter of proper algorithm design, not just a language implementation detail.

Before converting this modified algorithm into a new version of P-3.1, let's take a more general look at how information flows to and from subprograms. Figure 7.2 illustrates two examples of how programming languages *might* treat variables within a single source code file consisting of a main program and one or more subprograms.

In Figure 7.2(a), all variables are ***global variables***. As indicated by the "leaky" boxes surrounding the main program and subprograms, this means that all variables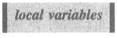
defined anywhere in the source code file, whether in the main program or in one of the subprograms, are available to the main program and any of the other subprograms contained in the source code file. There is no need for a subprogram to have a parameter list because, since all calculations are "global," there is no need to think about "input" and "output." This is the model used in early versions of BASIC, for example.

In Figure 7.2(b), the other extreme, ***local variables*** are available only to the main program or subprogram in which they are defined. Information is exchanged between
the main program and the subprograms, and among subprograms only along specific "paths." These paths can operate in one direction, as "input" or "output," or in both directions. This is close to the model used by Fortran.

At first, you might think that the arrangement of Figure 7.2(a) is simple and efficient because you can simply define variables anywhere you like and have them available everywhere else in your program. However, this defeats the purpose of program modularization. At the algorithm design level, each subprogram should be a self-contained solution to a particular part of a larger problem, with well-defined lines of communication with other parts of the program. This separation of tasks is nullified when the names of variables and the results of calculations in a subprogram are available globally to the rest of the program.

At the programming level, a lack of local variables means that you have to be careful never to duplicate variable names in the various parts of your program. This might not seem like much of a problem when your programs are small, but eventually you will make a mistake. When you do, the results can range from catastrophic to unnoticeable; the latter result is by far the more dangerous, as your program may appear to work properly even though it may sometimes, or always, produce incorrect answers.

(source code file)

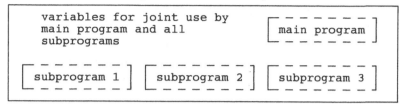

(a) All variables are global

(source code file)

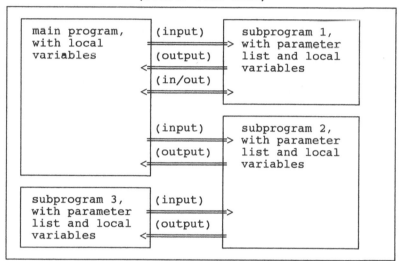

(b) All variables are local

Figure 7.2. Two models for controlling information flow between a program and one or more subprograms

Because of these potential problems, modern programming languages favor isolated subprograms with local variables and calculations and restricted communications with other parts of the program. Fortran has always provided strong support for this concept, and as we shall see, Fortran 90 provides new ways to define very specific interfaces between a program and its subprograms. In Fortran, subprograms can be implemented in two basic ways. We will discuss both implementations in considerable detail in this chapter.

If you still need to convince yourself of the importance of isolated program modules, imagine you are writing a program to solve a problem that requires a very lengthy and difficult calculation involving mathematical skills you don't yet have. Your instructor has already written a subprogram to perform this calculation and distributes a copy to each student. What is required for you to take advantage of this generous offer? Should you have to worry about the details of the calculations? Should you have to worry about what variable names your instructor used in the subprogram? Should you have to worry about whether variable names in your program will conflict with variable names in the subprogram? "No" is the answer to each of these questions. You should have to know *only* the number, data type, and purpose of each quantity in the parameter list of the subprogram.

A strictly controlled information interface is absolutely essential to the way Fortran is used in practice. Many of the professional uses of Fortran depend on subprogram libraries written by others, and there are many commercially available libraries of Fortran code for solving specific computational problems. Even in applications where programs are written entirely from "scratch," large programs often require the efforts of many individuals. In such circumstances, it should be clear that the potential for confusion in the situation depicted in Figure 7.2(a)—where every variable name is available globally—is unacceptable. Fortunately, Fortran supports the strict separation between program and subprogram units depicted in Figure 7.2(b). In fact, the model of completely global variables in Figure 7.2(a) doesn't even exist in Fortran.[3]

Assuming that this discussion has convinced you of the need for strictly controlled information interfaces between parts of a program, you should be aware that when subprograms are implemented in Fortran, there are ways to share information other than through the parameter list. However, this is an implementation issue and not an algorithm design issue. At the algorithm design level, all information flowing to and from a subprogram can be included in the parameter list.

7.2 Fortran Subroutines

Once the concepts of designing information interfaces with subprograms are clear, it is then possible to discuss the specifics of their implementation. The most important Fortran

subroutine

implementation of a subprogram is the **subroutine**. The keyword SUBROUTINE marks the beginning of a subroutine in the same way that the keyword PROGRAM begins a main program. An important difference is that although the PROGRAM keyword that begins the source code for a main program is optional, the SUBROUTINE keyword is required at the beginning of a block of source code intended to be a subroutine.

---

[3]It's possible to approximate such a model in Fortran, but it's such a bad idea that we won't even discuss it!

The general syntax for a SUBROUTINE **header statement** is

```
SUBROUTINE name [(parameter list)]

Example:
      SUBROUTINE Polar_to_Cartesian(r,theta,x,y)
```

Names for subroutines follow the same rules as Fortran variable names. As a matter of style, names should describe the purpose of the subroutine. Even though the brackets in the syntax definition imply that the parameter list is optional, it is almost always required. Subroutines used in this text will always require a parameter list.

Don't be confused by the similarity between the pseudocode command **SUBPROGRAM** and the Fortran reserved word SUBROUTINE. The former is just a generic way to define modularized calculations. The latter is one specific implementation of the subprogram concept in Fortran.

The general structure of a subroutine is similar to that of a main program:

```
SUBROUTINE name [(parameter list)]
   [specification statements]
   [executable statements]
[RETURN] [label or string constant]
END [SUBROUTINE [name]]
```

When subroutines are used by themselves in programs, only the END statement by itself is needed to terminate the subroutine. In some other circumstances, as we shall see later in this chapter, the last statement *must* contain END SUBROUTINE rather than just END, although the name is still optional.

When a subroutine is completed, it returns control to the (sub)program from which it was called. One or more RETURN statements are optional in a subroutine. Just as the STOP statement can be used to terminate a main program prior to the END statement, the RETURN statement provides an optional means of terminating a subroutine and returning control to the main program. Like the STOP statement, a RETURN statement may appear anywhere after the nonexecutable statements and may include a line label or a string constant that will be printed when the RETURN statement is executed. A RETURN statement may not appear anywhere in a main program.

To access a Fortran subroutine, use a CALL statement. This is a direct implementation of the pseudocode **CALL** command. Its syntax is

```
CALL name [(argument list)]

Example:
      CALL Polar_to_Cartesian(r,theta,x,y)
```

When you use the CALL statement, there must be a SUBROUTINE with the same name somewhere in your source code file.[4] Usually, subroutines follow the main program in the source code, but this isn't a requirement.

It is often the case that subroutines are CALLed in a program only from a main program. However, Fortran doesn't impose this as a restriction; subroutines can CALL other subroutines. That is the reason for the phrase "the calling (sub)program," used often in this chapter to indicate that a subprogram (including a subroutine) can be accessed from any other part of a program.

The number of items in a call to a subroutine must agree in number and data type with the items in the subroutine's parameter list. The quantities in the argument list may be (depending on the circumstances, as discussed below) variable names, constants, or functions. The requirement for matching data types in argument and parameter lists is extremely important and deserves closer examination. Consider code fragment P-7.1.

P-7.1 (fragment)

```
      . . .
      REAL x,y
      INTEGER z
      x=1.5
      y=3.5
      CALL Add(x,y,z)  !Not allowed!
      PRINT *,z
      . . .
!
      SUBROUTINE Add(x,y,z)
      REAL x,y,z
      z=x+y
      END
```

This code is *not* allowed in Fortran 90 because the data type of the variable z is different in the main program (INTEGER) and subroutine (REAL), no doubt due to a programming oversight (in either the main program or the subroutine).[5]

---

[4]Program units can also be "linked" to subroutines in other program units, but we will not address that topic now.

[5]However, this code *is* allowed in earlier versions of Fortran. Fortran 90's ability to trap this kind of programming error is another significant improvement over previous versions.

Suppose you "fix" this code by declaring z as REAL in the main program. The following code, with a different assignment to x, will work because of the integer-to-real type conversion performed in the first assignment statement:

```
x=3
y=3.5
CALL Add(x,y,z)
```

Now consider this "reasonable" call to Add, in which you ask the subroutine to perform a type conversion between the integer value in the argument list and the REAL variable in the parameter list:

```
y=3.5
CALL Add(3,y,z)  !Won't work!
```

This won't work, again because of the disagreement between data types.

We can now complete the conversion of P-3.1, using the pseudocode modifications presented so far in this chapter. Program P-7.2 produces the same output as P-3.1, but it uses a subroutine to calculate the area and circumference of the circle.

P-7.2 [CIRCLSUB.F90]

```
      PROGRAM CircleSub
!
! File name CIRCLSUB.F90.
! Calculate area and circumference of a circle, using
! a subroutine.
      IMPLICIT NONE
      REAL radius,area,circumference
!
      PRINT *,' What is the radius of the circle?'
      READ *,radius
      CALL CircleStuff(radius,area,circumference)
      PRINT 1000,area,circumference
1000  FORMAT(1x,2f10.3)
      END
!
      SUBROUTINE CircleStuff(radius,area,circumference)
!
! Do area and circumference calculations.
!
      IMPLICIT NONE
      REAL radius,area,circumference,pi
      INTENT(IN) radius
      INTENT(OUT) area,circumference
      PARAMETER (pi=3.14159)
!
      area=pi*radius*radius
      circumference=2.0*pi*radius
      END
```

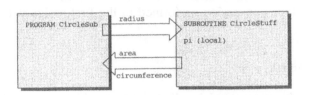
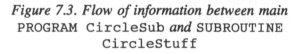

Figure 7.3. Flow of information between main
PROGRAM CircleSub *and* SUBROUTINE
CircleStuff

The flow of information between the main program CircleSub and the subprogram SUBROUTINE CircleStuff is shown in Figure 7.3. The details of SUBROUTINE CircleStuff are important and we will discuss them in detail.

7.2.1 Using Subroutines

The parameter list in SUBROUTINE CircleStuff defines how information flows between the main program and the subroutine. As indicated in Figure 7.3, the radius of a circle is the input to the subroutine, and the area and circumference of the circle are the output. Except for the fact that the programmer needs to be aware of the purpose of the three variables, area, circumference, and radius (the purposes are made clear by the choice of meaningful variable names), the main program is unaware of what happens in the subroutine, and vice versa.

As one consequence of the independence of a subroutine, the data types of parameters—radius, area, and circumference in this case—must be redeclared in the subroutine. This is how Fortran makes sure that there are no inconsistencies between the parameter list and the argument list in the calling (sub)program. You should include the IMPLICIT NONE statement in every subroutine for the same reasons you include it in every main program. The IMPLICIT NONE affects not just locally defined variables, but also all variables in the parameter list. Any variable name appearing in the parameter list, but not in a data declaration statement, will generate a compile-time error.

The names used in the parameter list of a subroutine don't have to be—and, in general, aren't—the same as the names used in the argument list when that subroutine is called. Only the number and data type of parameters and calling arguments must agree. The names in the formal parameter list define the *local* names by which the variables will be known and used inside the subroutine. In

P-7.2, the same names are used in the argument and parameter lists, but only because those names are reasonable and convenient. We could also start the subroutine like this:

```
SUBROUTINE CircleStuff(r,a,c)
```

This is OK, even if the variable names aren't very good choices as a matter of style, as long as we use those names appropriately for calculations within the subroutine.

The important point of this discussion about names is that the programmer doesn't have to worry about matching names between a CALL to a subroutine and the subroutine itself. All the programmer should need to know to use a subroutine is the data types and purposes of the items in the parameter list.

Even though Fortran will not allow you to become confused about the data types of variables, it's certainly possible to be confused about the *meaning* of parameters and arguments. Suppose a programmer accessed CircleStuff like this:

```
CALL CircleStuff(radius,circumference,area)
```

This is perfectly OK from Fortran's point of view, assuming all three variables are declared as REAL numbers, but in the context of P-7.2, this represents a fatal design error because the references to area and circumference are switched. These kinds of errors can be *very* difficult to find in programs, so be careful!

7.2.2 Controlling the Flow of Information

Expressing intent

In the general discussion of subprograms earlier in the chapter, we emphasized the importance of understanding how information flows between a subprogram and a calling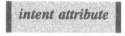
(sub)program. When you design subprograms, you need to know what constitutes "input" and "output," or to put it another way, which way the information flows. In Fortran 90, in contrast with earlier versions of Fortran and some other high-level languages, it's possible to make and enforce distinctions between input to and output from subprograms. This is done by giving variables an *intent attribute* using the INTENT keyword. The general syntax of an INTENT statement is

```
data_ type, INTENT(status) :: list of names from parameter list
  or
INTENT(status) list of names from parameter list

where status may be IN, OUT, or INOUT

Examples:

      REAL, INTENT(IN) :: x,y
      REAL, INTENT(OUT) :: r,theta

      REAL x,y,r,theta
      INTENT(IN) x,y
      INTENT(OUT) r,theta
```

In the first syntax form and the first example, data declarations are given in the same statement as the INTENT attribute. In the second form and the second example, the data declarations and INTENT attributes appear in separate statements. Some Fortran programmers have a strong preference for the first form, but either is OK. In the examples, the first group of two statements is equivalent to the second group of three statements.

Program P-7.2 contains two examples of INTENT statements. In SUBROUTINE CircleStuff, the statements

```
      INTENT(IN) radius
      INTENT(OUT) area,circumference
```

identify radius as "input" to CircleStuff and area and circumference as "output."

What are the implications of assigning the INTENT attribute? In P-7.2, the specification of area and circumference as INTENT(OUT) means that this statement *should* be unacceptable:

```
      CALL CircleStuff(3.0,4.0,5.0)
```

The first argument is OK because it's associated with the input quantity radius. However, constant values for the second and third arguments, associated with area and circumference, don't make sense. Why not? Because the corresponding quantities in SUBROUTINE CircleStuff's parameter list have been given the INTENT(OUT) attribute, which implies that the corresponding items in this argument list must be variables to "receive" the output.

Returning to the first value in the argument list, what is the implication of assigning radius the INTENT(IN) attribute in SUBROUTINE CircleStuff? There are two reasonable possibilities. The first is that changes can be made to radius inside CircleStuff, and those changes will be "invisible" to the calling (sub)program. For this interpretation to work, SUBROUTINE

CircleStuff will make a copy of radius and will make changes only to that copy. Regardless of what changes are made locally (inside the subroutine), the INTENT(IN) attribute protects the value originally assigned to radius in the calling (sub)program, whether it's a constant or a value held in a variable, because the information flow is a "one way street" *into* CircleStuff.

Another possibility is that a subroutine will have access to the original value passed through a parameter list, but the INTENT(IN) will prevent the value from being changed inside the subroutine. Thus in the case of SUBROUTINE CircleStuff, giving radius the INTENT(IN) attribute will prevent the value of radius from being changed inside CircleStuff. This implies that even though the information flow between a subprogram and its calling (sub)program is a "two way street," you may still wish, in some cases, to prevent changed values from flowing back to a calling (sub)program.

Which of these interpretations does Fortran 90 apply to an INTENT(IN) attribute? Even though the meaning of INTENT attributes seems clear from the algorithm design point of view—variables designed as "input" should not be changed in a subprogram and variables designed as "output" are, by definition, subject to change, it is worth thinking about the possibilities. With respect to the INTENT(IN) attribute, consider the code fragment in P-7.3(a):

P-7.3(a) (fragment, see INTENT.F90)

```
(main program)
. . .
      x=3.0
      CALL InTest(x)
      PRINT *,x
      END
!
      SUBROUTINE InTest(x)
      IMPLICIT NONE
      REAL x
      INTENT(IN) x
      x=2.0
      END
```

If Fortran subprograms make a copy of INTENT(IN) parameters, the code in P-7.3(a) should be allowed and x will still have a value of 3 when it is printed in the main program. However, Fortran does *not* apply this interpretation to treating INTENT(IN) parameters.

The alternative, which implies that Fortran subprograms have access to the original memory locations of parameters, is that the code in P-7.3(a) should *not* be allowed because, by specifying the INTENT(IN) attribute, you have asked your program to protect the original value of x. The compiler used to develop the programs in this text does, in fact, prevent reassignment of the value of an INTENT(IN) variable inside SUBROUTINE InTest; it generates a compilation error message. However, an earlier version of this same compiler printed only a *warning* that the INTENT(IN) attribute was being violated; it did not actually prevent the reassignment of x.

This behavior demonstrates that communication between a subprogram and its calling (sub)program *may* be a "two way street" even when the INTENT(IN) attribute is used. Such an interpretation can be confusing if you consider the possibility that violation of an INTENT(IN) attribute might force a compiler to try to "redefine" the value of a *constant* appearing in an argument; it can't do that, of course.[6]

What about violations of the INTENT(OUT) attribute? Consider the code in P-7.3(b).

P-7.3(b) (fragment, see INTENT.F90)

```
      (main program)
      ...
      CALL OutTest(3.0)
      END
!
      SUBROUTINE OutTest(x)
      IMPLICIT NONE
      REAL, INTENT(OUT) :: x
      x=2.0
      END
```

This code shouldn't be allowed because it apparently tries to "redefine" the value of the constant 3.0. However, even though the Fortran 90 standard is clear that arguments associated with INTENT(OUT) parameters *must* be variable names and not constants, it is not *required* that compilers check for such violations. The compiler used to develop the programs in this text executes without errors even though the code asks it to do something—assign an output value to a constant—that makes no sense.

Consequently, referring back to P-7.2, adding the statement CALL CircleStuff(3.0,4.0,5.0) may or may not generate an error. If no error message is generated, your program will continue to run, but you may not have the access to output quantities that you thought you would. This is yet another reason, not that more are needed, to be careful with the design of algorithms *before* they are incorporated into programs. It is always your responsibility to ensure that the tasks you ask a program to perform make sense independent of the implementation details of the programming language.

It's also possible to give quantities in a subroutine's parameter list an INTENT attribute of INOUT. In this case, values associated with variable names

---

[6]This possibility isn't as ridiculous as it seems. In some early versions of Fortran, it was actually possible to *change* the value of a constant, such as the integer value 3, in this way!

can flow in either direction between a subprogram and a calling (sub)program. Constants or function values should not be allowed as arguments in the CALL statement. However, the same compiler-dependent ambiguities exist with respect to enforcing these restrictions.

It's not always required to assign INTENT attributes to subroutine parameters. Any name in a parameter list that's not given an INTENT attribute will have INOUT status by default. The programs in this text will generally be consistent about explicitly assigning INTENT attributes. A final restriction is that only variable names appearing in the parameter list can be given an INTENT attribute; it doesn't make sense, and isn't allowed, to ascribe INTENT to a quantity defined and used only locally within a subprogram. Table 7.1 summarizes the restrictions on arguments appearing in calls to functions and subroutines.

Table 7.1 Restrictions on arguments based on their INTENT attribute

INTENT **Attribute**	**Allowed Argument**
IN	variable, constant, expression, function
OUT	variable
INOUT	variable

Enforcing intent

Considering the importance we have attached to specifying INTENT attributes in your program, you may be surprised to find that responses to intent violations may vary from compiler to compiler. You can protect yourself by following these two program design rules.

> **Intent Rule 1.** *Never* **change the value of an** INTENT(IN) **variable inside a subprogram.**

> **Intent Rule 2.** *Never* **use a constant value or a variable with the** PARAMETER **attribute as an argument to a subprogram in which that variable has** INTENT(OUT)**.**

In addition to following these rules, there are some important modifications you can make to programs containing subprograms that will improve the chances that intent violations will generate appropriate responses. P-7.4 gives another version of P-7.2.

P-7.4 [CIRCLSB2.F90]

```
      MODULE CircleSubs
!
      CONTAINS
!
      SUBROUTINE CircleStuff(radius,area,circumference)
!
! Do area and circumference calculations.
!
      IMPLICIT NONE
      REAL radius,area,circumference,pi
      INTENT(IN) radius
      INTENT(OUT) area,circumference
      PARAMETER (pi=3.14159)
!
      area=pi*radius*radius
      circumference=2.0*pi*radius
!
      END SUBROUTINE CircleStuff
!
      END MODULE
!-----------------------------------------------------
!
      PROGRAM CirclSub2
!
! File name CIRCLSB2.F90.
! Calculate area and circumference of a circle, using
! a subroutine.  Uses MODULE to enforce intent.
!
      USE CircleSubs
      IMPLICIT NONE
      REAL radius,area,circumference
!
      PRINT *,' What is the radius of the circle?'
      READ *,radius
      CALL CircleStuff(radius,area,circumference)
!
      PRINT 1000,area,circumference
!
1000  FORMAT(1x,2f10.3)
      END
```

The code in P-7.4 is nearly identical to the code in P-7.2. There are only two differences:

(1) SUBROUTINE CircleStuff is contained in a MODULE structure named CircleSubs that appears before the main program.

(2) The USE statement (printed in bold italics) gives the main program access to MODULE CircleSubs and, within this module, SUBROUTINE CircleStuff.

MODULEs are a new kind of program structure. A simplified syntax for MODULEs as they are used in P-7.4 is:

```
MODULE module name
  CONTAINS
   <one or more SUBROUTINEs or FUNCTIONs>
END [MODULE [module name]]

Example:
     MODULE SeveralSubs
        CONTAINS
        SUBROUTINE Sub1
         . . .
        END SUBROUTINE Sub1
        SUBROUTINE Sub2
         . . .
        END SUBROUTINE Sub2
!       (more subroutines)
        END MODULE SeveralSubs
```

The CONTAINS keyword appears whenever subprograms are included within a MODULE. The only difference in how subprograms are written when they appear within a MODULE is that the END statement *must* also contain the word SUBROUTINE or FUNCTION, as discussed in the next section. When subprograms appear by themselves, the word SUBROUTINE is optional. The name of the subprogram is still optional.

Because each MODULE has a name, your program can contain more than one MODULE. Unlike subroutines and functions, which can be included in any order along with a main program in a source code file, the source code for MODULE structures must appear *before* the main program. One simple explanation for this difference is that MODULEs can contain data declarations that are needed before the main program can be compiled.[7]

The contents of a MODULE are accessed with the USE statement. A simplified form of its syntax is:

```
USE module_name

Example:
     USE SeveralSubs
```

---

[7]It is unclear whether this restriction is part of the Fortran 90 standard. Therefore, it is possible that some Fortran 90 compilers will not enforce this requirement. It is also possible to access subroutines, functions, and MODULEs stored in other files. This topic will be discussed in Chapter Twelve.

In P-7.4, the subroutine has been "encased" in a module structure and the END statement has been replaced by END SUBROUTINE CircleStuff. The subroutine in the MODULE is accessed by inserting the USE CircleSubs statement before the type declarations statements in P-7.4. (That is, the USE statement must appear directly after the PROGRAM statement.)

The changes in P-7.4 might seem to serve no purpose other than adding yet another layer of programming overhead; after all, the main program had access to SUBROUTINE CircleStuff even before it was included in a MODULE. MODULEs might be pointless in this context *except* for the fact that the use of this structure should force your Fortran compiler to detect and respond appropriately to intent violations. The same compiler that allowed the INTENT(OUT) violation in P-7.3(b) to go unnoticed doesn't allow that same violation when a subprogram is defined in a MODULE and accessed through a USE statement. This additional protection is sufficient reason to use MODULE structures, but they will make even more sense when you learn some of their other uses later in this chapter.

Programming Tip

The source code files available for downloading from the World Wide Web site mentioned in Section i.5 of the Preface include program INTENT.F90, which contains the code fragments in P-7.3(a) and P-7.3(b), and some similar small subroutines contained within a MODULE structure. You should study the code and observe how your compiler responds to intent violations before you try to use INTENT attributes in your programs.

7.2.3 More About SUBROUTINE Syntax

Except for some differences in the data declaration statements, the structure of subroutines is similar to the structure of a main program. Remember that, except for information passed back and forth through the parameter list, what happens inside a subroutine is local to that subroutine. This means that you may reuse variable names and line labels even if they have been used elsewhere, either in the main program or in other subprograms. This is especially useful when you write large programs with many variable names and FORMAT statements. If you are in the habit of numbering FORMAT statements starting at 1000 (as is done in this text), you may restart this sequence in each subroutine. As another example, if you're in the habit of using i, j, k, and so forth, for loop control variables, you may reuse these variables in any subroutine without worrying about causing interference with loop calculations in other subroutines.

7.3 Fortran Functions

The other important Fortran subprogram is the function. Two kinds of Fortran functions have already been discussed in Chapter 4. One is the statement function, a one-line, user-defined calculation that can be referenced elsewhere in a program. (See P-4.4, for example.) The other kind is the Fortran intrinsic function. This section will extend the concept of the function to include user-defined subprograms that work like intrinsic functions.

The idea of treating program modules like "black boxes," as discussed earlier in this chapter, is especially evident in the use of intrinsic functions. In order to use an intrinsic function, you need to know the number and data type(s) of the required argument(s) and the data type of the value returned in the name of the function. What you don't need to know, and in the case of intrinsic functions, can't easily find out, is what happens inside the function; its calculations are completely isolated from the rest of your source code and, assuming you're confident that the intrinsic function works properly, of no interest to your program. In Fortran, you can write your own external functions that work just like intrinsic (internal) functions. The difference is that presumably you will understand how the function works.

As an example, P-7.5 provides yet another rewrite of P-3.1 so that the area and circumference of a circle are each calculated in separate user-defined Fortran functions.

P-7.5 [CIRCLFUN.F90]

```
      MODULE CircleFunctions
!
      CONTAINS
!--------------------------------
         REAL FUNCTION Area(radius)
!
! Do area calculation.
!
            IMPLICIT NONE
            REAL, PARAMETER :: pi=3.14159
            REAL, INTENT(IN) :: radius
!
            Area=pi*radius*radius
!
         END FUNCTION Area
!---------------------------------------------
         REAL FUNCTION Circumference(radius)
! Do circumference calculation.
            IMPLICIT NONE
            REAL, PARAMETER :: pi=3.14159
            REAL, INTENT(IN) :: radius
!
            Circumference=2.0*pi*radius
         END FUNCTION Circumference
!--------------------------------
```

```
      END MODULE
!=====================
      PROGRAM CirclFun
!
! Calculate area and circumference of a circle, using
! two functions.
!
      USE CircleFunctions, ONLY : Area,Circumference
      IMPLICIT NONE
      REAL radius
!
      PRINT *,' What is the radius of the circle?'
      READ *,radius
!
      PRINT 1000,Area(radius),Circumference(radius)
!
1000  FORMAT(1x,2f10.3)
      END
```

It is obvious that P-7.5 is a *much* longer solution to the problem of calculating the area and circumference of a circle than the original P-3.1. What has been gained? In fact, there isn't much justification for modularizing this simple program to this extent. However, it is the concepts illustrated in P-7.5 that are important, and we will discuss the code in detail.

The general syntax of the FUNCTION subprogram is

```
[data_type] FUNCTION name[(parameter list)]
[specification statements]
[executable statements]
[RETURN]
END [FUNCTION [name]]

Example of FUNCTION header:
      REAL FUNCTION DotProduct(x1,y1,z1,x2,y2,z2)
```

The data type specification is optional only if implicit data typing is used. That is, the data type of a function must be declared, either implicitly based on the first letter in its name or explicitly, just as though it were a variable. (Remember that implicit data typing is never used in this text.)

The structure of the code inside functions is the same as for subroutines; specification and other nonexecutable statements are followed by executable statements. The name of the function must appear at least once on the left side of an assignment statement in order to provide the value returned by the function to the calling (sub)program. The function ends with an END statement and may include one or more RETURN statements prior to the END statement.

P-7.5 contains a great deal of information about how to define and use functions, and it deserves careful study. It includes the functions Area and Circumference. They are called with the single argument radius and their values are printed at the end of the program. In P-7.5, the functions are contained in a MODULE, but this isn't necessary as a matter of Fortran syntax; they *could* simply follow the main program in the same way that SUBROUTINE CircleStuff follows the main program in P-7.2 earlier in this chapter. However, there are good reasons for including subroutines and functions in one or more MODULEs. A sufficient reason is to enforce intent attributes, as discussed in Section 7.2; other reasons will become clear later in this chapter.

Once a function has been defined, it can be used just like an intrinsic function within the program unit that contains its definition. It can appear on the right side of an assignment operator either alone or as part of an expression, or as a value to be printed. In P-7.5, the functions appear in a PRINT statement, but you could also assign them to other variable names:

```
area1=Area(radius)
circumference1=Circumference(radius)
```

assuming area1 and circumference1 are declared as REAL variables. However, you can't use functions like this:

```
CALL Area(radius)           ! NOT ALLOWED
Circumference(radius)=x      ! NOT ALLOWED
```

The first statement isn't allowed because a function can't be "CALLed" like a subroutine; functions return single values. The second statement isn't allowed because only variable names, not function names, can appear on the left side of assignment operators; a function is equivalent to a value, not a variable name.

As you can see from P-7.5, FUNCTION parameters can and should be given INTENT attributes for the same reasons that subroutine parameters should be given INTENT attributes. In fact, the rules are identical to those for expressing intent in subroutines.

7.4 Using Subroutines and Functions

7.4.1 Using the MODULE Structure for Passing Information to Subroutines and Functions

This chapter has introduced MODULE structures as a way to provide access to subroutines and functions in a way that allows Fortran to enforce intent attributes. The other important use of MODULEs is to make data definitions and values available to Fortran subprograms without having to include them in the formal parameter list. This has been done in P-7.5 to make the value of π available to the two functions and to assure that the same value of π is used in both; information can be passed to subroutines in the same way.

A simplified syntax of the MODULE structure for passing information, including data type definitions and declarations and values from PARAMETER statements, is

```
MODULE module_name
   [specification statements]
END [MODULE [module_name]]

Example:
     MODULE Constants
        REAL, PARAMETER :: pi=3.1415927,dr=0.0174532
        END MODULE Constants
```

As indicated in P-7.5, the same MODULE can also include subroutines following a CONTAINS statement.

Once again, access to the information in a MODULE structure is provided through the USE statement. The default condition is for all information in the MODULE to be available to the (sub)program containing a reference to the MODULE. However, it is possible to give access to only some of the information in the MODULE referred to in the USE statement. An expanded syntax for the USE statement is

```
USE module_name[, ONLY : list of included names,
                          separated by commas]

where each item in the ONLY list has the form
[local_name =>] module_name

Examples:
     USE Constants

     USE Constants, ONLY : pi, deg_to_rad => dr
```

The local_name => module_name option allows you to assign a different name locally within a (sub)program that uses data definitions and other information from a module. This makes it easier to reuse modules in several programs because you can write a new program, with its own variable names, without initially having to refer to the names in the module.

When variables or other names, such as function names, are USEd in a (sub)program, they shouldn't and can't be redeclared within that (sub)program; that defeats the purpose of defining them in a MODULE in the first place and will generate a compile-time error. This applies even when a quantity accessed from a MODULE has been given a local name.

You might reasonably ask why MODULEs should be used to pass information to subprograms, especially when those values then no longer appear in a subroutine's or function's argument list. Doesn't this violate the algorithm design principle that a subprogram's parameter list should completely define the information interface between the subprogram and its calling (sub)program?

In Fortran 90, MODULEs are essentially an implementation detail, albeit a relatively large and complicated detail. They are important because they provide new kinds of information interfaces among programs and their subprograms which were not available in earlier versions of Fortran. They should be used whenever they can make programs less prone to error or easier to modify and maintain. In fact, we will use MODULEs in this text whenever a program requires a subprogram. However, these capabilities don't have to affect the way your algorithms are designed. That, after all, is the point of having a "syntax free" way to design algorithms. You can still think of all information flowing through a subprogram's parameter list.

In small programs, the practical advantages of using MODULEs are marginal, but in large programs where many subprograms share common information, the use of MODULEs greatly reduces the possibility of errors. For example, remember that every variable appearing in a parameter list must be explicitly typed within the subprogram in which it appears. However, variables made available through a MODULE have to be declared only once, in the MODULE. When variables and other entities are made available in this way, it is good programming style to use the ONLY option to provide a list of the names of the entities even when *all* these entities are being USEd.

Programming Tip

In programs written with older versions of Fortran, you will often see the keyword COMMON. This keyword is used to define "common blocks" of values that can be shared among a main program and its subprograms by making them available "in common." Common blocks are still supported by Fortran 90, but we will not use them in this text. Why not? Because the information contained in common blocks is "storage associated" rather than "name associated." Without going into the details, suffice it to say that programs that use MODULEs to share information by name association are much less prone to errors than programs that use COMMON blocks to share information by storage association. This fact, coupled with the other advantages of MODULEs in Fortran 90, is sufficient reason for anyone learning Fortran for the first time to avoid using COMMON blocks. Nonetheless, because you will see COMMON blocks in older Fortran programs, a brief description of the syntax is given in Chapter 12.

7.4.2 Initializing Information in Subroutines and Functions

As discussed in this chapter, there are two basic mechanisms for making externally generated information available to a subprogram: its parameter list, through which a calling (sub)program can transmit values, and a MODULE, which can transmit information about data types and subprograms as well as values. What about information that is generated inside a subprogram? Consider this code fragment from a subroutine:

P-7.6 (fragment)

```
SUBROUTINE X(...)
...
INTEGER i
REAL z
DATA z/0./
DO i=1,10
  z=z+1.
END DO
RETURN
END
```

The first time this subroutine is called, z initially has a value of 0 because it appears in a DATA statement. When control is returned to the calling program, z has a value of 10. What is the value of z when the subroutine is called again during the same program? Because of the DATA statement, it is tempting to conclude that z will be reinitialized to 0 every time the subroutine is called. **However, this is *NOT TRUE!***

A DATA statement is not an executable statement, which means that values are assigned to variables in a DATA statement *before* the program starts to execute. As a result, the initialization performed in a DATA statement is performed only *once*.

In the above example, the "initial" value of z when the subroutine is called a second time is 10. If it is called yet again, its value is 20, and so forth. Note that this problem doesn't apply to variable names initialized as constants in PARAMETER statements because such values can't be changed while the program is running.

Subroutines and functions are often called more than once within the same program, which is one reason the subprogram was written in the first place. Also, subprograms often contain many internal variables that, if they appeared in a main program, could appropriately be initialized in a DATA statement to avoid writing many assignment statements. This situation represents a tempting but potentially fatal design trap that is very difficult to find after a program has been written.

Fortran issues no warning message because it might be reasonable to ask a subprogram to do what the code in P-7.6 does, but it is almost never what you intended!

The solution is to use an assignment statement to initialize z to 0. Assignment statements are executable, so the assignments will be made every time the subprogram is called. In P-7.6, the code should probably look like this:

```
INTEGER i
REAL z
z=0.
DO i=1,10
  z=z+1.
END DO
```

7.4.3 Using Subroutines and Functions in Argument and Parameter Lists

Suppose you have written a subroutine to print a table of values of sin(x). The intrinsic SIN function could be used in code something like that in P-7.7, assuming appropriate data declarations and assignments for all variables:

P-7.7 (fragment)

```
SUBROUTINE Printer(lo,hi,step)
...
x=first
DO i=lo,hi
  PRINT *,x,SIN(x)
  x=x+step
END DO
...
```

In order to "reuse" this subroutine to print values of a different function, you would have to rewrite the subroutine by replacing the SIN(x) in the PRINT statement with some other function; this other function could be a different intrinsic function or some function you defined yourself, such as x**3.

Especially if you consider this example in a broader context of using functions for more involved calculations in subprograms, you might wish to find a way to give a subprogram access to a function without having to define the function inside the subprogram. If you could do this, it would mean that the code in such subprograms could be written independently of the function itself.

In fact, it is possible for either a function or a subroutine to appear in the parameter list of a subprogram and therefore in its corresponding argument list. This means that you could use something similar to SUBROUTINE Printer in P-7.7 to print values of *any* function of one variable simply by representing the name of the function symbolically in SUBROUTINE Printer's parameter list and including the name of the actual function in the argument list when `Printer` is called. However, quite a bit of extra code is required to do this properly. Program P-7.8 shows how. This is an important code example and it is important to study it thoroughly.

P-7.8 [EXT_FUNC.F90]

```
      MODULE ExternalFunctions
      CONTAINS
!---------------------------
      REAL FUNCTION f_of_x(x)
      IMPLICIT NONE
      REAL, INTENT(IN) :: x
      f_of_x=x**2
      END FUNCTION f_of_x
!------------------------------------
      SUBROUTINE Print_f(lo,hi,step,f)
      IMPLICIT NONE
      INTEGER, INTENT(IN) :: lo,hi
      REAL, INTENT(IN) :: step
      REAL f,x
      INTEGER i
! Explicit function interface definition...
      INTERFACE
         REAL FUNCTION f(x)
           REAL, INTENT(IN) :: x
         END FUNCTION f
      END INTERFACE
      x=0.-step
      PRINT *,'   x            f(x)'
      DO i=lo,hi
        x=x+step
        PRINT 1000,x,f(x)
      END DO
1000  FORMAT(1x,2f10.5)
      END SUBROUTINE Print_f
!---------------------------
      SUBROUTINE f_of_x_sub(x,s)
      IMPLICIT NONE
      REAL, INTENT(IN) :: x
      REAL, INTENT(OUT) :: s
      s=SQRT(x)
      END SUBROUTINE f_of_x_sub
!------------------------------------
      SUBROUTINE Print_s(lo,hi,step,s)
      IMPLICIT NONE
      INTEGER, INTENT(IN) :: lo,hi
      REAL, INTENT(IN) :: step
      REAL x,y
      INTEGER i
! Explicit subroutine interface definition...
      INTERFACE
         SUBROUTINE s(x,y)
           REAL, INTENT(IN) :: x
           REAL, INTENT(OUT) :: y
         END SUBROUTINE
      END INTERFACE
```

```
!
       x=0.-step
       PRINT *,'    x           f(x)'
       DO i=lo,hi
         x=x+step
         CALL s(x,y)
         PRINT 1000,x,y
       END DO
1000   FORMAT(1x,2f10.5)
       END SUBROUTINE Print_s
!--------------------------------
       END MODULE ExternalFunctions
!================================
       PROGRAM Ext_Func
!
! Demonstrate how to pass a function or subroutine
! to a subprogram.
!
       USE ExternalFunctions, ONLY : f_of_x,f_of_x_sub, &
                                     print_f,print_s
       IMPLICIT NONE
       INTRINSIC SIN !for an intrinsic function
!
       CALL Print_f(1,11,.1,SIN) !uses an intrinsic function
       CALL Print_f(1,11,.1,f_of_x) !uses a user-defined function
       CALL Print_s(1,11,.1,f_of_x_sub) !uses a subroutine
!
       END
```

Running P-7.8

```
   x              f(x)
0.00000        0.00000
0.10000        0.09983
0.20000        0.19867
0.30000        0.29552
0.40000        0.38942
0.50000        0.47943
0.60000        0.56464
0.70000        0.64422
0.80000        0.71736
0.90000        0.78333
1.00000        0.84147
   x              f(x)
0.00000        0.00000
0.10000        0.01000
0.20000        0.04000
0.30000        0.09000
0.40000        0.16000
0.50000        0.25000
0.60000        0.36000
0.70000        0.49000
0.80000        0.64000
0.90000        0.81000
1.00000        1.00000
   x              f(x)
0.00000        0.00000
0.10000        0.31623
0.20000        0.44721
0.30000        0.54772
0.40000        0.63246
0.50000        0.70711
0.60000        0.77460
0.70000        0.83666
0.80000        0.89443
0.90000        0.94868
1.00000        1.00000
```

In P-7.8, the main program does nothing more than call subprograms to illustrate some Fortran implementation details. Consider the first CALL statement in the main program:

```
CALL Print_f(1,11,.1,SIN) !uses an intrinsic function
```

Clearly, the purpose of this call is to give SUBROUTINE Print_f access to the intrinsic SIN function by including the name of this function in the argument list when Print_f is called. In the parameter list of Print_f, the function is represented symbolically by the parameter f. As a result, Print_f prints a table of values of sin(x).

In the first call to Print_f in P-7.8, the critical question is this: "How does Fortran know to interpret the argument SIN as the intrinsic SIN function being passed to Print_f rather than as a variable named SIN?" The answer is that the name of the function is included in an INTRINSIC statement, which allows Fortran to make the association between the name SIN and the intrinsic funcion of this name. In P-7.8, the INTRINSIC statement is printed in bold italics. The general form of the INTRINSIC statement is

```
INTRINSIC list of external names, separated by commas
```

Now consider the second and third CALL statements in P-7.8.

```
CALL Print_f(1,11,.1,f_of_x)     !uses a user-defined function
CALL Print_s(1,11,.1,f_of_x_sub) !uses a subroutine
```

The first of these statements includes as an argument the name of the user-defined function f_of_x in the call to SUBROUTINE Print_f. The code in Print_f doesn't change, but as you can see by examining the code in REAL FUNCTION f_of_x, Print_f now evaluates and prints values of x^2. The critical question for this call is the same as before: "How does Fortran know to interpret the name f_of_x as a user-defined function being passed to Print_f rather than as a variable name?"

The answer to this question is somewhat more complicated than it is for intrinsic functions. The basic answer is that you must should provide Print_f with 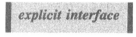 an *explicit interface* definition for the parameter that will be interpreted as a function, using an INTERFACE code block. This code is printed in bold italics in Print_f. The general syntax definition is:

```
INTERFACE
 <function or subroutine header>
   <data declaration statements>
 END <FUNCTION or SUBROUTINE> [name]
 ...
END INTERFACE
```

This code structure includes the first line (the "header") of a function or subroutine and the data declaration statements for all quantities appearing in its parameter list, but not the local declarations. The name of the function or subroutine must be the same as its name in the parameter list of the subprogram unit in which the INTERFACE block appears, but the names of the quantities in the header don't have to be the same as in the subprogram unit or in the function or subroutine that the INTERFACE block is describing. More than one function and subroutine can be included in an INTERFACE block.

The third CALL statement in P-7.8's main program references a different subroutine, Print_s, and the argument list now includes a subroutine that calculates the square root of x. A subroutine different from Print_f is necessary because the code required to access values returned from a subroutine is slightly different from the code required to use a value returned as the result of evaluating a function. The output from SUBROUTINE Print_s is similar to that from Print_f—it still performs the simple task of printing a table of calculated values. This time, however, the value comes as output from SUBROUTINE f_of_x_sub. Because there is only one value returned from f_of_x_sub, there is actually no compelling reason to use a subroutine to provide the square root of x; it could also have been defined as a function. It has been defined as a subroutine in this example only to illustrate how to include a subroutine in a parameter list.

For the same reason that a function name used in Print_f's parameter list was described in an INTERFACE block, a subroutine name appearing in Print_s's parameter list must also appear in an INTERFACE block. This code is also printed in bold italics in P-7.8.

Inside the subroutines Print_f and Print_s, the parameters are given INTENT attributes as usual, except for the parameter associated with the function or subroutine. Such a parameter can't have an INTENT attribute because it isn't a variable; it represents a different kind of entity that is accessible to the subprogram.

Even though the examples in P-7.8 involve only one function or subroutine used in a parameter list, it is certainly possible to have more than one such parameter in a list of several parameters. Several intrinsic functions can appear in the parameter lists of subprograms as long as the names of the intrinsic functions appear in INTRINSIC statements in the calling (sub)program. Several user-defined functions and subroutines can appear in the parameter lists of subprograms as long as the functions and subroutines are described in an INTERFACE block.

7.4.4 Choosing Between Subroutines and Functions

This chapter has described, among other things, several modifications of program P-3.1, all of which resulted in programs that are longer and more complex than the original. Were these attempts to modularize P-3.1 worth the effort? Perhaps not for the simple task involved. However, in general, any source code that occupies more than a page or so is a candidate for some kind of modularization. Beginning programmers often react inappropriately to the concept of modularization, either by creating subprograms for *every* calculation, even when it makes little sense to do so, or by refusing to break even large programs into more easily manageable pieces.

Between these extremes there are choices to be made. If two people independently solve the same reasonably complex programming problem, their programs often will not look the same, either in their details or in the overall structure as expressed through their choices of subroutines and functions. The programs in the rest of this text, hopefully, reflect reasonable approaches to the use of subroutines and functions. However, other equally reasonable approaches may also be possible.

Some decisions about using subroutines and functions can be based on the two important differences between these two kinds of subprograms:

(1) A subroutine can return multiple values, each associated with its own variable name. It is accessed through the CALL statement.

(2) A function returns a single value. It is accessed by name, just as any other variable name.

Obviously, if your subprogram needs to produce several output values, you must use a subroutine. If you need only a single value, then you have the option of using a function. However, if a single value that results from the same function call is needed more than once in a program, repeated use of a function with the same arguments to obtain this value represents redundant calculations that should be eliminated. A better approach in this case is either to use a subroutine or to use the function just once and assign the result to a variable name. If the same calculation needs to be done many times for different input arguments, then it makes sense to use a function.

Based on the material presented in this chapter, it may seem that a great deal of programming overhead is required to use Fortran subprograms. It's true, and these details can make small programs seem more trouble than they're worth. However, the ability to write completely isolated subprograms, assign INTENT attributes to control the flow of information, and make selected information available to different parts of a program, through the MODULE structure, makes Fortran an ideal language for developing large and complex programs that use combinations of commercial and custom subprograms. Because this is how Fortran is often used in practice, it is necessary to present many of these details even in an introductory course.

Program P-7.8, in particular, will require careful study before you can write similar programs on your own. It may seem like a *lot* of code to achieve relatively simple ends. However, it is worth the time required to understand this program because it shows how to write code that separates the task of manipulating functions from the functions themselves. This is important for science and engineering applications and is an essential part of Fortran program modularization.

7.5 Applications

7.5.1 Relativistic Mass and Speed of an Electron

This problem was discussed previously as an application in Chapters 3 and 5, so the preliminary problem-solving steps won't be dupicated here. Briefly, the problem requires a 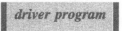 program that prompts a user to provide a voltage and then calculates the relativistic speed and mass of an electron accelerated by that voltage in an electron gun. Program P-7.9 will perform all the calculations inside a subroutine and will add some extra calculations in the main program. It will use a MODULE to provide access to the subroutine and to make available some physical constants, such as the speed of light, necessary for the calculations. After these constants are defined once in the MODULE, they can be used throughout the program. This minimizes the chance for errors. With this arrangement, the main program serves just as a *driver program* to test the operation of the subroutine. Once you're confident that the subroutine works properly, you shouldn't ever have to worry about writing code to do these particular calculations again.[8]

P-7.9 [RELMASS3.F90]

```
      MODULE ElectronConstants
        IMPLICIT NONE
        REAL, PARAMETER :: rest_mass=9.109e-31 !kg
        REAL, PARAMETER :: e=1.602e-19          ! electronic charge,
Coulomb
        REAL, PARAMETER :: c=2.9979e8           ! speed of light, m/s
      END MODULE ElectronConstants
!-------------------------------
      MODULE ElectronSubs
!
      CONTAINS
!
      SUBROUTINE Rel_E(voltage,rel_mass,speed)
!
! Calculates relativistic mass and speed of an electron.
! See Schaum's Outline of Theory and Problems of College Physics.
!
      USE ElectronConstants, Only : rest_mass,e,c
      IMPLICIT NONE
!
      REAL rel_mass ! kg
      REAL voltage  ! volts
      REAL speed    ! m/s
      INTENT(IN) voltage
      INTENT(OUT) rel_mass,speed
!
```

---

[8]You may also be pleased to hear that we will *not* return again to this problem.

```
      rel_mass=(voltage*e+rest_mass*c**2)/c**2
      speed=c*SQRT(1.-(rest_mass/rel_mass)**2)
!
      END SUBROUTINE Rel_E
!
      END MODULE ElectronSubs
!
      PROGRAM RelMass3
!
! Driver for subroutine to calculate relativistic mass and speed
! of electron.
!
      USE ElectronSubs, Only : Rel_E
      USE ElectronConstants, Only : rest_mass,speed_of_light => c
      IMPLICIT NONE
      REAL voltage,relativistic_mass,speed
!
      PRINT *,' Give electron gun voltage in volts: '
      READ *,voltage
      CALL Rel_E(voltage,relativistic_mass,speed)
!
      WRITE(6,1000)voltage
      WRITE(6,1001)rest_mass
WRITE(6,1002)relativistic_mass,speed,relativistic_mass/rest_mass
      WRITE(6,1003)speed/speed_of_light
!
1000  FORMAT('      For an electron gun voltage of: ',es10.4,' V')
1001  FORMAT('              rest mass of electron: ',es10.4,' kg')
1002  FORMAT('        relativistic mass and speed: ',es10.4,' kg',&
             es12.4,' m/s'/&
             ' ratio of relativistic to rest mass: ',es10.4)
1003  FORMAT('   ratio of speed to speed of light: ',es10.4)
      END
```

It is worth taking the time to study how the MODULE structure is used in P-7.9, as writing this kind of code requires a great deal of practice. Constants needed for the calculations are stored in MODULE ElectronConstants. Then SUBROUTINE Rel_E is defined in MODULE ElectronSubs. The USE statement in Rel_E provides access to the needed constants. In the main program, both MODULEs are needed. The ONLY option is used to clarify which values or subroutines are needed:

```
      USE ElectronSubs, Only : Rel_E
      USE ElectronConstants, Only : rest_mass,speed_of_light => c
```

Note how the variable name c used for the speed of light in the MODULE—that's the standard symbol used for this quantity in physics—is given the more descriptive name speed_of_light for its local use in the main program.

7.5.2 A Function Library for Converting Units

In science and engineering, it is always important to express quantities in appropriate units. In science, almost all calculations are units based on the metric system. In engineering, calculations are still done in a variety of units.

You can make your life as a science or engineering student a lot easier if you start now to accumulate a set of unit conversion functions that you can incorporate into  your programs. Such a collection of functions is referred to as a *function library*. The application in this section will show you how to develop your own function libraries.

1 *Define the problem.*

Write two functions, one of which converts inches to several other units of length and another that converts pressure, expressed in pounds per square inch, to several other units such as atmospheres and millibars.

2 *Outline a solution.*

This problem is conceptually simple. The function name itself should indicate the "source unit" and the input to the function should include the name of the "target unit" and the value of the quantity in the source unit. You can include both abbreviations and the full names of the target units. For example, a function for converting inches to some other unit of length could be called Inches_to. A call to such a function for the purpose of converting 12 inches to meters should allow either Inches_to('meters',12) or Inches_to('m',12) and should return a value of 0.3048, the number of meters in 12 inches.

Find the appropriate conversion factors in a table and check them carefully against at least one other source.

3 *Design an algorithm.*

SUBPROGRAM *Inches_to(IN: name of target unit as string;*
value as real)
CHOOSE *(based on name of target unit)*
(m or meters)

      ASSIGN *Inches_to = value•0.0254*
       (ft or feet)
      ASSIGN *Inches_to = value/12.0*
       (etc.)
(end **CHOOSE**)
(end **SUBPROGRAM**)

SUBPROGRAM *PSI_to(IN: name of target unit as string; value as real)*
CHOOSE *(based on name of target unit)*
     (mb or millibars): **ASSIGN** *PSI_to = value•68.95*
     (atm or atmospheres) : **ASSIGN**
                 (to Pascals, then to atm)
                 PSI_to = value•6895/101330
(end **CHOOSE**)
(end **SUBPROGRAM**)

This subprogram algorithm will become part of a complete program that can be used to test each of these conversions. It shouldn't be necessary to write pseudocode for the driver program.

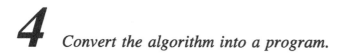

Convert the algorithm into a program.

P-7.10 [UNITS.F90]

```
    MODULE UnitSubs
    CONTAINS
!-------------------------------------
    REAL FUNCTION Inches_to(what,value)
!
    IMPLICIT NONE
    CHARACTER*(*), INTENT(IN) :: what
    REAL, INTENT(IN)      :: value
!
    SELECT CASE (what)
      CASE ('ft','feet')
        Inches_to=value/12.0
      CASE ('cm','centimeters')
        Inches_to=value*2.54 !definition
      CASE ('m','meters')
        Inches_to=value*.0254 !definition
      CASE ('yd','yards')
        Inches_to=value/36.0
      CASE DEFAULT
        STOP &
        'ERROR in InchesTo: Requested conversion does not exist.'
    END SELECT
    END FUNCTION Inches_to
!-------------------------------------
```

```
      REAL FUNCTION PSI_to(what,value)
!
      IMPLICIT NONE
      CHARACTER*(*), INTENT(IN) :: what
      REAL, INTENT(IN) :: value
      REAL, PARAMETER :: c=6894.757361 !PSI to newtons/sq-meter
!
      SELECT CASE (what)
        CASE ('Pa','Pascal')
          PSI_to=value*c
        CASE ('mb','millibars')
          PSI_to=value*c/100.
        CASE ('atm','atmospheres')
          PSI_to=value*c/1.01325e5
        CASE ('cm-Hg')
          PSI_to=value*c/1333.223874
        CASE ('in-Hg')
          PSI_to=value*c/1333.223874/2.54
        CASE DEFAULT
          STOP &
          'ERROR in PSI_to: Requested conversion does not exist.'
        END SELECT
      END FUNCTION PSI_to
!-------------------------------------
      REAL FUNCTION Watts_to(what,value)
      IMPLICIT NONE
      CHARACTER*(*), INTENT(IN) :: what
      REAL, INTENT(IN) :: value
!
      SELECT CASE (what)
        CASE ('Btu_per_s')
          Watts_to=value/1055.055863
        CASE ('cal_per_s')
          Watts_to=value/4.1868
        CASE ('ft-lb_per_s')
          Watts_to=value/1.355817948
        CASE ('hp','horsepower')
          Watts_to=value/746.0 !definition
        CASE DEFAULT
          STOP &
          'ERROR in Watts_to: Requested conversion does not exist.'
        END SELECT
      END FUNCTION Watts_to
!-------------------------
      END MODULE UnitSubs
!=========================
      PROGRAM Units
! Conversion functions.
! See James L. Cook, _Conversion Factors_, OUP 1990.
      USE UnitSubs, ONLY : Inches_to,PSI_to,Watts_to
      IMPLICIT NONE
!
      PRINT*,' Test Inches_to for 6"...'
      PRINT*,Inches_to('feet',6.0),Inches_to('ft',6.0),' feet'
      PRINT*,Inches_to('cm',6.0),Inches_to('centimeters',6.0),' cm'
      PRINT*,Inches_to('m',6.0),Inches_to('meters',6.0),' m'
      PRINT*,Inches_to('yd',6.0),Inches_to('yards',6.0),' yd'
      PRINT*,' Test PSI_to for 14.7 PSI...'
      PRINT*,PSI_to('Pa',14.7),PSI_to('Pascal',14.7),' Pa'
      PRINT*,PSI_to('mb',14.7),PSI_to('millibars',14.7),' mb'
```

```
      PRINT*,PSI_to('atm',14.7),PSI_to('atmospheres',14.7),' atm'
      PRINT*,PSI_to('cm-Hg',14.7),' cm-Hg'
      PRINT*,PSI_to('in-Hg',14.7),' in-Hg'
      PRINT*,' Test Watts_to for 1 kW...'
      PRINT*,Watts_to('Btu_per_s',1000.0),' Btu/s'
      PRINT*,Watts_to('cal_per_s',1000.0),' cal/s'
      PRINT*,Watts_to('ft-lb_per_s',1000.0),'ft-lb/s'
      PRINT*,Watts_to('hp',1000.0), &
             Watts_to('horsepower',1000.0),' hp'
      END
```

Running P-7.10

```
Test Inches_to for 6"...
 0.5000000     0.5000000    feet
15.2399998    15.2399998    cm
 0.1524000     0.1524000    m
 0.1666667     0.1666667    yd
Test PSI_to for 14.7 PSI...
 1.0135293E+05    1.0135293E+05   Pa
 1.0135293E+03    1.0135293E+03   mb
 1.0002756     1.0002756    atm
76.0209427    cm-Hg
29.9295044    in-Hg
Test Watts_to for 1 kW...
 0.9478171    Btu/s
 2.3884590E+02  cal/s
 7.3756219E+02 ft-lb/s
 1.3404826     1.3404826    hp
```

5 *Verify the operation of the program.*

It's important to be *very* careful with code like this because once you write functions for something as boring as converting units, you will probably never look at the code again. Use the driver program to test each function and make sure you perform every available conversion at least once. Check the results of each conversion with a calculator and against other printed sources! As a last resort, ask yourself, "Does this answer make sense?"

Problem Discussion

A few more conversions have been added to P-7.10 in addition to the ones given in Step 3. This is a simple matter in the context of the SELECT CASE construct. The values for the conversions have been taken from the book referenced in the main program. In some cases, the number of significant figures given for the conversion constants in this reference exceeds the accuracy of default Fortran REAL numbers. It is not always clear where the *physically* significant digits in conversion factors stop and the "artifacts" of mathematical operations begin. In any case, the presence of too many significant digits is not a problem from either the programming or the physical point of view. Fortran will simply ignore "extra" digits in constants and the accuracy of REAL numbers is more than adequate for these kinds of unit conversions.

One interesting point about the code in P-7.10 has to do with the use of a STOP statement in the CASE DEFAULT clause of each SELECT CASE construct. This is an attempt to respond to the possibility that an error in a calling argument might request a conversion that doesn't exist. However, simply stopping the program doesn't seem like a particularly graceful response. You might wonder why the choice has been made to terminate the program rather than print an appropriate message and keep the program running:

```
CASE DEFAULT
   PRINT *,' ERROR. The requested conversion does not exist.'
```

The reason has to do with a subtle restriction on the code allowed in FUNCTION subprograms. Recall that functions can be used just like constants or variables. This is why the function itself can appear in the PRINT statements in P-7.10, for example:

```
PRINT*,Inches_to('feet',6.0),Inches_to('ft',6.0),' feet'
```

However, because of the way PRINT statements are implemented in Fortran,

> A PRINT or WRITE **statement cannot be used in any** FUNCTION **subprogram that is called from a** PRINT **or** WRITE **statement.**

The mere presence of a PRINT or WRITE statement won't cause a problem inside a function, but the program will crash if such a statement is actually executed. Rather than restrict the use of the functions in PRINT or WRITE statements, it is better never to include PRINTs or WRITEs inside the final version of a function. (It is often helpful to include some output statements inside a function while it is being debugged. However, the presence of these statements precludes the use of the function in an output statement in the calling (sub)program while the function is being tested.) Including a message as part of a STOP statement is a way to provide an informative message without using a PRINT or WRITE.

Because of this restriction, you might wish to consider other ways of "trapping" inappropriate input. One obvious way is to use a subroutine instead of a function. Then both the converted value and an "error flag" can be included in the parameter list. The error flag could be an integer assigned a value of 0 or 1, for example, or it could be a LOGICAL variable. Then, of course, you will have to modify the code in the driver program. This approach is left as an end-of-chapter exercise.

Another interesting feature of P-7.10 is the use of variably sized character strings. The statement CHARACTER*(*) in the conversion functions allows a string of any allowed length to be passed as input. Its operation is analogous to using variably sized arrays. In this case, the variable-length string is the name of the desired output unit, used to select the appropriate conversion in the SELECT CASE construct.

7.5.3 A Simple Character-Based Function Plotter

1 Define the problem.

Even though there are many computer applications that can provide sophisticated plotting capabilities, it is sometimes convenient to be able to provide a "quick and dirty" representation of a function directly from a Fortran program. Write a subprogram that accepts as input a function f(x), the lower and upper limits at which it should be evaluated, and the step size by which to increment the independent variable x. The subroutine should produce a text-based "graphical" representation of the function. Test this subprogram with a driver program.

2 Outline a solution.

1. Pass all information to a subprogram, including the name of the function.
2. Determine the largest and smallest values of f(x) within the specified range.
3. Determine a scaling factor to apply such that the value of the function can be "plotted" by printing an appropriate character, such as an asterisk, along the x-axis. A reasonable choice is to restrict the "plot" to no more than 50 spaces:

$$\text{scaling factor} = 50/(\text{largest-smallest})$$

4. Generate values of f(x). Convert each value to an integer position from 1–50. If, for example, this position is 25, print 24 blank spaces followed by an asterisk.

3 Design an algorithm.

This algorithm is more dependent on the specific capabilities of Fortran than is usually the case. In particular, it depends on the availability of the advance='no' option in the WRITE statement.

SUBPROGRAM *Plot(IN: lo,hi,step; f(x))*
DEFINE/DECLARE *(smallest, largest, scale, value as REAL,n as # of steps,*
max_points as max # of spaces along x-axis,
i as loop counter, "where" as integer position)

Determine the number of intervals and initialize some variables.

ASSIGN *n = (hi – lo)/step*
INITIALIZE *smallest = 0*
largest = 0

Find the largest and smallest values of f(x).

LOOP *(for i = 0 to n)*
    IF *(f(x) > smallest)* **THEN** *smallest = f(x)*
    IF *(f(x) < largest)* **THEN** *largest = f(x)*
END LOOP

Set the scaling factor and assign maximum number of points.

ASSIGN *scale = max_points/(largest-smallest)*
max_points = 50

Generate values of f(x) and "plot" them.

LOOP *(for i = 0 to n)*
    ASSIGN *value = f(lo + i•step)*
            where = (value – smallest)•scale
                    (Round to nearest integer.)
    WRITE *(i, no line feed) (Could print x instead.)*
    WRITE *(where – 1 spaces, no line feed)*
    WRITE *("*", with line feed)*
END LOOP

4 *Convert the algorithm into a program.*

P-7.11 [PLOTTER.F90]

```fortran
      MODULE PlotSubs
      CONTAINS
!---------------------------------
      SUBROUTINE Plot(lo,hi,step,f,u)
! Create a crude plot of a function.
      IMPLICIT NONE
      REAL, INTENT(IN) :: lo,hi,step
      INTEGER, INTENT(IN) :: u !output unit
      REAL f,largest,smallest,value,scale
      REAL max_x
      INTEGER i,j,n,where
      PARAMETER (max_x=50.) !# of spaces for plot along x-axis
      n=NINT((hi-lo)/step) !# of points to plot
      smallest=1e10
      largest=-1e10
! Find smallest and largest values.
      DO i=0,n
        value=f(lo+REAL(i)*step) !evaluate the function
        IF (value<smallest) smallest=value !find smallest...
        IF (value>largest) largest=value    !and largest values
      END DO
      scale=max_x/(largest-smallest) !calculate scaling factor
      IF (u/=6) OPEN(u,file='c:\ftn90.dir\plot.out')
      DO i=0,n
! Where does the plotting symbol go?
      where=NINT((f(lo+REAL(i)*step)-smallest)*scale)
! Print the step.
      WRITE(u,1000,advance='no')i
! Print where-1 blank characters.
      WRITE(u,1010,advance='no')(' ',j=1,where-1)
! Finally, print the plotting character.
      WRITE(u,*)'*'
      END DO
      IF (u/=6) CLOSE(u)
1000  FORMAT(i3)
1010  FORMAT(50a1)
      RETURN
      END SUBROUTINE Plot
!-----------------------
      END MODULE PlotSubs
!=========================
      PROGRAM Plot_it
! Create crude plot of a user-specified function.
      USE PlotSubs, ONLY : Plot
      IMPLICIT NONE
      INTEGER u
      CHARACTER*1 where
      INTERFACE
        REAL FUNCTION F_of_x(x)
          REAL, INTENT(in) :: x
        END
      END
```

```
!
      PRINT *,' Output to (s)creen or (f)ile? '
      READ *,where
      IF (where=='f') THEN
        u=1
      ELSE
        u=6
      END IF
      CALL Plot(0.,10.,.5,F_of_x,u)
      END
!
      REAL FUNCTION F_of_x(x)
      REAL, INTENT(IN) :: x
      F_of_x=x**2-50.
      RETURN
      END
```

Running P-7.11

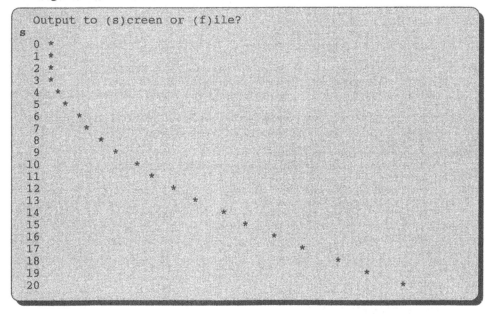

5 *Verify the operation of the program.*

The output from SUBROUTINE Plot can be verified by testing it with a simple function whose appearance you already understand. As you can see from examining the code, the output from P-7.11 is for the function $f(x) = x^2\text{-}50$.

Problem Discussion

Program P-7.11 contains a great deal of useful information about how to use functions and subroutines. The MODULE PlotSubs and SUBROUTINE Plot are written so that they can be used easily in other programs. In particular, the function being plotted appears in Plot's parameter list rather than being "hard coded" into the subroutine so that different functions can be plotted without changing any of Plot's code. The only restriction is that f(x) must return a REAL value. This kind of reusability is very important in Fortran programming. In this case, the somewhat limited usefulness of the "graph" produced by Plot would hardly justify writing the code more than once.

The loop to generate blank spaces before printing the asterisk is contained in an implied DO. . . loop in a WRITE statement. This step has been defined only as **WRITE (where – 1 spaces, with no line feed)** in the algorithm design. Note how the advance='no' option has been used to produce the desired result; a new line is started only after the asterisk is printed at the end of the line. When this kind of implied loop appears inside another loop, it's important to remember to define a different loop counter, in this case, something other than i.

The code in P-7.11 has been expanded a little beyond the problem statement. The main program asks the user to indicate whether the output should go to a monitor screen, the default output device, or be saved in a file. If the latter selection is made, then an output file called PLOT.OUT is created in SUBROUTINE Plot. If default output is desired, unit 6 is used and no file is opened.

7.6 Debugging Your Programs

7.6.1 Programming Style

Any source code that is more than a page or so long should be modularized so that each subroutine or function performs one clearly defined task. MODULEs are always used when subprograms are required. In some cases, the parameter list of each subprogram will contain all the input values required by the subprogram. In other cases, some of the input values may be obtained by USEing definitions from a MODULE. Quantities that can be defined locally within a subprogram should never appear in a parameter list.

An INTENT attribute should be given explicitly for every quantity appearing in a subprogram's parameter list.

Comments in each subprogram should clearly state its purpose and define the quantities in the parameter list. When a USE statement appears in a main program or subprogram, the ONLY option should be used to define the information being obtained from a referenced MODULE.

7.6.2 Problems with Programs

1. There are two basic reasons to modularize your programs. The first is to simplify and clarify the design and implementation of a large program. The second is to avoid having to reinvent important and perhaps complicated algorithms every time you need them. (We will deal with several such algorithms in Chapter 10.) In either case, the approach often taken by students—and professionals who should know better—when they create subprograms is this: (1) write the code; (2) debug it with one or two sets of input values; (3) use it and forget it.

If you follow this approach, eventually you will be sorry! Especially when you write code for reuse in other programs under different conditions, it is imperative to attempt to check the output of subprograms under *all* possible input conditions! Even if you don't know what "all" conditions might be, you should at least verify the operation of subprograms under conditions that you don't actually expect to encounter in practice.

2. Problems with variable definitions and declarations can arise when you use MODULEs. Let's review the possible sources of information used by a subprogram.

(a) The parameter list. This list includes input to and output from the subprogram.
(b) Locally defined variables. These include values that are needed within the subprogram, but are of no interest to the calling (sub)program. Beginning programmers often put variables in the parameter list that should be defined only locally.
(c) Information from one or more MODULEs. This includes information that would otherwise be defined locally as well as functions and subroutines needed for the subprogram to do its job. This method of sharing information is useful when several subprograms need the same values or when a subprogram uses code that has previously been written for some other purpose.

Remember that variables and function names made available through a USE statement in a (sub)program cannot be redeclared within that (sub)program.

7.7 Exercises

7.7.1 Self-Testing Exercises

Exercise 1. Describe in your own words the two most important concepts you have learned from this chapter.

Exercise 2. Describe in your own words how you could use in your own programs a problem-solving skill demonstrated in a program discussed in this chapter.

Exercise 3. Explain in your own words the difference between a subroutine and a function.

Exercise 4. Explain in your own words how Fortran subroutines and functions control the flow of information between various parts of a program.

Exercise 5. Explain in your own words some reasons for using MODULEs.

Exercise 6. Consider the following lines from a subroutine and a CALL statement to access the subroutine from a main program:

```
SUBROUTINE X(d,e,f,a,b,c)
IMPLICIT NONE
REAL, INTENT(OUT) :: a,b,c
INTEGER, INTENT(IN) :: d,e,f
...
PROGRAM XX
...
CALL X(a,b,c,d,e,f)
```

(a) What data types must a, b, c, d, e, and f have in the main program that CALLs SUBROUTINE X?

(b) Which of these CALLs to SUBROUTINE X are allowed, assuming that x, y, and z are declared as REAL and i, j, and k are declared as INTEGER?

```
CALL X(10,20,30,x,y,z)
CALL X(a,b,c,3.3,4.4,5.5)
CALL X(ROUND(SIN(x)),ROUND(SIN(y)),ROUND(SIN(z)),x,y,z)
CALL X(x,y,z,x,y,z)
CALL X(i,j,k,i,j,k)
```

7.7.2 Basic Programming Exercises

Where appropriate, functions and subroutines written for these exercises should be tested by including them in appropriate driver programs.

Exercise 7. The area of a triangle for which the length of two sides a and b and the angle α between the sides are known is

$$\text{area} = a \bullet b \bullet \sin(\alpha)$$

Write a FUNCTION to perform this calculation.

Exercise 8. The total cost for a production run of items equals the startup cost S plus the number of items n times the materials cost M and labor cost L per item:

$$\text{total cost} = S + n \cdot (M + L)$$

Write a FUNCTION to perform this calculation.

Exercise 9. Suppose a car travelling v m/s requires d meters to stop. Write a SUBROUTINE to calculate the time t and deceleration a required to stop within that distance, assuming that the deceleration is constant. The formulas are

$$t = 2d/v \qquad a = v/t$$

Exercise 10. (a) Add at least one additional conversion function to P-7.10.
(b) Modify program P-7.10 so that the conversion functions are replaced with subroutines. Each subroutine should have an "error flag" in its parameter list that will tell the calling program whether the requested conversion was performed successfully. (See the Problem Discussion of P-7.10.)

Exercise 11. Modify program P-7.11 so that
(a) a description of the function is printed at the top of the "graph";
(b) the value of x is printed in the left margin instead of the loop counter;
(c) a different symbol is printed for positive and negative values of f(x);
(d) the program user can specify the name of the output file.

Exercise 12. Based on material from other courses you are taking, state a computational problem and write a complete program to solve it. Your program should take the form of one or more functions and subroutines, with a driver program to test them.

7.7.3 Programming Applications

Each of the programs in these exercises should be written with the goal of building a library of "portable" subprograms. Even if the problem statement is not specific about this point, the source code for each exercise should include a driver program that tests the subprogram(s). In some cases, such as the exercises that deal with calendar and date calculations, you may be able to write one driver program that tests subprograms for several exercises.

Exercise 13. Write a program that calls a subroutine that accepts as input the month (as a character string), year (in the range 1899–2099), number of days in the month, and the day of the week (integer values 1–7 for Sunday through Saturday) on which the month starts. The output from the subroutine should be a printed calendar that looks something like this:

```
                April 1995

      Sun Mon Tue Wed Thu Fri Sat
      ---------------------------
                                1
       2   3   4   5   6   7   8
       9  10  11  12  13  14  15
      16  17  18  19  20  21  22
      23  24  25  26  27  28  29
      30
      ---------------------------
```

Depending on the length of the month and the day of the week on which it starts, no less than four lines (for a nonleap-year February starting on Sunday) and up to six lines may be required to print all the days. Be sure your program will work for all combinations of month lengths and starting days.

Hint: the major problem in this program is formatting the output. You may find an implied DO . . . loop used with the advance='no' option and a colon (:) control character in the FORMAT statement helpful for filling in blank spaces on the first line of the calendar, before day 1 is printed. You may have to think carefully about how to avoid an extra blank line between the last line of days and the row of dashes printed as the last row of the calendar in the example.

Extra Credit

Modify this program so that the only user input required is the year and the month. This means that your program must be able to provide the number of days in a month (these values could be contained in a DATA statement) and determine on what day of the week a specified month starts. Use these two facts:

(1) If a year is evenly divisible by 4 and not divisible by 100, or if a year is evenly divisible by 400, then it's a leap year. In leap years, February has 29 days instead of 28.
(2) January 1, 1899, was a Sunday.

This part of the problem will involve adding more subprograms to your program. If you haven't included the subroutine for the basic part of this exercise in a MODULE, you should certainly do so for all the subprograms required to complete this version of the problem. [CALENDAR.F90]

Exercise 14. The modern civil calendar system (the Gregorian calendar) is inconvenient for scientific purposes because, historically, different civil calendars have been used in different places at different times, and even when events are consistently recorded on the modern calendar it is not easy to count the number of days between two events.

The complexity of calendars—the fact that not all months have the same number of days and that extra days, such as leap years, are required to keep seasons in sync with the calendar—is basically due to the fact that the mean solar year—the time required for the earth to make one complete revolution around the sun—is not an integer number of mean solar days, where a mean solar day is defined as the time required for the earth to complete one revolution around its own axis relative to a fictitious sun that moves along the equinoctial (the projection of the equator on the celestial sphere) at a constant rate equal to the *average* apparent rate of motion of the actual sun. (If you think you understood this paragraph without reading it several times, you're just not paying attention. The celestial sphere is an imaginary sphere surrounding the earth on which the stars appear to be embedded and on the surface of which the sun, moon, and planets appear to move.)

A simpler time-tracking alternative is a system that assigns a unique identifier to every mean solar day of recorded history. The Julian date system, which starts with a value of 1 at noon on Gregorian date November 25, 4714 B.C., provides a simple and unambiguous way to record events. Without such a system, errors in the timing of events can result because not all countries converted to the Gregorian calendar at the same time. The English-speaking world didn't convert to the Gregorian calendar until 1752, for example. The Julian date system was invented by English astronomers at the Greenwich Observatory on the Thames River near London.[9] It was convenient to assign the same Julian date to an entire night of observations, which is why a Julian day starts at noon Greenwich time.

The following formula can be used to convert a date expressed in the Gregorian calendar to its corresponding Julian date:

```
temp = <(month-14)/12>
Julian Date = day - 32075 + <1461*(year+4800+temp)/4> +
              <367*(month-2-temp*12)/12> - <3*<(year+4900+temp)/100>/4>
```

where < . . . > means to truncate the enclosed expression.

Use this formula to write a function that accepts as input the Gregorian month, day, and year and returns the corresponding Julian date. Test the function with a driver program. The Julian date for Greenwich noon on January 1, 1995,

---

[9]These astronomers also defined the longitude system, which is why 0° longitude, the Greenwich meridian, passes through the Greenwich Observatory.

is 2449719.0. Be careful with historical dates before the mid-eighteenth century, as they may not be expressed in the Gregorian calendar.

Hint: the Julian date can be stored as either a real or an integer number. Although it is generally a good idea to avoid mixed-mode expressions, it would be OK in this case to assign the integer result of evaluating the above formula as a REAL number.

Also, because of the way Fortran handles arithmetic operations with integers, note that these two statements are equivalent, assuming that month is an integer variable:

```
temp = INT((month-14.)/12.)
temp = (month-14)/12
```

That is, the result of dividing two integer values or expressions, as in the second expression, is an integer equal to the truncated quotient. This is equivalent to performing a real arithmetic division and truncating the result, as in the first expression. You can force a Fortran expression to perform real division by using a real number or variable for at least one of the values in the expression. This expression is legal but redundant because the argument itself already has the desired truncated integer value:

```
temp = INT((month-14)/12)
```

When you write this program, you could try translating the formula in two different ways. The first way should express the numbers in the formula as real values (14. rather than 14, for example) and should use the INT function to truncate the expression. The other way should express all numbers as integers and will not require use of the INT function. The second way is a more "clever" solution that makes use of specific implementation details in Fortran that wouldn't apply to the same calculation done in another language. [CALENDAR.F90]

Extra Credit

Write a subroutine that converts a Julian date to its corresponding calendar date. Use these calculations:

```
TempA = JD + 68569.
TempB = <4•TempA/146097>
TempA = TempA - <(146097•TempB + 3)/4>
year = <4000•(TempA + 1)/1461001>
TempA = TempA - <1461•year/4> + 31
month - <80•TempA/2447>
day = <TempA - <2447•month/80>>
TempA = <month/11>
month = <month + 2 - 12•TempA>
year = <100•(TempB - 49) + Year + TempA>
```

Exercise 15. Another way of expressing dates is as $1000 \cdot (\text{year} - 1900)$ plus the number of the day in the year. Thus March 7, 1992, is day 31+29+7 of 1992 (a leap year), so the date can be represented as 92067. January 1, 2000, is 100001.

This system has the advantage of requiring only five or six characters to specify a date, and it simplifies calculations that involve knowing the number of days between two dates in the same way as the use of Julian dates. The values in this system are sometimes referred to as Julian days, but they are not the same as the Julian dates defined in the previous exercise.

Write a function that accepts as input a calendar date and returns the value defined here. If you did the extra credit part of the previous exercise, you may be able to reuse some of that code. Test the function in a driver program. [CALENDAR.F90]

Exercise 16. It is often necessary to estimate values based on engineering tables. If the tabulated values are not too far apart, a decision that depends on your application, linear interpolation may provide a sufficiently accurate approximation of a desired value. If a table contains two values, x_1 and x_2, of an independent variable x and two corresponding values, y_1 and y_2, of a dependent variable y, then a linearly interpolated estimate for y for a value x in the range $[x_1, x_2]$ is given by

$$y = y_1 + [(x - x_1)/(x_2 - x_1)] \cdot (y_2 - y_1)$$

Write a function or subroutine that accepts as input values for x, x_1, x_2, y_1, and y_2 and returns as output the linearly interpolated value of the dependent variable y corresponding to x.

Here are some sample values you can use to test your subprogram. (Refer to the file INTERPOL.DAT, which is included in the data files available for downloading from the World Wide Web site mentioned in Section i.5 of the Preface.)

x	y
5.0	5.9
10.0	6.6
15.0	7.1
20.0	8.3
25.0	10.0
30.0	12.2

As an example, if the value of the independent variable is 7.5, then the linearly interpolated value y is

$$y = 5.9 + [(7.5 - 5.0)/(10.0 - 5.0)](6.6 - 5.9) = 6.25$$

Should you use an interpolation formula for extrapolating past the ends of a table? Should your program include some protection against "unreasonable" use of an interpolation formula? [INTERPOL.F90]

Extra Credit
Here are formulas for higher order interpolations, in the form of Lagrange polynomials. The requirement on x is that it must lie within the range $[x_0,x_2]$ for quadratic interpolation and $[x_0,x_3]$ for cubic interpolation. Modify your program so the user can specify linear, quadratic, or cubic interpolation.

Quadratic interpolation:

$$y = y_0\frac{(x-x_1)(x-x_2)}{(x_0-x_1)(x_0-x_2)} + y_1\frac{(x-x_0)(x-x_2)}{(x_1-x_0)(x_1-x_2)} + y_2\frac{(x-x_0)(x-x_1)}{(x_2-x_0)(x_2-x_1)}$$

Cubic interpolation:

$$y = y_0\frac{(x-x_1)(x-x_2)(x-x_3)}{(x_0-x_1)(x_0-x_2)(x_0-x_3)} + y_1\frac{(x-x_0)(x-x_2)(x-x_3)}{(x_1-x_0)(x_1-x_2)(x_1-x_3)}$$

$$+ y_2\frac{(x-x_0)(x-x_1)(x-x_3)}{(x_2-x_0)(x_2-x_1)(x_2-x_3)} + y_3\frac{(x-x_0)(x-x_1)(x-x_2)}{(x_3-x_0)(x_3-x_1)(x_3-x_2)}$$

Exercise 17. Even scientists and engineers sometimes need to take out loans. Typically, a loan is made at a specified annual interest rate and must be repaid in a specified number of equal monthly payments. The formula for calculating the monthly payment is

$$\text{payment} = \frac{\text{amount}{\bullet}(r/12)}{1 - (1+r/12)^{-n}}$$

where r is the interest rate expressed as a decimal fraction, not as a percent.

When a payment is made at the end of any month, the interest accrued on the loan balance during that month is added to the balance at the beginning of the month (interest = balance${\bullet}$r/12). Then the payment is subtracted from the sum of the balance plus the interest to yield a new balance. For example, the interest due after one month on a $1000 loan at 8 percent is 1000{\bullet}$.08/12=$6.67. If the monthly payment were $90, then the new balance would be $916.67.

Write a subroutine that accepts as input the amount of a loan, the annual interest rate, and the number of payments. Calculate the monthly payment and print a loan repayment table that gives the interest accrued each month, the new balance after making a payment, and the total amount paid on the loan to date. Test the subroutine with several sets of user-supplied values. [FINANCAL.F90]

Extra credit
Because of roundoff errors in real arithmetic calculations, the balance at the end of the loan repayment period may not be exactly $0.00. Modify your program so that it recalculates the final payment to give a balance of $0.00, to the nearest cent.

Exercise 18. "Congratulations! You have just won the Megabucks Lottery Grand Prize of $1,000,000!" Naturally, this would be good news no matter how cynical you are. However, you have read the fine print, which states that the prize has an "annuity value" (not a cash value) of $1,000,000 and will be paid in equal installments of $50,000 per year, starting immediately and continuing for a total of 20 annual payments.

This method of paying a prize is equivalent to an "annuity due." In order to guarantee that money for the payments will be available, enough money must be set aside now to cover the first and all subsequent payments. However, assuming that the account will earn interest at an annual rate r, expressed as a decimal fraction, the "present value" of the annuity is not equal to the total of the payments, but some smaller amount, given by

$$\text{present value} = \frac{\text{payment} \cdot [1 - (1+r)^{-n}]}{r}(1+r)$$

where n is the number of annual payments, including the payment made immediately. A prize with an "annuity value" rather than a "cash value" is a good deal for the prize-giver because the present value is substantially less than the annuity value; the present value of a $1,000,000 annuity to be paid in 20 yearly installments of $50,000, assuming that the annuity account earns 8 percent annually, is about $530,000. It is a bad deal for the recipient because the effects of inflation erode the value of future payments.

Write a subroutine that will calculate the present value of an "annuity due" for an assumed annual interest rate and will print a table showing the value of the account each year until the final payment is made. Test the subroutine with several sets of user-supplied values. [FINANCAL.F90]

Exercise 19. You work for a progressive company that appreciates the value of investing in future research. Management has decided that it wants to invest money now for a major research program that will start 10 years from now and will cost $1,000,000. You have been asked to determine the amount of 10 equal annual payments your company should make into an interest-bearing account every year for the next 10 years, starting now, in order to have the required $1,000,000 at the end of 10 years.

This is a variation of the previous exercise and is equivalent to calculating the future value of an annuity. The formula is

$$\text{future value} = \text{payment} \cdot \frac{(1+r)^n - 1}{r}(1+r)$$

Write a subroutine that will accept as input the desired future amount and an interest rate, and will calculate the annual payment required to produce the specified future amount at the end of n years. Print a table showing the value of the account at the end of each year. Test the subroutine with several different interest rates. [FINANCAL.F90]

Using Arrays to Organize Information

This chapter begins with a typical data collection problem to illustrate the utility of and Fortran syntax for defining and using arrays. Topics covered include one-dimensional and multidimensional arrays, arrays as parameters in functions and subroutines, allocatable arrays, strings as "arrays" of characters, user-defined record types, and arrays of records.

8.1 Arrays in Structured Programming

Up to now, this text has discussed only data types for which a variable name corresponds to a single value and a single location in memory.[1] It is possible, and very desirable in structured programming, to define other kinds

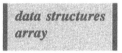

data structures
array

of *data structures* that lead to more convenient and compact ways of organizing information in a program. The most important user-defined data structure is the *array*. Basically, an array is a collection of related values organized under a single name. In this section, we will develop the basic concepts of arrays by posing a specific data management problem and examining how best to organize the information required to solve that problem.

Suppose you are conducting an experiment to monitor the concentration of tropospheric ozone, a federally regulated air pollutant. You have in place equipment that produces one measurement per hour for 24 hours. You would like to store these measurements and then write a program to process the data. How should your program handle this task? One way would be to associate each ozone measurement with its own variable name:

```
Ozone1
Ozone2
Ozone3
Ozone4
. . .
Ozone23
Ozone24
```

---

[1]This simple concept is adequate as long as we recognize that a single memory "location" will contain as many bytes as required to hold the variable, based on its data type declaration.

This seems a little awkward, but it will become much worse if you decide that what you really need is hourly measurements for 10 days. Suddenly you're faced with creating another 216 variable names!

Fortunately, there's an easier way: define a single variable name—Ozone—and an indexing system that can be used to address all the ozone measurements under this single variable name. Symbolically, each measurement could be addressed like this:

```
Ozone(1)
Ozone(2)
Ozone(3)
Ozone(4)
...
Ozone(23)
Ozone(24)
```

The interpretation of this system is the obvious one: Ozone(1) is the measurement at the first hour, Ozone(2) is the measurement at the second hour, and so forth. If you need more measurements, all you have to do is increase the value of the largest index, from 24 to 240, for example:

```
Ozone(1)
Ozone(2)
Ozone(3)
Ozone(4)
...
Ozone(239)
Ozone(240)
```

When it's translated into a programming language, this kind of data representation is called an array. The name of the array will be something obvious and descriptive, like Ozone. The number in parentheses is the **array index**. The value associated with each index is called an **array element**.

array index
array element
extent

The number of elements is called the **extent** (or size) of the array. For an array holding 24 ozone measurements per day for 10 days, the extent would be 240. For the above example, the notation Ozone(26) will refer to the 26th element—the second measurement on the second day—in the array named Ozone. This notation seems perfectly straightforward, and as we will see, it is just the notation that Fortran uses.

One-dimensional arrays are often associated with vectors, in the physical sense, or with **vector data** in a somewhat more generalized sense, as opposed to **scalar data**. This is a distinction that should be familiar from an

vector data
scalar data

introductory physics course. To cite some examples, the speed of a moving object is represented by a single number and is a scalar quantity. The velocity of a moving object is a vector quantity that describes both speed and direction with components in each of three coordinates in physical space. Mass is a scalar quantity, but weight, or force, is a vector quantity.

The association of arrays with vectors is especially relevant in problems in mathematics, science, and engineering, but the use of arrays in programs isn't restricted to applications that can be physically or mathematically associated with vectors. In programming, arrays are organizational tools for managing large amounts of related information. Basically, you should use an array any time you need to manipulate collections of related values, regardless of whether that use is associated with some kind of "vector" operation. Clearly, the problem of managing ozone measurements has no "vector" significance, but it is nonetheless a natural candidate for an array representation. Perhaps you could think of the ozone data as a vector in "data space" rather than in physical space.

It's worth pointing out here that it is easy to confuse the meaning of "dimension" when that word is applied to arrays. In physics, a "three-dimensional" vector might refer to the position or velocity of an object in space because space has three dimensions.[2] However, such a vector is represented by a rank one (one-dimensional) array in Fortran. To put it another way, the dimensionality of arrays, in the programming use of that term, describes not their "size" (for example, in terms of the number of vector components), but their "shape." A physical vector has a "shape" of one regardless of how many components it has, but a table with several rows and columns, for example, has a "shape" of two regardless of how many rows and columns it has.

Arrays can represent data in more than one *dimension*. | **dimension** |
Suppose your experiment expands to include hourly measurements every day for a month. This could require up to
$31 \times 24 = 744$ values. In the same way that an array with 240 elements can hold 24 hourly measurements for up to 10 days, you could represent monthly data with an array the indices of which can take values from 1 to 744. However, in terms of organizing this information, it makes more sense to define a two-dimensional array—essentially, a table of values. One index—from a programming point of view, it doesn't matter which one—will represent a day of the month, and the other will represent an hour in the day. Assume that the first index represents the day and the second the hour:

On day 1:   `Ozone( 1, 1)`   On day 31:   `Ozone(31, 1)`
             `Ozone( 1, 2)`   `Ozone(31, 2)`
             `. . .`   `. . .`
             `Ozone( 1,24)`   `Ozone(31,24)`
On day 2:   `Ozone( 2, 1)`
             `Ozone( 2, 2)`
             `. . .`

---

[2]Note to physics students: this statement refers to the properties of space as described by Newtonian mechanics.

```
Ozone( 2,24)
```

This two-dimensional array of size (31,24) contains the same number of elements as a one-dimensional array of size 31×24=744, but the two-dimensional arrangement is a more natural way of storing and accessing information for this problem.

As you can see from this example, the dimensionality of an array is associated with the number of array indices required to access values in the array. A two-dimensional array requires two indices. The dimensionality of an array is called its **rank**. A two-dimensional array is a rank two array. The ozone array has extent 31 in its first dimension and extent 24 in its second dimension.

Fortran supports arrays of up to seven dimensions (rank seven). Figure 8.1 should help you visualize the structure of arrays up to rank three. Starting with the simplest case, you can think of a rank one array as a "line" of boxes. For example, you could imagine a single row of mailboxes in a post office named, unimaginatively, "A." Each mailbox corresponds to an element of a rank one array (array A in Figure 8.1). The number on each mailbox at post office "A" corresponds to its array index. In Figure 8.1, the arrow from array A points to the seventh "box." Although you wouldn't be likely to confuse the contents of a mailbox with the address of that mailbox, it is nonetheless easy to confuse an array and its elements with the indices to that array. Just remember that an index corresponds to the "address" of a mailbox and an element corresponds to the "contents" of a mailbox.

You can easily expand this "post office" image to visualize rank two (two-dimensional) arrays as several rows of mailboxes (array B in Figure 8.1). One array dimension represents rows and the other represents columns. However, in a real post office, boxes are likely to be numbered consecutively. In array notation, the addresses of the mailboxes are identified by a row and column. In Figure 8.1, the arrow from array B points to the "box" in column seven of the fourth row.

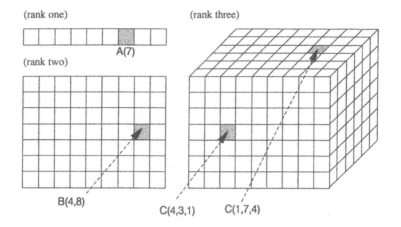

Figure 8.1. Structure of arrays with rank one (array A), rank two (array B), and rank three (array C)

You may have to abandon the post office image to visualize a rank three array (array C in Figure 8.1); you might identify the three dimensions as row, column, and "layer." Arrows in Figure 8.1 point to array elements in row four, column three, layer one, and row one, column seven, layer four. Arrays with more than three dimensions are harder to visualize, but their treatment in Fortran remains fundamentally the same. There are many applications of arrays in mathematics, science, and engineering, so it is not surprising that Fortran has always provided strong support for arrays. Fortran 90 has added some important new features in support of arrays, which we will discuss in this chapter.

8.2 Basic Array Implementation

This section presents the basics of using arrays in Fortran by developing a program for a simple problem. We will return to the ozone data problem later in this chapter.

8.2.1 Example: Testing a Random Number Generator

1 *Define the problem.*

Recall that the radiation testing application in Chapter 6 made use of Fortran's built-in random number generator to simulate a radiation exposure experiment. During the development of that application, we simply assumed that the random number generator works as advertised—that is, that it produces uniformly distributed real numbers over the range [0.0,1.0).

How can you be sure it works? Basically, the random number generators found in programming languages are no more than algorithms that produce values that *appear* to be random; an algorithm-based random number generator cannot produce an infinite series of truly random numbers. A convincing statistical proof of randomness is beyond the scope of this text. However, as an intuitively simple test, you might devise this experiment. Convert 1000 uniformly distributed real numbers in the range [0.0,1.0) to 1000 integers in the range [1,10]. Let the real numbers in the range [0,0.1) correspond to an index of 1, those in the range [0.1,0.2) to an index of 2, and so forth. If the real numbers are uniformly distributed over the range [0.0,1.0), then each integer in the range [1,10] is equally probable. Thus there should be, on the average, 100 ones, 100 twos, and so forth.

Write a program that implements this experiment and displays the results.

2 Outline a solution.

1. Create an array of size 10. Initialize all its elements to 0.
2. Inside a loop, generate 1000 random integers in the range 1–10.
3. If the integer is a 1, increment the contents of array element 1 by 1. If the integer is a 2, increment the contents of array element 2 by 1, and so forth.
4. When you're done, the array will contain the total number of ones, twos, and so forth. The sum of the values in each element of the array will be 1000, and there should be approximately 100 ones, 100 twos, and so forth. This array is called a "count histogram." One such histogram is shown in Figure 8.2.

3 Design an algorithm.

This problem sounds more complicated than it actually is. The pseudocode is very simple.

DEFINE *(integer array (histogram) of size 10, loop counter, array_index)*
INITIALIZE *all array elements to 0*
LOOP *(counter = 1 to 1000)*
    ASSIGN *array_index = random integer in range [1,10]*
    INCREMENT *histogram(array_index) = histogram(array_index) + 1*
END LOOP
WRITE *(histogram)*

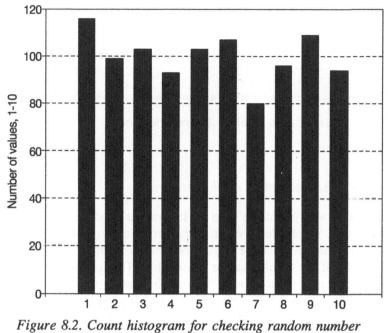

Figure 8.2. Count histogram for checking random number generator

4 Convert the algorithm into a program.

P-8.1 [RANDTEST.F90]

```
      PROGRAM RandTest
!
! Generate count histogram from random number generator.
! (Demonstrate 1-D arrays.)
      IMPLICIT NONE
      INTEGER A(0:9),i,index
      INTEGER Count(1) ! for random number generator
      REAL x
!
!     Initialize array.
!
      A = 0
!
!     Generate count histogram.
!
      CALL System_Clock(Count(1))
      CALL Random_Seed(Put=Count)
      DO 10 i=1,1000
        CALL Random_Number(x)
        index = INT(x*10.)
        A(index) = A(index) + 1
10    CONTINUE
```

```
PRINT*,A
END
```

Running P-8.1

```
117 99 103 93 103 107 80 96 109 93
```

WWe will discuss P-8.1 in detail in the next section.

5 *Verify the operation of the program.*

You can verify that the sum of the values produced by the program is 1000—if it isn't, you made an error in the programming—but it isn't otherwise easy to verify the operation of Fortran's random number generator except by asking yourself if the results appear reasonable. This count histogram program simply reports results without providing any indication of what they mean.

Even if you run P-8.1 many times, you will probably never find a case for which the value of every element of A is equal to 100. If the contents of one or more elements in your histogram array are consistently considerably greater or less than 100, you might suspect a problem. However, such a problem would almost certainly be within your source code rather than within the generator itself because even a statistically poor random number generator can easily pass the "test" we've devised here. A standard statistical test that can be applied to the results from P-8.1 is presented in Exercise 17 at the end of this chapter.

8.2.2 Declaring Arrays

P-8.1 contains a great deal of information about using arrays in Fortran, and we will discuss it in detail. First consider the declaration of an array data structure. When variables associated with scalar values are declared, the only information required is the data type. When an array is declared, both the data type of the array elements—the contents of the array—and the number of elements—the size and shape of the array—must be specified. There are several ways this can be done in Fortran 90, but we will use only syntax forms in which the size and data type of an array are specified in a single statement:

```
data_type name(spec)[,name(spec)]...
data_type, DIMENSION(spec)[,name(spec)]... :: name[,name]...
where (spec) is (low:high[,low:high]...) or (size[,size]...)]

Examples:
     REAL A(0:9)
     INTEGER B(10,3,2),C(-2:2,3,0:99)
     REAL, DIMENSION(10,20) :: x,y

     INTEGER, PARAMETER :: n1=-5,n2=5,n3=10
     REAL C(n1:n2),D(n3)
```

Names for arrays are subject to the same rules as other Fortran variables. A size specifier (*spec*) gives the lower and upper bounds for each array index or simply the size of a one-dimensional array, in which case the lower index is 1 by default. These index boundaries must be of type INTEGER; they can be either integer constants or named values declared as INTEGER and given the PARAMETER attribute. (This is another way of saying that only integers can serve as array indices.) A statement assigning the PARAMETER attribute must appear before the statement requiring the values.

The *data_type* specifier refers to the contents of the array, not its indices; arrays can contain values of any data type, including INTEGER and REAL numbers, CHARACTERs, and LOGICALs.

A simple specification for a one-dimensional array is REAL A(50). This means that the array named A contains 50 elements of type REAL and that these 50 elements are accessed through the INTEGER array indices 1–50. In P-8.1, the size specifier is given as 0:9. This is an array with 10 elements (that is, with extent 10), accessed with indices 0–9 rather than 1–10. Why? Because the statement in P-8.1 that generates the index (printed in bold italics) produces integer values in the range [0,9] rather than [1,10]. This is a programming detail that need not affect your algorithm design.

Negative array indices are also allowed. An array with the specifier (-5:5) has size (extent) 11, and not 10, because the element with an index of 0 is included. As noted above, arrays may contain up to seven dimensions. Each dimension requires its own size specifier.

Programming Tip

In programs written in earlier versions of Fortran, you will see the rank and size of an array declared in a separate statement using the DIMENSION keyword. If the array is explicitly typed, that declaration will be in a previous statement. Hence the array specification REAL A(0:9) could also be given as

```
REAL A
DIMENSION A(0:9)
```

However, there is no reason to use this syntax form in Fortran 90.

The arrays we have described are *statically allocated arrays*. This means that once their size is set as part of their declaration, that size cannot be changed while the program is running. Consequently, you must know ahead of time—while you're writing your source code—the maximum number of array elements your program will need. If you allocate more space than you need, the extra space is, in some sense, "wasted." The total amount of array space available to a program is limited by your Fortran compiler and, ultimately, by your computer's resources. However, this is rarely a problem in practice and will never be a problem for the programs discussed in this text.

If you try to access array elements beyond the declared boundaries, your program *should* crash.[3] It might also print an informative message, although Fortran compilers may not be as helpful in this situation as some other programming environments are.

Here is another important point about arrays. It should be clear from the syntax of array definitions that

> **Every element in an array must contain the same *kind* of value.**

If an array is declared as type INTEGER, then all its elements must contain integers. If the array has more than one dimension, the elements in all dimensions must have the same data type. In Section 8.6, we will discuss a way to circumvent this restriction by defining a new kind of data type that can be used as an element in an array. It will then be possible to define an array the elements of which all have this user-defined data type. This will meet the restriction that each element of an array must hold the same data type, while allowing the user-defined data type to hold several different kinds of values.

8.2.3 Assigning Values to Arrays

After arrays have been declared, they need to be given values in your program. There are several ways to accomplish this important task.

---

[3]Author's note: I use the word "should" rather than "will" because of a general wariness that results from observing significant differences in the way compilers and other languages respond to array references beyond the defined boundaries. Tests for array boundary violations aren't made in C, for example.

Assigning a value to an entire array or part of an array

Here is an executable statement that assigns a single value to every element in an array:

```
X=17.7
```

This statement sets every element of the apparently REAL array X to a value of 17.7, regardless of the size or dimension of X. Although this statement looks like a simple assignment of a number to a scalar variable, your compiler "knows" that X is an array because of its data declaration. Consequently, you can think of this statement as a kind of implied DO... statement that initializes all the elements of X. This is a very useful way of manipulating the contents of arrays, which did not exist in older versions of Fortran.

It's also possible to assign the same value to just some of the elements in an array. The statements

```
REAL x(-10,10)
. . .
X(-4:4)=0.
```

result in a value of 0 being assigned to the nine elements from X(-4) through X(4). This can be tricky with multidimensional arrays. The statements

```
REAL Z(10,10)
. . .
Z(1,1:3)=1.
Z(:,1)=1.
Z(2,1:10:2)=0.
```

are all possible. Assume that the first dimension represents rows and the second represents columns. In the first assignment, columns 1–3 of row 1 are assigned a value of 1. In the second, the entire first column is assigned a value of 1. In the third example, the :2 in the specification means that every second column of row 2, starting with the first, that is, columns 1, 3, 5, 7, and 9, is assigned a value of 0. These "shorthand" means of assigning array elements may sometimes be convenient, but they are never required. When you use this kind of syntax in your own programs, be sure to test the code thoroughly![4]

---

[4]There are, in fact, even more "shorthand" ways to assign values to subsections of arrays. If you're interested, consult a Fortran 90 language reference manual such as the one referenced in the Preface to this text.

Assigning array elements with count-controlled loops

Consider a one-dimensional array A(-5:5), all of whose elements need to be assigned a value of zero. Based on the previous subsection, all that is required is the statement A=0. However, it is also possible to construct an explicit DO... loop:

```
DO i=-5,5
  A(i)=0.
END DO
```

If the array is multidimensional, use nested loops. For B(2,3,4),

```
DO i=1,2
  DO j=1,3
    DO k=1,4
      B(i,j,k)=0.
    END DO
  END DO
END DO
```

Array elements are referenced by following the array name with the array index or indices enclosed in parentheses. The index references may be integer constants or variables, or expressions or functions that return integer values.

For the purpose of simply assigning values to all or some of an array's elements, there is little justification for writing explicit loops. However, you will often see such loops in programs written in older versions of Fortran, which provided no alternatives.

Assigning values to individual array elements

You can assign values to individual array elements. Assuming appropriate type declarations, these are typical assignments:

```
B(1,1,1)=B(1,1,1)+B(0,1,1)
A(3)=B(1,1,1)
```

Remember that *individual* array elements are treated just like scalar variables. That's why it's OK to assign an element of one array to an element of another regardless of whether the two arrays have the same rank and extent(s). However, the same caveats about mixed-mode expressions and type conversions that apply to assignments involving scalar variables (for example, assigning a REAL value to an INTEGER variable) also apply to assignments involving array elements. Therefore, you should avoid mixed-mode expressions involving array elements.

Using a DATA statement to initialize arrays

If an array must be initialized at the beginning of a program, the DATA statement provides a convenient method. Syntax forms of the DATA statement suitable for initializing arrays are

```
DATA (name(i),i=n1,n2)/constant[,constant].../
DATA (name(i),i=n1,n2)/n*constant/
DATA name/n*constant/
DATA name(element)[,name(element)]/constant[,constant].../
DATA name(element)[,name(element)]/n*constant/

Examples:
      INTEGER i,j
      REAL A(10),B(11:20),C(0:9,0:19)
      INTEGER D(10)
      DATA A/10*1./,(B(i),i=11,15)/5*0./,(B(i),i=16,20)/5*-1./
      DATA ((C(i,j),i=0,9),j=0,9)/-1./
      DATA D(1),D(3),D(5),D(7),D(9)/1,2,3*3/
```

The integers *n1* and *n2* refer to the first and last elements to be initialized in *name*, and *n* is a repetition value no greater than the total number of elements in the array to which it refers. The values *n*, *n1*, and *n2* can be either integer constants or values given the PARAMETER attribute prior to their use. As the examples imply, it's not necessary to initialize the entire array to the same value, or even at all, although that is usually what you would wish to do. These forms of the DATA statement can be intermixed with forms used to assign constant values to scalar variables.

The first two DATA statement syntax forms use an implied DO... loop, as discussed in Chapter 6. The DATA statement for a REAL array A,

```
DATA (A(i),i=1,5)/0./
```

may appear equivalent to the statement A=0 or the explicit DO... statement,

```
DO i=1,5
  A(i)=0.
END DO
```

However, the difference—and it's a very important one—is that the DATA statement is nonexecutable and can appear only at the beginning of your program. That is, the DATA statement can't be used to reinitialize an array later in your program.[5]

---

[5]This is an especially important point to remember if you use a DATA statement in a function or procedure, as discussed in Chapter Seven.

Implied DO... loops in DATA statements can be nested. For an appropriately declared two-dimensional array with a size specifier of at least (1:10,1:5), this is a perfectly reasonable statement by which to initialize the INTEGER array A:

```
DATA ((A(i,j),j=1,10),i=1,5)/50*10/
```

The third syntax form of the DATA statement indicates that it is possible to initialize an entire array without using an implied DO... loop and without specifically referring to each array element. This applies to multidimensional arrays as well as one-dimensional arrays. Here's an example:

```
REAL A(0:4:0:9)
DATA A/50*0./
```

The REAL array A has 50 elements altogether, and it's not necessary to know the order in which these elements are stored to initialize them all to zero.

Using elemental intrinsic functions

Another important Fortran 90 innovation allows many Fortran intrinsic functions to be called with arrays as arguments. In fact, all the mathematical functions

elemental functions

listed in Table 4.1 are *elemental functions* that will accept either scalar or array arguments of the appropriate data type and will return identically typed and sized arrays as output. For example, the statement

```
B=SIN(A)
```

is valid regardless of whether A and B are scalar variables or arrays. If A and B are arrays, they must have the same size. Program P-8.2 uses elemental functions to calculate "vectors" of sines and cosines.

P-8.2 [SINCOS.F90]

```
      PROGRAM SinCos
!
! Illustrate the use of elemental functions for array assignments.
!
      IMPLICIT NONE
      REAL X(0:18),Y(0:18),Z(0:18),pi
      INTEGER i
!
      pi=4.*ATAN(1.)
!
! Create array of angles...
      DO i=0,18
        X(i)=5.*REAL(i)*pi/180.
      END DO
! Calculate trig functions for entire array...
      Y=SIN(X)
      Z=COS(X)
!
      PRINT 1000,(i*5,Y(i),Z(i),i=0,18)
1000  FORMAT(1x,i3,2f6.3)
      END
```

Running P-8.2

```
  0 0.000 1.000
  5 0.087 0.996
 10 0.174 0.985
 15 0.259 0.966
 20 0.342 0.940
 25 0.423 0.906
 30 0.500 0.866
 35 0.574 0.819
 40 0.643 0.766
 45 0.707 0.707
 50 0.766 0.643
 55 0.819 0.574
 60 0.866 0.500
 65 0.906 0.423
 70 0.940 0.342
 75 0.966 0.259
 80 0.985 0.174
 85 0.996 0.087
 90 1.000 0.000
```

Remember that angles must be converted to radians before you can use Fortran trigonometric functions. The code

```
DO i=0,18
  X(i)=5.*REAL(i)*pi/180.
END DO
Y=SIN(X)
Z=COS(X)
```

is equivalent to

```
DO i=0,18
  X(i)=5.*REAL(i)*pi/180.
  Y(i)=SIN(X(i))
  Z(i)=COS(X(i))
END DO
```

The statement that assigns values to X could be written as

```
X(i)=5*i*pi/180.
```

but using a specific type conversion is better programming style.

8.2.4 Displaying the Contents of Arrays (Implied DO . . . Loops)

There are several ways to display the contents of arrays. The simplest and least flexible is simply to PRINT or WRITE the array. If A and B are arrays,

```
PRINT *,A
WRITE(*,*)B
```

will display the entire contents of the A and B arrays, one element at a time. This is perfectly straightforward if A and B are one-dimensional arrays. However, the results are not so obvious when A and B are multidimensional arrays because the order in which elements of multidimensional arrays are stored isn't obvious. Consider P-8.3, the only purpose of which is to demonstrate how array elements are stored.

P-8.3 [ROWCOL.F90]

```
      PROGRAM rowcol
!
      IMPLICIT NONE
      INTEGER B(3,4),row,col
!
      DO row=1,3
        DO col=1,4
          B(row,col)=row*10+col
        END DO
      END DO
      PRINT 1000,((B(row,col),col=1,4),row=1,3)
      PRINT *
      PRINT *,B
1000  FORMAT(1x,4i4)
      END
```

Running P-8.3

```
11  12  13  14
21  22  23  24
31  32  33  34

11  21  31  12  22  32  13  23  33  14  24  34
```

The two dimensions of B are associated with rows and columns in a table. The assignments in the nested DO... loop produce the values shown in the first three lines of output. The value 34, for example, is in column four of the third row. In the PRINT 1000 statement, B is printed row by row by using a nested implied DO... loop. This implied DO... loop displays the contents of B in the same order in which the contents were created, with columns in the inner loop and rows in the outer loop. Because an array can have a maximum dimension of seven, implied DO... loops can be nested seven levels deep.

What happens when the B array is printed in the statement PRINT *,B? In this case, the programmer no longer exerts control over how the array elements are printed. Instead the values are printed in the order in which they are stored in memory, which is column by column and *not* row by row.

What you can learn by generalizing the output from P-8.3 is that in a two-dimensional array where the first index is thought of as specifying a row and the second index as specifying a column, the array is stored not row by row, but column by column; that is, row 1, column 1 is stored first, row 2, column 1 is stored second, etc. The association of dimensions in a two-dimensional array with "rows" and "columns" is artificial, of course. It could just as well be the other way around, but in either case Fortran doesn't care. When you declare indices for arrays, it's up to you to assign meaningful names and use them properly in a program.

To generalize to arrays of higher rank, values associated with cycling the leftmost dimension of multidimensional arrays are contiguous in memory. A three-dimensional array A declared as A(i,j,k) is stored like this:

```
A(1,1,1)  ┌─>A(1,2,1)  ┌─>..  ┌─>A(1,j,1)  ┌─>A(1,1,2)  ┌─>..  ┌─>A(1,j,k)
A(2,1,1)  │  A(2,2,1)  │      │  A(2,j,1)  │  A(2,1,2)  │      │  A(2,j,k)
...       │  ...       │      │  ...       │  ...       │      │  ...
A(i,1,1)─┘  A(i,2,1)─┘      ─┘  A(i,j,1)─┘  A(i,1,2)─┘      ─┘  A(i,j,k)
```

One way to remember how elements are stored is to think of an automobile odometer. The way array elements cycle when they're displayed in their stored order is the *opposite* order from the way the ones, tens, and hundreds mileage indicators cycle; that is, the elements cycle from left to right rather than from right to left.

Because of the frequency with which two-dimensional arrays are used in programs to represent tables in a row-and-column format, it is often inconvenient to display them in their "natural" column-wise order. With arrays of more than two dimensions, you will almost always want to exert direct program control over the order in which the elements are displayed. (Alternatively, you can define the array indices so they will naturally print in the desired order.) In any case, your code will usually be easier to understand if you use DO. . . loops (either explicit or implied) to control the display of arrays.

A final point of interest in P-8.3 is the FORMAT statement. The 4i4 format specifier always displays four numbers per row of output. The PRINT statement keeps "reusing" this format as long as there are values left to print. This format was chosen to display this particular table of values because the array was considered as representing three rows of four columns each. Whether the row and column values are actually displayed in their proper positions depends on how the array elements are accessed, not on the format specifier itself.

Study Tip

Create a program whose only purpose is to declare, define, and display several arrays using the syntax presented so far in this chapter. Later on, if you're having trouble with array syntax or are unsure whether a particular syntax will work, try it in this test program.

8.2.5 Example: Monthly Ozone Summary

At the beginning of this chapter, we discussed the problem of managing a series of ozone measurements. In this section, we will develop a program for storing and manipulating one month of ozone data in a two-dimensional array.

1 Define the problem.

An ozone monitoring station stores a measurement every hour for one month. Write a program that stores these data and calculates averages for each day and for the monthly hourly average.

2 Outline a solution.

1. Read the data and store them in a two-dimensional array. Let the first index represent up to 31 days and the second index hours 1 through 24.
2. For each day, calculate the daily average ozone value.
3. For each hour, calculate the monthly average ozone value at that hour.

4. Display the ozone measurements with the daily average in the rightmost column and the monthly hourly averages as an additional row at the bottom of the table.

The major difficulty for this problem is gaining access to the ozone measurements. Such data would usually be read from an external data file, a process we will discuss in detail in Chapter 9. For the present, we will simply hardcode a subset of the data—five hours for each of three days—into a DATA statement. This is an unacceptable way to provide data in general, but it will suffice for the purpose of this program, which is to illustrate some interesting Fortran 90 capabilities for processing arrays. We will return to a "full-size" version of this problem in Chapter 9.

3 *Design an algorithm.*

Here is a loop-intensive algorithm design for this problem.

DEFINE *(ozone array of real numbers, dimensioned 31×24;*
daily and monthly hourly averages as real numbers;
number of hours in a day and days in a month as integers;
loop counters as integers)
READ *(data into array)*
(get daily averages...)
LOOP *(for days = 1 to number of days)*
    INITIALIZE *daily_avg = 0*
    LOOP *(for hours = 1 to number of hours)*
        INCREMENT *daily_avg = daily_avg + ozone(day,hour)*
    END LOOP
    ASSIGN *daily_avg = daily_avg/number of hours*
END LOOP
(get monthly hourly averages...)
LOOP *(for hours = 1 to number of hours)*
    INITIALIZE *hourly_avg = 0*
    LOOP *(for days = 1 to number of days)*
        INCREMENT *hourly_avg = hourly_avg + ozone(days,hours)*
    END LOOP
    ASSIGN *hourly_avg = hourly_avg/number of days*
END LOOP

4 *Convert the algorithm into a program.*

In earlier versions of Fortran, you would have to translate this algorithm directly, with its explicit loop structures. However, because of Fortran 90's advanced array management capabilities, the algorithm is trivial to implement!

P-8.4 [OZONE.F90]

```
      PROGRAM OzoneData
!
! File name OZONE.F90
! Process monthly ozone data
! (short version for 3 days with 5 hours in each day)
!
      IMPLICIT NONE
      REAL ozone(31,24)
      INTEGER n_hours,n_days,hours,days
      DATA ozone(1,1:5)/3.2,3.3,3.1,2.9,3.4/, &
           ozone(2,1:5)/2.9,2.8,2.7,3.0,4.0/, &
           ozone(3,1:5)/2.8,2.6,2.5,2.9,3.1/, &
           n_hours,n_days/5,3/
!
! Get daily averages...
      PRINT 1010,((ozone(days,hours),hours=1,n_hours), &
         SUM(ozone(days,1:n_hours))/n_hours,days=1,n_days)
! Get hourly averages...
      PRINT 1020,
         (SUM(ozone(1:n_days,hours))/n_days,hours=1,n_hours)
!
1010  FORMAT(1x,5f5.1,f5.2)
1020  FORMAT(1x,5f5.2)
      END
```

Running P-8.4

```
   3.2  3.3  3.1  2.9  3.4 3.18
   2.9  2.8  2.7  3.0  4.0 3.08
   2.8  2.6  2.5  2.9  3.1 2.78
  2.97 2.90 2.77 2.93 3.50
```

In P-8.4, it is apparent that the Fortran 90 function SUM has taken over the work of setting up loops to accumulate components of the data

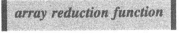
array reduction function

vector ozone. SUM is an example of an *array reduction function* that requires an array as its input argument and returns a scalar value. The general syntax is:

```
SUM(array_name[(spec[,spec]...)])
```

where *spec* has the same interpretation as it does for array declarations. That is, it specifies the low and high limits on a range of array elements. When the name of an array appears by itself, SUM returns the sum of all elements in the array. When a range specifier is included, just the elements within the range are summed. In P-8.4, the function call SUM(ozone(days,1:n_hours)) calculates the sum of elements 1 through n_hours for the current value of days in the implied DO... loop. This and several other array reduction functions are described in more detail in Chapter 12.

5 *Verify the operation of the program.*

The advantage of working with a small subset of an entire month's worth of data is that you can check the calculations by hand with a calculator.

Problem Discussion

The availability of "high-level" array functions such as SUM in Fortran 90 suggests that detailed pseudocode can be abandoned for these kinds of operations. It isn't necessary to do so, but it is certainly reasonable and often allows both the pseudocode and the resulting source code to be significantly shorter than they would otherwise be.

In P-8.4, no separate variables are set aside for the daily and monthly hourly averages. Instead the averages are calculated and printed "on the fly" with the aid of implied DO... loops in the PRINT statements. In some other context, it might be desirable to save these values. One way to do this would be to expand the array declaration to 32×25. Then the 25th column could hold the daily averages and the 32nd row could hold the monthly hourly averages.

8.3 Using Statically Allocated Arrays in Subprograms

As you should recall from the discussion earlier in this chapter, arrays are statically allocated. That is, the amount of space reserved for an array is set when it is defined in the block of nonexecutable statements at the beginning of a (sub)program. It is often the case that although the data type and rank of an array are known when a program is being written, the required number of elements is not. For example, you might know that a one-dimensional array will hold measurements of a physical quantity, so the elements of the array should be REAL numbers, but you don't know how many measurements there will be. To put this situation in programming jargon, you know the rank and data type of the array at "compile time," but you would like to be able to defer the sizing of the array until "run time." With statically declared arrays, you can't do this. Instead you have to declare the array in your main program with the maximum number of elements your program will need.

Another typical example might be a program that includes a subroutine to perform an operation on two vectors. At the time the program is written, you know that the vectors will be represented by one-dimensional arrays of real numbers. However, you won't know ahead of time how many components the vectors will have.

A static array solution to this kind of problem is to declare one-dimensional arrays in your main program so that they will accommodate the largest number of components you will ever need to use with the program. However, what happens in subprograms? How do they "know" when the actual number of elements used in an array is less than the declared size? Must subprograms be rewritten if the maximum array size changes? No, because Fortran allows you to declare arrays in subprograms with variable dimensions, using a symbolic representation for the *actual* number of array elements to be used by the subprogram. The values containing this information will be calculated by the calling (sub)program and passed to the subprogram through its parameter list.

Here is a problem that illustrates this approach.

1 *Define the problem.*

In mathematics, a "set" describes a nonordered collection of "things" on which certain operations can be performed. The "union" of two sets A and B is a new set that contains every element that appears in **either** A or B. The "intersection" of two sets A and B is a new set that contains every element that appears in **both** A and B. We can represent sets as arrays for the purpose of forming the union and intersection. We will further specify that the sets represented by the arrays are "proper sets" (to use the mathematical terminology), which means that no duplicate values are allowed in either the initial or the result sets.

Consider these sets:

$$A = \{1,5,9,3\}$$
$$B = \{5,3,8\}$$

(Note that the values do not have to be in any particular order, and there is no requirement that the sets must contain the same number of values.) The union of A and B, $A \cup B$, is $\{1,3,5,8,9\}$. The intersection of A and B, $A \cap B$, is $\{3,5\}$.

Clearly, this is a calculation for which the size of the resulting array cannot, in general, be determined ahead of time (that is, at "code writing" time).

The maximum number of elements required for A∪B is the sum of the number of elements in A and B. The maximum number for A∩B is the number of elements in the smaller of the two sets.

Write a subroutine that returns as output the union of two sets A and B and the number of elements in the union. (Writing a subroutine that returns the intersection is left as an end-of-chapter exercise.)

2 *Outline a solution.*

1. Specify the maximum size for each of the "input" arrays: that is, the maximum number of members in each set. Specify the maximum size of the "output" array as the sum of the sizes of the two input arrays.
2. Define a subprogram that includes in its parameter list the names of the arrays and the actual number of members in the set each array represents; these values must be no greater than the maximum declared sizes. Provide the total number of members in the intersection set as output from the subprogram.
3. Initialize the array representing the intersection set to some value that will never be found in either of the input sets. For this program, assume that the members of the set will be non-negative integers, so the intersection array can be initalized to any negative number.
4. Suppose the first n_A elements of the array A contains values representing members of one of the input sets. Set the first n_A elements of the output array C to these values because the intersection set will contain at least these values.
5. For each element of the array representing members of the second input set, check to see if that value is also present in the first input set. If it is, don't add it to the intersection set (because the intersection can't contain duplicate values). If it isn't present, add it to the intersection set.

3 *Design an algorithm.*

This algorithm requires a great deal of care to assign elements properly in the array holding the intersection of the two input sets.

DEFINE *(Arrays A, B, and C as arrays of integers with sizes n_A, n_B, and n_C = n_A + n_B. n_set as an integer holding the numer of elements in the intersection set represented by C.)*
ASSIGN *(values to n_A and n_B)*
ASSIGN *(values to A(1:n_A) and B(1:n_B))*
CALL *Union(IN: A and B; OUT C and n_set)*
WRITE *(n_set and all values of C)*

SUBPROGRAM *Union(IN: Arrays A, B, n_A, n_B, n_C; OUT: C, n_set)*
DEFINE *(local variables: i, j as loop counters; "add" as boolean)*
INITIALIZE *C = -1 (a value that won't be found in either set)*
ASSIGN *C(1:n̄_A) = A (The intersection will contain at least these values.)*
LOOP *(for i = 1 to n_B) (Search through B...)*

> **ASSIGN** *add = true*
> **INITIALIZE** *j = 1*
> **LOOP** *(while j <= n_A) and (add is true)*
>
>> **IF** *B(i) = A(j)* **THEN ASSIGN** *add = false (Looking for*
>>> *duplicates...)*
>>
>> **INCREMENT** *j = j + 1*
>
> **END LOOP**
> **IF** *(add is true)* **THEN** *(add new values if not duplicates...*
>
>> **INCREMENT** *n_set = n_set + 1 (Increment union counter.)*
>> **ASSIGN** *C(n_set) = B(i)*
>
> *(end IF...)*
> **END LOOP**

END LOOP
(end subprogram)

4

Convert the algorithm into a program.

P-8.5 [UNION1.F90]

```
      MODULE SetStuff
!
      CONTAINS
!-----------------------------------------------
      SUBROUTINE Union(A,B,C,n_A,n_B,n_C,n_set)
      IMPLICIT NONE
      INTEGER, INTENT(IN) :: n_A,n_B,n_C
      INTEGER, INTENT(OUT) :: n_set
      INTEGER, INTENT(IN) :: A(n_A),B(n_B)
      INTEGER, INTENT(OUT) :: C(n_C)
      INTEGER i,j
      LOGICAL add
!
      C=-1 !Initialize union "set" to negative value.
      C(1:n_A)=A !Now set union to A...
      n_set=n_A !and initialize union counter to # values in A.
      DO i=1,n_B !Search through B...
        add=.TRUE.
        j=1
        DO WHILE ((j <= n_A) .AND. (add))
          IF (B(i) == A(j)) add=.FALSE. !looking for duplicates...
          j=j+1
        END DO
```

```
      IF (add) THEN !add new values if not duplicates...
        n_set=n_set+1 !increment union counter.
        C(j)=B(i)
      END IF
    END DO
    END SUBROUTINE Union
!-----------------------
    END MODULE SetStuff
!=========================


    PROGRAM UnionDemo
!
! Calculate union of two proper sets stored in arrays.
!
    USE SetStuff, ONLY : Union
    IMPLICIT NONE
    INTEGER A(10),B(10),C(20)
    INTEGER n_A,n_B,n_C,n_set,i
!
    n_A=4
    n_B=3
    n_C=n_A+n_B
!
    A=(/1,5,9,3,0,0,0,0,0,0/)
    B=(/5,3,8,0,0,0,0,0,0,0/)
    CALL Union(A,B,C,n_A,n_B,n_C,n_set)
    PRINT *,' Elements in A: ',A
    PRINT *,' Elements in B: ',B
    PRINT *,' Elements in union: ',n_set
    PRINT *,(C(i),i=1,n_C)
!
    END
```

Running P-8.5

```
Elements in A:  1 5 9 3 0 0 0 0 0 0
Elements in B:  5 3 8 0 0 0 0 0 0 0
Elements in union:  5
 1 5 9 3 8 -1 -1
```

5 Verify the operation of the program.

You can verify the results with these small sets by inspection. However, you should also test the program with other sets of values, including sets that have no members in common and identical sets. Will you allow empty sets? If not, how will you exclude them?

Problem Discussion

The statements involving the array declarations in the main program and subroutine are printed in bold italics. In the main program, arrays A and B are declared with 10 elements accessed by indices 1 through 10. Because it is possible that array C will need to contain all the elements of A and B, it is declared with 20 elements. However, within the program, the actual numbers of values used are assigned values of 4 and 3 for the A and B arrays. This information is passed through the argument list when SUBROUTINE Union is called from the main program. The array holding the union is initialized to a value of -1.

How does SUBROUTINE Union make use of the information passed to it from the main program? In the subroutine's declaration statements, the sizes of the arrays | *automatic array* | appearing in the parameter list are represented symbolically by the parameters n_A, n_B, and n_C, which appear in the parameter list and have already been declared as integers. Thus, the subroutine does not need to know at "code writing" time (or, more officially, at compile time) what the size of the arrays eventually will be. This fact is critical for making efficient use of modularized code. Arrays defined this way, with variable dimensions, are sometimes called *automatic arrays*.

It's important to realize that arrays associated with names in a subroutine's parameter list don't require a new allocation of space by the compiler. Rather, the fact that the array names appear in the parameter list means that the subroutine can use some or all of the space originally allocated in the calling program. Thus, it is not allowed to pass as an argument a value for a parameter appearing in an array declaration statement that is larger than the originally allocated size. In P-8.5, this means that values corresponding to n_A, n_B, and n_C can have values no larger than 10, 10, and 20.

8.4 Allocatable Arrays

In Fortran 90, there is another solution to the problem of writing programs that include arrays whose size is unknown until run time; that is, until the program is | *allocatable arrays* | executing. That solution is to use *allocatable arrays* instead of statically allocated arrays. To illustrate their use, we will rewrite the main program of P-8.5 with minor modifications. The MODULE in P-8.6 is the same as in P-8.5, so the code isn't reprinted. (The fact that the MODULE doesn't have to be rewritten is, in itself, significant.) The program output is the same, too, so that won't be reprinted either.

P-8.6 [UNION2.F90]

```
! Put MODULE SetStuff here...
      PROGRAM UnionDemo !allocatable array version
!
! Calculate union of two proper sets stored in arrays.
!
      USE SetStuff, ONLY : Union
      IMPLICIT NONE
      INTEGER, ALLOCATABLE :: A(:),B(:),C(:)
      INTEGER n_A,n_B,n_C,n_set
!
      n_A=4
      n_B=3
      n_C=n_A+n_B
      ALLOCATE(A(n_A),B(n_B),C(n_C))
!
      A=(/1,5,9,3/)
      B=(/5,3,8/)

      CALL Union(A,B,C,n_A,n_B,n_C,n_set)
      PRINT *,' Elements in A: ',A
      PRINT *,' Elements in B: ',B
      PRINT *,' Elements in union: ',n_set
      PRINT *,C
!
      END
```

The difference between P-8.5 and P-8.6 is in the array declarations. The relevant statements are printed in bold italics. In P-8.6, the statement

```
      INTEGER, DIMENSION(:), ALLOCATABLE :: A,B,C
```

defines the arrays A, B, and C as allocatable arrays. The general syntax (assuming use of the IMPLICIT NONE statement) is

```
data_type, ALLOCATABLE :: name(:[,:])[,name(:[,:])]...
```

Once an array has been given the ALLOCATABLE attribute, it can't be used until its size has been specified in an ALLOCATE statement. The general syntax of the ALLOCATE statement is

```
ALLOCATE(name(spec)[,name(spec)]...[,STAT=status])

where (spec) has the syntax ([lo:]hi) and
status is an integer variable
```

When the STAT= option is present, the variable *status* is given a value of 0 if the allocation is successful or a positive value if it isn't. The common reason for an unsuccessful allocation is insufficient memory space for the array. If STAT= isn't present and an allocation can't be executed successfully, your program will crash. Only the size (extent) of an array can be defined with an ALLOCATE statement. The rank (dimension) of the array is set (permanently) in the ALLOCATABLE statement. That is, the rank of an array is set at "compile time," but its size is set at "run time."

The specifiers A(:), B(:), and C(:) in the array declaration statement in P-8.6 define arrays A, B, and C as one-dimensional arrays of undetermined size. A few lines later, the statement

```
ALLOCATE(A(n_A),B(n_B),C(n_C))
```

(also printed in bold italics) defines the size of the arrays. The allocation could also be done in separate statements:

```
ALLOCATE(A(n_A))
ALLOCATE(B(n_B))
ALLOCATE(C(n_C))
```

In P-8.6, the values of n_A, n_B, and n_C come from an assignment statement, but they could also come from a DATA statement, a PARAMETER, a constant, or an integer-valued expression. The point, though, is that in a "real" problem, the array sizes are provided by the program user at the time the program is executing. So it doesn't make much sense to get this value from a PARAMETER statement because, by definition, such a value can't be changed while the program is running.

The purpose of these discussions has been to show how to pass variably sized arrays to subprograms. What has been gained by using allocatable arrays? For the problem solved in P-8.5 and P-8.6, the answer is, "Not much." However, this is *only* because the arrays are one-dimensional. To understand this conclusion, which certainly isn't obvious, here is another problem that involves rank two (two-dimensional) arrays.

1 *Define the problem.*

Given a matrix **A**, write a subroutine that replaces each element of **A** with the square of that element. For example, if the original matrix is

$$A = \begin{vmatrix} 3.3 & 4.7 & 5.4 \\ 2.9 & 1.7 & 0.6 \end{vmatrix}$$

then the new matrix would be

$$A = \begin{vmatrix} 10.89 & 22.09 & 29.16 \\ 8.41 & 2.89 & 0.36 \end{vmatrix}$$

The subroutine shouldn't be restricted just to 2×3 matrices.

2 Outline a solution.

This is a conceptually simple problem that requires only two steps to solve.
1. Define a two-dimensional array for the matrix.
2. Multiply each element of the matrix by itself and replace the original value with this new value.

3 Design an algorithm.

The algorithm design seems straightforward. First, write a driver program to test the subroutine. Because the subroutine can't be restricted to 2×3 matrices, we will declare the two-dimensional array as 5×5.

DEFINE (5×5 array A of real numbers;
  row and col counters for printing row-by-row)
INITIALIZE all elements of A to 0
ASSIGN values to first three columns in the first two rows
WRITE (original values in A)
CALL GetSquare(A, n_rows, n_cols)
WRITE (new values in A)

SUBPROGRAM GetSquare(IN/OUT: A; IN: n_rows, n_cols)
DEFINE (A locally as n_rows × n_cols; r and c as counters for printing A)
WRITE (A, row-by-row)
ASSIGN each element of A equal to original element squared
(end GetSquare)

4 *Convert the algorithm into a program.*

The code to implement this algorithm, given in P-8.7, is even easier than you think. Because operators can be applied to arrays as "whole objects," the code to square all the elements in an array A can be written simply as

```
A=A*A
```

Clearly, this means that you don't really need a subroutine for this array operation. However, we will still write a subroutine to demonstrate an important point about passing multidimensional arrays through the parameter list of a subprogram.

P-8.7 [`MAT_SQ1.F90`]

```
      MODULE MatrixStuff
!----------------------
      CONTAINS
!-----------------------------------
      SUBROUTINE GetSquare(A,row,col)
      IMPLICIT NONE
      INTEGER row,col,r,c
      REAL A(row,col)
!
      PRINT *,'from GetSquare...'
      DO r=1,row
        PRINT *,(A(r,c),c=1,col)
      END DO
      A=A*A
      END SUBROUTINE GetSquare
!----------------------------
      END MODULE MatrixStuff
!===========================
      PROGRAM Mat_sq1
!
      USE MatrixStuff, ONLY : GetSquare
      IMPLICIT NONE
      REAL, ALLOCATABLE :: A(:,:)
      INTEGER row,col
!
      ALLOCATE(A(2,3))
      A=RESHAPE( (/3.3,2.9,4.7,1.7,5.4,0.6/), (/2,3/) )
      DO row=1,2
        PRINT *,(A(row,col),col=1,3)
      END DO
      CALL GetSquare(A,2,3)
      PRINT *
      DO row=1,2
        PRINT *,(A(row,col),col=1,3)
      END DO
!
      END
```

Running P-8.7

```
     3.300000      4.700000      5.400000
     2.900000      1.700000      0.600000
from GetSquare...
     3.300000      4.700000      5.400000
     2.900000      1.700000      0.600000

    10.889999     22.089998     29.160002
     8.410001      2.890000      0.360000
```

5 *Verify the operation of the program.*

The results should be checked by hand using the values coded in the main program.

P-8.7 uses an allocatable array so that the size of A can be set at run time rather than compile time. The two statements required to do this (printed in bold italics) are

```
REAL, ALLOCATABLE :: A(:,:)
...
ALLOCATE(A(2,3))
```

Why are allocatable arrays preferred over statically allocated arrays for the problem addressed in P-8.7? In general, what can we learn from P-8.7 about the kinds of programming problems that lend themselves to the use of allocatable rather than statically declared arrays?

Suppose P-8.7 is modified to use static arrays. This involves changes only in the main program, as shown in P-8.7(a).

P-8.7(a) [MAT_SQ2.F90]

```
      MODULE MatrixStuff
!---------------------
      CONTAINS
!-------------------------------
      SUBROUTINE GetSquare(A,row,col)
      IMPLICIT NONE
      INTEGER row,col,r,c
      REAL A(row,col)
!
      PRINT*,'from GetSquare...
      DO r=1,row
        PRINT *,(A(r,c),c=1,col)
      END DO
      A=A*A
!
      END SUBROUTINE GetSquare
```

```
!- - - - - - - - - - - - - - - - - - - - - - - - - - - -
      END MODULE MatrixStuff
!=============================
      PROGRAM Mat_Sq2
!
! THIS PROGRAM WILL NOT WORK PROPERLY!!
!
      USE MatrixStuff, ONLY : GetSquare
      IMPLICIT NONE
      REAL A(5,5)
      INTEGER row,col
      DATA A/25*0/
!
      A(1,1)=3.3
      A(1,2)=4.7
      A(1,3)=5.4
      A(2,1)=2.9
      A(2,2)=1.7
      A(2,3)=0.6
      DO row=1,2
        PRINT *,(A(row,col),col=1,3)
      END DO
      CALL GetSquare(A,2,3)
      PRINT *
      DO row=1,2
        PRINT *,(A(row,col),col=1,3)
      END DO
!
      END
```

Running P-8.7(a) **(NOTE: These values are wrong!)**

```
   3.3000000    4.6999998    5.4000001
   2.9000001    1.7000000    0.6000000
from GetSq...
   3.3000000    0.0000000E+00    0.0000000E+00
   2.9000001    0.0000000E+00    4.6999998

 10.8899994   22.0899982    5.4000001
   8.4100008    1.7000000    0.6000000
```

The ALLOCATABLE and ALLOCATE statements have been removed, and the array is statically defined as 5×5; that is, with a maximum of five rows and five columns.

You may be surprised to see that P-8.7(a) runs without error, but as is clear from the program output, it does *not* produce the correct answers! This code represents a common and very serious programming error, and it is important to understand it. The problem lies in the way statically declared arrays are interpreted when they are passed to subprograms as variably dimensioned arrays.

In the main program of P-8.7(a), a statically declared array of five rows and five columns has set aside 5×5=25 locations. The entire array is initialized to zero in the DATA statement. Later, when values are assigned to the first three columns in the first two rows, the array looks like this when it is printed row by row:

```
3.3   4.7   5.4   0.0   0.0
2.9   1.7   0.6   0.0   0.0
0.0   0.0   0.0   0.0   0.0
0.0   0.0   0.0   0.0   0.0
0.0   0.0   0.0   0.0   0.0
```

When the subroutine in P-8.7(a) is passed the values 2 and 3 for the number of rows and columns, it accesses the space originally set aside for the 5×5 array defined in the main program. However, it doesn't use the "upper lefthand corner" of the array, as printed above in a row-by-row format. Instead, it uses the first six elements in the 25 locations that have been defined in the main program **in the order in which those locations are stored internally**. What is that order? Two-dimensional arrays are stored column-wise rather than row-wise, so the values for array A in the main program are stored in memory in this order:

Column 1	Column 2	Column 3	Column 4	Column 5
3.3	►4.7	►5.4	►0.0	►0.0
2.9	1.7	0.6	0.0	0.0
0.0	0.0	0.0	0.0	0.0
0.0	0.0	0.0	0.0	0.0
0.0	0.0	0.0	0.0	0.0

When the program asks the subroutine to use six values (2•3=6), **it uses the first six values, in the order in which they are stored in the original array.** Based on these values, the local array contains the following values, as PRINTed row-by-row inside GetSquare:

```
3.3   0.0   0.0
2.9   0.0   4.7
```

Obviously, these are not the intended values, so a subroutine that performs operations on these values can't possibly work correctly.

What, in this case, is the result of the statement A=A*A? This statement causes the first six values in the original array to be multiplied by themselves. Thus, the values 3.3, 2.9, 0.0, 0.0, 0.0, and 4.7 are squared, but the rest are unchanged. The results are PRINTed from the main program, after the call to GetSquare; the values 1.7 and 0.6 remain unchanged.

A different approach is required to produce the correct answer to this programming problem in earlier versions of Fortran, which did not support allocatable arrays. Variably dimensioned arrays with more than one dimension had to be given the maximum sizes for each dimension of the array as defined in the main program. This required that both the maximum and "actual" array sizes be passed to the subroutine. The required modifications are shown in P-8.7(b):

P-8.7(b) (fragment – see MAT_SQ3.F90)

```
...
SUBROUTINE GetSquare(A,row,col,maxrow,maxcol)
IMPLICIT NONE
INTEGER r,c
INTEGER, INTENT(IN) :: row,col,maxrow,maxcol
REAL, INTENT(INOUT) :: A(maxrow,maxcol)
...
PROGRAM Mat_Sq3
...
CALL GetSquare(A,2,3,5,5)
...
```

Note that the parameter list of GetSquare has been enlarged to include maxrow and maxcol. This is a "pre-Fortran 90" solution only in the conceptual sense of how it treats arrays in subroutines because it still uses Fortran 90 features such as MODULEs and INTENTs. Similar modifications are required in MatrixPrint as well.

The solution in P-8.7(b) still makes these kinds of general-purpose subroutines portable from one program to another, but it is conceptually awkward because it requires that both the maximum and actual array sizes appear in the parameter list. Consequently (and this is the point of this entire protracted discussion),

> Allocatable arrays are the best choice whenever array sizes need to be determined at run time rather than at compile time, prior to any statement that needs to access the array elements.

It is not always possible to use allocatable arrays because it is sometimes necessary to perform operations on arrays before their final size can be determined. In that case, the approach used in P-8.7(b) can still be used.

Allocatable arrays provide an additional benefit that make them useful even when they are not used to solve problems of passing variably sized arrays to subprograms. It is possible to "re-use" allocated array names while a program is running by deallocating the arrays and then reallocating them with different sizes. The syntax of the DEALLOCATE statement is

```
DEALLOCATE(name[,name]...)
```

Allocatable arrays are especially useful in programs that use large arrays. Every Fortran implementation imposes a limit on the amount of memory available for arrays, even though you may only rarely be aware of those limits. If the total array space needed by a program exceeds this limit, it may be possible to arrange the program so that the large arrays are needed sequentially, rather than all at once. Then you can ALLOCATE and DEALLOCATE array space as needed. P-8.8 demonstrates how to allocate and deallocate arrays.

P-8.8 [ALLOCAT.F90]

```
      PROGRAM Allocat
!
! Demonstrate syntax for allocatable arrays.
!
      IMPLICIT NONE
      REAL, ALLOCATABLE :: A(:,:)
      INTEGER i,j,n
!
      n=2
      ALLOCATE(A(n,2*n))
      DO i=1,n
        DO j=1,2*n
          A(i,j)=i*j
        END DO
      END DO
      PRINT *,((A(i,j),j=1,2*n),i=1,n)
      DEALLOCATE(A)
      ALLOCATE(A(n,3*n))
      DO i=1,n
        DO j=1,3*n
          A(i,j)=i*j
        END DO
      END DO
      PRINT *,((A(i,j),j=1,3*n),i=1,n)
!
      END
```

Running P-8.8

```
  1.0000000    2.0000000    3.0000000    4.0000000    2.0000000
  4.0000000    6.0000000    8.0000000
  1.0000000    2.0000000    3.0000000    4.0000000    5.0000000
  6.0000000    2.0000000    4.0000000    6.0000000    8.0000000
 10.0000000   12.0000000
```

The statements that allocate, deallocate, and then reallocate the array A are printed in bold italics.

8.5 Treating Strings of Characters as Arrays of Characters

In Fortran, every character variable, regardless of whether it is a single character or a "string" of characters, is given the CHARACTER data type. Table 4.2 in Chapter 4 presented some functions for manipulating character strings. This section will examine strings again in light of what you have learned about arrays.

You already know that for an array A containing numbers, n elements of A can be accessed in sequence like this:

```
DO i=1,n
  PRINT *,A(i)
END DO
```

Now suppose B is declared as a character variable. It is possible to access the individual characters of B in this "array-like" fashion:

```
DO i=1,LEN_TRIM(B)
  PRINT *,B(i:i)
END DO
```

The LEN_TRIM function (see Table 4.2 in Chapter 4) sets the upper limit on the DO. . . loop at what is usually the desired position in the B "array," the position (numbered from the left) of the first nonblank character, counting from the right. That is, the DO. . . loop accesses the characters of B from left to right and ignores the trailing blanks. (The LEN function provides access to the entire string, as specified in its CHARACTER declaration, and specifically *includes* trailing blanks.) For example, for the string 'DAVIDｂｂｂｂ', LEN returns a value of 9, but LEN_TRIM returns a value of 5. Counting in from the right, the first nonblank character is D, which is in the fifth position of the string.

In fact, it is possible to access any subset of a CHARACTER variable (assuming that it contains more than one character) by using a (lo: hi) notation to specify the boundaries of the substring. The specifiers may be constants, variables, or expressions.

Another "array-like" property of character strings becomes evident when they are passed as parameters to subprograms. In the same way that arrays appearing in parameter lists can have variable dimensions when they are declared in a subroutine or function, so can character strings have variable length. Consider the following code fragment:

```
CHARACTER*20 s
...
CALL Sub(s)
...
END !main program
!
SUBROUTINE Sub(s)
CHARACTER*(*) s
```

The declared length of the variable s in SUBROUTINE Sub is 20, its declared length in the main program. The length doesn't have to appear as a variable in the parameter list, as it would for an array, because the length of the string used in the subprogram is obtained directly from the actual length of the string s that is passed to the subprogram. This is true regardless of whether the corresponding argument is a variable or a string constant. The CHARACTER*(*) syntax has been used previously in Chapter 7's program P-7.10.

The CHARACTER*(*) can also be written CHARACTER([LEN=]*), and it can also appear in a main program in this context:

```
CHARACTER(*), PARAMETER :: 'This is a string constant.'
```

Here, also, the defined length of the string is determined by the actual length of the string constant (26 characters).

8.6 The TYPE Statement, Records, and Arrays of Records

In the previous sections of this chapter, array elements have consisted of Fortran implicit data types such as REAL or INTEGER numbers. However, the full power of arrays is realized only when the definition of an array is expanded to include elements that consist of user-defined data structures.

In arrays as defined previously, the elements of the arrays can be thought of as entries in a table. Each position in the table—an array element—contains one entry. All entries have the same data type. Now consider a box of file cards. Suppose the file contains information about suppliers of materials to your manufacturing facility. Each card in the file contains the supplier's name, address, contact person, telephone number, and up to three products that you obtain from that supplier. Each card constitutes one *record*, and each record consists of seven *fields*. It would be convenient to be able to define a data structure whose elements were records, each of which could contain several values, rather than a single value. These two kinds of data structures are illustrated in Figure 8.3.

This "file card" structure *could* be represented by five arrays of simple variables:

```
CHARACTER name(100)*20,address(100)*40,contact(100)*30
CHARACTER phone(100)*15,product(100,3)*20
```

An array containing
simple data types

An array containing
user-defined records

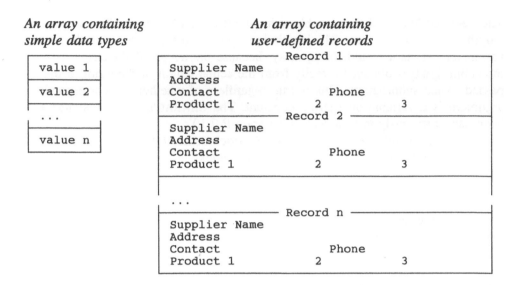

| value 1 |
| value 2 |
| . . . |
| value n |

Figure 8.3. Array structures containing simple data types and user-defined
records.

Because the data declaration for each product name is the same, the product names can be stored in a two-dimensional array rather than three separate one-dimensional arrays. The 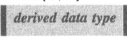 representation for all of these data uses ***parallel arrays***. In general, parallel arrays all have the same length, and an element in any of the arrays is associated with those elements having the same index in the other arrays. For example, record 6 in the file card box is represented by `name(6)`, `address(6)`, `contact(6)`, `phone(6)`, `product(6,1)`, `product(6,2)`, and `product(6,3)`.

It's certainly possible to manipulate information this way (and there was no alternative in earlier versions of Fortran), but it's not very convenient. It would be better to be able to create a single array, each of whose elements contains an entire data record. This is an example of a ***derived data type***, which you can create in Fortran 90 with a `TYPE` definition. Its general syntax is

```
TYPE type_name
  field_type name
  [field_type name]...
END TYPE type_name

Example:
     TYPE Student_Info
        CHARACTER*20 name
        CHARACTER*11 student ID
        INTEGER credit_hours
        REAL GPA
     END TYPE Student_Info
```

The example describes a record that contains information about a student. With this syntax, it's possible to bypass the restriction that array elements in multidimensional arrays must all contain the same kind of values. For the supplier file problem, and in general, an array whose elements are a derived data type is still one-dimensional, with a single data type for its elements. However, each element can contain several different kinds of information.

In order to associate a name with a user-defined type, use a TYPE declaration. Its general syntax is

```
TYPE (type_name) variable_name[,variable_name]...

Example:
     TYPE (Student_Info) freshmen, all_students
```

Let's return now to the materials supplier problem as an illustration of how to incorporate an appropriate record structure into a program. Instead of declaring five parallel arrays to hold the seven fields from the materials suppliers records, combine all the fields into a single record and then declare an array to hold these records. P-8.9 shows how this can be done.

P-8.9 (fragment)

```
PROGRAM...
IMPLICIT NONE
TYPE supplier_fields
  CHARACTER*20 name
  CHARACTER*40 address
  CHARACTER*30 contact
  CHARACTER*15 phone
  CHARACTER*15 product1,product2,product3
END TYPE supplier_fields
TYPE(supplier_fields) supplier_data(100)
...
```

The TYPE construct is used to define
a record to hold all the information about a
particular supplier. Individual fields within

component selector character

each record are accessed by giving the name of the record, followed by the
component selector character %, followed by the name of the field. For example,
the contact field in the sixth element of the temp_data array is referred to
as supplier_data(6)%contact.

As another example, recall the ozone measurement problem discussed at
the beginning of this chapter. Suppose you wish to augment your data collection
to include other data, such as temperature, wind speed, cloudiness, etc., such that
now there is a total of 10 measurements taken every hour, during every day of the
month. One way to represent these data is with a three-dimensional array:

```
REAL Measurements(31,24,10)
```

With this representation, it can be confusing to keep track of the meaning
of each array index. Also, it is difficult to change the structure of the data
representation, and it is impossible to include additional data that might need to
be represented by something other than real numbers. (For example, the cloudiness
might be better represented with an integer value.) However, you can make use
of the fact that the fields in records created with a TYPE structure don't have to
be scalar; a field can also be an array. For this problem, better alternatives might
be to define a record including a 10-element array as its data field:

```
REAL MeasurementArray(10)
TYPE Measurements
  MeasurementArray
END TYPE Measurements
TYPE (Measurements) MonthlyData(31,24)
```

or a record with 10 separately named fields:

```
        TYPE Measurements
          REAL ozone,temperature
          INTEGER wind_speed, wind_direction
          INTEGER ozone
!         ... (etc.)
        END TYPE Measurements
        TYPE (Measurements) MonthlyData(31,24)
```

The advantage of creating a record structure with TYPE is its flexibility. With this
approach, it is easy to add additional fields to the Measurements record (and
hence to the elements of the MonthlyData array), no matter what data type is
required.

The advantage of easy expandability also applies to the materials supplier
problem discussed earlier in this section. Suppose the supplier has more than three
products. In that case, it might be desirable to replace the fields product1,

product2, and product3 with an array of product descriptions. Such a change is easily accomplished by modifying the fields defined in the TYPE structure; this is left for an exercise at the end of the chapter.

Although this text has described records in the context of arrays of records, it's not necessary to associate records with arrays. It's sometimes convenient to define records of related information even when you don't need an array. However, it's certainly true that the most common use of records is as elements in arrays of records. As an example of using an array of records, consider this problem.

1 *Define the problem.*

Predicting power demand is important for electric utilities. In a cold winter, this demand may be driven by space heating requirements. Widely used measures of heating demand are heating degrees and heating degree days. These quantities can be predicted based on forecasted high and low temperatures and compared to values calculated from past temperature histories. The number of heating degrees is equal to the number of degrees the average temperature is below 65°F. It is approximately equal to 65 minus the average of the high and low temperatures for the day, 65-(high+low)/2, or 0, whichever is larger. Heating degrees can't be negative. (Average daily temperatures above 65°F generate cooling degrees, but we won't consider them in this problem.) The sum of all heating degrees over several days gives the number of heating degree days for that time period. The average heating degrees is the total heating degree days, including zeros, divided by the number of days.

Write a program that prompts the user to supply the high and low temperature predictions for the next week and then calculates the heating degrees for each day, the daily average heating degrees, and the total heating degree days for the week. Display all results for the week. Print an asterisk after each day with heating degrees above the average for the period.

2 *Outline a solution.*

1. Prompt the user to provide the input in a count-controlled loop.
2. Store the data in an array of records. Inside the loop, calculate the daily heating degrees and store the value as a calculated field in the array of records. Be sure to assign a value of 0 to days with negative heating degrees. Increment the total number of heating degree days, including the 0 values.
3. When the loop is complete, calculate the average heating degrees. Be sure to count all days, even those with 0 heating degrees.

4. In another loop, print all fields in the array, with an asterisk to mark days with heating degrees above the average.
5. At the end, print the total heating degree days for the week.

It's the requirement to print an asterisk after data for some of the days that provides the motivation to store data in an array. This is because you don't know which days will have asterisks until all the data have been processed. As long as the data are available in an array, you can access all the values as many times as you need them without re-entering any of the data.

3 *Design an algorithm.*

DEFINE *(array of records to hold high and low temperatures and*
    heating_degrees; total_heating_degree_days;
    day (loop control variable); n_days=7)
INITIALIZE *total_heating_degree_days = 0*
ASSIGN *n_days = 7*
LOOP *(day = 1 to n_days)*
  WRITE *("Enter daily high and low, deg F:")*
  READ *(high(day) and low(day))*
  ASSIGN *heating_degrees(day) = 65 − (high(day) + low(day))/2*
  IF *heating_degrees(day) < 0* **THEN**
    ASSIGN *heating_degrees(day)=0*
    INCREMENT *total_heating_degree_days =*
      total_heating_degree_days + heating_degrees(day)
END LOOP
ASSIGN *average = total_heating_degree_days / n_days*
LOOP *(day = 1 to n_days)*
  WRITE *(all fields of array) (no line feed)*
  IF *heating_degrees(day) > average* **THEN**
    WRITE *("*")*
  ELSE
    WRITE *(new line)*
  END IF
END LOOP
WRITE *(average, total heating degree days)*

4 *Convert the algorithm into a program.*

P-8.10 [DEGDAYS.F90]

```
      PROGRAM DegDays
!
! Calculate heating degree days for a week.
! Demonstrate arrays of records.
!
      IMPLICIT NONE
! Declare a record...
      TYPE temp_data_type
         REAL high,low,heating_deg
      END TYPE temp_data_type
      INTEGER days,n_days
      PARAMETER (n_days=7)
! and declare an array of these records.
      TYPE(temp_data_type) temp_data(n_days)
      REAL heating_deg_days,average
! Gather and process data.
      heating_deg_days=0.
      DO days=1,n_days
         PRINT 1000,days
         READ *,temp_data(days)%high,temp_data(days)%low
         temp_data(days)%heating_deg=65.-(temp_data(days)%high &
                                +temp_data(days)%low)/2.
         IF (temp_data(days)%heating_deg < 0.) &!set neg. value to 0
           temp_data(days)%heating_deg=0.
         heating_deg_days= &
           heating_deg_days+temp_data(days)%heating_deg
      END DO
      average=heating_deg_days/n_days
! Display results
      PRINT *,' Day high  low  heating degrees'
      PRINT *,'-----------------------------'
      DO days=1,n_days
         WRITE(*,1010,advance='no')                          &
           days,temp_data(days)%high,temp_data(days)%low,&
           temp_data(days)%heating_deg
         IF (temp_data(days)%heating_deg > average) THEN
           WRITE(*,*)' *'
         ELSE
           WRITE(*,*)
         END IF
      END DO
      PRINT 1020,average,heating_deg_days
!
1000  FORMAT(' Enter high and low temperature (F) for day ',i1)
1010  FORMAT(1x,i4,2f5.1,f6.1)
1020  FORMAT(' Average heating degree days = ',f5.1/&
             '    Total heating degree days = ',f5.1)
      END
```

Running P-8.10

```
 Enter high and low temperature (F) for day 1
 62 49
 Enter high and low temperature (F) for day 2
 63 51
 Enter high and low temperature (F) for day 3
 65 50
 Enter high and low temperature (F) for day 4
 70 61
 Enter high and low temperature (F) for day 5
 60 58
 Enter high and low temperature (F) for day 6
 66 54
 Enter high and low temperature (F) for day 7
 70 62
  Day high  low  heating degrees
 ---------------------------------
     1 62.0 49.0   9.5  *
     2 63.0 51.0   8.0  *
     3 66.0 50.0   7.0  *
     4 70.0 61.0   0.0
     5 60.0 58.0   6.0  *
     6 66.0 54.0   5.0
     7 70.0 62.0   0.0
 Average heating degree days =   5.1
   Total heating degree days =  35.5
```

It's important to study P-8.10 carefully to make sure you understand how arrays of records and their fields are used; the syntax can be confusing. The field name comes *after* the array element reference. Writing temp_data%high(days) instead of temp_data(days)%high is a common mistake that will generate a syntax error message. The pseudocode in Step 3 might add to the confusion. Remember that an "array of records" is a Fortran implementation detail, and it's not necessary to try to include this kind of structure in your pseudocode. You might wish to include comments in your pseudocode solutions that indicate how you will handle the implementation.

Also, note the use of the WRITE statement with the advance='no' option to allow the printing of an asterisk at the end of some of the lines. This task could also have been accomplished by having two separate FORMAT statements, one of which would include the asterisk as a string constant. The latter approach would have been required in earlier versions of Fortran, which did not support the advance option.

Problem Discussion

In this problem, an array of records provides significant organizational advantages. Although a two-dimensional array could have been used to hold the values, the one-dimensional array allows us to assign meaningful field names to the two temperatures and the calculated value for heating degrees. Despite the fact that this solution involves more typing, the resulting code is more self-documenting and less prone to errors.

5 Verify the operation of the program.

Check the program's calculations by hand. This program requires some care to make sure you've treated days with no heating degrees properly. It's easy to forget that you can't have negative heating degrees.

8.7 Applications

8.7.1 Vector Operations

1 Define the problem.

Arrays are an obvious way to represent vectors in three-dimensional space. Many problems in physics and mathematics involve calculating the scalar (or "dot") product and vector (or "cross") product of two vectors. The scalar and vector products of two vectors **A** and **B** are:

$$\mathbf{A} \cdot \mathbf{B} = A_x B_x + A_y B_y + A_z B_z$$
$$\mathbf{A} \times \mathbf{B} = \mathbf{C}$$

where
$$C_x = A_y B_z - B_y A_z$$
$$C_y = A_z B_x - B_z A_x$$
$$C_z = A_x B_y - B_x A_y$$

Note that $\mathbf{A} \times \mathbf{B} = -\mathbf{B} \times \mathbf{A}$.

The dot product is related to the cosine of the angle θ between **A** and **B**:

$$\mathbf{A} \cdot \mathbf{B} / (\,|\,\mathbf{A}\,|\ \ |\,\mathbf{B}\,|\,) = \cos(\theta)$$

As their names imply, $\mathbf{A} \cdot \mathbf{B}$ is a scalar value and $\mathbf{A} \times \mathbf{B}$ is a vector with x, y, and z components as shown.

Write subroutines that will calculate the dot product and angle between two three-dimensional vectors, and the cross product of two vectors. Assume that the calculations apply only to three-dimensional vectors (rank-one arrays with three components), so there is no need to use variably dimensioned arrays in the subroutines.

2 *Outline a solution.*

1. Define three three-component vectors **A**, **B**, and **C**.
2. Assign components to **A** and **B**.
2. Calculate the scalar product and angle between **A** and **B** and the components of the cross product vector according to the formulas given.

The magnitude of $|\mathbf{A}|$ (for example) is $\sqrt{A_x^2 + A_y^2 + A_z^2}$.

3 *Design an algorithm.*

SUBPROGRAM Dot(IN: A_x, A_y, A_z, B_x, B_y, B_z;
                    OUT: dot_product, angle (rad))
ASSIGN dot_product = $A_x B_x + A_y B_y + A_z B_z$
        angle = $\cos^{-1}[(dot\_product)/(A_x^2 + A_y^2 + A_z^2)^{1/2} \cdot (B_x^2 + B_y^2 + B_z^2)^{1/2}]$
(end)
SUBPROGRAM Cross(IN: A_x, A_y, A_z, B_x, B_y, B_z;
            OUT: C_x, C_y, C_z)
ASSIGN C_x= (See Step 1 of the problem definition.)
        C_y=
        C_z=
(end)

4 *Convert the algorithm into a program.*

P-8.11 [VECTOROP.F90]

```
!------------------------------------------------
      MODULE VectorSubs
        CONTAINS
!
        SUBROUTINE Dot(a,b,DotProduct,angle)
!
! Calculate the scalar (dot) product of two 3-D vectors and the
! angle between them.
        IMPLICIT NONE
        INTEGER i
        REAL, INTENT(IN) :: a(3),b(3)
        REAL, INTENT(OUT) :: DotProduct,angle
```

```
!
            DotProduct=DOT_PRODUCT(a,b) !an intrinsic function
            angle=ACOS(DotProduct/SQRT(a(1)**2+a(2)**2+a(3)**2)/ &
                  SQRT(b(1)**2+b(2)**2+b(3)**2))
         END SUBROUTINE Dot
!
         SUBROUTINE Cross(a,b,c)
!
! Calculate the cross product of two vectors.
!
         IMPLICIT NONE
         REAL, INTENT(IN) :: a(3),b(3)
         REAL, INTENT(OUT) :: c(3)
!
         c(1)=a(2)*b(3)-b(2)*a(3)
         c(2)=a(3)*b(1)-b(3)*a(1)
         c(3)=a(1)*b(2)-b(1)*a(2)
         END SUBROUTINE Cross
!
      END MODULE
!--------------------------------------------------
      PROGRAM VectorOperations
!
! File name: VECTOROP.F90
! Calculate and display vector dot and cross products.
!
      USE VectorSubs
      IMPLICIT NONE
      REAL DotProd,angle,pi
      INTEGER i
      REAL a(3),b(3),c(3)
!
      pi=4.*ATAN(1.)
      PRINT *,' Give 3 components for a, 3 for b: '
      READ *,(a(i),i=1,3),(b(i),i=1,3)
      CALL Dot(a,b,DotProd,angle)
      PRINT 1000,DotProd,angle*180.0/pi
      CALL Cross(a,b,c)
      PRINT 1010,c
!
1000  FORMAT(1x,'dot product and angle (deg): ',2f8.3)
1010  FORMAT(1x,'cross product: ',3f8.3)
      END
```

Running P-8.11

```
 Give 3 components for a, 3 for b:
3.3 4.4 1.1 5.2 4.2 7.9
   44.330   40.205
   30.140  -20.350   -9.020
```

Programming Tip

P-8.11 highlights once again some vector terminology that is easy to confuse with array terminology. The vectors used in the application are called "three-dimensional" vectors because they have three components. In physics, for example, they could represent a position in three-dimensional space. However, these three-dimensional vectors are represented in Fortran by rank-one (one-dimensional) arrays; each element represents one component of the vector.

To clarify this point further, suppose the three-dimensional vector represents the position of an object in three-dimensional space. You would add additional *vector* dimensions to represent values in a higher-order space of more than three dimensions. You could add additional *array* dimensions to hold additional three-dimensional vectors. For example, by adding a second dimension to an array, you could represent both the three-dimensional position and velocity of the object. By adding yet another dimension, you could represent position, velocity, and acceleration.

Another interesting feature of P-8.11 is its use of the intrinsic DOT_PRODUCT function, which requires as arguments two rank-one arrays of the same size. Thus, a specific implementation of the **LOOP** structure defined in the algorithm design isn't required in Fortran.

5 *Verify the operation of the program.*

Check all calculations with a hand calculator. Try to find values of **A** and **B** that constitute "special cases." When is the dot product 0? What happens to the cross product vector when the vectors **A** and **B** are parallel? If **A** and **B** lie entirely in the x-y plane (that is, if their z-components are 0), in which direction does the cross product vector point? Make sure that **A•B=B•A** and **A×B=-B×A**?

8.7.2 Cellular Automata and Sierpinski Triangles

1 *Define the problem.*

A computer science topic that is also of interest in biology and engineering is the study of artificial "organisms" called automata. These are essentially artificial life forms that, with the aid of a set of rules for "dying" and "reproducing" themselves, appear to be self-organizing. When these rules are incorporated into a computer program, they can lead to surprising patterns, some of which can also be derived from fractal theory. One interesting pattern is the "Sierpinski triangle," illustrated in Figure 8.4.

When a single "cell"—represented by an asterisk in a CHARACTER*1 array initialized to blank spaces—is given an appropriate set of organizing rules, it will propagate into multiple cells in a pattern that resembles a Sierpinski triangle. The rules are:

> For cell i, if cell i-1 is occupied and cells i and i+1 are not, or if cell i-1 is empty and cell i+1 is occupied, then an organism will appear in cell i in the next generation. Otherwise, the cell will be empty.

Write a program that will use these rules to produce a pattern that looks like a Sierpinski triangle.

2 *Outline a solution.*

1. Consider an array of cells. The content of each cell is represented by a single character. When a cell is "alive," it will contain an asterisk; when it's not, it will contain a blank space. Start with an initial "population" that consists of a single "live" cell somewhere near the middle of the array. Display this state by printing the contents of the array as a single line of output.
2. Now apply the organizing rules, encoded as boolean expressions, to get from the initial state to the next state.
3. Display this new state.
4. Repeat Steps 2 and 3 for a specified number of generations.

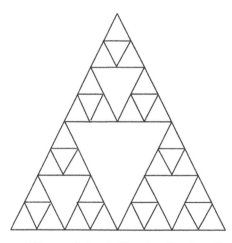

Figure 8.4. A Sierpinski triangle

3

Design an algorithm.

There is one tricky part to implementing this algorithm: The tests to determine the contents of a cell in the next generation must be applied to a *copy* of the current generation. Otherwise, a cell that will not be occupied until the next generation may be modified so that it will already appear to be populated in the current generation, or a cell that will be empty in the next generation will no longer be occupied in the current generation, thereby affecting the evaluation of adjacent cells.

```
DEFINE (logical arrays cell(41), old_cell(41); character array ch(41);
         # of generations; i and j as loop counters)
INITIALIZE arrays cell = false
           ch = ' '
ASSIGN cell(21) = true (Put an organism in the middle.)
       ch(21) = '*'
WRITE (0 and ch) (Display generation 0.)
 ASSIGN  n = 15 (number of generations)
LOOP (for j = 1 to n)
(Apply the propagation rules.)
     ASSIGN old_cell = cell (Make temp copy.)
     LOOP (for i = 2 to 40 ) (Avoid range violations.)
           (Apply rules...)
           IF (old_cell(i-1) & not(old_cell(i)) & not(old_cell(i+1)))
           OR (not(old_cell(i-1)) & old_cell(i+1))
           THEN
                 cell(i) = true
           ELSE
                 cell(i) = false
     END LOOP
     (Display new generation.)
     LOOP (for i = 1 to 41)
           IF (cell(i) = true) THEN ch(i) = '*'
      ELSE ch(i) = ' '
     END LOOP
     WRITE (j and ch)
END LOOP
```

4 Convert the algorithm into a program.

P-8.12 [SIERPINS.F90]

```fortran
      PROGRAM Sierpinski
!
! Program name SIERPINS.F90
! One-dimensional cellular automata with rule that generates a
! Sierpinski triangle.
!
      IMPLICIT NONE
      INTEGER size
      PARAMETER (size=60)
      LOGICAL a(60),old_a(60),a_1,a0,a1
      CHARACTER*1,b(60)
      INTEGER i,j,cycle,n_cycles
      DATA n_cycles,a,b/15,size*.FALSE.,size*' '/
!
      cycle=0
      a(size/2)=.TRUE. !start with a single live cell...
      b(size/2)='*'
      WRITE(*,1000)cycle,b
!
! Generate more cycles...
!
      DO i=1,n_cycles
        old_a=a
        DO j=2,size-1
          a_1=old_a(j-1)
          a0=old_a(j)
          a1=old_a(j+1)
          a(j)=(a_1.AND.(.NOT. a0).AND.(.NOT. a1)) &
            .OR. ((.NOT. a_1).AND.a1)
        END DO
        DO j=1,size
          IF (a(j)) THEN
            b(j)='*'
          ELSE
            b(j)=' '
          END IF
        END DO
        WRITE(*,1000)i,b
      END DO
!
1000  FORMAT(1x,'(',i2,')',60a1)
      END
```

Running P-8.12

```
Generation  0                             *
Generation  1                           *  *
Generation  2                         *      *
Generation  3                       *  *  *  *
Generation  4                     *            *
Generation  5                   *  *        *  *
Generation  6                 *     *     *     *
Generation  7               *  *  *  *  *  *  *  *
Generation  8             *                       *
Generation  9           *  *                    *  *
Generation 10         *     *                 *     *
Generation 11       *  *  *  *              *  *  *  *
Generation 12     *           *           *           *
Generation 13   *  *        *  *        *  *        *  *
Generation 14 *     *     *     *     *     *     *     *
Generation 15 *  *  *  *  *  *  *  *  *  *  *  *  *  *  *  *
```

5 *Verify the operation of the program.*

The printed output of P-8.12 will either look like a Sierpinski triangle or it won't. An incorrect implementation of the propagation rules will yield some other (perhaps equally interesting) pattern.

Problem Discussion

This problem presents an ideal opportunity to use boolean data types. There are only two possible states for a cell—occupied or empty. By representing the "organism array" as LOGICAL, these states are represented by the values true or false. This makes applying the propagation rules easier. Instead of using an IF...THEN... statement, as was done in the algorithm design, it is easier to use a statement that simply assigns the result of evaluating the expression incorporating the propagation rules.

It may seem amazing that such a well-organized pattern can be created just by following two simple rules. It would be interesting to apply these rules to different starting configurations containing more than one organism, or to change the propagation rules.

8.7.3 Probability Analysis for Quality Control of Manufacturing Processes

This application makes use of Fortran's ability to treat strings of characters as "arrays" of characters, as described in Section 8.5.

1 *Define the problem.*

A manufacturer's experience has shown that 10 percent of all integrated circuits (ICs) will be defective. Because of this high failure rate, a quality control engineer monitors the manufacturing process by testing random samples every day. What is the probability that:
(a) Exactly two ICs in a sample of 10 will be defective?
(b) At least two will be defective?
(c) No more than two will be defective?

2 *Outline a solution.*

You are not expected to know how to solve this problem, even in principle, unless you have had a probability and statistics course. However, you should be able to write the source code once you know what the solution is.
(a) The probability that a particular sample of 10 will contain exactly two defective ICs is $(0.1)^2(0.9)^8 = 0.004305$. However, there are $_{10}C_2 = 45$ possible combinations of two defective and eight good ICs. From probability theory, the number of combinations of n things taken k at a time is

$$_nC_k = n!/[k!(n-k)!]$$

where ! indicates the well-known factorial function. Therefore, the probability that a sample of 10 will contain exactly two defects is

$$P(=2) = {}_{10}C_2(0.1)^2(0.9)^8 = (45)(0.004305) = 0.1937$$

(b) The probability of finding at least two defective ICs is equal to 1 minus the probability of finding 0 defective ICs minus the probability of finding 1 defective IC:

$$P(\geq 2) = 1 - {}_{10}C_0(0.1)^0(0.9)^{10} - {}_{10}C_1(0.1)^1(0.9)^9 = 0.2639$$

(Remember that $0!=1$ by definition.)

(c) The probability of finding no more than two defective ICs is

$$P(\leq 2) = {}_{10}C_0(0.1)^0(0.9)^{10} + {}_{10}C_1(0.1)^1(0.9)^9 + {}_{10}C_2(0.1)^2(0.9)^8 = 0.9298$$

There are several approaches that could be taken to writing a program to solve this problem. One solution would be simply to "hard code" the required calculations. This program would need to include, as a minimum, a user-defined function to calculate the factorial function.

However, in the context of Fortran's string manipulation capabilities discussed in this chapter, there is a more elegant solution. The program described here will include user-defined functions for calculating combinations *and* a function for calculating factorials. Then the user will type a character string that can be "parsed" to yield values to use as arguments for function calls and for the other calculations that are required. For example, for part (b) of the problem, the user could type

```
1-c(10,0,.1)-c(10,1,.1)
```

This character string would result in the evaluation of the expression $P(\geq 2)$ as given above. The first two values inside the parentheses will be used as arguments for a function to calculate the combinations of n things taken k at a time. The third value is the probability of a defective IC. The probability of a good IC (0.9) is just 1 minus this value.

The key to the program is to enclose the desired numerical values inside parentheses. If your program then searches for a left parenthesis and its matching right parenthesis, the characters inside that set of parentheses can be "read" and converted to numerical values. This probably sounds more difficult than it actually is. (As you will see, the Fortran code needed to do this isn't really very hard.)

Note that such a program doesn't "know" how to solve probability problems. It just performs the required calculations based on user input. Also, because the magnitude of n! grows rapidly with n, there are some rather restrictive limits on the size of the sample if default INTEGER data types are used for n and k; a sample of size 10 can be handled comfortably. (See Exercise 17 in Chapter 4 for a way to estimate n! for large values of n.)

3 *Design an algorithm.*

DEFINE (character string (a); integers: length of string, loop counter (i),
n and k, sign (+1 or -1), location of a left parenthesis;
probability, prob a (real numbers)

(NOTE: prob_a is probability that a single unit will be defective.
"probability" is the probability that the event defined by the string will
occur.)
WRITE *(Prompt user for string. Give "syntax" example.)*
READ *(a)*
ASSIGN *length = length of a, no trailing blanks*
INITIALIZE *probability = 0*
         sign = 1
(Values in parentheses after string variable refer to character position,
using Fortran notation.)
IF *a(1:1) = '1'* **THEN ASSIGN** *probability = 1*
LOOP *(through the string, one character at a time)*
         IF *a(i:1) = '+'* **THEN** *sign = 1*
         IF *a(i:1) = '-'* **THEN** *sign = -1*
         IF *a(i:1) = '('* **THEN** *left = i*
         IF *a(i:1) = ')'* **THEN** *(process substring)*
                 READ *(from substring a(left+1:i-1), n,k,prob_a)*
                 INCREMENT *probability = probability+sign•C(n,k)•prob_a^k•*
                                       (1 - prob_a)$^{(n-k)}$
                 WRITE *(n,k,C(n,k) (optional)*
         (end IF...)
END LOOP
WRITE *(probability)*

When it refers to a range of characters within the string a, this algorithm appears to violate the usual style rule that algorithms shouldn't require the use of syntax from a particular programming language. However, it's necessary to use some kind of notation, and it seems better to use Fortran's notation than to invent something arbitrarily different.

4

Convert the algorithm into a program.

P-8.13 [PROB.F90]

```
      MODULE ProbFunctions
!
      CONTAINS
!----------------------------
      INTEGER FUNCTION Fact(x)
!
! Calculate x! as long as x! not too large for default integer type.
!
      IMPLICIT NONE
      INTEGER, INTENT(IN) :: x
      INTEGER prod,i
```

```
!
      prod=1
      DO i=2,x
        prod=prod*i
      END DO
      Fact=prod
      RETURN
      END FUNCTION Fact
!--------------------------
      INTEGER FUNCTION C(n,k)
!
! Calculate combinations of n things taken k at a time.
!
      IMPLICIT NONE
      INTEGER, INTENT(IN) :: n,k
!
      C=Fact(n)/Fact(k)/Fact(n-k)
      RETURN
      END FUNCTION C
!--------------------------
      END MODULE ProbFunctions
!=============================
      PROGRAM prob
!
! Evaluate probabilities by parsing a string expression and
! performing the implied calculations.
!
      USE ProbFunctions, ONLY : C
      IMPLICIT NONE
      CHARACTER*80 a
      INTEGER i,n,k,length,sign,left
      REAL probability,prob_a
!
      PRINT*,'Type expression to be evaluated (no syntax checking).'
      PRINT*,'Example: 1-c(10,0,.2)-c(10,1,.2)'
      READ(*,1020)a
!
      length=LEN_TRIM(a)
      probability=0.
      IF (a(1:1)=='1') probability=1.
      sign=1 !a leading + sign is optional
      DO i=1,length
        IF (a(i:i)=='+') sign=1
        IF (a(i:i)=='-') sign=-1
        IF (a(i:i)=='(') left=i
        IF (a(i:i)==')') THEN
          READ(a(left+1:i-1),*)n,k,prob_a
          probability=probability+ &
                    sign*C(n,k)*prob_a**k*(1.-prob_a)**(n-k)
          PRINT 1030,n,k,C(n,k)
        END IF
      END DO
      PRINT 1010,probability
1000  FORMAT(a1)
1010  FORMAT(1x,'probability = ',f10.4)
1020  FORMAT(a80)
1030  FORMAT(1x,'C(',i2,',',i2,') = ',i5)
      END
```

Running P-8.13 (three times, for three different input strings)

```
Type expression to be evaluated (no syntax checking).
Example: 1-c(10,0,.2)-c(10,1,.2)
c(10,2,.1)
  C(10,  2) =      45
  probability =       0.1937

Type expression to be evaluated (no syntax checking).
Example: 1-c(10,0,.2)-c(10,1,.2)
1-c(10,0,.1)-c(10,1,.1)
  C(10,  0) =       1
  C(10,  1) =      10
  probability =       0.2639

Type expression to be evaluated (no syntax checking).
Example: 1-c(10,0,.2)-c(10,1,.2)
c(10,0,.1)+c(10,1,.1)+c(10,2,.1)
  C(10,  0) =       1
  C(10,  1) =      10
  C(10,  2) =      45
  probability =       0.9298
```

5 *Verify the operation of the program.*

P-8.13 needs to be checked carefully by hand to ensure both that the user-defined functions work properly and that the character string is interpreted correctly. It's easy to be confused by probability calculations, so it is difficult to achieve a high level of confidence in the answers produced by this program except by comparing them against other sources in which you already have a high level of confidence.

Problem Discussion

The key to P-8.13 is the READ statement printed in bold italics:

```
READ(a(left+1:i-1),*)n,k,prob_a
```

This statement demonstrates that even though it certainly isn't obvious, it's possible to treat a string as an "input device" from which values can be read. Essentially, the contents of the indicated subrange of the string a are treated just as though they had been typed at a keyboard. This is called an "internal file." We will discuss this feature again in the broader context of Chapter 9.

This program allows you to do each of the probability calculations specified in the problem statement, as well as others. Both the required values and the algebraic form of the calculations are given as user input, which makes the program very versatile. By forcing the user to specify how the user-defined combination function (C) is to be used, the program is actually simplified. Instead of having to "know" a lot about probability calculations, all the program has to do is use the general-purpose functions in a user-specified way. Note that although the cs in the suggested user-response string (as in c(10,1,.1)) make the input look more "algebraic," they are optional. Only the balanced left and right parentheses are required for the program to work.

The program doesn't perform any "syntax checking" on the user's input. In particular, it assumes that every left parenthesis is matched by a right parenthesis and that the characters inside a set of parentheses can be read as three numerical values using only list-directed input.

8.8 Debugging Your Programs

8.8.1 Programming Style

Programs that use arrays should do so either because there is no reasonable alternative or because the use of arrays simplifies the organization of a problem that doesn't actually require arrays.[6] Especially when multidimensional arrays are used, the names of the indices should be descriptive, such as "row" or "column" rather than "i" or "j."

In many cases, information that might otherwise require a multidimensional array should be organized instead into a one-dimensional array of records, using the TYPE structure. The fields in such a structure should always have meaningful names that make the source code more self-documenting.

8.8.2 Problems with Programs That Use Arrays

There are several common problems that you may encounter when working with arrays:

1. Attempting to reference an array element that lies outside the defined limits
   No programming environment should allow this!

2. Confusing index references in multidimensional arrays
   An especially important case is a two-dimensional array that represents a table. Using meaningful names such as "row" and "column" for the array indices will minimize potential problems.

---

[6]Author's note: as hard as it is to believe, my experience is that students sometimes go to the trouble of using arrays even when they're not needed or even when they make a program more difficult to write!

3. Inappropriate use of multidimensional arrays passed to a subprogram as variably dimensioned arrays

Recall the lengthy discussion of this topic in Section 8.4. One way to minimize this problem is to use allocatable arrays whenever possible. Then the "working" size of an array can be the same as its declared size.

4. Inappropriate placement of an array index in an array of records.

The required syntax is typically `A(i)%field`, not `A%field(i)`. However, the latter syntax might be OK if one field in a record is an array. The reference `B%field(j)` implies that `B` is a record rather than an array of records. Also, the syntax `X(i)%field(j)` would be OK if `X` is an array of records and `field` is also an array.

8.9 Exercises

8.9.1 Self-Testing Exercises

Exercise 1. Describe in your own words the two most important concepts you have learned from this chapter.

Exercise 2. Describe in your own words how you could use in your own programs a problem-solving skill demonstrated in a program described in this chapter.

Exercise 3. What is the *total* number of elements in each of these arrays? What are the allowed ranges of indices for accessing the contents of these arrays?

(a) `A(2,3,4)`
(b) `A(50,-10:10)`
(c) `A(2,3,4,5,0:4,0:3,0:2)`

Exercise 4. Define arrays and, where appropriate, data types to hold the specified information:

(a) A two-dimensional array with these specifications: Its first dimension has a lower index value of 0 and holds 20 elements. Its second dimension has a lower index value of -10 and holds 15 elements.

(b) The temperatures at which a sample of 100 resistors failed when they were subjected to destructive testing and their resistances at 90 percent of their failure temperature

(c) A database of the elements including the name, symbol, and atomic weight of each element

(d) The x-y coordinates and depths of a 100-km² seabed surface surveyed on a 1-km square grid

Exercise 5. What are the values returned by `LEN` and `LEN_TRIM` for these strings?

(a) `'␢Fortran␢'`

(b) `'Fortran 90 is fun!'`

8.9.2 Basic Programming Exercises

Exercise 6. (a) Write a `DO...` loop that prints every other element of a one-dimensional array of integers.
        (b) Write a `DO...` loop that prints all positive elements of a one-dimensional array of integers.

Exercise 7. (a) Write a `DO...` loop that prints every other row of a two-dimensional array of real numbers.
        (b) Write a `DO...` loop that prints every other column of a two-dimensional array of real numbers.
        (c) Write a `DO...` loop that prints the top-right-to-bottom-left diagonal of a two-dimensional array that has the same number of rows as columns. That is, the array represents a square matrix.

Exercise 8. Write a `DO...` loop that sums the rows and columns of a two-dimensional array of real numbers and prints the results after the last column and row.

Exercise 9. Assign the values shown to a 2×4×3 array of real numbers. Consider the first two dimensions as representing rows and columns and the third dimension as representing "layers." Print the layers in the following formats:

```
(a)    1.1  1.9  2.3  4.1
       2.2  3.3  4.4  5.5

       0.9  0.8  0.7  0.6
       1.1  1.2  1.3  1.4

       2.9  2.9  2.6  2.5
       7.1  7.2  7.4  5.5
```

(b) 1.1 1.9 2.3 4.1   0.9 0.8 0.7 0.6   2.9 2.9 2.6 2.5
     2.2 3.3 4.4 5.5   1.1 1.2 1.3 1.4   7.1 7.2 7.4 5.5

Exercise 10. Write a DO... loop that prints every second character in a character string, starting with (a) the first character; (b) the second character.

Exercise 11. Write a DO... loop that prints only the *letters* in a character string. That is, it ignores spaces, punctuation, and other characters, such as digits.

Exercise 12. Modify P-8.10 so that it calculates both heating degree days and cooling degree days. Cooling degrees are equal to the number of degrees the average temperature is above 65°F. Use the same approximation as for heating degrees, as shown in the original problem statement for P-8.10. Instead of an asterisk after days for which heating degrees exceed the average, print an H. Print a C after days for which cooling degrees exceed the average.

Exercise 13. Suppose you wish to represent the position, velocity, and acceleration of an object. Write a program that defines a three-dimensional array for this purpose. In the same program, define a one-dimensional array that will store the same information, using a record containing three fields. The purpose of this program is simply to practice the syntax of defining, declaring, and using array structures. Therefore, your program doesn't have to do anything more than assign and display values for all vector components. Usually, fields in a record don't all have the same data type. They can, however, and in this problem all the fields are REAL numbers. Be sure to compile your program to check it for syntax errors.

Exercise 14. Modify the code fragment in P-8.9 so that the three fields product1, product2, and product3 are replaced with an array that will hold the names of up to 10 products. Include your new definition in a program "shell" and let your compiler check it for syntax errors.

Exercise 15. An interesting mathematical recreation is designing magic squares. A magic square of size n contains the integers from 1 to n^2. Each value appears only once. The sum of the integers in each row and column and along both diagonals must be the same. Here's a 3×3 magic square, for which the values in each row, column, and diagonal must add up to 15:

6	1	8
7	5	3
2	9	4

Write a program that will prompt a user to enter values for an n×n square one row at a time and determine if it's a magic square. The program does *not* have to design magic squares. (That's a lot harder!)

Exercise 16. For a two-dimensional array declared as REAL A(5,5), initialize the elements so that they form an identity matrix; that is, all the elements are 0 except for the elements along the top-left to bottom-right diagonal, which are 1. Use assignment statements, not a DATA statement.

```
1 0 0 0 0
0 1 0 0 0
0 0 1 0 0
0 0 0 1 0
0 0 0 0 1
```

Exercise 17. Modify P-8.1 so that you can easily change both the total number of random numbers generated and the number of bins to which the numbers are assigned. For example, 10,000 random numbers could be assigned to 20 bins numbered 0–19. **Hint:** use PARAMETERs, or let the user provide the values when the program runs.

Extra Credit
How can you tell whether a random number generator is working? One way is to compare the actual contents of the bins in P-8.1 or your modification of it to the expected contents. For example, if 10,000 numbers are randomly assigned to 20 bins, on average there should be 500 numbers in each bin; this is the expected content of each bin.

This comparison can be quantified by using the well-known χ^2 distribution from nonparametric statistics:

$$\chi^2 = \sum_{i=1}^{n} \left(\frac{O_i - E_i}{E_i} \right)^2$$

where O_i and E_i are the observed and expected contents of each of the n bins.

Add a calculation of the χ^2 statistic to your program and compare the resulting value to values in a table of χ^2 values. For n bins, you should use values in the $(n-1)^{st}$ row of such a table. Consult a statistics text for an interpretation of the values. You will probably find that according to this test, the random number generator is not very convincingly random. It is beyond the scope of this text to discuss whether this means that the χ^2 test is inappropriate or the random number generator is actually not very good.

Exercise 18. Using P-8.5 as a guide, add a subroutine that calculates the intersection of two sets.

Exercise 19. Modify P-8.11 so that the two (three-component) vectors **A** and **B**, their dot product, the angle between them, and their cross product (**C**) are all defined as part of a TYPE structure. Modify the subroutines to use this structure.

Exercise 20. Based on material from another course you are taking, state a computational problem and write a complete program to solve it. Your program must include an appropriate use of arrays to store and manipulate information.

8.9.3 Programming Applications

Exercise 21. A bored postal employee is playing with a row of mailboxes. Initially, all the boxes are closed. Then, starting with the 2nd box, the employee opens every 2nd box. Then, starting with the 3rd box, she opens every 3rd box if it's closed and closes it if it's open. Then, starting with the 4th box, etc. When the employee gets to the end of the line of mailboxes, which ones are still closed?

　　Hint: use an array of LOGICALs to represent the boxes; 40 or so elements are sufficient to see the pattern. Initialize the array to .TRUE. in a DATA statement and assume that .TRUE. corresponds to a closed box. Use a logical operator that will "toggle" the state of each box. Print the results with an L format. [MAILBOX.F90]

Exercise 22. Refer to Exercise 16 in Chapter 7. In that problem, you were asked to create a function that performs linear interpolation between two values in a table. Often, you can hold an entire table of values in an array of records (or in two parallel arrays). Suppose an array X holds n values of an independent variable and an array Y holds n values of the tabulated dependent variable. Write a program that will accept a value of an independent variable x, where $X(1) \leq x \leq X(n)$, and then calculates a linearly interpolated value of y for that value of x.

　　You should put the necessary subprograms in a MODULE and access them with a driver program. You may assume that when the program user provides a value of x, it is within the limits of the values of the independent variable in the table. You can use either two parallel arrays or a single array that has elements defined in a TYPE structure. Use these x and y values to test your program:

x	y
5.0	5.9
10.0	6.6
15.0	7.1
20.0	8.3
25.0	10.0
30.0	12.2

Hint: separate this problem into two parts. First, determine the two positions in the table between which the interpolation will be done. Then do the interpolation.

Make sure to test your program for values of x at each end of the table. For the data shown here, test the program when x=5 and when x=30, as well as at intermediate values of x. [INTERPOL.F90]

Extra Credit

If you would like to look ahead to Chapter 9, you could try reading the data for this problem from the file INTERPOL.DAT, which is among the files available for downloading from the World Wide Web site mentioned in Section i.5 of the Preface.

Exercise 23. When a time sequence of measurements is made on a "noisy" system, it is often desired to "smooth" the data so that trends are easier to spot. One simple smoothing technique is a so-called unweighted moving average. Suppose a data set consists of n values. These data can be smoothed by taking a moving average of m points, where m is some number significantly less than n. The average is "unweighted" because "old" values count just as much as newer values. The formula for calculating the ith smoothed value S_i is

$$S_i = \left(\sum_{j=i-m+1}^{i} x_j \right)/m , \quad i \geq m$$

Figure 8.5 shows an unweighted moving average with m=10 for a data set of 100 random numbers in the range [0,200]. A moving average does "smooth" these data, but because the data are random, by definition there shouldn't be any "trend" to spot.

The algorithm for calculating a moving average over m values for a data set containing n values is:

1. Calculate the sum of the first m points. The first average is sum/m.
2. For i=m+1 to n, add the ith value to the sum and subtract the $(i-m)^{th}$ value. Then calculate the average for this new sum.
3. Repeat Step 2 until i=n.

If the data set contains n points, there will be n-m+1 moving average calculations.

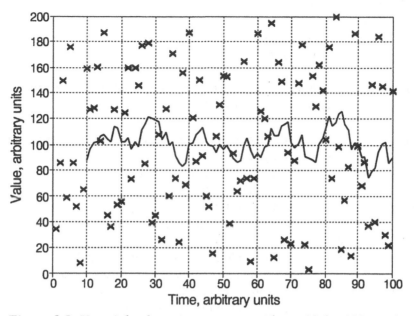

Figure 8.5. Unweighted moving average with m=10 for 100 random values

Write a subroutine that calculates and displays a moving average over a specified number of points for a one-dimensional array of specified size. Store the results in a second array of the same size. For a moving average over m points, the first m-1 elements of the second array should be set to 0. Test the subroutine in a program that generates an array of random numbers and smoothes that array with the moving average subroutine. [MOVE_AVG.F90]

Exercise 24. It is often of interest in simulation problems to be able to select values randomly from a predefined set of values. This is a trivial problem if the same value can be used more than once. More care is required if each value in a set of n values can be used only once, or to put it another way, if it is required that after n values have been used, every value in the set has been used once. The latter problem is analogous to dealing cards randomly from a deck.

Suppose a deck of cards is represented by the integer values 1–52. Create an array holding the values 1–52. One way to "shuffle" this deck is to construct a loop for i = 1 to 52 and swap the ith card with a randomly chosen card. It is of no concern that occasionally the card will be swapped with itself. The swapping algorithm looks like this:

ASSIGN *temp = card(i)*
        index = random #, 1-52
        card(i) = card(index)
        card(index) = temp

Incorporate this algorithm into a complete program that will deal four random "hands" of 13 cards each. [CARDDECK.F90]

Exercise 25. The game of Life provides a simple model of how organisms are born, survive, and die. It is played on a two-dimensional board with m rows and n columns. The game is started by establishing an initial distribution of organisms in a small region of the board. The distribution of the next generation of the population is calculated according to three rules:
(1) A new organism will appear in the next generation in any empty square with exactly three living neighbors.
(2) An organism in a square surrounded by less than two neighbors will die from loneliness in the next generation, and an organism in a square surrounded by more than three neighbors will die from overcrowding in the next generation.
(3) An organism with two or three neighbors will survive into the next generation.
        Write a program that plays this game. A 20×20 board is certainly large enough. You should produce output for several generations using at least the following initial population distributions, where an X indicates that an organism occupies that square:

```
(1)     - - - - - - -          - - - X - -
        - - XXX - -            - - - - X -
        - - - X - - -          - - XXX -
```

Some initial configurations die out, some form patterns that grow, oscillate, or become stable, and others form patterns that reproduce themselves and move across the board. The second of the two initial configurations shown above is called the "glider," for reasons that are apparent from following it through four generations:

```
(2)     - - X -        - - - -          - - - -          - - - - -          - - - - -
        - - - X        - X - X          - - - X          - - X - -          - - - X -
        - XXX   -->    - - XX   -->     - X - X   -->    - - - XX   -->    - - - - X
        - - - -        - - X -          - - XX           - - XX -          - - XXX
```

Question: What happens to two gliders that start from opposite sides of the board and "collide" in the middle?
        Hint: you can simplify the code by assuming that any organism occupying a row or column at the "edge" of the game board simply disappears in the next generation. This means that the rules for the game apply only to (m-1)×(n-1)

squares on the board. One way to apply the rules is to create an intermediate board configuration that marks births and deaths for the next generation. This is necessary because organisms don't die immediately when you detect that they have less than two or more than three neighbors. They stay there until all the rules have been applied to all squares on the board for the current generation. Similarly, new organisms aren't born until the start of the next generation, so they can't count as neighbors during the current generation. [LIFE.F90]

Exercise 26. A terrain map is stored in digital form as integers in a two-dimensional array. Write a program to examine the array and find high and low spots in the terrain. The criterion for a high or low spot will be a user-specified amount above or below the average of the eight surrounding values.

For the purposes of this program, you can assume that the values are in the range 0-9. Print the original array and, next to it, an array that has high and low spots marked with the letter H or L. A 20×20 array is large enough. You can use a random number generator to create the original array. Some sample output is shown in Figure 8.6.

```
           Look for differences >     4.0000000
80049726420096732609      +-----------------+
98993765555866751665      | H               |
92963649758076007267      |L         L     H |
42656156372985104461      |L    L            |
69703872560985655139      |H L       LH      |
06873874745619060247      |          L L L   |
56372675111978597581      |        L LH   H  |
82801839947613638148      |  L  L    L     L |
37453949894019191082      |          L H H LH|
05868892687760244491      |        L        H|
32891669863529244108      |    L        H   LL|
87356395794731439382      |                H H|
54575719084038623368      |      L L    H    |
74996174932405620873      |        H   L  L  |
77624904068377508883      |     HL L         |
22254284728657164754      |      H H      L  |
90601530345986559496      |L L           H H|
89647213209988943141      |          L   H L |
66029884073921148437      |  L    L          |
42958575844660457699      +-----------------+
```

Figure 8.6. Sample output from the terrain map program

Hint: you can't look for high and low spots in the rows and columns at the edges of the map because you must look at all eight surrounding values. [TERRAIN.F90]

Exercise 27. An engineer designing a new computer chip is concerned about operating temperatures within the chip. Tests show it is possible to design heat sinks that, when attached to the sides of the rectangular chip, will maintain each edge of the chip at a suitable temperature. Write a program to determine the temperature distribution within the chip.

One way to solve this problem is to divide the rectangular area into a two-dimensional grid. (See Figure 8.7.) Initialize the grid nodes at each edge of the chip to specified temperatures; in general, each edge can have a different temperature. Initialize the "interior" nodes to some other value; a good choice would be the average of all the edge temperatures. Then, using an iterative loop, recalculate the temperature of each interior node as the average of the temperatures of the four surrounding nodes. Terminate the iteration when the difference between the current temperature and the next iteration is less than some specified small amount for *every* node.

Hint: the conditional loop to conduct the iteration could be in the main program. It should call a subroutine whose purpose is to recalculate the node temperatures and return a "flag" value that indicates whether the terminating conditions for the iteration have been met.

One obvious verification for your program is to set each edge temperature to the same value. Then a successful iteration should result in all the interior nodes reaching this temperature. In this case, it would not be helpful to initialize the interior temperatures to the average of the edge temperatures because then no iteration would be necessary. Try a different initial value, such as half the edge temperature. [CIRCT_BD.F90]

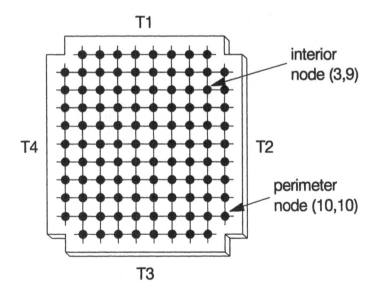

Figure 8.7. Nodes on a circuit board, as defined for determining interior temperature distribution

Using Formatted Sequential Access and Internal Files

This chapter discusses the concept of a formatted text file and presents the syntax of the OPEN, READ, WRITE, and CLOSE statements required to access and create such files. The important scenario in which a READ statement appears in a conditional loop structure to control the reading of a data file of unknown length is discussed in detail. The syntax for writing formatted files is described. Internal files are presented as a way to store records in a temporary buffer for processing.

9.1 The Text File Concept

Up to now, you have made external input available to your programs by typing values on your keyboard or hardcoding them within a program. Obviously, this will be inadequate for many problems involving large amounts of data. Fortran provides extensive support for reading data from external data files in a variety of formats. In this chapter, the only kind of file considered is a *text file*.

text file
sequential access file
end-of-line mark
end-of-file mark

A text file is a line-oriented file consisting of printable characters, including digits. Each line, which can be interpreted as one or more data fields, is terminated by a system-dependent *end-of-line* mark. A file is always terminated by a system-dependent *end-of-file* mark. Typically, a text file is treated as a *sequential access file* that is accessed one record at a time, starting at the beginning.

Suppose you create a file of student names and grades. It might look like the data in Table 9.1. These data can be found in the file GRADES.DAT, which can be downloaded from the World Wide Web site mentioned in Section i.5 of the Preface. Table 9.1 obviously represents a "text" file in the sense that the *header lines* (the first two lines in this particular file) and names consist of "text" in the form of letters and dashes. It is less obvious that the apparent numbers in the file, corresponding to the grades, are also

header line

Table 9.1. A sample text file

```
Name        Grade
- - - - - - - - - - - - - -
Adams        99.3
Brown       100.0
Carter       77.9
Jones        81.1
Smith        66.6
```

just "text." That is, numbers are represented in the file by a sequence of digits plus a decimal point.

This might seem like a trivial point because it's easy for you to interpret the data records in this file as a name and a number. In particular, it's easy to interpret a series of digits such as 99.3 as a number. However, computers don't store numbers this way. In order for a Fortran program to interpret the characters 99.3 as the number 99.3, it must convert this *external representation* of a number to its *internal representation*.

external representation
internal representation

How can you force your program to interpret the characters 99.3 as a number or, more generally, to make an appropriate interpretation of any set of characters? The basic answer is that Fortran will interpret characters in a text file any way you like as long as you tell it what to do. To put it another way, there is no *inherent* interpretation for the characters in any record of a text file. Consider the third line of the file:

```
          1
123456789012345
Adams       99.3
```

The column "ruler" isn't part of the file. It's there just to help keep track of where the data are located. It appears reasonable to conclude that the names in this file are right-justified in columns 1–6. The nine columns 7–15 contain what appears to be a number right-justified in those columns.

By creating a format specification, using the same syntax developed in Chapter 5 for creating formatted output, you can force your Fortran program to interpret this line of text in an appropriate way—as one character field and one numerical field. The required statements are

```
       CHARACTER*6 name
       REAL grade
       ...
       READ(1,1000) name,grade
       ...
1000   FORMAT(a6,f9.1)
```

Note that it's not necessary for you to understand what the internal representation of a REAL number is. All you need to understand is that formatted input allows you to impose your own interpretation on the data in the file.

There are critical pieces missing from this brief code fragment. Before you can READ from the file, you must include the statements required to make the file containing these records available. An explanation of the READ statement syntax is also needed. The next section will discuss the details of reading sequential access text files and show how to incorporate this code fragment into a complete program.

First, however, consider some alternate ways of interpreting the data in the file. It's possible to interpret every line in the file shown in Table 9.1 as consisting entirely of characters:

```
       CHARACTER*15 one_line
       . . .
       READ(1,1000) one_line
       . . .
1000   FORMAT(a15)
```

In this case, all 15 characters become part of the CHARACTER variable one_line. This is OK for the header lines, but if the third and subsequent lines are read with this format, the numerical information contained in the file is at least temporarily lost because Fortran hasn't been told to interpret the digits as the external representation of a number.

Here's another possible, although not very likely, interpretation of the data in the file:

```
       CHARACTER*3 n1,n2
       INTEGER a
       REAL b
       . . .
       READ(1,1000) n1,n2,a,b
       . . .
1000   FORMAT(a3,a3,i7,f2.1)
```

This format divides the six columns occupied by the name in half. It then interprets the blanks and characters to the left of the decimal point as an integer and the remaining two characters as a REAL number. For the first line of data, a and b will have values of 99 and 0.3.

Neither of these possibilities seems to be a reasonable interpretation of the contents of the file shown in Table 9.1. The point of showing them is to demonstrate that even though humans may assign certain "obvious" interpretations to text files, Fortran must be told specifically how to interpret the contents of such files.

As a result of this discussion, you should now understand FORMAT statements in a more general way: they tell Fortran how to translate quantities back and forth between their internal and external representations. When formats are used with a READ statement, they tell your program how to interpret characters in a text file in the same sense that formatted output tells your program how to display output. Throughout the rest of this chapter, we will make extensive use of formats for reading information in text files. Fortunately, there isn't much new to learn if you have a thorough understanding of how to use FORMAT statements to create formatted output.

P-9.1 gives a more complete code fragment for providing a reasonable interpretation of the first three records in the file shown in Table 9.1.

P-9.1 (fragment)

```
      . . .
      CHARACTER*6 name,heading*15
      REAL grade
!
! (statements to make the file available for reading...)
!
      READ(1,1000) heading
      PRINT *,heading
      READ(1,1000) heading
      PRINT *,heading
      READ(1,1010) name,grade
      PRINT *,name,grade
!
1000  FORMAT(a15)
1010  FORMAT(a6,f9.1)
      . . .
```

If access to the records shown in Table 9.1 is to be restricted to "sequential access," the implication is that the contents of the file must be read in order, starting at the beginning. Your program can stop anywhere before the end of the file, but it can't skip ahead or backward. This means that before P-9.1 can read the data in the first data record of the file shown in Table 9.1, which is the first line containing data, it must first read past the first two header lines. In this example, the header lines have been assigned a variable name and printed; this is entirely optional, and it is also acceptable to use two PRINT* statements simply to read past these header lines.

For some kinds of problems involving file operations, sequential access imposes a severe restriction, but for now, sequential files will be adequate. The next section shows how to implement sequential access text files in Fortran.

9.2 OPEN, READ, and CLOSE Statements for Sequential File Access

In Chapter 2, the **OPEN**, **READ**, and **CLOSE** pseudocode commands were briefly introduced as symbolic tools to access data files. These same words are keywords in Fortran, and this section will explore their syntax in the context of a complete program to read the name and grade data file from Table 9.1.

9.2.1 Reading a File Containing Student Names and Grades

1 Define the problem.

A data file contains a list of student names and grades. (See Table 9.1.) Write a program that reads the file and calculates the average of all grades in the file.

2 Outline a solution.

1. Examine the file to make sure you understand its contents. In this case, the file includes two header lines lines that describe what is in the file.
2. Read the two header lines.
3. Read the data in the file one line at a time, in a loop that will stop at the end of the file. Increment a sum and a line counter inside the loop.
4. When the loop terminates, close the file.
5. The average is the sum divided by the line counter.

3 Design an algorithm.

DEFINE *(name, header as string; grade, sum, average as real;*
             counter as integer)
OPEN *(file containing the data)*
INITIALIZE *sum = 0*
                counter = 0
READ *(first header line)*
WRITE *(first header line)*
READ *(second header line)*
WRITE *(second header line)*
LOOP *(as long as there are data in the file)*
        READ *(name,grade)*
        WRITE *(name,grade)*
        INCREMENT *sum = sum + grade*
                       counter = counter + 1
END LOOP
CLOSE *(file)*
ASSIGN *average = sum/counter*
WRITE *(average)*

4 Convert the algorithm into a program.

P-9.2 [GRADES_F.F90]

```fortran
      PROGRAM Grades_f
!
! Calculate average grade from a file of names and grades.
! Demonstrates use of sequential access text files.
!
      IMPLICIT NONE
      CHARACTER*6 name,heading*15
      REAL grade,avg
      INTEGER n_grades
      DATA avg,n_grades/0.0,0/
!
      OPEN(1,file='c:\ftn90.dir\grades.dat',action='read')
!
      READ(1,1000)heading
      PRINT *,heading
      READ(1,1000)heading
      PRINT *,heading
!
! Start READ loop
!
10    READ(1,1010,END=999)name,grade
      WRITE(*,1020)name,grade
      avg=avg+grade
      n_grades=n_grades+1
      GO TO 10
!
! End READ loop
!
999   CLOSE(1)
      IF (n_grades > 0) THEN
        avg=avg/n_grades
      ELSE
        avg=0.
      END IF
      WRITE(*,1030)avg
!
1000  FORMAT(a15)
1010  FORMAT(a6,f9.1)
1020  FORMAT(1x,a6,f9.1)
1030  FORMAT(1x,'Average grade = ',f6.1)
      END
```

Running P-9.2

```
   Name      Grade
- - - - - - - - - - - - - - -
   Adams      80.0
   Brooks    100.0
   Carter     77.3
   Nixon      33.3
   Mason      66.6
   Smith      55.9
   Turner     92.1
Average grade =    72.2
```

This program will be discussed in detail below, particularly the loop formed by the READ statement in the line labelled 10 and the statement GO TO 10. (The statements in this loop are printed in bold italics.)

5 *Verify the operation of the program.*

Verify the program by calculating the average by hand. This might not be practical with a long data file. In that case, read just a few records in the file, using a DO... loop instead of a conditional loop.

Problem Discussion

As demonstrated by P-9.2, the process of reading data from an external file consists of three steps. These steps and their associated Fortran keywords are given in Table 9.2. As usual, the names of the keywords are closely associated with their functions.

Table 9.2. Three steps required to read a data file.

Required Step	Fortran Statement
Open the file.	OPEN
Read the file one record at a time, starting at the beginning.	READ
Close the file.	CLOSE

Program P-9.2 is based on the assumption that the data file containing names and grades actually exists and contains information in the format illustrated in Table 9.1. As we will see later in this chapter, it is possible to provide some protection against files that do not meet a program's expectations, but P-9.2 contains no such protections. What will happen if, for example, the two header lines are missing? In that case, P-9.2 won't crash, but it will treat the first two data lines as header lines, so these data won't be included in the calculation of the grade average. Also, P-9.2 won't crash if the file contains the two header lines, but no name and grade data. This is because the IF...THEN...ELSE... statement near the end of P-9.2 tests the value of n_grades before calculating the average. If n_grades is zero, then the average is assigned a value of zero; you might choose some other value instead, such as a negative number.

9.2.2 The OPEN and REWIND Statements

A partial syntax for the OPEN statement is

```
OPEN([UNIT=]u,optional specifiers)

where u is a unit number and the optional specifiers include:
  ACCESS=
    The possible values are 'SEQUENTIAL' and 'DIRECT'
  ACTION=
    The suggested values for sequential access files are
    'READ' or 'WRITE'
  BLANK=
    The possible values are 'NULL' or 'ZERO'.
  ERR=statement label
    Program control will be transferred to statement label if
      the OPEN statement generates an error.
  FILE=path and file name
    The full path and file name for the file to be opened.
      If the file name appears directly after the unit number,
      the specifier is optional.
  FORM=
    The possible values are 'FORMATTED' and 'UNFORMATTED'.
  IOSTAT=integer variable
    OPEN returns a zero if there are no errors and a positive
      value otherwise.
  POSITION=
    The suggested values for writing to a sequential access
      file are 'REWIND' and 'APPEND'.  'REWIND' positions an
      existing file at the beginning, causing exising data to
      be overwritten.  'APPEND' positions the file at the end,
      allowing new data to be appended to existing data.
  STATUS=
    The possible values are 'OLD', 'NEW', 'REPLACE',
    'SCRATCH', and 'UNKNOWN'.

Example:
      OPEN(1,'a:grades.dat',err=99,action='read')
```

In Fortran, files must be associated with a unit number—the symbolic "name" by which the file is referenced in the program. If the unit number is given first, the UNIT= specifier is optional. The association between a unit number and a physical file on your computer's hard drive or a diskette is made in the OPEN statement, either directly after the unit number or elsewhere in the statement following the FILE= specifier. The allowed range of possible unit numbers is system dependent. Unit numbers 5 and 6 are usually reserved for standard input and output devices, but the other values between 1 and 10 are probably good choices.

There are many optional specifiers available in the OPEN statement, only a few of which will be of interest now. The programs in this chapter require only the unit number, the file name, and a value for the ACTION= specifier. In some cases, you may also wish to include ERR= specifier. For text files, FORM='FORMATTED' and ACCESS='SEQUENTIAL' are the default values, so these specifiers are unnecessary.

As usual in Fortran, the names of the options and the character string values assigned to them are case-insensitive. Thus action='read' is equivalent to ACTION='READ' and action='READ'. The actions 'read' and 'write' mean "read only" and "write only." That is, you can either read from or write to a sequential access text file, but you can't do both at the same time. For now, programs will read from data files. Options for writing to a file will be discussed later in the chapter.

OPEN statements can appear anywhere in a program after the nonexecutable statements and before the referenced unit number is required in a READ or WRITE statement. However, it is good programming practice to group all OPEN statements together near the beginning of your program if this is otherwise appropriate because file name information provided in OPEN statements may not be compatible from one system to another. If these statements are all in one place, the required changes are easier to make. However, it might *not* be appropriate to group all OPEN statements together if the opening of a file depended on some other part of your program being executed first.

It is sometimes the case that you would like to read part or all of a file more than once. One option is to CLOSE the file (see Section 9.2.4) and OPEN it again. However, this isn't necessary. Using the syntax

```
REWIND unit
  or
REWIND([unit=]unit)
```

positions the open file associated with *unit* back at the beginning.

It is poor programming practice to use the REWIND statement unless it's absolutely necessary. It is usually better to store data in an array when you need repeated access to the values, because operations taking place in memory are more efficient than read/write operations on files.[1]

9.2.3 The READ and BACKSPACE Statements

The READ statement, previously used to access input from the keyboard, has a more complicated syntax when it is used to access the contents of a text file. Its general syntax is

```
READ([UNIT=]u,[FMT=]format specifier[,IOSTAT=integer variable]
     [,ERR=line_label][,END=line_label]) list of variables

where:
u is a unit number, format specifier is a label for a
     line containing a FORMAT statement
IOSTAT returns implementation-dependent integer values for
     various abnormal conditions
ERR= directs program control to a labelled line if an error
     occurs while reading the file
END= directs program control to a labelled line when the end
     of the file is encountered.
The list of variables to be read can take several forms,
     similar to the possibilities with formatted WRITE and
     PRINT statements.

Examples:
     READ(5,*)a,b,c !reads from standard input device
     READ(3,*)a,b,c
     READ(1,1000,END=999,ERR=998)(A(i),B(i),i=1,10)
```

The first example is a simple statement that reads three values using list-directed input. However, it doesn't read a text file, even though it appears to do so, because of the presence of a unit number. By default on most systems, unit 5 is permanently associated with your computer's keyboard. Because unit 5 isn't an external file, even though it appears to be, it doesn't have to be opened or closed.

The second and third examples are intended to read data from an external file. They assume that their units (1 and 3) have previously been OPENed. The third example refers to a format and includes directions, through the END= and

---

[1]Author's note: the REWIND statement has its roots in Fortran at a time when large data files were stored on magnetic tape. In that case, REWIND caused the physical rewinding of the tape reel, which could be very time-consuming. On modern systems, the REWIND statement simply reinitializes an electronic "pointer" to the beginning of a file stored, typically, on your computer's hard drive. This does not take long. However, my own personal style is still to avoid using REWIND.

ERR= options, about where to transfer program control when the end of the file is reached or an error is detected.

Now return to P-9.2. The data file GRADES.DAT has a typical structure. It contains header lines that describe the contents of the file; these are not necessary, but they are useful for clarifying the structure of the file and making its contents more easily accessible to a human reader. Then the file contains a typically unknown number of lines of data, all of which use the same format. In this situation, the header lines must be read first in order to get to the data, even if the information in the header lines isn't needed for anything. Then all the identically formatted data records can be read inside a conditional loop.

In P-9.2, the loop to read the file begins with the labelled line containing the READ statement (line 10) and ends at the line containing the GO TO 10 statement, which transfers program control back to the READ statement. The syntax of the GO TO statement is

```
GO TO line_label
```

Modern programming style generally disparages the use of "go to" statements and labelled lines, no matter what the language.[2] Indeed, we will use it for no other purpose in this text. What are the alternatives for a program such as P-9.2? One alternative is to determine ahead of time how many grade listings are in the file. Then the file can be read in a DO... loop. This "record count" could be "hard coded" into the source code or it could be given as a separate record at the beginning of the file. The second alternative is to add a "sentinel value" to the end of the file and use this value to terminate a conditional loop. For example, the line

```
nomore        0.0
```

could be added to the end of the data in Table 9.1.

In this text, we will generally not use the first of these alternatives, and we will never use the second. Why not? The first alternative imposes an unnecessary burden on a programmer, if the record count is hard coded into the program, or on the creator of the file if the record count is given as a value at the beginning of the file. However, the tactic of including the record count in the file itself can sometimes be useful, and it at least has the advantage that the source code itself does not need to be changed if records are added or deleted from the file.

---

[2]Author's note: this is somewhat of an understatement according to some Fortran 90 programmers, who will, in my purely personal opinion, go to unreasonable lengths to avoid the use of GO TO statements.

The second alternative imposes an unnecessary burden on the creator of a file; there is no good reason to require the addition of an extra record that might be useful for a Fortran program, but a nuisance for some other use of the file. It seems a bad idea, in principle, to require that the creator of a data file have detailed knowledge of how the file will be used in the future by a program written in a particular programming language.

There are no good reasons to accept either of these alternatives. We will instead use the "implied" conditional loop structure made possible by the END= specifier in the READ syntax, even at the risk of using the much-maligned GO TO statement.

As you know, every conditional loop requires a terminating condition. In this case, the terminating condition is found inside the READ statement. Every text file includes an end-of-file mark at the end of the file, which is automatically put there when the file is created. The END= specifier enables the READ statement to "look ahead" for this mark before the read operation actually takes place. When the end-of-file mark is found, the loop terminates and transfers program control to the line with the specified label (999 in P-9.2). It is not allowed actually to read the end-of-file mark. Without the END= specifier, a program will crash when it tries to read data past the end of the file. As shown in P-9.2, the usual action to take when the loop terminates is to close the file and continue with the rest of the program.

The presence of the terminating condition inside the READ statement implies that the conditional loop in P-9.2 is a pre-test loop. As a result, your program won't crash if you ask it, presumably not on purpose, to read an empty file. If the input file doesn't even exist, you won't get this far because your program will crash when it tries to OPEN a nonexistent file, unless you have used the IOSTAT= specifier in the OPEN statement (see the syntax summary for the OPEN statement) to recover from such errors more gracefully.

P-9.2 implicitly assumes that there will be no data errors in the file, or if they do exist, that you will simply fix them and run the program again. If you need a more sophisticated way of recovering from file errors, you can include the ERR= option in the READ statement. As a general rule,

> It is easier to edit data files so that their contents are predictable than to write a program that will keep running no matter what it finds, or doesn't find, in a file.

There are many opportunities for errors when you're writing programs that involve reading external data files. It's important to provide an appropriate format for the data records in the file and to be aware of how many lines, if any, must be read as header lines. It is also important that the file being read meet the program's expectations. Once an input format is specified within your program, all the data in the file must adhere to that format. If any does not, your program will crash, or even worse, your program will continue to run, but will produce answers that are wrong. If your program uses list-directed input, then the formatting conditions imposed on the file are not so strict (for example, numbers don't need to line up in columns), but that may place limitations on how information in the file can be interpreted.

Note that it's not required for every line in a file, other than the header lines, to have the same format. However, it *is* necessary to know the structure and arrangement of every line. One common situation involves a data record that requires more than one line in a file. Then each data record in the file must be extracted by reading a group of lines, with each line in the group having having its own format.

It may sometimes *seem* necessary to reread a record. For example, you may wish to reinterpret a value in a record based on a value found elsewhere in that same record. The statement

```
BACKSPACE unit
   or
BACKSPACE([unit=]unit)
```

skips back one record in the file associated with unit number *unit*. As a matter of style, you should not make a habit of using this statement. If you really can't process a file sequentially, then you shouldn't be using a sequential access file. (Alternative file structures are discussed in Chapter 12.) Anything you wish to accomplish with a BACKSPACE can more reasonably be achieved by reading a record into an internal file, as discussed below in Section 9.4.2. The BACKSPACE statement is mentioned here only because you may sometimes encounter it in programs.[3]

9.2.4 The CLOSE Statement

A CLOSE statement is required to close each file that you have OPENed in your program. The results of not closing a file depend on how the file is being used and may be system-dependent. In any event, you should always be careful to include a CLOSE statement for every open file even if a program seems to work

---

[3]Author's note: the BACKSPACE statement has its roots in Fortran at a time when data files were stored on magnetic tape, in which case a BACKSPACE could require physical movement of the tape on its reel. On modern systems, data being read from a file are typically held in an input buffer that may be large enough to hold many data records at once. In that case, a BACKSPACE may actually be quite efficient. Nonetheless, my personal style is still to avoid its use.

without it (for example, if you forget to put a CLOSE statement in a program and nothing bad happens). The syntax of the CLOSE statement is

```
CLOSE(unit)
```

9.3 Files and Arrays

This is an extremely important section because it brings together two of the most important features of any programming language, file processing and arrays. Once you understand this material, you will be able to write a large percentage of the programs you will ever need.

In Chapter 8, the need for arrays was discussed in the context of managing collections of related values. However, what was missing from that discussion was a clear idea of how those values could be transmitted to your program when they couldn't be generated within the program itself. The obvious solution is to store the required input values in a data file that can be accessed by your program. Depending on the application, you might also wish to store the data in an array defined within your program. Remember that information in an external file represents "permanent" data storage—as long as your hard drive keeps working— whereas an array in your program is temporary in the sense that it is a data structure that lasts only as long as your program is running. The techniques will be presented in the context of specific examples.

Table 9.3. High and low temperatures during January 1994

01/01/94	43	24
01/02/94	51	31
01/03/94	37	33
01/04/94	35	30
01/05/94	38	24
01/06/94	32	24
01/07/94	33	30
01/08/94	37	18
01/09/94	28	17
01/10/94	29	17
01/11/94	40	21
01/12/94	39	36
01/13/94	41	36
01/14/94	39	31
01/15/94	17	6
01/16/94	15	4
01/17/94	34	14
01/18/94	33	8
01/19/94	6	-5
01/20/94	15	0
01/21/94	34	5
01/22/94	33	15
01/23/94	33	24
01/24/94	51	31
01/25/94	48	32
01/26/94	34	21
01/27/94	33	11
01/28/94	58	33
01/29/94	42	34
01/30/94	36	29
01/31/94	37	22

1 Define the problem.

Given a data file containing the date and high and low temperatures for every day in a month, write a program that will calculate the average temperature for the month and will then print the high and low temperatures for each day on which the average temperature was below the average temperature for the month. The average temperature for the month is defined as the average of the daily averages. The daily average temperature is defined as half the sum of the low and high temperatures for that day. The sample data given in Table 9.3 can be found in file JANUARY.DAT, which may be downloaded from the World Wide Web site mentioned in Section i.5 of the Preface.

2 *Outline a solution.*

1. Read the data file and store the dates and measurements in an array. The array is necessary because all the measurements will be needed again, after the monthly average has been calculated.

2. While reading the data file, calculate the average temperature for each day and sum up those average temperatures. (Assume the daily average is, in fact, equal to the average of the high and low temperatures.)

3. Calculate the average temperature for the month by dividing the sum of the daily average temperatures by the number of days in the month.

4. Loop through the contents of the array and print out all data for a day when the average temperature is below the average temperature for the month.

3 *Design an algorithm.*

DEFINE *(array containing the date, high and low temperatures, and daily*
average temperature for each day of the month;
a loop counter (i); number of days (n_days); monthly_average)
OPEN *(data file)*
READ *(header lines, if any)*
WRITE *(header lines – optional or for testing)*
(Read the data.)
INITIALIZE *n_days = 0*
monthly_average = 0
LOOP *(through all the data)*
　　INCREMENT *n_days = n_days + 1*
　　READ *(from the file: date(n_days), high(n_days), low(n_days)*
　　WRITE *(all data – optional or for testing)*
　　ASSIGN *daily_average(n_days) = (high(n_days) + low(n_days))/2*
　　INCREMENT *monthly_average = monthly_average*
　　　　　　　　　　　　　+ daily_average(n_days)
END LOOP
CLOSE *(data file)*

```
(Decrement loop counter.)
INCREMENT n_days = n_days – 1
(Calculate monthly average.)
ASSIGN monthly_average = monthly_average/n_days
(Print desired data.)
LOOP (for i = 1 to n_days)
        IF (daily_average(i) < monthly_average) THEN
                WRITE (all data for that day)
END LOOP
```

You should study this algorithm carefully because it illustrates an essential model for reading a data file and storing its contents in an array. The first question to ask yourself is, "Do I understand precisely why an array is needed to store the data within this program?" For this problem, the reason is that you must first calculate the monthly average and then read back through all the data again to print the desired values (those days for which the average temperature is less than the monthly average temperature).

In principle, you could achieve this goal without storing the measurements in the array, but that would involve REWINDing the file and reading it again from the beginning (or closing and re-opening the file). However, there is no reason to take this approach. In general, you should always favor storing the contents of a data file in an array instead of reading the file more than once because operations on data in a file are much slower than operations taking place in memory.

Note that the variable n_days is initialized to 0 outside the loop and incremented inside the loop before the **READ** statement. This is done because the first array index is needed in the **READ** statement so that values in the data file can be associated directly with elements in an array as they are read from the file. When the loop terminates, n_days must be decremented by 1 because it was incremented *before* the end of the file was detected.

Here's an alternative way to read and store the data. Its only disadvantage is that it requires additional variables; you can assume that each of the three temporary variables in this algorithm is associated with an appropriate data type. This is a useful, and perhaps essential, algorithm if you have any reason to test values in a data file *before* you store them in an array.

```
...
INITIALIZE n_days = 0
          monthly_average = 0
LOOP (until the end-of-file)
        READ (from the file: temp1,temp2,temp3)
        WRITE (all data – optional or for testing)
        INCREMENT n_days = n_days + 1
```

```
        ASSIGN date(n_days) = temp1
               high(n_days) = temp2
               low(n_days) = temp3
               daily_average(n_days) = (temp2 + temp3)/2
        INCREMENT monthly_average = monthly_average +
                        daily_average(n_days)
END LOOP
CLOSE (data file)
...
```

In this code, n_days is incremented only after the **READ** has been completed and the values have been examined. In other circumstances, you could make incrementing of an index dependent on the values read from the file.

For the data file shown in Table 9.3, there is yet another way to read and store the data that takes advantage of the fact that the array index is available in the file itself as part of the date string. For example, in the string 01/01/94, the numerical value for the day (1) is contained in the characters 01 in columns 4 and 5. Similarly, numerical values for the month and year are also available, and all these values may be accessed in Fortran:

```
...
INITIALIZE monthly_average = 0
LOOP (until the end-of-file)
        READ (from file: mon,d,year(d),high(d),low(d))
        ASSIGN month(d) = mon
                day(d) = d
        WRITE (all data – optional or for testing)
        ASSIGN daily_average(d) = (high(d) + low(d))/2
        INCREMENT monthly_average = monthly_average +
                                    daily_average(d)
END LOOP
CLOSE (data file)
...
```

In this version of the algorithm, the date is defined not as a string, but as three numerical values for the month, day, and year. This implementation imposes some special conditions on the contents of the data file. It requires that all the days of the month be present so that the array index d, starting at one, is available in the file itself. Using the **READ** command in this way implies that it's possible to read a value and use it immediately in the same **READ** command. As we will see, this is, in fact, allowed in Fortran. Because it's obviously not possible to use the value *before* it's read, the month and day array elements must be assigned after the **READ** command.

We will use the original version of the algorithm because it is more typical code than the others. A modification of the program that uses the "clever" approach for getting the array index from the date will be left for an end-of-chapter exercise.

4 *Convert the algorithm into a program.*

There are some choices to be made about how to implement the arrays required by this algorithm. One way is to define separate arrays for each daily quantity. Another is to define one array for the date and a second multidimensional array for the numerical values, all of which can, and should, be real numbers. The third and best choice in this and many similar problems is to define a one-dimensional array of records using a TYPE construct. Each record will contain the date (stored as three numerical values for the month, day, and year), the high and low temperatures, and the daily average temperature. The last of these fields will be calculated, and all the rest will be obtained directly from the file. This approach is an example of good programming style that uses Fortran 90's capabilities to manage several related variables.

P-9.3 [AVG_TEMP.F90]

```
      PROGRAM avg_temp
!
! Process high and low temperatures for one month.
!
      IMPLICIT NONE
      TYPE hi_lo_type
         CHARACTER*8 date
         REAL hi,lo,daily_average
      END TYPE hi_lo_type
!
      TYPE(hi_lo_type) hi_lo(31)
      INTEGER n_days,d
      REAL monthly_average
!
      OPEN(1,file='c:\ftn90.dir\january.dat')
! Initialize ...
      monthly_average=0.0
      n_days=0
! Read data file...
10    n_days=n_days+1
         READ(1,1000,end=20)hi_lo(n_days)%date,hi_lo(n_days)%hi, &
                            hi_lo(n_days)%lo
         hi_lo(n_days)%daily_average= &
           (hi_lo(n_days)%hi+hi_lo(n_days)%lo)/2.
         monthly_average= &
                 monthly_average+hi_lo(n_days)%daily_average
!        PRINT *, &
!            hi_lo(n_days)%date,hi_lo(n_days)%hi,hi_lo(n_days)%lo
      GO TO 10
```

```
! End of READ loop...
20    CONTINUE
      CLOSE(1)
! Decrement loop counter by 1...
      n_days=n_days-1

! Calculate average...
      monthly_average=monthly_average/n_days
! Print contents days for avg. T < monthly avg. T
      WRITE(*,1002)monthly_average
      WRITE(*,1003)
      WRITE(*,1005)
      DO d=1,n_days
        IF (hi_lo(d)%daily_average < monthly_average) &
          WRITE(*,1010)hi_lo(d)%date, &
                       NINT(hi_lo(d)%hi),NINT(hi_lo(d)%lo), &
                       hi_lo(d)%daily_average
      END DO
!
1000  FORMAT(a8,2f4.0)
1002  FORMAT(' Monthly average temperature = ',f6.2)
1003  FORMAT(' These days have below-average temperature:')
1005  FORMAT(1x,'   Date  hi low   avg' &
             /1x,'----------------------')
1010  FORMAT(1x,a8,2i4,f6.1)
      END
```

Running P-9.3

```
Monthly average temperature =   28.02
These days have below-average temperature:
   Date  hi low   avg
----------------------
 1/ 6/94  32   24   28.0
 1/ 8/94  37   18   27.5
 1/ 9/94  28   17   22.5
 1/10/94  29   17   23.0
 1/15/94  17    6   11.5
 1/16/94  15    4    9.5
 1/17/94  34   14   24.0
 1/18/94  33    8   20.5
 1/19/94   6   -5    0.5
 1/20/94  15    0    7.5
 1/21/94  34    5   19.5
 1/22/94  33   15   24.0
 1/26/94  34   21   27.5
 1/27/94  33   11   22.0
```

5 *Verify the operation of the program.*

Check some daily averages by hand. It might seem unreasonable to ask you to check the entire monthly average by hand, but you can at least ask yourself if the value makes sense. Does your program's output look reasonable?

Problem Discussion

You should examine carefully how the READ loop is implemented. As mentioned during the algorithm design, it is necessary to decrement n_days after the loop terminates because this value is incremented before the READ statement detects the end-of-file.

Even though the temperature values have been read as REAL numbers, they are printed as integer values by using the NINT function in the WRITE statement. This is because a REAL number can't be printed without a decimal point. For example, an F4.0 format would print a value of 24 as "24." and not "24". Why bother to read the temperatures as REAL numbers in the first place? Because calculating the average daily temperature is a real, as opposed to an integer, arithmetic calculation, and it's better programming style to consider the high and low temperatures as REAL values even though a mixed-mode calculation would work in this case.

Even if you quite reasonably conclude that the average temperature should be expressed only to the nearest degree, reflecting the precision of the original data, it would still be better style to treat the data as REAL numbers and convert the final output to an integer value with NINT.

9.4 More About Formatted READ Statements

9.4.1 FORMAT *Statements and Standard Field Descriptors*

Ideally, when you create data files for use in your own programs, you will design them so they are easy to read, perhaps requiring no more than list-directed input. However, you will often have to use files that haven't been created specifically to make them easy to use in Fortran programs. In that case, it's necessary to have a thorough understanding of how to use formatted input to decipher the contents of files. Here is an example.

1 *Define the problem.*

The file BAROM.DAT, which can be downloaded from the World Wide Web site mentioned in Section i.5 of the Preface, contains the date and four barometric pressure readings at 6:00 am, 12:00 noon, 6:00 pm, and midnight for an entire month. The reading consists of the numerical value followed directly by the letter f, s, or r, depending on whether the value is lower (falling), the same as (steady), or higher (rising) than the reading at the previous hour. There are no header records. The first two data records look like this:

```
01/01/94 29.97f 29.97s 30.00s 30.01r
01/02/94 30.00s 30.00f 29.99f 29.98s
```

Write a program that will read and print the information in this file. In particular, your program must separate the numerical value of the barometric pressure from the character following the numerical value.

2 *Outline a solution.*

1. Open the data file for reading.
2. Read each record in the file, separating the f, s, or r from the numerical value for barometric pressure.
3. Print the results.

3 *Design an algorithm.*

DEFINE (date (as string); four sets of pressure and flag values)
OPEN (barometric pressure data file)
LOOP (until end of file)
    READ (date and four sets of pressure/flag values)
    WRITE (date and pressure/flag values)
END LOOP
CLOSE (data file)

4 *Convert the algorithm into a program.*

In this case, the algorithm is simple because the objective of the program is very simple. However, this is an example of a problem for which the implementation details in a particular language are very important.

P-9.4 [BAROM.F90]

```
      PROGRAM barometer
!
! File name BAROM.F90
! Interpret file of daily barometric pressure readings.
!
      IMPLICIT NONE
      CHARACTER*8 date
      REAL at_6am,at_noon,at_6pm,at_midnight
      CHARACTER*1 flag_6am,flag_noon,flag_6pm,flag_midnight
!
      OPEN(1,file='c:\ftn90.dir\humidity.dat')
!
10    READ(1,1000,end=20)date,at_6am,flag_6am,at_noon,flag_noon, &
                        at_6pm,flag_6pm,at_midnight,flag_midnight
      WRITE(*,1010)date,at_6am,flag_6am,at_noon,flag_noon, &
                   at_6pm,flag_6pm,at_midnight,flag_midnight
      GO TO 10
!
20    CLOSE(1)
!
1000  FORMAT(a8,4(f6.0,a1))
1010  FORMAT(1x,a8,4(f8.2,1x,a1))
      END
```

Running P-9.4

```
01/01/95   29.92 f   29.89 f   29.90 r   29.85 f
01/02/95   29.81 r   29.95 r   30.09 r   30.23 r
01/03/95   30.33 r   30.30 f   30.25 f   30.15 f
01/04/95   30.11 f   30.09 f   30.11 f   30.27 r
01/05/95   30.35 r   30.39 f   30.36 s   30.31 f
01/06/95   30.30 f   30.20 f   30.06 f   30.00 f
01/07/95   29.48 r   29.61 r   29.77 r   29.93 r
01/08/95   30.07 r   30.13 f   30.13 r   30.17 s
01/09/95   30.17 r   30.18 f   30.19 r   30.32 r
01/10/95   30.40 r   30.43 f   30.42 r   30.42 f
01/11/95   30.43 r   30.40 f   30.35 r   30.29 f
01/12/95   30.22 s   30.15 f   30.09 s   30.11 s
01/13/95   30.13 r   30.19 f   30.20 r   30.10 f
01/14/95   30.22 s   30.21 f   30.14 f   30.14 s
01/15/95   30.01 f   29.92 f   29.84 s   29.84 s
01/16/95   29.82 r   29.82 f   29.87 r   29.91 s
01/17/95   29.94 r   30.01 f   30.08 r   30.16 r
01/18/95   30.21 r   30.28 s   30.27 r   30.25 f
01/19/95   30.19 f   30.10 f   30.00 s   29.45 f
01/20/95   29.45 f   29.24 f   29.21 f   29.31 r
01/21/95   29.41 r   29.49 s   29.57 r   29.35 r
01/22/95   29.71 r   29.77 f   29.83 r   29.35 r
01/23/95   29.91 r   29.90 f   29.88 s   29.83 f
01/24/95   29.84 r   29.85 r   29.92 r   29.99 s
01/25/95   30.05 r   30.07 f   30.03 s   30.04 s
01/26/95   30.05 r   30.05 f   30.05 r   30.05 s
01/27/95   30.07 s   30.08 f   30.05 s   30.05 s
01/28/95   30.09 f   30.11 f   30.01 f   30.10 r
01/29/95   30.13 r   30.21 f   30.20 s   30.17 f
01/30/95   30.09 s   29.97 f   29.83 s   29.82 r
01/31/95   29.85 r   29.85 f   29.75 r   29.75 s
```

In this case, the desired information cannot be retrieved with list-directed input because the character "flag" appears directly after a numerical value. To separate these values, you must tell your program which columns contain which kind of information. That is, you must use a FORMAT statement to impose a field structure on each record.

5 *Verify the operation of the program.*

It is easy to verify the operation of P-9.4 by comparing the printed output with the original file. Note that when programs rely on formatted input, they must assume that data will always be in the desired format. So part of the program verification in this case is to make sure your data file is properly formatted.

Program P-9.4 is a straightforward application using formatted input. In many ways, input is much easier than output because you will probably be able to do everything you need to do with just four format specifiers: A, F, I, and X. There is not much new to learn. When you use these specifiers for output, they create a column-by-column image of how you want your output to look. When you use them for input, they impose a column-by-column "overlay" on the characters in your data file that tells your program how to translate what it finds there. Consider this statement from P-9.4:

```
1000   FORMAT(a8,4(f6.0,a1))
```

This tells your program that the first eight characters on a line are to be treated as a string. Next there are four groups of seven characters. In each group, the first six are to be treated as a REAL number and the seventh is a single character. Note that the number actually contains only five characters, but it is right-justified in a field six characters wide; there is nothing wrong with having blanks to either the left or the right of a numerical value.[4]

The f6.0 specifier in this statement may be puzzling. As you can see from the data file itself, this seems an inappropriate input format for a number such as 29.97, which has two digits to the right of the decimal point. The applicable rule for using formatted input is this:

Rule 1. When a value to be read and associated with a REAL variable includes a decimal point, the position of that decimal point overrides the position implied by the d field in an fw.d specifier.

That is, as long as the number contains a decimal point, the only part of the fw.d specifier that matters is the w field. In the above case, an f6.2 specifier would work, but so would any other fw.d specifier with w=6.

Here are a few more rules for using formatted input:

Rule 2. When a value to be read and associated with a REAL variable does not include a decimal point, the position of that decimal point can be implied by the d field in an fw.d specifier.

Rule 3. When a value to be read is not right-justified in the field implied by an i or f specifier, the trailing blanks (to the right of the digits) are interpreted by default as blanks and not zeros.

---

[4]However, see the Programming Tip following the discussion of P-9.5.

> **Rule 4. When a value to be read and associated with a REAL variable is written in scientific notation, an f specifier will correctly interpret that value.**

P-9.5 is a simple program that demonstrates these rules. The file READTEST.DAT, which can be downloaded from the World Wide Web site mentioned in Section i.5 of the Preface, looks like this:

```
1    22222
1.3e21
99999
```

P-9.5 [READTEST.F90]

```
      PROGRAM ReadTest
!
! Test program for formatted READ.
!
      IMPLICIT NONE
      INTEGER a,b
      REAL x,y
!
      OPEN(1,file='c:\ftn90.dir\readtest.dat')
      READ(1,1000)a,b
      READ(1,1010)x
      READ(1,1020)y
      PRINT*, a,b
      PRINT*,x,y
      CLOSE(1)
!
1000  FORMAT(2i5)
1010  FORMAT(f6.0)
1020  FORMAT(f5.3)
      END
```

Running P-9.5

```
1 22222
  1.3000001E21   99.9990005
```

Ignoring the small inaccuracies that creep into these values simply because they're stored as REAL variables, you can see that the 1 is translated as 1 and not as 10000, the scientific notation is interpreted correctly, and the 99999 is translated as 99.999 because of the f5.3 format in line 1020.

In the case of the 99999, the result is completely equivalent to writing 99.999 in the data file and reading the value with an f6.0 format. This may seem a rather odd feature of Fortran. Why not just store the number as 99.999

in the first place and avoid possible confusion? The explanation is that in the early days of Fortran, everything, including data files too short to justify creating a magnetic tape, had to be stored on 80-column punch cards, and space was at a premium. If it was possible to store the value 99.999 as the characters 99999 and find a way to interpret those characters appropriately, then the column saved on the punch card could be used for something else. If you actually wanted to interpret the characters 99999 as the number 99999, you could use an integer format or an f5.0 specifier if you still wanted it to be treated as a real number.

Programming Tip

It is possible to use formatted, but not list-directed, input to change the way Fortran interprets trailing blanks in a numerical field. Refer to the OPEN syntax in Section 9.2.2 and the BLANK= option. The default condition is to treat trailing blanks in a field as nulls (equivalent to including BLANK='null'). (However, a completely blank field will be interpreted as a zero.) If you include the BLANK='zero' option in an OPEN statement, trailing blanks will be interpreted as zeros. In the above example, 1ɸɸɸɸ could be interpreted as a value of 10000 rather than 1. You should avoid using this option, as it may result in an unexpected interpretation of the contents of text files. The option exists mainly to allow compatibility with older programs.

9.4.2 Reading Internal Files

Returning now to P-9.4, this program is based not only on the assumption that the data are consistently formatted, but also on the assumption that there are no missing data. This is not always a good assumption, and an appropriate response depends greatly on the circumstances. Here is one possible circumstance and an approach for dealing with it. Assume that the first few records of the data file used in P-9.4 look like this:

```
01/01/95  29.92f  29.89f  29.90r  ------
01/02/95  29.81r  29.95r  30.09r  30.23r
01/03/95  30.33r  30.30f  30.25f  30.15f
```

This is just like the original file except that the first line is missing barometric pressure data for midnight and the field is filled with dashes. The problem this situation poses is that your program can no longer count on being able to read the fields as a numerical value followed by a character. Instead it's necessary to read the six characters in each entry and then decide what to do based on whether those six characters include dashes. Although the idea behind a solution is generally applicable, a solution for this particular data file will be just an *ad hoc* approach to dealing with the contents of this particular file.

There is no need to redesign the algorithm to solve this problem, as it's a Fortran implementation problem that must be solved rather than an algorithm design problem. Therefore, we will proceed directly to the program, P-9.6.

P-9.6 [BAROM2.F90]

```
      PROGRAM barom2
!
! Interpret file of barometric pressure readings when data
! are missing.
!
      IMPLICIT NONE
      CHARACTER*8 date
      CHARACTER*6 temp
      REAL barom_value
      CHARACTER*1 flag
      CHARACTER*80 buffer !temporary string storage
      INTEGER i
!
      OPEN(1,file='c:\ftn90.dir\barom2.dat')
!
10    READ(1,1000,end=20)buffer
! Read and write date...
         date=buffer(1:8)
         WRITE(*,1010,advance='no')date
! Check and interpret the four barometer fields...
         DO i=1,4
            temp=buffer(3+7*i:9+7*i)
            IF (temp == '------') THEN
              WRITE(*,1020,advance='no')
            ELSE !do internal read on substring
              READ(temp,1025)barom_value,flag
              WRITE(*,1030,advance='no')barom_value,flag
            END IF
         END DO
         WRITE(*,1040) !Write a "line feed"
      GO TO 10
!
20    CLOSE(1)
!
1000  FORMAT(a80) !to hold the temporary string
1010  FORMAT(1x,a8) !to read the date
1020  FORMAT(1x,'-------') !output for missing barometer field
1025  FORMAT(f5.0,a1) !for internal read on substring
1030  FORMAT(f6.2,1x,a1) !output for data
1040  FORMAT() !line feed after advance='no'
      END
```

Running P-9.6

```
01/01/95 29.92 f 29.89 f 29.90 r --------
01/02/95 29.81 r 29.95 r 30.09 r 30.23 r
01/03/95 30.33 r 30.30 f 30.25 f 30.15 f
01/04/95 30.11 f 30.09 f 30.11 f 30.27 r
01/05/95 30.35 r 30.39 f 30.36 s 30.31 f
01/06/95 30.30 f 30.20 f 30.06 f --------
01/07/95 29.48 r 29.61 r 29.77 r 29.93 r
01/08/95 30.07 r 30.13 f 30.13 r 30.17 s
01/09/95 30.17 r 30.18 f 30.19 r 30.32 r
01/10/95 30.40 r 30.43 f 30.42 r 30.42 f
01/11/95 30.43 r 30.40 f 30.35 r 30.29 f
01/12/95 30.22 s 30.15 f 30.09 s 30.11 s
01/13/95 30.13 r 30.19 f 30.20 r --------
01/14/95 30.22 s 30.21 f 30.14 f --------
01/15/95 30.01 f 29.92 f 29.84 s 29.84 s
01/16/95 29.82 r 29.82 f 29.87 r 29.91 s
01/17/95 29.94 r 30.01 f 30.08 r 30.16 r
01/18/95 30.21 r 30.28 s 30.27 r 30.25 f
01/19/95 30.19 f 30.10 f 30.00 s --------
01/20/95 29.45 f 29.24 f 29.21 f --------
01/21/95 29.41 r 29.49 s 29.57 r --------
01/22/95 29.71 r 29.77 f 29.83 r --------
01/23/95 29.91 r 29.90 f 29.88 s 29.83 f
01/24/95 29.84 r 29.85 f 29.92 r 29.99 s
01/25/95 30.05 r 30.07 f 30.03 s 30.04 s
01/26/95 30.05 r 30.05 f 30.05 r 30.05 s
01/27/95 30.07 s 30.08 f 30.05 s --------
01/28/95 30.09 f 30.11 f 30.01 f --------
01/29/95 30.13 r 30.21 f 30.20 s 30.17 f
01/30/95 30.09 s 29.97 f 29.83 s 29.82 r
01/31/95 29.85 r 29.85 f 29.75 r --------
```

The most notable feature of P-9.6 is that it is a lot more complicated than P-9.4 because the programming burden of responding to missing data is substantial. In fact, you could argue that it might be worth modifying the data file rather than writing this code. For example, missing barometric pressure values could be given a value of 0 and the single character field could be left as a dash. Then the code in P-9.4 would work without modification. However, large data files aren't always easy to modify, and in any event, it may still be necessary to respond differently to certain kinds of entries in the file.

The solution in P-9.6 is first to read each line of the data file as a string of characters (named `buffer`). The contents of the four sets of six columns that may contain
barometric pressure values are then extracted from `buffer`, by reading each of them into a substring, and examined one at a time, using the variable name `temp`

inside the DO i=1,4... loop. If they contain dashes, they are simply printed as part of the output. Otherwise, those columns are processed as an *internal file*.[5]

Internal files are used just like unit numbers in a READ statement, as you can see by referring to the READ(temp,1025)... statement in P-9.6 (printed in bold italics). This has the effect of treating the CHARACTER variable temp as a temporary "buffer" holding data to be read. You can perform a formatted READ on the contents of the internal file just as you would for data being read directly from a file or typed at the keyboard. In general, you can also perform a list-directed READ on an internal file, but that won't work in this case because list-directed input won't allow you to separate the "flag" character from the numerical value.

In summary, P-9.6 has performed some "error checking" to look for missing data and has used an internal file to extract fields from a record. Internal files are also useful when the interpretation of part of a record depends on the contents of some other part. Data stored in an internal file can be read as many times as you like, and you can even apply more than one interpretation to the same record. Although it's possible to read a record in a text file more than once using BACKSPACE, it is usually better style to store a record in a temporary CHARACTER variable and then perform one or more internal READs on that variable.

9.5 Writing Text Files

It shouldn't surprise you to find that Fortran can be used to create text files as well as to read them. In fact, the same WRITE statements that display output on a monitor screen or printer will also send output to a file. The only difference is the choice of unit numbers. On most systems, 6 is the default unit for a monitor screen. This represents a "file" that, essentially, is "open" all the time and doesn't have to be opened in your program.

Only WRITEs (and not PRINTs) can be used to direct output to a text file. Therefore, if there is any chance that you will want a program to write its output to an external file, you should use only WRITEs in that program even when the output is sent initially to your computer monitor. On the other hand, you can use PRINTs for the parts of a program's output that you *don't* want to appear in an external file. For example, you could use PRINTs for prompts to provide keyboard information in a program that sends calculated output to a text file.

---

[5]The use of the variable name buffer for these series of characters implies that they are not really stored in a "file," but are instead held in a temporary location, or buffer, in computer memory. However, the term makes sense because the syntax for extracting information from this "internal file" buffer is identical to the syntax for reading information from an external file.

If your program uses WRITE statements, all you have to do to direct output to a file instead of to your monitor is to OPEN an appropriate unit number, provide an appropriate file name, and specify that the file is to be "write only" (ACTION='WRITE'). If the unit number is specified as a variable, nothing in the WRITE statements themselves needs to be changed. Depending on the application, you may need to include other information in the OPEN statement, using the STATUS= and POSITION= options. (See Section 9.2.2.) Some possible values of these options are given in Table 9.4.

Table 9.4. Some options in the OPEN statement applicable to writing text files

Option Specifier	Description
ACTION='write'	File is "write only."
POSITION='rewind'	For "write only" file, positions file to the beginning (default value).
POSITION='append'	For "write only" file, positions file to the end, just before the end-of-file mark. New data are written on the end of an existing file.
STATUS='new'	File must not exist when the OPEN statement is executed. A new file with the specified name is created.
STATUS='old'	File must already exist when OPEN statement is executed.
STATUS='replace'	If file does not exist, it is created. If it already exists, the old file is deleted and a new one with the same name is created.
STATUS='scratch'	File is created, but cannot be kept as a permanent file when the program terminates.
STATUS='unknown'	Status of file is system-dependent, based on how file is used in program. This is the default status.

STATUS='scratch' and STATUS='new' files are rarely needed during program development. In fact, you will only rarely need to supply any values other than the default values for any of these options.

9.6 Applications

9.6.1 Exponential Smoothing of Data

1 *Define the problem.*

When noisy data are collected as a result of an experiment, some kind of data smoothing algorithm is sometimes applied as a way to spot trends and predict future values. A common technique is "exponential smoothing." Suppose a set of data X are collected as a function of time; it isn't necessary that time be the independent variable, but this is often the case. For time interval i = 1, let the "forecasted" value equal the actual value. For i > 1, the forecasted value F_i is estimated by

$$F_i = F_{i-1} + A[X_{i-1} - F_{i-1}] \, , \, i \geq 2$$

where A is some arbitrarily chosen "smoothing parameter" between 0 and 1. This calculation requires only one historical value. However, it is a subjective calculation because there is no "rule" for selecting the value for A. As A approaches 1, the forecasted value approaches the previous data value. As A approaches 0, the forecasted value approaches the previous forecasted value, which means that all the forecasted values will equal X_i. In general, you should try different values of A and then apply some statistical criterion to determine the value of A that best forecasts historical trends in a data set. (See the Problem Discussion below and Exercise 12 in Section 9.8.2.)

Write a subroutine that calculates and displays exponential smoothing of data in a one-dimensional array X of specified size. Store the results in a second array of the same size. Set the first element in the second array to the first element in X.

Note that exponential smoothing is supposed to be a "forecasting" technique and not just a "smoothing" technique. It will not work well with random data because it assumes that there is a relationship between a previous value and the current value, an assumption that, by definition, is not true for random values. (To put it another way, a past history of random numbers is of no value for predicting the next random number.) To provide a more realistic test of exponential smoothing, you could write a subroutine to provide a data set that has random noise imposed on a trend. For example, a "noisy" linear relationship would look like this:

$$X_i = A + Bt_i + random \ component$$

You could also use the data file SP500.DAT, which can be downloaded from the World Wide Web site mentioned in Section i.5 of the Preface, to test your program. That file contains a historical record of the Standard & Poor's 500 stock index. (See Problem Discussion below.)

2 *Outline a solution.*

The exponential smoothing equation is contained in the problem statement, so all that is required here are the steps for implementing this definition.

1. Open the data file for reading and store the data in an array. Alternatively, let the program create a set of data as described in Step 1. Although an array isn't actually required to implement the exponential smoothing algorithm, the problem statement requests that both the original data and the smoothed values be stored in an array.
2. Call a subroutine to apply the exponential smoothing algorithm to the data for a user-specified value of A.
3. Display the original array and the smoothed array.

3 *Design an algorithm.*

The design of the algorithm to read and store the original data is straightforward. Therefore, only the subroutine design will be presented here.

SUBPROGRAM *ExpSmooth(X – the data array; size – the # of points;*
weight – value of the smoothing parameter;
F – the forecast array)
DEFINE/DECLARE *i – local counter variable*
ASSIGN *F(1) = X(1)*
LOOP *(for i = 2 to size)*
    F(i) = F(i-1) + weight•[X(i-1) – F(i-1)]
END LOOP

4 *Convert the algorithm into a program.*

P-9.7 [SMOOTH.F90]

```fortran
      MODULE Forecasting
!
      IMPLICIT NONE
      REAL a(100),b(100)
      REAL b1,b2,b3,rand
      DATA b1,b2,b3/5.,15.,50./
      INTEGER size
      CONTAINS
!------------------------
      SUBROUTINE ExpSmooth(weight)
!
! Apply exponential smoothing with specified weight.
      IMPLICIT NONE
      REAL, INTENT(IN) :: weight
      INTEGER i
!
      b(1)=a(1)
      DO i=2,size
        b(i)=b(i-1)+weight*(a(i-1)-b(i-1))
      END DO
      END SUBROUTINE ExpSmooth
!---------------------------
      SUBROUTINE MakeData
!
! Create array = b1+b2*x+b3*random
!
      INTEGER Count(1),i
!
      CALL System_Clock(Count(1))
      CALL Random_Seed(Put=Count)
!
      size=20
      DO i=1,size
        CALL Random_Number(rand)
        a(i)=b1+b2*REAL(i)+b3*(rand-.5)
!        PRINT 1000,a(i)
      END DO
1000  FORMAT(f8.3)
      END SUBROUTINE MakeData
!---------------------------
      END MODULE Forecasting
!---------------------------
```

```
      PROGRAM Smooth
!
! Demonstrate exponential smoothing.
!
      USE Forecasting, ONLY : ExpSmooth,MakeData,a,b,size,b1,b2
      IMPLICIT NONE
      INTEGER i,u
      REAL weight,sum,diff_sq
      CHARACTER*20 filename,date*9
!
      PRINT *,' Give input file name or "none":'
      READ *,filename
      PRINT *,' Give output destination 6 (monitor) or 1 (file):'
      READ *,u
      PRINT *,' Give smoothing factor 0-1:'
      READ *,weight
      IF (filename /= 'none') THEN
        OPEN(1,file=filename,action='read')
        READ(1,*) !read past two header lines
        READ(1,*)
        size=1
10      READ(1,*,end=20)date,a(size)
          PRINT *,size,a(size)
          size=size+1
        GO TO 10
20      CLOSE(1)
        size=size-1
      ELSE
        CALL MakeData !get array a
      END IF
      CALL ExpSmooth(weight)
      IF (u==1) OPEN(1,file='smooth.out',action='write')
      sum=0.
      DO i=1,size
        diff_sq=(a(i)-b(i))**2
        sum=sum+diff_sq
        WRITE(u,1000)i,a(i),b(i),diff_sq
      END DO
      WRITE(u,1010)sum
      IF (u==1) CLOSE(1)
1000  FORMAT(i3,3f10.3)
1010  FORMAT(' Sum of squares = ',f10.3)
      END
```

Running P-9.7

```
   Give input file name or "none":
none
   Give output destination 6 (monitor) or 1 (file):
6
   Give smoothing factor 0-1:
.3
    1      9.824      9.824      0.000
    2     54.172      9.824   1966.740
    3     69.944     23.128   2191.680
    4     57.119     37.173    397.848
    5     73.238     43.157    904.899
    6     99.575     52.181   2246.171
    7    100.705     66.399   1176.883
    8    104.008     76.691    746.239
    9    133.562     84.886   2369.379
   10    159.407     99.489   3590.191
   11    193.214    117.465   5738.043
   12    199.738    140.190   3546.041
   13    204.254    158.054   2134.416
   14    209.510    171.914   1413.448
   15    207.576    183.193    594.551
   16    268.348    190.508   6059.065
   17    266.530    213.860   2774.151
   18    275.097    229.661   2064.414
   19    265.264    243.292    482.782
   20    316.217    249.883   4400.153
Sum of squares =   44797.098
```

This output is for a case in which the program generates its own test data rather than reading data from an external data file.

P-9.7 adds one additional feature that is not required by the problem statement: it calculates and displays the sum of the squares of the differences between the predicted and actual values. (See the problem discussion below.)

5   Verify the operation of the program.

It is easy to check a few of P-9.7's calculations by hand.

Problem Discussion

Some analysts believe that exponential smoothing and related techniques can be used to predict the future course of the stock market. This optimism is based on the observation that although the stock market contains a large random component, that "noise" is superimposed on a long-term upward trend. However, because short-term price fluctuations tend to be random, you should not expect this technique to be successful at predicting the short-term behavior of individual stocks or of the stock market as a whole. Even if long-term stock prices show a trend, short-term fluctuations tend to be random, in which case exponential smoothing does little more than "chase" the previous stock price. Indeed it is hard to believe that this technique, which at each step relies on just a single historical value, actually has much reliability as a forecasting technique.

When stock analysts use exponential smoothing, they try to select a value of A that works best for forecasting historical trends in the price of particular stocks or in overall market performance. Figure 9.1 shows some stock prices (the heavy line) and exponential smoothing with four values of the parameter A.

One measure of the quality of forecasts is to calculate the sum of the squares of the differences between all the forecasted and actual values. For the prices shown in Figure 9.1, A = 0 (a value not shown on the figure) provides the smallest sum of squares value, which means that none of the forecasts is better than assuming that the price at every future time will be equal to the price at the first time interval. Clearly, this is not a very useful forecast! You should try the same calculation for yourself on long-term stock price or market index trends (see Exercise 12 in Section 9.8.2.)

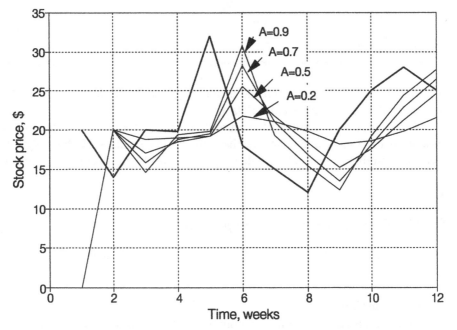

Figure 9.1. Exponential smoothing applied to short-term stock price fluctuations

9.6.2 Billing Program for an Urban Water Utility

In this application, an external data file is used to provide test data for a calculation with many different branches. All the possible branches must be tested systematically, and it would be very time-consuming to enter the required data by hand.

1 *Define the problem.*

You have been hired by a large urban water utility to develop a billing program based on its published rate structure. The customers' quarterly bills depend on the size of their incoming water line, as described by a meter code, and the type of customer, ranging from residential to industrial. Table 9.5 gives the rate structure.

Table 9.5. Rate structure for an urban water utility

Meter Code	Minimum Quarterly Charge	Quarterly Allowance, Gallons
1	$ 16.80	1500
2	25.50	1500
3	43.50	1500
4	88.50	1500
5	124.98	1500
6	253.38	0
7	411.54	0
8	850.26	0
9	1488.03	0
0	2199.00	0

Customer Class	Consumption Code	Quarterly Consumption from	Rate to	Rate per 1000 Gal
Residential and Public	R1	allowance	100,000	$3.787
	R2	100,001	more	2.710
Other Utilities	U1	allowance	100,000	3.787
	U2	100,001	1,000,000	2.710
	U3	1,000,001	more	2.247
Commercial	C1	allowance	30,000	3.787
	C2	30,001	100,000	3.350
	C3	100,001	1,000,000	2.710
	C4	1,000,001	more	2.247
Industrial	I1	allowance	30.000	3.787
	I2	30,001	100,000	3.350
	I3	100,001	1,000,000	2.710
	I4	1,000,001	10,000,000	2.247
	I5	10,000,001	more	2.088

2 *Outline a solution.*

1. Create a version of the rate structure table that can be read more easily by a Fortran program. This might mean, for example, eliminating the $ sign in the Minimum Quarterly Charge column of the table and removing the commas from the Quarterly Consumption columns. The file H2O_RATE.DAT, which can be downloaded from the World Wide Web site mentioned in Section i.5 of the Preface, includes these changes.

2. Define appropriate data structures for holding the rate data. Create one record structure to hold the information related to the meter code and another record structure to hold the information related to customer consumption. This is an implementation-related step.

3. Read file H2O_RATE.DAT and store meter- and customer-related information in two separate arrays. The four customer classes (r, u, c, and i) can be combined with quarterly consumption levels to provide a total of 14 different rate structures, i.e., r1, r2, u1, u2, u3, and so forth, as shown in Table 9.5. For example, a "U3" customer is a utility that consumes more than 1,000,000 gallons in a quarter.

4. Read a file of input data consisting of the customer class (residential, utility, commercial, or industrial), meter code, and actual consumption. For each set of values, calculate and print the bill. The data in Table 9.6 provide a partial test for a complete program. These data are available in file WATER.DAT, which can be downloaded from the World Wide Web site mentioned in Section i.5 of the Preface. The first column is a consumer code: r for residential, u for other utilities, c for commercial, and i for industrial. Columns 2–3 contain the meter code. Columns 4–13 contain the quarterly consumption. Information to the right of column 13 is just for documentation and should be ignored by your program.

Table 9.6. Test file for water utility program (P-9.8)

```
r  1           50 Check minimum charges according to meter code.
r  2           50
r  3           50
r  4           50
r  5           50
r  6            0
r  7            0
r  8            0
r  9            0
r10            0
r  1         2000 Residential
r  1       200000
u  5         1000 Utility
u  5        20000
u  5       200000
u  5      1000005
c  6        15000 Commercial
c  6        40000
c  6       200000
c  6      2000000
i  9        15000 Industrial
i  9        40000
i  9       200000
i  9      2000000
i  9     11000000
```

3 *Design an algorithm.*

This is a relatively large program, and it demands careful thought before you start to write code. The main program controls interpretation of the rate file and customer data contained in a test file.

(main program)
OPEN *(rate file)*
CALL *MeterCodeData(IN: rate file; OUT: meter data)*
WRITE *(data for 10 meter classes)*
CALL *CustomerClassData(IN: rate file;*
                                  OUT: rate data for 14 customer classes - e.g., r1, c3)
WRITE *(rate data)*
CLOSE *(rate file)*
OPEN *(test data file)*
LOOP *(until no more records)*
        READ *(customer class code (r, u, c, or i), meter type,*
                gallons consumed)

> ***CALL*** *CalculateBill(IN: customer class code, meter type,*
> *gallons consumed;*
> *meter and rate data;*
> *OUT: quarterly bill, rate index (1–14))*
> ***WRITE*** *("echo" input, quarterly bill, class code corresponding to rate*
> *index)*
>
> ***END LOOP***
> ***CLOSE*** *(test data file)*
> *(end main program)*

This subprogram calculates a quarterly bill based on customer class (r, u, c, or i), meter code, and gallons consumed. Representative pseudocode is shown only for the "u" classification, which returns a rate index in the range 3–5. The ***ASSIGN*** statement for the quarterly bill will have to be expanded in Fortran to calculate how much should be charged at each consumption level.

> ***SUBPROGRAM*** *CalculateBill(IN: customer class code,meter,*
> *gallons consumed;*
> *meter and rate data;*
> *OUT: quarterly bill, rate index (1-14))*
>
> *...*
> *(sample billing calculation)*
> ***CHOOSE*** *(based on customer class code)*
> *'u'*
> ***ASSIGN*** *index = 3*
> ***IF*** *(gallons consumed > max U1 level)* ***THEN ASSIGN*** *index=4*
> ***IF*** *(gallons consumed > max U2 level)* ***THEN ASSIGN*** *index=5*
> ***IF*** *(gallons consumed > quarterly min for this meter code)* ***THEN***
> ***ASSIGN*** *quarterly bill = minimum charge +*
> *excess amount at U1 rate +*
> *amount at U2 rate +*
> *amount at U3 rate*
>
> *(and so forth)*

4 *Convert the algorithm into a program.*

P-9.8 does the basic calculations required by the problem statement, but it doesn't print output in an acceptable "Invoice" format. This is left as an end-of-chapter exercise.

P-9.8 [WATER.F90]

```
      MODULE WaterBillDefinitions
!
      TYPE MeterCode
        REAL MinCharge
        INTEGER allowance
      END TYPE
      TYPE CustomerClass
        CHARACTER*2 ClassCode
        INTEGER min,max
        REAL Per1000Gallons
      END TYPE
!
      CONTAINS
!-------------------------------------------
      SUBROUTINE MeterCodeData(MeterData)
!
! Read H2O_RATE.DAT and extract billing information that
! depends on meter code.
!
      USE WaterBillDefinitions, ONLY : MeterCode
      IMPLICIT NONE
      TYPE (MeterCode), INTENT(OUT) :: MeterData(10)
      INTEGER i,code
!
! Read 4 header lines...
      DO i=1,4
        READ(1,*)
      END DO
!
! Read meter code data...
      DO i=1,10
        READ(1,*)code,MeterData(code)%MinCharge, &
                 MeterData(code)%allowance
      END DO
      END SUBROUTINE MeterCodeData
!-------------------------------------------
      SUBROUTINE CustomerClassData(ClassData)
!
! Read H2O_RATE.DAT and extract rate information that depends
! on customer class.
!
      USE WaterBillDefinitions,  ONLY : CustomerClass
      IMPLICIT NONE
      TYPE (CustomerClass) ClassData(14)
      INTEGER i
      CHARACTER a*78,b*10
!
```

```
! Read 4 header lines...
      DO i=1,4
        READ(1,*)
      END DO
!
! Read class data...
      DO i=1,14
        READ(1,1000)a
!       PRINT *,a
        ClassData(i)%ClassCode=a(26:27)
        READ(a(33:40),*)ClassData(i)%min
        b=a(45:52)
        IF (b(5:8)=='over') THEN
          ClassData(i)%max=HUGE(1)
        ELSE
          READ(a(45:52),*)ClassData(i)%max
        END IF
        READ(a(57:61),*)ClassData(I)%Per1000Gallons
      END DO
!
1000  FORMAT(a78)
      END SUBROUTINE CustomerClassData
!-------------------------------------------------------------
      SUBROUTINE CalculateBill(code,meter,gallons,MeterData, &
                              RateData,QuarterlyBill,index)
!
      USE WaterBillDefinitions, ONLY : MeterCode,CustomerClass
      IMPLICIT NONE
      CHARACTER, INTENT(IN) :: code
      INTEGER, INTENT(IN) :: gallons,meter
      TYPE (MeterCode), INTENT(IN) :: MeterData(10)
      TYPE (CustomerClass), INTENT(IN) :: RateData(14)
      REAL, INTENT(OUT) :: QuarterlyBill
      INTEGER, INTENT(OUT) :: index
      INTEGER MinimumGallons
!
! Based on meter code...
      QuarterlyBill=MeterData(meter)%MinCharge
      MinimumGallons=MeterData(meter)%allowance
!
! Based on customer class and consumption...
      SELECT CASE (code)
        CASE ('r')
          index=1
          IF (gallons>RateData(1)%max) index=2
          IF (gallons>MinimumGallons) &
            QuarterlyBill=QuarterlyBill+ &
  MIN(RateData(1)%max-MinimumGallons,gallons-MinimumGallons)/1e3* &
            RateData(1)%Per1000Gallons+ &
            MAX(gallons-RateData(1)%max,0)/1e3* &
            RateData(2)%Per1000Gallons
        CASE ('u')
          index=3
          IF (gallons>RateData(3)%max) index=4
          IF (gallons>RateData(4)%max) index=5
          IF (gallons>MinimumGallons) &
            QuarterlyBill=QuarterlyBill+ &
  MIN(RateData(3)%max-MinimumGallons,gallons-MinimumGallons)/1e3* &
            RateData(3)%Per1000Gallons+ &
            MIN(RateData(4)%max-RateData(3)%max, &
```

```
                  MAX(gallons-RateData(3)%max,0))/1e3* &
                RateData(4)%Per1000Gallons+ &
                MAX(gallons-RateData(4)%max,0)/1e3* &
                RateData(5)%Per1000Gallons
          CASE ('c')
            index=6
            IF (gallons>RateData(6)%max) index=7
            IF (gallons>RateData(7)%max) index=8
            IF (gallons>RateData(8)%max) index=9
            IF (gallons>MinimumGallons) &
            QuarterlyBill=QuarterlyBill+   &
MIN(RateData(6)%max-MinimumGallons,gallons-MinimumGallons)/1e3* &
                RateData(6)%Per1000Gallons+ &
                MIN(RateData(7)%max-RateData(6)%max, &
                  MAX(gallons-RateData(6)%max,0))/1e3* &
                RateData(7)%Per1000Gallons+ &
                MIN(RateData(8)%max-RateData(7)%max, &
                  MAX(gallons-RateData(7)%max,0))/1e3* &
                RateData(8)%Per1000Gallons+ &
                MAX(gallons-RateData(8)%max,0)/1c3* &
                RateData(9)%Per1000Gallons
          CASE ('i')
            index=10
            IF (gallons>RateData(10)%max) index=11
            IF (gallons>RateData(11)%max) index=12
            IF (gallons>RateData(12)%max) index=13
            IF (gallons>RateData(13)%max) index=14
            IF (gallons>MinimumGallons) &
            QuarterlyBill=QuarterlyBill+ &
 MIN(RateData(10)%max-MinimumGallons,gallons-MinimumGallons)/1e3* &
                RateData(10)%Per1000Gallons+ &
                MIN(RateData(11)%max-RateData(10)%max, &
                  MAX(gallons-RateData(10)%max,0))/1e3* &
                RateData(11)%Per1000Gallons+ &
                MIN(RateData(12)%max-RateData(11)%max, &
                  MAX(gallons-RateData(11)%max,0))/1e3* &
                RateData(12)%Per1000Gallons+ &
                MIN(RateData(13)%max-RateData(12)%max, &
                  MAX(gallons-RateData(12)%max,0))/1e3* &
                RateData(13)%Per1000Gallons+ &
                MAX(gallons-RateData(13)%max,0)/1e3* &
                RateData(14)%Per1000Gallons
      END SELECT
      END SUBROUTINE CalculateBill
!
      END MODULE WaterBillDefinitions
!=======================================
```

```fortran
      PROGRAM WaterBill
!
! File name WATER.F90.
! Billing program for water service.
!
      USE WaterBillDefinitions, ONLY : MeterCode,CustomerClass, &
        MeterCodeData,CustomerClassData,CalculateBill
      IMPLICIT NONE
      TYPE (MeterCode) MeterData(10)
      TYPE (CustomerClass) RateData(14)
      INTEGER i,meter,gallons,RateIndex
      REAL QuarterlyBill
      CHARACTER code
!
      OPEN(1,file='c:\ftn90.dir\h2o_rate.dat',action='read')
! Get meter code data.
      CALL MeterCodeData(MeterData)
      DO i=1,10
        PRINT 1000,i,MeterData(i)%MinCharge,MeterData(i)%allowance
      END DO
!
! Get customer class data.
      CALL CustomerClassData(RateData)
      DO i=1,14
        PRINT 1010,RateData(i)%ClassCode,RateData(i)%min, &
                   RateData(i)%max,RateData(i)%Per1000Gallons
      END DO
      CLOSE(1)
!
! Read test data file.
      OPEN(1,file='c:\ftn90.dir\water.dat',action='read')
10    READ(1,1050,end=900)code,meter,gallons
        CALL CalculateBill(code,meter,gallons,MeterData,RateData, &
                   QuarterlyBill,RateIndex)
        PRINT 1060,code,meter,gallons,QuarterlyBill, &
                   RateData(RateIndex)%ClassCode
      GO TO 10
900   CLOSE(1)
!
1000  FORMAT(i3,f10.2,i6)
1010  FORMAT(a3,2i12,f8.3)
1050  FORMAT(a1,i2,i10)
1060  FORMAT(a2,i3,i10,f10.2,a3)
      END
```

Running P-9.8 (This output is for the data given in Table 9.6)

```
   1      16.80  1500
   2      25.50  1500
   3      43.50  1500
   4      88.50  1500
   5     124.98  1500
   6     253.38     0
   7     411.54     0
   8     850.26     0
   9    1488.03     0
  10    2199.00     0
R1            0     100000   3.787
R2       100001  2147483647   2.710
U1            0     100000   3.787
U2       100001    1000000   2.710
U3      1000001  2147483647   2.247
C1            0      30000   3.787
C2        30001     100000   3.350
C3       100001    1000000   2.710
C4      1000001  2147483647   2.247
I1            0      30000   3.787
I2        30001     100000   3.350
I3       100001    1000000   2.710
I4      1000001   10000000   2.247
I5     10000001  2147483647   2.088
r   1        50      16.80 R1
r   2        50      25.50 R1
r   3        50      43.50 R1
r   4        50      88.50 R1
r   5        50     124.98 R1
r   6         0     253.38 R1
r   7         0     411.54 R1
r   8         0     850.26 R1
r   9         0    1488.03 R1
r  10         0    2199.00 R1
r   1      2000      18.69 R1
r   1    200000     660.82 R2
u   5      1000     124.98 U1
u   5     20000     195.04 U1
u   5    200000     769.00 U2
u   5   1000005    2937.01 U3
c   6     15000     310.18 C1
c   6     40000     400.49 C2
c   6    200000     872.49 C3
c   6   2000000    5287.49 C4
i   9     15000    1544.84 I1
i   9     40000    1635.14 I2
i   9    200000    2107.14 I3
i   9   2000000    6522.14 I4
i   9  11000000   26586.14 I5
```

5 *Verify the operation of the program.*

Suppose a water utility has actually contracted with you to write this program. The contracting officer will demand that your code be tested rigorously and that the results of those tests be presented in writing as a condition for payment. If errors are found, especially if they aren't found until after the utility discovers billing problems with its customers, you could be in serious financial trouble because the utility will attempt to hold you liable for its losses.

The best way to protect against errors is to compare the calculations in *every* possible program branch against calculations done with a calculator. As indicated above, the only practical way to perform such large-scale testing is to create one or more data files containing many sets of meter code, customer class, and consumption data. Table 9.6 shows part of such a test file, but it does not provide a complete test for the program.

Problem Discussion

P-9.8 is a relatively long program, and there is no way to avoid writing a lot of code. Note the use of the MAX and MIN functions in SUBROUTINE CalculateBill. These have been used to eliminate the longer, but more obvious code required to implement the calculations using IF...THEN... statements, such as, "If the consumption is greater than 100,000 gallons and less than or equal to 1,000,000 gallons, then...." In this application, the MAX and MIN functions require significantly less code than Fortran IF...THEN... statements. If you feel less comfortable with the resulting calculations, it becomes even more important to test all the code.

Another interesting feature of this program concerns the contents of the test file, as shown in Table 9.6. The comments included in the file, following the three columns of data, are ignored by the code that reads the file because a READ statement reads past the end-of-line mark even if there is more information on the line than the READ statement is asked to process.

Finally, note the use of the HUGE intrinsic function in SUBROUTINE CustomerClassData to assign a numerical upper limit on water consumption. This facilitates later calculations and is much better than having an unspecified upper limit.

9.6.3 Merging Sorted Lists

1 *Define the problem.*

A common data management problem involves merging two lists of data. Write a program that will merge two lists of numbers.

In a practical science or engineering problem, this problem might involve two sets of measurements made with two different instruments over the same period. If the data include the time of each measurement, it might be desirable to merge the two sets into a single set of measurements in chronological order.

It's certainly possible simply to append one set of measurements to the other and sort the resulting combined set of measurements by time. In fact, algorithms for doing this will be discussed in the next chapter. However, assuming that each set of measurements is already arranged in time sequence, it is more efficient to merge the two sets rather than sort the combined set. This is especially true if the combined set of measurements is very large; for example, too large to be stored in memory in an array.

The programming applications in this text have generally presented practical science and engineering problems. In this case, however, the abstract process of merging two lists must be considered carefully, and it will be easier to develop the algorithm without being distracted by the details of a particular practical problem. Therefore, we will consider the simple problem of merging two lists of integers, assuming that each list is sorted in ascending order. In order to make this problem more easily applicable to a practical situation, we will store the lists of integers in two files, and we will operate directly on the contents of the files rather than storing their contents in arrays within the program. This will allow us to apply the solution to lists that are too large to be stored in arrays.

This is an excellent example of a programming problem that needs careful thought and a modular approach. It will also provide additional practice in operating on external data files. The program will use the two lists of integers shown in Table 9.7. These lists can be found in files LISTA.DAT and LISTB.DAT, which can be downloaded from the World Wide Web site mentioned in Section i.5 of the Preface.

Table 9.7. Data for a list-merging algorithm

lista	listb
1	3
3	5
5	5
7	6
7	6
9	7
11	7
17	8
21	9
21	11
22	12
22	13
	14
	15
	16
	17
	18
	22
	24
	25
	26
	27

These two lists have several characteristics that are important for developing and testing a merge algorithm: they are of different lengths, each list contains some duplicate values, and the lists have some values in common.

2 Outline a solution.

It's easy to see how to start the process of merging the two lists, but you will have to be especially careful toward the end of each list. You can assume that each list contains at least one value; the algorithm will be implemented in a Fortran subroutine, and there is no point in even calling such a subroutine if one of the lists is empty.

Also, you can assume that an instruction to "print" a value will initially mean nothing more than displaying that value on your monitor screen. Once you're convinced that the algorithm is working properly, you can replace this instruction with an instruction that writes a value into a new file.

1. Read one value from each list.
2. Compare the values. If one value is smaller than the other, print the smaller value and read another number from the same list. If both values are the same, print both values and read another number from each list.
3. Eventually, you will come to the end of one of the lists. Be sure the last value from that list is printed. If there are still numbers in the other list, they will be larger than all the numbers printed so far. Read the remaining numbers and print them all. Note that you will not necessarily reach the end of the shorter list first; when you reach the end of a list is determined not by its length, but by its contents.

This solution outline doesn't include the details of what to do when you reach the end of a list. The best way to develop a complete algorithm is to work through the sample lists given above:

```
Operation            Value:      Compare        Output
                     a    b
-------------------------------------------------------
read a               1
read b                    3
(now we are inside a loop)
                                 a<b (1<3)
print a                                         1
read a               3
                                 a=b (3=3)
print a and b                                   3
                                                3
read a and b         5    5
                                 a=b (5=5)
print a and b                                   5
                                                5
read a and b         7    5
                                 a>b (7>5)
print b                                         5
read b                    6
                                 a>b (7>6)
print b                                         6
read b                    6
                                 a>b (7>6)
print b                                         6
read b                    7
                                 a=b (7=7)
print a and b                                   7
                                                7
read a and b         7    7
                                 a=b (7=7)
print a and b                                   7
                                                7
read a and b         9    8
                                 a>b (9>8)
print b                                         8
   .
   .
   .
                     22   22
                                 a=b (22=22)
print a and b                                   22
                                                22
read a and b         22   24
                                 a<b (22<24)
print a                                         22
(end of "a" list and end of loop)
```

Now that the algorithm has reached the end of the "a list," what remains to be done? The current value of b (24) hasn't yet been printed. Therefore, the algorithm must print that value and then read and print the rest of the b list.

As you know from previous discussions, you have to be careful not to read past the end of a file. You will have to incorporate a test for the end-of-file when you design the merging algorithm.

Study Tip

To make sure you understand these operations, fill in the missing steps in the list of merge operations above.

3 *Design an algorithm.*

DEFINE *("a" and "b" lists; a and b values;*
            end_a and end_b as logical variables)
OPEN *("a" and "b" lists)*
READ *(a and b from "a" and "b" lists)*
LOOP *(as long as there are data in both lists)*
    IF *(a < b)* **THEN**
        WRITE *(a)*
        IF *(NOT end_a)* **CALL** *ReadOne(from "a",a,end_a)*
        IF *(end_b)* **WRITE** *(b)*
    ELSE IF *(a = b)* **THEN**
        WRITE *(a,b)*
        IF *(NOT end_a)* **CALL** *ReadOne(from "a",a,end_a)*
        IF *(NOT end_b)* **CALL** *ReadOne(from "b",b,end_b)*
    ELSE
        WRITE *(b)*
        IF *(NOT end_b)* **CALL** *ReadOne(from "b",b,end_b)*
        IF *(end_a)* **WRITE** *(a)*
    (end IF...)
END LOOP
IF *(NOT end_a)* **THEN**
    LOOP *(to end of "a")*
        READ *(from "a",a)*
        WRITE *(a)*
    END LOOP
(end IF...)
IF *(NOT end_b)* **THEN**
    LOOP *(to end of "b")*
        READ *(from "b",b)*
        WRITE *(b)*
    END LOOP
(end IF...)

Study Tip

Write pseudocode for subprogram ReadOne and for a subprogram to read
to the end of a file, as required at the end of the algorithm (after the main loop).
Try to do this before you study the actual code in Step 4.

4   *Convert the algorithm into a program.*

P-9.9 [MERGE.F90]

```
      MODULE MergeData
!
      IMPLICIT NONE
      TYPE fields
         INTEGER x
      END TYPE fields
!
      CONTAINS
!-------------------------------------------
      SUBROUTINE ReadOne(unit,value,end_file)
!
! Read one value and return to program; set an e-o-f flag.
!
      USE MergeData, ONLY : fields
      IMPLICIT NONE
      INTEGER, INTENT(IN) ::  unit
      TYPE (fields), INTENT(OUT) :: value
      LOGICAL, INTENT(OUT) :: end_file
!
      end_file=.false.
      READ(unit,*,END=20)value%x
      RETURN
20    end_file=.true.
      END SUBROUTINE ReadOne
!---------------------------
      SUBROUTINE ReadAll(unit)
!
! Read to end of file.
!
      IMPLICIT NONE
      INTEGER, INTENT(IN) :: unit
      TYPE (fields) value
!
10    READ(unit,*,END=20)value%x
         PRINT*,value%x
      GO TO 10
20    CONTINUE
      END SUBROUTINE ReadAll
!-------------------------------------------
```

```
      SUBROUTINE MergeLists(unit_a,unit_b)
!
      USE MergeData, ONLY : fields
      IMPLICIT NONE
      INTEGER, INTENT(IN) :: unit_a,unit_b
      TYPE (fields) list_a,list_b
      LOGICAL end_a,end_b
      DATA end_a,end_b/2*.false./
!
      CALL ReadOne(unit_a,list_a,end_a)
      CALL ReadOne(unit_b,list_b,end_b)
10    CONTINUE
        IF (list_a%x .LT. list_b%x) THEN
          PRINT*,list_a%x
          IF (.NOT. end_a) CALL ReadOne(unit_a,list_a,end_a)
          IF (end_b) PRINT*,list_b%x
        ELSE IF (list_a%x .EQ. list_b%x) THEN
          PRINT*,list_a%x
          PRINT*,list_b%x
          IF (.NOT. end_a) CALL ReadOne(unit_a,list_a,end_a)
          IF (.NOT. end_b) CALL ReadOne(unit_b,list_b,end_b)
        ELSE
          PRINT*,list_b%x
          IF (.NOT. end_b) CALL ReadOne(unit_b,list_b,end_b)
          IF (end_a) PRINT*,list_a%x
        END IF
      IF ((.NOT. end_a) .AND. (.NOT. end_b)) GO TO 10
      IF (.NOT. end_a) THEN
        PRINT*,list_a%x
        CALL ReadAll(unit_a)
      END IF
      IF (.NOT. end_b) THEN
        PRINT*,list_b%x
        CALL ReadAll(unit_b)
      END IF
      END SUBROUTINE MergeLists
!----------------------------
      END MODULE MergeData
!=========================
      PROGRAM merge
! Merge two sorted lists of integers.
!
      USE MergeData, ONLY : MergeLists
      IMPLICIT NONE
      INTEGER unit_a,unit_b
      DATA unit_a,unit_b/1,2/
!
      PRINT *,' opening list a...'
      OPEN(unit_a,file='c:\ftn90.dir\lista.dat')
      PRINT *,' opening list b...'
      OPEN(unit_b,file='c:\ftn90.dir\listb.dat')
!
      CALL MergeLists(unit_a,unit_b)
!
      CLOSE(unit_a)
      CLOSE(unit_b)
!
      END
```

Running P-9.9

```
opening list a...
opening list b...
 1  3  3  5  5  5  6  6  7  7  7  7  8  9  9 11 11 12 13 14 15 16 17 17 18
21 21 22 22 22 24 25 26 27
```

(To save space, the output values are listed horizontally across the output box. In the actual program output, the values are listed one per row.)

5 Verify the operation of the program.

It is not a trivial matter to verify the operation of this program under *all* possible input conditions! As a minimum, you need to test situations where the "a" or "b" list has only one value, where the values in one or both lists are all the same, and where all the values in one list are larger (or smaller) than all the values in the other list. If you use the program on real data of your own, be sure to test it with a subset of the data that is small enough to verify by hand.

Problem Discussion

Program P-9.9 associates the "a" and "b" lists with units 1 and 2; this is an arbitrary but reasonable choice. The major difficulty in writing the code is keeping track of the end-of-file status of each file. Recall that the READ command includes the END= option, which transfers control of the program to a labelled statement when an end-of-file is detected. In order to make use of this option conveniently, the program includes SUBROUTINE ReadOne, which reads a value from a file if one is available and returns a LOGICAL value of .true. if the end of the file is detected.

Note the use of the RETURN statement in SUBROUTINE ReadOne to control the exit from the subroutine when a value is read. This statement hasn't previously been used in this way in this text. The file unit number, which can be passed as a variable as well as a constant, is used to tell the subroutine which file to read.

The other required subroutine, ReadALL, is used to read any remaining values in a file that haven't been read inside the loop.

Remember that this is just a demonstration program. In a real application, an output file will be opened and the unit number will be replaced with some value other than 6, so the merged file will be saved to a new permanent file.

9.6.4 Creating a "Quote-and-Comma-Delimited" Input File for Spreadsheets

Fortran is an ideal language for doing many kinds of complex calculations, but graphical displays and simple data analysis can often be performed more efficiently with other computing applications. The most versatile PC application is the spreadsheet. Many of the figures in this text were produced by implementing programming algorithms in a spreadsheet.

It is very useful to be able to share output from Fortran programs by generating output files that can be

quote-and-comma-delimited text file

read by a spreadsheet and other applications. Although Fortran can't produce output in a spreadsheet's "native" format, all spreadsheets have the ability to "import" text files. When output files contain mixtures of character strings— "labels" in spreadsheet terminology—and numbers, the most reliable way to import data is to create a *quote-and-comma-delimited text file*. In this kind of file, all character strings are enclosed in quotation marks and all values are separated by commas. The presence of quotation marks around character strings removes ambiguity about where the character string ends. For example, the string `Brooks, David` will be interpreted by a spreadsheet as two separate character strings, separated by a comma. However, assuming that you want the entire string to be treated as a single label, `"Brooks, David"` would be interpreted correctly.

1 *Define the problem.*

The purpose of this application is to write a program that will create a quote-and-comma-delimited text file that can be imported directly into a spreadsheet.

2 *Outline a solution.*

As a simple example, use the `JANUARY.DAT` file shown in Table 9.3. Read this file one record at a time and copy the values into a quote-and-comma-delimited text file that treats each date as a character string.

3 Design an algorithm.

The algorithm solution to this problem is trivial and interesting only in its Fortran implementation.

4 Convert the algorithm into a program.

P-9.10 [JAN-QCD.F90]

```
      PROGRAM January_QCD
!
! Create a quote-and-comma-delimited ASCII text file for
! use by a spreadsheet.
!
      IMPLICIT NONE
      CHARACTER*8 date
      REAL hi,lo
!
      OPEN(1,file='c:\ftn90.dir\january.dat',action='read')
      OPEN(2,file='c:\ftn90.dir\january.qcd',action='write')
!
10    READ(1,1000,end=900)date,hi,lo
      PRINT 1010,'"',date,'"',',',hi,',',lo
      WRITE(2,1010)'"',date,'"',',',hi,',',lo
      GO TO 10
900   CLOSE(1)
      CLOSE(2)
1000  FORMAT(a8,2f4.0)
1010  FORMAT(1x,a1,a8,a1,a1,f4.0,a1,f4.0)
      END
```

Running P-9.10 (partial output)

```
"01/01/94", 43., 24.
"01/02/94", 51., 31.
"01/03/94", 37., 33.
. . .
```

5 Verify the operation of the program.

Try importing the file into a spreadsheet.

Problem Discussion

P-9.10 sends identical output to the screen and the output file; the output statements of interest are printed in bold italics. The optional PRINT statement displays the output on the screen and the WRITE statement creates the JANUARY.QCD file with the same format. Single-quote character-string delimiters are used to print the double quotes in the output file.

9.7 Debugging Your Programs

9.7.1 Programming Style

When programs use or create external data files, the OPEN command should specify the allowed use (action='read' or action='write') for each file. When otherwise appropriate, OPEN commands are grouped together near the beginning of the source code file so that the names of files are easy to find. Unit numbers for output files typically should be declared as variables. While a program is being developed, the unit number can be assigned to the default output device so that WRITE statements direct output to the screen for testing.

Internal READs should be used whenever repeated access to a particular record is required; this approach is always favored over using REWIND and BACKSPACE statements.

List-directed READs should be used on input files whenever practical. However, formatted WRITEs should usually be used to improve the appearance and readability of output files.

When file records contain large numbers of fields, and especially if the information must be stored in an array, the TYPE structure, as discussed in Chapter 8, should be used to define record types that help organize the data.

Finally, files should always be CLOSEd when a program no longer needs them.

9.7.2 Problems with Programs That Access External Data Files

When your program reads an external data file, problems can arise either from mistakes in programming or from problems with the file itself. One common problem involves extra blank lines at the beginning or end of text files. These empty lines are "invisible" when you examine the file with a text editor or word processor, but they can still cause crashes when your program tries to read such a file.

The problem with blank lines at the beginning of a file is that unless you are aware of their presence and skip past them with READ statements, your program won't find what it is looking for. Blank lines at the end of a file are a particular hazard. Suppose a READ statement contains an END= option to search for the end-of-file mark. If a data file contains a blank line at the end, the end-of-file mark won't be detected and your program will try to read the blank line. It won't find what it was looking for, and instead it will try to read the end-of-file mark, which will cause it to crash.

Another obvious source of problems is a misunderstanding about the contents of the file. Your program can't work properly if you ask it to read information that doesn't actually exist in a file. Especially when formatted input is needed, it is essential to be sure you have a complete understanding of the contents and format of the file. In some cases, it may be worth the effort to rewrite a file in a more suitable format. (See Exercise 19 at the end of this chapter.)

It is certainly possible to destroy the contents of data files under Fortran control. If you do not specify `action='read'` in the OPEN statement, it is possible to WRITE *to* a file rather than READ *from* it. If you open a file with write access and your program crashes before it has completed its task, that file may be empty and unusable. This might not be too serious if the file in question was intended to be an output file; the worst that can happen is that you will have to fix the errors in your program and run it again. But what if the file in question is an input file that was inadvertently opened with write access? That file may now be corrupted beyond recovery.

This potential for disaster explains why you should always include the `action='read'` option for any file to be used as input. Also, just to be on the safe side,

---
> **It is always good practice to make copies of critical data files *before* you access them from a Fortran program.**

There are many options available for the OPEN statement, including several not discussed in this chapter. The values assigned to some of these options depend on having other values set appropriately. Inappropriate combinations of OPEN options can cause program crashes. You can experiment with various combinations of options and values, but not all of them are intended to work with the formatted sequential access files described in this chapter; some other possibilities are discussed in Chapter 12.

One way to avoid problems with files is to set a simple initial goal for any program that reads a file:

> **If your program needs to process data from an external file, make sure it can read the file in its entirety without producing any errors *before* writing any other part of the program.**

This is an easy rule to forget, especially because the completed programs shown in this text are, by definition, past this stage in their development.

You may also wish your program to display part or all of the file contents as it reads through the file. If the structure of the data is complicated, it may be worthwhile initially to treat each record as a string; this may even be required in your final program if you need to do an internal READ to interpret any of the data in a record. In any event, until your program can achieve this simple goal, there is no point in writing more source code. Failure to complete this simple task may indicate that there are problems with the file itself, rather than with your program.

Another way to avoid problems with files is to use the conditional loop structure described in this chapter, which uses the END= option in a READ statement. It may seem easier to determine ahead of time how many records a file contains and read it with a DO . . . loop. However, in "real world" problems, the size of a data file is always subject to change. Your program should reflect this fact by using code that can respond to files of varying length. An exception to this rule could occur when you are developing a program that uses a very long file. Then, to speed up the code development process, you could *temporarily* replace the conditional loop with a DO . . . loop that reads just the first few records in the file.

9.8 Exercises

9.8.1 Self-Testing Exercises

Exercise 1. Describe in your own words the two most important concepts you have learned from this chapter.

Exercise 2. Describe in your own words how you could use in your own programs a problem-solving skill demonstrated in a program described in this chapter.

Exercuse 3. In your own words, describe the characteristics that are required for a file to be treated as a "text file" in a Fortran program.

Exercise 4. Using an appropriate file name syntax for your computer, such as "c:\mydata\practice.dat" for MS-DOS systems, write OPEN statements for

(a) A file to be opened for reading on unit 3

(b) A file to be opened for writing on unit 2

(c) An existing file to be opened for writing on unit 1, to which new records will be appended

(d) A file to be opened for writing on unit 1, but only if that file does not already exist

Exercise 5. Give appropriate READ statements to interpret these records in a reasonable way, including type declaration and FORMAT statements as appropriate:

(a)			(b)		
	January	31		1991a	$1000000
	February	28		1991b	$ 873000
	March	31		1991c	$1002000
	April	30		1991d	$ 777000
	May	31			
	June	30			
	July	31	(c)	1e6 -0.17e-9 14 19.3	
	August	31			
	September	30			
	October	31	(d)	1,999,017	
	November	30		15,765,333	
	December	31		43,000,000	

Exercise 6. For parts (a)–(c), make some reasonable assumptions about the contents of each record in the file.

(a) Write the code required to read the first 10 records in a file on unit 1.

(b) Write the code required to read all the records in a file of unknown length, with program control transferring to statement 999 when the end-of-file mark is detected.

(c) The same as (b), except include an option to transfer program control to statement 888 if an error is found in the file

Exercise 7. Assume that a file contains a large amount of data stored in groups of three records. Make some reasonable assumptions about the contents of the records and write the code required to read all the records.

9.8.2 Basic Programming Exercises

Exercise 8. Create a data file consisting of several records of three real numbers each. Write a program to read this file and print its contents:

(a) assuming that the values don't need to be stored in an array

(b) assuming that the values can be read immediately into an array, using either a two-dimensional array or a one-dimensional array with an appropriate TYPE structure

(c) assuming that the values must first be tested before they are stored in an array, using either a two-dimensional array or a one-dimensional array with an appropriate TYPE structure

You may include all these options in a single program, or you may write three separate programs.

Exercise 9. Modify P-9.2 so that it does these three things:

(a) prints an asterisk in front of a student's name if his or her GPA is greater than or equal to 3.0

(b) prints names left-justified in a field of width 10

(c) prints a letter grade assigned according to these rules:
    90-100 = A
    80-89 = B
    70-79 = C
    60-69 = D
    <60 = F

Exercise 10. (a) Modify P-9.3 so that it uses the "clever" solution discussed in the algorithm design that reads the day of the month directly from the file and then uses this value as the index for the rest of the values in each line of the file. That is, instead of considering the date as a string of eight characters, think of it as three integers separated by two "/" separators.

(b) Modify P-9.3 so that it will also calculate and print the number of heating degrees for each day and, at the end of the daily output, the total number of heating degree days for the month. "Heating degrees" for a particular day are defined as 65° minus the daily average temperature. Instead of printing data just for days whose daily average temperature is below the average, print data and the results from calculations for all days. Print an asterisk after the heating degrees if they are higher than the average, and print an asterisk after the daily average temperature if it is below the monthly average. (See P-8.10 in Chapter 8 for a similar problem involving heating degree days.)

Exercise 11. Modify P-9.4 so that it calculates the monthly average barometric pressure at each of the four reported times.

Extra Credit

Include calculations of standard deviation and monthly minimum and maximum barometric pressure for each measurement time.

Exercise 12. Refer to program P-9.7 and apply this program to the Standard & Poor's 500 stock index, using the file SP500.DAT, which can be downloaded from the World Wide Web site mentioned in Section i.5 of the Preface. (The section of code in P-9.7 that reads a specified file is compatible with the format of SP500.DAT.) Is there a better value for A than the suggested value of 0.5? Calculate the sum of the squares of the differences between forecasted and actual S&P 500 values. Then try different values of A to see if the sum of the squares goes up or down. You do not have to write code that seeks to optimize the value of A in some formal way. This would be a much more difficult problem!

Extra Credit

Write code that optimizes the value of A for the S&P 500 index based on finding the minimum sum of squares value.

Exercise 13. Add a subroutine to program P-9.8 that prints a customer invoice in an attractive and easily readable format. Include the customer's code (R1, U2, and so forth), the water consumed in each applicable category, and the cost associated with each category.

Exercise 14. The two files, BIRDS1.DAT and BIRDS2.DAT, which can be downloaded from the World Wide Web site mentioned in Section i.5 of the Preface, contain bird sightings on two different days. Modify P-9.9 so that it merges these files to produce a list of sightings that doesn't contain any duplicate bird names.

Exercise 15. Based on material from other courses you are taking, state a computational problem that involves the use of one or more external data files, and write a complete program to solve it.

9.8.3 Programming Applications

Exercise 16. The R100 is a light rail line that runs for 13.4 miles from the western edge of Philadelphia through the northwest suburbs. Distance markers are placed along the track at intervals of usually 0.1 miles. The time at which these markers were passed on a typical outbound afternoon trip has been recorded, estimated to the nearest second. Stops along the way are indicated by the presence of the words "stop," "go," and "end" in the distance column. Table 9.8 contains a sample of the measurements. The complete file, R100.DAT, can be downloaded from the World Wide Web site mentioned in Section i.5 of the Preface.

Table 9.8. Partial listing of R100 file	
miles	time
------	-------
0.0	16:55:04
0.3	16:55:34
0.4	16:56:05
0.5	16:56:26
...	
3.4	17:00:11
stop	17:00:23
go	17:01:05
3.5	17:01:09
3.6	17:01:20
...	
13.3	17:21:47
13.4	17:22:01
end	17:22:02

Write a program that uses these data to calculate the average speed between each pair of markers and the cumulative average speed along the R100 line. What is the speed resolution when the times between 0.1-mile markers are recorded only to the nearest second? [R100.F90]

Exercise 17. A large engineering project consists of many separate tasks. Some can be done simultaneously, but others depend on the completion of previous tasks. When a collection of tasks that can be done simultaneously has been completed, a "milestone" has been reached. All the tasks required to reach a particular milestone must be completed before work toward reaching the next milestone can begin. The time needed to reach a particular milestone is equal to the time required to complete the longest task associated with that milestone. The total time to complete the project is the sum of the times required to reach all milestones. This is illustrated symbolically in Figure 9.2.

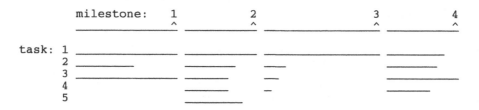

Figure 9.2. Symbolic illustration of a project with tasks and milestones

As project engineer, one of your jobs is to examine time estimates for all tasks on a project and try to find the most likely places to save time and hence money. Identify the longest task and the average time required to complete all tasks within a milestone. Whenever the longest task requires a specified percentage more than the average time for all tasks within a milestone, mark that task as one that needs to be examined in detail. (The goal is to determine whether the task can be subdivided into two or more tasks that can be done simultaneously rather than sequentially.) In Figure 9.2, task 1 for milestone 3 is an obvious candidate for close examination.

Assume that data about the project's tasks have been entered in a data file in no particular order. The sample data file shown in Table 9.9, PROJECT.DAT, can be downloaded from the World Wide Web site mentioned in Section i.5 of the Preface. These tasks are ordered by milestone, but they don't have to be.

The number on the second line of the file (1.25) is a multiplying factor. If a particular task takes more than this value times the average task time for a milestone, that task should be flagged.

Write a program to read this or a similar file and produce a task report for the project that includes identification of the longest and average task times for each milestone and "flags" tasks that take too long. When you write your program, make some reasonable assumptions about the total number of milestones in a project and the maximum number of tasks per milestone and define your array(s) accordingly. (This problem is not a good candidate for allocatable arrays. Why not?)

Although you can simply look at this sample file and determine the total number of project milestones (4) and the maximum number of tasks for any single milestone (5), you should write your program so that it can determine these values when it reads the data file.

Save all program output in a data file, in addition to displaying it on your monitor screen. [PROJECT.F90]

Table 9.9. Task and milestone data

task	milestone	time
1.25		
1	1	10
2	1	6
3	1	10
1	2	8
2	2	6
3	2	4
4	2	4
5	2	7
1	3	12
2	3	3
3	3	2
4	3	1
1	4	6
2	4	5
3	4	7
4	4	4

Exercise 18. A highway contractor is bidding on a project to prepare a roadbed by leveling the ground where the road will be built. This involves cutting dirt from high spots along the roadway and filling low spots. To prepare the bid, the contractor uses data from surveys conducted by the state highway department. These data consist of estimated cross-sectional areas for cut and fill measured at approximately 50-foot intervals along the roadway. Some sample data are given in Table 9.10; these values can be found, without the headings, in file GRADING.DAT, which can be downloaded from the World Wide Web site mentioned in Section i.5 of the Preface.

Table 9.10. Cross-sectional cut and fill data for a highway right-of-way

Station+Feet		Cut	Fill
		(feet²)	
107	50	0	0
108	0	62.3	1.8
108	50	188.4	0
109	0	192.7	11.8
109	50	121.9	34.6
109	98.33	36.7	89.2
110	52.33	12.0	187.3
111	6.33	27.0	267.6
111	50	77.8	402.5
112	0	262.1	487.6
112	50	408.5	554.3
112	77.33	447.4	617.7
113	25	486.5	799.0
113	75	422.4	936.3

Cross section estimates are given relative to numbered surveying stations that are 100 feet apart; these are given in the first column of Table 9.10. The second column gives the number of feet from the station at which the cross section was estimated. Obstructions sometimes prevent the estimates from being made at the desired intervals of exactly 50 feet.

To estimate the total cut volume between any two cross sections i and j, the contractor adds the ith and j^{th} cut cross-sectional areas, divides by 2, and multiplies by the distance between the ith and j^{th} station. This same calculation is performed with the fill cross sections. The total cut and fill volumes are the sums of these volumes.

Write a program that uses the data in Table 9.10 to calculate the total estimated cut and fill volumes in cubic feet and cubic yards. The file GRADING.DAT, which can be downloaded from the World Wide Web site mentioned in Section i.5 of the Preface, contains a copy of the data in the table. (It does not include the table headings.)

Note: if you have had a calculus or numerical analysis course, you may recognize this calculation as similar to Trapezoidal Rule numerical integration. The only difference is that the intervals in this problem are not all the same, as is required to apply the Trapezoidal Rule. [GRADING.F90]

Exercise 19. Often data are not arranged conveniently for reading in a Fortran program. The file of stock indices and stock prices shown in Table 9.11 are available as file STOCK.DAT, which can be downloaded from the World Wide Web site mentioned in Section i.5 of the Preface.

Table 9.11. Stock and market index prices (original form)

```
Date,DJIA,S & P 500,Nike,Reebok,S & P 100,Boston Chicken
3/22/95,4083.000 ,495.656 ,74.125 ,34.000 ,465.031 ,17.000
3/21/95,4072.500 ,495.063 ,73.750 ,34.375 ,464.250 ,16.875
3/20/95,4083.750 ,496.156 ,75.750 ,34.875 ,465.406 ,17.125
3/19/95,4073.750 ,495.531 ,76.250 ,35.000 ,464.844 ,16.688
3/18/95,4069.125 ,495.406 ,78.000 ,34.875 ,465.313 ,16.375
3/17/95,4038.375 ,491.875 ,76.375 ,34.625 ,461.250 ,15.625
3/16/95,4048.750 ,492.875 ,75.875 ,35.000 ,462.344 ,16.000
3/15/95,4025.250 ,490.063 ,77.375 ,35.125 ,459.719 ,16.313
3/14/95,4035.625 ,489.563 ,76.500 ,35.250 ,459.375 ,16.625
3/13/95,3983.375 ,483.156 ,75.000 ,34.875 ,452.281 ,16.750
3/12/95,3979.250 ,483.125 ,74.875 ,35.500 ,451.781 ,16.875
3/11/95,3962.625 ,482.125 ,73.250 ,35.375 ,451.313 ,17.000
3/10/95,3997.500 ,485.625 ,73.875 ,36.125 ,453.938 ,17.063
3/9/95,3989.625 ,485.406 ,74.375 ,36.125 ,453.313 ,17.375
3/8/95,3979.875 ,485.125 ,74.125 ,36.000 ,453.281 ,17.500
3/7/95,3994.750 ,485.656 ,72.875 ,36.500 ,453.844 ,18.000
```

The date string sometimes has seven characters and sometimes six. If the month were 10, 11, or 12 and the day were 10 or greater, then the date string would have eight characters. Because of this, the numerical values do not always appear in the same columns. Also, the commas after the numerical fields don't appear directly after the number. These irregularities mean that the file in its present form can't be read conveniently with either formatted or list-directed READs.

Write a program to create a new file that contains this information in a consistent format that is easier for a Fortran program to read. It should look something like this:

```
Date,DJIA,S & P 500,Nike,Reebok,S & P 100,Boston Chicken
03/22/95 4083.000  495.656   74.125   34.000  465.031   17.000
03/21/95 4072.500  495.063   73.750   34.375  464.250   16.875
03/20/95 4083.750  496.156   75.750   34.875  465.406   17.125
03/19/95 4073.750  495.531   76.250   35.000  464.844   16.688
03/18/95 4069.125  495.406   78.000   34.875  465.313   16.375
03/17/95 4038.375  491.875   76.375   34.625  461.250   15.625
03/16/95 4048.750  492.875   75.875   35.000  462.344   16.000
03/15/95 4025.250  490.063   77.375   35.125  459.719   16.313
03/14/95 4035.625  489.563   76.500   35.250  459.375   16.625
03/13/95 3983.375  483.156   75.000   34.875  452.281   16.750
03/12/95 3979.250  483.125   74.875   35.500  451.781   16.875
03/11/95 3962.625  482.125   73.250   35.375  451.313   17.000
03/10/95 3997.500  485.625   73.875   36.125  453.938   17.063
03/09/95 3989.625  485.406   74.375   36.125  453.313   17.375
03/08/95 3979.875  485.125   74.125   36.000  453.281   17.500
03/07/95 3994.750  485.656   72.875   36.500  453.844   18.000
```

Now the date string always contains exactly eight characters and the numerical values are neatly tabulated so that they always line up.

Hint: to solve this programming problem, you will need to make use of the INDEX function, Fortran's ability to access any subset of a string variable, and the concatenation operator. Read the entire line into a string so you can treat it as an internal file. Extract the date string by looking for the first comma in the line. Then "fix" this date string so that it always contains exactly eight characters. Then extract the characters to the right of the first comma. Build a new string that doesn't contain any commas. This string will contain values for the six prices and can be read with list-directed input. [STOCKFIX.F90]

Exercise 20. It is widely believed by climatologists that significant global warming will occur sometime during the next century, largely as a result of humankind's dependence on fossil fuels as a source of energy. When fossil fuels are burned, they release CO_2 into the atmosphere. As a result, CO_2 levels in the atmosphere are increasing at a very rapid rate compared to historical fluctuations inferred from ice core and other climate records.

Ice core records give reliable CO_2 levels back to roughly the mid-eighteenth century, and the modern record of direct atmospheric observations begins in 1958 at the Mauna Loa Observatory in Hawaii. The data file CO2.DAT, which can be downloaded from the World Wide Web site mentioned in Section i.5 of the Preface, contains both ice core and Mauna Loa measurements. Taken together, these data sets provide continuous coverage from well before the start of the Industrial Revolution, near the end of the nineteenth century, up to the present.

In the few centuries prior to the start of the Industrial Revolution, CO_2 levels increased slowly—perhaps as a result of natural fluctuations and perhaps partly due to the presence of a relatively slowly growing, pre-industrial human population. Population growth is usually modeled as exponential growth even when the increases are small. Following the Industrial Revolution, not only did population continue to grow exponentially, but per capita energy consumption also started to grow exponentially. That is, the *rate* at which growth in CO_2 levels occurred also started to increase exponentially. This situation has led to the current compound exponential growth in atmospheric CO_2.

In a discrete implementation of this model, the CO_2 concentration for year i, prior to the Industrial Revolution, is given in terms of the concentration in the previous year:

$$CO_2(i) = CO_2(i - 1) \cdot (1 + r_o), \text{ year} \leq 1880$$

After the Industrial Revolution, starting in approximately 1880, the annual growth rate is no longer constant:

$$r(i) = r(i - 1) \cdot (1 + g_r), \text{ year} > 1880$$
$$CO_2(i) = CO_2(i - 1) \cdot [1 + r(i)], \text{ year} > 1880$$

where r_o is the initial yearly growth rate and g_r is the constant yearly increase in the growth rate.

Write a program that allows the user to provide values for the constant initial growth rate r_o, the year at which compound exponential growth is assumed to start, and the rate g_r at which the growth increases after that year. Then use the model to predict values for CO_2 through the year 2050. Use the sum of the squares of the differences between the measured and modeled values to determine how well your model fits the existing data. Try several different values until you believe a satisfactory fit has been obtained. A value often used to compare CO_2 prediction models is the year in which the level will increase to twice its preindustrial level of about 275 ppm. In what year does your model predict that this will happen?

Figure 9.3 shows one forecast based on the kind of model suggested in this exercise. These modeled values slightly underestimate CO_2 levels in the early part of the twentieth century, but they match the measured levels very well after the 1950s. According to this model, the 550-ppm level will be reached in 2035, a prediction that is widely regarded as reasonable. [CO2MODEL.F90]

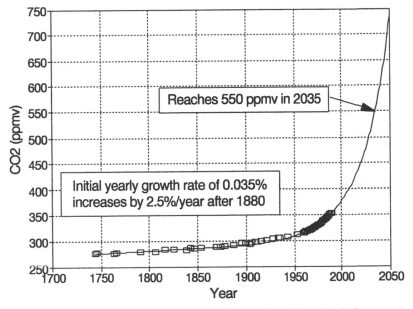

Figure 9.3. CO₂ forecasting model based on historical data

Exercise 21. Consider the file JANUARY.DAT. (See Table 9.3.) Copy this file to a new file called YEARLY.DAT. Create a similar file called FEBRUARY.DAT. (You can simply make up the data.) Write a program that opens YEARLY.DAT and *appends* the data in FEBRUARY.DAT to this file. That is, when you're done, the file YEARLY.DAT should contain all the information in both JANUARY.DAT and FEBRUARY.DAT.

Extra Credit

(1) Modify your program so that it prompts the user to provide the name of the monthly data file to be appended to YEARLY.DAT and then checks to make sure that file exists before it opens YEARLY.DAT. If it doesn't, the program should print an informative message and stop. Test your program by temporarily moving or renaming FEBRUARY.DAT so that your program won't be able to find it.

(2) Create a text file that contains a record of all updates to a file. When your program runs, it should open this "history" file and print the contents before prompting for the name of a new file to be appended. This file would look like this after the files FEBRUARY.DAT and MARCH.DAT were appended to YEARLY.DAT:

```
On 19950320 FEBRUARY.DAT was appended to YEARLY.DAT.
On 19950411 MARCH.DAT was appended to YEARLY.DAT.
```

The date strings (e.g., 19950320) are available from the intrinsic subroutine DATE_AND_TIME(date). (See **Appendix 4** for additional information about this and related subroutines.) [UPDATE.F90]

Exercise 22. It is always to a manufacturer's advantage to minimize the size of its raw materials inventory, consistent with being able to satisfy customer demand for its product. In your role as a production management engineer, you have implemented a cost-cutting approach that involves setting minimum allowed material stock levels and automatically reordering a predetermined amount of that item whenever stocks fall below this level. Your goal is to set minimum and reorder levels that will minimize current inventories without encountering "out of stock" situations.

You have created a "master materials inventory" file containing a material ID code, the current amount in stock, the amount below which additional material should be reordered, and the amount that will be reordered. One or more transaction files contain information about materials use. Each of these files is processed by updating the master materials inventory file and generating a reorder report. If any transaction asks for more material than is available, include an "out-of-stock" report and request an emergency reorder. (Based on the out-of-stock reports, you will want to make recommendations to your production manager for adjusting the minimum and reorder amounts in order to avoid future problems.

"Emergency reorders" cost more than regular reorders. If too many out-of-stock reports result from miscalculations on your part, you should start looking for a new job.)

Write a program to implement and test this inventory management system. There are several worthwhile simplifications you can make. First of all, consider the material ID codes to be integers just because they are less trouble to process than character strings. In the master materials inventory file, store the information in order by ID code. The transaction data file should contain an ID code and the amount used. Not all ID codes have to be present in a transaction file, but those that are should be ordered by ID code. Assume that every ID code in the transaction file corresponds to an ID code in the master inventory file; that is, the transaction file will never contain any mistakes in its ID code references.

Being able to assume these characteristics for the files will greatly simplify the code you need to write. For example, for each ID code in the transaction file, you will have to find the corresponding ID code in the master inventory file. This is easy if you know that the ID codes in both files are in order. Finally, you can assume that all reorder requests are filled immediately, so the processing of each transaction file includes the addition of reordered material to the inventory.

Table 9.12 gives two sample files, INSTOCK.DAT and USE_STK1.DAT, which can be downloaded from the World Wide Web site mentioned in Section i.5 of the Preface. The header line is included in each file. The physical units for the quantities are unimportant from the point of view of writing the program, as long as they are consistent.

Table 9.12. Data files for an inventory management program

(INSTOCK.DAT)

ID	stock	min.	reorder
1000	10000	750	15000
1001	5000	1000	6500
1002	8000	500	8500
1003	9050	600	12000
1004	11500	1000	14000
1005	80	50	750
1006	275	200	1000
1007	15000	3000	20000
1008	850	750	1000
1009	900	75	1000
1010	8730	450	10000

(USE_STK1.DAT)

ID	used
1000	8000
1001	4500
1003	2700
1005	140
1006	100
1007	10000
1009	500
1010	1700

Note that the data shown in Table 9.12 will result in routine reorders of items 1001 and 1006 and an "emergency reorder" of item 1005 because the amount used (140) is greater than the amount in stock (80).

Your program should create as output a third file, INSTOCK.OUT, that contains the updated inventory file. To process the inventory again with another file, the original and output files should be renamed. INSTOCK.DAT should be renamed INSTOCK.OLD, and INSTOCK.OUT (which will be the input file for the next set of transactions) should be renamed INSTOCK.DAT. [INSTOCK.F90]

Some Essential Programming Algorithms

This chapter deals with the Fortran implementation of some common algorithms from computer science that have many applications in science and engineering. These include algorithms for searching and sorting lists of data and algorithms for recursively defined functions. These algorithms are implemented as subroutines and functions in MODULEs so that they can be incorporated into your own programs even if you don't spend much time understanding the details of their operation.

10.1 Introduction

There are many algorithms basic to computing in any discipline, including science and engineering. Some of these are routinely included as part of an introductory computer science course. Some are of interest to particular areas of science and engineering. Others fall under the general category of numerical analysis algorithms; these will be covered separately in Chapter 11.

It is important for any programmer to have some sense of these general-purpose algorithms to avoid "reinventing the wheel" whenever certain programming problems arise. In this chapter we will discuss *searching algorithms*, *sorting algorithms*, and *recursive algorithms*.

searching algorithms
sorting algorithms
recursive algorithms

Searching and sorting algorithms are important because in many computer applications, a great deal of time is spent "looking for things." As we will see, the efficiency of searching algorithms can be improved dramatically by performing the search on a list of things that are in order. For a list of numbers, for example, "in order" means that the numbers appear in the list in either ascending or descending order. For a list of words, "in order" means that the words are alphabetized as they would be in a dictionary.

Sorting algorithms are therefore of great practical interest because it's so often necessary to reorganize lists of things into a more useful order. We will discuss three different sorting algorithms in this text.[1] They vary greatly in their

---

[1] A fourth algorithm, which applies in special cases, appears as an exercise at the end of this chapter.

efficiency when they're applied to lists originally in random order, but each of them is a reasonable choice in certain circumstances.

Recursive algorithms provide an efficient approach to solving certain kinds of problems. This chapter will show how to evelute some mathematical functions that are important in science and engineering and whose definitions lend themselves to recursive evaluation. Discussions of recursive algorithms have not previously appeared in Fortran programming texts for the simple reason that Fortran 90 is the first version of Fortran to support recursion as part of the standard language.[2]

Except for the Fortran-specific implementation details of recursive algorithms, the material in this chapter isn't about Fortran *per se*, but about its application to important computing problems. You should be able to use the algorithms presented in this chapter in your own programs even if you don't spend a great deal of time understanding the details of their operation. Consider, for example, an algorithm to search for all occurrences of a specified value in an array. That algorithm has been written as a Fortran subroutine, which has then been incorporated into a driver program that tests and demonstrates its operation. In order to use that subroutine in your own programs, you need only understand how it is used in the driver program. Then you can simply copy the source code for the subroutine into your own program; in some cases, you may need to make minor modifications to meet specific needs.

The driver programs for testing the searching and sorting algorithms have made certain assumptions about the contents of the list being searched or sorted. This is necessary not because the algorithm demands data of a certain type, but because every Fortran variable requires a specific data type. How can you customize these algorithms so they will work with data types other than the ones for which they were originally written?

There is no entirely general answer to this question. However, it is possible to minimize the effort required to modify the data types used in the subprograms presented in this chapter. Information about data used by subprograms is included in a MODULE that is USEd in the main program and all subprograms associated with the algorithm. This means that much of the information about data types can conveniently be found in one place.

Consider this example. With a searching algorithm, the quantities of interest are an array to hold the items being searched, an integer specifying the size of the list, the value being searched for, and possibly another integer specifying the position of an item in the list. The array elements and the value being searched for can have any intrinsic or derived data type. If these quantities are defined in a MODULE, then the data type of the array and of any value in the list can easily be redefined in the MODULE when that source code is used in a

---

[2]Some Fortran 77 compilers support recursion, but only as an extension of the standard

program. A complete program example is given in Section 10.6, the Applications section of this chapter.

There are some potential disadvantages to using MODULEs in this way. First of all, when a variable from a MODULE is used in a subprogram, that variable can't be passed to a subprogram in its parameter list. In other words, a variable can appear either in the parameter list or in a USE statement, but not in both places. This makes the information flow between the subprogram and its calling (sub)program less clear. It's possible to compensate somewhat for this loss of information by using the ONLY option in the USE statement specifically to name the variable (and subprogram) names being used in that particular (sub)program, even though this isn't required.

Second, subprograms that would otherwise be able to make use of variably dimensioned arrays can no longer do so because variable array dimensions aren't allowed in MODULE data declarations. Third, variables shared among several subprograms can't have different intent (for example, IN in one subprogram and OUT in another) because the INTENT attribute is part of the data declaration that is made in the MODULE. A variable's data declaration can't be split between the MODULE, where a data type would be given, and a subroutine that USEs that module, where you might otherwise wish to declare its intent. Therefore, any variable declared in a MODULE that you wish to use as input to one subprogram and output from another will need to have INOUT intent.

Even with these potential problems, it's still a good idea to use MODULEs whenever possible to share data declarations when subprograms need access to data types that can change from application to application.

10.2 Searching Algorithms

Suppose you need to write a program for finding chemical names in a list of chemicals. Assume the chemicals are in alphabetical order. The program will contain a menu of options that might include these choices:

1. Find a chemical whose name starts with "methyl."
2. Find a chemical whose name includes "oxide."
3. Find all occurrences of chemicals whose names start with "methyl."
4. Find all occurrences of chemicals whose names include "oxide."

Each of these requests forces the program to search through the directory, but not in the same way. The first two options aren't even completely clear. Suppose there is more than one chemical starting with "methyl." Do you wish your program to find the *first* occurrence of "methyl," or will you be happy with *any* chemical starting with "methyl?" It appears that the last two options will force you to search through the entire directory because they specifically ask for *all* occurrences of a specified value. (At least, if the list is in alphabetical order, all the chemicals beginning with "methyl" will be together.)

For now, suppose either that there are no duplicate names in the list or that it is sufficient to find the first occurrence of a specified name. Assume that the list is held in an array. The simplest algorithm for searching an array uses a loop structure:

LOOP *(until we find what we're looking for or we get to the end of the list)*
(compare an element of the array to what we're looking for and store result as "yes" or "no.")
END LOOP

The details of this algorithm, even at the pseudocode level, depend on what you're looking for and on how you will ask the algorithm to find it. Note, however, that the terminating condition should, in general, account for the possibility that the list doesn't contain the sought-after value.

10.2.1 Linear Searches

Let's solve a specific problem that involves looking for something in a list.

1 Define the problem.

Find the first occurrence of a specified chemical name in a list of names or determine that the name doesn't appear in the list.

2 Outline a solution.

1. Start at the beginning of the list and compare each item in the list against the specified name. Store the result of the comparison as "yes" or "no."
2. Stop when you find what you're looking for—when the comparison yields a "yes"—or when you get to the end of the list.

Incorporate this solution in a subprogram. The output from the subprogram should be the position of the item in the list, or a zero if the item isn't found in the list.

3 *Design an algorithm.*

The algorithm can be simplified because the comparison against an array element and the specified name can be used to control the execution of the loop. The only action that must be taken inside the loop is incrementing the array index.

SUBPROGRAM *FindOne(IN: array, size, search_value;*
             OUT: where (position of item found))
INITIALIZE *where = 1*
LOOP *(while array(where) ≠ search_value and counter < size)*
  INCREMENT *where = where + 1*
END LOOP
IF *array(where) ≠ search_value* **THEN ASSIGN** *where = 0*

If you find the name you're looking for, the variable where contains its position in the array. If you don't find it, where has a value of 0.

  This algorithm will require, on the average, n/2 tries to find an item in a randomly ordered list, assuming that the item actually exists in the list. This means that the time required to find something in a list is linearly proportional to the length of the list. A list containing 1,000,000 items in random order will require, on the average, 500,000 tries.

4 *Convert the algorithm into a program.*

P-10.1 contains the source code for a subroutine that implements this algorithm.

P-10.1 (see SEARCH.F90)

```
        SUBROUTINE FindFirst(size,where)
! Linear search of list for first occurrence of target value.
        USE Setup, ONLY : a,target
        IMPLICIT NONE
        INTEGER, INTENT(IN) :: size
        INTEGER, INTENT(OUT) :: where
        where=1
        DO WHILE ((a(where) /= target) .AND. (where < size))
          where=where+1
        END DO
        IF (a(where) /= target) where=0
!
        END SUBROUTINE FindFirst
```

The code given here is a subroutine that will become part of a MODULE that will be incorporated into a driver program for testing this and other searching algorithms. The data array and "target" value will be defined in another MODULE (MODULE Setup). Unless you look at this second MODULE (you can find it in the program SEARCH.F90, which can be downloaded from the World Wide Web site mentioned in Section i.5 of the Preface, or listed later in the chapter in P-10.4), you have no way of knowing what kinds of data are being searched; it's important to understand that the code within SUBROUTINE FindFirst is the same regardless of the data type of the array a.

5 *Verify the operation of the program.*

As just noted, subroutine P-10.1 needs to be incorporated into a driver program that should be used to test the subroutine on a list whose contents you know. It will be helpful to search for several items, including one at the beginning and one at the end of the list, as well as one that doesn't exist in the list. If your list contains some duplicate names, you will be able to reuse it to test the subroutine discussed in the next section.

Problem Discussion

Proper termination of the search loop is a potential trouble spot in P-10.1. Consider this code from SUBROUTINE FindFirst:

```
where=1
DO WHILE ((a(where) ≠ target) .AND. (where < size))
  where=where+1
END DO
```

An easily overlooked mistake would be to initialize where to 0 instead of 1—because 0 is a typical initial value for a variable that will be incremented inside a loop. This is a problem because when the DO WHILE... loop tests the terminating condition, it will attempt to examine the contents of a(0) even though this array element doesn't exist. Your Fortran environment should issue at least a warning message when it encounters this kind of "range violation" error.

Here's a slightly different problem.

1 *Define the problem.*

Find all occurrences of a specified name in a list of names. Keep count of how many occurrences are found.

2 *Outline a solution.*

The main difference between this problem and the previous one is that now the loop will be count-controlled rather than conditional because it is always necessary to search through the entire list.

3 *Design an algorithm.*

Here is the critical part:

```
INITIALIZE how_many = 0
LOOP (for counter = 1 to array size)
      IF search_name = array(counter) THEN
            WRITE (array(counter))
            INCREMENT how_many = how_many + 1
      (end IF...)
END LOOP
```

4 *Convert the algorithm into a program.*

P-10.2 contains source code for a subroutine that implements this algorithm. A driver program containing this subroutine will be discussed later in this chapter. (See P-10.4.)

P-10.2 (see SEARCH.F90)

```
        SUBROUTINE FindAll(size,how_many)
!
! Linear search of a list for all occurrences of
! specified target value.
!
        USE Setup, ONLY : a,target
        IMPLICIT NONE
        INTEGER i
        INTEGER, INTENT(IN) :: size
        INTEGER, INTENT(OUT) :: how_many
!
        how_many=0
        DO i=1,size
          IF (a(i) .EQ. target) THEN
            PRINT *,target,' at position ',i
            how_many=how_many+1
          END IF
        END DO
!
        END SUBROUTINE FindAll
```

---

5 *Verify the operation of the program.*

SUBROUTINE FindAll should be included in a driver program that tests its performance on a list whose contents you know.

10.2.2 Binary Search

Recalling the options discussed earlier in the chapter for a program that searches for a chemical name, suppose that chemicals beginning with the word "methyl" are of interest. If the names are sorted in alphabetical order, then all the chemicals starting with "methyl" will be together in the list. Otherwise, they will appear in random locations throughout the list. In the latter case, the only way to find the word "methyl" is to start at the beginning of the list and continue until you find what you're looking for or get to the end of the list. This is OK for short lists, but seems inefficient for large lists. Is there any way to take advantage of a list in alphabetical order to develop a more efficient searching algorithm?

If a list is sorted in order—alphabetically, as in this example—then, in fact, a much more efficient algorithm exists. Let's investigate the possibilities by playing a simple game:

1. You will pick an integer between 1 and 100.
2. I will guess the number.
3. You will tell me whether the number I have guessed is too big or too small relative to the number you've picked.

How many tries will I need to guess your number?

Here's one way to play the game. You pick 33.

My Guess	Your Response
50	too big
25	too small
37	too big
31	too small
34	too big
32	too small
33	you guessed it!

Obviously, another way to play the game is to use a linear search of the numbers from 1 to 100. On the average, if you pick a number randomly from this range, it will take 50 tries to guess the number. For the above example, it will take 33 tries. However, the solution here requires only seven guesses! In fact, it should never require more than seven guesses to find a number in the range 1–100.

This solution requires that guesses be chosen in a particular way. My first guess of 50 is in the middle of the range of possible numbers. When you tell me that 50 is too big, then I know that the number must be in the range 1–49. Therefore, my next guess is 25, the number in the middle of the range 1–49. When you tell me that 25 is too small, I select 37, a number in the middle of the range 26–49. By continuing in this way I must eventually arrive at the number you have selected.

This algorithm is called a binary search. By selecting a value that is at the midpoint of the remaining range at each step, this algorithm guarantees that you can find any value in an *ordered* list—or determine that the value doesn't exist in the list—in no more than $\log_2(n)$ guesses. This is a significant improvement over a linear search. Suppose you have to find a value in a list containing 1,000,000 values. Recall that a linear search will require an average of 500,000 comparisons. However, a binary search on such a list will require no more than 20 comparisons because $2^{20} \approx 1,000,000$.

The number guessing game is a simplified version of the general search problem because if everybody follows the rules of the game, the number to be guessed is guaranteed to exist within the numbers 1–100. In general, a binary searching algorithm must also account for the possibility that the requested value doesn't exist in the list of available values. Here's an appropriate problem statement and a complete solution.

1 *Define the problem.*

Given a list of values in order, find one occurrence of a specified value in the list or determine that the value doesn't exist in the list.

2 *Outline a solution.*

The outline of a solution should implement the steps used in the number-guessing game.

1. Select a value in the middle of the possible range.
2. If that value is the desired value, stop.
3. If the value is smaller than the desired value, reset the lower boundary of the possible range to the middle position plus 1.
4. If the value is larger than the desired value, reset the upper boundary of the possible range to the middle position minus 1.
5. Repeat steps 1–4 until the desired value is found or until the lower boundary is larger than the upper boundary.

In order to use a binary search, the exact statement of the problem is important. First of all, the list must be in order; it makes no conceptual sense to do a binary search on a randomly ordered list! A binary search will find only one occurrence of a specified value. If that value appears more than once in the list, you have no way of knowing which occurrence the binary search will locate. However, because the list must be in order, you could use a binary search to find one occurrence and then look forward and backward in the list to find additional occurrences.

3 *Design an algorithm.*

SUBPROGRAM *BinarySearch(IN: array (A),*
                    lo and hi as array boundaries, desired value;
                    OUT: found, as boolean value, or
                    position in array)
DEFINE *(midpoint, as integer array index)*

ASSIGN found = false (alternate: position = 0)
LOOP (while (lo ≤ hi) and (not found))
       (alternate: while (lo ≤ hi) and (position = 0))
    ASSIGN midpoint = (lo + hi)/2
    IF A(mid) = desired value *THEN*
        ASSIGN found = true (alternate: position = mid)
    ELSE IF A(mid) < desired value *THEN*
        ASSIGN hi = midpoint − 1
    ELSE ASSIGN lo = midpoint + 1
END LOOP

By specifying the low and high boundaries of an array in the parameter list rather than just its size (with an implied lower boundary of 1), this algorithm can be used to search just part of a list, if desired. For example, you could search an electronic dictionary just for words beginning with the letter b if you know where the first and last word beginning with b are located in the dictionary.

4   *Convert the algorithm into a program.*

P-10.3 contains source code for a subroutine that implements this algorithm. A driver program for subroutine will be discussed in the next section. (See P-10.4.)

P-10.3 (see `SEARCH.F90`)

```
        SUBROUTINE Binary(low,high,where)
!
! Binary search of an ordered list for one occurrence of
! specified target value.  Assumes low < high, i.e., there is
! something in the list to look for.
!
        USE Setup, ONLY : a,target
        IMPLICIT NONE
        INTEGER mid,lo,hi
        INTEGER, INTENT(OUT) :: where
        INTEGER, INTENT(IN) :: low,high
!
        lo=low  !Assign these values locally so...
        hi=high !INTENT(IN) on low and high won't be violated.
        where=0
        DO WHILE ((lo .LE. hi) .AND. (where .EQ. 0))
          mid=(lo+hi)/2
          IF (a(mid) .EQ. target) THEN
            where=mid
          ELSE IF (a(mid) .GT. target) THEN
            hi=mid-1
          ELSE
            lo=mid+1
```

```
      END IF
   END DO

   END SUBROUTINE Binary
```

5 Verify the operation of the program.

Test this algorithm in a driver program that searches for values in a list whose contents you know. Be sure to search for values at the beginning and end of the list, as well as for values that don't exist in the list.

Problem Discussion

Table 10.1. Data file for use with searching algorithms

```
Alice
Allen
Bob
Carla
David
Evelyn
Frank
Frank
Grace
Grace
Grace
Hal
Laura
Susan
Ted
Wanda
```

Algorithms such as these are deceptively simple. It's easy to write code that looks OK and works *most* of the time. Clearly, this is unacceptable. For example, suppose you use P-10.3 to search a list of names in alphabetical order, as shown in Table 10.1. Now ask your program to find the name David in the list in Table 10.1. For the purposes of observing the operation of the algorithm, insert the statement PRINT*,lo,mid,hi,a(mid) just after the statement mid=(lo+hi)/2 in the DO WHILE... loop in the subroutine. Your program should now produce the following output:

```
1   8   16   Frank
1   4    7   Carla
5   6    7   Evelyn
5   5    5   David
```

It correctly locates David in the fifth position in the list. However, if the .LE. relational operator in the statement

```
DO WHILE ((lo .LE. hi) .AND. (where .EQ. 0))
```

is changed to .LT., the loop will terminate prematurely and the subroutine will incorrectly report that David can't be found in the list. With this change, the algorithm will work correctly only part of the time. When you're thinking about the design of an algorithm, it's easy to assume that a small detail such as the difference between "less than" and "less than or equal to" won't be very important. In this case, you would be wrong![3]

10.2.3 Comparing Searching Algorithms

As indicated earlier in the chapter, linear searching algorithms are required under some circumstances. In particular, if a list isn't sorted in any useful order, then a linear search is required. Linear searching algorithms are referred to as "order N" algorithms, represented in what is known as "big O" notation as O(N) algorithms. For any O(N) algorithm, the number of operations required to complete the algorithm is directly proportional to N. Because "operations" on your computer translate directly into time, doubling the size of the list means that the search will take twice as long for an O(N) algorithm.

On the other hand, the binary search algorithm is an O(log$_2$N) algorithm, which means that the number of operations grows only as the log to the base 2 of N. As noted above, this represents a tremendous increase in efficiency for large lists, with a binary search taking only about 20 comparisons to find a value in a list of 1,000,000 items, rather than the average of 500,000 comparisons required by a linear search.

The savings represented by a binary search are so significant that it is often worth the extra effort to devise algorithms that combine binary and linear searching techniques. For example, you know that a binary search finds only one occurrence of a specified value even if that value occurs several times in a list. In the list of names appearing in the Problem Discussion following P-10.3, the name Grace appears three times. You can use a binary search to locate one occurrence of Grace, but you won't know whether it's the first, second, or third. Therefore, once you have found one occurrence of Grace, you can do a linear search forward and backward to find additional occurrences. Since the list is in order, you can stop the search in either direction when you find a name other than Grace.

This hybrid algorithm might seem like a waste of time for a short list, but it makes sense as an efficient way to search a large list. (See Exercise 15 at the end of this chapter.)

10.2.4 A Driver Program for Testing Searching Algorithms

The three algorithms discussed above and implemented as subroutines in P-10.1, P-10.2, and P-10.3 all need to be tested. As noted in Section 10.1, the subroutines

---

[3]An incorrect version of this algorithm has, in fact, been published in at least one Fortran text

have been designed to make it easy to change the type of data being searched. Progam P-10.4 shows how the subroutines have been incorporated into a driver program. The data type is CHARACTER, and the data file SEARCH.DAT, which can be downloaded from the World Wide Web site mentioned in Section i.5 of the Preface, contains the names shown in Table 10.1. You can learn a lot from this program about how to use MODULEs to make your programs easy to maintain and modify. The type of the data being searched is defined in MODULE Setup; a subroutine to create the list is also included in Setup. The searching subroutines are included in MODULE SearchSubs. The subroutines themselves haven't been duplicated here because they are identical to those already listed in P-10.1, P-10.2, and P-10.3. However, the program SEARCH.F90, which can be downloaded from the World Wide Web site mentioned in Section i.5 of the Preface, contains all the code and is "ready to run."

P-10.4 [SEARCH.F90]

```
       MODULE Setup
         IMPLICIT NONE
         CHARACTER(20) a(100),target
!
         CONTAINS
!
         SUBROUTINE GetList(size)
!
         IMPLICIT NONE
         INTEGER, INTENT(INOUT) ::  size
!
         OPEN(1,file="c:\ftn90.dir\search.dat")
         size=1
10       READ(1,*,END=900)a(size)
            size=size+1
         GO TO 10
900      size=size-1
         CLOSE(1)
!
         PRINT *,'# of items in list = ',size
         END SUBROUTINE GetList
       END MODULE Setup
!======================
       MODULE SearchSubs
         CONTAINS
!
! (Insert code for FindFirst here.)
!
! (Insert code for FindAll here.)
!
! (Insert code for Binary here.)
!
         END MODULE SearchSubs
!===========================
```

```
      PROGRAM Search
!
! Driver program to test linear and binary search algorithms.
!
      USE Setup ! array and target specifications
      USE SearchSubs ! various searching subroutines
      IMPLICIT NONE
      CHARACTER YesNo,choice
      INTEGER size,where,how_many
!
      CALL GetList(size) !Build list to search.
!
10    CONTINUE !START LOOP
        PRINT *,' What name would you like to look for?'
        READ *,target
        PRINT *,'Linear search for (f)irst, (a)ll, or (b)inary?'
        READ *,choice
        SELECT CASE (choice)
          CASE ('a') !linear search for all occurrences
            CALL FindAll(size,how_many)
            IF (how_many .GT. 0) THEN
              PRINT *,how_many,' occurrences found'
            ELSE
              PRINT *,target,' not found'
            END IF
          CASE ('b') !binary search for one occurrence
            CALL Binary(1,size,where)
            IF (where .GT. 0) THEN
              PRINT *,target,' found at position',where
            ELSE
              PRINT *,target,' not found'
            END IF
          CASE ('f') !linear search for first occurrence
            CALL FindFirst(size,where)
            IF (where .GT. 0) THEN
              PRINT *,target,' found at position',where
            ELSE
              PRINT *,target,' not found'
            END IF
        END SELECT
        PRINT *,' Try again (y/n)?'
        READ *,YesNo
      IF (YesNo .EQ. 'y') GO TO 10
!
      END
```

Running P-10.4

```
# of items in list =  16
What name would you like to look for?
David
Linear search for (f)irst, (a)ll, or (b)inary?
f
David                found at position 5
Try again (y/n)?
y
What name would you like to look for?
Grace
Linear search for (f)irst, (a)ll, or (b)inary?
a
Grace                at position  9
Grace                at position  10
Grace                at position  11
3  occurrences found
Try again (y/n)?
y
What name would you like to look for?
Grace
Linear search for (f)irst, (a)ll, or (b)inary?
b
Grace                found at position 10
Try again (y/n)?
n
```

Problem Discussion

The output from this program is just a demonstration and isn't sufficient to test the code thoroughly. Note that the binary search happened to find the second of Grace's three occurrences in the list.

10.3 Sorting Algorithms

The discussion of binary and linear searching in Section 10.2 makes clear the importance of putting lists in sorted order for efficient searching. In this section, we will develop algorithms for two different "intuitive" methods of sorting lists of data contained in arrays.

10.3.1 Selection Sort

1 *Define the problem.*

Start with an array of integers in random order and sort it in ascending order. (The extension of the problem statement to sort the array in descending order or to sort arrays of other data types is straightforward.)

2 *Outline a solution.*

It will help to use a specific example for describing the solution. Suppose this list of seven integers is stored in an array A:

$$17 \ 4 \ 11 \ 9 \ 13 \ 3 \ 5$$

1. Assume that the value in the first element of the array is the smallest value in the entire list.

Assume that the smallest value = $A(1)$ = 17.

2. Starting at the second element, compare all the remaining elements with the first element. If you find a smaller one, mark it as the smallest element.

Assign new smallest = $A(6)$ = 3.

3. When you have found the position of the smallest remaining element, exchange this element with the first element. Now the smallest element is where it belongs.

This operation looks like this:

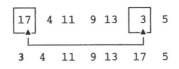

In this and following steps, the integers in bold type indicate values that have been put in their proper position in the array.

4. Repeat steps 1–3 starting at the second, third, and so on, positions, up to the (n - 1)st position.

This is what the array looks like after each of the five repetitions of steps 1–3:

(2nd repetition)   3 **4** 11 9 13 17 5 (no exchange required)

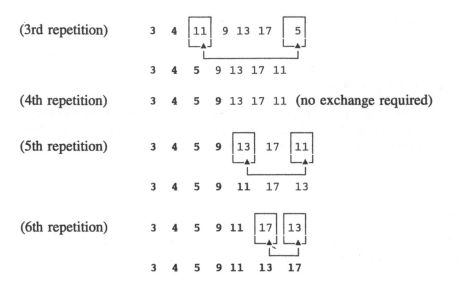

Note that in some cases, the element initially chosen as the smallest remains the smallest. Then it's not necessary to exchange a pair of elements.

3 *Design an algorithm.*

```
SUBPROGRAM Selection(IN/OUT: array (A); IN: size)
DEFINE (current, test, smallest, as integers)
LOOP (current = 1 to size-1)
        ASSIGN smallest = current
        LOOP (test = current + 1 to size)
                IF (A(test) < A(smallest)) THEN
                        ASSIGN smallest = test
        END LOOP
        IF (A(current) ≠ A(smallest)) THEN
                CALL Swap(A(current),A(smallest))
END LOOP
(end of subprogram)
SUBPROGRAM Swap(IN/OUT: a, b as integers)
DEFINE (temp as integer)
ASSIGN temp = a
        a = b
        b = temp
(end of subprogram)
```

We will reuse the *Swap* subprogram in subsequent algorithms.

4 Convert the algorithm into a program.

P-10.5 contains source code for a subroutine that implements the Selection Sort algorithm.

P-10.5 (see SORT.F90)

```
          SUBROUTINE Selection(size)
!
          USE SortSetup, ONLY : a => array,Swap
          IMPLICIT NONE
          INTEGER, INTENT(IN) :: size
          INTEGER current_cell,i,smallest
!
            DO current_cell=1,size-1
              smallest=current_cell
              DO i=current_cell+1,size
                IF (a(i) .LT. a(smallest)) smallest=i
              END DO
            IF (a(current_cell) .NE. a(smallest)) &
              CALL Swap(a(current_cell),a(smallest))
            END DO
          END SUBROUTINE Selection
```

5 Verify the operation of the program.

It is easy to verify the operation of such an algorithm for any list, but it's not so easy to be confident that it will work correctly for *every* list. A driver program to test this subroutine should allow you to produce random lists, lists already in order, lists that are backwards, and lists the contents of which are all the same value. Note that the DO... loop won't execute at all for a list of length 1.

Problem Discussion

Selection Sort has the advantage that elements are exchanged only when the final location of an element is known. It performs the same number of comparisons regardless of the initial order of values in the array. This isn't necessarily a disadvantage in most circumstances. However, if the list is initially almost in order, Selection Sort performs a lot of unnecessary comparisons. In the next section, we will describe an algorithm that performs substantially better than Selection Sort if an array is already almost in order.

10.3.2 Insertion Sort

Insertion Sort is another "intuitive" sorting algorithm. Suppose you're being dealt a hand in a card game such as bridge. Every time you're given a new card, you automatically insert it into its proper place. The same kind of process can apply to sorting an array.

1 Define the problem.

Start with an array of integers in random order and sort it into ascending order.

2 Outline a solution.

Again, it will help to use a specific example. Suppose the array contains these values:

$$17 \quad 4 \quad 11 \quad 9 \quad 13 \quad 3 \quad 5$$

1. Find the smallest element and exchange it with the value in the first position.

Now we know that we won't find any value smaller than the first element, and we also know that the second element is at least as large as the first element. The values in bold type represent a subset of the array that is sorted.

2. Determine whether the third element is in its proper place relative to the preceding elements.

3   4 11   9 13 17   5   (3rd element is in place)

3. Repeat step 2 until you get to the end of the list.

3 4   11   9   13 17   5   (4th element is out of place)

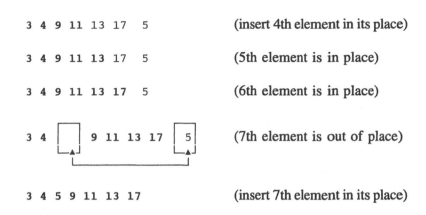

3 4 9 11 13 17 5	(insert 4th element in its place)
3 4 9 11 13 17 5	(5th element is in place)
3 4 9 11 13 17 5	(6th element is in place)
3 4 ⬚ 9 11 13 17 ⬚5⬚	(7th element is out of place)
3 4 5 9 11 13 17	(insert 7th element in its place)

The instruction in step 2 is vague and must be translated into more specific pseudocode. Consider the last step in the sorting of the list illustrated above, in which the seventh element of the array was put in its proper place. We will take these specific steps:

1. Save the seventh element in a temporary variable.
2. Compare the temporary variable with the sixth element. If the temporary variable is less than the sixth element, move the sixth element up one position.
3. Repeat step 2 with successive elements until an element is less than or equal to the temporary variable.
4. Insert the temporary variable just after this position.

3 *Design an algorithm.*

SUBPROGRAM *Insertion(IN/OUT: array A; IN: size)*
DEFINE *(counter, count2, min, as integers;*
        temp, same type as element of array)

(Find the smallest element and put it where it belongs.)

ASSIGN *min = 1*
LOOP *(for counter = 2 to size)*
        IF A(counter) < A(min) **THEN**
                ASSIGN *min = A(counter)*
END LOOP

(Check additional elements starting with third.)

```
LOOP (for counter = 3 to size)
        ASSIGN temp = A(counter)
        INITIALIZE count2 = counter
        LOOP (while temp < A(counter – 1))
                ASSIGN A(count2) = A(counter2 – 1)
                INCREMENT count2 = count2 – 1
        END LOOP
        ASSIGN A(count2) = temp
END LOOP
```

It's easy to design an insertion algorithm that doesn't work under all conditions! Note particularly the inner loop that operates as long as *temp* is less than *A(counter – 1)*. This loop will terminate properly only if *temp* is never less than the first element in the array. Otherwise, the loop will eventually try to access *A(0)*. This is why the algorithm first selects the smallest value in the array and places it in the beginning of the list.

4 *Convert the algorithm into a program.*

P-10.6 contains source code for a subroutine that implements the Insertion Sort algorithm.

P-10.6 (see SORT.F90)

```
        SUBROUTINE Insertion(size)
! Assumes size>=3
        USE SortSetup, ONLY : a => array,save_value,Swap
        IMPLICIT NONE
        INTEGER, INTENT(IN) :: size
        INTEGER current,smallest,test
!
! Find smallest element...
        smallest=1
        DO current=2,size
          IF (a(current)<a(smallest)) smallest=current
        END DO
!
! and swap it if necessary to get it into 1st position.
        IF (a(1) .NE. a(smallest)) CALL Swap(a(1),a(smallest))
!
! Check remaining elements, starting a position 3.
        DO current=3,size
          save_value=a(current)
          test=current
```

```
!  (DO WHILE... will always terminate because smallest element
!  is in position 1.)
            DO WHILE (save_value .LT. a(test-1))
              a(test)=a(test-1)
              test=test-1
            END DO
            a(test)=save_value
          END DO
!
        END SUBROUTINE Insertion
```

Problem Discussion

Don't be misled by the fact that the Insertion Sort code is longer than the Selection Sort code. These algorithms are both $O(N^2)$ algorithms, and the Insertion Sort code really is more efficient in some circumstances. The efficiency of an algorithm is not necessarily related to the length of the code required for its implementation.

5 *Verify the operation of the program.*

See Step 5 of the Selection Sort problem. The same verification procedures apply.

10.3.3 Efficiency of Sorting Algorithms

Recall that in Section 10.2.3, we identified linear and binary search algorithms as $O(N)$ and $O(\log_2 N)$ algorithms. We can characterize sorting algorithms in the same way, to determine the relationship between the number of operations required to perform a sort and the size of the list being sorted.

Note that the Selection Sort algorithm contains nested DO... loops. For an array of size N, the statements inside the outer loop are executed approximately N times and the statements inside the inner loop are executed, on average, approximately N/2 times each time the inner loop is executed. Altogether, then, each operation inside the inner loop is executed approximately N*N/2 times. If n = 100, the IF statement is executed roughly 10,000/2 = 5,000 times. If N = 200, the IF statement is executed roughly 20,000 times, a factor of four increase. In general, if the size of the array increases, the number of operations required to sort the array with a Selection Sort algorithm increases as the square of the factor by which the array size increases.

This relationship between array size and performance characterizes an $O(N^2)$ algorithm. An N^2 dependence on array size represents a severe performance penalty for large values of N, with the result that neither the Selection Sort nor the Insertion Sort algorithm is very efficient for large arrays. Although computer scientists and programmers may not be happy with a theoretically inefficient algorithm, acceptable performance is largely a matter of perception, depending on your own definition of a "severe performance penalty."

The Selection Sort algorithm requires the same number of comparison operations regardless of the original state of the list being sorted. On the other hand, the performance of the Insertion Sort depends strongly on the original state of the list. If the list is backwards, for example, the Insertion Sort is very inefficient. However, if the list is originally almost in order, the Insertion Sort is very efficient—because it makes only about N comparisons and no exchanges if the list is already in order. If the list is in random order, the Insertion Sort is still an $O(N^2)$ algorithm. In this case, a conditional loop is nested inside a DO... loop.

In summary, the Selection Sort is a reasonable choice for small lists that are originally in random order, but the Insertion Sort is better if the list is originally almost in sorted order. Later in the chapter, we will use a version of the Insertion Sort algorithm as part of a program to add new items to a list that is already in order.

10.3.4 A Driver Program for Testing Sorting Algorithms

P-10.7 is a driver program for testing the Selection Sort and Insertion Sort subroutines. The program file SORT.F90, which can be downloaded from the World Wide Web site mentioned in Section i.5 of the Preface, also includes the Quicksort algorithm discussed later in this chapter.

P-10.7 [SORT.F90]

```
      MODULE SortSetup
        IMPLICIT NONE
        INTEGER array(100),save_value
!  (see also declarations for a, b, and temp in Swap)
!
        CONTAINS
!---------------------------
        SUBROUTINE Swap(a,b)
!
        IMPLICIT NONE
        INTEGER, INTENT(INOUT) :: a,b
        INTEGER temp
!
           temp=a
           a=b
           b=temp
        END SUBROUTINE Swap
!----------------------------------
```

```
        SUBROUTINE GetList(size)
        IMPLICIT NONE
        INTEGER, INTENT(OUT) :: size
        INTEGER i
        INTEGER Count(1) ! for random number generator
        REAL x
!
          CALL System_Clock(Count(1))
          CALL Random_Seed(Put=Count)
          DO i=1,size
            CALL Random_Number(x)
            array(i)=x*100+1
          END DO
        END SUBROUTINE GetList
!-------------------------------
        SUBROUTINE PrintList(size)
        IMPLICIT NONE
        INTEGER, INTENT(IN) :: size
        INTEGER i
!
          PRINT *,(array(i),i=1,size)
!
        END SUBROUTINE PrintList
!----------------------------
      END MODULE SortSetup
!=========================
      MODULE SortSubs
        CONTAINS
!
! (Insert SUBROUTINE Selection code here.)
!
! (Insert SUBROUTINE Insertion code here.)
!
      END MODULE SortSubs
!=========================
      PROGRAM Sort
!
! Test and demonstrate several sorting algorithms.
!
      USE SortSetup, ONLY : a => array,GetList,PrintList
      USE SortSubs
      IMPLICIT NONE
      INTEGER size
      CHARACTER choose,YesNo
!
      size=15
!
10    PRINT *,' Choose sorting algorithm: '
      PRINT *,' Insertion (i), Quicksort (q), Selection (s)'
      READ *,choose
      CALL GetList(size)
      SELECT CASE (choose)
        CASE ('i')
          CALL Insertion(size)
        CASE ('q')
          CALL QuickSort(1,size)
        CASE ('s')
          CALL Selection(size)
      END SELECT
      CALL PrintList(size)
```

```
      PRINT *,' Again (y/n)?'
      READ *,YesNo
   IF (YesNo == 'y') GO TO 10

   END
```

Running P-10.7

```
Choose sorting algorithm:
Insertion (i), Quicksort (q), Selection (s)
s
 6  7  15  21  28  29  30  38  48  61  70  88  88  93  99
Again (y/n)?
n
```

10.4 Recursive Algorithms

The word "recursive" comes from the Latin word for "run back." In languages that support recursive algorithms, subprograms can "run back" on themselves by calling themselves repeatedly. Fortran 90 is the first version of Fortran to support recursion as part of the standard.

As an introduction to the motivation behind defining recursive algorithms, consider n!, the well-known factorial function.

1 Define the problem.

The factorial function n! can be defined like this (for non-negative values of n):

$$n! = 1, 0 \leq n \leq 1$$
$$n! = n \bullet (n - 1) \bullet (n - 2) \bullet \cdots \bullet (2), n \geq 2$$

For example, $5! = 5 \bullet 4 \bullet 3 \bullet 2 = 120$. An alternative definition of n! is:

$$n! = 1, 0 \leq n \leq 1$$
$$n! = n \bullet (n - 1)!, n \geq 2$$

In the second definition, which is completely equivalent to the first, n! is defined in terms of n and (n-1)!. When a function is defined in terms of itself in this way, it is called a recursively defined function.

Write a Fortran function that will use a recursive algorithm to calculate n!.

2 *Outline a solution.*

In this case, the problem definition itself defines the solution.

3 *Design an algorithm.*

The first definition of n! can easily be implemented as a count-controlled loop:

```
SUBPROGRAM Fact1(IN: n; OUT: n!)
ASSIGN n! = 1
IF (n > 1) THEN
        LOOP (for i = 2 to n)
                ASSIGN n! = n!*n
        END LOOP
(end subprogram)
```

The second definition can be implemented as a conditional loop:

```
SUBPROGRAM Fact2(IN: n; OUT: n!)
ASSIGN n! = 1
LOOP (while n > 1)
        ASSIGN n! = n!*n
                n=n – 1
END LOOP
(end subprogram)
```

Both of these algorithms are iterative algorithms because of their loop structures. They aren't recursive because neither of the subprograms references itself. However, the second algorithm can easily be converted into a recursive algorithm.

```
SUBPROGRAM Factorial(IN: n)
IF (n ≤ 1) THEN
        ASSIGN Factorial = 1
ELSE
        ASSIGN Factorial=n*Factorial(n – 1)
END
(end subprogram)
```

Note that this algorithm is a direct implementation of the recursive definition of n!. Because the subprogram doesn't have any separate output value in the parameter list, the implication is that it will be implemented as a Fortran function in which the name of the function contains the output value.

4 *Convert the algorithm into a program.*

Just for comparison purposes, P-10.8 contains Fortran implementations of each of the pseudocode implementations. Of these, RECURSIVE INTEGER FUNCTION Factorial is the one of most interest because it is the implementation of the recursive algorithm.

P-10.8 [FACTORAL.F90]

```
      MODULE FactorialSubs
!-----------------------
      CONTAINS
!----------------------------
      INTEGER FUNCTION Fact1(n)
      IMPLICIT NONE
      INTEGER, INTENT(IN) :: n
      INTEGER i,factorial
!
      factorial=1
      IF (n .GT. 1) THEN
        DO i=2,n
          factorial=factorial*i
        END DO
      END IF
      Fact1=factorial
      END FUNCTION Fact1
!----------------------------
      INTEGER FUNCTION Fact2(n)
      IMPLICIT NONE
      INTEGER, INTENT(IN) :: n
      INTEGER factorial,temp
!
      temp=n ! use temp to avoid violating INTENT(IN) on n
      factorial=1
      IF (temp > 1) THEN
        DO WHILE (temp > 1)
          factorial=factorial*temp
          temp=temp-1
        END DO
      END IF
      Fact2=factorial
      END FUNCTION Fact2
!------------------------------------------------------------
```

```
      RECURSIVE INTEGER FUNCTION Factorial(n) RESULT(n_Fact)
      IMPLICIT NONE
      INTEGER, INTENT(IN) :: n
!
      IF (n <= 1) THEN
        n_Fact=1
      ELSE
        n_Fact=n*Factorial(n-1)
      END IF
      END FUNCTION Factorial
!--------------------------
      END MODULE FactorialSubs
!==============================
      PROGRAM n_Factorial
!
! File name FACTORAL.F90
! Use factorial function to demonstrate recursive algorithms.
!
      USE FactorialSubs
      IMPLICIT NONE
      INTEGER n
!
      PRINT *,' Give an integer: '
      READ *,n
      PRINT *,' Using a DO... loop, ',n,'! = ',Fact1(n)
      PRINT *,' Using a WHILE... loop, ',n,'! = ',Fact2(n)
      PRINT *,' Using a recursive function, ',n,'! = ',Factorial(n)
      END
```

Running P-10.8

```
 Give an integer:
 8
Using a DO... loop,  8 ! =  40320
Using a DO WHILE... loop,  8 ! =  40320
Using a recursive function,  8 ! =  40320
```

5

Verify the operation of the program.

Check the results with a calculator.

Problem Discussion

The recursive function Factorial differs from a direct translation of the pseudocode because of some Fortran requirements. The RECURSIVE qualifier keyword is required for recursive functions and subroutines. In the case of a recursive function that calls itself directly, an additional variable name is required to hold the result of the function evaluation. That is, this code is *NOT* allowed:[4]

```
IF (n <= 1) THEN
   Factorial=1
ELSE
   Factorial=n*Factorial(n-1)
```

The required extra variable name, which can be any convenient name, is defined in the RESULT clause in the heading of the function.

The recursive implementation works in the following way. Suppose n = 5. When the function is first called from another program, the ELSE branch of the IF... statement is executed. However, the code Factorial(n-1) is interpreted as another call to the same function. As a result of that call, the local value of n in the function becomes 4. This process continues until, finally, n = 1. Then the assignment n_Fact=1 can be carried out. However, the Fortran environment "remembers" all the previous calls to Factorial in which the requested calculations couldn't be carried out. First it is able to complete the calculation n*Factorial(n-1)=2*1 when n = 2. Then it is able to complete n*Factorial(n-1) = 3*2 when n = 3, 4*6 = 24 when n = 2, and 5*24 when n = 5. Only when the final calculation is complete is control returned to the program that originally called the function.

There isn't really any compelling reason to use a recursive definition for the factorial function. We have done so in this section only because the recursive definition of n! is so easy to understand and translate into Fortran. In fact, recursive algorithms often require more computing resources and execute more slowly than their iterative counterparts. It is also a fact that any algorithm that can be written recursively can be written iteratively, and *vice versa*. However, recursive algorithms are sometimes very simple to write relative to their iterative equivalents. Consequently, speed and computing resources usually are not a problem, and recursive algorithms are often preferred over iterative ones. In the next section, we will discuss a sorting algorithm that is so easy to define recursively that an interative version is rarely seen.

---

[4]This code is shown only because in some other languages that support recursion, it *would* be allowed.

10.5 The Recursive Quicksort Algorithm

1 *Define the problem.*

Recall that the sorting algorithms discussed earlier in this chapter were both $O(N^2)$ algorithms. This means that sorting operations performed on large lists can take a very long time. Find a sorting algorithm that is more efficient and write a program that implements this algorithm.

2 *Outline a solution.*

This is *not* a problem you are expected to solve on your own. First consider Table 10.2, which shows the "effort" required to sort a list containing 128 items and then to sort that list if it can be subdivided into two or more sublists. The initial size of 128 is significant only because it can be evenly subdivided down to size 1. The effort required to sort the original and subdivided lists is an arbitrary measure of computer operations or elapsed time. If an $O(N^2)$ algorithm is used to sort the various sublists, this effort is proportional to N^2 and, for the purposes of this discussion, this value will simply be set equal to N^2. On modern PCs, the actual time required to sort lists of a few hundred items is no more than a second or so, even with $O(N^2)$ algorithms, but lists containing thousands of items can take many seconds to sort. Whether this is of any practical concern depends on the application.

Table 10.2. "Effort" to sort lists with an $O(N^2)$ algorithm, relative units

Number of Lists	"Effort" Required to Sort List(s)
1	$1 \cdot 128 = 16,384$
2	$2 \cdot 64^2 = 8,192$
4	$4 \cdot 32^2 = 4,096$
8	$8 \cdot 16^2 = 2,048$
16	$16 \cdot 8^2 = 1,024$
32	$32 \cdot 4^2 = 512$
64	$64 \cdot 2^2 = 256$
128	$128 \cdot 1^2 = 128$

Listing the time required to sort 128 lists of size 1, as given in Table 10.2, might appear to be pointless because no sorting actually has to be done. However, as we shall soon see, this limiting case isn't as irrelevant as it seems.

The message of Table 10.2 is that it should take only half as long to sort two lists of size N/2 as it does to sort a list of length N, one quarter as long to sort four lists of size N/4, and so forth. Is there some way to take advantage of these savings? Suppose we arbitrarily divide a list of length N into two lists of length N/2; this is an operation that can be done for "free." Can we save time—or operations—simply by sorting these two lists? No, because then the two individually sorted lists have to be merged again and that operation carries its own computational cost that offsets the savings achieved by sorting two shorter lists.

However, suppose we could subdivide a list into two parts so that one sublist, or *partition,* contains "little" values and the other contains "big" values. To do this, select one value in the original list, called the *pivot value,* and use this value to subdivide the list into two partitions, one that contains values less than or equal to the pivot value and the other that contains values greater than or equal to the pivot value:

<= pivot value	>= pivot value

Although the "less than or equal to" and "greater than or equal to" phrases appear to create overlapping lists, this definition is required to account for the special situation where all values in the list are the same.

If we now sort these two partitions, the result is equivalent to sorting the entire list. The algorithm can be stated in three steps.

(1) Divide a list into two partitions, one containing "little" values and the other containing "big" values.
(2) Sort the lefthand partition if it contains more than one value.
(3) Sort the righthand partition if it contains more than one value.

If we can construct the partitions with no computational cost, it's obvious that even if we use an $O(N^2)$ sorting algorithm, we have devised a more efficient approach to sorting a list. Of course, the partitioning can't be done "for free." However, we don't actually have to worry about selecting a sorting algorithm. All we have to do is continue to subdivide these partitions. Eventually, every partition will contain no more than one value. When this occurs, the entire list will be sorted. In effect, the apparently trivial final entry in Table 10.2, sorting 128 lists of size 1, will become a reality. Essentially, we have traded "partitioning effort" for "sorting effort." As it turns out, this will be an excellent trade!

3 *Design an algorithm.*

An approach that involves repetitively performing the same operations until a terminating condition is reached is most naturally expressed as a recursive algorithm:

```
SUBPROGRAM Quicksort(IN/OUT: array; IN: lower,upper)
DEFINE left,right
CALL Partition(array,lower,upper,left,right)
IF first < right THEN CALL Quicksort(array,lower,right)
IF left < last THEN CALL Quicksort(array,left,upper)
```

This is called a Quicksort algorithm. The values *lower* and *upper* arc the boundaries of the original list, or during recursive calls, the subset of the list currently being sorted. In the original call to the subprogram, *lower* and *upper* would typically be 1 and n for a list containing n values. The values *left* and *right* are the lower and upper boundaries of the "righthand" and "lefthand" partitions returned from the *Partition* subprogram:

(original list)

lower   *upper*

```
┌─────────────────────────────────────────────────┐
│                                                 │
└─────────────────────────────────────────────────┘
```

(partitioned list)

lower   *right*   *left*   *upper*

```
┌──────────────────────┐  ┌───────────────────────┐
│                      │  │                       │
└──────────────────────┘  └───────────────────────┘
```

Of course the Quicksort algorithm doesn't sort a list "for free" because, as noted above, the partitioning itself requires computational resources. The first step is to select the pivot value. Table 10.2 implies that the best results will be achieved if each partitioning operation divides a list into equal halves (plus or minus one, depending on whether the list contains an odd or even number of values). Ideally, then, the pivot value should be the median value in the list. However, the median can't be calculated without sorting the list first!

If the list is originally "almost" in order, or in reverse order, a good approximation to the median is the element in the middle of the list. If the list is originally in random order, then there is no "free" way to find the median and, in fact, no way to pick a pivot value that is better than any other value without performing time-consuming operations on the list. Thus, an element in the middle of the list is still as reasonable a choice as any other. The middle element between two specified limits *lower* and *upper* is simply the element (*lower* + *upper*)/2 (assuming integer division).

To illustrate the partitioning process, consider this list of seven random integers:

```
10 -1 14 9 3 11 13
```

The pivot value 9, element $(1 + 7)/2 = 4$, is printed in bold type. Our task is to create two partitions, one that contains elements less than or equal to 9 and the other that contains values no less than 9. How can we produce these two partitions "in place," using the memory locations occupied by the original list?

The answer to this question may not be immediately obvious. Start at the left end of the list and move a "list pointer," which will become an array index in the Fortran implementation, to the right as long as the element is less than 9. Save its location. Now start at the right end of the list and move to the left as long as 9 is less than the element. Save its location. For this example, the left pointer doesn't move at all because the first element (10) doesn't belong in the lower partition. Moving down from the right, the first element that is out of place is 3.

```
L           R
↓           ↓
10 -1 14 9 3 11 13
```

Now exchange these two elements. Increment the left pointer by one position and decrement the right pointer by one position.

```
L       R
↓       ↓
3 -1 14 9 10 11 13
```

Move the left pointer to the right as long as the element is less than 9 and move the right pointer to the left as long as 9 is less than the element. Save the locations. For this example, the right pointer doesn't move at all.

```
L R
↓ ↓
3 -1 14 9 10 11 13
```

Exchange the elements and advance the pointers:

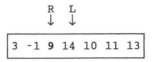

At this point, the right pointer is less than the left pointer, and this is a terminating condition that defines the first two partitions:

Note that the two partitions haven't been sorted because that's not the purpose of creating the partitions. All that has happened is that they are divided into "little" and "big" partitions. Continue to apply this algorithm on the partitions. In each case, the pivot value is printed in bold type.

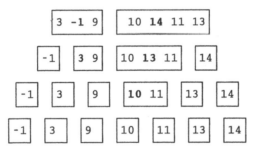

The translation of this process into a complete algorithm requires a great deal of care to ensure that it will produce the appropriate partitions regardless of the size or contents of the sublist being partitioned. There are several problems that can occur when the left and right pointers meet "in the middle" of the list, and it is *very* easy to come up with an algorithm that looks reasonable, but won't work under all conditions. Here is the complete pseudocode for a partitioning algorithm:

```
SUBPROGRAM Partition(IN: array, lower, upper; OUT: left, right)
DEFINE (pivot)
ASSIGN left = lower
       right = upper
       pivot = a[(lower + upper)/2] (use integer division)
LOOP (until right ≤ left)
  (Move up from the left as long as the element is less than pivot.)
```

LOOP (while a(left) < pivot)
          INCREMENT left = left + 1
     END LOOP
(Move down from the right as long as pivot is less than the element.)
          LOOP (while pivot < a(right))
               INCREMENT right = right – 1
          END LOOP
     (Swap if required and increment/decrement pointers.)
          IF (left <= right) THEN
                    IF (left ≠ right) THEN CALL Swap(a(left),a(right))
                    INCREMENT left = left + 1
                              right = right – 1
     (end IF...)
END LOOP

The partitioning part of the Quicksort algorithm is a binary process because it repeatedly divides the list into two parts, and therefore is an $O(\log_2 N)$ algorithm for the same reason that the binary search algorithm is an $O(\log_2 N)$ algorithm. The operations required to form each partition are $O(N)$ because they involve a single rather than a nested loop. Therefore, the Quicksort algorithm is an $O(N\log_2 N)$ algorithm. This is a *major* improvement over $O(N^2)$ algorithms. Consequently, Quicksort is the favored algorithm for general-purpose sorting tasks.

4 *Convert the algorithm into a program.*

The partitioning and Quicksort subprograms can now be combined in a complete program. P-10.9 includes MODULEs plus a driver program that allows testing with small arrays typed at the keyboard. Because Quicksort is the best general-purpose sorting algorithm, it is important that it be as portable as possible. Consequently, the data type of the list to be sorted is defined in a MODULE so multiple code changes won't be required to sort different kinds of lists. The QuickSort and Partition subroutines are also included in the SORT.F90 driver program discussed earlier in the chapter.

P-10.9 [QUIKSORT.F90]

```
      MODULE Quick_Sort
!
      INTEGER a(100),pivot,temp
      CONTAINS
!---------------------------------------------------
      SUBROUTINE Partition(lower,upper,left,right)
!
      IMPLICIT NONE
      INTEGER,INTENT(IN) :: lower,upper
      INTEGER, INTENT(INOUT) :: left,right
!
      left=lower ! Start at bottom and top of list.
      right=upper
      pivot=a((lower+upper)/2)
! Begin post-test loop.
10    CONTINUE
        DO WHILE (a(left)<pivot)
          left=left+1
        END DO
        DO WHILE (pivot<a(right))
          right=right-1
        END DO
        IF (left<=right) THEN
          IF (left/=right) THEN !exchange elements
            temp=a(left)
            a(left)=a(right)
            a(right)=temp
          END IF
          left=left+1
          right=right-1
        END IF
      IF (right>left) GO TO 10
! End post-test loop.
      END SUBROUTINE Partition
!---------------------------------------------------
      RECURSIVE SUBROUTINE QuickSort(lower,upper)
!
      IMPLICIT NONE
      INTEGER left,right
      INTEGER, INTENT(IN) :: lower,upper
!
      CALL Partition(lower,upper,left,right)
      IF (lower<right) CALL QuickSort(lower,right)
      IF ( left<upper) CALL QuickSort(left,upper)
!
      END SUBROUTINE QuickSort
!---------------------------
      END MODULE Quick_Sort
!=============================
```

```
!
      PROGRAM QuikSort
!
! Demonstrate the recursive QuickSort algorithm.
!
      USE Quick_Sort, ONLY : x => a, QuickSort
      IMPLICIT NONE
      INTEGER i,n
!
      PRINT *,' How many values to sort (<=100)? '
      READ *,n
      PRINT*,'Type ',n,' integers...'
      READ*,(x(i),i=1,n)
      PRINT*,(x(i),i=1,n)
!
      CALL QuickSort(1,n)
      PRINT*,(x(i),i=1,n)
      END
```

5 *Verify the operation of the program.*

It is necessary to test this program rigorously under several different conditions. The recursive sorting subroutine is straightforward. However, the partitioning subroutine must be tested to make sure it creates proper partitions for

a. lists already in ascending order
b. lists originally in descending order
c. lists for which all the values are the same
d. small lists containing two or three values

It's easy to observe the results of using the Quicksort program as implemented in P-10.9; either the resulting list is sorted or it's not. However, it is difficult to *guarantee* that the program will work under all circumstances.

Problem Discussion

If a list is consistently subdivided into partitions that aren't of roughly equal size, Quicksort can deteriorate into an $O(N^2)$ algorithm as a result of the work required to partition long lists. As noted above, the optimum dividing point for any list is the median value in the list. However, the median isn't available until the list is sorted, and as a practical matter, the middle value in the list is usually a good compromise.

As a programming detail, note that the *Swap* subprogram in the algorithm design, for exchanging two array elements, is implemented in the code directly within SUBROUTINE Partition. (See the three lines printed in bold italics.)

This is done to minimize the number of variables that have to be redefined if the data type of the array being sorted changes.

Even though Quicksort *could* be implemented as an iterative algorithm (as all recursive algorithms can), this would be a lot more trouble than it's worth. Consequently, even though Quicksort is generally regarded as the best all-purpose sorting algorithm, you will rarely find it discussed in texts devoted to earlier versions of Fortran. Why? Because, as noted earlier, earlier versions of Fortran didn't support recursive functions and subroutines as part of the language standard.

10.6 Applications

10.6.1 Keeping a List of Words in Alphabetical Order

1 Define the problem.

Consider a file containing a list of words sorted in alphabetical order. Assuming that the list is short enough to be stored in an array, write a program that will allow you to add and delete words from the list. Whenever you add a word, the list should be maintained in alphabetical order.

2 Outline a solution.

Deleting an element from an array is straightforward. The problem of maintaining an array in alphabetical order when a new item is added can be solved with a version of the Insertion Sort discussed earlier in this chapter. Basically, all that's required is to add the new word to the end of the list and then determine where it belongs in the list. Be sure to take into account the trivial situation where the new word stays at the end of the list.

The program should be organized as a menu-driven main program that calls subprograms to add and delete words from the list.

3 Design an algorithm.

We include here the design for subprograms to determine the position of a new value in an existing array, to add a new value, and to delete a value.

```
SUBPROGRAM GetPosition(IN: A size; OUT: where)
IF (A(size) ≤ A(1)) THEN
        where = 1
ELSE
        ASSIGN where = size - 1
        LOOP (while A(where) > A(size))
                INCREMENT where = where - 1
        END LOOP
        INCREMENT where = where + 1
(end IF...)
(end GetPosition)


SUBPROGRAM Add(IN/OUT: A, size; IN: new_value)
INCREMENT size = size + 1
ASSIGN A(size) = new_value
IF (A(size) < A(size-1)) THEN
        CALL GetPosition(A,size,where)
        LOOP (for i = size down to where+1)
                ASSIGN A(i) = A(i-1)
        END LOOP
        ASSIGN A(where) = new_value
(end IF...)
(end Add)


SUBPROGRAM Delete(IN/OUT: A, size; IN: where)
LOOP (for i = where to size-1)
        ASSIGN A(i) = A(i+1)
END LOOP
INCREMENT size = size – 1
(end Delete)
```

4 Convert the algorithm into a program.

In contrast to the usual practice in this text, this program doesn't completely solve the stated problem because it is only a demonstration program that operates on numbers typed at the keyboard. Its purpose is to test the required subroutines for solving the original problem. Conversion of this program into the intended application is left as an end-of-chapter exercise.

P-10.10 [INSERT2.F90]

```
      MODULE DataDef
        IMPLICIT NONE
        INTEGER size,where,max_size
        REAL a(22),value
        PARAMETER (max_size=22)
!
      END MODULE DataDef
!
      MODULE InsertSubs
        CONTAINS
!
      SUBROUTINE GetPosition
      USE DataDef, ONLY : a,size,where
      IMPLICIT NONE
!
      IF (a(size) .LE. a(1)) THEN
        where=1
      ELSE
        where=size-1
        DO WHILE (a(where) .GT. a(size))
          where=where-1
        END DO
        where=where+1
      END IF
      PRINT*,' Put ', a(size),' in position ',where
      END SUBROUTINE GetPosition
!--------------------------------
      SUBROUTINE Add
! Inserts a value in an array at a specified location.
!
      USE DataDef, ONLY : a,size,value,where
      IMPLICIT NONE
!
      size=size+1
      a(size)=value
      IF (a(size) .LT. a(size-1)) THEN
        CALL GetPosition
        a(where+1:size)=a(where:size-1)
        a(where)=value
      ENDIF
!
      END SUBROUTINE Add
!------------------------
      SUBROUTINE Remove
!
! Removes an element at specified location.
!
      USE DataDef, ONLY : a,size,where
      IMPLICIT NONE
!
      a(where:size-1)=a(where+1:size)
      size=size-1
!
      END SUBROUTINE Remove
!
      END MODULE InsertSubs
!============================
```

```fortran
      PROGRAM Insert
!
! MS-DOS file name INSERT2.F90.
! Demonstrate an insertion algorithm that keeps a list sorted.
!
      USE DataDef
      USE InsertSubs
      IMPLICIT NONE
      INTEGER i
      CHARACTER choice
! Create an array of integers in ascending order.
      size=20
      DO i=1,size
        a(i)=2*i
      END DO
      CALL PrintList
      choice=' '
!
      DO WHILE (choice .NE. 'q')
        PRINT*,'(a)dd or (r)emove value, or (q)uit?'
        READ*,choice
        SELECT CASE (choice)
        CASE ('a')
          IF (size .LT. max_size) THEN
            PRINT*,' Give a number to add to this list:'
            READ*,value
            CALL Add
            CALL PrintList
          ELSE
            PRINT*,"Can't add a number to this list."
          END IF
        CASE ('r')
          PRINT*,' Give position of a number to remove from list'&
                  ,' between 1 and ',size
          READ*,where
          IF ((where .GE. 1) .and. (where .LE. size)) THEN
            CALL Remove
            CALL PrintList
          ELSE
            PRINT*,'Position is out of range.'
          END IF
        CASE ('q')
        CASE DEFAULT
          PRINT*,'INPUT ERROR - THIS CHOICE NOT AVAILABLE'
        END SELECT
      END DO
!
      CONTAINS ! internal subroutine
      SUBROUTINE PrintList
        IMPLICIT NONE
        INTEGER j
        DO j=1,size
          WRITE(*,1000,advance='no')a(j)
        END DO
        PRINT *
1000    FORMAT(f5.1)
      END SUBROUTINE PrintList
      END PROGRAM
```

Running P-10.10

```
   2.0  4.0  6.0  8.0 10.0 12.0 14.0 16.0 18.0 20.0 22.0 24.0 26.0
28.0 30.0 32.0 34.0 36.0 38.0 40.0
 (a)dd or (r)emove value, or (q)uit?
a
  Give a number to add to this list:
13
  Put    13.000000  in position  7
   2.0  4.0  6.0  8.0 10.0 12.0 13.0 14.0 16.0 18.0 20.0 22.0 24.0
26.0 28.0 30.0 32.0 34.0 36.0 38.0 40.0
 (a)dd or (r)emove value, or (q)uit?
r
  Give position of a number to remove from this list between
 1 and   21
5
   2.0  4.0  6.0  8.0 12.0 13.0 14.0 16.0 18.0 20.0 22.0 24.0 26.0
28.0 30.0 32.0 34.0 36.0 38.0 40.0
 (a)dd or (r)emove value, or (q)uit?
a
  Give a number to add to this list:
41
   2.0  4.0  6.0  8.0 12.0 13.0 14.0 16.0 18.0 20.0 22.0 24.0 26.0
28.0 30.0 32.0 34.0 36.0 38.0 40.0 41.0
 (a)dd or (r)emove value, or (q)uit?
q
```

5 *Verify the operation of the program.*

Test P-10.10 by adding and deleting elements at each end and at the middle of the list.

Problem Discussion

Subroutines Add and Remove in P-10.10 use some "shorthand" Fortran 90 array manipulation techniques to reassign elements of the array. The relevant statements, which allow assignments to be made to all or part of an array without writing explicit loops, are printed in bold italics. Array manipulation functions will be discussed in more detail in Chapter 12.

10.6.2 Evaluating Legendre Polynomials

1 *Define the problem.*

A special set of functions called Legendre polynomials are sometimes required in science and engineering applications. Table 10.3 gives the Legendre polynomials $P_n(x)$ for $0 \leq n \leq 7$.

Table 10.3. The first eight Legendre polynomials

n	$P_n(x)$
0	1
1	x
2	$(3x^2 - 1)/2$
3	$(5x^3 - 3x)/2$
4	$(35x^4 - 30x^2 + 3)/8$
5	$(63x^5 - 70x^3 + 15x)/8$
6	$(231x^6 - 315x^4 + 105x^2 - 5)/16$
7	$(429x^7 - 693x^5 + 315x^3 - 35x)/16$

Legendre polynomials of any order n>2 can be generated with a recursion relation:

$$R_n(x) = \frac{2n-1}{n} x R_{n-1}(x) - \frac{n-1}{n} R_{n-2}(x)$$

Write a recursive function to evaluate the Legendre polynomial for any value of n and x, where n > 0

2 *Outline a solution.*

The solution involves implementing the recursive relationship and testing it with a driver program.

3 *Design an algorithm.*

SUBPROGRAM *Legendre(IN: n and x)*
IF *n = 0* **THEN ASSIGN** *Legendre(0,x) = 1*
ELSE IF *n = 1* **THEN ASSIGN** *Legendre(1,x) = x*
ELSE ASSIGN *Legendre(n,x) = ... (see problem statement for*
                              recursive definition)

4 *Convert the algorithm into a program.*

P-10.11 includes hard-coded evaluations for the first eight Legendre polynomials, to help verify correct operation of the function.

P-10.11 [LEGENDRE.F90]

```
      MODULE Poly
!
      CONTAINS
!
      RECURSIVE REAL FUNCTION Legendre(n,x) RESULT(LegendrePoly)
      IMPLICIT NONE
      INTEGER, INTENT(IN) :: n
      REAL, INTENT(IN) :: x
!
      IF (n==0) THEN
        LegendrePoly=1.
      ELSE IF (n==1) THEN
        LegendrePoly=x
      ELSE
        LegendrePoly=(2.*REAL(n)-1.)/REAL(n)*x*Legendre(n-1,x)- &
                (REAL(n)-1.)/REAL(n)*Legendre(n-2,x)
      END IF
      END FUNCTION Legendre
! - - - - - - - - - - - - - - - - - - - - - - -
      END MODULE Poly
! ================================
```

```
      PROGRAM LegendreTest
!
! MS-DOS file LEGENDRE.F90
! Calculate Legendre polynomials using a recursive relationship.
!
      USE Poly, ONLY : Legendre
      IMPLICIT NONE
      INTEGER i
      REAL x
      x=.5
      PRINT *,'n=0-7 from recursive function, x=0.5'
      DO i=0,7
         PRINT *,Legendre(i,x)
      END DO
! Check against the first 8 functions (from tables)
      PRINT *,'n=0-7 from tabulated polynomials, x=0.5'
      PRINT *,0.
      PRINT *,1.
      PRINT *,(3.*x**2-1.)/2.
      PRINT *,(5.*x**3-3.*x)/2.
      PRINT *,(35.*x**4-30*x**2+3.)/8.
      PRINT *,(63.*x**5-70.*x**3+15.*x)/8.
      PRINT *,(231.*x**6-315.*x**4+105.*x**2-5.)/16.
      PRINT *,(429.*x**7-693.*x**5+315.*x**3-35.*x)/16.
!
      END
```

Running P-10.11

```
 n=0-7 from recursive algorithm, x=0.5
  1.0000000
  0.5000000
 -0.1250000
 -0.4375000
 -0.2890625
  8.9843750E-02
  0.3232422
  0.2231445
 n=0.7 from tabulated polynomials, x=0.5
  1.0000000
  0.5000000
 -0.1250000
 -0.4375000
 -0.2890625
  8.9843750E-02
  0.3232422
  0.2231445
```

5 *Verify the operation of the program.*

Compare program output with polynomials evaluated using tabulated values. This comparison has been included in P-10.11, but the code still should be checked against tabulated listings of the functions.

10.7 Debugging Your Programs

10.7.1 Programming Style

The ideal program always takes advantage of previously written code whenever possible. Even if existing code sometimes needs minor revisions, it is usually preferable to make these revisions than to start "from scratch." This policy helps to minimize errors in algorithms that originally may have required a great deal of thought and careful coding. Whenever possible, existing algorithms should be incorporated into your program through MODULE structures.

10.7.2 Problems With Programs

As indicated at the beginning of this chapter, it's possible to use the subroutines and functions discussed in this chapter even if you don't completely understand them. However, you *do* need to test each of them thoroughly in the context of your own application. The MODULE and USE statements make it relatively easy to incorporate these subprograms into your own programs. Especially with the searching and sorting subroutines, changes in the types of data you are using may cause problems. However, these are easy to spot because data type inconsistencies will cause syntax errors. Make sure you understand the data type and purpose of any parameter in a call to a subroutine or function.

As always, it's a good idea to apply any program you write to familiar data. If your program needs to search for something in a list, ask it to search for a value you know is there. Does it find it? Ask your program to search for a value you know isn't there. Does it respond in a useful way? If you're sorting a list, try your program initially on several short lists in various orders and check the results carefully.

If you've written a FUNCTION, recursive or otherwise, to evaluate a mathematical function, be sure to test your program by calculating values that can be checked against at least one other source, such as a published tabulation of values for the function.

By the time you reach this chapter, you should be reasonably proficient at finding syntax and obvious logical errors in programs. Do not be lulled into complacency by the ease with which you can now write programs that don't crash! No matter how proficient a programmer you become, you will *always* need to be concerned about the performance of your programs. This attitude is especially important when you write subprograms that will be reused in other programs, often without additional thought about their performance. Your best safeguard is a permanently suspicious attitude toward any answer provided by a computer program.

10.8 Exercises

10.8.1 Self-Testing Exercises

Exercise 1. Describe in your own words the two most important concepts you have learned from this chapter.

Exercise 2. Describe in your own words how you could use in your own programs a problem-solving skill demonstrated in a program described in this chapter.

Exercise 3. Show a "worst case" binary search scenario for guessing an integer value between 1 and 130.

Exercise 4. Here are two examples of an array of integers followed by the modifications performed on the contents after several "trips" through the outer loop of a sorting algorithm. Which algorithm has been used in each case? Complete the implied steps until the array is sorted.

(a)
```
13.3 7.9 2.2 33.0 0.9 4.5 18.6
0.9 7.9 2.2 33.0 13.3 4.5 18.6
0.9 2.2 7.9 33.0 13.3 4.5 18.6
0.9 2.2 4.5 33.0 13.3 7.9 18.6
(and so on)
```

(b)
```
13.3 7.9 2.2 33.0 0.9 4.5 18.6
0.9 7.9 2.2 33.0 13.3 4.5 18.6
0.9 2.2 7.9 33.0 13.3 4.5 18.6
0.9 2.2 7.9 33.0 13.3 4.5 18.6
0.9 2.2 7.9 13.3 33.0 4.5 18.6
(and so on)
```

Exercise 5. Using the original array from the previous exercise, show how a Quicksort algorithm would partition the array to produce an array that is sorted in *descending* order.

10.8.2 Basic Programming Exercises

Exercise 6. Modify P-10.1 so that it returns a LOGICAL value of .true. or .false. depending on whether the target value is found.

Exercise 7. The searching algorithms implemented in this chapter are case-sensitive when they look for words. That is, if the word "Zebra" is in the list, the algorithm will not find the word "zebra." Modify the linear and binary searching algorithms so they will perform a case-insensitive search for words in a list.

Exercise 8. Here is some pseudocode for the "Bubble Sort" algorithm, a very inefficient $O(N^2)$ algorithm. Write a subroutine that applies this algorithm to n elements of an array a. This is just a programming exercise. The Bubble Sort algorithm is inferior to the others described in this chapter, and there is no reason actually to use it.

```
LOOP (j = n down to 2)
     LOOP (i = 2 to j)
          IF a(i) < a(i-1) THEN CALL Swap(a(i),a(i-1))
     END LOOP
END LOOP
```

Exercise 9. Write a driver program to test the Selection Sort and Insertion Sort subroutines in P-10.5 and P-10.6.

Exercise 10. Rewrite the three sorting algorithms and their corresponding subroutines in this chapter so that they sort a list in descending rather than ascending order.

Extra Credit
Modify one or more of the sorting subprograms so that a "flag" in the parameter list allows the user to indicate whether she wants the list sorted in ascending or descending order.

Exercise 11. Generate a list of words and apply the three sorting algorithms in this chapter to the list. As the sorting subroutines are currently written, the result of sorting words will be case-sensitive. That is, the word "Zebra" will come before the word "aardvark" because uppercase "Z" comes before lowercase "a" in the ASCII collating sequence. When you sort your list of words, do you want the result to be case-insensitive or case-sensitive? Make sure your program implements your choice correctly.

Extra Credit

Modify one or more of the sorting subroutines so you can pass a "flag" in the parameter list to tell the subprogram when you're sorting a list of words and whether you want the result to be case-sensitive or case-insensitive.

Exercise 12. Referring to the application in Section 10.6.1, keeping a list of words in sorted order, modify P-10.10 so that it completes this application. Create your own list of a dozen or so words in alphabetical order and then add and delete several words from that list. Remember that the algorithm is case-sensitive unless you write code to convert words to all uppercase or all lowercase before you compare them.

Exercise 13. Based on material from other courses you are taking, state a computational problem that requires one or more of the subprograms described in this chapter. Write a complete program to solve the problem, using one or more of the subroutines or functions given in this chapter. Describe any modifications you make to whatever subprograms you use.

10.8.3 Programming Applications

Exercise 14. A database of drugs contains the name of the drug, the recommended maximum daily dose, and the recommended maximum cumulative dose. In some cases, both the daily and cumulative maximums are assumed to be proportional to body weight and are given in the database for a 150-pound individual of either gender. In some cases, drugs may be approved for only men or only women. The maximum dose for a drug that is not approved is given as 0.

Proposed treatments for patients are also available in a database. The information includes the proposed drug, the gender and weight of the patient, the proposed daily dose, and the number of days the treatment will last.

Write a program that will read and store drug information in an array and will then read and process a file containing information about proposed treatments. Search through the drug file for the drug name given in a proposed treatment. If the proposed treatment exceeds either the maximum daily or the cumulative dose, print an appropriate message. Assume that the daily dose remains constant throughout the treatment. Account for the possibility that one or more proposed treatments will include drugs that are not yet entered into the drug database.[5]

Sample data files, which can be downloaded from the World Wide Web site mentioned in Section i.5 of the Preface, include DRUGBASE.DAT (the drug

---

[5]This problem was inspired by a widely reported incident in 1995 in which a breast cancer patient at a major cancer treatment center died because chemotherapy drugs were administered at several times the approved dose. I *hope* the drug names I have made up don't actually exist!

database) and `DRUGBASE.IN` (the treatment database). You should add records to `DRUGBASE.IN` to ensure that all program branches are tested. (That is not currently the case.) [`DRUGBASE.F90`]

`DRUGBASE.DAT`

	Maximum dose: P = weight-dependent, with value for 150 lb			
Drug Name	Daily (M)	Cum (M)	Daily (F)	Cum (F)
abracap	P2.3	100	3.0	100
betalit	0.5	10	0.5	100
deproved	P0.01	0.05	0	0
ethicoo	P0	0	500	5000
gonagain	1.5	15	1.5	10
heptez	0.001	0.05	0.0005	0.025

`DRUGBASE.IN`

drug	wt.	daily, mg	days
abracap	M 300	900	10
gonagain	F 120	.1	200
newdrug	F 135	100	20

Exercise 15. In Section 10.2.3, it was suggested that a binary search could be combined with a linear search to find all the occurrences of a specified value in the list. Using a sorted list that contains some duplicate values (the data type of items in the list can be whatever you like), write a subroutine that uses a binary search to find one occurrence of a value and then searches backward and forward in the list to find all occurrences of that value. [`BIN_SRCH.F90`]

Exercise 16. Especially if a large sorted list contains many duplicate values, it may make sense to construct an index to values in the array. An index array will hold this kind of information in a `TYPE` structure:

value	first location	number of values
17	1	10
19	11	41
22	52	13
33	65	17
(and so on)		

For the value 19, for example, the index array indicates that the first 19 is in element 11 and that there are 41 values of 19 altogether.

Create a data file based on these and a few additional values. Then write a program that generates an index array and uses the array to search for and display all occurrences of a specified value. When you test your program, be sure to include a test for a value that doesn't exist in the array. The assumption is that the index array is small compared to the array being searched. If so, you could justify using a linear search of the index array. However, as long as the indexed values (the left-hand column in the example) are sorted, you can also apply a binary search to this array. [INDEX_TO.F90]

Exercise 17. Under special conditions, it's possible to devise an O(N) sorting algorithm. Suppose you wish to sort a large list of lowercase letters initially in random order and stored in an array A. There are only 26 possible values, a number that is assumed to be much smaller than the number of letters to be sorted. A Counting Sort takes advantage of this situation. Here is an outline of the algorithm.

1. Define an index array with 26 elements, one for each letter of the alphabet.

2. Read through the array of letters A. Convert each letter to an integer in the range 1–26 and increment the corresponding element of the index array by one. When you're done, the index array will contain the number of a's, b's, and so on.

3. Read through the index array from positions 2–26 and set each element equal to itself plus the previous element. When you're done, the index array will contain the last position occupied by each letter in a new sorted array. For example, if the original list contains 23 a's, 33 b's, and 41 c's, the first three elements of the index array will be 23, 56, and 97.

4. Read through the original array of letters. Convert each letter to an integer in the range 1–26 and use this value to access the corresponding element in the index array. Put the letter into its indicated position in the B array, which will hold the sorted data. Then decrement the value in the index array by 1. Consider the example in step 3. Here's what will happen in this loop:

```
Letter in A  Letter in B  1st 3 Components of Index Array
                          23  56  97 (original contents)
a            B(23)=a      22  56  97
a            B(22)=a      21  56  97
b            B(56)=b      21  55  97
b            B(55)=b      21  54  97
b            B(54)=b      21  53  97
c            B(97)=c      21  53  96
```

The first letter in the A array is an "a." It goes in element 23 of the B array. The first element in the index array is decremented by 1, from 23 to 22. The next letter in A is also an "a." It goes in element 22 of the B array, and the first element in the index array is decremented again. The third letter in the A array is a "b." It goes in element 56 of the B array, and the second element of the index array is decremented by 1. This continues until all the letters have been placed in the B array.

5. Print the list of sorted letters.

Hint: use this statement function to convert a lowercase letter to an integer in the range 1–26:

```
LetterIndex(letter)=IACHAR(letter)-IACHAR('a')+1
```

Note that this algorithm doesn't contain any nested loops; that's why it's an O(N) algorithm. Also, it should be clear that the second array B isn't actually required to sort letters because a sorted array of letters can easily be created just by overwriting the original A array with the appropriate number of a's, b's, and so on. However, the algorithm has been written this way, with two arrays, in order to make possible the Extra Credit part of this problem, in which all the original values in the A array must be saved.

Extra Credit

Create an array of words in random order. (The "words" could just be random combinations of letters.) Use a Counting Sort to put all words starting with "a" together, all words starting with "b" together, and so forth. You can use the index array to determine the first and last positions for words beginning with "a," "b," and so on. Then use Quicksort to sort words beginning with the same letter. This is an efficient way to sort a large list of words. [KNT_SORT.F90]

Exercise 18. Write a complete program that uses a recursive function to calculate the nth value in the Fibonacci series. The Fibonacci numbers are defined like this for positive values of n:

$$F(n)= 1, n=1 \text{ or } n=2$$
$$F(n)=F(n-1)+F(n-2), n>2$$

This gives values 1, 1, 2, 3, 5, 8, 13,.... Some botanists have suggested that the growth pattern of leaves around the stem of a plant or the pattern of seeds in a sunflower head can be described by the Fibonacci series. Also, the growth in rabbit populations, for example, has been modeled using the Fibonacci series.

Extra Credit

The irrational number $(\sqrt{5}-1)/2 \approx 0.6180339$ is the so-called "golden ratio" that plays a role in attempts to ascribe a mathematical definition to the concept of "beauty" in nature and architecture. The sides of a standard 3"×5" index card have approximately this ratio (0.6). The golden ratio appears often in the proportions of classical Greek architecture, and speculation about the role of this ratio in nature and its relationship to the Fibonacci series was popular in the nineteenth century.

1. Verify that the golden ratio is the result of dividing a straight line into two segments such that the ratio of the longer segment to the total length of the line is identical to the ratio of the shorter segment to the longer segment: BC/AB = AB/AC. (This is an algebra program, not a programming problem!)

```
A          B      C
•—————————•———————•
```

2. Use the function you have written to verify that the sequence formed by the ratio of successive Fibonacci numbers, 1/1, 1/2, 2/3, 3/5, 5/8, 8/13, ... approaches the golden ratio for large n. [FIBONACI.F90]

Exercise 19. The binary search algorithm lends itself to a recursive implementation. Create a modification of P-10.3 that performs a recursive binary search. From the point of view of the calling (sub)program, this function should perform identically to P-10.3. [BIN_RCUR.F90]

Exercise 20. Bessel functions are sometimes encountered in advanced engineering and science mathematics (for example, to describe electric charge configurations in cylindrical coordinates). Write a function to calculate what are referred to as "ordinary Bessel functions of the first kind" for orders 0 and 1. A definition for these functions is

$$J_0(x) \approx \left(1 - \frac{u^2}{1 \cdot 1}\left(1 - \frac{u^2}{2 \cdot 2}\left(1 - \frac{u^2}{3 \cdot 3}\left(1 - \dots - \frac{u^2}{n \cdot n}\right)\right)\right)\right)\dots$$

$$J_1(x) \approx u\left(1 - \frac{u^2}{1 \cdot 2}\left(1 - \frac{u^2}{2 \cdot 3}\left(1 - \frac{u^2}{3 \cdot 4}\left(1 - \dots - \frac{u^2}{n \cdot (n+1)}\right)\right)\right)\right)\dots$$

where $u = x/2$. Figure 10.1 illustrates these functions.

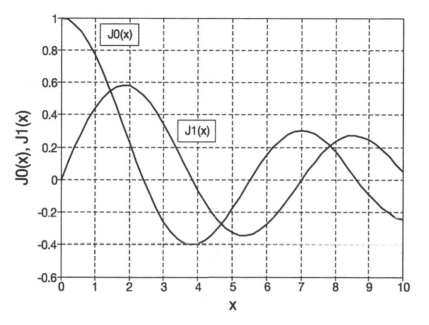

Figure 10.1. Bessel functions of order 0 and 1

The most straightforward way to evaluate the nested multiplications in the definition of the Bessel functions is to use a recursive algorithm. Use these two functions:

```
REAL FUNCTION BesselFunction(order,x)

RECURSIVE REAL FUNCTION BesselCalc(order,u,k,n)
```

The first of these functions is called from the (sub)program that needs the Bessel function. The parameter list includes only the order (0 or 1) and the value of x at which the function is to be evaluated. The first function calls the second, which recursively evaluates n terms inside the large brackets in the definition and then multiplies the result by 1 or u (u^{order}). The larger the value of n, the more terms are evaluated.

The second of these two functions, the recursive one, does the "bookkeeping" for the recursive calls, which is of no interest to the calling (sub)program. The argument needed directly for the calculation is u rather than x, and the parameter k keeps track of which of the n terms is currently being evaluated. The first call to `BesselCalc` from inside `BesselFunction` is with k = 1. The terminating branch of the recursive function evaluates the innermost term when k = n; for example, $1 - u^2/(n \cdot n)$ for $J_0(x)$.

Note: it is important to verify the limitations on the numerical accuracy of this method of evaluating Bessel functions. It should be clear from examining the definitions for these functions that, for fixed n, they will become more inaccurate as x increases. With increased precision for REAL numbers (in excess of 12 significant digits) and 100 terms in the series expansion, it is possible to obtain values accurate to about six significant digits for values of x up to no more than 10. For a discussion of how to increase the precision of REAL numbers, see Chapter 12. [BESSEL.F90]

Extra credit
Higher-order Bessel functions of the first kind may be obtained with the recursive relation

$$J_{n+1}(x) = \frac{2n}{x} J_n(x) - J_{n-1}(x)$$

Write another recursive function to return the value of Bessel functions of the first kind for a specified order. Be sure to investigate the computational limitations on this method.

Exercise 21. Maze traversal is a common recursive algorithm discussed in programming courses. Although this is "just a game," it is a very useful problem because it requires a different way of thinking about algorithms and problem solving, and it illustrates the power of recursive algorithms to solve certain kinds of computing problems.

Suppose a maze is represented as a two-dimensional array of "walls" and "corridors." Enter the maze at the upper-left ("northwest") corner. The only exit from the maze is in the lower-right ("southeast") corner.

An algorithm that will find its way out from any point in the maze M(row,col), assuming that such a path exists, can be expressed like this:[6]

IF (M(row,col) is the southeast corner) THEN
    done
ELSE
    Mark M(row,col) as trial step along the path out of the maze.
    Now try all four directions.
    IF *M(row,col) is not on right boundary* **THEN**
        travel to the right
    IF *(not done) and (M(row,col) not on lower boundary)* **THEN**
        travel down

---

[6]This algorithm follows the one described in W. Findlay and D. A. Watt's 1978 text, *PASCAL: An Introduction to Methodical Programming* (Computer Science Press).

> **IF** (not done) and (M(row,col) not on left boundary) **THEN**
>   travel left
> **IF** (not done) and (M(row,col) not on top boundary) **THEN**
>   travel up

(end IF...)
IF done **THEN**
    Mark M(row,col) as a final step on the path out of the maze.

The phrases "travel to the right," "travel down," and so forth., mean "If the next square in the indicated direction is not a wall, then move to that square and find a path out of the maze from that square."

However, "find a path out of the maze from that square" is identical to the original problem, starting from the new square. Therefore, all these calculations should be done in a procedure that calls itself at the appropriate points. [MAZE.F90]

Exercise 22. The Towers of Hanoi problem is another famous programming exercise that is often presented as a striking example of the power of recursive algorithms. In theory, an algorithm that is written iteratively can also be written recursively, and *vice versa*. However, one implementation is often conceptually simpler than the other.

The Towers of Hanoi problem can be stated as follows. Suppose ten rings, graduated in size from largest on the bottom to smallest on top, are stacked on a pole. Nearby are two other poles. The object is to move the stack of ten rings from their original pole to one of the other poles, using the third pole as a "working space" during the transfer. There are only two rules governing how the rings can be moved.

(1) Only one ring at a time may be moved.
(2) At no time can a larger ring be moved onto a smaller ring.

It takes some thought and planning to figure out how the transfers should be made. Consider a simpler problem involving only four rings. If the original pole is numbered A, the destination pole is C, and the intermediate pole is B, the required transfers are shown in Table 10.4.

Table 10.4. Transfers for the Towers of Hanoi problem when n=4

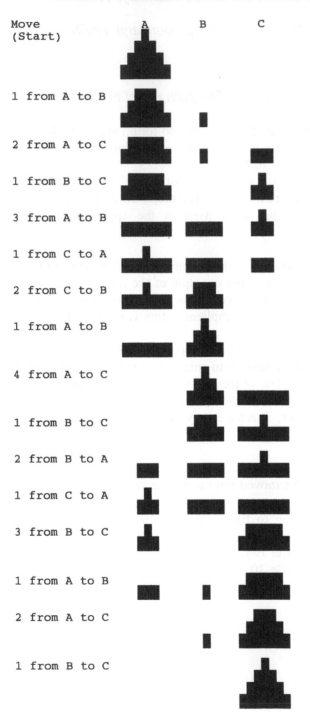

Move (Start)	A	B	C
1 from A to B			
2 from A to C			
1 from B to C			
3 from A to B			
1 from C to A			
2 from C to B			
1 from A to B			
4 from A to C			
1 from B to C			
2 from B to A			
1 from C to A			
3 from B to C			
1 from A to B			
2 from A to C			
1 from B to C			

This transfer requires 15 moves. In general, moving n rings from one pole to another requires $2^n - 1$ moves.

Although it might not be obvious how to instruct a program to make a large number of moves in what seems like a complicated pattern, it is actually easy to write an algorithm for moving n rings in a programming language that supports recursion. Consider this statement of the problem of moving n rings from A to C.

1. Move n-1 rings from A to B.
2. Move the nth ring from A to C.
3. Move n-1 rings from B to C.

This solution takes a typical recursive approach of defining one level of a problem's solution in terms of a previous level. Specifically, the problem of moving n rings is stated in terms of the problem of moving n-1 rings. If the algorithm makes successive recursive calls with argument n-1, the problem of moving n rings can be reduced to the point that, eventually, the only problem the algorithm needs to "solve" directly is the trivial problem of moving one ring! The algorithm design looks like this:

DEFINE *(n as initial number of rings, start, aux, and final as strings)*
INITIALIZE *start = 'start'*
            aux = 'aux'
            final = 'final'
CALL *MoveRings(n, start, aux, final)*
(end of program)

SUBPROGRAM *MoveRings(n, start, aux, final)*
IF *n_rings > 0* **THEN**
        CALL *MoveRings(n_rings-1, start, final, aux)*
        WRITE *("Transfer ring ", n_rings, "from'",start, "to ", final)*
        CALL *MoveRings(n_rings-1,aux,start,final)*
ELSE
        WRITE *("Transfer ring ", n_rings, "from", start, "to", final)*
(end IF)
(end SUBPROGRAM)

The Fortran subroutine header could look like this:

```
RECURSIVE SUBROUTINE MoveRings(n,start,aux,final)
```

Using this algorithm as a guide, write a complete program to solve the Towers of Hanoi problem. The printed output from the program should consist of a series of messages, similar to those in Table 10.4, that indicate which ring will be moved from which initial position to which final position.

You may find it hard to believe that such an apparently difficult problem can be solved with so little code, but this is typical of recursive algorithms. Such algorithms work because of the way recursive calls to subroutines keep track of the local values of their parameters.[7] The variables start, aux, and final are initially given the values 'start', 'aux', and 'final', but these values change when the recursive calls are made. Remember that start, aux, and final are CHARACTER variables. Don't confuse their names with values assigned to these variables. [TOWERS.F90]

Exercise 23. As director of a wildlife tracking project, one of your jobs is to collect field reports of radio tracking data and enter them in a database. Each report consists of a tracking number for each animal, the date, and two coordinates. For the purposes of this problem, the coordinates are arbitrary real numbers. A small sample set of reports might look like this:

```
101    05/05/95    55.3   44.8
101    05/06/95    57.1   43.4
102    05/05/95    66.0   13.3
102    06/01/95    66.8   22.1
102    06/05/95    69.0   25.7
101    06/01/95    50.0   50.9
```

Note that the tracking reports for a particular animal aren't necessarily consecutive, but all reports for each animal are in chronological order. Assume that the tracking reports file will eventually be too large to be held in an array.

Write a program that will perform these three functions.

1. Add reports to the database.
2. Print out all the tracking reports for a specified animal.
3. Print all reports for a specified date.

One way to do this is to maintain the file as a so-called "linked list" for both dates and animals. In the Fortran implementation of this problem, define a TYPE structure like this:

---

[7]This information is maintained on the "runtime stack." To find out more about this, consult a text that would be used to teach programming or data structures (usually in C or C++) in an introductory computer science course.

```
TYPE TrackType
  INTEGER ID
  CHARACTER*8 date
  REAL x,y
  INTEGER SameAnimal,SameDate
END TYPE TrackType
```

The variables `SameAnimal` and `SameDate` are "pointers"[8] that point to the next report on the same animal and the next report on the same date. If the reports are maintained in a binary date file, then the pointers are file indices. For example, in the above example, the first mention of animal 101 is in the first record of the file. Additional references are found in records 2 and 6. Animal 102 is found in records 3, 4, and 5. The date 05/05/95 appears in record 1 and again in record 3.

To construct this linked database, create two additional files: an index file for animals and an index file for dates. In each file, the first index is for the *first* occurrence of that animal or date and the second index is for the *last* occurrence. These files, which can be text files, could look like this for the above example, which has reports for two animals and four different dates:

(animal index file)			(date index file)		
000	0	0	00/00/00	0	0
101	1	6	05/05/95	1	3
102	3	5	05/06/95	2	2
			06/01/95	4	6
			06/05/95	5	5

The "dummy record" at the head of each file allows us to create these index files even before the first tracking reports are processed. This will simplify programming because the index files can always be assumed to exist. Your program can also assume that these index files will always be small relative to the tracking reports file, and that their contents can be held in two arrays in memory; use an appropriate `TYPE` definition for each array.

To add a new report to the database, add the report to a new record at the end of the file and look for the animal code in the animal index file. If it doesn't exist, add the new code and set both index values to the record where the new report will be stored. If the animal code already exists, go to the record holding the last previous entry and update the pointer to point to the new record. Then update the "last pointer" value in the animal index file to point to the new record. Follow the same procedure for updating the date index file.

To print all reports for a specified animal, first look for its code in the animal index file. Then use the first index (the value in the second column of the file) to locate the first report. Use the pointer from the `SameAnimal` field in the

---

[8]Although the concept is similar, this use of the word "pointers" is not the same as the programming implementation of this term in languages such as Fortran 90, C, and Pascal. The implementation of pointers as part of a programming language is not discussed in this text.

record to locate the next record. To find all records for the specified animal, follow the pointers through the file. When the pointer to the next record is 0, then you are at the end of the list of reports for that animal. Follow the same procedure to print all reports for a specified date. [WILDLIFE.F90]

Basic Statistics and Numerical Analysis With Fortran

Statistical and numerical analysis are among the most important applications of Fortran. In this chapter, algorithms are presented for calculating basic descriptive statistics and some typical problems in numerical analysis, including differentiation and integration, solving systems of linear equations, finding roots of equations, and numerical solutions to differential equations. The code for many of the algorithms is incorporated into a MODULE that you can use in your own programs. Each of the sections includes a typical application and is independent of the other sections.

11.1 Introduction

This chapter will describe algorithms for basic descriptive statistics and for some standard problems in numerical analysis. These include

✗ mean, standard deviation, and linear regression

✗ numerical differentiation and integration

✗ finding the roots of a function

✗ solving systems of linear equations

✗ numerical solutions to differential equations

The topics in this chapter require a greater degree of mathematical sophistication than earlier material. Although the text does not presume to provide all the necessary background, the discussion of each topic includes at least a sketchy mathematical introduction.

It is an extreme understatement to point out that there are several possible approaches to the numerical analysis problems discussed in this chapter, which are quite properly the subject of entire texts and courses. For each of these problems, this text will discuss just one simple approach and will present a complete solution in the form of an algorithm and a complete MODULE that you can include in your own programs.

In this chapter, applications are included with each section of the chapter rather than at the end. In this way, each section is independent of the others. For example, if you understand algebraic equations, you should be able to understand the section that deals with solving systems of linear equations, which does not rely on calculus, even if you bypass the sections on numerical differentiation and integration, which do require some understanding of calculus. To further underscore the independence of each section, equations are numbered starting with (1) within each section.

Although the algorithms discussed in this chapter will work satisfactorily for a wide range of problems, it is a mistake to apply them blindly. For many kinds of realistic problems, more robust algorithms will be needed to minimize computational problems.[1] It is extremely important to remember that *all* numerical methods have inherent limitations. Quantification of those limitations is largely absent from the discussions in this chapter not because it is unimportant, but because an appropriate treatment lies well beyond the scope of this text. In spite of this *caveat*, it is equally true that it never hurts to try the relatively simple algorithms presented here, as long as you are willing to retain a healthy skepticism about the results.

11.2 Basic Descriptive Statistics

Statistical characterization of data is essential in all areas of science and engineering. Hence some basic algorithms for this task are essential tools for any programmer. This section is restricted to the statistics of normal distributions and linear regression. The results will not be derived, but will simply be stated in a way that facilitates their computation.

11.2.1 The Sample Mean and Standard Deviation

Consider a collection of measurements x that are *assumed* to be drawn from a normally distributed population. These measurements can be characterized by two quantities: their **arithmetic mean** and their **standard deviation**. The arithmetic mean, what is commonly called the average, m of n such measurements is defined as

arithmetic mean
standard deviation
variance

$$m = \frac{\sum x_i}{n} \tag{1}$$

---

[1]There is an entire software industry built around the development of Fortran subroutines to solve difficult problems in numerical analysis. In fact, the continued popularity of Fortran as a language for scientists and engineers is due in large part to these subroutine libraries.

The standard deviation s is a measure of the variability in the data. It is defined as the square root of the *variance* s^2:

$$s^2 = \frac{\sum (x_i - m)}{n - 1} \tag{2}$$

This definition can be put into a form that is easier to calculate and doesn't require that the mean be calculated ahead of time:

$$s^2 = \frac{\sum x_i^2 - (\sum x_i)^2/n}{n - 1} \tag{3}$$

The standard deviation has the property that approximately 68 percent of all normally distributed measurements of a quantity will be within $\pm s$, 95 percent within $\pm 2s$, and 98 percent within $\pm 3s$. The "plus or minus three standard deviations" rule is sometimes used as a basis for discarding measurements lying outside these limits; this may or may not be a good idea, depending on the application and the nature of the quantity being measured.[2]

Because tables of cumulative probabilities are based on the standardized normal variable z, having a mean of 0 and a standard deviation of 1, it is often desirable to transform the mean and standard deviation of a set of measurements into the corresponding standardized normal variable. For any measurement x,

$$z = \frac{x - m}{s} \tag{4}$$

Figure 11.1 illustrates the standard normal distribution, which for obvious reasons, is referred to as the "bell curve."

---

[2]The existence of the now-famous Antarctic "ozone hole" was confirmed in the 1980s only after scientists rewrote satellite data analysis algorithms to accept measurements that had previously been rejected by such a statistical test.

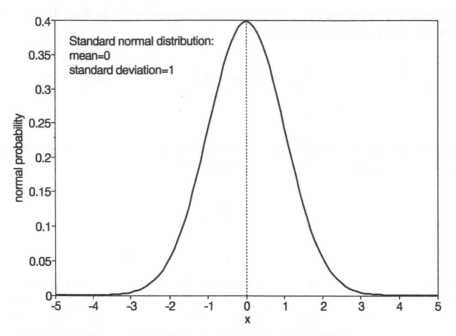

Figure 11.1. The standard normal distribution

Especially for small sets of data, it is important to distinguish between the *sample* mean and standard deviation m and s and the *population* mean and standard deviation, usually denoted by μ and σ. The former are available from direct observation, but the latter are usually unknown; it is often assumed that sample statistics are the same as population statistics. The n − 1 in the denominator of the formula for standard deviation is there specifically because s is the sample standard deviation and not the population standard deviation. For small data sets, this has the effect of increasing the sample standard deviation compared to the population standard deviation. To put it another way, the smaller the sample, the greater the uncertainty about the properties of the entire population from which the sample is drawn.

11.2.2 Linear Regression and the Linear Correlation Coefficient

Assume that a collection of measurements has been taken of a quantity y that is a function of an independent variable x. Assume that these data can be represented by an equation of form

$$y(x) = a + bx \tag{5}$$

where a and b are the intercept and slope of a straight line called the **regression line**. In general, this linear relationship will be an imperfect representation of both the *observed* and the *actual* relationship between x and y, either because there is noise in the system or because the relationship is not really linear. Linear regression attempts to determine the values of a and b that *best* represent the data, assuming that a linear relationship is a reasonable choice for the data being examined.

The usual definition of the "best" representation uses the **sum of squares**, defined as the sum of the squares of the differences between measured and modeled values of y:

$$\text{sum of squares} = \Sigma(y_i - y_{model})^2 \tag{6}$$

The method of least squares assumes that the best values of a and b are those that minimize the sum of squares for a particular set of measurements. These parameters are given by

$$a = \frac{(\sum y_i)(\sum x_i^2) - (\sum x_i)(\sum x_i y_i)}{n\sum x_i^2 - (\sum x_i)^2}$$

$$b = \frac{n\sum x_i y_i - (\sum x_i)(\sum y_i)}{n\sum x_i^2 - (\sum x_i)^2} \tag{7}$$

The **standard error of estimate** of y on x is a measure of the variability about the regression line. It is obtained from

$$s_{y,x}^2 = \frac{\sum y_i^2 - a\sum y_i - b\sum x_i y_i}{n - 2} \tag{8}$$

The value n − 2 in the denominator once again reflects the fact that this statistic is calculated from a sample of measurements rather than an entire population. The standard error of estimate of y on x has properties similar to the standard deviation. If lines are drawn parallel to and at vertical distances $s_{y,x}$, $2s_{y,x}$, and $3s_{y,x}$ above and below the best-fit regression line, 68 percent, 95 percent, and 99.7 percent of the measurements will fall within these lines.

One quantitative measure of the applicability of a linear regression model is given by the **correlation coefficient** *correlation coefficient*. This is a dimensionless quantity in the range [-1,+1] that is equal to the ratio of the explained variation in a set of data to the total variation, with respect to the best-fit regression line:

$$r = \pm\sqrt{\frac{\text{explained variation}}{\text{total variation}}} = \pm\sqrt{1 - s_{y,x}^2/s_y^2} \tag{9}$$

The explained variation is equal to the total variance s_y^2 of all the measurements calculated using equation (2) or (3) from Section 11.2.1, minus the square of the standard error of estimate $s_{y,x}$. When r is +1, all the data lie exactly along the regression line, with positive slope. A negative value of r denotes a regression line with negative slope. When r equals 0, y and x are totally unrelated to each other; that is, a value of x provides *no* information about what the corresponding value of y might be. Intermediate values of r indicate that a linear relationship is only partially successful as a model to explain the behavior of y as a function of x. Note that a linear model for data with a strong *random* component, as opposed to an inherently nonlinear relationship, can still be reasonable even if the correlation coefficient isn't close to 1.

When, as is often the case, a regression line is forced to pass through the coordinates (0,0) (*i.e.*, it is required that y=0 when x=0), the slope is the only coefficient required for the model

$$b = \frac{\sum y_i}{\sum x_i} \tag{10}$$

and the standard error of estimate of y on x is given by

$$s_{y,x}^2 = \frac{\sum y_i^2 - 2b\sum x_i y_i + b^2\sum x_i^2}{n - 2} \tag{11}$$

We can now develop algorithms and a program.

1 *Define the problem.*

Create one or more subprograms for calculating the basic descriptive statistics described above.

2 *Outline a solution.*

The solution should include one subprogram for calculating mean and standard deviation and another for performing linear regression on a set of data. In each case, the data will be held in one or more appropriate arrays.

3 *Design an algorithm.*

We will create two algorithms, one for the mean and standard deviation and the other for linear regression. In the first algorithm, we will include a test on the variance as a precaution to make sure it is non-negative *before* taking the square root to calculate the standard deviation. However, the variance should never be less than 0. If the data have a standard deviation of 0, which requires all the measurements to be the same, then it is possible for arithmetic roundoff errors to produce a very small negative value for the variance.

We will also include in the first algorithm a provision for calculating either the population or the sample standard deviation, as specified by a user-supplied character "flag." For experimental data, as noted above, the sample statistic is generally accepted as the appropriate choice.

SUBPROGRAM *NormalStats(IN: A (array of real numbers),*
n (# of elements), flag (character);
OUT: avg, std_dev)
DEFINE *sum, sum_sq, variance, i (loop counter)*
ASSIGN *sum = (sum elements of A)*
sum_sq = (sum elements of A^2)
CHOOSE *(between flag= 'p' for population stats and 's' for sample stats)*
'p': **ASSIGN** *variance = (sum_sq + sum^2/n)/n*
's': **ASSIGN** *variance = (sum_sq + sum^2/n)/(n-1)*
IF *variance ≥ 0* **THEN**
ASSIGN *std_dev = $variance^{1/2}$*
ELSE
WRITE *(appropriate message?)*
ASSIGN *std_dev = some "error" value (optional?)*
(end IF...)
ASSIGN *avg = sum/n*

For the linear regression analysis, there are two choices to be made: one for population or sample statistics and the other for a regression line that either is or isn't forced through (0,0). This subprogram requires *NormalStats* as part of the calculations for the correlation coefficient. Note that the intercept parameter *a* is declared as an *IN/OUT* variable. This is because its value on input is used to determine whether the regression should be forced through (0,0); if that value is other than 0, a "full" regression is assumed. Note that the standard error of estimate is also included in the output.

SUBPROGRAM *LinearRegression(IN: x, y (arrays), n, flag (character);*
IN/OUT: a; OUT: b, s_yx, r)
DEFINE *sum_x, sum_y, sum_xy, sum_xx, sum_yy, temp, avg, std_dev*
i (loop counter)
ASSIGN *sum_x = (sum elements of x)*
sum_y = (sum elements of y)
sum_xy = (sum elements of x•y)
sum_yy = (sum elements of y•y)
(Get regression parameters.)
IF *(a ≠ 0)* **THEN** *(calculate full regression)*
ASSIGN *temp = n•sum_xx - sum_x²*
a = (sum_y•sum_xx-sum_x•sum_xy)/temp
b = (n•sum_xy - sum_x•sum_y)/temp
s_yx = ((sum_yy-a•sum_y-b•sum_xy)/n)¹ᐟ²
ELSE *(just calculate slope)*
ASSIGN *b = sum_y/sum_x*
s_yx = ((sum_yy – 2•b•sum_xy + b²•sum_xx)/n)¹ᐟ²
IF *(flag = 's')* **THEN ASSIGN** *s_yx = s_yx•(n/(n-2))¹ᐟ² (for sample stats)*
(Get correlation coefficient.)
CALL *NormalStats(y,n,flag,avg,std_dev)*
ASSIGN *r = [1 – (s_yx/std_dev)²]¹ᐟ² (assume std_dev is OK)*

Several sums over the components of data vectors, as defined in equations (7), (8), (10), and (11), are required in this algorithm. For reasons that will become clear when the code is written, these sums are represented with "shorthand" **ASSIGN** statements in the algorithm.

4 Convert the algorithm into a program.

P-11.1 packages these algorithms in a MODULE that also includes a subroutine to generate data from a linear relationship with a superimposed "noise signal." To save space, this code isn't included in the program listing, but it can be found in the STATS.F90 source code file, which can be downloaded from the World Wide Web site mentioned in Section i.5 of the Preface.

P-11.1 [STATS.F90]

```
      MODULE DescriptiveStats
!
      CONTAINS
!----------------------------------------------------
      SUBROUTINE NormalStats(a,n,flag,avg,std_dev)
!
! Basic descriptive statistics for normally distributed data.
! Calculates either sample or population statistics.
! Sets std_dev = -1 if error condition is detected.
!
      IMPLICIT NONE
      INTEGER, INTENT(IN) :: n
      REAL, INTENT(IN) :: a(n)
      CHARACTER, INTENT(IN) :: flag ! 'P' or 'S' statistics
      REAL, INTENT(OUT) :: avg,std_dev
      REAL sum_,sum_sq,variance
!
      sum_=SUM(a)
      sum_sq=DOT_PRODUCT(a,a)
      SELECT CASE (flag)
        CASE ('p','P')
          variance=(sum_sq-sum_**2/n)/n
        CASE ('s','S')
          variance=(sum_sq-sum_**2/n)/(n-1)
        CASE DEFAULT
          PRINT *," FROM NormalStats: FLAG ERROR, 'P' assumed"
          variance=(sum_sq-sum_**2/n)/n
      END SELECT
      IF (variance < 0.) THEN !an error condition exists
        PRINT *,' FROM NormalStats: NEGATIVE VARIANCE', variance
        std_dev=-1
      ELSE
        std_dev=SQRT(variance)
      END IF
      avg=sum_/n
!
      END SUBROUTINE NormalStats
!-----------------------------------------------------------
      SUBROUTINE LinearRegression(x,y,n,flag,a,b,s_yx,r)
!
! For data to be represented by y=a+bx, calculates linear
! regression coefficients, sample standard error of y on x, and
! sample correlation coefficient.  Sets r=0 if error condition
! exists.  If the intercept coefficient a is set to 0 on input,
! the regression is forced through (0,0).
!
      IMPLICIT NONE
      INTEGER, INTENT(IN) :: n
      REAL, INTENT(IN) :: x(n),y(n)
      CHARACTER, INTENT(IN) :: flag !'P' or 'S' statistics
      REAL, INTENT(OUT) :: b,s_yx,r
      REAL, INTENT(INOUT) :: a
      REAL avg,std_dev
      REAL sum_x,sum_y,sum_xy,sum_xx,sum_yy,temp
!
```

```fortran
      sum_x=SUM(x)
      sum_y=SUM(y)
      sum_xy=DOT_PRODUCT(x,y)
      sum_xx=DOT_PRODUCT(x,x)
      sum_yy=DOT_PRODUCT(y,y)
      IF (a /= 0.) THEN !calculate full regression
        temp=n*sum_xx-sum_x**2
        a=(sum_y*sum_xx-sum_x*sum_xy)/temp
        b=(n*sum_xy-sum_x*sum_y)/temp
        s_yx=SQRT((sum_yy-a*sum_y-b*sum_xy)/n)
      ELSE !just calculate slope
        b=sum_y/sum_x
        s_yx=SQRT((sum_yy-2.*b*sum_xy+b*b*sum_xx)/n)
      END IF
      SELECT CASE (flag)
        CASE ('p','P')
        CASE ('s','S')
          s_yx=s_yx*SQRT(REAL(n)/REAL(n-2))
        CASE DEFAULT
          PRINT *," FROM LinearRegression: FLAG ERROR, 'P' assumed"
      END SELECT
!   Use NormalStats to get standard deviation of y.
      CALL NormalStats(y,n,flag,avg,std_dev)
      IF (std_dev > 0.) THEN
        temp=1.-(s_yx/std_dev)**2
        IF (temp >= 0.) THEN
          r=SQRT(temp)
        ELSE ! an error condition exists
          r=0.
          PRINT *,'FROM LinearRegression: ERROR CONDITION',temp
        END IF
      ELSE ! an error condition exists
        r=0.
      END IF
      END SUBROUTINE LinearRegression
!--------------------------------
      SUBROUTINE NormalArray(a,n)
!
! Generates an array of normal random numbers from
! pairs of uniform random numbers in range 0<=x<1.
!
      IMPLICIT NONE
      INTEGER, INTENT(IN) :: n
      REAL, INTENT(OUT) :: a(n)
      INTEGER i
      INTEGER Count(1) ! for random number generator
      REAL pi,u1,u2
      PARAMETER (pi=3.1415927)
!
      CALL System_Clock(Count(1))
      CALL Random_Seed(Put=Count)
      CALL Random_Number(a) !fills array with uniform random
      DO i=1,n,2
        u1=a(i)
        u2=a(i+1)
        IF (u1 == 0.) u1=1e-15 ! u must not be 0
        IF (u2 == 0.) u2=1e-15
        a(i)  =SQRT(-2.0*LOG(u1))*COS(2.0*pi*u2)
        a(i+1)=SQRT(-2.0*LOG(u2))*SIN(2.0*pi*u2)
      END DO
```

```
        IF (MOD(n,2) /= 0) THEN !there's one extra element
          IF (a(n) == 0.) a(n)=1e-15
          a(n)=SQRT(-2.0*LOG(a(n)))*SIN(2.0*pi*a(n))
        END IF
!
        END SUBROUTINE NormalArray
!----------------------------
        END MODULE
!=====================
        PROGRAM Stats
!
        USE DescriptiveStats
        IMPLICIT NONE
        REAL x(500),y(500),avg,std_dev
        REAL a,b  ! intercept and slope for linear regression
        REAL s_yx ! standard error of estimate of y on x
        REAL corr ! correlation coefficient
        INTEGER n ! # of points in array
        INTEGER i
        DATA n/100/
!
! Test basic statistics...
        CALL NormalArray(x,n)
        CALL NormalStats(x,n,'p',avg,std_dev)
        PRINT *,' population mean and std dev: ',avg,std_dev
        CALL NormalStats(x,n,'s',avg,std_dev)
        PRINT *,' sample mean and std dev: ',avg,std_dev
! Test linear regression...
        CALL NormalArray(y,n)
! Create a linear relationship with "noise"...
        DO i=1,n
          x(i)=i
          y(i)=2.*i+10.*y(i)
        END DO
! Set a /= 0 for full regression analysis.
        a=1.
        CALL LinearRegression(x,y,n,'s',a,b,s_yx,corr)
        PRINT *,' FOR FULL REGRESSION...'
        PRINT *,'                regression coefficients: ',a,b
        PRINT *,' standard error of estimate of y on x : ',s_yx
        PRINT *,'                correlation coefficient: ',corr
! Set a=0 for regression forced through (0,0)
        a=0.
        CALL LinearRegression(x,y,n,'s',a,b,s_yx,corr)
        PRINT *,' FOR REGRESSION FORCED THROUGH (0,0)...'
        PRINT *,'                regression coefficients: ',a,b
        PRINT *,' standard error of estimate of y on x : ',s_yx
        PRINT *,'                correlation coefficient: ',corr
!
        END
```

Running P-11.1

```
population mean and std dev:     0.2155715   0.9041344
sample mean and std dev:     0.2155715   0.9086893
FOR FULL REGRESSION...
        regression coefficients:     4.1518574  1.9581977
        standard error of estimate of y on x : 9.2461329
        correlation coefficient:     0.9870095
FOR REGRESSION FORCED THROUGH (0,0)...
        regression coefficients:     0.0000000E+00   .0404127
        standard error of estimate of y on x :     9.5518789
        correlation coefficient:     0.9861301
```

5 *Verify the operation of the program.*

The code in P-11.1 contains some safeguards against potential problems with the calculations—primarily taking the square root of a negative number. However, these safeguards don't test the code itself. The only way to verify the accuracy of all the code is to check it carefully and compare results against an example worked through by hand. Even though normal statistics aren't intended to be applied to very small samples, the calculations themselves can be checked adequately with a data set of only three or four "measurements."[3]

Programming Tip

An important feature of this program is its use of the implicit function DOT_PRODUCT, used previously in the vector operations application in Section 8.7.1, and the SUM function, which returns a scalar value equal to the sum of the elements of its array arguments. The availability of these functions greatly reduces the amount of code and pseudocode that would otherwise be required to initialize sums and increment them inside loops.

Use of the SUM function explains the otherwise rather odd variable name sum_. If you *didn't* use the SUM function in P-11.1, then it would be OK to call a variable sum. That is, a local definition will override the association of the word "sum" with a Fortran intrinsic function of the same name. This holds true in general, so you can redefine the name of *any* Fortran intrinsic function in a program. This doesn't seem like a very good idea!

---

[3]If you have access to a spreadsheet, it should include built-in functions for performing these calculations. Make sure you understand whether your spreadsheet calculates population or sample statistics; some spreadsheets have separate functions for each.

11.3 Numerical Differentiation

11.3.1 Newton's and Stirling's Formulas

Consider the function f(x). The derivative f'(x) is the rate of change of f(x) with respect to x. Although the derivatives of analytic functions are usually available without much difficulty,[4] rates of change are often required for experimental data. For example, you might collect data as a function of time and then require an estimate of rates of change with respect to time based on those data. In either case, an estimate of a function's rate of change can be obtained by calculating the slope between two evaluations of the function at two closely spaced values of x. Here are three intuitive formulas based on a simple graphical interpretation of the derivative as the slope of a function:

$$f'(x) \approx [f(x+\Delta x) - f(x)]/\Delta x \qquad \text{(Newton's forward formula)} \qquad (1)$$

$$f'(x) \approx [f(x+\Delta x) - f(x-\Delta x)/]/(2\Delta x) \qquad \text{(Stirling's formula)} \qquad (2)$$

$$f'(x) \approx [f(x) - f(x-\Delta x)]/\Delta x \qquad \text{(Newton's backward formula)} \qquad (3)$$

where Δx is a small interval. The second of these formulas averages the calculation in the forward and backward directions and seems generally the best choice. Note that it does not matter whether a function has been evaluated analytically at $x \pm \Delta x$ or whether the Δx's correspond to some interval between experimental data.

These formulas are trivial to implement in Fortran. However, there are reasons to be cautious in their application. They and similar higher order versions are basically polynomial approximations. Even if the difference between f(x) and its polynomial approximation is small, there is no guarantee that the same is true of the difference between an analytic derivative and the polynomial approximation to that derivative. Additionally, for functions whose derivatives can become large (in absolute magnitude), it is important to select appropriately small values of Δx; the criteria may not always be obvious.

If the formulas are used to approximate rates of change for experimental data, the dominant error source is most likely the data themselves, through the independent or dependent variable or some combination of the two. Suppose measurements are taken as a function of time so that the interval Δx becomes Δt. In general, you would expect that the best approximation to the derivative would be obtained when Δt is small. However, because Δt appears in the denominator,

---

[4]The availability of symbolic algebra systems such as Maple V means that even "difficult" analytic derivatives can be obtained with little effort.

small errors in measuring time intervals can produce approximations to the derivative that are wildly in error. (For an example of the problems that can arise with time measurements, recall Exercise 16 in Chapter 9. In that problem, estimates of the speed of a commuter train were in error because time intervals between 0.1–mile distance markers were measured only to the nearest second.)

In some experimental situations, therefore, it might be preferable to approximate the data with a well-behaved analytic function whose derivative can be calculated analytically; this is a tradeoff between representing accurately all measurements of a dependent variable and "smoothing" the numerically generated rates of change of that variable. (An end-of-chapter exercise explores this process.) In other situations, a numerical derivative is actually the desired result. Suppose production cost data are available monthly for a manufacturing facility. A backward formula using this month's and last month's costs gives the true rate of change in sales from last month to this month; there is no reason to think of this value as an approximation.

Table 11.1 Distance and speed as a function of time

time	distance	speed
0	0.00	0
1	4.90	9.80
2	19.60	19.60
3	44.10	29.40
4	78.40	39.20
5	122.50	49.00
6	176.40	58.80
7	240.10	68.60
8	313.60	78.40
9	396.90	88.20
10	490.00	98.00
11	592.90	107.80
12	705.60	117.60
13	828.10	127.40
14	960.40	137.20
15	1102.50	147.00
16	1254.40	156.80
17	1416.10	166.60
18	1587.60	176.40
19	1768.90	186.20
20	1960.00	196.00

11.3.2 Application. Estimating the Speed of a Falling. Object

1 *Define the problem.*

Table 11.1 gives time, distance, and speed for an object accelerating under the influence of gravity (9.8 m/s^2), ignoring air resistance. (See the file FALLING.DAT, which can be downloaded from the World Wide Web site mentioned in Section i.5 of the Preface.) Suppose time and distance are measured. Distance is measured accurately, but time is measured with an error in the range ±0.2 s. Write a program that simulates such measurements and uses them to estimate the speed as a function of time using an appropriate approximation formula.

2 *Outline a solution.*

When an object is accelerating, a backward approximation formula will underestimate the true speed. For example, using the values for distance at t = 0 and t = 1, the estimated speed is 4.9/ = 4.9 m/s—half the true value. For the same reason, a forward formula will overestimate the speed. Therefore, Stirling's formula is the best choice from the three possibilities previously discussed. If the acceleration is constant and there are no errors in any of the measurements, this formula will yield the actual speed.

The solution to this problem should include a general-purpose subprogram that approximates the derivative using Stirling's formula. (See Equation (2) above.) Its implementation is straightforward. However, note that the original definition of Stirling's formula assumes that the interval Δx between f(x) and its forward and backward values is the same. This is an unnecessary assumption and one that may not be true when experimental data are being used. (In this problem, the true time intervals are equal, but because of the random component, the measured time intervals will not be equal, in general.) Therefore, replace the definition of Stirling's formula with:

$$f'(x_2) = \frac{[f(x_2)-f(x_1)]/(x_2-x_1) + [f(x_3)-f(x_2)]/(x_3-x_2)}{2} \qquad (4)$$

The main program should read the data file and use the subprogram to calculate the speed, assuming that there is a random error in the time measurement. It will be adequate for this problem to assume that time errors are linearly distributed over the range ±0.2 s.

3 *Design an algorithm.*

The design of a subprogram to implement this version of Stirling's formula is trivial.

SUBPROGRAM *Stirling(IN: $x_1, x_2, x_3, y_1, y_2, y_3$; OUT: derivative)*
ASSIGN *derivative=[($y_2 - y_1$)/($x_2 - x_1$)+($y_3 - y_2$)/($x_3 - x_2$)]/2*

The design of the driver program is straightforward, and no algorithm design should be required.

4 *Convert the algorithm into a program.*

P-11.2 [FALLING.F90]

```
      MODULE Numerical_Differentiation
!
      CONTAINS
!-------------------------------------------------
      REAL FUNCTION Stirling(x1,x2,x3,y1,y2,y3)
!
      IMPLICIT NONE
      REAL, INTENT(IN) :: x1,x2,x3,y1,y2,y3
!
      Stirling=((y2-y1)/(x2-x1)+(y3-y2)/(x3-x2))/2.
      END FUNCTION Stirling
!-------------------------------------------------
      END MODULE Numerical_DIfferentiation
!=================================================
      PROGRAM Falling
!
! Driver for numerical differentiation routines.
!
      USE Numerical_Differentiation, ONLY : Stirling
      IMPLICIT NONE
      TYPE fall_data
        REAL true_time
        REAL true_distance
        REAL measured_time
      END TYPE fall_data
      TYPE(fall_data) fall(0:20)
      REAL g,x,true_speed,speed
      INTEGER i,n,Count(1)
      PARAMETER (g=9.8) !m/s**2 (gravitational acceleration)
!
      OPEN(1,file='c:\ftn90\source\falling.dat')
!
! Get data...
!     (Read past 1 header line.)
      READ(1,*)
      CALL System_Clock(Count(1))
      CALL Random_Seed(Put=Count)
      n=-1
10    n=n+1
        READ(1,*,end=900)fall(n)%true_time,fall(n)%true_distance
        CALL Random_Number(x)
        fall(n)%measured_time=fall(n)%true_time+x*.4-.2
        PRINT 1000,fall(n)%true_time,fall(n)%true_distance, &
                   fall(n)%measured_time
      GO TO 10
900   CLOSE(1)
      n=n-1
! Calculate numerical derivative...
      PRINT *,'  true meas.      true        true'
      PRINT *, &
  '  time  time  distance      speed      speed speed/(true speed)'
```

```
        DO i=1,n-1
          speed=Stirling(fall(i-1)%measured_time, &
                         fall(i  )%measured_time, &
                         fall(i+1)%measured_time, &
                         fall(i-1)%true_distance, &
                         fall(i  )%true_distance,&
                         fall(i+1)%true_distance)
          true_speed=Stirling(fall(i-1)%true_time, &
                              fall(i  )%true_time, &
                              fall(i+1)%true_time, &
                              fall(i-1)%true_distance, &
                              fall(i  )%true_distance,&
                              fall(i+1)%true_distance)
          PRINT 1010,fall(i)%true_time,fall(i)%measured_time, &
                     fall(i)%true_distance,true_speed,speed, &
                     speed/true_speed
        END DO
!
1000    FORMAT(1x,f6.2,2f10.3)
1010    FORMAT(1x,2f6.2,3f10.3,f10.2)
        END
```

Running P-11.2

```
 0.00      0.000     -0.025
 1.00      4.900      1.028
 2.00     19.600      1.989
 3.00     44.100      2.891
 4.00     78.400      3.836
 5.00    122.500      5.049
 6.00    176.400      6.075
 7.00    240.100      6.859
 8.00    313.600      7.951
 9.00    396.900      9.153
10.00    490.000     10.026
11.00    592.900     11.015
12.00    705.600     12.015
13.00    828.100     12.879
14.00    960.400     13.977
15.00   1102.500     14.863
16.00   1254.400     15.800
17.00   1416.100     17.095
18.00   1587.600     17.817
19.00   1768.900     18.919
20.00   1960.000     20.163
true meas.        true          true
time time    distance         speed       speed speed/(true speed)
 1.00  1.03      4.900         9.800       9.977      1.02
 2.00  1.99     19.600        19.600      21.224      1.08
 3.00  2.89     44.100        29.400      31.726      1.08
 4.00  3.84     78.400        39.200      36.330      0.93
 5.00  5.05    122.500        49.000      44.449      0.91
 6.00  6.07    176.400        58.800      66.873      1.14
 7.00  6.86    240.100        68.600      74.250      1.08
 8.00  7.95    313.600        78.400      68.316      0.87
 9.00  9.15    396.900        88.200      88.001      1.00
10.00 10.03    490.000        98.000     105.319      1.07
11.00 11.02    592.900       107.800     108.320      1.00
12.00 12.02    705.600       117.600     127.282      1.08
13.00 12.88    828.100       127.400     131.184      1.03
14.00 13.98    960.400       137.200     140.462      1.02
15.00 14.86   1102.500       147.000     161.244      1.10
16.00 15.80   1254.400       156.800     143.435      0.91
17.00 17.10   1416.100       166.600     181.278      1.09
18.00 17.82   1587.600       176.400     201.073      1.14
19.00 18.92   1768.900       186.200     159.018      0.85
```

5 *Verify the operation of the program.*

These calculations are easy to verify with a calculator.

Problem Discussion

The array in P-11.2 has been dimensioned $0:20$ because $t = 0$ is the first value. Because Stirling's formula requires values from one step backward and one step forward, the loop to calculate and display speed starts at $i = 1$ and ends at $n - 1$. There is no loss of information at $t = 0$ because the speed is zero. However, the speed at the final time step cannot be calculated using this method.

The code in P-11.2 applies to experimental data taken at discrete values of an independent variable, even though the data for this particular problem have been generated with an analytic function so that results from the numerical procedure can be evaluated. In general, experimental data may not correspond to an analytic function, so there may not even *be* an analytic derivative for comparison.

However, suppose you wish to estimate the derivative of an analytic function—one whose value exists and can be calculated *everywhere* over a range of interest. (You may also wish to require that the analytic derivative of the function exists as well, and that it can be calculated everywhere over the range, even though you don't know what it is.) Then a function that calculates Stirling's formula can take a slightly different form,

```
REAL FUNCTION Stirling_f(F,dx)
```

where F is the name of a function passed from the calling program and dx is the interval over which the backward and forward values are to be calculated. The implementation of Stirling_f is left as an end-of-chapter exercise.

11.4 Numerical Integration

11.4.1 Polynomial Approximation Methods

It is often the case that functions cannot be integrated analytically. Such functions don't even have to be very complicated. (See the next Application in this Section.) In such a situation, numerical integration techniques must be used. There are several widely used methods, including those that use polynomials to "piece together" an approximation of a function $y = f(x)$. We will develop algorithms for three closely related polynomial approximation methods: the Rectangular Rule, the Trapezoidal Rule, and Simpson's Rule. These all have in common the fact that the integration range of the independent variable is divided into many intervals of equal size.

The Rectangular Rule is the easiest algorithm to understand because it has a simple graphical interpretation. Assume the value of $y = f(x)$ is known for any value of x in the range $[x_1,x_2]$. The integral of $f(x)$ over the range x_i to x_f can be approximated by dividing the range into n equal segments of length Δx and taking the sums of the function evaluated at the midpoints of each segment,

$$\int_{x_1}^{x_2} f(x)\,dx \approx \left(\sum_{i=1}^{n} f(x_i - \Delta x/2) \right) \Delta x \tag{1}$$

where $x_i = x_1 + i \cdot \Delta x$. This process is illustrated in Figure 11.2, although in practice many more than eight subdivisions of the integration interval would be used.

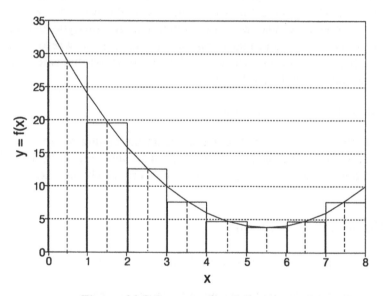

Figure 11.2 Rectangular Rule integration

Trapezoidal Rule integration also has a simple graphical interpretation. The integral of a function $y = f(x)$ between two closely spaced points x and $x + \Delta x$ can be approximated by the area of the trapezoid formed by the points $(x,0)$, $(x,f(x))$, $(x + \Delta x, f(x + \Delta x))$, and $(x + \Delta x, 0)$. To put it another way, the integral can be approximated by the average of $f(x)$ evaluated at x and $x + \Delta x$, multiplied by Δx:

$$\int_{x}^{x+\Delta x} f(x)\,dx \approx \frac{[f(x) + f(x+\Delta x)]\Delta x}{2} \tag{2}$$

Hence, assuming that the range $[x_1,x_2]$ is divided into n equal intervals of size Δx, the integral of $f(x)$ over that range can be approximated by

$$\int_{x_1}^{x_2} f(x)\,dx \approx \left(\sum_{i=0}^{n-1} [f(x_i)+f(x_i+\Delta x)]\right)\frac{\Delta x}{2} = \frac{[f(x_1) + f(x_2)]\Delta x}{2} + \Delta x\sum_{i=1}^{n-1} f(x_i) \qquad (3)$$

where $x_i = x_1 + i\cdot\Delta x$. (See Exercise 25 and Figure 2.13 in Chapter 2.)

Simpson's Rule integration is similar in principle to the other two; it approximates the integral of $f(x)$ over the range from $x-\Delta x$ to $x+\Delta x$ by a second-order polynomial. For the range x_1 to x_2 divided into n equal intervals of size Δx, where n must be an even number, it can be shown that

$$\int_{x_1}^{x_2} f(x)\,dx \approx \left(\sum_{i=2,4,6,\dots}^{n} [f(x_{i-2}) + 4f(x_{i-1}) + f(x_i)]\right)\frac{\Delta x}{3}$$

$$= \left(f(x_1) + f(x_2) + 4\sum_{i=1,3,5,\dots}^{n-1} f(x_i) + 2\sum_{i=2,4,6,\dots}^{n-2} f(x_i)\right)\frac{\Delta x}{3} \qquad (4)$$

where $x_i = x_1 + i\cdot\Delta x$.

1 *Define the problem.*

Write a subprogram that integrates functions that can't be integrated analytically.

2 *Outline a solution.*

Write a driver program for testing Simpson's Rule integration using a function whose analytic integral is known or whose numerically integrated values are tabulated.

3 *Design an algorithm.*

Algorithms for Rectangular Rule and Trapezoidal Rule integration are left as end-of-chapter exercises. The algorithm for Simpson's Rule is this:

SUBPROGRAM (IN: F, x_1, x_2, n_steps; OUT: integral)
DEFINE (odd sum, even sum, i)
ASSIGN $\Delta x = (x_2 - x_1)/n\_steps$
INITIALIZE odd sum = 0
            even sum = 0
LOOP (for i = 1 to n_steps-1, steps of 2)
        INCREMENT odd sum = odd sum + F(x_1 + i•Δx)
END LOOP
LOOP (for i = 2 to n_steps-2, steps of 2)
        INCREMENT even sum = even sum + F(x_1 + i•Δx)
END LOOP
ASSIGN integral = [F(x_1) + F(x_2) + 4•(odd sum) + 2•(even sum)]•Δx/3

4

Convert the algorithm into a program.

P-11.3 contains code for a function that implements this algorithm. The function can be found in the MODULE that is part of program NUM_INT.F90, which can be downloaded from the World Wide Web site mentioned in Section i.5 of the Preface.

P-11.3 (see NUM_INT.F90)

```
      MODULE NumericalIntegration
!
      CONTAINS
!----------------------------------------------------
      REAL FUNCTION SimpsonsRule(F,x1,x2,n_steps)
!
! Does numerical integration using Simpson's Rule.
!
      IMPLICIT NONE
      REAL, INTENT(IN) :: x1,x2
      REAL sum_odd,sum_even
      INTEGER, INTENT(IN) :: n_steps
      REAL dx
      INTEGER i
!---------------------------
      INTERFACE
        REAL FUNCTION F(x)
          REAL, INTENT(IN) :: x
        END FUNCTION F
      END INTERFACE
!---------------------------
      dx=(x2-x1)/n_steps
      sum_odd=0.
      DO i=1,n_steps-1,2
        sum_odd=sum_odd+F(x1+REAL(i)*dx)
      END DO
      sum_even=0.
```

```
        DO i=2,n_steps-2,2
          sum_even=sum_even+F(x1+REAL(i)*dx)
        END DO
        SimpsonsRule=(F(x1)+F(x2)+4.*sum_odd+2.*sum_even)*dx/3.
!
        END FUNCTION SimpsonsRule
!----------------------------
        END MODULE NumericalIntegration
!====================================
        MODULE FunctionDefinition
!
        CONTAINS
!-------------------------
        REAL FUNCTION FofX(x)
!
! This is the cumulative probability function for the
! normal function. Its integral doesn't have an analytic form.
!
        IMPLICIT NONE
        REAL, INTENT(IN) :: x
        REAL pi
        pi=4.*ATAN(1.)
        FofX=EXP(-x*x/2.0)/SQRT(2.0*pi)
        RETURN
        END FUNCTION FofX
!-----------------------------------
        END MODULE FunctionDefinition
!====================================
        PROGRAM Num_Int
!
! Performs numerical integration on specified function.
!
        USE NumericalIntegration, ONLY : SimpsonsRule
        USE FunctionDefinition, ONLY : FofX
        IMPLICIT NONE
        REAL z
        PRINT *,' Integrate normal function to z = '
        PRINT *,' (Appropriate values in range -10 to +10.)'
        READ *,z
        IF (z /= 0.0) THEN
          PRINT *," With Simpson's Rule..."
          PRINT 1000,SimpsonsRule(FofX,0.,z,100)+.5
        ELSE
          PRINT 1000,0.5
        END IF
!
1000    FORMAT(1x,f8.5)
        END
```

In program NUM_INT.F90, which can be downloaded from the World Wide Web site mentioned in Section i.5 of the Preface, the example used to test the subroutine is the integral under the normal distribution curve. This example has been chosen because it is easy to find tabulated values against which to check the results; look in any statistics text. A sample output from the program is

```
Integrate normal function to z =
(Appropriate values in range -10 to +10.)
1.6
With Simpson's Rule...
   0.94520
```

5 *Verify the operation of the program.*

It is often the case that numerical integration is used to replace tabulated values, as has been done in the driver program for P-11.3. If so, then the output can be tested by selecting several known tabulated values. If the results are correct, it is then reasonable to assume that results for other values will also be correct, assuming that they are within the range of the table.

Problem Discussion

This is a typical use of an externally defined function passed as an argument to a subprogram. In P-11.3, the function FofX is defined in a module separate from the module containing numerical integration routine. Note how the INTERFACE block, printed in bold italics. is used in FUNCTION SimpsonsRule. It isn't necessary for the function used in a subprogram to have the same name as the function in which it is defined. In FUNCTION SimpsonsRule, the function is named just F, rather than FofX.

11.4.2 Application: Evaluating the Gamma Function

Once you have developed a computer algorithm and satisfied yourself that it works for several cases of interest, you are likely to trust it in the future. That trust is easily misplaced, as this application will demonstrate.[5] The mathematical details of this application won't make much sense if you haven't had a course in integral calculus, but the code itself isn't very difficult to follow.

---

[5]Author's note: In fact, I should be ashamed of myself for including this example, which is full of traps for the mathematically unsophisticated programmer.

1 *Define the problem.*

The gamma function appears in physics problems involving wave functions and probabilities; it is defined for positive values of n in terms of an integral:

$$\Gamma(n) = \int_0^\infty e^{-x} x^{n-1} dx \tag{5}$$

When n is an integer,

$$\Gamma(n) = (n - 1)! \tag{6}$$

That is, the gamma function is just a generalization of the factorial function to noninteger numbers. Gamma functions for noninteger values of n are defined through a recursion relationship:

$$\Gamma(n + 1) = n\Gamma(n) \tag{7}$$

The integral that defines the gamma function can't be evaluated analytically except in special cases, so numerical integration is required to calculate the gamma function for noninteger values of n. Write a program that will evaluate the gamma function for any positive value of n.

2 *Outline a solution.*

At first, this problem might appear hopeless because one of the limits on the integral is infinity. Fortunately, the integrand—the function being integrated—decreases rapidly toward zero as x increases. Figure 11.3 shows the integrand as a function of x for n = 0.5, 1.5, and 2.5, for x from 0 to 5. At x = 20, the value of the integrand for n = 2.5 is about 1.8×10^{-7}. This suggests that it should be possible to obtain a useful approximation to $\Gamma(n)$ by limiting the range over which a numerical integration is done.

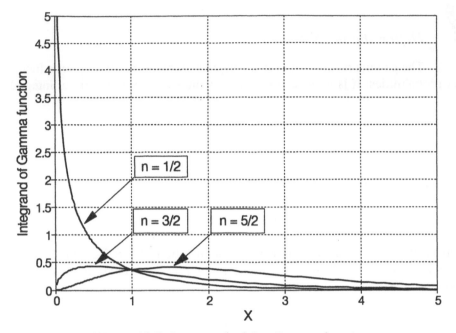

Figure 11.3. Integrand of the Gamma function

Furthermore, once the integral has been evaluated for $0 \le n \le 1$, the recursion relationship can be used to evaluate the gamma function for all other values of n. It will be helpful to know that, as a special case, the integral for $\Gamma(1/2)$ can be evaluated analytically; it yields a value of $\pi^{1/2}$.

3 *Design an algorithm.*

The algorithm is straightforward: incorporate Simpson's Rule into a subprogram and include it in a driver program that evaluates the integrand $e^{-x}x^{n-1}$. In this case, the gamma function is defined as a statement function inside FUNCTION Gamma and Simpson's Rule integration is carried out specifically for this function, rather than making use of the general-purpose Simpson's Rule function described previously in this section.

4 Convert the algorithm into a program.

P-11.4 [GAMMA.F90]

```
      MODULE Gamma_Calc
!
      CONTAINS
!
      REAL FUNCTION Gamma(n)
      IMPLICIT NONE
      REAL x,n,z,f,dx,x_max,sum
      INTEGER i,n_terms
      f(x,z)=EXP(-x)*x**(z-1.0)
      DATA dx,x_max/0.001,10.0/
!
      n_terms=NINT(x_max/dx)
      PRINT*,n_terms
      sum=0.0
      DO i=2,n_terms-2,2
        sum=sum+2.0*f(i*dx,n)
      END DO
      DO i=1,n_terms-1,2
        sum=sum+4.0*f(i*dx,n)
      END DO
      sum=(sum+f(x_max,n))*dx/3.0
      Gamma=sum
!
      END FUNCTION Gamma
!----------------------
      END MODULE
!==========================
      PROGRAM Gamma_Function
!
! Evaluate the Gamma function.
!
      USE Gamma_Calc, ONLY : Gamma
      IMPLICIT NONE
      REAL n,x
!
      PRINT*,'Give 0<n<1: '
      READ*,n
      x=Gamma(n)
      PRINT 1000,x
!
1000  FORMAT(1x,f15.8)
      END
```

Running P-11.2

```
 Give 0<n<1:
.5
 10000
    1.73261499
```

5 *Verify the operation of the program.*

If you test this program for n = 1/2, you can compare the results to the known value of $\pi^{1/2}$ = 1.772454. The program returns Γ(n) = 1.732615. Even though the intervals used in the Simpson's Rule calculation seem very small, the numerical result is not very close to the right answer. Why not? Can the accuracy be improved by increasing the number of steps? In fact, the accuracy will improve somewhat for a step size of 0.0001. However, examine Figure 11.3 again and note that for n = 1/2, the integrand approaches infinity as x approaches 0; to put it in mathematical terminology, the integrand has a singularity at x = 0 for any n in the range $0 \leq n < 1$.

The significance of this application should now be clear. Even though the numerical integration algorithm *appears* to work, and even produces an answer that isn't too far from the correct one, the entire process is fatally flawed because of the nature of the function we have tried to evaluate.

Fortunately, because of the recursion relationship that applies to the gamma function, we can salvage the situation. Whereas $x^{1/2-1} = x^{-1/2} = 1/x^{1/2}$ has a singularity at x = 0, $x^{3/2-1} = x^{1/2}$ does not. This means that we can evaluate Γ(1/2) by first evaluating Γ(3/2) and then applying the recursion relationship. This strategy will work for any value of n in the range $0 \leq n < 1$. However, it is still prudent to be concerned about the behavior of the function. For reasons that are beyond the scope of this text, some functions are better candidates for Simpson's Rule integration than others, and we will need to develop some confidence from independent sources before we start using FUNCTION Gamma without worrying about the results! Table 11.2 shows some results of applying FUNCTION Gamma and the recursion relationship to evaluate Γ(0.1), Γ(0.5), and Γ(0.9).

Of the three cases examined, the only value that can be obtained directly is Γ(0.5)=$\pi^{1/2}$; this value is given in bold type. (Additional values for Γ(3/2), Γ(5/2), and so on, can be obtained to arbitrarily high accuracy using forward recursion.) As an example of how to interpret the values in the table, the first "backward" recursive evaluation of n = 0.1 comes from using the numerical evaluation n = 4.1 to calculate the value for n = 3.1 (by dividing 6.812444 by 3.1) and using that value to calculate the value for n = 2.1, and so on. Other values for n = 0.1 come from starting at numerically integrated values for 3.1, 2.1, and 1.1. Each of these calculations yields a slightly different result, and it is clear that there is no reason to assume that the gamma function can be evaluated accurately beyond about four or five significant figures, which is considerably less than the potential seven-digit accuracy available for REAL numbers.[6] For many purposes, this will be sufficient, but it is important not to lose sight of the fact that

---

[6]This number of available significant figures may differ from compiler to compiler.

numerical integration is not a substitute for an analytic solution; it is, at best, *never* more than just an approximation that will be better in some circumstances than in others.[7]

Table 11.2. Gamma functions evaluated directly and by using a recursion relationship

n	Direct Evaluation	Recursive Evaluation			
0.1		9.513257	9.513303	9.513300	9.512023
1.1	0.9512023	0.9513257	0.9513303	0.9513303	
2.1	1.046463	1.046458	1.0464633		
3.1	2.197573	2.197563			
4.1	6.812444				
0.5	1.7724539 [1]	1.772402	1.772415	1.772423	1.772412
1.5	0.8862059	0.8862011	0.8862074	0.8862113	
2.5	1.329317	1.329302	1.3293112		
3.5	3.323278	3.323254			
4.5	11.63139				
0.9		1.068607	1.068606	1.068606	1.068608
1.9	0.9617471	0.9617464	0.9617457	0.9617457	
2.9	1.827317	1.827318	1.8273169		
3.9	5.299219	5.299223			
4.9	20.66697				

[1] This integral has a value of $\pi^{1/2}$.

---

[7]For additional information about evaluating the gamma function, see, for example, William. H. Press, *et al.*, *Numerical Recipes: The Art of Scientific Computing*. Cambridge University Press, New York, 1986.

Problem Discussion

In P-11.4, the step size used in the Simpson's Rule algorithm (0.001) has been hard coded within the function. If you wish, you can require this value to be provided as input by the user or by the calling program. It might be a good idea to do this while you're testing the function. However, in the same sense that a programmer shouldn't have to worry about the details of how Fortran evaluates the SIN function, you shouldn't have to ask the user of this function to provide values that are relevant only to the internal details of how the gamma function will be evaluated.

You should make sure you understand the recursion relationship for gamma functions by comparing the values of $\Gamma(3/2)$, $\Gamma(5/2)$, and so on, with their calculated values.

11.5 Solving Systems of Linear Equations

11.5.1 Linear Equations and Gaussian Elimination

The behavior of many physical systems can be represented, or at least approximated, by a system of linear equations. In this section, we will present one technique for solving such a system.

1 Define the problem.

Consider the following system of three equations, linear in x:

$$\begin{align}
x_1 a_{11} + x_2 a_{12} + x_3 a_{13} &= c_1 \\
x_1 a_{21} + x_2 a_{22} + x_3 a_{23} &= c_2 \\
x_1 a_{31} + x_2 a_{32} + x_3 a_{33} &= c_3
\end{align} \tag{1}$$

In vector notation, this system is expressed as $AX = C$. Develop a subprogram that will solve this system of equations for x_1, x_2, and x_3. The method should be easy to generalize to larger systems.

2 Outline a solution.

One widely used tehnique for solving a system of linear equations is Gaussian elimination. Suppose system (1) could be replaced with the following system:

$$
\begin{aligned}
x_1 + x_2 a'_{12} + x_3 a'_{13} &= c'_1 \\
x_2 + x_3 a'_{23} &= c'_2 \\
x_3 &= c'_3
\end{aligned}
\tag{2}
$$

The matrix formed by the terms to the left of the = sign in system (2) is called an **upper triangular matrix**, in which all the coefficients below the

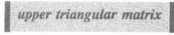
upper triangular matrix

left-to-right, top-to-bottom diagonal are 0. (We will henceforth refer to this particular diagonal simply as the diagonal.) The coefficients along the diagonal are 1. We now claim, without proof or additional discussion, that a solution for system (2) is equivalent to a solution for system (1). We further claim that for many systems of equations related to properly formulated problems of physical interest, it is possible to convert a set of system (1) equations into a set of system (2) equations. This process is called "triangularizing the matrix."[8]

It should be clear that if such a system can be found, it is then possible to solve for the all the x's, using a process called **backsubstitution**:

backsubstitution

$$
\begin{aligned}
x_3 &= c'_3 \\
x_2 &= c'_2 - x_3 a'_{23} \\
x_1 &= c'_1 - x_2 a'_{12} - x_3 a'_{13}
\end{aligned}
\tag{3}
$$

We will now work through the calculations required to convert system (1) into the upper triangular form (2). It will be easier to follow the calculations if we use a numerical example with coefficients that can be expressed as rational numbers. (Rational coefficients are used *only* for demonstration purposes and do *not* affect the general applicability of the method.) Consider this system of equations:

$$
\begin{aligned}
x_1 \cdot (1/3) + x_2 \cdot (1/2) + x_3 \cdot (1/4) &= 6 \\
x_1 \cdot (2) + x_2 \cdot (1/3) - x_3 \cdot (1/4) &= 6 \\
x_1 \cdot (1/4) - x_2 \cdot (1/8) + x_3 \cdot (1) &= 8
\end{aligned}
\tag{4}
$$

The coefficients along the diagonal are called **pivots**. The first step in the solution is to find the row with the largest coefficient (in absolute magnitude) in the first column and interchange that row with

pivots

the top row in system (4). In this example, the largest coefficient in the first column occurs in the second row. Therefore, you should interchange the first and second rows:

$$
\begin{aligned}
x_1 \cdot (2) + x_2 \cdot (1/3) - x_3 \cdot (1/4) &= 6 \\
x_1 \cdot (1/3) + x_2 \cdot (1/2) + x_3 \cdot (1/4) &= 6 \\
x_1 \cdot (1/4) - x_2 \cdot (1/8) + x_3 \cdot (1) &= 8
\end{aligned}
\tag{5}
$$

---

[8]For further discussion, see any text on numerical analysis.

The next step is to divide row one by the coefficient in the first column. The result is that the first pivot will have a coefficient of 1:

$$
\begin{array}{llll}
x_1 \cdot (1) & + \; x_2 \cdot (1/6) & + \; x_3 \cdot (-1/8) & = \; 3 \\
x_1 \cdot (1/3) & + \; x_2 \cdot (1/2) & + \; x_3 \cdot (1/4) & = \; 6 \\
x_1 \cdot (1/4) & + \; x_2 \cdot (-1/8) & + \; x_3 \cdot (1) & = \; 8
\end{array}
\tag{6}
$$

The next step is to multiply the first row by the coefficient in column one of the second row and subtract row one from row two. Then multiply the original first row by the coefficient in column one of the third row and subtract row one from row three. This produces a reduced system of equations:

$$
\begin{array}{lll}
x_1 \cdot (1) + x_2 \cdot (1/6) & + x_3 \cdot (-1/8) & = \; 3 \\
x_2 \cdot (1/2 - 1/18) & + x_3 \cdot (1/4 + 1/24) & = \; 5 \\
x_2 \cdot (-1/8 - 1/24) & + x_3 \cdot (1 + 1/32) & = \; 29/4
\end{array}
\tag{7}
$$

$$
\begin{array}{lll}
x_1 \cdot (1) & + \; x_2 \cdot (1/6) & + \; x_3 \cdot (-1/8) & = \; 3 \\
& x_2 \cdot (8/18) & + \; x_3 \cdot (7/24) & = \; 5 \\
& x_2 \cdot (-4/24) & + \; x_3 \cdot (33/32) & = \; 29/4
\end{array}
$$

Of the remaining coefficients in column two of rows two and three, 8/18 is larger in magnitude than -4/24, so these rows don't need to be interchanged. Divide row two by the coefficient of the second pivot:

$$
\begin{array}{lll}
x_1 \cdot (1) & + \; x_2 \cdot (1/6) & + \; x_3 \cdot (-1/8) & = \; 3 \\
& x_2 \cdot (1) & + \; x_3 \cdot (21/32) & = \; 45/4 \\
& x_2 \cdot (-4/24) & + \; x_3 \cdot (33/32) & = \; 29/4
\end{array}
\tag{8}
$$

Now multiply row two by -4/24 and subtract row two from row three:

$$
\begin{array}{lll}
x_1 \cdot (1) & + \; x_2 \cdot (1/6) & + \; x_3 \cdot (-1/8) & = \; 3 \\
& x_2 \cdot (1) & + \; x_3 \cdot (21/32) & = \; 45/4 \\
& & + \; x_3 \cdot (73/64) & = \; 219/24
\end{array}
\tag{9}
$$

Finally, divide row three by the coefficient of x_3:

$$
\begin{array}{lll}
x_1 \cdot (1) & + \; x_2 \cdot (1/6) & + \; x_3 \cdot (-1/8) & = \; 3 \\
& x_2 \cdot (1) & + \; x_3 \cdot (21/32) & = \; 45/4 \\
& & + \; x_3 \cdot (1) & = \; (219/24) \cdot (64/73) \; = \; 8
\end{array}
\tag{10}
$$

This immediately gives $x_3 = 8$ for one of the solutions. Now substitute x_3 into row two,

$$
x_2 \; = \; 45/4 \; - \; (21/32) \cdot 8 \; = \; 6
\tag{11}
$$

and x_1 and x_2 into row one.

$$x_1 = 3 - 6/6 + 8/8 = 3 \qquad\qquad (12)$$

3 *Design an algorithm.*

Using the example from Step 2, we can outline an algorithm. The sequence of operations is sufficiently involved that it is worth designing the algorithm first in outline form and then in more detail. Here is an outline.

1. Define an array to hold the coefficients (a) and the constants (c).
2. Read a data file containing a value for n and the $(n) \cdot (n+1)$ elements of A.
3. Triangularize the matrix.

LOOP *(through each row)*
> a. *For each row below current row, look for a coefficient A(row,current_row) that is larger in absolute magnitude than the coefficient A(current_row, current_row).*
> b. *If a larger coefficient exists, exchange that row with current_row.*
> c. *Divide all columns in the current row of A by A(current_row,current_row)*
> d. *For all rows below current_row, multiply the coefficients in (original) current_row by the first coefficient in the row and subtract from the corresponding coefficient in row.*

END LOOP

4. Backsubstitute to find solutions.

> a. Solve directly for last root.
> b. Substitute in previous row, continuing to first row.

Here is the algorithm in more detail.

DEFINE *(array of real numbers A with n rows and n+1 columns and array of size n to hold roots)*

OPEN *(data file)*
READ *(n)*
READ *(n•(n+1) elements of A)*
(Triangularize the matrix.)
LOOP *(for row = 1 to n_rows)*
> *(Search for row with larger pivot.)*
> **IF** *(row < n_rows)* **THEN ASSIGN** *PivotRow=row*

```
LOOP (for i = row+1 to n_rows)
            IF /A(i,row)/>/A(PivotRow,PivotRow)/
            THEN ASSIGN PivotRow = i
END LOOP
      {Swap rows if required.)
IF (PivotRow ≠ row) THEN
      LOOP (for col = row to n_cols)
            ASSIGN temp = A(PivotRow,col)
                  A(PivotRow,col) = A(row,col)
                  A)row,col) = temp
      END LOOP
      (end IF...)
(end IF...)
(Divide all coefficients in row by pivot.)
ASSIGN DivideBy = A(row,row)
LOOP (for col  = row to n_cols)
ASSIGN A(row,col) = A(row,col)/DivideBy
END LOOP
(Reduce the (row)th column to 0.)
IF (row < n_rows) THEN
      LOOP (for i = row+1 to n_rows)
            LOOP (for col = row+1 to n_cols)
                  ASSIGN A(i,col) = A(i,col – A(row,col)•A(i,row)
            END LOOP
            ASSIGN A(i,row) = 0
      END LOOP
(end IF...)
(optional for testing: print reduced matrix)
END LOOP
(Backsolve for roots.)
ASSIGN roots(n_rows) = A(n_rows,n_cols)
LOOP (for row = n_rows-1 (down) to 1)
      ASSIGN roots(row) = A(row,n_cols)
      LOOP (for i = row+1 to n_rows)
            ASSIGN roots(row) = roots(row) – A(row,i)•roots(i)
      END LOOP
END LOOP
```

4 *Convert the algorithm into a program.*

Program P-11.5 uses the data file GAUSS.DAT, which can be downloaded from the World Wide Web site mentioned in Section i.5 of the Preface.

P-11.5 [GAUSS.F90]

```
!-------------------------------------------------------------
      MODULE LinearSystemSubs
!
      CONTAINS
!
      SUBROUTINE GaussianElimination(a,n_rows,n_cols,solutions)
!
! Solves system of linear equations using Gaussian
! elimination with partial (row) pivoting.
!
      IMPLICIT NONE
      INTEGER, INTENT(IN) :: n_rows,n_cols
      REAL, INTENT(INOUT) :: a(n_rows,n_cols)
      REAL, INTENT(OUT)   :: solutions(n_rows)
      INTEGER row,col,PivotRow,i
      REAL DivideBy,temp
!
      DO row=1,n_rows
!
! Search for pivot row.
         IF (row < n_rows) THEN
           PivotRow=row
           DO i=row+1,n_rows
             IF ( ABS(a(i,row)) > ABS(a(PivotRow,row)) ) PivotRow=i
           END DO
!
! Swap pivot row if required.
           IF (PivotRow /= row) THEN
             PRINT*,'swapping pivot row...'
             DO col=row,n_cols
               temp=a(PivotRow,col)
               a(PivotRow,col)=a(row,col)
               a(row,col)=temp
             END DO
           PRINT*,'swap done...'
           CALL PrintMatrix(a,n_rows,n_cols)
           END IF
         END IF !IF (row < n_rows) ...
!
! Divide by pivot.
         DivideBy=a(row,row)
         a(row,row:n_cols)=a(row,row:n_cols)/DivideBy
!
```

```
! Reduce the (row)th column to 0
      IF (row < n_rows) THEN
        DO i=row+1,n_rows
          a(i,row+1:n_cols) &
            = a(i,row+1:n_cols)-a(row,row+1:n_cols)*a(i,row)
          a(i,row)=0.
        END DO
      END IF
!
! Print reduced matrix.
      CALL PrintMatrix(a,n_rows,n_cols)
    END DO
!
! Backsolve for solutions.
    solutions(n_rows)=a(n_rows,n_cols)
    DO row=n_rows-1,1,-1
      solutions(row)=a(row,n_cols)
      DO i=row+1,n_rows
        solutions(row)=solutions(row)-a(row,i)*solutions(i)
      END DO
    END DO
!
    RETURN
    END SUBROUTINE GaussianElimination
!
    SUBROUTINE PrintMatrix(a,n_rows,n_cols)
!
    IMPLICIT NONE
    INTEGER, INTENT(IN) :: n_rows,n_cols
    REAL, INTENT(IN)    :: a(n_rows,n_cols)
    INTEGER rows,cols
!
!     PRINT*,'from PrintMatrix...'
    DO rows=1,n_rows
      DO cols=1,n_cols
        WRITE(*,1000,advance='no')a(rows,cols)
      END DO
      WRITE(*,1010)
    END DO
!
1000  FORMAT(f7.2)
1010  FORMAT()
!
    RETURN
    END SUBROUTINE PrintMatrix
!
    END MODULE
!-----------------------------------------------------
    PROGRAM Gauss
!
! Driver program for LinearSystemSubs,
! including Gaussian elimination with partial pivoting.
!
    USE LinearSystemSubs
    IMPLICIT NONE
    REAL, DIMENSION(:,:), ALLOCATABLE :: a
    REAL, DIMENSION(:),   ALLOCATABLE :: solutions
    INTEGER n_rows,n_cols,rows,cols
!
```

```
      OPEN(1,file='c:\ftn90\source\gauss.dat')
!
      READ(1,*)n_rows ! number of equations
      n_cols=n_rows+1
      ALLOCATE(a(n_rows,n_cols),solutions(n_rows))
!
      DO rows=1,n_rows
        READ(1,*)(a(rows,cols),cols=1,n_cols)
        PRINT*,(a(rows,cols),cols=1,n_cols)
      END DO
!
! Print original matrix.
      CALL PrintMatrix(a,n_rows,n_cols)
!
! Solve system.
      CALL GaussianElimination(a,n_rows,n_cols,solutions)
      WRITE(*,1020)(solutions(rows),rows=1,n_rows)
!
1000  FORMAT(f7.2)
1010  FORMAT()
1020  FORMAT(e15.5)
      END
```

Running P-11.5

```
 3.0000000E+02    0.0000000E+00   -2.0000000E+02    0.0000000E+00
 0.0000000E+00    5.5000000E+02   -2.5000000E+02    6.0000000
-2.0000000E+02   -2.5000000E+02    6.0000000E+02    0.0000000E+00
 300.00     0.00-200.00    0.00
   0.00 550.00-250.00    6.00
-200.00-250.00 600.00    0.00
 300.00     0.00-200.00    0.00
   0.00 550.00-250.00    6.00
-200.00-250.00 600.00    0.00
   1.00     0.00   -0.67    0.00
   0.00 550.00-250.00    6.00
   0.00-250.00 466.67    0.00
   1.00     0.00   -0.67    0.00
   0.00     1.00   -0.45    0.01
   0.00     0.00 353.03    2.73
   1.00     0.00   -0.67    0.00
   0.00     1.00   -0.45    0.01
   0.00     0.00     1.00    0.01
   0.51502E-02
   0.14421E-01
   0.77253E-02
```

5 *Verify the operation of the program.*

For the example used to develop the algorithm, the intermediate calculations with fractions all cancel out to give exact solutions in terms of integer values. However, in general, the potential loss of accuracy as a result of cumulative errors involving real arithmetic on computers is always a concern in any algorithm that involves many calculations. For reasons that aren't obvious, the algorithm we have used seeks to minimize arithmetic errors by searching for the row with the largest coefficient in the pivot column and interchanging it with the current row.[9] However, there is still no guarantee that unacceptable errors won't accumulate. If the physical problem represented by the equations is poorly defined, it is possible that the algorithm will give answers that look OK, but in fact are wrong. (This can happen with so-called "ill-conditioned matrices." A famous example is presented in Exercise 11 at the end of this chapter.) In extreme cases, divisions by zero can occur, and the program will crash. This might be distressing, but it is a better result than obtaining wrong answers with a program that doesn't crash.

In any algorithm involving many calculations with real numbers, you should *NEVER* assume that the results are correct until you have checked them thoroughly. This is not always easy to do! One test you can perform is to substitute the x values into the original equations. In Exercise 7 at the end of this chapter, you are asked to modify P-11.5 to include calculation of a "residual" vector. Each component of the residual vector should be very close to zero for a "good" solution. However, this is what mathematicians call a "necessary but insufficient condition" to guarantee a "good" solution. Ill-conditioned matrices can result in solutions for which the residuals are small even though the solution is not correct. Such matrices may not even have a "good" solution.

11.5.2 Application: Current Flow in a DC Circuit with Multiple Resistive Branches

1 Define the problem.

Consider the DC circuit shown in Figure 11.4. It consists of a voltage source connected to several resistive branches. Kirchoff's Laws state that the voltage drop around any closed branch of such a network of resistances must be zero. This fact leads directly to a series of linear equations that describe the current flow in the three branches of this circuit:

---

[9]It is also possible to interchange both columns and rows to move the absolutely largest coefficient in the reduced system to the pivot position. However, it can be shown that this results in relatively small improvements in the overall accuracy of the method. Such a solution is called "Gaussian elimination with full pivoting." The solution described here is called "Gaussian elimination with partial pivoting."

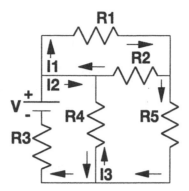

Figure 11.4. Current flow in a DC circuit with resistive branches

$$(R_1 + R_2)I_1 \qquad\qquad\qquad\quad - R_2I_3 = 0$$
$$(R_3 + R_4)I_2 \qquad\quad - R_4I_3 = E$$
$$-R_2I_1 \qquad\quad - R_4I_2 + (R_2 + R_4 + R_5)I_3 = 0$$

Solve this equation for these values:

R1 = 100 Ω R4 = 250 Ω
R2 = 200 Ω R5 = 150 Ω
R3 = 300 Ω   E = 6 V

2 *Outline a solution.*

In a physics course, you would probably be asked to derive the equations yourself, which is the only difficult part of this problem. Note that the direction of current flow is normally considered positive in the direction from the "+" terminal of a battery (or other voltage source) to the "-" terminal. If you guess wrong about the direction of flow in a particular branch of the circuit, the current will have a negative value in the solution.

3 *Design an algorithm.*

There is no need to design an algorithm for this problem, as it is a straightforward application of subroutines already written.

4 *Convert the algorithm into a program.*

There is also no need to write any new code to solve this problem. Simply create an appropriate data file in the same format as GAUSS.DAT, as used by P-11.5, and run GAUSS.F90.

5 *Verify the operation of the program.*

This is a problem that should not cause significant numerical difficulties. It is relatively easy to check the value for I_2 by noting that R_1 and R_2 are in parallel. Then the resistance of this parallel combination plus R_5 is in parallel with R_4. Finally, this parallel combination is in series with R_3. If you do these calculations by hand, you should find that I_2 is approximately 14.4 mA.

11.6 Finding the Roots of Equations

Consider a function $y = f(x)$. A common problem in mathematics is finding the value(s) of x for which the equation $f(x) = 0$. As a simple example, consider the polynomial

$$f(x) = x^2 - 8x + 15$$

It is easy to determine the values of x for which this function equals zero because the polynomial can be factored by inspection:

$$f(x) = (x - 5)(x - 3)$$

The values x=5 and x=3 are called the roots of the function.

In general, it is not this easy to find the roots of a function. For example, although there are standard methods for finding the roots of a quadratic equation, there are no comparable methods for high-order polynomials. Consequently, numerical methods are often needed. In this section we will develop one intuitively simple numerical method. Often it is of interest to find all real roots over a specified range, so that is how we will formulate the problem.

1 *Define the problem.*

Write a subprogram that will estimate the real roots for the equation $f(x) = 0$ over the range $[x_a, x_b]$.

2 *Outline a solution.*

The approach we will discuss is called the bisection method. How can we tell whether there are any roots in the range $[x_a, x_b]$? Suppose that the sign of $f(x_a)$ is different from the sign of $f(x_b)$. The obvious interpretation of this fact is that the function has crossed the x-axis at least once in the range $[x_a, x_b]$. It is also possible that the function crossed the x-axis more than once, in which case the total number of crossings must be odd. This means that $f(x)$ must have at least one real root in the range $[x_a, x_b]$.

A second possibility is that the sign of $f(x_a)$ is the same as the sign of $f(x_b)$. This means that there may be no roots or that the function has crossed the x-axis an even number of times, so that $f(x)$ must have either no roots or an even number of roots in the range $[x_a, x_b]$.

A third possibility, which is applicable in either of the above two situations, is that $f(x)$ just touches the x-axis without crossing it. This is true for the function

$$f(x) = x^2 - 6x + 9 = (x - 3)(x - 3)$$

This function, which never crosses the x-axis, has two identical real roots. Such possibilities complicate the search for a generally applicable root-finding algorithm. Figure 11.5 illustrates these three possibilities.

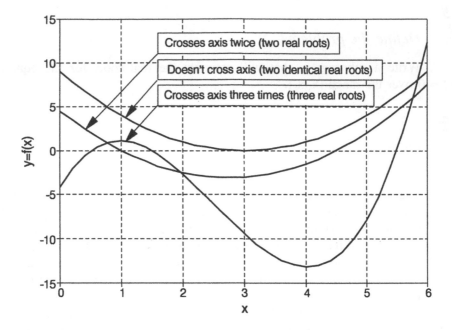

Figure 11.5. Polynomials with one or more real roots

In any case, we will proceed on the assumption that roots can be found by identifying the places where a function crosses the x-axis. (That is, we will ignore the third possibility mentioned above.) Assume that the range $[x_a, x_b]$ is subdivided into intervals sufficiently small that each interval contains either one root or no roots. If $f(x)$ at the left boundary x_L of the interval is different from the sign at the right boundary of the subinterval x_R, we will assume that the interval contains one real root. Otherwise, we will assume that the interval contains no roots. It is important to realize that this is just an assumption, and there is no way to guarantee whether the assumption is justified.

Now divide the interval $[x_L, x_R]$ in half. There are three possibilities, which take into account the fact that if $f(x_L) \cdot f(x_R) < 0$, then the function crosses the x-axis somewhere in the interval $[x_L, x_R]$:

(1) $f(x_{mid}) = 0$
(2) $f(x_L) \cdot f(x_{mid}) < 0$
(3) $f(x_{mid}) \cdot f(x_R) < 0$

If (1) is true, then x_{mid} will be accepted as a root. It isn't quite accurate to say that x_{mid} is a root because of the limitations on real arithmetic. However, as a practical matter, we can usually assume that x_{mid} is sufficiently close to the "real" root.

Also as a practical matter, it is unlikely that the value $f(x_{mid})$ will ever equal exactly zero (recalling the discussion of real-number arithmetic and IF. . . tests in Chapter 6).

If (2) is true, then the root must lie in the interval $[x_L, x_{mid}]$. Let $x_R = x_{mid}$ and repeat the test. If (3) is true, then the root must lie in the interval $[x_{mid}, x_R]$. Let $x_L = x_{mid}$ and repeat the test. As a result of repeatedly halving the interval in this way, $[x_L, x_R]$ will eventually become smaller than some specified small value. At that point, we can assume that the algorithm has converged and that the root is located at x_{mid}. It is also possible to terminate the algorithm based on the absolute magnitude of $f(x_{mid})$.

3 *Design an algorithm.*

As usual, it is important to specify the input to and output from the algorithm and to isolate the algorithm in a subprogram that can be applied in a variety of circumstances.

SUBPROGRAM Bisect(IN: x_L, x_R, F; OUT: root, final_interval)
DEFINE (x_{mid}, hit (logical), epsilon_f, epsilon_x (values to test for
        convergence))
ASSIGN epsilon_f = ?
        epsilon_x = ?
        x_{mid} = (x_R + x_L)/2
        hit = false
LOOP (while $/x_R - x_L/$ > epsilon_x and $/F(x_{mid})/$ > epsilon_f and not hit)
    IF $F(x_{mid})$ = 0 *THEN* hit = true (found "exact" root)
    ELSE IF $F(x_L) \cdot F(x_{mid})$ < 0 *THEN* x_R = x_{mid} (root in left half)
    ELSE $F(x_R) \cdot F(x_{mid})$ < 0 *THEN* x_L = x_{mid} (root in right half)
    ASSIGN x_{mid} = (x_L + x_R)/2
END LOOP
ASSIGN root = $f(x_{mid})$
        final_interval = $/x_R - x_L/$

This algorithm assumes that the values against which convergence will be tested can be hard-coded into the subprogram. You might instead wish to supply them as parameters. (See Exercise 5 in Basic Programming Exercises at the end of this chapter.) Note that *Bisect* returns the length of the final subinterval as well as the estimated root. This gives the calling (sub)program an additional chance to decide whether to accept the root.

Bisect will typically be called from another subprogram that divides the original range $[x_a, x_b]$ into a specified number of intervals and calls *Bisect* once for each such interval. The design of this subprogram is straightforward. The expectation is that some of these intervals will contain a root and some won't. One way to store the results is to create an array to hold a value for each of the specified intervals. When control is returned to the calling program, each element of this array will hold either a root or an initial value chosen such that it can't be mistaken for a root.

4 *Convert the algorithm into a program.*

P-11.6 [ROOTS.F90]

```fortran
        MODULE RootSubs
!
        TYPE RootType
          REAL root,f_root,interval
        END TYPE RootType
!
        CONTAINS
!-----------------------------------------------------
        SUBROUTINE Bisection(F,XL,XR,n_intervals,roots)
!
! Set up intervals for finding roots with bisection method.
!
        IMPLICIT NONE
        REAL, INTENT(IN) :: XL,XR
        INTEGER, INTENT(IN) :: n_intervals
        TYPE (RootType), INTENT(OUT) :: roots(n_intervals)
        REAL dx,xa,xb
        INTEGER i
!-----------------------------------
        INTERFACE
          REAL FUNCTION F(x)
            REAL, INTENT(IN) :: x
          END FUNCTION F
        END INTERFACE
!-----------------------------
!
        dx=(XR-XL)/n_intervals
        DO i=1,n_intervals
          xa=XL+REAL(i-1)*dx
          xb=XL+REAL(i)*dx
          IF (F(xa)*F(xb) < 0.) THEN
            CALL Bisect(F,xa,xb,roots(i)%root,roots(i)%f_root, &
                     roots(i)%interval)
          ELSE
            roots(i)%root=0.; roots(i)%f_root=0.; roots(i)%interval=0.
          END IF
        END DO
!
        END SUBROUTINE Bisection
!-----------------------------------------------------------
```

```
      SUBROUTINE Bisect(F,xa,xb,x_mid,f_mid,final_interval)
!
      IMPLICIT NONE
      REAL, INTENT(INOUT) :: xa,xb
      REAL, INTENT(OUT) :: x_mid,f_mid,final_interval
      LOGICAL hit
      REAL, PARAMETER :: epsilon_x=1e-5,epsilon_f=1e-5
!----------------------------
      INTERFACE
        REAL FUNCTION F(x)
          REAL, INTENT(IN) :: x
        END FUNCTION F
      END INTERFACE
!----------------------------
      x_mid=(xb+xa)/2.
      hit=.false.
      f_mid=F(x_mid)
      DO WHILE (((xb-xa) > epsilon_x).AND. &
            (ABS(f_mid) > epsilon_f).AND.(.NOT. hit))
        IF (f_mid == 0.) THEN
          hit=.true.
        ELSE IF (F(xa)*f_mid < 0) THEN
          xb=x_mid
        ELSE IF (F(xb)*f_mid < 0) THEN
          xa=x_mid
        ELSE
          PRINT *,' Unexplained error!'
        END IF
        x_mid=(xb+xa)/2.
        f_mid=F(x_mid)
        final_interval=xb-xa
      END DO
!
      END SUBROUTINE Bisect
!-------------------------
      END MODULE RootSubs
!===============================
      MODULE FunctionDefinition
!
      CONTAINS
!-----------------------
      REAL FUNCTION F(x)
!
      IMPLICIT NONE
      REAL x
!
      F=5.*x**3-2.*x**2+3.
      END FUNCTION F
!-----------------------------------
      END MODULE FunctionDefinition
!===================================
```

```
      PROGRAM GetRoots
!
! MS-DOS file name ROOTS.F90
!
      USE RootSubs, ONLY : RootType,Bisection
      USE FunctionDefinition, ONLY : F
      IMPLICIT NONE
      INTEGER, PARAMETER :: n_intervals=10
      TYPE (RootType) roots(n_intervals)
      INTEGER i
!
      CALL Bisection(F,-10.,0.,n_intervals,roots)
      DO i=1,n_intervals
         PRINT *,i,roots(i)%root,roots(i)%f_root,roots(i)%interval
      END DO
!
      END PROGRAM
```

Running P-11.6

```
 0.0000000E+ 00   0.0000000E+00    0.0000000E+00
 0.0000000E+00    0.0000000E+00    0.0000000E+00
 0.0000000E+00    0.0000000E+00    0.0000000E+00
 0.0000000E+00    0.0000000E+00    0.0000000E+00
 0.0000000E+00    0.0000000E+00    0.0000000E+00
 0.0000000E+00    0.0000000E+00    0.0000000E+00
 0.0000000E+00    0.0000000E+00    0.0000000E+00
 0.0000000E+00    0.0000000E+00    0.0000000E+00
 0.0000000E+00    0.0000000E+00    0.0000000E+00
-0.7290001    1.4424324E-05    7.6293945E-06
```

5 *Verify the operation of the program.*

The results from any root-finding algorithm can always be tested directly by substituting the estimated root back into the original function. The result should differ from zero by no more than some specified tolerance. It is assumed that this subroutine Bisect will be called *only* when the function changes sign over the original interval supplied in the parameter list. As long as this is true, the algorithm is guaranteed to converge as long as the specified tolerance is reasonable relative to the accuracy with which real arithmetic is performed; a tolerance of 10^{-15} is unreasonable when real arithmetic is performed only to seven or eight significant figures!

Once the bisection algorithm has converged, you should check values of the function in the vicinity of the root to examine its slope—essentially, its numerical derivative. If the derivative is very small, it means that the root returned by the algorithm will be very sensitive to the criteria you have chosen for terminating the bisection algorithm.

Although it is possible to test the roots returned by the bisection method, it is not so easy to guarantee that *all* the roots in the original range have been found. For any interval supplied to the parameter list, the bisection method will find *one* root, because, by design, the function changes sign in that interval. In the previous discussion of this method, we have *assumed* that when the original range of x values is divided into intervals, each interval will contain either one root or no roots. However, it may be true that more than one root lies within an interval. As implemented, the algorithm searches first for a sign change in the left half of the original interval. If it finds one, it thereafter ignores the right half of the original interval. An additional root that lies within the right half will remain undetected.

11.7 Numerical Solutions to Differential Equations

There are several numerical techniques for solving differential equations of various kinds. In general, the technique must be matched carefully with the problem. In this section, we will focus on a particular class of second-order differential equations that demonstrate clearly how mathematics can tie together apparently unrelated physical concepts. The equations we will discuss here all have analytic solutions, and we will give those solutions for the purpose of comparing them with the numerical calculations. However, you are not expected to be able to derive the solutions yourself unless you have had a course in differential equations. In general, the mathematical sophistication required to understand these results goes beyond that required in any other part of this text.

We will begin by presenting a particular problem. It may seem that this problem is more like an "application" than a general approach to solving a class of differential equations, but associating the results with a simple physical system will make the mathematics easier to follow. In addition, the solutions to this conceptually simple physical problem are broadly and directly applicable to other important problems in science and engineering.

11.7.1 Motion of a Damped Mass and Spring

Consider a mass hanging from the end of a massless spring. If this system is in static equilibrium—that is, if nothing is moving—the spring is stretched and the force due to gravity acting on the mass is counterbalanced by a restoring upward force provided by the spring. If the displacement in the spring is small, then according to Hooke's Law, the restoring force provided by the spring is proportional to the displacement:

$$mg - kL = 0 \tag{1}$$

where k is a spring constant that can be determined experimentally by measuring the displacement resulting from hanging a known weight on the spring (mg = mass times the gravitational acceleration).

Now suppose that the mass is displaced from its equilibrium position in the downward (assumed positive) direction by an amount ℓ. As long as the total displacement L+ℓ is still small (i.e., as long as Hooke's Law still applies) the restoring force is still proportional to the displacement. If the mass is now released, it will vibrate around its equilibrium position. If damping forces are ignored, the equation of motion for the mass is

$$md^2\ell/dt^2 = mg - k[L + \ell(t)] \tag{2}$$

Because mg = kL, this equation reduces to

$$md^2\ell/dt^2 + k\ell(t) = 0 \tag{3}$$

The solution to this solution is a cosine-shaped curve with period T,

$$\ell(t) = A\cos(\omega_o t) + B\sin(\omega_o t) = R\cos(\omega_o t - \delta) \tag{4}$$

where $T = 2\pi/\omega_o = 2\pi(m/k)^{1/2}$, $A = R\cos(\delta)$, $B = R\sin(\delta)$, $R = (A^2 + B^2)^{1/2}$, and the phase angle $\delta = \tan^{-1}(B/A)$. The quadrant of δ must be determined from the signs of $\cos(\delta)$ and $\sin(\delta)$. The initial conditions for the system determine values for the constants. In a typical situation where the mass is initially displaced downward (in the positive direction) by an amount L and released, A=L, the initial velocity equals 0, and B and δ are both equal to 0.

Because this motion is undamped, the amplitude of the oscillation does not decrease as a function of time. This is a physically unrealistic situation. Therefore, suppose that the motion is damped by having the spring move in a resisting medium. The resistance could be provided incidentally just by air or it could be an intentional part of the system, through the addition of a mechanical damping device, sometimes called a "dashpot," for example. Such situations can be modeled by adding another term to the equation of motion, proportional to velocity,

$$md^2\ell/dt^2 + Dd\ell/dt + k\ell = 0 \tag{5}$$

where D is a damping coefficient. For the interesting case of "small" damping, it can be shown that $D^2 - 4km$ must be less than 0. Then the general solution is

$$\ell(t) = e^{-Dt/2m}[A\cos(\mu t) + B\sin(\mu t)] \tag{6}$$

where $\mu = \sqrt{4km - D^2}/2m$. It is at least qualitatively clear that this solution has the desired properties. The sine and cosine terms provide the oscillating component and the exponential term guarantees that the amplitude of the oscillation will approach zero as time approaches infinity, no matter what its initial amplitude.

The presence of damping changes the period previously derived for undamped motion. This new "quasiperiod" T' still gives the time between successive maxima or minima of the function,

$$T' = 4\pi m/\sqrt{4km - D^2} \tag{7}$$

which approaches the period for undamped motion as D approaches 0. This value is important when applying numerical methods because in order to characterize the behavior of the motion, it is of course necessary to use step sizes that are small compared to the period for undamped motion or to this "quasiperiod" for damped motion.

A standard technique for solving a second-order differential equation in the form of (5) is to rewrite it as a system of two first-order equations. For the mass-and-spring problem, the result is especially easy to understand because of the simple physical nature of the problem. Because velocity v is the time derivative of position (v=dx/dt) and acceleration is the time derivative of velocity $(d^2\ell/dt^2=dv/dt)$,

$$d\ell/dt = v(t)$$
$$dv/dt = a(t) = -[Dv(t) + k\ell(t)]/m \tag{8}$$

There are several numerical methods applicable to equations such as these, having the general form dy/dx = f(x,y). They all involve, in some fashion, selecting a small interval Δx and estimating the value of y for this "future" value of x. (Again, this concept is easy to grasp when the independent variable is time, as is the case for the equations of motion we are discussing.) We will use the well-known Runge-Kutta method, which has the advantage that no higher order derivatives are required. In general,

$$\kappa_1 = \Delta t \bullet f(x,y)$$
$$\kappa_2 = \Delta t \bullet f(x+\Delta x/2, y+k_1/2)$$
$$\kappa_3 = \Delta t \bullet f(x+\Delta x/2, y+k_2/2) \tag{9}$$
$$\kappa_4 = \Delta t \bullet f(x+\Delta x, y+k_3)$$
$$y(x+\Delta x) \approx y(x) + (\kappa_1 + 2\kappa_2 + 2\kappa_3 + \kappa_4)/6$$

For the equations of motion in (8),

$$
\begin{aligned}
\kappa_{1,\ell} &= \Delta t \cdot v(t) \\
\kappa_{2,\ell} &= \Delta t \cdot [v(t+\Delta t/2)] = \Delta t \cdot [v(t) + a(t)\Delta t/2] \\
\kappa_{3,\ell} &= \Delta t \cdot [v(t) + a(t)\Delta t/2] \\
\kappa_{4,\ell} &= \Delta t \cdot [v(t) + a(t)\Delta t] \\
\kappa_{1,v} &= -\Delta t \cdot [Dv(t) + k\ell(t)]/m \\
\kappa_{2,v} &= -\Delta t \cdot \{D[v(t) + \kappa_{1,v}/2] + k\ell(t+\Delta t/2)\}/M \\
&= -\Delta t \cdot \{D[v(t) + \kappa_{1,v}/2] + k[\ell(t)+v(t)\Delta t/2]\}/M \\
\kappa_{3,v} &= -\Delta t \cdot \{D[v(t) + \kappa_{2,v}/2] + k[\ell(t)+v(t)\Delta t/2]\}/M \\
\kappa_{4,v} &= -\Delta t \cdot \{D[v(t) + \kappa_{3,y}] + k[\ell(t)+v(t)\Delta t]\}/M
\end{aligned}
$$

(10)

(11)

from which

$$
\begin{aligned}
\ell(t+\Delta t) &= \ell(t) + \kappa_{1,\ell} + 2\kappa_{2,\ell} + 2\kappa_{3,\ell} + \kappa_{4,\ell})/6 \\
v(t+\Delta t) &= v(t) + \kappa_{1,v} + 2\kappa_{2,v} + 2\kappa_{3,v} + \kappa_{4,v})/6
\end{aligned}
$$

(12)

These kinds of numerical solutions suffer from several sources of error. Even if it can be assumed (which it can't) that there is no error due to the limitations of real arithmetic on computers, there remains an inherent *discretization error*. This is due to the fact that estimated values one step "into the future" are used as the initial conditions for the next step. However, these conditions are, by definition, estimates and not the true values. For each step, therefore, there is a local discretization error that propagates over the rest of the solution as accumulated discretization error. These errors can be analyzed (a topic that is beyond the scope of this text), but they are unavoidable whenever methods such as these are used. As always, therefore, it is necessary to be extremely cautious when applying numerical methods to real problems.

| discretization error |

11.7.2 Application. Current Flow in a Series LRC Circuit

As mentioned earlier in this section, the equations of motion used to describe the motion of a mass attached to a spring can also be used to describe other physical systems.

1 Define the problem.

An electrical circuit contains a resistor R (ohms) and an inductor L (henrys) in series with a source of constant (DC) voltage V (volts). A switch is initially opened and is then closed at time t = 0. What is the current flow in the circuit after the switch is closed? How does the addition of a capacitor C (farads) in series with the resistor and inductor change the current flow? See Figure 11.6.

2 Outline a solution.

The generally applicable equation for this problem is

$$L d^2 q/dt^2 + R dq/dt + q/C = V \tag{13}$$

where the current i is the time derivative of the charge q. This equation has the same form as the equation of motion for a damped mass-and-spring problem. The correspondence between the variables is

$$
\begin{aligned}
m &\to L \\
D &\to R \\
k &\to 1/C \\
\ell &\to q \\
v &\to dq/dt = i \\
f(t) &\to V(t)
\end{aligned}
$$

The first part of the problem, with $1/C=0$ and V a constant, is a special case of the general problem. The second-order equation reduces immediately to a single first-order equation:

$$di/dt = (V - Ri)/L \tag{14}$$

The solution is

$$i(t) = V/R(1 - e^{-Rt/L}) \tag{15}$$

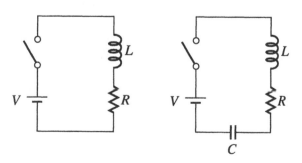

Figure 11.6 LR and LRC circuits

There is no oscillating component because there is no "spring constant" term. The solution satisfies the condition that $i = 0$ and $di/dt = V/L$ at $t = 0$ and that $i \rightarrow V/R$ (from Ohm's Law) as $t \rightarrow \infty$.

For the second part of the problem, which adds capacitance to the circuit, assume that $4L/C - R^2 > 0$. Then the solution for charge q is

$$q(t) = CV\left[1 - e^{\frac{-Rt}{2L}} \cos\left(\frac{\sqrt{4L/C - R^2}t}{2L}\right)\right] \qquad (16)$$

This solution is a damped oscillation that exhibits the desired properties. At $t = 0$, $q = 0$. As $t \rightarrow \infty$, $q \rightarrow CV$. It is also true that the current ($i = dq/dt$) approaches 0 as $t \rightarrow \infty$, as required by the fact that the voltage V is constant.

3 Design an algorithm.

One property of these calculations is that it is easier to calculate the Runge-Kutta coefficients in the context of a specific problem. It may not be worth the trouble required to write a "general purpose" Runge-Kutta integration routine. We will first design an algorithm that can be used to solve "mass-and-spring-like" problems such as the one in this application.

SUBPROGRAM *MassAndSpring(IN: D, K, M, F, dt; OUT x, v)*
DEFINE *k1_x, k2_x, k3_x, k4_x, k1_v, k2_v, k3_v, k4_v*
(Calculate Runge-Kutta coefficients.)
    ASSIGN *k1_x = v*
                *k2_x = v + AofT(x, v, D, K, M, F)•dt/2 (see **SUB.** AofT)*
                k3_x = v + AofT(x, v, D, K, M, F)•dt/2
                k4_x = v + AofT(x, v, D, K, M, F)•dt
                k1_v = AofT(x, v, D, K, M, F)
                k2_v = AofT(x + v•dt/2, v + k1_v•dt/2, D, K, M, F)
                k3_v = AofT(x + v•dt/2, v + k2_v•dt/2, D, K, M, F)
                k4_v = AofT(x + v•dt, v + k3_v•dt, D, K, M, F)
(Propagate solution.)
    ASSIGN *x = x + (k1_x + 2•k2_x + 2•k3_x + k4_x)•dt/6*
                v = v + (k1_v + 2•k2_v + 2•k3_v + k4_v)•dt/6

Because of the way *AofT* is used, make a note in the algorithm that it should be implemented as a Fortran function.

SUBPROGRAM *(Fortran function) AofT(IN: x, v, D, K, M, F)*
    ASSIGN *AofT = -(-F + D•v + K•x)/M*

Now design the algorithm for solving the first part of the problem: $Ldi/dt + Ri = V$.

WRITE *(prompt for input)*
READ *(V, L, R, t_final,n)*
INITIALIZE *i = 0*
       t = 0
ASSIGN *dt = t_final/n*
LOOP *(for j = 1 to n)*
(Calculate Runge-Kutta coefficients.)
    ASSIGN *k1_i = (V - R•i)/L*
        k2_i = [V -R•(i + k1_i•dt/2)]/L
        k3_i = [V - R•(i + k2_i•dt/2)]/L
        k4_i = [V - R•(i + k3_i•dt)]/L
(Propagate solution.)
    INCREMENT *i = i + (k1_i + 2•k2_i + 2•k3_i + k4_i)•dt/6*
       t = t + dt
    WRITE *(t, i, (V/R)•(1 - $e^{-Rt/L}$) (Include analytic solution.)*
END LOOP

Finally, solve the second part of the problem: $Ld^2q/dt^2 + Rdq/dt + q/C = V$. Include the analytic solution for q.

WRITE *(prompt for input)*
READ *(V, L, R, C, t_final, n)*
INITIALIZE *q = 0*
       i = CVR/(2L)
       t=0
ASSIGN *dt=t_final/n*
LOOP *(for j = 1 to n)*
    CALL *MassAndSpring(q, i, R, 1/C, L, V, dt)*
    INCREMENT *t = t + dt*
    WRITE *(t, q, i, CV[1 - $e^{-Rt/(2L)}\cos(\dfrac{\sqrt{4L/c - R^2}\,t}{2L})$])*

END LOOP

4

Convert the algorithm into a program.

P-11.7 [CIRCUIT.F90]

```
      MODULE RungeKutta
!
      CONTAINS
!----------------------------------
      REAL FUNCTION AofT(x,v,D,K,M,F)
! Calculate acceleration for "mass and spring" problem.
      IMPLICIT NONE
      REAL, INTENT(IN) :: x,v,D,K,M,F
      AofT=-(-F+D*v+K*x)/M
      END FUNCTION AofT
!-------------------------
      SUBROUTINE MassAndSpring(x,v,D,K,M,F,dt)
! Calculate motion for mass and spring problem with constant force
term.
      IMPLICIT NONE
      REAL,INTENT(INOUT) :: x,v
      REAL, INTENT(IN) :: D,K,M,F,dt
      REAL k1_x,k2_x,k3_x,k4_x,k1_v,k2_v,k3_v,k4_v
!
! Runge-Kutta coefficients...
      k1_x=v
      k2_x=v+AofT(x,v,D,K,M,F)*dt/2.
      k3_x=v+AofT(x,v,D,K,M,F)*dt/2.
      k4_x=v+AofT(x,v,D,K,M,F)*dt
      k1_v=AofT(x,v,D,K,M,F)
      k2_v=AofT(x+v*dt/2.,v+k1_v*dt/2.,D,K,M,F)
      k3_v=AofT(x+v*dt/2.,v+k2_v*dt/2.,D,K,M,F)
      k4_v=AofT(x+v*dt,v+k3_v*dt,D,K,M,F)
! Propagate solution...
      x=x+(k1_x+2.*k2_x+2.*k3_x+k4_x)*dt/6.
      v=v+(k1_v+2.*k2_v+2.*k3_v+k4_v)*dt/6.
      END SUBROUTINE MassAndSpring
!----------------------------------
      END MODULE RungeKutta
!===========================
      PROGRAM Circuit
!
! Use Runge-Kutta method to solve LRC circuit problems.
! Variable equivalences with mass-and-spring problem:
! V    => force F
! q    => displacement x
! i    => velocity v
! L    => mass m
! R    => damping constant D
! 1/C  => spring constant K
      USE RungeKutta, ONLY : MassAndSpring
      IMPLICIT NONE
      REAL i,q,L,C,R,V,t,dt,t_final
      REAL k1_i,k2_i,k3_i,k4_i
      INTEGER j,n
      CHARACTER*1 choice
!
```

```
! Choose circuit type...
!
      PRINT *,' Specify [o]scillating or [n]o oscillating term...'
      READ *,choice
      SELECT CASE (choice)
      CASE ('o','O')
! Ld^2q/dt^2+Rdq/dt+q/C=V
10      PRINT *,' Give V, L, R, C (4L/C-R^2) > 0:'
        READ *,V,L,R,C
        PRINT *, &
          ' one period at t=',4*3.14159*L/SQRT(4.*L/C-R*R),' s'
        PRINT *,' Give t_final and number of points:'
        READ *,t_final,n
        IF ((4.*L/C-R*R) <= 0.) GO TO 10
        q=0.; i=C*V*R/2./L; t=0. !Initial values
        dt=t_final/REAL(n)
        PRINT *,'          time             q            i  analytic q'
        DO j=1,n
          CALL MassAndSpring(q,i,R,1./C,L,V,dt)
          t=t+dt
          PRINT 1000, &
          t,q,i,C*V*(1.-EXP(-R*t/2./L)*COS(SQRT(4.*L/C-R*R)*t/2./L))
        END DO
1000    FORMAT(1x,es12.6,3es12.4)
!
      CASE ('n','N')
! Ldi/dt+Ri=V (no oscillating term)...
        PRINT *,' Give V, L, R:'
        READ *,V,L,R
        PRINT *,' time constant at t=',L/R,' s'
        PRINT *,' Give t_final and number of points:'
        READ *,t_final,n
        i=0.; t=0. !Initial values
        dt=t_final/REAL(n)
        PRINT *,'          time             i         analytic 1'
        DO j=1,n
! Runge-Kutta coefficients...
          k1_i=(V-R*i               )/L
          k2_i=(V-R*(i+k1_i*dt/2.))/L
          k3_i=(V-R*(i+k2_i*dt/2.))/L
          k4_i=(V-R*(i+k3_i*dt)   )/L
! Propagate solution...
          i=i+(k1_i+2.*k2_i+2.*k3_i+k4_i)*dt/6.
          t=t+dt
          PRINT 1000,t,i,V/R*(1.-EXP(-R*t/L))
        END DO
!
      CASE DEFAULT
        PRINT *,' No such choice.  Try again...'
      END SELECT
!
      END
```

Running P-11.7 (LR circuit)

```
    Specify [o]scillating or [n]o oscillating term...
n
  Give V, L, R:
100 .02 25
  time constant at t=   7.9999998E-04  s
  Give t_final and number of points:
.001 20
        time            i           analytic 1
  5.000000E-05  2.4235E-01  2.4235E-01
  1.000000E-04  4.7001E-01  4.7001E-01
  1.500000E-04  6.8388E-01  6.8388E-01
  2.000000E-04  8.8480E-01  8.8480E-01
  2.500000E-04  1.0735E+00  1.0735E+00
  3.000000E-04  1.2508E+00  1.2508E+00
  3.500000E-04  1.4174E+00  1.4174E+00
  4.000000E-04  1.5739E+00  1.5739E+00
  4.500000E-04  1.7209E+00  1.7209E+00
  5.000000E-04  1.8590E+00  1.8590E+00
  5.500000E-04  1.9887E+00  1.9887E+00
  6.000000E-04  2.1105E+00  2.1105E+00
  6.500001E-04  2.2250E+00  2.2250E+00
  7.000001E-04  2.3326E+00  2.3326E+00
  7.500001E-04  2.4336E+00  2.4336E+00
  8.000002E-04  2.5285E+00  2.5285E+00
  8.500002E-04  2.6176E+00  2.6176E+00
  9.000002E-04  2.7014E+00  2.7014E+00
  9.500002E-04  2.7801E+00  2.7801E+00
  1.000000E-03  2.8540E+00  2.8540E+00
```

Figure 11.7 shows more of the solution.

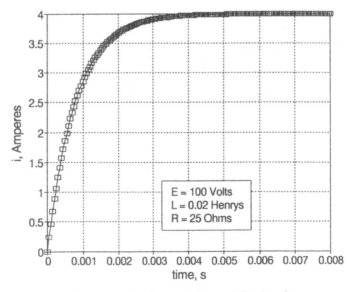

Figure 11.7. Current in an LR circuit

Running 11.7 (LRC circuit)

```
  Specify [o]scillating or [n]o oscillating term...
o
  Give V, L, R, C (4L/C-R^2) > 0:
100 .02 25 1e-6
  one period at t=    8.9206733E-04  s
  Give t_final and number of points:
.001 20
          time            q              i    analytic q
 5.000000E-05    9.2773E-06    2.9723E-01    9.0252E-06
 1.000000E-04    2.9345E-05    4.8089E-01    2.8413E-05
 1.500000E-04    5.7054E-05    5.9355E-01    5.5211E-05
 2.000000E-04    8.8488E-05    6.2533E-01    8.5756E-05
 2.500000E-04    1.1950E-04    5.7706E-01    1.1616E-04
 3.000000E-04    1.4623E-04    4.5952E-01    1.4278E-04
 3.500000E-04    1.6560E-04    2.9151E-01    1.6266E-04
 4.000000E-04    1.7562E-04    9.7026E-02    1.7382E-04
 4.500000E-04    1.7559E-04   -9.8052E-02    1.7545E-04
 5.000000E-04    1.6612E-04   -2.6931E-01    1.6794E-04
 5.500000E-04    1.4894E-04   -3.9674E-01    1.5273E-04
 6.000000E-04    1.2667E-04   -4.6702E-01    1.3212E-04
 6.500001E-04    1.0238E-04   -4.7476E-01    1.0891E-04
 7.000001E-04    7.9233E-05   -4.2269E-01    8.6037E-05
 7.500001E-04    6.0056E-05   -3.2088E-01    6.6222E-05
 8.000002E-04    4.7010E-05   -1.8499E-01    5.1659E-05
 8.500002E-04    4.1362E-05   -3.4040E-02    4.3775E-05
 9.000002E-04    4.3378E-05    1.1222E-01    4.3111E-05
 9.500002E-04    5.2352E-05    2.3577E-01    4.9309E-05
 1.000000E-03    6.6750E-05    3.2253E-01    6.1210E-05
```

Figure 11.8 shows more of this solution.

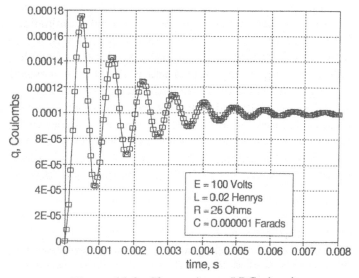

Figure 11.8. Charge in an LRC circuit

5 *Verify the operation of the program.*

The code in P-11.7 includes the analytic solution, which can be compared side-by-side with the numerical solution. Even though this problem is identical to the mass-and-spring problem discussed earlier, it is important to test the program with physically reasonable values. It is easy to imagine a mass on the order of a few hundred grams or so bouncing up and down at the end of a spring, with a period on the order of a second. For LRC circuits in radio circuits, for example, the magnitudes of the quantities are much different. Millihenrys, microfarads or picofarads, kilo- or mega-ohms, and megahertz frequencies are typical working units for quantities in such circuits. When you select values for testing, make sure that the time step is appropriately chosen so that it is much less than one oscillating period; $\Delta t = t_{osc}/100$ would be reasonable.[10]

For this problem, we can "cheat" in the sense that we know the analytic solution. In the code, the user is asked to input V, L, and R for the non-oscillating circuit, or V, L, R, and C for the oscillating circuit. In the former case, the program displays the time constant L/R to give an idea of the decay time. In the latter case, the program displays the oscillating period $t = 4\pi L/\sqrt{4L/C - R^2}$.

Problem Discussion

Of the numerical analysis problems presented in this chapter, solutions to differential equations pose the greatest difficulties. The Runge-Kutta algorithm has been chosen because it is a "classic" and is relatively simple to implement. However, it is in no sense a generally applicable technique or one that can always be depended upon to produce reliable results. Additional examination of this topic lies beyond the scope of this text. In contrast, Simpson's Rule integration, as discussed earlier in this chapter, will generally produce predictable and reliable results for functions without singularities and is therefore a reasonable working tool for evaluating many kinds of nonanalytic integrals.

For the LRC circuit treated in P-11.7 (and other oscillating systems), it is easy to pick values that don't work. If you don't have some idea of the oscillating period of the system, it is hard to pick time units and step sizes that will give a reasonable depiction of the motion. It is possible, for example, to pick a time step that produces what looks like the periodic motion of your system, but which in

---

[10]Author's note: I confess to working out this problem on a spreadsheet before writing the Fortran program because it is easier to try different values for the circuit and, of course, a spreadsheet has graphics capabilities built in, making it easier to examine the results of calculations.

fact is sampling from periodic motion taking place on a much smaller time scale. In other cases, your program will simply crash.

11.8 Exercises

(Because this chapter doesn't describe any new Fortran syntax, there are no self-testing exercises.)

11.8.1 Basic Programming Exercises

Exercise 1. The "plus or minus three standard deviations" rule mentioned in Section 11.2.1 can also be applied to linear regression models.

(a) Modify P-11.1 so that it prints a report of all data values that fall more than three standard deviations above or below the regression line.

(b) Include an additional modification that replaces all such "outlying" data values with the modeled value.

Exercise 2. Referring to the Problem Discussion following P-11.2 in Section 11.3.2, write a function `Stirling_f` that implements Stirling's formula for an analytic function whose derivative you know. Test this function with a driver program.

Exercise 3. Refer to the Application discussed in Section 11.3.2 and the measured distances and "measured" times (the ones generated with random errors) in Table 11.1. Assume a functional relationship between time t and distance D: $D = at^2/2$ for constant acceleration a. Calculate the acceleration value that best fits the data by determining which value produces the smallest sum of squares of the differences between true and "measured" distances; a trial-and-error approach is OK. Determine the speed v at each measured time by taking the analytic derivative of your model: $v = dD/dt = at$. Are these values closer to the true values than the values obtained using Stirling's formula to estimate the speed?

Exercise 4. Write subprograms for Rectangular Rule and Trapezoidal Rule integration. For a function whose integral is known, compare the results from these two subprograms with the results from Simpson's Rule integration as implemented in P-11.3.

Exercise 5. Modify P-11.6 so that the convergence criteria are specified by the user and supplied to the subroutine. One possibility might be to specify the criterion for the size of the interval as a fraction of the original interval.

Exercise 6. The Regula-Falsi method is a simple modification of the bisection method for finding roots that attempts to speed convergence to a root by making an informed guess about where the "midpoint" x_{mid} that subdivides an interval should be. The bisection method puts this point in the middle of the current subinterval. The Regula-Falsi method puts this point at the place where a straight line joining $f(x_L)$ and $f(x_R)$ crosses the x-axis. Modify P-11.6 to implement this modification.

Exercise 7. Modify P-11.5 so that it calculates a residual vector $\mathbf{R} = \mathbf{AX} - \mathbf{C}$. It is necessary, but not necessarily sufficient, that the residual vector be small before the vector $\mathbf{X}$ can be considered a "good" solution for the system.

11.8.2 Programming Applications

Exercise 8. The bisection method of finding roots was discussed in Section 11.6. Its advantage is that it doesn't require calculus to understand and implement this method.

> A basic understanding of differential calculus is required.

Its disadvantage is that it is relatively inefficient and may be unreliable. Newton's method is an alternative that may work better in some cases. Its potential disadvantage is that both $f(x)$ and its derivative $f'(x)$ are required.

To implement Newton's method, guess a root and recalculate x_{root} using the two-step algorithm

$$x_{old} = x_{root}$$
$$x_{root} = x_{root} - f(x_{root})/f'(x_{root})$$

Continue to recalculate x_{root} until $|f(x_{root})|$ or $|x_{old} - x_{root}|$ is less than some specified value.

There are some situations in which this algorithm fails; for example, whenever $f'(x)$ equals zero for an initial guess or any subsequent estimate of a root. Therefore, it is a good idea to limit the maximum number of iterations. Note that in contrast with the bisection method, a root found by Newton's algorithm may lie far from an initial guess and not necessarily within an initially specified range of x values. [NEWTON.F90]

Exercise 9. A manufacturer of laminated panels wishes to mold some ripple-shaped panels. The finished size of the sheet is 4'×8', with the ripples running along the 8' side. Assume that

> A basic understanding of integral calculus is required.

the ripples are in the shape of a sine curve, with a specified amplitude ±b and length L; for example, ±0.5" and 3". (See Figure 11.9.) How long must the original sheet of material be to produce a finished panel with a length of 8'?

Figure 11.9. Parameters for a rippled panel

The length of a segment ds along a curve formed by a function $y(x)$ is

$$ds = \sqrt{dx^2 + dy^2} = \sqrt{1 + \left(\frac{dy}{dx}\right)^2}\, dx$$

For a sine curve of amplitude b and length L,

$$ds = \sqrt{1 + \left[\frac{2\pi b}{L}\cos\left(\frac{2\pi x}{L}\right)\right]^2}\, dx$$

The length of the material required to make L inches of panel is the integral of ds from 0 to L. This integral cannot be evaluated analytically. Use Simpson's Rule to evaluate the integral for user-specified values of b and L. [RIPPLE.F90]

Extra Credit

If b << L, ds can be approximated by a series expansion, the terms of which can be integrated analytically. Use the first two terms in the binomial series for $(1 + x)^{1/2}$ to verify the results of Simpson's Rule integration as b approaches 0.

Exercise 10. This chapter has discussed the Gaussian elimination method for solving systems of linear equations. Another method, one of a class of so-called relaxation methods, is Gauss-Seidel iteration. To illustrate, let's consider a system of three equations:

$$x_1 a_{11} + x_2 a_{12} + x_3 a_{13} = c_1$$
$$x_1 a_{21} + x_2 a_{22} + x_3 a_{23} = c_2$$
$$x_1 a_{31} + x_2 a_{32} + x_3 a_{33} = c_3$$

Make an initial estimate for the unknowns (x_1, x_2, x_3); (1, 1, 1) is a reasonable choice. Then solve the first equation for x_1 in terms of x_2 and x_3, the second for x_2 in terms of x_1 and x_3, and the third for x_3 in terms of x_1 and x_2:

$$x_1 = \frac{c_1 - a_{12}x_2 - a_{13}x_3}{a_{11}} \qquad x_2 = \frac{c_2 - a_{21}x_1 - a_{23}x_3}{a_{22}} \qquad x_3 = \frac{c_3 - a_{31}x_1 - a_{32}x_2}{a_{33}}$$

Repeat this process iteratively until convergence criteria are met. Note that the newest estimated value is always used in subsequent calculations. That is, the first iteration on x_2 uses the new estimate of x_1 and the original estimate of x_3 because a new estimate of x_3 isn't yet available.

Convergence can be either relative or absolute. If absolute convergence is required, for all values of x_i on the kth iteration:

$$\left| x_i^{\,k} - x_k^{\,k-1} \right| < \epsilon$$

If relative convergence is acceptable, for all values of x_i on the kth iteration,

$$\frac{\left| x_i^{\,k} - x_i^{\,k-1} \right|}{\left| x_i^{\,k} \right|} < \epsilon$$

where ϵ is some user-specified small number.

This method is trivial to generalize to larger systems, and it is relatively easy to program. However, for a variety of reasons that are beyond the scope of this text, the iteration will not converge for all systems of equations. One obvious requirement is that all the diagonal coefficients must be nonzero. Chances for convergence are good for "diagonally dominant" matrices of coefficients. Therefore, it is a good idea to arrange the equations so that, if possible, the diagonal terms are larger than all the others. It may also be helpful to normalize all the equations by dividing each equation by the diagonal coefficient so that the diagonal coefficients are all equal to 1. If the off-diagonal terms are all small compared to 1, then chances for convergence are good.

Because of possible convergence problems, your program should set a maximum number of iterations as one of the terminating conditions in the loop that controls the iterations.

Here is a system of equations for which Gauss-Seidel iteration will converge:

$$\begin{aligned}
56x_1 + 22x_2 + 11x_3 - 18x_4 &= 34 \\
17x_1 + 66x_2 - 12x_3 + 7x_4 &= 82 \\
3x_1 - 5x_2 + 47x_3 + 20x_4 &= 18 \\
11x_1 + 16x_2 + 17x_3 + 10x_4 &= 26
\end{aligned}$$

Note that the diagonal terms are largest in all but the last equation. [GAUS_SEI.F90]

Exercise 11. In Section 11.5.1, it has been stated that some matrices are "ill conditioned" and resist attempts at solution with Gaussian elimination. One well-known example is the Hilbert matrix. Here is a 5×5 Hilbert matrix for $AX = C$.

$$A = \begin{pmatrix} 1 & 1/2 & 1/3 & 1/4 & 1/5 \\ 1/2 & 1/3 & 1/4 & 1/5 & 1/6 \\ 1/3 & 1/4 & 1/5 & 1/6 & 1/7 \\ 1/4 & 1/5 & 1/6 & 1/7 & 1/8 \\ 1/5 & 1/6 & 1/7 & 1/8 & 1/9 \end{pmatrix} \quad C = \begin{pmatrix} 1 \\ 0 \\ 0 \\ 0 \\ 0 \end{pmatrix}$$

Express the decimal fractions with seven significant digits (*e.g.*, .3333333). What is the solution when you apply Gaussian elimination to this matrix? What is the solution if you express the decimal fractions with only four significant digits (*e.g.*, .1667)?

Extra Credit

Refer to Section 12.3 in Chapter 12 and modify your Gaussian elimination subroutine so that it uses extended precision arithmetic. Express the coefficients of the A matrix with an appropriate number of digits, based on your data declarations for extended precision variables. What happens to the solution to the Hilbert matrix?

Exercise 12. Consider a radioactive particle inside a cube-shaped block. What is the probability, as a function of its original location, that the particle will exit the block on a particular side? Assuming that travel in all directions is equally probable, an answer to a simplified version of this question can be obtained by modeling the problem in two dimensions. Set up a grid of possible locations. Three rows of three locations are sufficient to set up the problem:

```
┌─┬─┬─┐
├─1─2─3─┤
├─4─5─6─┤
├─7─8─9─┤
└─┴─┴─┘
```

What is the probability that a particle will escape through a specified face of the grid? Suppose the bottom is chosen. The probability can be expressed as a system of equations in which P_n is the probability that a particle at position n will escape through the bottom of the grid. This probability is one-fourth the sum of the probabilities that a particle in the four locations surrounding n will escape through the bottom:

$$P_1 = (0 + P_2 + P_4 + 0)/4 \qquad P_2 = (0 + P_3 + P_5 + P_1)/4 \qquad P_3 = (0 + 0 + P_6 + P_2)/4$$
$$P_4 = (P_1 + P_5 + P_7 + 0)/4 \qquad P_5 = (P_2 + P_6 + P_8 + P_4)/4 \qquad P_6 = (P_3 + 0 + P_9 + P_5)/4$$
$$P_7 = (P_4 + P_8 + 1 + 0)/4 \qquad P_8 = P_5 + P_9 + 1 + P_7)/4 \qquad P_9 = (P_6 + 0 + 1 + P_8)/4$$

Rewrite these equations in the form $AP = C$ and solve for P. Try both Gaussian elimination as described earlier in this chapter and Gauss-Seidel iteration as described in Exercise 10. For Gauss-Seidel iteration, are the results sensitive to the initial reasonable guesses for P?

One test of your program's output is the fact that the probability of a particle initially in the center of the grid escaping through any specified side of the grid should be exactly 0.25. [ESCAPE.F90]

12

A Closer Look

The purpose of this chapter is to provide some additional insight into various Fortran 90 features. Each section is self-contained. There are several complete programs, but in contrast to previous chapters, there are no applications or exercises.

12.1 Introduction

The topics presented in this chapter have in common only the fact that they may be considered optional. It is, in fact, possible to do a great deal of programming without studying any of the topics in this chapter.

Each section in this chapter is completely self-contained and is intended as a guide to a topic you may wish to explore in more depth on your own. For more complete information, you will need to refer to a Fortran 90 reference manual (see Section i.3 in the Preface to this text) or the documentation for whatever version of Fortran you are using. Also, there are no exercises at the end of this chapter. This is based on the assumption that, if your instructor has asked you to study one or more of the topics in this chapter, she or he already has a very specific goal in mind.

The first topic, incorporating multiple source code and precompiled files into a program, contains material that your instructor may believe is very important even in an introductory course because of the way Fortran is used in practice. For example, your instructor may wish to provide you with certain problem-solving capabilities in the form of source code or precompiled files to use in your own programs, even though the writing of that code might be beyond your current capabilities.

The second topic deals with the internal representation of numbers and how the properties of INTEGER and REAL numbers can be controlled. This may be of interest in programming applications that require very small or very large numbers, or that require a more thorough understanding of the process of real arithmetic as it is performed by Fortran. A more advanced course in numerical analysis is one place where these questions are important because, for example, arithmetic roundoff errors arising from limited accuracy in individual calculations with REAL numbers are often cumulative.

There is a tendency for students to believe that all problems with arithmetic calculations in numerical analysis can be fixed simply by using numbers with more significant digits. In fact, this is typically not the case. Problems traceable to a loss of accuracy in numerical calculations are inherent in the methods themselves. Although the accumulation of unacceptable errors can be postponed, such errors cannot actually be eliminated just by carrying extra significant digits in calculations. If accumulated roundoff errors are causing difficulties with a particular calculation, it may be more useful to examine alternate means of posing and solving the problem at hand.

The third topic in this chapter addresses the many array-handling capabilities provided by Fortran 90. In previous chapters, we have occasionally used these capabilities to eliminate source code that would have been required in earlier versions of Fortran (and in other procedural languages, for that matter). The most important capabilities allow us to write simple statements that perform operations on arrays that would previously have required loop structures, with their accompanying variable initializations and assignment statements.

The fourth topic introduces alternate ways to construct and use files. Most importantly, this discussion includes random access binary files, which provide a much more flexible means of storing and manipulating information in files. With random access to files, we can extend to files some of the algorithms originally applied in this text to arrays. Thus we can contemplate dealing with collections of data that are too large to be held in arrays in memory.

The fifth topic is a very brief introduction to the COMPLEX data type. Although support for complex numbers is an important part of Fortran because of its mathematical heritage, this text assumes that you will not develop the mathematical sophistication required to make good use of complex numbers until well after taking an introductory programming course. For now, it is sufficient simply to know that this data type exists. You can give it more attention later when a real need arises.

For the final topic, we will return to the COMMON block, discussed briefly in Chapter 7. Even though Fortran 90 provides much better ways of sharing information among programs and subprograms, the COMMON block deserves some additional attention because it is a familiar feature in older Fortran programs.

12.2 Using More Than One Program Unit

Throughout most of this text, we have emphasized the importance of modularized program design. In Fortran, there are several ways to write modularized programs. Early in the text, we used simple statement functions. Later, we used functions and subroutines to accomplish the goal of writing structured "top-down" code that divides a large program's multiple tasks into several smaller and, hopefully, more manageable tasks. We included functions and subroutines in MODULEs, and we often USEd those subprograms in driver programs whose only purpose was to test the subprograms. Once they have been thoroughly tested, the MODULEs are available for use in other programs.

The programs presented previously in this text share one common feature: all the source code for a program is contained in a single file. Each such file is a single program unit. However, many Fortran applications require that subprograms be assembled from several program units. There are two basic ways to accomplish this. At the source code level, a compiler can be directed to use source code from other files—essentially to copy source code from an existing file into the new source code. The contents of these other source code files then become part of the executable program when it is compiled.

The second way to add code to a program is by linking together program units after they have been compiled. In this case, you can use compiled program units even though you may have no access to, or understanding of, the source code itself.

The first option works essentially like a "text merge" operation in a word processor. If the program unit into which another source code file is being merged contains a main program, the only restriction is that the merged source code can contain only subprograms; a Fortran program can have only one main program. Of course the merged source code must make sense, just as it would if it had originally been written in a single source code file. Typically, merged source code contains one or more subroutines in one or more MODULEs.

The second option—linking two or more previously compiled source code files—is possible because Fortran source code can be compiled even if it doesn't contain a main program. That is, it is possible to compile a source code file containing just subprograms, even though the resulting compiled (binary) code can't be executed because it doesn't include a main program.

The ability to link a main program (with or without "local" subprograms) with one or more previously compiled program units is critical to the professional use of Fortran. With this capability, subprogram "packages" to perform highly specialized tasks can be added to your own programs even though you don't understand (or have never even seen) the source code in those specialized subprograms. All you need to know is what the information interface looks like for each subprogram so you can provide appropriate input to obtain a clearly defined output. This is a familiar algorithm and program design requirement that has been stressed throughout the text. Remember that in Fortran 90, the information interface is implemented by assigning IN, OUT, or INOUT attributes to subroutine and function parameters.

To demonstrate how to create a program from several units, we will return to the subprograms and driver program for numerical differentiation developed in Chapter 11. The code is simple and numerical differentiation is an appropriate choice because it is in the area of numerical analysis that you will most likely need to use specialized subprograms from other sources in your own programs.

12.2.1 Merging Source Code

First recall program P-11.2, FALLING.F90, the purpose of which was to test a function that uses Stirling's approximation to a function's derivative—in this case to approximate the speed of a falling object. In that program, the main program and the MODULE containing the function were included in a single program unit. However, it is not necessary to do this.

Program P-12.1 is similar to P-11.2, but renamed DERIVATV.F90 to avoid confusion with the program in Chapter 11.

P-12.1 [DERIVATV.F90]

```
      MODULE Numerical_Differentiation
!
      CONTAINS
!-------------------------------------------------------
      REAL FUNCTION derivative_2(x1,x2,x3,y1,y2,y3)
!
      IMPLICIT NONE
      REAL, INTENT(IN) :: x1,x2,x3,y1,y2,y3
!
      derivative_2=((y2-y1)/(x2-x1)+(y3-y2)/(x3-x2))/2.
      RETURN
      END FUNCTION derivative_2
!-------------------------------------------------------
      END MODULE Numerical_DIfferentiation
!
      PROGRAM Derivative
!
! Driver for numerical differentiation routines.
! File name DERIVATV.F90.
!
      USE Numerical_Differentiation
      IMPLICIT NONE
      TYPE distance_data
        REAL true_time
        REAL true_distance
        REAL true_speed
        REAL measured_time
      END TYPE distance_data
      TYPE(distance_data) distance(0:20)
      REAL g
      INTEGER i
      PARAMETER (g=9.8) !m/s**2 (gravitational acceleration)
!
      OPEN(1,file='derivatv.dat')
! Get data...
!     (Read past 2 header lines.)
      READ(1,*)
      READ(1,*)
      DO i=0,20
        READ(1,*)distance(i)%true_time,distance(i)%true_distance,&
                distance(i)%true_speed,distance(i)%measured_time
        PRINT *,distance(i)%true_time,distance(i)%true_distance
      END DO
```

```
        CLOSE(1)
! Calculate numerical derivative...
        DO i=0,20
          IF ((i==0) .OR. (i==20)) THEN
            PRINT 1000, &
               distance(i)%true_time,distance(i)%true_distance, &
               distance(i)%true_speed,distance(i)%measured_time
          ELSE
            PRINT1000, &
               distance(i)%true_time,distance(i)%true_distance, &
               distance(i)%true_speed,distance(i)%measured_time,&
                       derivative_2(distance(i-1)%true_time, &
                                    distance(i)  %true_time, &
                                    distance(i+]%true_time, &
                                    distance(i-1)%true_distance, &
                                    distance(i)  %true_distance, &
                                    distance(i+1)%true_distance)
          END IF
        END DO
!
1000    FORMAT(1x,f4.1,5f10.3)
        END
```

It is left for the diligent reader to run this program with its accompanying data file, DERIVATV.DAT, because the point of this discussion is not the source code, but to look at alternative ways to produce the executable code for this program. One possibility is shown in program P-12.1(a).

P-12.1(a) [DERIVAT2.F90]

```
INCLUDE 'c:\ftn90.dir\deri_mod.f90'
      PROGRAM Derivative
!
! Driver for numerical differentiation routines.
! File name DERIVAT2.F90.
(and so forth)
```

P-12.1(a) is functionally identical to P-12.1. It differs only in its assumption that MODULE Numerical_Differentiation has been saved as a separate file. The main program source code is identical and is not reproduced here. The line

```
INCLUDE 'c:\ftn90.dir\deri_mod.f90'
```

appearing at the top of the source code results in the MODULE code in the MS-DOS file c:\ftn90.dir\deri_mod.f90 being *physically* copied into the source code file at compile time.

The general syntax of the INCLUDE statement, which instructs the compiler to insert the referenced file into the source code, is

> INCLUDE *string constant containing file name, including path*

The INCLUDE line is *not* a Fortran statement. It is properly referred to as a ***compiler directive***. The 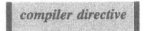 INCLUDE directive is similar to a "merge" function in a word processor except that you don't actually see the complete merged source code file. (If you want or need to see it, you should simply physically copy all the source code rather than use an INCLUDE directive.) You can have more than one INCLUDE directive, so your program can access code from many different source code files.

The file DERI_MOD.F90 referred to in the above INCLUDE directive is, as you should expect, a source code file containing just the MODULE for numerical differentiation. This file can be downloaded from the World Wide Web site mentioned in Section i.5 of the Preface.

What has been accomplished by using an INCLUDE statement? Remember that P-12.1 is just a test program for the numerical differentiation subprograms. Once the testing is complete, the MODULE can be saved separately—in this case as DERI_MOD.F90; this file can now be INCLUDEd in any program that needs the capabilities provided by the subprogram.

Although it is common in Fortran 90 to use INCLUDE lines to access existing MODULEs, the included code doesn't *have* to be a MODULE. INCLUDE directives can appear anywhere in your program. So you can also include subprograms that aren't part of a MODULE, typically after the main program, or even sections of code in the main program. The only restriction is that you must be aware of the contents of the code so that it will make sense wherever it is INCLUDEd.

12.2.2 Merging Object Code

As indicated above, it is not even necessary to have the source code for the numerical differentiation subprograms in order to use them. An alternative is to compile separately the main program from P-12.1 and the MODULE DERI_MOD.F90 and then link the two resulting binary (object) files together. In this case, the main program's source code still USEs the Numerical_Integration module, but it doesn't need to contain any reference to the source code file that contains this module. Source code for the main program of P-12.1 is stored as DERIVAT3.F90; it can be downloaded from the World Wide Web site mentioned in Section i.5 of the Preface. The point of doing this is the same as for using an INCLUDE directive for source code: the capabilities included in the numerical differentiation subprograms are now available to any program that needs them.

Where do the two object files come from? Depending on what kind of computer system and Fortran compiler you are using, you may be more or less aware of the creation of separate object files as an intermediate step to producing an executable file. There is not really any motivation to keep track of these intermediate files when you are creating an executable file from a single source code file.

Although systems differ in details, the general principle is always the same. After compiling your source code file to create an object file, a linker program combines this object file with required Fortran library files and, if you request it, other pre-existing object files; this process has been shown symbolically in Figure 3.4 in Chapter 3.

Here are the steps necessary to compile the main program DERIVAT3.F90 and the MODULE contained in DERI_MOD.F90 and link these two object files together to produce a single executable file, using the compiler employed to develop the programs in this text (the NAG/Salford FTN90 compiler for MS-DOS and Windows systems). Other systems will differ in detail, but the principle will be the same.

```
ftn90 derivat3.f90
ftn90 deri_mod.f90
link77
$ load derivat3
$ load deri_mod
$ file derivat3
derivat3
```

The first two lines separately compile the main program DERIVAT3 and the MODULE subprogram DERI_MOD.F90. The third line executes a linker program, called LINK77 in this case; this program (apparently left over from earlier versions of Fortran) is part of the Fortran environment provided with the FTN90 compiler. The LINK77 commands following the $ prompt, which is provided by LINK77 and is not typed, assume that source code files have an .F90 extension, compiled binary files have an .OBJ extension, and the resulting executable file has an .EXE extension; these are the usual extensions and there is no reason to change them. However, you might wish to give the executable file a name different from any of its components. You may link together several .OBJ files, in any order. The file... statement, which creates an executable file containing all the linked object files, terminates the LINK77 program. The optional final line derivat3 executes the newly created program.

Although the two source code files in this example have been compiled and linked together in a single sequence of steps, this isn't necessary. You can link *any* object files created with the compiler, no matter when they were created. However, you can't mix object files created on different computer systems or, possibly, even on the same system with different Fortran compilers. That is why no .OBJ files can be downloaded from the World Wide Web site mentioned in Section i.5 of the Preface.

When binary files are linked together to form an executable (.EXE) file, the importance of understanding the information interface between subprograms and a calling (sub)program becomes abundantly clear. Suppose you wished to let someone use subprograms you had created, but you did not wish them to have access to the source code. As we have just demonstrated, you can give them one or more .OBJ files containing the compiled subprograms, which they can then link to their own programs. However, because they can't determine the nature of the information interface by looking at your source code, you must provide them with details of how to use the subprograms. Suitable documentation for DERI_MOD.OBJ might look like this:

> The object file DERI_MOD.OBJ contains function derivative_2 for approximating numerical derivatives. Function derivative_2 is a type REAL function that calculates rates of change for tabulated data by averaging the "forward" and "backward" differences relative to the second of three data pairs. Its parameters are all REAL with INTENT(IN). Use of this function implies that an analytic description of tabulated data is either not known or doesn't exist and therefore that its derivative cannot be calculated analytically. The function is called like this,
>
> derivative_2(x1,x2,x3,y1,y2,y3)
>
> where all arguments are type REAL. The intervals x_2-x_1 and x_3-x_2 need not be equal.

12.3 The Internal Representation of Numbers and Extended Precision

12.3.1 Internal Representation of Numbers

As noted in previous discussions about INTEGER and REAL variables, integers and real numbers are stored differently in Fortran. We have also noted that, because computers are basically binary devices, integers can be stored exactly, but real numbers cannot, in general. In this section, we will briefly describe the internal format of numbers. You can pursue this topic in more detail on your own computer system by writing numbers into unformatted (binary) files (see Section 12.5) and then using a byte-level editing program to examine the contents of these files.

Integers

The familiar way of expressing integers is in a base 10 system, where each digit represents multiplication by a power of 10, starting on the right with 10^0. Thus the integer number 125 is a representation of $1\bullet10^2 + 2\bullet10^1 + 5\bullet10^0$. Such a system requires 10 distinct characters (the digits 0–9) to represent all possible values.

Integers can be represented in this way using any base. For computers, base 2 is convenient because only two characters, 0 and 1, which can be associated with "off" and "on" states in a computer, are required. The integer number 125 can be represented in base-2 (binary) notation as $1\bullet2^6 + 1\bullet2^5 + 1\bullet2^4 + 1\bullet2^3 + 1\bullet2^2 + 0\bullet2^1 + 1\bullet2^0 = 64 + 32 + 16 + 8 + 4 + 1$.

Another common representation uses a hexadecimal (base 16) system, with the integers 0–9 and the letters A–F representing the sixteen base-10 values 0–15. In hexadecimal notation, the decimal value 15 is represented as 0F and 125 is represented as 7D ($7\bullet16 + 13\bullet1$)

To see how this representation is used for the internal storage of integers, consider the statement

```
WRITE(1) 32767,-32767,1,-1
```

that writes integers to a file opened as unformatted (binary). A byte-level disk editor reveals that these values are stored in the following sequence of bytes, using their hexadecimal representation:

```
FF 7F 00 00 01 80 FF FF 01 00 00 00 FF FF FF FF
```

First of all, note that there are 16 bytes in all, from which you can conclude that each integer occupies four bytes. You might be tempted to think that the amount of storage is related to the size of the integer value—that is, that a value of 1 should take more storage than a value of 32767. However, this is not true. Every INTEGER value requires the same amount of space because the space allocated to store an integer is determined only by its data type.

The easiest place to start interpreting the byte pattern for the four digits is with the value 1. This is the third of the four values to be written to the file, so it must be stored in bytes 9–12: 01 00 00 00.

Positive integers are stored internally as their binary equivalent, which means that 1 should be stored as 00 00 00 01. The fact that the bytes seem to be stored "backwards" in the file is due to the fact that bytes are often stored in "low byte to high byte" order, rather than the natural "high byte to low byte" order that you might expect. If the four bytes used to store the value 1 are numbered,

```
 1  2  3  4
00 00 00 01
```

the order in which they are stored internally is probably

```
 4  3  2  1
01 00 00 00
```

Next consider the value 32767. Its four-byte binary equivalent is

```
00000000 00000000 01111111 11111111
```

In hexadecimal notation, this is 00 00 7F FF. However, Fortran stores these "backwards," as FF 7F 00 00, as shown in bytes 1–4 in the above file.

What about negative integers? A typical approach is to use a "twos complement" algorithm.

1. Convert the absolute value of a number to its binary equivalent.
2. Take the complement, which means to replace every 0 with a 1, and vice versa.
3. Add 1.

Thus −1 is stored as

```
00000000 00000000 00000000 00000001 (binary equivalent)
11111111 11111111 11111111 11111110 (complement)
11111111 11111111 11111111 11111111 (add 1)
```

Thus −1 would be stored as FF FF FF FF.

Similarly, −32767 would be represented as

```
00000000 00000000 01111111 11111111 (binary equivalent of 32767)
11111111 11111111 10000000 00000000 (complement)
11111111 11111111 10000000 00000001 (add 1)
```

Thus, -32767 would be stored as FF FF 80 01, or in low-high format, as 01 80 FF FF.

Although these conventions for storing integers might not seem to make much sense to humans, their purpose is to facilitate integer arithmetic, and the fact that they are efficient from a computer's point of view is all that matters. (You can find more information about twos complement arithmetic in any text on computer mathematics.)

Real Numbers

Storage of real numbers, including irrational numbers, is complicated by the fact that all values must somehow be stored in a binary format. There are several possibilities. One common format is the IEEE standard for floating-point numbers. Suppose a real number is stored in four bytes. The 32 bits, labeled right to left as bits 0 through 31, are divided into three fields, starting at the left.

Bit 31:   a sign bit, with 1 = negative and 0 = positive
Bits 23–30:   an exponent of 2 increased by 127
Bits 0–22:   the magnitude of the mantissa or fractional part related to the
               number

Values are encoded in this "normalized floating-point" form according to the
expression

$$(-1)^S \; 2^{(E-127)} \; (1.0 + F)$$

Consider the real number 20.0, as opposed to the integer 20. Although it's perhaps
not obvious how to arrive at this representation in general, 20.0 can be expressed
as 16•1.25 or 2^4•1.25. Thus the quantity F in the above expression is 0.25.
Fractions can be represented in binary form as a series having the general form

$$b_0/2 + b_1/2^2 + b_3/2^3 + \cdots$$

where the b's are binary digits (0 or 1). For the fractional value 0.25, the exact
representation is $0/2 + 1/4 + 0/8 + \cdots$.
     Thus the real number 20.0 can be represented as

0 (sign bit)
10000011 (131 = 127 + 4)
0100000000000000000000 (representation for 0.25)

or, arranged in a four-byte pattern,

01000001 10100000 00000000 00000000

In low-high hexadecimal notation, this is

00 00 A0 41

     The number 20 has the advantage that it can be represented exactly in this
format. In general, this is not true. Consider the number 33 1/3, or
33.3333333333.... The sign bit for this positive number will be 0. Since 2^5 is the
largest number represented as a power of 2 that is less than 33 1/3, the exponent
5 must be represented as 5 + 127 = 132. Dividing by 32, 33.33333333/32 =
1.0416666666.... The 1 is implied and the fractional part is represented by the first
23 terms in an infinite series:

$$0/2 + 0/2^2 + 0/2^3 + 0/2^4 + 1/2^5 + 0/2^6 + 1/2^7 + 0/2^8 + 1/2^9 + \cdots$$

Thus the representation of 33 1/3 is

0 (sign bit)
10000100 (exponent)
00001010101010101010101 (representation for .0416666666...)

or in bytes,

01000010 00000101 01010101 01010101

In low-high hexadecimal notation,

55 55 05 42

12.3.2 Specifying Precision for Numerical Variables

It's not necessary for most Fortran programmers to understand the details of how numbers are stored; these matters are more appropriate to computer science courses. However, Fortran 90's support for a user-specified precision number of significant digits in number representations is an important addition to the language that gives users more control over the accuracy of arithmetic calculations.

In Fortran 90, certain attributes of data types can be specified at the time they are declared by using the KIND parameter. We will discuss here the KIND parameters that are applicable to REAL and INTEGER data types.

Suppose you need an integer that will contain at least a specified number of digits. The intrinsic function Selected_Int_Kind returns an integer that can be used with a KIND parameter to declare an integer that meets the specified requirements. To declare an integer with at least 15 digits,

```
INTEGER, PARAMETER :: long_int=Selected_Int_Kind(15)
INTEGER(KIND=long_int) big_integer
```

In the type declaration, KIND= is optional, so you could also write INTEGER(long_int) big_integer.

Similarly, the function Selected_Real_Kind returns a parameter that can be used to declare a real number with at least a specified number of significant digits and a specified exponent range, as a power of 10. (The default exponent range is often ±38.) The general syntax is

```
Selected_Real_Kind([r][,k])
```

where r is the number of significant digits and k is the exponent. Both parameters are optional. To specify a real number with at least 15 digits of precision and an exponent range of $10^{\pm99}$,

```
INTEGER, PARAMETER :: long_real=Selected_Real_Kind(15,99)
REAL(KIND=long_real) x
```

As before, the KIND= is optional.

It's not difficult to find calculations that require more than the seven or eight significant digits supported by the default REAL data type. One example is the Julian date, which is typically used for astronomical calculations and calculations involving orbiting satellites. At least 13 significant digits are required to specify the Julian date to the nearest second on any calendar day.

How did earlier versions of Fortran provide additional precision for numerical variables? The Fortran 77 standard supports a data type for real numbers called DOUBLE PRECISION, which doubles the number of bytes used to store a real number—from four to eight, for example. Fortran 90 still supports this data type, which often appears in older Fortran source code, but its use is discouraged. (Why? Basically, because the actual precision available with DOUBLE PRECISION variables is system-dependent.) For integers, many Fortran 77 compilers support at least two additional data types. If the standard INTEGER data type occupies four bytes, then the compiler may support "regular" integers (INTEGER*4) as well as "short" and "long" integers (INTEGER*2 and INTEGER*8). However, this notation is nonstandard, so it can't be used in Fortran 90 programs even if it were otherwise a good idea.

Here is a problem statement that uses Julian date calculations and therefore requires extended precision variables.

1 Define the problem.

Time must be specified accurately and unambiguously in calculations used in astronomy or for describing the motion of orbiting satellites. The system commonly used is Julian time. The Julian day, which starts at noon, Greenwich Mean Time (GMT), assigns a unique integer value for every day, with an origin dating back to several thousand years BC. The Julian date for noon, January 1, 1995, is 2449719. Time, in fractions of a day, is measured from Greenwich noon. (This is because the system was originated by British astronomers who wished all observations during a single night to have the same Julian date.) Thus 6:00 p.m. GMT on 01/01/95 is Julian time 2449719 + 6/24 = 2449719.25.

Suppose you need to specify Julian time to the nearest second. There are 86,400 seconds in a day, so at least six digits are required to express Julian time to the nearest second. Thus at least 13 significant digits—seven for the day and six for the fractional day—are required to represent Julian time with full precision. Although it is sufficient for some purposes to store the day separately, as an integer, from the fractional part, it would be simpler just to store the entire Julian time value, including the day, as a single real number.

The formula for converting a specified calendar date to its corresponding Julian date is not obvious because of the complexities of the calendar system, including months of different lengths and leap years. Here it is for a specified day, month, and year,

temp=<(mon-14)/12>
Julian day = day - 32075 + <1461*(year + 4800 + temp)/4> +
           <367*(mon - 2 - temp*12)/12> - <3*<(year + 4900 + temp)/100>/4>

where <...> indicates that the value of the enclosed expression should be truncated (not rounded).

2 Outline a solution.

1. Convert a specified day, month, and year to Julian day as indicated in the problem statement. (Use a function for this calculation.)
2. Convert a specified time, expressed as hours, minutes, and seconds (including fractional seconds if needed), to fraction of a day from GMT noon according to this formula:

$$\text{fraction of day} = (\text{hour} - 12)/24 + \text{min}/1440 + \text{sec}/86400$$

3. Add the Julian day to the day fraction. The variable that holds this sum must have a precision of at least 13 decimal digits.

3 Design an algorithm.

The pseudocode is a straightforward implementation of Step 2.

(Get calendar date)
CALL *Calendar_to_Julian(day, month, year, Julian day)*
(Get time relative to GMT noon)
CALL *DayFraction(hr, min, sec, fraction)*

SUBPROGRAM *Calendar_to_Julian(IN: day, month, year; OUT: Julian day (integer))*
ASSIGN *temp = <(mon - 14)/12>*
      Julian day = day - 32075 + <1461•(year + 4800 + temp)/4> +
            <367•(mon - 2 - temp•12)/12> -
            <3•<(year + 4900 + temp)/100>/4>
(end Calendar_to_Julian)

SUBPROGRAM *DayFraction(IN: hr, min, sec;*
                        OUT: fraction of a day (real))
ASSIGN *fraction of a day = (hr – 12)/24 + min/1440 + sec/86400*
(end DayFraction)

4 *Convert the algorithm into a program.*

P-12.2 [JULIAN_T.F90]

```
      PROGRAM Julian_t
!
! Tests a function to calculate Julian time to the nearest
! second for a specified GMT on a specified calendar day.
!
      IMPLICIT NONE
      INTEGER mon,day,year,hh,mm,ss
      INTEGER Calendar_to_Julian !function to get Julian date
      REAL DayFraction
      INTEGER, PARAMETER :: long=Selected_Real_Kind(14)
      REAL(kind=long) JulianTime
!
      PRINT *,' Give a calendar date in the format mm dd yyyy:'
      READ *,mon,day,year
      JulianTime=REAL(Calendar_to_Julian(mon,day,year))
      PRINT 1000,JulianTime
      PRINT *,' Give clock time as hh mm ss, GMT:'
      READ *,hh,mm,ss
      JulianTime= JulianTime + DayFraction(hh-12,mm,ss)
      PRINT 1010,JulianTime
1000  FORMAT(' The Julian date at 12h00m00s GMT is ',f10.1)
1010  FORMAT(' The Julian time is               ',f16.7)
!
      END
!
      INTEGER FUNCTION Calendar_to_Julian(mon,day,year)
!
! Converts Gregorian calendar date to a Julian date.
! Test value: 01/01/1995 = 2449719 (Greenwich noon).
!
      IMPLICIT NONE
      INTEGER, INTENT(IN) :: mon,day,year
      INTEGER temp
!
```

```
        temp=(mon-14)/12
        Calendar_to_Julian=day-32075+1461*(year+4800+temp)/4+ &
                     367*(mon-2-temp*12)/12-                   &
                     3*((year+4900+temp)/100)/4
        RETURN
        END FUNCTION Calendar_to_Julian
!
        REAL FUNCTION DayFraction(hh,mm,ss)
!
! Converts hours, minutes, and seconds into a fraction of a day.
!
        IMPLICIT NONE
        INTEGER, INTENT(IN) :: hh,mm,ss
!
        DayFraction=REAL(hh)/24.+REAL(mm)/1440.+REAL(ss)/86400.
        RETURN
        END FUNCTION DayFraction
```

Running P-12.2

```
Give a calendar date in the format mm dd yyyy:
07 10 1996
 The Julian date at 12h00m00s GMT is  2450275.0
 Give clock time as hh mm ss, GMT:
14 30 00
 The Julian time is                   2450275.1041667
```

5 Verify the operation of the program.

The Julian date can be verified by consulting a table of Julian dates, which can be found in texts and reference books on astronomy. (One test date is given in the internal documentation for Calendar_to_Julian.) Note that such tables often give the Julian date corresponding to the calendar date at 0.5 GMT; this means noon on the *previous* calendar day. Thus a tabulated value of 2449718 will be given for January 0.5, 1995. This is a convenience for calculating the Julian date corresponding to noon on any day of the month; just add the day number to the tabulated value.

The fractional part of the day can be checked by hand. Remember that the time is relative to noon, not midnight. This is why the argument in the call to DayFraction is hh−12 rather than hh.

Problem Discussion

The critical step in this program is using a KIND parameter to ensure that the variable holding the Julian time has enough significant digits. The argument 14 in the call to the Fortran 90 function Selected_Real_Kind returns a KIND parameter that can be used to define a REAL number with at least 14 significant digits. In this example, the second parameter can be omitted because the default exponent range (typically 10^{-38} to 10^{+38}) is usually much larger than required. The Fortran compiler responds to KIND parameters by increasing or decreasing the number of bytes associated with a REAL variable. Since only whole bytes can be allocated, the *actual* number of digits may be even more than you requested. A call to the Fortran 90 function Precision will verify the actual number of significant digits that are available; when this program is executed on the compiler used to develop the programs in this text, Precision returns a value of 15.

Note that the INT function is not required to truncate the expressions. This is because each constant value or variable in the truncated expressions, all of which involve a division, is an integer. When both numerator and denominator of a division expression are integers, the quotient is a truncated integer.

12.4 Array Operations and Array Inquiry and Reduction Functions

Fortran 90's major development in array processing is its ability to treat arrays as objects that can be manipulated in their entirety rather than as a collection of elements that must be manipulated one at a time. One consequence that has already been discussed in Chapter 4 is that the arguments of the intrinsic functions, listed in Table 4.1, are so-called elemental functions that can accept, in addition to scalar arguments, array arguments whose elements are of an appropriate data type. It is never required to use the intrinsic functions in this way, but doing so can often save significant amounts of code; element-by-element array operations always require explicit or implicit loop structures.

Although it is less obvious, and less important to beginning programmers, the ability to treat arrays as objects can be important when Fortran programs are written for high-performance parallel processing computers. Using a syntax that deals with arrays in their entirety rather than one element at a time means that access to parallel processing capabilities, in which operations on the elements of an array are carried out in parallel (all at once) rather than in series (one at a time), is incorporated into the Fortran 90 language standard. The following subsections will explore some of the syntax possibilities.

12.4.1 Intrinsic Array Operations

The treatment of arrays as objects rather than as a collection of elements extends *all* the intrinsic operators as well. Thus, for example, it is possible to write

conformable array

```
A = B*C
```

where A, B, and C are ***conformable arrays*** rather than scalar variables. Conformable arrays must have the same shape; that is, the ranks and extents of each dimension must be the same.

Intrinsic operations on arrays apply to each element of the array. If you keep this in mind, you don't need to worry about the definition of conformable arrays. The statement A = B*C is allowed only if the arithmetic operation(s) make sense in an algorithm design context; that is, if there are corresponding elements in all of the arrays A, B, and C.

One additional fact that might not be obvious is that, by definition, a scalar variable is conformable with any array whose elements have the same (or a compatible) data type as that scalar variable. That is, in the statement A = B*C, either B or C may be a scalar variable. (It should be clear that A must be an array if either B or C is an array.)

In considering the statement A = B*C, it is important to remember that A is *not* the dot product of the vectors B and C even though the notation looks similar to the vector notation **A = B•C**; the dot product is a scalar value, not an array. (In the next subsection, you will see that Fortran 90 includes a function for calculating the dot product of two vectors.)

12.4.2 Array Functions

In addition to intrinsic operations on conformable arrays, Fortran 90 includes several intrinsic functions that deal specifically with arrays. Table 12.1 lists some of these functions.

Array manipulation functions have in common the fact that they each require at least one array-typed argument. Most of them allow one or more optional arguments. The names of the three possible arguments, ARRAY, DIM, and MASK, can appear in calls to these functions, followed by an = sign. These names must be used as given, although they are case-insensitive; they are not "variable names" that are user-selectable. If the names do not appear, the optional arguments must be given in the order shown, with an extra comma separating the first and third arguments if all three arguments are not given.

Table 12.1. Array multiplication, inquiry, and reduction functions

Function Name	Function
Multiplication Functions	
`DOT_PRODUCT(VECTOR_A,VECTOR_B)`	Calculates the dot product of two vectors.
`MATMUL(MATRIX_A,MATRIX_B)`	Calculates the product of two matrices.
Inquiry Functions	
`LBOUND(ARRAY[,DIM])`	Returns an integer containing the lower bound of the indices for `ARRAY`, optionally for the specified dimension of a multidimensional array.
`SHAPE(ARRAY)`	Returns a rank one integer array holding the shape of `ARRAY`. If `ARRAY` is a scalar, the result is zero.
`SIZE(ARRAY[,DIM])`	Returns an integer that is the size of `ARRAY`, optionally for the specified dimension of a multidimensional array.
`UBOUND(ARRAY[,DIM])`	As for `LBOUND`, except for the upper bound
Reduction Functions	
`ALL(MASK[,DIM])`	Returns `.TRUE.` if all elements of `MASK` are true, `.FALSE.` otherwise optionally for the specified dimension of a multidimensional array.
`ANY(MASK[,DIM])`	Returns `.TRUE.` if any elements of `MASK` are true, `.FALSE.` otherwise, optionally for the specified dimension of a multi-dimensional array.
`COUNT(MASK[,DIM])`	Returns number of elements for which `MASK` equals `.TRUE.`, optionally for the specified dimension of a multidimensional array.
`MAXVAL(ARRAY[,DIM][,MASK])`	Returns maximum value in specified dimension of `ARRAY`.
`MINVAL(ARRAY[,DIM][,MASK])`	Returns minimum value in specified dimension of `ARRAY`.
`PRODUCT(ARRAY[,DIM][,MASK])`	Returns product of all elements of a specified dimension of `ARRAY`.
`SUM(ARRAY[,DIM][,MASK])`	Returns sum of all elements of a specified dimension of `ARRAY`.

Array multiplication functions

The functions DOT_PRODUCT and MATMUL are array multiplication functions. DOT_PRODUCT calculates the (scalar) dot product of two rank-one arrays, both of which must have the same number of elements. MATMUL calculates the product of two matrices, where the number of columns of MATRIX_A must equal the number of rows of MATRIX_B and the number of rows of MATRIX_A must equal the number of columns of MATRIX_B.

Array inquiry functions

The functions LBOUND and UBOUND return a rank-one integer array holding the lower or upper bounds on the *indices* of ARRAY, not on the values of the *elements* of ARRAY. Function SHAPE returns a rank-one integer array holding the number of elements (the array shape) of each dimension in ARRAY. Function SIZE returns a default integer that equals the total number of elements in ARRAY. Functions LBOUND, SIZE, and UBOUND may include an optional second dimension, DIM. In that case, the functions return a scalar integer result along the specified dimension of ARRAY. For the array A(2,0:5,10), LBOUND returns the vector (1,0,1) and UBOUND returns (2,5,10). SHAPE returns (2,6,10) and SIZE returns 120.

Array reduction functions

These are called "reduction functions" because they return a result that "collapses" an array of rank n to an array of rank n-1. This includes reducing a rank-one array to a scalar that, in this context, is considered to be a "rank-zero" array.

To see how much code array reduction functions can eliminate, consider the simple problem of summing all the elements in a rank-one array A of dimension n. Code using a DO . . . loop would look like this:

```
sum_array=0.
DO i=1,n
  sum_array=sum_array+A(i)
END DO
```

However, this same result can be achieved with a single call to the function SUM:

```
sum_array=SUM(A)
```

Here is another example that performs a more sophisticated task. Count the number of elements in an array that are larger than some specified value:

```
GT_zero=0.
DO i=1,n
  IF (A(i)>0.) GT_zero=GT_zero+1
END DO
```

This result can also be achieved with a single function call:

```
GT_zero=COUNT(mask=A>0.)
```

Program P-12.3 demonstrates functions described in Table 12.1. This is a program to study just for the syntax, as it doesn't do anything meaningful.

P-12.3 [ARAYFUNC.F90]

```
      PROGRAM ArrayFunctions
!
! MS-DOS file name ARAYFUNC.F90.
! Demonstrate array manipulation functions.
!
      IMPLICIT NONE
      REAL a(3),b(3)
      REAL x(3,4),y(4,3),z(3,3)
      INTEGER row,col
! Here's one way to initialize an array.
      DATA x/1.1,2.1,3.1,1.2,2.2,3.2,1.3,2.3,3.3,1.4,2.4,3.4/
      DATA y/10.1,20.1,30.1,40.1,10.2,20.2,30.2,40.2, &
             10.3,20.3,30.3,40.3/
!
      a=(/1.,2.,3./)
      b=(/2.,3.,4./)
      PRINT *,'a=',a
      PRINT *,'b=',b
      PRINT *,'DOT PRODUCT(a,b)=',DOT_PRODUCT(a,b)
```

```
! Here's an alternate way to assign values to an array.
! Don't use both!
      x=RESHAPE((/1.1,2.1,3.1,1.2,2.2,3.2,1.3,2.3,3.3, &
               1.4,2.4,3.4/),(/3,4/))
      PRINT *,'LBOUND(x)=',LBOUND(x),'UBOUND(x)=',UBOUND(x), &
             'SHAPE(x)=',SHAPE(x),'SIZE(x)=',SIZE(x)
      y=RESHAPE( (/10.1,20.1,30.1,40.1,10.2,20.2,30.2,40.2, &
               10.3,20.3,30.3,40.3/), (/4,3/) )
      PRINT *,'LBOUND(y,1)=',LBOUND(y,1),'LBOUND(y,2)=', &
             LBOUND(y,2),'SHAPE(y)=', &
             SHAPE(y),'SIZE(y,1)=',SIZE(y,1), &
             'SIZE(y,2)=',SIZE(y,2)
! Using the "mask" parameter.
      PRINT  ,'ALL(mask=(x>30.0))',ALL(mask=(x>30.0))
      PRINT *,'ANY(mask=(x> 3.0))',ANY(mask=(x> 3.0))
      PRINT *,'COUNT(mask=(x>3.0))',COUNT(mask=(x>3.0))
! Finding max and min values.
      PRINT *,'MAXVAL(x)=',MAXVAL(x),' MINVAL(x)=',MINVAL(x)
! Finding product and sum of array elements.
      PRINT *,'Product across columns of x for each row.'
      PRINT *,'PRODUCT(x,2)',PRODUCT(x,2)
      PRINT *, &
      'Product across columns of x for each row for which an element'
      PRINT *,'is greater than 3.'
      PRINT *,'PRODUCT(x,2,mask=(x>3.0))',PRODUCT(x,2,mask=(x>3.0))
      PRINT *,'Sum of all elements in y.'
      PRINT *,'SUM(y)=',SUM(y)
      z=MATMUL(x,y)
      PRINT *,'x'
      PRINT 1000,((x(row,col),col=1,4),row=1,3)
      PRINT *,'y'
      PRINT 1010,((y(row,col),col=1,3),row=1,4)
      PRINT *,'z'
      PRINT 1010,((z(row,col),col=1,3),row=1,3)
! You can apply DOT_PRODUCT to one dimension of a vector.
      PRINT *,DOT_PRODUCT(x(1,1:4),y(1:4,1))
!
1000  FORMAT(1x,4f8.2)
1010  FORMAT(1x,3f8.2)
      END
```

Running P-12.3

```
a=      1.000000    2.000000    3.000000
b=      2.000000    3.000000    4.000000
DOT_PRODUCT(a,b)=     20.000000
LBOUND(x)= 1 1 UBOUND(x)= 3 4 SHAPE(x)= 3 4 SIZE(x)= 12
LBOUND(y,1)= 1 LBOUND(y,2)= 1 SHAPE(y)= 4 3 SIZE(y,1)= 4
SIZE(y,2)= 3
ALL(mask=(x>30.0))  F
ANY(mask=(x> 3.0))  T
COUNT(mask=(x>3.0))  4
MAXVAL(x)=        3.400000   MINVAL(x)=       1.100000
Product across columns of x for each row.
PRODUCT(x,2)      2.402400    25.502399   1.1130241E+02
Product across columns of x for each row for which an element
is greater than 3.
PRODUCT(x,2,mask=(x>3.0))     1.000000     1.000000
1.1130241E+02
Sum of all elements in y.
SUM(y)=    3.0239999E+02
x
      1.10      1.20      1.30      1.40
      2.10      2.20      2.30      2.40
      3.10      3.20      3.30      3.40
y
     10.10     10.20     10.30
     20.10     20.20     20.30
     30.10     30.20     30.30
     40.10     40.20     40.30
z
    130.50    131.00    131.50
    230.90    231.80    232.70
    331.30    332.60    333.90
    1.3050000E+02
```

Here is a more practical problem that makes use of some of Fortran 90's array reduction functions.

1 *Define the problem.*

Given a table containing monthly average temperatures for n years, write a program that calculates the yearly average temperature for each of the n years and the 12 monthly average temperatures over the years 1960–1990. A table of temperatures from Philadelphia for 1960 to 1990 is contained in file TEM_PHIL.DAT, which can be downloaded from the World Wide Web site mentioned in Section i.5 of the Preface. The first few records look like this:

```
Average Temperature for Philadelphia (deg F)
60    34.2 35.4 32.7 56.7 61.2 70.6 73.3 74.5 67.3 54.8 45.5 27.6
61    25.0 34.0 43.1 49.8 58.6 69.9 75.6 73.5 71.5 55.7 45.2 31.0
62    30.0 30.4 40.5 52.0 64.1 71.7 72.0 72.0 63.1 56.3 42.1 31.0
```
(and so on)

2 Outline a solution.

1. Store the temperature values in a two-dimensional array.
2. Average the temperatures over twelve months for each year.
3. Average the temperatures over all years for each month.

3 Design an algorithm.

Here is an algorithm that appears to be short on details. However, it can be implemented quite directly in Fortran 90.

DEFINE (2-D array to hold temperatures, two 1-D arrays to hold averages)
OPEN (data file containing temperatures)
READ (temperature values and store in 2-D array)
AVERAGE (across all months to get yearly_average)
AVERAGE (across all years to get monthly_average)

This algorithm appears to violate our usual rule of making pseudocode sufficiently detailed to translate it directly into any procedural programming language—even one that doesn't include Fortran's array manipulation features. However, this might be a reasonable simplification of the algorithm design for an experienced programmer, regardless of the language, because it shouldn't be necessary to spell out in detail the loop structures necessary to achieve the desired results.

4 Convert the algorithm into a program.

Although a loop structure is still required to read and store the temperature values in a two-dimensional array, Fortran 90's array reduction functions can be used to implement this algorithm without using any programmed loop structures to calculate the averages. Program P-12.4 shows how to do it.

P-12.4 [TEM_PHIL.F90]

```
      PROGRAM temp_phil
!
! file name TEM_PHIL.F90
! Determine average annual and monthly temperatures, using
! array reduction functions.
!
      IMPLICIT NONE
      INTEGER year,month
      REAL temp(60:90,12),monthly_avg(12),yearly_avg(60:90)
!
      OPEN(1,file='c:\ftn90.dir\tem_phil.dat',action='read')
!
      READ(1,*)
10    READ(1,*,end=900)year,(temp(year,month),month=1,12)
      GO TO 10
900   CLOSE(1)
!
! Get monthly and yearly averages.
      monthly_avg=SUM(array=temp,dim=1)/31.
      yearly_avg=SUM(array=temp,dim=2)/12.
      PRINT *,' Monthly averages'
      PRINT 1000,monthly_avg
      PRINT *,' Yearly averages'
      PRINT 1000,yearly_avg
!
1000  FORMAT(1x,6f10.1)
      END
```

Running P-12.4

```
 Monthly averages
      30.5      33.0      42.1      52.5      62.8      71.7
      76.6      75.5      68.2      56.3      46.4      35.5
 Yearly averages
      52.8      52.7      52.1      51.9      54.1      53.0
      53.0      53.3      54.1      53.8      54.5      55.6
      54.1      56.4      55.3      56.1      54.2      54.3
      53.5      54.5      54.5      53.7      54.2      54.8
      53.8      54.9      55.3      55.4      54.5      54.4
      57.5
```

5 *Verify the operation of the program.*

It is easy to get confused about the interpretation of array dimensions in problems such as this. Because the required calculations are carried out "transparently" by the array reduction functions without any programming on your part, it is especially important to check the results by doing some of the calculations by hand.

Problem Discussion

In P-12.4, the array reduction functions (see the two statements printed in bold italics) have eliminated several lines of code. In the context of the Fortran 90 language, it is perfectly reasonable to take advantage of the existence of these functions by inventing a pseudocode command such as **AVERAGE** *(array over specified dimension)*. Because the loop structure code required to average array elements is essentially the same in all procedural languages, and because you should now be able to write such code without difficulty, you could use this "high level" command regardless of whether the language in which you will implement the algorithm supports array reduction functions.

Note how the lower and upper limits of the two-dimensional array have been set to the values of the 31 years in the table (60:90). This is an *ad hoc* approach to this specific problem, based on an examination of the contents of the data file TEM_PHIL.DAT.

12.5 Direct Access and Unformatted (Binary) Files

12.5.1 Introduction to File Types

In Chapter 9 and briefly in Chapter 5, the concept of using external files for storing information needed by or produced by a program was introduced, and the syntax of using a sequential access formatted file was covered in detail. This section will discuss other kinds of files and other modes of file access.

First let's review briefly some important properties of the sequential access formatted ("text") files used in Chapters 5 and 9.

1. Formatted files contain characters that can be interpreted either as "text" or as numbers.

The interpretation of characters as "text" or numbers is based on a description of the file contents contained in a FORMAT statement. For example, an A format is used to interpret text as characters. List-directed access can also be used when information in text files can be interpreted unambiguously without user-supplied format information. (This means that list-directed input is often unsuitable for reading text files containing character strings either by themselves or in combination with numbers.)

The fact that formatted files represent numbers as a string of characters means that your program must translate back and forth between internal and external representations of information. This process is transparent at the programming level except for the need to provide a FORMAT (either explicitly or implicitly with list-directed I/O) to impose the desired translation on each record in the file.

2. When sequential access files are read, they are accessed in order, starting at the beginning. When they are written, they are written from the beginning.

This restriction can be relaxed through the BACKSPACE and REWIND statements, although their use has been discouraged.

3. Sequential access text files are "line oriented," which means that every record in the file is terminated by a system-dependent end-of-line mark.

The end-of-line mark is written into a file or output device whenever a WRITE statement is executed without an advance='no' option, in which case the writing of an end-of-line mark is suppressed.

4. Sequential access text files are opened with *either* read or write access, with action='read' or action='write' specifiers.

In the applications discussed so far, sequential access files have been used for either reading or writing, but not for both within the same program.

Although these limitations pose no problems in a large number of programming situations, they can sometimes be restrictive in significant ways. To cite just one example, to which we will return later in this chapter, it is impossible to conduct a binary search on a file that is restricted to sequential access. This means that the binary search algorithm discussed in Chapter 10 is restricted to files that are small enough to be held in an array in memory. This may not appear to be a restriction of any practical consequence; after all, it is more efficient to perform operations on arrays held in memory than on the same information held in an external file. However, it is on the largest files that a binary search algorithm confers the greatest potential advantage, and it is, in fact, not uncommon to have data files that are too large to be stored in arrays.

Fortunately, Fortran provides ways to create and use files that overcome many of the restrictions on sequential access formatted files as used so far in this text. For these purposes, there are three kinds of file properties that can be specified by choosing options in the OPEN statement: file format, means of access, and read/write permission. Each of these properties can be specified independently, so there are several different possibilities. Table 12.2 shows the options in the OPEN statement available for establishing these properties.

As always, Fortran is case-insensitive, so the specifiers and their values given in Table 12.2 may be entered with any combination of lowercase or uppercase letters.

Table 12.2. Options for the OPEN statement.

OPEN **Specifier**	**Values**	**Default Value**
FORM=	'FORMATTED', 'UNFORMATTED'	'FORMATTED' for sequential access, 'UNFORMATTED' for direct access
ACCESS=	'SEQUENTIAL', 'DIRECT'	'SEQUENTIAL' for formatted files, 'DIRECT' for unformatted files
ACTION=	'READ', 'WRITE', 'READWRITE'	System dependent
POSITION=	'ASIS', 'REWIND', 'APPEND'	'ASIS' (applicable only to sequential access files)
RECL=	*record_length*	none (see text - applicable only to direct access files)

We will now discuss each of the specifiers in detail.

1. FORM=

Previously, the files created and used in Chapters 5 and 9 were formatted sequential access files opened with 'READ' or 'WRITE' status. The 'FORMATTED' property is the default condition when both the FORM= and the ACCESS= options are absent from an OPEN statement.

The other possibility for the FORM= option is the 'UNFORMATTED' property. To understand its importance, recall that formatted files contain external representations of values. For example, the real number 33.3 is stored in a formatted file as the *characters* 33.3 rather than in its internal format, as previously discussed in Section 12.3. As a result, a program must translate back and forth between internal and external representations of information when it reads from or writes to a text file. There is a price—file processing time—associated with this translation.

An unformatted file, also called a binary file, contains information that has simply been copied from its internal storage locations, without translation of any kind. The implication of this difference is that unformatted files *should* allow faster file processing and, in some cases, should produce smaller data files. These differences are important in some applications, although there are no programs in the previous chapters of this text for which file processing time or file size should have any impact on program design.

When unformatted files are accessed with a READ or WRITE statement, no format specifier of any kind is allowed, including an asterisk for list-directed input or output. This makes sense because, by definition, unformatted files require no translation to or from an external representation.

One important advantage of doing away with formats is that entire records defined with a TYPE structure may be read and written as a whole, rather than being broken down into component fields. In fact, individual records can't be extracted during a READ operation because this would require a format.

Some Fortran programmers prefer to use unformatted files unless there are specific requirements that a file be easily transportable to some other computing environment. Clearly, such a requirement exists if a program needs to access input information generated outside the program. This text has used formatted files because it's important for beginning programmers to be able to view and print the contents of files easily.

There are some other possible disadvantages to using unformatted files. They can be generated only under program control, and for all practical purposes, they can be read only under program control. A program that reads an unformatted file created by another program must know the record structure of the information written by that other program. Whereas it is usually possible to interpret a text file just by looking at it, equivalent information about an unformatted file can be obtained only with great effort and a thorough understanding of how information is stored internally in your computer. Also, binary files created on one computer system will not be portable to a different kind of computer system. Formatted files, on the other hand, are easily transportable with no or only minor modifications even among different kinds of computer systems.

Another possible impact on program design is that the ADVANCE= specifier isn't allowed for writing unformatted files. This could have a design impact on programs that use this feature.

Finally, binary files are required to have a fixed record length, for reasons that are discussed under the ACCESS= option. This is not a restriction for formatted files, in which each record, or line, of a file may have a different length and may contain different kinds of information. Because binary files are record-oriented, there is no equivalent of a line-by-line structure. When a problem requires that the records of a file contain different kinds of information, it may not be at all convenient to create fixed-length binary files to hold that information.

2. ACCESS=

All the files used so far in this text have been ACCESS='SEQUENTIAL' files. This is Fortran's default for formatted files unless overridden by option specifiers. As you should recall, sequential access means that, when files are opened for reading, a pointer is positioned at the beginning of the file and the file can be read one record at a time, in order, with the exceptions provided by REWIND and BACKSPACE. When they are opened for writing, the records must be created in sequence, starting at the beginning.

With the ACCESS='DIRECT' option, *any* record in a file may be accessed at any time. However, keeping track of the location of all records in a file could impose a substantial burden on the programming environment. To minimize this burden, direct access files are required to have fixed record lengths. In this way, it is easy to "index" the file for the purposes of locating a particular record. The required record length information is included in the RECL=*record_length* option, which is required for direct access files and is described below.

One typical use of a direct access file is to open a file with read/write access (see the ACTION= option below), read a record, decide that some values need to be changed, and then overwrite this record. Hence whenever a program needs to examine and possibly modify records in a file, direct access files are the appropriate choice.

Direct access is the default condition for unformatted files. It is also possible, but not recommended for beginning programmers, to specify direct access for formatted files.

3. ACTION=

For sequential access files, the allowed action should be either 'READ' or 'WRITE'. 'READWRITE' access should *not* be specified for a sequential access file, even though it is allowed in principle. There are good reasons for this restriction. Consider this code fragment that appears to read a record and then change the values in the record:

```
      ...  !won't work!
10    READ(1,*,END=900)a,b,c
      PRINT *,a,b,c
      BACKSPACE(1)
      WRITE(1,*)a+2,b+2,c+2
      GO TO 10
      ...
```

This might look like a reasonable way to use BACKSPACE, but (without belaboring the details) it will not work. In general, only direct access files should be opened as 'READWRITE'.

4. POSITION=

When sequential access files are opened, the *file pointer* can be either at the beginning or at the end. In the default ('ASIS') condition, the file pointer is always at the beginning when a file is first opened for either reading or writing. The purpose of the 'APPEND' property is to position the file pointer at the end of an existing file so that new records can be added to the end. Usually, the 'REWIND' option is not needed. This option can be used only with sequential access files.

5. RECL=*record_length*

For a sequential access file, RECL= specifies the maximum length of a record; it is system-dependent and optional. For a direct access file, this specifier is *mandatory*. If the file is formatted, *record_length* contains the number of characters in the record, *including the end-of-line mark*. If the file is unformatted, *record_length* contains the number of bytes required to represent the information in the record; this is a system-dependent value.

12.5.2 Using Other File Types

Program P-12.5 illustrates how to use the OPEN statement to create formatted and unformatted files with direct access. It performs the following tasks.

1. Read an existing text file (FILETEST.DAT) and create a random access binary file (FILETEST.BIN).
2. Read FILETEST.BIN file backwards and print the contents.
3. Read FILETEST.DAT again and create a new formatted file (FILETEST.FIX) with a specified fixed record length.
4. Read FILETEST.FIX backwards and print the contents.

P-12.5 [FILETEST.F90]

```
      PROGRAM FileTest
!
! Test syntax of various file options.
!
      IMPLICIT NONE
      INTEGER i,n,a,b,c,n_bytes
!
      OPEN(1,file='c:\ftn90\source\filetest.dat',action='read')
      INQUIRE(iolength=n_bytes)a,b,c
      OPEN(2,file='c:\ftn90\source\filetest.bin', &
           form='unformatted',action='readwrite', &
           access='direct',recl=n_bytes)
! Read text file and use it to create direct access binary file.
      n=0
      PRINT *,'Read original file and create new binary file.'
10    READ(1,*,end=900)a,b,c
        PRINT *,a,b,c
        n=n+1
        WRITE(2,rec=n)a,b,c
      GO TO 10
900   CLOSE(1)
```

```
! Read binary file backwards.
      PRINT *,'Read binary file backwards.'
      DO i=n,1,-1
        READ(2,rec=i)a,b,c
        PRINT *,a,b,c
      END DO
      CLOSE(2)
!
! Now create a formatted file for direct access.
      OPEN(1,file='c:\ftn90\source\filetest.dat',action='read')
      OPEN(2,file='c:\ftn90\source\filetest.fix',action='write', &
          form='formatted',status='replace')
      n=0
      PRINT *,'Create formatted (fixed-length records) file.'
20    READ(1,*,end=910)a,b,c
        PRINT 1000,a,b,c
        n=n+1
        WRITE(2,1000)a,b,c !Do NOT use list-directed output.
      GO TO 20
910   CLOSE(1)
      CLOSE(2)
! Open this formatted file for random access.
      PRINT *,'Open for random access and read every other record.'
! Open file with n_bytes+2 to allow for CR/LF characters.
      OPEN(1,file='c:\ftn90\source\filetest.fix',action='read', &
          recl=n_bytes+2,access='direct',form='formatted')
      DO i=1,n,2
        READ(1,1000,rec=i)a,b,c !List-directed input not allowed.
        PRINT *,a,b,c
      END DO
      CLOSE(1)
1000  FORMAT(3i4)
      END
```

Running P-12.5

```
Read original file and create new binary file.
3 4 6
0 -1 4
17 16 15
11 20 -3
4 2 1
33 14 9
-5 -1 0
-5 -4 -3
1 2 3
6 7 8
Read binary file backwards.
6 7 8
1 2 3
-5 -4 -3
-5 -1 0
33 14 9
4 2 1
11 20 -3
17 16 15
0 -1 4
3 4 6
Create formatted (fixed-length records) file.
   3   4   6
   0  -1   4
  17  16  15
  11  20  -3
   4   2   1
  33  14   9
  -5  -1   0
  -5  -4  -3
   1   2   3
   6   7   8
Open for random access and read every other record.
3 4 6
17 16 15
4 2 1
-5 -1 0
1 2 3
```

P-12.5 is a deceptively simple program that bears close examination. The first part of the program, reading an existing formatted file, is straightforward. However, the creation of the unformatted file raises a question. The RECL= option is required for the direct access file. But what value should you use? How many bytes does it take to store three integers? If you know that the default integer data type takes four bytes, you might guess correctly that the answer is 12 bytes. However, for other data types, including derived data types, the answer might be less obvious.

The solution is to use the Fortran 90 INQUIRE statement, which is printed in bold italics in P-12.5. This statement examines the proposed output list (a, b, c in this case) and returns the required number of bytes in the variable n_bytes. A partial syntax is

```
INQUIRE(iolength=n) I/O_list
```

where n is a user-supplied variable name and I/O list is a list of variables to be written in the record. Note that it's not necessary for a, b, and c to have values yet because it is only their data type that is of interest for this purpose.

Once the record length has been established with the INQUIRE statement in P-12.5, the file can be created. When it's time to read the contents of this new binary file, that fact that it has been opened as a direct access file means that it's not necessary to close it and open it again, or to "rewind" it in order to read the contents. All that is required is to specify the record number with the REC= option in the READ statement. Because this is an unformatted file, every READ or WRITE statement that accesses the file must include a record index:

```
READ(unit,REC=n,...)
WRITE(unit,REC=n,...)
```

Remember that I/O statements cannot include a format specifier when they are accessing a binary file.

The third step in P-12.5 reads FILETEST.DAT again and creates a new formatted file, FILETEST.FIX. This file contains the same information as FILETEST.DAT, but it is written with a FORMAT statement so that all the records will have the same length; the values in FILETEST.DAT aren't lined up in columns so the records don't all have the same length. This is done in anticipation of reopening this file for direct access. In that case, a record length must be specified and all the records should have the same record length. Because the format specifier is 3I4, the three values occupy 12 bytes in each record.

Finally, step four opens FILETEST.FIX as a formatted direct access file and reads it backwards. Because it is a direct access file, the OPEN statement once again requires that the record length be specified. What is the appropriate value this time? Every record in FILETEST.FIX includes an end-of-line mark. In DOS text files, the end-of-line mark requires two characters—a carriage return and a line feed. Thus the value that must appear in the OPEN statement is 12+2, or 14 bytes. Note that this value is system-dependent because the end-of-line mark on some computer systems (Macintosh, for example) requires only one byte.

If you are motivated to examine other uses of the INQUIRE statement in a Fortran reference manual, you might try to use it to determine the number of bytes in the fixed-length records of an existing formatted file *before* the file is opened. However, this is not possible; INQUIRE will return only the maximum *allowed* record length for a file of this type, and obtaining even that information requires that the file already be open. In general, it would also be useful if an INQUIRE could determine the number of records in a formatted file. Why? Because the END= option in the READ statement is not allowed when a file is opened for direct access. This is inconvenient when reading through direct access files of unknown length. (In P-12.5, the number of records was already known from operations earlier in the program.) However, it isn't possible to use INQUIRE for this purpose, either.

Although Fortran has extensive capabilities to create files that meet many different needs, the details of P-12.5 should convince you to stick to the basics unless you have a very unusual requirement. In particular, it is a good idea to restrict your use of formatted files to sequential access and to use unformatted files for direct access. This should serve your needs in nearly all the programs you will write yourself.

12.5.3 Example: Binary Search of a File

A binary search algorithm applied to an array of sorted values was discussed in Chapter 10 and that algorithm was implemented in P-10.3. In this section, we will discuss a program, P-12.6, that modifies P-10.3 so that it can be used to perform a binary search on a file. This has obvious advantages for files that are too large to be stored in an array. It should be clear that in order for a binary search to work, such a file must be treated as a direct access file. Because a file-based searching algorithm makes sense only for large files, it also makes sense to assume that the data are stored in an unformatted file because of the reduced processing time associated with such files.

P-12.6 [SRCHFILE.F90]

```
      MODULE FileSearch
      IMPLICIT NONE
      TYPE filefields
        INTEGER x
      END TYPE filefields
      INTEGER search_key
!
      CONTAINS
!-------------------------------------------------
      SUBROUTINE Bin_Search_F(u,n_rec,where)
!
! Binary search of an ordered list for one occurrence of
! specified target value.
!
      USE FileSearch, ONLY : FileFields,target => search_key
      IMPLICIT NONE
      INTEGER mid,lo,hi
```

```
      INTEGER where
      INTEGER, INTENT(IN) :: u,n_rec
      TYPE (FileFields) file
!
      lo=1
      hi=n_rec
      where=0
      DO WHILE ((lo .LE. hi) .AND. (where .EQ. 0))
        mid=(lo+hi)/2
        READ(u,rec=mid)file
        IF (file%x .EQ. target) THEN
          where=mid
        ELSE IF (file%x .GT. target) THEN
          hi=mid-1
        ELSE
          lo=mid+1
        END IF
      END DO
!
      END SUBROUTINE Bin_Search_F
!----------------------------
      END MODULE FileSearch
!===========================
      PROGRAM SearchFile
!
! MS-DOS file name SRCHFILE.F90
! Binary search on unformatted direct-access file.
!
      USE FileSearch, ONLY : Bin_Search_F,FileFields, &
                             what => search_key
      IMPLICIT NONE
      INTEGER i,u,n_rec,n_bytes,where
      TYPE (FileFields) file
      DATA u,n_rec,file%x/1,10,0/
!
      INQUIRE(iolength=n_bytes)file
      OPEN(u,file='c:\ftn90.dir\srchfile.bin',access='direct', &
           form='unformatted',recl=n_bytes,action='readwrite')
!
! Fill file with even integers.
      DO i=1,n_rec
        file%x=2*i
        WRITE(1,rec=i)file
        PRINT *,file%x
      END DO
!
10    PRINT *,' Search for what, 999 to quit?'
      READ *,what
      CALL Bin_Search_F(1,n_rec,where)
      IF (what/=999) PRINT *,where
      IF (what/=999) GO TO 10
!
      CLOSE(1)
      END
```

Running P-12.6

```
2
4
6
8
10
12
14
16
18
20
Search for what, 999 to quit?
6
 3
Search for what, 999 to quit?
5
 0
Search for what, 999 to quit?
999
```

Problem Discussion

P-12.6 has been implemented using a MODULE so that both the subroutine to do the binary search and the data type definition associated with file records, which in this example contain only one field, are as portable as possible and easy to modify. The basic difference between Bin_Search_F and Bin_Search from Chapter 10 is that array references are replaced by READs of specified records in the file.

It should be clear that Bin_Search_F can be applied to *any* binary file for which the record structure is known. It is necessary only to include an appropriate TYPE definition and refer to the field on which the search is being conducted.

12.6 The COMPLEX Data Type

Because of the importance of complex numbers in scientific and engineering computing, Fortran supports a separate data type for manipulating complex numbers and variables. The general syntax is

```
COMPLEX variable list

Example:
COMPLEX root_1,root_2
```

The complex number a + b*i* is specified as (a,b); that is, with the real and imaginary components enclosed in parentheses and separated by a comma. Both components must always be present even if one value is zero. The components can be either REAL or INTEGER, and they don't both have to have the same data type.

Complex values can be read and written with either list-directed or formatted I/O. Assume C1 and C2 are declared as COMPLEX. To respond to the statement

```
READ *,C1,C2
```

type, for example,

```
(1.,-.5) (-1.,-2.)
```

The statement

```
PRINT *,C1,C2
```

produces compiler-dependent output that will look something like this:

```
(1.000000,  -0.500000)        (-1.000000,  -2.000000)
```

Formatted I/O requires a separate format specifier for each component of the complex number. Here's an example:

```
      READ 1000,C1,C2
      PRINT 1010,C1,C2
1000  FORMAT(4f5.1)
1010  FORMAT(2('(',f5.1,',',f5.1,')'))
```

The format specifiers for the real and imaginary components don't have to be the same. Assignments of constants to a COMPLEX variable can be made like this:

```
C1=(1.,2.)
```

However, assignments involving one or more variables must use the intrinsic CMPLX function:

```
x=1.
y=2.
C1=(x,y)
C2=(0.5,y)
```

The syntax of the CMPLX function is

```
CMPLX(x[,v][,KIND])
```

If y is not present, x must be of type COMPLEX.

Fortran supports arithmetic operations on complex numbers. Table 12.3 shows the results of these operations.

Table 12.3. Operations on complex numbers

Fortran Operation	Real Component	Imaginary Component
CMPLX(a,b)+CMPLX(c,d)	a+c	b+d
CMPLX(a,b)-CMPLX(c,d)	a-c	b-d
CMPLX(a,b)*CMPLX(c,d)	ac-bd	ad+bc
CMPLX(a,b)/CMPLX(c,d)	$(ac+bd)/(c^2+d^2)$	$(bc-ad)/c^2+d^2)$

P-12.7 is a short program that illustrates some of the syntax associated with using COMPLEX variables.

P-12.7 [COMPLEX.F90]

```
      PROGRAM Complex
!
! Demonstrate operations with COMPLEX data.
!
      IMPLICIT NONE
      REAL x,y,a,b
      COMPLEX c1,c2
!
      x=1.
      y=2.
      a=0.5
      b=3.
      c1=CMPLX(x,y)
      c2=CMPLX(a,b)
      PRINT *,c1,c2,c1+c2,c1*c2,c1/c2
      PRINT *,REAL(c1),AIMAG(c1)
      END
```

Running P-12.7

```
( 1.0000000, 2.0000000) ( 0.5000000, 3.0000000)
( 1.5000000, 5.0000000) ( -5.5000000, 4.0000000)
( 0.7027027, -0.2162162)
  1.0000000  2.0000000
```

As another example, P-12.8 calculates the roots of the quadratic equation $ax^2 + bx + c = 0$ with real or imaginary roots. Previously, it would have been required that the discriminant be positive to guarantee real roots. However, if the discriminant is less than zero, -b plus and minus the square root of the negative of the discriminant are the numerators of the imaginary components of two complex roots.

P-12.8 [QUADRAT2.F90]

```fortran
      PROGRAM Quadrat2
!
! Calculates solutions to the quadratic equation.
!
      IMPLICIT NONE
      REAL a,b,c          ! coefficients of ax^2+bx+c=0
      COMPLEX root1,root2 ! two roots
      REAL discriminant
!
      PRINT*,' Give coefficients of ax^2+bx+c: '
      READ*,a,b,c
!
! Test for existence of one or more roots.
!
      discriminant=b*b-4.0*a*c
      SELECT CASE (discriminant>0.)
        CASE (.TRUE.)
          root1=CMPLX((-b+SQRT(discriminant))/2./a,0.)
          root2=CMPLX((-b-SQRT(discriminant))/2./a,0.)
          PRINT*,' The two real roots are ',root1,root2
        CASE (.FALSE.)
          IF (ABS(discriminant)<1e-7) THEN !assume discriminant=0
            root1=-b/2./a
            PRINT*,' The single real root is ',root1
          ELSE
            root1=CMPLX(-b/2./a,SQRT(-discriminant)/2/a)
            root2=CMPLX(-b/2./a,-SQRT(-discriminant)/2./a)
            PRINT*,' The two complex roots are ',root1,root2
          ENDIF
      END SELECT
      END
```

Running P-12.8

```
 Give coefficients of ax^2+bx+c:
1 2 3
  The two complex roots are  ( -1.0000000,  1.4142135)
 ( -1.0000000, -1.4142135)
```

12.7 Data Sharing with COMMON Blocks

In Chapter 7, the MODULE was introduced as a way of sharing information among a main program and its subprograms. At the same time, it was noted that in older versions of Fortran, COMMON blocks were used for this purpose. There is no reason to use COMMON blocks in new programs written in Fortran 90. However, because COMMON blocks are often found in older programs, a brief discussion may be helpful.

The need for COMMON blocks, or some other information-sharing mechanism, arises because variables defined within any Fortran program or subprogram are local just to that program or subprogram. To put it another way, there is no concept in Fortran of "global variables" that are automatically accessible to all units within a program.

The basic way to share information among parts of a Fortran program is to pass variables through an argument list, a principle that has been followed throughout this text. However, recall program P-7.4, in which a MODULE was used to define the value of π and make it available to FUNCTION Area. Program P-12.9 is a version of P-7.4 that uses a COMMON block instead of a MODULE to make the value of π available to the function. (The MODULE is still used to contain the subprograms, thereby making this a "hybrid" program that, just for demonstration purposes, uses a "pre-Fortran-90" method of sharing the value of π.)

P-12.9 [CIRCLCOM.F90]

```
      MODULE CircleFunctions
!
      CONTAINS
!
         REAL FUNCTION Area(radius)
!
! Do area calculation.
!
            IMPLICIT NONE
            REAL radius,pi
            INTENT(IN) radius
            COMMON pi
!
            Area=pi*radius*radius
!
         END FUNCTION Area
!
         REAL FUNCTION Circumference(radius)
!
! Do circumference calculation.
!
            IMPLICIT NONE
            REAL radius,pi
            INTENT(IN) :: radius
            COMMON pi
!
            Circumference=2.0*pi*radius
!
         END FUNCTION Circumference
      END MODULE
!---------------
```

```
      PROGRAM CirclCom
!
! Calculate area and circumference of a circle, using
! two functions.
!
      USE CircleFunctions, ONLY : Area,Circumference
      IMPLICIT NONE
      REAL radius,pi
      COMMON pi
!
      pi=4.*ATAN(1.)
      PRINT *,' What is the radius of the circle?'
      READ *,radius
!
      PRINT 1000,Area(radius),Circumference(radius)
!
1000  FORMAT(1x,2f10.3)
      END
```

In P-12.9, the variable `pi` is defined in the main program. Its value is then made available to the `Area` and `Circumference` functions through a COMMON statement. This use of COMMON is also called "unnamed" or "blank" COMMON.

It's also possible to give names to one or more COMMON blocks. In this way, variables can be grouped together depending on how they are used in other program units. This is called "named" COMMON. The general syntax for defining COMMON blocks is

```
COMMON [/name/] list of variables
```

Program P-12.10 illustrates some interesting properties and potential pitfalls of using COMMON blocks and storage rather than name association. In the main program, an array of 20 REAL numbers is stored in a blank COMMON block. As a result, an area of memory is set aside that is large enough to hold 20 REAL numbers.

In SUBROUTINE com_test, the information in this memory area is associated with *two* arrays of 10 REAL numbers each, rather than a single array of 20 REAL numbers. This works, as is clear from the first set of output values from P-12.10, because information in COMMON blocks is "storage associated" rather than "name associated."

In SUBROUTINE com_test_2, values in the COMMON block are associated with an array of 20 INTEGERs rather than 20 REAL numbers. The second set of output values from P-12.10 shows the result of this association. Fortran is perfectly willing to interpret the information in the COMMON block (the bytes required to store six REAL numbers) in a different way. Again, this is possible because information in COMMON blocks is storage associated.

P-12.10 [COM_TEST.F90]

```
      MODULE com_blk_subs
      CONTAINS
!----------------------
      SUBROUTINE com_test
      IMPLICIT NONE
      REAL A(10),B(10)
      INTEGER i
      COMMON A,B
!
      DO i=1,10
        PRINT 1000,A(i),B(i)
      END DO
1000  FORMAT(2f10.2)
      END SUBROUTINE com_test
!-------------------------
      SUBROUTINE com_test_2
      IMPLICIT NONE
      INTEGER A(20)
      INTEGER i
      COMMON A
!
      DO i=1,20
        PRINT 1000,A(i)
      END DO
1000  FORMAT(i20)
      END SUBROUTINE com_test_2
!--------------------------
      END MODULE com_blk_subs
!===========================
      PROGRAM com_blk
!
! Demonstrates use (and possible misuse) of COMMON blocks.
!
      USE com_blk_subs, ONLY : com_test,com_test_2
      IMPLICIT NONE
      REAL A(20)
      INTEGER i
      COMMON A
!
      DO i=1,20
        A(i)=i*10.
      END DO
      CALL com_test
      CALL com_test_2
      END
```

Running P-12.10

```
 10.00    110.00
 20.00    120.00
 30.00    130.00
 40.00    140.00
 50.00    150.00
 60.00    160.00
 70.00    170.00
 80.00    180.00
 90.00    190.00
100.00    200.00
        1092616192
        1101004800
        1106247680
        1109393408
        1112014848
        1114636288
        1116471296
        1117782016
        1119092736
        1120403456
        1121714176
        1123024896
        1124204544
        1124859904
        1125515264
        1126170624
        1126825984
        1127481344
        1128136704
        1128792064
```

Both uses of COMMON blocks in P-12.10 are potential sources of major programming problems. The first use, in SUBROUTINE com_test, might seem like a "neat" Fortran feature that can be used to advantage in some circumstances. The second, in SUBROUTINE com_test_2, is much more likely to result from a mistake (declaring the array as INTEGER rather than REAL) on the part of the programmer.

In fact, the implications of storage association are often exploited by "clever" Fortran programmers. However, the fact that Fortran doesn't care how information in a COMMON block is interpreted when it is used in a subprogram is a programming disaster just waiting to happen, especially in large programs that are written by more than one programmer. Without exception, programs written in Fortran 90 should avoid the use of COMMON blocks and should take advantage of the security provided by the name association of MODULEs.

Appendix 1. Table of ASCII Characters for IBM-Compatible PCs

Dec	Hex		Dec	Hex		Dec	Hex		Dec	Hex	
0	0		32	20		64	40	@	96	60	
1	1	☺	33	21	!	65	41	A	97	61	a
2	2	☻	34	22	"	66	42	B	98	62	b
3	3	♥	35	23	#	67	43	C	99	63	c
4	4	♦	36	24	$	68	44	D	100	64	d
5	5	♣	37	25	%	69	45	E	101	65	e
6	6	♠	38	26	&	70	46	F	102	66	f
7	7	•	39	27	'	71	47	G	103	67	g
8	8	◘	40	28	(	72	48	H	104	68	h
9	9	○	41	29	)	73	49	I	105	69	i
10	A	◎	42	2A	*	74	4A	J	106	6A	j
11	B	♂	43	2B	+	75	4B	K	107	6B	k
12	C	♀	44	2C	,	76	4C	L	108	6C	l
13	D	♪	45	2D	-	77	4D	M	109	6D	m
14	E	♫	46	2E	.	78	4E	N	110	6E	n
15	F	☼	47	2F	/	79	4F	O	111	6F	o
16	10	►	48	30	0	80	50	P	112	70	p
17	11	◄	49	31	1	81	51	Q	113	71	q
18	12	↕	50	32	2	82	52	R	114	72	r
19	13	‼	51	33	3	83	53	S	115	73	s
20	14	¶	52	34	4	84	54	T	116	74	t
21	15	§	53	35	5	85	55	U	117	75	u
22	16	▬	54	36	6	86	56	V	118	76	v
23	17	↨	55	37	7	87	57	W	119	77	w
24	18	↑	56	38	8	88	58	X	120	78	x
25	19	↓	57	39	9	89	59	Y	121	79	y
26	1A	→	58	3A	:	90	5A	Z	122	7A	z
27	1B	←	59	3B	;	91	5B	[	123	7B	{
28	1C	∟	60	3C	<	92	5C	\	124	7C		
29	1D	↔	61	3D	=	93	5D	]	125	7D	}
30	1E	▲	62	3E	>	94	5E	^	126	7E	~
31	1F	▼	63	3F	?	95	5F		127	7F	⌂

Dec	Hex		Dec	Hex		Dec	Hex		Dec	Hex	
128	80	Ç	160	A0	á	192	C0	└	224	E0	α
129	81	ü	161	A1	í	193	C1	┴	225	E1	ß
130	82	é	162	A2	ó	194	C2	┬	226	E2	Γ
131	83	â	163	A3	ú	195	C3	├	227	E3	π
132	84	ä	164	A4	ñ	196	C4	─	228	E4	Σ
133	85	à	165	A5	Ñ	197	C5	┼	229	E5	σ
134	86	å	166	A6	ª	198	C6	╞	230	E6	µ
135	87	ç	167	A7	º	199	C7	╟	231	E7	τ
136	88	ê	168	A8	¿	200	C8	╚	232	E8	Φ
137	89	ë	169	A9	⌐	201	C9	╔	233	E9	θ
138	8A	è	170	AA	¬	202	CA	╩	234	EA	Ω
139	8B	ï	171	AB	½	203	CB	╦	235	EB	δ
140	8C	î	172	AC	¼	204	CC	╠	236	EC	∞
141	8D	ì	173	AD	¡	205	CD	=	237	ED	φ
142	8E	Ä	174	AE	«	206	CE	╬	238	EE	ε
143	8F	Å	175	AF	»	207	CF	╧	239	EF	∩
144	90	É	176	B0	▓	208	D0	╨	240	F0	≡
145	91	æ	177	B1	█	209	D1	╤	241	F1	±
146	92	Æ	178	B2	█	210	D2	╥	242	F2	≥
147	93	ô	179	B3	│	211	D3	╙	243	F3	≤
148	94	ö	180	B4	┤	212	D4	╘	244	F4	⌠
149	95	ò	181	B5	╡	213	D5	╒	245	F5	⌡
150	96	û	182	B6	╢	214	D6	╓	246	F6	÷
151	97	ù	183	B7	╖	215	D7	╫	247	F7	≈
152	98	ij	184	B8	╕	216	D8	╪	248	F8	°
153	99	Ö	185	B9	╣	217	D9	┘	249	F9	·
154	9A	Ü	186	BA	║	218	DA	┌	250	FA	·
155	9B	¢	187	BB	╗	219	DB	█	251	FB	√
156	9C	£	188	BC	╝	220	DC	▄	252	FC	ⁿ
157	9D	¥	189	BD	╜	221	DD	▌	253	FD	²
158	9E	Pt	190	BE	╛	222	DE	▐	254	FE	■
159	9F	ƒ	191	BF	┐	223	DF	▀	255	FF	

Note: 0 is a null character, 32 is a space, obtained by pressing the space bar, and 255 is a blank.

Appendix 2. Summary of Pseudocode Commands and Fortran Statement Syntax

Appendix 2.1 Pseudocode Commands

For a detailed discussion of these pseudocode commands, see Chapter Two.

ASSIGN
Set a variable equal to another variable, constant value, or expression. See also the **INCREMENT** and **INITIALIZE** commands.

CALL subprogram_name (list of parameters)
Invoke another set of commands that, given a particular set of input values, executes a list of instructions and produces a particular set of output values.

CHOOSE (from a list of possibilities)
From a list of possible courses of action, select just one action based on the value of a single variable or expression.

CLOSE (data file)
Close an external data file when you're done with it.

DEFINE (list of variables and/or data structures)
Define the names and kinds of variables your program will need.

IF (something is true) THEN (action) ELSE (a different action)
Take one course of action or another based on the value of a boolean (logical) expression.

INCREMENT
This special case of an assignment command is for assignments such as $x = x + 1$.

INITIALIZE
This special case of an assignment command is used to emphasize the necessity of initializing the value of variables before they can be incremented.

LOOP (terminating conditions)...END LOOP
Define a structure inside of which lists of instructions can be executed repetitively until (or as long as) certain conditions are met.

OPEN (data file)
Open an external data file for use within a program.

READ *(list of values)*

Provide input for a program from a keyboard or some other input device.

SUBPROGRAM *(list of input and output parameters)*

Contains an algorithm to produce one or more output values using one or more specified input values.

WRITE *(list of values)*

Display output from a program, typically on a monitor screen, or save output to some other device.

Appendix 2.2 Fortran Statement Syntax

For a detailed discussion of the syntax and use of these Fortran statements, see the referenced chapter.

Chapter 8

```
ALLOCATE(name(spec)[,name(spec)]...[,STAT=status])

where (spec) has the syntax ([lo:]hi) and
status is an integer variable
```

Chapter 3 (assignment statement)

```
variable_name = expression consisting of constants,
                variables, functions, and operators
```

Chapter 9

```
BACKSPACE unit
  or
BACKSPACE([unit=]unit)
```

Chapter 7

```
CALL name [(argument list)]

Example:
      CALL Polar_to_Cartesian(r,theta,x,y)
```

Chapter 3

```
CHARACTER[([LEN=]n)] variable_name[*n][, variable_name[*n]]...
CHARACTER[*n] variable_name[*n][, variable_name[*n]]...
   where n is an integer constant.

Examples:
      CHARACTER a, b, c, d*3
      CHARACTER*10 name1, name2
      CHARACTER*20 Name, Street*30, City*25, State*2
      CHARACTER(20) Name, Street*30, City*25, State*2
```

Chapter 9

```
CLOSE(unit)
```

Chapter 12

```
COMMON [/name/] list of variables
```

Chapter 12

```
COMPLEX variable list

Example:
COMPLEX root_1,root_2
```

Chapter 3

```
DATA variable_list/constant for each variable,
     separated by commas/
DATA variable_list/n*constant/
DATA variable_name/constant/[,variable_name/constant/] ...

   where n is an integer that specifies the number
   of repetitions of the constant

Examples:
      DATA x,y,z/1.1,2.2,3.3/
      DATA x/1.1/,y/2.2/,z/3.3/
      DATA a,b,c/0,0,0/
      DATA a,b,c/3*0/
```

Chapter 8

```
DATA (name(i),i=n1,n2)/constant[,constant].../
DATA (name(i),i=n1,n2)/n*constant/
DATA name/n*constant/
DATA name(element)[,name(element)]/constant[,constant].../
DATA name(element)[,name(element)]/n*constant/

Examples:
      INTEGER i,j
      REAL A(10),B(11:20),C(0:9,0:19)
      INTEGER D(10)
      DATA A/10*1./,(B(i),i=11,15)/5*0./,(B(i),i=16,20)/5*-1./
      DATA ((C(i,j),i=0,9),j=0,9)/-1./
      DATA D(1),D(3),D(5),D(7),D(9)/1,2,3*3/
```

Chapter 3 (data declarations)

```
data_type[, attributes] [::] <list of variables,
                                separated by  commas>
```

```
REAL [::] variable_name[, variable_name] ...
INTEGER variable_name[, variable_name]

Examples:
      REAL x_value, y_value, radius, angle
      INTEGER i,j,k
```

Chapter 8

```
data_type name(spec)[,name(spec)]...
data_type, DIMENSION(spec)[,name(spec)]... :: name[,name]...
where (spec) is (low:high[,low:high]...) or (size[,size]...)]

Examples:
      REAL A(0:9)
      INTEGER B(10,3,2),C(-2:2,3,0:99)
      REAL, DIMENSION(10,20) :: x,y

      INTEGER, PARAMETER :: n1=-5,n2=5,n3=10
      REAL C(n1:n2),D(n3)
```

Chapter 8

```
data_type, ALLOCATABLE :: name(:[,:])[,name(:[,:])]...
```

Chapter 8

```
DEALLOCATE(name[,name]...)
```

Chapter 6

```
Syntax
form
(1)      [name:] DO n = limit1,limit2[,step]
                   statement block
                 END DO [name]

(2)              DO label n = limit1,limit2[,step]
                   statement block, except for...
           label     last line of statement block

(3)              DO label n = limit1,limit2[,step]
                   statement block
         label CONTINUE
```

```
[name:] DO WHILE (relational/logical expression)
          statement block
        END DO [name]
```

Chapter 3

```
END [PROGRAM [program_name]]
```

Chapter 5

```
label FORMAT(format descriptors)

Example:
1000  FORMAT(1x,'x and y: ',2f6.2)
```

Chapter 4

```
function_name(one or more "dummy" parameters) = expression

Example:
      REAL BoxVolume,l,w,h
      BoxVolume(l,w,h)=l*w*h
```

Chapter 7

```
[data_type] FUNCTION name[(parameter list)]
[specification statements]
[executable statements]
[RETURN]
END [FUNCTION [name]]

Example of FUNCTION header:
      REAL FUNCTION DotProduct(x1,y1,z1,x2,y2,z2)
```

Chapter 9

```
GO TO line_label
```

Chapter 6

```
Syntax
form

(1)   IF (logical expression) action_statement

(2)   [name:] IF (logical expression) THEN
                 statement block
           END IF [name]

(3)   [name:] IF (logical expression) THEN
                 statement block
              ELSE [name]
                 statement block
              END IF [name]

(4)   [name:] IF (logical expression) THEN
                 statement block
              [ELSE IF (logical expression) THEN [name]
                 statement block]...
              [ELSE [name]
                 statement block]
              END IF [name]
```

Chapter 3

```
IMPLICIT NONE
```

Chapter 12

```
INCLUDE string constant containing file name, including path
```

Chapter 12

```
INQUIRE(iolength=n)I/O_list
```

Chapter 7

```
data_ type, INTENT(status) :: list of names from parameter list
  or
INTENT(status) list of names from parameter list

where status may be IN, OUT, or INOUT

Examples:

      REAL, INTENT(IN) :: x,y
      REAL, INTENT(OUT) :: r,theta

      REAL x,y,r,theta
      INTENT(IN) x,y
      INTENT(OUT) r,theta
```

Chapter 7

```
INTERFACE
 <function or subroutine header>
   <data declaration statements>
 END <FUNCTION or SUBROUTINE> [name]
 ...
END INTERFACE
```

Chapter 7

```
INTRINSIC list of external names, separated by commas
```

Chapter 3

```
LOGICAL variable_name[, variable_name]
```

Chapter 7

```
MODULE module name
  CONTAINS
   <one or more SUBROUTINEs or FUNCTIONs>
END [MODULE [module name]]

Example:
      MODULE SeveralSubs
        CONTAINS
        SUBROUTINE Sub1
         ...
        END SUBROUTINE Sub1
        SUBROUTINE Sub2
         ...
        END SUBROUTINE Sub2
!       (more subroutines)
      END MODULE SeveralSubs
```

Chapter 7

```
MODULE module_name
  [specification statements]
END [MODULE [module_name]]

Example:
      MODULE Constants
         REAL, PARAMETER :: pi=3.1415927,dr=0.0174532
      END MODULE Constants
```

Chapter 9

```
OPEN([UNIT=]u,optional specifiers)

where u is a unit number and the optional specifiers include:
   ACCESS=
     The possible values are 'SEQUENTIAL' and 'DIRECT'
   ACTION=
     The suggested values for sequential access files are
     'READ' or 'WRITE'
   BLANK=
     The possible values are 'NULL' or 'ZERO'.
   ERR=statement label
     Program control will be transferred to statement label if
        the OPEN statement generates an error.
   FILE=path and file name
     The full path and file name for the file to be opened.
        If the file name appears directly after the unit number,
        the specifier is optional.
   FORM=
     The possible values are 'FORMATTED' and 'UNFORMATTED'.
   IOSTAT=integer variable
     OPEN returns a zero if there are no errors and a positive
        value otherwise.
   POSITION=
     The suggested values for writing to a sequential access
        file are 'REWIND' and 'APPEND'.  'REWIND' positions an
        existing file at the beginning, causing exising data to
        be overwritten.  'APPEND' positions the file at the end,
        allowing new data to be appended to existing data.
   STATUS=
     The possible values are 'OLD', 'NEW', 'REPLACE',
     'SCRATCH', and 'UNKNOWN'.

Example:
      OPEN(1,'a:grades.dat',err=99,action='read')
```

Chapter 3

```
PARAMETER (variable_name=value[, variable_name=value] ...)
data_type,PARAMETER :: variable_name=value
                       [, variable_name=value] ...

Examples:
(using a PARAMETER statement)
      INTEGER MaxSize
      PARAMETER (MaxSize=1000)
(using the PARAMETER attribute)
      REAL,PARAMETER :: pi=3.1415927, Deg_to_Rad=0.0174532
```

Chapter 3

```
PRINT *[,list of variables, expressions, functions,
          or constants, separated by commas]
Examples:
      PRINT*,'This prints a string constant.'
      PRINT* ! This prints a blank line.
      PRINT*, 'The two sides are ',x,' and ',y, &
             '.  The hypotenuse is ',hypotenuse,'.'
      PRINT*,'The average of x and y is ',(x+y)/2.0
```

Chapters 5 and 6

```
PRINT *[, list of variables, expressions, functions,
          or constants, separated by commas]
PRINT label[, list...]
PRINT format string[, list...]

PRINT *,loop
PRINT fffff,loop
WRITE(*,*)loop
WRITE(*,fffff)loop

where loop is
  (variable_name,variable_name=lower,upper,step)
or
  (array_name(index),index=lower,upper,step)
and fffff is
  format label or format description in the form of
  a string constant
```

Chapter 3

```
PROGRAM program_name

Examples:
      PROGRAM Model_1

      PROGRAM My_Program
!
!     This program is stored in file MY_PROG.F90
```

Chapter 3

```
[PROGRAM name]
[specification statements]
[executable statements]
END [PROGRAM [name]]
```

Chapter 3

```
READ *[, list of variable names, separated by commas]

Example:
      READ *,a,b,c
```

Chapter 9

```
READ([UNIT=]u,[FMT=]format specifier[,IOSTAT=integer variable]
     [,ERR=line_label][,END=line_label]) list of variables

where:
u is a unit number, format specifier is a label for a
      line containing a FORMAT statement
IOSTAT returns implementation-dependent integer values for
      various abnormal conditions
ERR= directs program control to a labeled line if an error
      occurs while reading the file
END= directs program control to a labeled line when the end
      of the file is encountered.
The list of variables to be read can take several forms,
      similar to the possibilities with formatted WRITE and
      PRINT statements.

Examples:
      READ(5,*)a,b,c  !reads from standard input device
      READ(3,*)a,b,c
      READ(1,1000,END=999,ERR=998)(A(i),B(i),i=1,10)
```

Chapter 6

```
[name:] SELECT CASE (expression)
        [CASE (list of nonoverlapping values and ranges
                with same data type as expression) [name]
           statement block]...
        [CASE DEFAULT
           statement block]
        END SELECT [name]
```

Chapter 9

```
REWIND unit
  or
REWIND([unit=]unit)
```
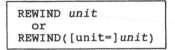

Chapter 3

```
STOP
STOP ddddd
STOP 'string constant'
```

Chapter 7

```
SUBROUTINE name [(parameter list)]

Example:
      SUBROUTINE Polar_to_Cartesian(r,theta,x,y)
```

Chapter 7

```
SUBROUTINE name [(parameter list)]
  [specification statements]
  [executable statements]
[RETURN] [label or string constant]
END [SUBROUTINE [name]]
```

Chapter 8

```
SUM(array_name[(spec[,spec]...)])
```

Chapter 8

```
TYPE type_name
  field_type name
  [field_type name]...
END TYPE type_name

Example:
      TYPE Student_Info
        CHARACTER*20 name
        CHARACTER*11 student ID
        INTEGER credit_hours
        REAL GPA
      END TYPE Student_Info
```

Chapter 8

```
TYPE (type_name) variable_name[,variable_name]...

Example:
      TYPE (Student_Info) freshmen, all_students
```

Chapter 7

```
USE module_name

Example:
      USE SeveralSubs
```

Chapter 7

```
USE module_name[, ONLY : list of included names,
                         separated by commas]

where each item in the ONLY list has the form
[local_name =>] module_name

Examples:
      USE Constants

      USE Constants, ONLY : pi, deg_to_rad => dr
```

Chapter 5

```
WRITE(u,*)[list of variables, expressions, functions,
           or constants, separated by commas]
WRITE(*,*)[list...]
WRITE(u,[FMT=]label,[ADVANCE='NO'])[ list...]
WRITE(u,[FMT=]format string,[ADVANCE='NO'])[ list..]
```

Appendix 3. Source Code File Name Summary

This appendix contains the source code file name and a brief description of each complete program in the text, listed by chapter starting with Chapter 2. Source code files, which have been created in an MS-DOS environment, have a .F90 file name extension. Some numbered programs in the text contain code fragments rather than complete programs and they are so noted. Program numbers marked with an asterisk appear in the Applications section of their chapter. In those cases where data files are required by a program, including programming problems found in the end-of-chapter exercises, the names of those files are also given. Source code and data files can be downloaded from Springer-Verlag's World Wide Web site:

http://www.springer-ny.com/supplements/dbrooks

Chapter 2

WINDCHIL	1	Calculate wind chill temperature.

Chapter 3

CIRCLE	1	Calculate area and circumference of a circle.
CIRCLE1A	1(a)	
BOX	2	Calculate surface area and volume of a rectangular box.
NAMES	3	Display name and age.
(fragment)	4	
(fragment)	5	
MIXED	6	Demonstrate results of mixed-mode calculations.
AVERAGE	7	Calculate average of three numbers.
(fragment)	8	
(fragment)	9	
(fragment)	10	
BEAM	11*	Calculate deflection of a beam under a central load.
REL_MASS	12*	Calculate relativistic mass and speed of an electron.

Chapter 4

(fragment)	1	
STRING	2	Demonstrate string concatenation.
POLAR	3	Polar to Cartesian coordinate transformations.
RING	4	Calculate area of a circular ring.
REFRACT	5*	Calculate refraction of light.

| PLOTTER | 11* | Generate character-based function "plotter." |
| INTENT | - | (No number—to check compiler's handling of INTENT attributes.) |

Chapter 8

RANDTEST	1	Generate count histogram for random integers.
SINCOS	2	Use elemental functions for array assignments.
ROWCOL	3	Demonstrate order in which 2-D array elements are stored.
OZONE	4	Calculate vector scalar product with variably sized arrays.
UNION1	5	Calculate union of two proper sets (static arrays).
UNION2	6	Calculate union of two proper sets (allocatable arrays).
MAT_SQ1	7	Calculate square of a matrix (allocatable arrays).
MAT_SQ2	7(a)	Calculate square of a matrix (improper use of static arrays).
MAT_SQ3	7(b)	Calculate square of a matrix (proper use of static arrays).
ALLOCAT	8	Demonstrate ALLOCATE and DEALLOCATE.
(fragment)	9	
DEGDAYS	10	Calculate heating degree days.
VECTOROP	11*	Calculate vector dot (scalar) and cross products.
SIERPINS	12*	Generate Sierpinski triangle.
PROB	13*	Probability calculations for manufacturing quality control.

| INTERPOL.DAT | | Data file for extra credit part of Exercise 22 |

Chapter 9

(fragment)	1	
GRADES_F	2	Calculate average grade from file. (GRADES.DAT)
AVG_TEMP	3	Calculate average temperatures from file. (JANUARY.DAT)
BAROM	4	Extract barometric pressure values from file. (BAROM.DAT)
READTEST	5	Demonstrate formatted READ from file. (READTEST.DAT)
BAROM2	6	Extract barometric pressure values from file when data are missing (using internal READ). (BAROM2.DAT)
SMOOTH	7*	Exponential smoothing of data from file. (SP500.DAT)
WATER	8*	Water utility billing. (H2O_RATE, DAT, WATER.DAT)
MERGE	9*	Merge two sorted data files. (LISTA.DAT, LISTB.DAT)
JAN_QCD	10*	Generate quote-and-comma-delimited text file.

Additional data files for exercises:

BIRDS1.DAT, BIRDS2.DAT, R100.DAT, PROJECT.DAT, GRADING.DAT, STOCKS.DAT. CO2.DAT. INSTOCK.DAT. USE STK1.DAT

Chapter 10

SEARCH	1	(SUBROUTINE FindFirst) find first occurrence of specified value. (SEARCH.DAT)
SEARCH	2	(SUBROUTINE FindAll) find all occurrences of specified value.
SEARCH	3	(SUBROUTINE Binary) binary search on ordered list.
SEARCH	4	Driver program for searching subroutines P-10.1–P-10.3.
SORT	5	(SUBROUTINE Selection) Selection Sort
SORT	6	(SUBROUTINE Insertion) Insertion Sort.
SORT	7	Driver program for sorting subroutines P-10.5 and P-10.6.
FACTORAL	8	Calculate factorial function, with recursion.
QUIKSORT	9	Recursive Quicksort.
INSERT2	10*	Keep a list in order.
LEGENDRE	11*	Recursive evaluation of Legendre polynomials.

Additional data files for exercises:

DRUGBASE.DAT, DRUGBASE.IN

Chapter 11

STATS	1	Basic descriptive statistics.
FALLING	2*	Estimate speed of a falling object.
NUM_INT	3	Simpson's rule integration.
GAMMA	4*	Evaluate the gamma function (a failed application of Simpson's rule.)
GAUSS	5	Gauss-Jordan elimination for solving linear systems. (GAUSS.DAT)
ROOTS	6	Bisection algorithm for finding roots.
CIRCUIT	7*	Calculate charge in a series LRC circuit.

Chapter 12

DERIVATV	1	Demonstrate numerical differentiation. (DERIVATV.DAT)
DERIVAT2	1(a)	Use INCLUDE for subroutines. (Uses DERI_MOD.F90)
DERIVAT3		Link object files.
JULIAN_T	2	Convert calendar date to Julian date.
ARAYFUNC	3	Demonstrate array manipulation syntax.
TEM_PHIL	4	Demonstrate use of array reduction functions. (TEM_PHIL.DAT)
FILETEST	5	Demonstrate various file options. (FILETEST.DAT)
SRCHFILE	6	Binary search of direct access file.

COMPLEX	7	Demonstrate COMPLEX syntax and arithmetic.
QUADRAT2	8	Find real and imaginary roots of quadratic equation.
CIRCLCOM	9	Demonstrate use of COMMON blocks.
COM_TEST	10	Demonstrate "misuse" of COMMON blocks.

Appendices

| DATETIME | 1 | Demonstrate access to system date and clock. |

Appendix 4. Accessing the System Time and Date

Fortran 90 assumes that your computer can provide information about the time and date, and it provides two intrinsic subroutines for accessing this information from a program. Their use is illustrated in the following program.

P-A.1 [DATETIME.F90]

```
      PROGRAM DateTime
!
! Demonstrate use of intrinsic date and time procedures.
!
      IMPLICIT NONE
      CHARACTER date*8,time*10,zone*5
      INTEGER values(8),count,count_rate,count_max
!
      CALL DATE_AND_TIME(date,time,zone,values)
      PRINT 1000,date,time,zone,values
!
      CALL SYSTEM_CLOCK(count,count_rate,count_max)
      PRINT 1010,count,count_rate,count_max
1000  FORMAT(a9,a11,a6,8i10)
1010  FORMAT (3i10)
      END
```

The variables have the following interpretation:

date	CHARACTER*8 variable holding calendar date in yyyymmdd format
time	CHARACTER*10 variable holding time in hhmmss.sss format
zone	CHARACTER*5 variable holding difference between local time and Greenwich Mean Time (GMT) in format Shhmm, where S is a + or - sign
values	INTEGER array of size 8 holding year, month, day, time difference relative to GMT, hour, minutes, seconds, milliseconds
count	INTEGER holding current value of system clock

count_rate   INTEGER holding number of system clock counts per second

count_max   INTEGER holding maximum value of count (before it recycles
             to zero)

The output from PROGRAM DateTime might look like this for an MS-DOS
system:

```
19950512  145802.000
    1995         5       12**********
      14        58        2                0
53891246      1000  86399999
```

The interpretation of the output is that this computer system doesn't know about
time zones relative to GMT and that it returns clock time only to the nearest
second (although milliseconds are available from count). The system clock
"recycles" after 86,400 seconds, the number of seconds in a day.

The information returned by these subroutines is only as good as the
information in a computer's system clock. For example, DOS system clocks don't
always keep accurate time and they may not automatically convert back and forth
between standard and daylight savings time.[1] If it is important for a program to
return an accurate time, it is easy to reset the date or time on a DOS system by
typing date or time at a DOS prompt.

---

[1]Author's note: when I purchased a new Windows 95 PC in the summer of 1996, I was
surprised to find that it automatically reset its clock to Eastern Standard Time on the appropriate
day in October.

Ch.	Term	Definition
1	account ID	A unique and public identifier for the user of a computer system.
2	algorithm	A step-by-step solution to a computing problem.
8	allocatable array	An array whose rank is specified when it is declared, but whose index bounds are specified while the program in which the array is declared is executing.
1	Apple II	The first widely distributed and commercially successful personal computer.
4	argument list	A list of one or more values, variables, or expressions passed to a subprogram when it is called.
11	arithmetic mean	The sum of a collection of values divided by the number of values.
2	arithmetic operator	A symbol in source code that represents operations such as addition, subtraction, multiplication, and division.
4	arithmetic overflow	A condition in which a calculation a program is asked to perform involves numbers larger than the program can support.
8	array	A data structure that provides access to a number of related values through one or more indices. In scientific and mathematical programming applications, arrays are often associated with vectors and matrices.
8	array dimension	The storage space represented by one of the one or more pairs of lower and upper indices in an array. Arrays are accessed by one subscript per dimension.
8	array element	One value in an array, accessed through an array index.
8	array extent	The number of elements along a particular array dimension.
8	array index	The integer value that identifies a particular array element.
8	array rank	The number of dimensions (subscripts) of an array. (See array dimension.) Vectors and matrices are represented as rank-one and rank-two arrays, respectively.

8	array reduction function	A function that returns as output an array of lower rank than an array appearing as an input argument.
2	ASCII collating sequence	A code for representing characters, as defined by the American Standard Code for Information Exchange.
3	assignment operation	See assignment statement.
3	assignment operator	The operator that is used to define an assignment operation.
2	assignment statement	A statement that alters the value of a variable.
8	automatic array	An array appearing in a subprogram with dummy values used to declare the extent of its indices.
11	backsubstitution	A process of calculating roots starting from the last row in an upper triangular matrix.
2	binary file	Any file whose contents are not representations of characters.
3	binary operator	An operator that requires two operands, typically one to the left of the operator and one to the right.
10	binary search	An algorithm that searches for an item in an ordered list by continuously dividing the list into partitions of, ideally, approximately equal size, one of which may contain the desired value and the other of which cannot contain that value.
1	bit	Binary digit. The smallest unit of information in a computer, represented electronically, magnetically, or optically by an "on-off" state and numerically by the values 0 and 1.
2	boolean value	A logical value of true or false.
2	bug	A mistake in a computer program. (See debugging.)
1	byte	A group of eight bits, forming a single computer "word."
2	calling argument	Values, variables, or expressions passed to a subprogram when it is called.
5	carriage return	A character that causes the return of a printer or file pointer to the beginning of a line.
1	central processing unit (CPU)	The electronic component that controls all the calculating functions of a computer.
1	centralized computing	A computing system characterized by mainframe computers managed by a professional staff.
3	character variable	A variable representing one or more characters. In the latter case, it may be called a string variable.
2	character (text) string	A sequence of characters that are interpreted as "text" rather than as one or more numbers.

4	collating sequence	The order in which coded characters are stored within a programming environment. (See ASCII collating sequence.)
3	comment line	Text within a program unit that documents and explains source code, and that is ignored by the compiler.
2	compiler	A program that converts source code into machine-level instructions.
12	compiler directive	An instruction that conveys information to a source code compiler, but is not part of the source code itself. In Fortran, INCLUDE is a compiler directive.
3	compile-time error	An error, usually a syntax error, that is detected during the compilation process.
8	component selector	The character used to specify a particular field in a character record. In Fortran, the component selector is the character %.
1	computer algebra software	Software that is able to perform symbolic manipulation in areas of mathematics such as algebra and calculus.
4	concatenation operator	A binary operator that appends one character or character string to the end of another.
6	conditional loop	A repetition (loop) structure in which the number of repetitions is determined while the loop is executing.
2	conditional (statement)	A statement that evaluates the "truth" of a specified relational/logical expression.
12	conformable arrays	Two arrays having the same shape.
2	control structure	A program statement or statements defining or modifying the order in which other program statements are executed.
6	convergence criterion	A programmer- or user-specified condition for terminating an iterative calculation in a conditional loop.
11	correlation coefficient	A dimensionless value between 0 and 1 that is a measure of how well a regression line represents data.
6	count-controlled loop	A repetition (loop) structure in which the number of repetitions is specified prior to the start of the loop.
1	data analysis and statistics software	Software designed specifically for the statistical analysis of data.
2	data file	A file containing information that can be used by, or has been produced by, a computer program.

8	data structure	A user-defined data representation that is built from the intrinsic data types, such as an array.
2	debugging	The act of looking for and correcting errors in a computer program. (See bug.)
1	decentralized computing	A computing system consisting of many widely distributed computers and peripherals, controlled by individuals and small groups of users.
8	derived data type	Any user-defined data structure consisting of intrinsic data types and other user-defined data structures.
11	discretization error	The typically cumulative error that results from the fact that real number arithmetic in a program is only an approximation.
7	driver program	A program whose sole purpose is to verify the operation of one or more subprograms.
1	electronic computer	A programmable calculating device that uses electronic rather than mechanical components.
8	elemental function	A function that can accept either a scalar or array variable as an input argument.
9	end-of-file mark	One or more characters that mark the end of a file, and that can be detected by a program.
9	end-of-line mark	One or more characters that mark the end of a line in a text file, and that can be detected by a program.
2	executable file	A binary file containing instructions that can be interpreted and executed directly by a computer.
2	executable instruction	An instruction that can be interpreted and executed directly by a computer.
3	executable statement	A statement that directs a computer to take some action while a program is executing.
7	explicit interface	A code construct that permits a compiler to check for consistency between a subprogram parameter list and the argument list when that subprogram is called.
3	explicit typing	A process by which every variable name is given a specific data type.
2	external input	Information provided to a program while it is executing, typically by the user from a keyboard or from an external data file.
9	external representation	Typically, a character-based representation for numerical and other data, as opposed to its internal (binary) representation.

1	e-mail	Electronic messages that can be sent and received via computer networks.
8	field	One piece of information in a data record.
5	field width	The number of characters allocated for a particular output or input format.
12	file pointer	A value maintained by a programming environment that keeps track of a location within a file. Reading or writing values in a file typically increments or decrements the file pointer.
3	fixed format	Referring to a language that requires that parts of a statement appear only in specified locations on a line. Older versions of Fortran are fixed-format languages.
2	flowchart	A visual means of representing an algorithm using a set of standard symbols.
5	format descriptor	Programmer-supplied information about how to interpret or display information.
5	format specifier	Programmer-supplied information for determining the appearance of output or the interpretation of input.
5	formatted output	Output whose appearance is specified by programmer-supplied instructions.
3	free format	Referring to a language that accepts statements without regard to their specific location in a line of source code. Fortran 90 is a free-format language.
7	function library	A collection of functions that can be included in other programs at either the source code or object code level.
7	global variable	A variable that is available to a main program and all its subprograms.
1	graphical interface	A computer operating system that is based on images rather than text, especially an operating system that relies on a mouse or other pointing device rather than typed commands.
2	hard coded	Numerical or text values written directly into code rather than being expressed as variables.
9	header line	A line at the beginning of a text file that, typically, describes the contents of data appearing after the header line(s) in the manner of a column heading.
7	header statement	The statement that contains the name and parameter list for a subprogram.

1	high-level programming language	A programming language that uses symbols and English-like words to implement algorithms and solve computing problems. It must be converted into machine language before it can be understood by a computer (see compiler).
1	IBM clone	Any personal computer not manufactured by IBM that adheres to the hardware and software standards of the IBM-PC computer and its descendants such as the XT and AT.
1	IBM-compatible	Any personal computer that is compatible with the IBM-PC and its descendents. (See IBM clone.)
1	IBM-PC	The personal computer introduced by IBM in 1981 in response to the Apple II personal computer.
3	implicit typing	A process by which a language assumes a data type for a variable based on the variable's name.
6	implied DO... loop	A count-controlled loop that is initiated by one or more forms of syntax "shorthand."
6	infinite loop	A conditional loop that executes indefinitely because its terminating conditions are never met.
2	integer	A whole number, and a data type for representing such numbers.
3	integer variable	A variable representing an integer number.
7	intent attribute	A designation of a subprogram parameter as "input," "output," or "input/output."
2	interactive program	A program that requires user input at the time the program executes.
9	internal file	An internal buffer for temporary storage of information that can be accessed with file-like statements.
2	internal representation	The form in which information is stored in a computer, as opposed to a character-based external representation.
9	internal representation	The manner in which information is stored in computer memory, as opposed to its external representation.
1	Internet	A worldwide computer network for the electronic exchange of information.
3	intrinsic data type	A data type that is part of the standard that defines a programming language.
4	intrinsic function	A built-in function that is supported by a language standard.

6	iterative calculation	A calculation that must be repeated indefinitely inside a conditional loop until a specified terminating condition is met.
3	keyword	Combinations of characters ("words") that have a specific meaning to a language compiler.
2	language syntax	The rules governing the writing of source code.
5	line feed	A character that advances a printer or file pointer by one line.
5	line label	A label for identifying a line in Fortran source code, in the format of an integer from 1 to 99999.
10	linear search	A searching algorithm that examines each item in a list, starting typically at the beginning of the list.
2	linker	Software that joins ("links") several machine-language (binary) files together to produce a complete program.
3	list-directed input	A form of input in which a programming language determines how to interpret input.
3	list-directed output	A form of output in which the programming language determines the appearance of the output.
3	literal constant	A value hard coded (as a constant) into source code.
7	local variable	A variable that is available only to the main program or subprogram in which it is declared.
6	logical expression	An expression containing one or more logical operators.
2	logical operator	A symbol in source code that represents the logical operations and, or, and not, for example, on one or more quantities.
1	logoff	The process of terminating a connection with a remote computer.
1	logon	The process of establishing a connection with a remote computer.
6	loop counter variable	A variable that controls the execution of a count-controlled loop. The counter is automatically incremented by a specified amount every time statements inside the loop are executed.
1	machine language	A low-level programming language that uses instructions understood directly by computers.
1	mainframe computer	A powerful multiuser computer around which a centralized computing system is organized.
8	matrix	A mathematical entity represented by a rank-two array.

1	microcomputer	A computer containing a CPU and associated electronics on a single circuit board.
1	minicomputer	A multiuser computer powerful enough for many kinds of computing tasks, but small enough to be managed by its users as part of a decentralized computing environment.
3	mixed-mode expression	An expression that contains more than one data type.
1	MS-DOS	Microsoft's text-based operating system for IBM-compatible personal computers, and the *de facto* standard operating system for such computers.
1	multitasking	An operating environment in which a single computer can perform more than one task nearly simultaneously, or in parallel.
3	named constant	A value associated with a name. Unlike a variable, its value cannot be changed while a program is executing.
1	network	A collection of computers interconnected electronically to allow them to share tasks and data.
3	nonexecutable statement	A statement that defines some aspect of a programming environment before the program executes.
3	nonstandard extension	Language features that are not part of the applicable standard for that language
4	numeric inquiry function	An intrinsic function that returns information about the allowed range for a specified numerical data type.
2	object file	The binary file produced by a compiler, and the first step toward producing an executable file.
1	operating system	The software that controls the basic functions and user interface of a computer.
6	ordinal value	A variable that keeps track of the number of repetitions in a count-controlled loop.
8	parallel array	An array whose elements are related to identically indexed elements in another array.
3	parallel port	An I/O path along which information flows in "packets" of one or more bytes, rather than one bit at a time.
4	parameter list	A list of the "local names" of one or more variables used as input or produced as output by a subprogram.

10	partition	A subdivision of a list formed by applying a user-defined algorithm.
1	password	A unique and private identification for the user of a computer system.
1	peripherals	Equipment in addition to basic computer hardware, *e.g.*, printers and CD-ROM drives.
1	personal computer	A single-user computer and its peripherals, controlled by an individual.
11	pivot	A value that determines how rows or columns in a system of linear equations are interchanged.
10	pivot value	The value used to separate a list into two partitions.
1	portable language	A standardized high-level language that will run on any computer that contains a compiler for that language.
6	post-test loop	A conditional loop in which the test for termination is made at the end of the loop.
6	pre-test loop	A conditional loop in which the test for termination is made at the beginning of the loop.
2	program modularization	The act of writing a program that solves a large task by breaking it into several smaller tasks, each with a well-defined information interface.
3	program unit	A main program or subprogram; in Fortran, any separately compilable main program, subroutine, function, or MODULE.
2	pseudocode	A shorthand means of expressing an algorithm that does not depend on the syntax of a formal programming language
6	pseudorandom numbers	A sequence of numbers that appear to be random even though they are generated by an algorithm.
9	quote-and-comma-delimited text file	A text file in which character information is enclosed in quotation marks and all fields are separated by commas. Such a file can be imported into the rows and columns of a spreadsheet.
1	random access memory (RAM)	Memory locations in a computer that can be read from or written to under program control.
6	random number generator	An algorithm that generates pseudorandom numbers.
1	read-only memory (ROM)	Memory locations in a computer system that may be read from, but not written to, by a program or operating system.
3	real variable	A variable representing a real (floating point) number.

2	real (floating point) number	A number with a fractional part.
8	record	A collection of related information, consisting of one or more data fields.
10	recursive algorithm	An algorithm that calls itself.
11	regression line	A statistically derived "best fit" line through a collection of data.
2	relational operator	A symbol in source code that represents a comparison of two quantities.
2	repetition structure	A means of repetitively executing a group of statements.
3	run-time error	An error that occurs when a compiled program is executing.
8	scalar data	Data that are represented with scalar (non-array) variables.
3	scientific notation	A way of expressing numbers using powers of 10.
10	searching algorithm	An algorithm designed to find a specified value in a list of values.
2	selection structure	A means of executing some statements and not others based on the evaluation of a relational/logical expression.
2	sequence structure	A series of program instructions carried out in sequence.
9	sequential access file	A file, typically a text file, that can be accessed only one record at a time, starting at the beginning.
3	significant figures	The number of digits that are actually maintained by the internal representation of a number.
10	sorting algorithm	An algorithm designed to reorder a list of items into descending or ascending order in the numerical or alphabetic sense.
2	source code	A text file containing instructions written in a high-level programming language.
1	spreadsheet	A computer application for performing certain kinds of "two-dimensional" calculations in tabular form.
11	standard deviation	A statistical measure of the variability of values in a collection of values; the square root of the variance.
11	standard error of estimate	A statistical measure of the extent to which a model represents values in a collection of data.
3	standard output device	The destination to which program output is sent by default, usually a monitor screen.
3	statement	An instruction written in a high-level language.

4	statement function	A user-defined function that exists only within the program unit in which it is defined.
8	statically allocated array	An array defined in a nonexecutable data declaration statement.
2	stepwise refinement	The iterative process of improving an algorithm by testing parts of a program and refining the algorithm based on these intermediate results.
2	structured programming	An approach to programming that stresses simple execution paths between program modules and clearly specified information interfaces for each module.
2	subprogram	A separate program module that accepts input, solves a specific problem, and returns output.
7	subroutine	A Fortran subprogram that accepts one or more values as input and returns one or more values as output.
11	sum of squares	Typically, the sum of the squares of the differences between all individual values in a data sample minus the mean of all values in the sample.
1	supercomputer	A large mainframe computer characterized by multiple processors, very high execution speeds, large amounts of memory, and specialized languages for highly specialized applications.
9	text file	A file containing information encoded in character ("external") format, as opposed to binary ("internal") format.
1	text-based interface	A user interface that relies entirely on character-based information, especially one that requires typed commands.
1	throughput	A measure of the ability of a computer or computer system to process information.
3	token	One or more characters that are interpreted as a single unit by a compiler.
2	top-down design	The process of solving a computing problem by subdividing a large problem into several smaller problems. (See structured programming.)
1	turnaround time	The time required to complete a computing task and return results to the user.
3	type conversion	A process that converts one data type to another.
3	type declaration	The process by which variable names are associated with a specific data type.

3	unary operator	An operator that requires one operand, typically to the right of the operator.
3	uninitialized variable	A variable that has not been assigned a value before it is used.
5	unit number	An integer identifier that specifies the association of an I/O statement with a physical device or file.
1	UNIX	A popular operating system for workstations and minicomputers.
11	upper triangular matrix	A matrix that has been manipulated so that all values below the left-to-right, top-to-bottom diagonal are zero.
2	variable	A quantity that can be represented symbolically in a high-level language and manipulated by a computer program.
11	variance	A statistical measure of the variability of values in a collection of values; the square of the standard deviation.
8	vector data	Data that are represented in a program by using array notation.
1	Windows	Microsoft's graphical operating environment for personal computers based on Intel and Intel-compatible CPUs.
1	workstation	A computer designed to operate in a graphics-intensive environment, intermediate in its capabilities between PCs and minicomputers.
1	World Wide Web	An information resource on the Internet for publishing and exchanging information.

Index

Command keywords, such as PRINT, and important specifiers, such as ACCESS, are individually indexed. Summaries of pseudocode commands and Fortran command syntax are organized alphabetically in Appendix 2 and are not indexed. All referenced intrinsic functions are indexed under "functions" and do not have separate entries. Format control and edit descriptors are indexed under "edit descriptors." Page references to glossary definitions are not indexed.

CPSIA information can be obtained at www.ICGtesting.com
Printed in the USA
LVOW021741280413

331269LV00007B/160/P